Developing Management Skills

What Great Managers Know and Do

Timothy T. Baldwin
Indiana University

William H. Bommer
Cleveland State University

Robert S. Rubin
DePaul University

McGraw-Hill Irwin

Boston   Burr Ridge, IL   Dubuque, IA   New York   San Francisco   St. Louis
Bangkok   Bogotá   Caracas   Kuala Lumpur   Lisbon   London   Madrid   Mexico City
Milan   Montreal   New Delhi   Santiago   Seoul   Singapore   Sydney   Taipei   Toronto

McGraw-Hill Irwin

DEVELOPING MANAGEMENT SKILLS: WHAT GREAT MANAGERS KNOW AND DO

Published by McGraw-Hill/Irwin, a business unit of The McGraw-Hill Companies, Inc., 1221 Avenue of the Americas, New York, NY, 10020. Copyright © 2008 by The McGraw-Hill Companies, Inc. All rights reserved. No part of this publication may be reproduced or distributed in any form or by any means, or stored in a database or retrieval system, without the prior written consent of The McGraw-Hill Companies, Inc., including, but not limited to, in any network or other electronic storage or transmission, or broadcast for distance learning.

Some ancillaries, including electronic and print components, may not be available to customers outside the United States.

This book is printed on acid-free paper.

5 6 7 8 9 0 QDB/QDB 12 11

ISBN 978-0-07-722595-7
MHID 0-07-722595-3

Editorial director: *John E. Biernat*
Executive editor: *John Weimeister*
Senior developmental editor: *Christine Scheid*
Senior marketing manager: *Anke Braun*
Project manager: *Jim Labeots*
Production supervisor: *Gina Hangos*
Designer: *Cara David*
Lead media project manager: *Cathy L. Tepper*
Cover design: *Aesthetic Apparatus*
Interior design: *Maureen McCutcheon*
Typeface: *10/12 New Aster*
Compositor: *Laserwords Private Limited*
Printer: *Quad/Graphics*

Library of Congress Cataloging-in-Publication Data
Baldwin, Timothy T.
    Developing management skills : what great managers know and do / Timothy Baldwin,
William Bommer, Robert Rubin.
      p. cm.
    Includes index.
    ISBN-13: 978-0-07-292010-9 (alk. paper)
    ISBN-10: 0-07-292010-6 (alk. paper)
    1. Management—Study and teaching. I. Bommer, William. II Rubin, Robert S. III. Title.
HD30.4.B355 2008
658.4'07124—dc22
                                                                                2006100869

www.mhhe.com

To JoEllen, Matt, Pop, and the memory of Mom—the greatest people manager I will ever know.

Tim Baldwin

For Meg—you will be missed always.

Bill Bommer

For Leah and Yonah—my best friends.

Bob Rubin

About the Authors

Timothy (Tim) T. Baldwin is Professor of Management at the Indiana University Kelley School of Business where he is also the Faculty Director of the Leadership Development Institute and co-director of the MBA Sports & Entertainment Academy. Professor Baldwin holds a Ph.D. in Organizational Behavior from Michigan State University and an MBA from MSU as well. He has published his research work in leading academic and professional outlets including the *Academy of Management Journal*, *Journal of Applied Psychology*, *Personnel Psychology* and *Academy of Management Executive*. He has won several national research awards including eight Best Paper awards from the Management Education & Development division of the Academy of Management. He has twice been the recipient of the Richard A. Swanson Excellence in Research Award presented by the American Society for Training & Development (ASTD). He is the co-author of *Improving Transfer Systems In Organizations* (Jossey Bass: 2003) and his current research interests include factors that impact the transfer of trained skills to the workplace and methods of leadership development.

In his time at Indiana University, Tim has been recognized for teaching excellence including eight MBA Teaching Awards, the Eli Lilly Alumni Teaching Award, the FACET All-University Teaching Award, and the Dow Innovation in Teaching Fellowship.

Tim's background includes consultation with Cummins Engine, Eli Lilly, FedEx, Whirlpool, and a variety of other organizations in both the public and private sector. He has also designed and delivered numerous executive education seminars in the US and abroad including the Kelley School's Asia-Pacific Management Development program. He serves on the Board of Directors of Paul I. Cripe, Inc., a professional services firm based in Indianapolis.

Tim is married with one son, one dog, one cat, and until recently, one gerbil (sad story and the cat is implicated). His interests include coaching youth sports, golf, basketball, gardening, and a little amateur magic.

William (Bill) H. Bommer earned his master's degree in organizational development from Bowling Green State University and his Ph.D. in organizational behavior from Indiana University. He is currently an associate professor and the Nance Distinguished Professor of Organizational Behavior and Development at Cleveland State University's Nance College of Business Administration. He has also been on the faculties of Bowling Green State University, Southern Illinois University at Edwardsville, and Georgia State University.

Bill has published widely in the management area in journals including the *Academy of Management Journal*, *Academy of Management Learning & Education*, *Leadership Quarterly*, *Organizational Behavior and Human Decision Processes*, *Personnel Psychology*, *Journal of Applied Psychology*, *Journal of Management*, *Journal of Vocational Behavior*, and *Organization Science*. His current research interests include transformational leadership, organizational and personal change, and the linkage between attitudes and behavior.

Prior to entering academia, Bill worked as a financial analyst and as a group process consultant in private industry. Bill has remained active in his business relationships and has designed and led numerous executive education programs over the last decade. In support of his research interests, he has served as a trainer and consultant to a large number of manufacturing companies across the United States and has had a long-term relationship with the Centers for Disease Control. In this capacity, Bill has designed corporate universities for his clients. Bill is also president of Academic Behavior Assessments, a company that builds management skills assessment tools and consults with university business schools in support of their learning objectives and complicence with accreditation standards. When not involved with teaching, researching, or consulting, Bill enjoys traveling, hiking, eating, and working out (the last activity is the direct result of the third).

Robert (Bob) S. Rubin is an Assistant Professor of Management in the Kellstadt Graduate School of Business at DePaul University. He received his B.A. in Psychology from Indiana University, his M.A. in Industrial-Organizational Psychology from Southern Illinois University at Edwardsville, and his Ph.D. in Organizational Psychology from Saint Louis University.

Bob specializes in Human Resource Management and Organizational Behavior at DePaul were he is an avid teacher committed to advancing the field of management science. He has been nationally recognized for his dedication to management pedagogy and scholarship including two best paper awards from the MED Division of the Academy of Management. His research interest centers on individual differences and their role in effective leadership and management development and includes forays into aspects of transformational leadership, managerial assessment and development, academic assessment centers, and emotions at work. Bob has published his work in leading academic journals such as *Academy of Management Journal, Academy of Management Learning & Education, The Leadership Quarterly, Journal of Organizational Behavior, Human Resources Management Journal, and Journal of Management Education*. Currently, Bob is an editorial board member of two journals, the *Academy of Management Learning & Education* and *Leadership and Organizational Studies*. Further, Bob frequently serves as a reviewer for journals and national meetings and has been recognized by the national Academy of Management as an outstanding reviewer in the Management Education Division.

"The great thing about having a Ph.D. is when people do not understand you, they think it's them."
—Henry Kissinger

In addition to his academic work, Bob has been an active human resources and organization development consultant to a variety of industries including biotechnology, healthcare, dentistry and transportation including organizations. His consulting work has spanned employee selection, management and team development. Bob also frequently serves as a coach for purposes of management skill development. When he's not engaged in managing his more senior textbook coauthors (Note: he had a full head of hair prior to beginning this book project), Bob enjoys playing music, travel, and hiking.

Chapter Overviews

I. Personal Skills

Chapter 1: Personal Effectiveness

Effective management has a strong personal dimension. Great managers are good learners, have a high level of self-awareness, and manage their stress and time well. This chapter presents a model of self-management and highlights the essential dimensions of "knowing oneself" related to personal and management style. A synthesis of the best ideas for effectively managing stress and time is also provided. The charge to learners is to get beyond hope and *take action* to improve their personal effectiveness.

Chapter 2: Communication

While great managers need not be highly charismatic or gifted speakers, they are able to deliver a persuasive message either in person or in print. They have also learned to process information and translate it into coherent messages that others can easily understand. They listen well, speak assertively and are alert to typical communication obstacles. This chapter focuses on models for creating and presenting persuasive messages, practicing active listening, and overcoming common barriers to effective communication.

Chapter 3: Problem Solving and Ethics

Critical thinking and decision making are always at the very top of any list of skills for great management. Moreover, it is impossible to be a great manager without a firm ethical foundation. This chapter presents proven problem-solving models and strategies for overcoming the most common traps and biases that often hinder effective decisions. The coverage of ethics focuses on the importance of a personal commitment to ethical behavior and on how to frame and make tough decisions in an ethically conscious and competent way.

II. Interpersonal Skills

Chapter 4: Motivation

Our belief is that motivation is not so much something you do as it is something you discover about others. Great managers discover what inspires those around them and use both intrinsic and extrinsic rewards to maximize that drive. This chapter includes diagnostic models for framing motivational challenges and a synthesis of the enormous volume of work that has explored how to create the most motivational of relationships and workplaces. We frame motivation as having three major sources: the employee, the manager, and the task or job. By leveraging this simple framework, students can learn to diagnose and attack motivation problems from a well-grounded systems perspective.

Chapter 5: Performance Management

Effective management is always tied to the performance of followers. Therefore, the selection, evaluation, and coaching of followers are all essential performance management skills. The best managers find and select good people to work with, rigorously evaluate their performance, and provide frequent feedback to help them continually improve. This chapter integrates the best human resource frameworks for selection and performance appraisal with the growing literature on feedback and development to provide a foundation for learners to become skilled coaches.

Chapter 6: Power and Influence

Effective managers are able to navigate within the political reality of their environments and utilize the power available to them to influence their superiors ("managing up") and to get things accomplished. The models and frameworks in this chapter are designed to help students understand the sources of power and how to increase their own influence and empower others. Specific tactics for building professionalism and establishing trust and respect in a management role are also highlighted.

Chapter 7: Leadership

In the words of Winston Churchill, leadership involves taking people in a direction they would not otherwise go. Great managers help people see what can be accomplished and provide the spark, inspiration, and direction to help them get there. An almost infinite number of leadership ideas are in print these days, but we believe effective leadership can be boiled down to a handful of key skills and behaviors, particularly for those thinking about or moving into their first leadership role. By utilizing such skills, which are based on both transactional and transformational leadership models (Full-Range Leadership), effective leaders can help move people in new and productive directions.

III. Group and Organizational Skills

Chapter 8: Team Effectiveness and Diversity

Teams are a paradox in that they have enormous potential but frequently flounder. Team members often face difficult issues such as how to deal with free-riders and how to energize a team that gets along well but has low performance. Further, in today's increasingly diverse workplace, teams often consist of members from very different backgrounds and professional experiences, accentuating the need for effective team skills. The models in this chapter are designed to help students understand the fundamental disciplines of high-performance teams, how to value and manage diversity in productive ways, and how to actively contribute as a productive team player.

Chapter 9: Conflict and Negotiation

Anything of importance in organizations today will inevitably involve some conflict. A reasonable level of conflict is desirable and healthy, but too little or too much can paralyze productive work. Great managers are skilled at recognizing and diagnosing conflict situations and managing them in productive ways. Particular emphasis in this chapter is given to the negotiation and mediation strategies useful to achieving win-win outcomes in conflicting situations.

Chapter 10: Making Change

In today's workplace, organizational change is not just a senior-level job but an increasingly necessary skill for people at all levels. Managers are frequently confronted with challenges that require them to be change agents or internal consultants. This chapter is designed to help students learn the conditions required for effective change and then understand how to overcome resistance to implement and support change initiatives.

Conclusion: Building High Performance Organizations and Great Places to Work

Since real management problems rarely fit neatly into a single skill category, the concluding chapter illustrates how skilled management translates into productive organizations. It is through engaging in the skills emphasized in this book that managers are able to lead companies toward the accomplishment of great outcomes resulting in high-performance organizations that are also healthy and engaging places to work. Examples of the organizational practices that stem from great management, and illustrations of those firms that are exemplary in executing those practices, are provided throughout.

Our Philosophy

We like to think that our "partners" in writing this book were the many students and practicing managers who have been in our courses, completed our surveys, and shared with us the ideas, tools, quotations, and "little gems" that helped them develop and refine their own managerial skills. Indeed, over the last few years we have asked our students to interview practicing managers and to find out how those managers would evaluate the management courses they took in college. In doing so, the managers frequently pointed out that courses focused a lot of attention on principles and concepts but, in their view, focused too little on relevant *skills*. They were challenged most by the "people problems" in their work, and yet felt their management education had not emphasized, nor adequately prepared them for, that component of their job.

For example, team effectiveness sounds like a very applied topic. But most textbook chapters so titled deal exclusively with the different types of teams, comparisons of individual and team decision-making, theories of team development and conflict, and so on. In most cases, the information is interesting and accurate, but it leaves students absolutely no better prepared to work effectively in a team. Similarly, chapters on motivation and leadership often trace the history of research and theory in those areas but end up not directly addressing the skills and behaviors a student needs to actually motivate others or lead a group or change project.

In fact, because of that lack of applied focus, we stopped using a textbook in our management courses years ago. But our customized reading packets always seemed fragmented and were not student favorites. So we wanted to create a learning package (the book being just one element) that we could use in our own courses. To work for us, the book would have to be one students would find engaging and that would meet our learning objectives for a skill-based management course.

So our charge was to create a book that would inform, illuminate, and inspire. We wanted to *inform* students of the best and most current knowledge about management skills. We wanted to *illuminate* those concepts with the most vivid and memorable examples and illustrations. And we wanted to *inspire* learners by capturing and conveying the challenge and excitement and even playfulness involved in managing and working with people.

Of course, we are hardly the first to recognize the importance of an applied skills-based approach, and, indeed, we owe a debt of gratitude to Dave Whetten, Kim Cameron, Steve Robbins, Phil Hunsaker, and others who have pioneered in this area.[1] Their prior work has influenced us significantly and helped direct us to several features that are central to our choice of content, organization, and features of this book.

> "Ideal management education should reorient its priorities and focus on skill training. A great deal is known about inculcating such skills, but the knowledge does not typically make its way into the business curriculum."
>
> —Henry Mintzberg,
> McGill University

---

[1] Robbins, S.P., & Hunsaker, P.L. (1996). *Training in interpersonal skills: Tips for managing people at work*. Upper Saddle Ridge, NJ: Pearson Prentice Hall. Hunsaker, P.L. (2001). *Training in management skills*. Upper Saddle Ridge, NJ: Pearson Prentice Hall. Robbins, S.P. (2003). *The truth about managing people*. Upper Saddle Ridge, NJ: Pearson Prentice Hall. Whetton, D.A., & Cameron, K.S. (2005).

Content and Organization of the Book

One question we were asked in the process of writing this book was why only 10 chapters and why these particular ones? First, it is only 10 chapters but hardly just 10 skills. For example, the chapter on *personal effectiveness* includes stress and time management and self-awareness, the *performance management* chapter deals with selection, appraisal, and feedback skills, managing the star performer and so on. Second, our goal was to include those skills, and *only* those skills, that might be labeled "mission critical." The book is relatively short in order to do a few things well, rather than attempt to superficially cover the waterfront.

In recent years we have also come to understand much more about how students actually consume textbook material. For example, in selecting the content for each chapter in this book, we did *not* start by looking at all the accumulated knowledge about that topic. Rather, we began with the key questions, problems, and challenges people face in, say, managing their time, communicating a persuasive message, overcoming resistance to change, or dealing with a problem team member, and then built the chapter around those problems.

Indeed, as we wrote each chapter, we adopted a position akin to editors of *Consumer Reports* magazine. That is, we tried to test assumptions about what students *really read and consume*, and what instructors *really use* from a textbook. And we asked ourselves: What do *we* want to use? What material connects with students? What are the best readings and exercises? What material do we rarely or never use?

In addition, our experience has been that management skills vary on a dimension that might be called "teachability." In this vein, we have often heard the question, "Can management (or leadership) really be taught?" (*The New Yorker* comic below is a clever takeoff on that). The appropriate answer is that management is not just one thing, but represents multiple dimensions of personal and interpersonal competence. It is certainly true that some very important managerial characteristics simply do not lend themselves to classroom instruction. They are instead products of genetics, years of experience, or acquired wisdom. On the other hand, the majority of management skills can unquestionably be strengthened and enhanced with the right models and practice. In this book we have sought to include mainly those skills we thought inexperienced students in traditional learning contexts could reasonably be expected to acquire and improve. Put simply, many management skills can be taught, but some skills are much more conducive to teaching and learning than others.

Another fundamental lesson is that the most "learner-centered" content is clearly not long sections of dense text. Rather, it is relatively short bites of information punctuated with examples, quotations, and illustrations. We have tried to adhere to that lesson in how we present material in this book. The order of the chapters is based on a hierarchy from personal to interpersonal to organizational skills, though we concede those concepts can overlap. Our hope is that instructors using this text will feel the chapters are sufficiently free-standing to use in any order they prefer.

Finally, in the course of writing this book we were often asked how our book would differ from popular-press books on management skills. In responding to that we are always quick to clarify that we certainly do not consider popular to be synonymous with *bad*. Indeed, there are some wonderful and useful popular works that we draw from in this book. We do, however, think the distinction between this book and many of the popular-press books on similar topics is pronounced and critically important. In our view, any book targeted to students in a university context must provide exposure to the "whys," that is, the conceptual

"To be honest—I'm not sure that accounting can be taught."

foundation of skills. We think this book's defining value is its practicality and usefulness but we contend that it is so *because* it is based on good theory and research, not because we *avoided* the important conceptual grounding.

Features of the Book

Manage *What?*

One of our favorite teaching colleagues is an accounting professor who enjoys pointing out to us that, while every organization has an accounting, information systems, and marketing department, he has *never* heard of a corporation that has a management department. He further chides us that having a degree in management invites the question, *"Management of what?"* In reality, he is a passionate advocate for improving the management skills of his accounting students and even pushed us to write this text. But his observation raises an important issue.

One of the legitimate criticisms of management courses and textbooks, even those with a stated skills focus, is they tend to be rather abstract about what is really being managed. There is often a curious lack of focus on the specifics of what managers are challenged to do, and on how great professionals might respond to those challenges.

With that in mind, we decided to open each chapter with a section we call Manage *What?* The Manage *What?* section consists of several fundamental and specific questions or challenges related to the skill focus of that chapter. For example, in the chapter on *team effectiveness* (Chapter 8), one scenario poses a challenge regarding how to deal with members who are not pulling their weight. In the *motivation* chapter (Chapter 4), one of the scenarios addresses how to diagnose and deal with a person who shows little desire to do better work, and so on. In the instructor's manual we offer critiques or debriefings of how a skilled manager might have proceeded on each of the questions/scenarios posed as a Manage *What?* Those critiques can be distributed to students at any point, though we like to make them available right in the midst of learning a chapter or sometimes as the key when we use the Manage *What?* scenarios as exam questions.

Taken together the Manage *What?* scenarios comprise a set of the most fundamental of management skills. They are hardly comprehensive—there is clearly much more to learn about management (and in the book) than how to handle just those scenarios—but the set is a concrete start toward isolating the mainstream and recurring things that great managers do well.

Our accounting professor friend likes to heighten student interest by pointing out how his course material is good preparation to become a CPA (certified public accountant). We would contend that an understanding and mastery of the Manage *What?* scenarios would likewise constitute a good step toward becoming a hypothetical CPM or "certified people manager." No such certification actually exists, but we have sought to include the recurring skills we would expect someone to demonstrate to be certified as a great manager if there were such an assessment. Those skills are the focus of the Manage *What?* scenarios.

Management Live

We doubt there is a management instructor alive who would deny the critical importance of illustration and examples in helping students develop the skills of great managers. So, in addition to liberally sprinkling examples into the text itself, we also have created a separate feature designed to highlight the most vivid and engaging illustrations, stories, and short cases we could find. We call

"Example is not the main thing in influencing others. It is the only thing."

—Albert Schweitzer

the section Management Live to capture the spirit of those illustrations, which is expressly to enliven the text and bring to life the concepts in ways meaningful and memorable to learners.

Learning theorists have begun using the term "stickiness" to describe learning stimuli that ultimately stay with learners, and that very much captures the spirit of this feature of the book. Our experience is that our students often recall specific cases and examples long after they have forgotten lectures and text. So our goal was to infuse each chapter with Management Live examples that catch attention, strike imagination, and really do "stick" with students as examples and guides.

True to our desire to maintain an evidence-based orientation, some Management Live examples are brief research summaries. To suggest that students want nothing to do with research would be both inaccurate and condescending. Indeed, our experience is that students *do* want to know the origins of what they are being taught—provided the research does help bring concepts to life. For example, a fascinating recent study found that monkeys will turn down very desirable food if they know that *other* fellow monkeys are getting even more desirable food. In our view, this is a terrific illustration of the intense power of equity perceptions, and something that is likely to stick with students in their study of motivational concepts.

Tool Kits

An irrefutable aspect of applying skills is to have a good set of tools. In our executive education work we have been struck by how much participants appreciate "takeaways" like self-assessments, good forms, quick checklists, and so on. Although we have never been particularly focused on such takeaways for our younger undergraduate students, it occurred to us such tools would be useful for *anyone* trying to improve his or her management skills.

We therefore include several Tool Kits at the end of each chapter. For example, the *performance management* chapter (Chapter 5) has Tool Kit boxes for developing behavioral interviews, choosing the right performance evaluation method, analyzing a performance problem and terminating or reassigning an employee, the *motivation* chapter (Chapter 4) has a quick guide to rewarding effectively, the *conflict* chapter (Chapter 9) includes a checklist for effective mediation, and so on. The Tool Kit boxes are presented at the conclusion of each chapter in a way that students can copy and actually make use of them now or in the future. Taken collectively, the Tool Kit boxes comprise something of a management skills manual. We make no claims that these are original or novel or provocative or anything fancy at all. However, they are the things that make their way on to managers' office doors, desktop frames, purse cards, and so on.

Ancillaries

It is hardly provocative to suggest that the ways students learn today have changed rather dramatically from a generation ago. Just as CDs and DVDs and iPods have changed the way music is delivered and consumed, so too has the Internet, wireless technology, and portable video capability transformed the way learners consume education. Moreover, learning researchers have long recognized that students have different learning styles: some favoring reading and reflection, and others engaged more by visual depictions and hands-on experience.

The instructional implication is that the most successful courses will be those that expose learners to *multiple* educational stimuli. With that in mind, we have supplemented this text with a set of supporting resources designed to facilitate the learning of management skills in multiple ways. Central to these support materials are our Web page and a sterling Instructor's Manual (special thanks to Carol Moore), which include:

- **Lecture and Discussion Aids** The Web page includes a full set of professionally crafted PowerPoint slides for each chapter of the text. The slides can be modified to include video clips from our Video Forum (see below) or any other customized material. Debriefings (solutions) to all Manage *What?* scenarios are also provided, as well as supplemental readings for students who may want to expand their knowledge and dig deeper into a particular topic.

- **Experiential Exercises** Management skills lend themselves to experiential education, and we have included a select set of exercises (with relevant support material, keys, and scoring) with each chapter. The exercises include popular staples of management and organizational behavior classes (e.g., group survival decision tasks, prisoner's dilemma, negotiation simulation), as well as an in-basket exercise and group discussion exercises commonly used in corporate assessment centers and behavioral evaluations of managers. While there has been a proliferation of exercises in recent years, our focus was to target those exercises that have been time-tested and have a track record of success in the classroom or corporate training contexts.

- **Video Forum** We would particularly call your attention to an exciting ancillary resource we call our Video Forum. While we are all familiar with the power of video to entertain, it is also a formidable teaching tool. Indeed, based on our own collective experience using video to illustrate management skill topics, we would contend that, if a picture is worth a thousand words, the moving image of video might be worth a million. Recent generations of students are particularly engaged with electronic media illustrations and examples.

"Happiness is coming to class and seeing the video projector set up."

—Charlie Brown

As we note throughout the text, even those who have mastered management theories often have trouble *implementing* them. Video is uniquely suited to show the subtleties, the emotions, and the context of behavior, and management is a subject matter particularly amenable to its use. Put simply, video can show management *as it really is*.

In our Video Forum we have identified many different kinds of video clips from many different sources. Some are from well-known feature films (*Dead Poets Society, Apollo 13*), others from news programs ("60 Minutes," "Primetime") and others from popular TV shows ("Lost," "The Office," "Seinfeld"). Some could be considered classic illustrations likely familiar to experienced instructors, while others are more representative of popular culture and dare we say "edgy". Our goal was to identify a broad and diverse array of options that capture the excitement, tension, and humor of management as only video can, but to let each instructor select those that fit his or her particular style and preference. Toward that end, a brief description and its relation to the text concepts accompany each identified clip.

To give credit where it is due, the idea of the Video Forum stemmed from the pioneering work of Bob Marx, Joe Champoux, Steve Meisel and other colleagues from the Organizational Behavior Teaching Conference.[2] They have led the quest for the most powerful and lasting illustrations of management concepts on film. Several of the best clips in our Video Forum resource section were first identified and class-tested by Bob and his colleagues of master teachers from the OBTC.

---

[2] Marx, R., Jick, T.D., & Frost, P.J. (1991). *Management live: The video book.* Englewood Cliffs, NJ: Prentice Hall. Champoux, J.E. (2005). *Our feature presentation: Organizational behavior.* Mason, OH: Southwestern Publishing.

Perhaps the most exciting feature of our Video Forum is that it is an ongoing work in progress. Our intent is to regularly update the collection, and we are eager to discover and include new clips (fully credited) that others have found to be particularly powerful illustrations of the concepts in this text. Please contact us to "talk video" regarding clips you think bring management skills to life.

In summary, we have tried to translate our own experiences in the classroom into a package of learning stimuli that will both appeal to and challenge young students of management. Although sometimes characterized as being elementary or common sensical, great management is neither common nor easy, and the existence of so many ineffective managers and toxic organizations attests to that. We firmly believe that many aspects of management can be learned but it takes a focus on skills and a more concerted effort to bring those skills to life than many of our traditional learning materials provide. Our hope is that this text and set of ancillaries will be useful in that regard – but we consider it all a work in progress. We actively invite your input as we all try to foster better-managed organizations and healthy and engaging places to work.

Acknowledgments

We'd also like to thank our many reviewers for their helpful feedback and suggestions. Our gratitude goes out to the following:

Dr. Richard Allen
University of Tennessee-Chattanooga

Joseph S. Anderson
Northern Arizona University

Charles E. Beck
University of Colorado-Colorado Springs

Mary Jo Boehms
Jackson State Community College

Dana C. D'Angelo
Drexel University

David Elloy
Gonzaga University

David J Glew
University of North Carolina-Wilmington

Barry A. Gold
Pace University

Patricia Hedberg
University of St. Thomas

Diane Holtzman
Richard Stockton College of New Jersey

Deborah Erdos Knapp
Kent State University

Michael Mazzarese
New York University

Arlyn Melcher
Southern Illinois University-Carbondale

Tanya Menon
University of Chicago

Stephen Peters
Clarkson College

Thomas Reading
Ivy Tech Community College

Brian D. Schmoldt
Madison Area Technical College

Christina Stamper
Western Michigan University

Fred A. Ware Jr.
Valdosta State University

Special thanks also go to Indiana University colleagues: Michael Metzger, for his contribution to our coverage of decision-making biases in Chapter 3. Brian Blume, Jason Pierce, Ross Peterson-Veatch, and Halden Williams, for their sterling and creative assistance on the ancillaries and other elements of the book. Carolyn Wiethoff, for her continuing collegial inspiration and substantive contributions to our coverage of diversity, communication, and conflict management. Keith Dayton, for his devotion to the cause of teaching management skills to young people, his willingness to put many of our ideas to test in his own courses, and his indomitable spirit.

Lastly, we would also like to thank Ed Miles of Georgia State University for his work on negotiations.

Finally, we would like to recognize John Weimeister and Chipper Scheid of McGraw-Hill who have shepherded this project competently, persistently, and patiently (sort of) and made it far better than it otherwise would have been.

List of Manage *What?* Scenarios and Tool Kits

The Manage *What?* Scenarios

The Tool Kits

PART ONE Personal Skills

PART TWO Interpersonal Skills

PART THREE Group and Organizational Skills

Management Skills for Career Success

The goal of this text is to focus on those skills, and only those skills, which are critical for any manager's success. These skills range from inherently personal competencies like stress management and decision making, to interpersonal capabilities such as motivation and performance management, to even broader organizational skill-sets dealing with teams and conflict and change management. Not only are all the skills covered in this text critical for future success, mastering the skill will have immediate impact on your performance.

What Do Managers Manage Anyway?

Every chapter opens with the *Manage What?* feature consisting of several fundamental and specific questions or challenges related to the skill focus of the chapter. These scenarios and questions are great for class discussions or written assignments and focus on recurring skills that are fundamental to any manager's success.

Manage **What**?

1. Making a Personal Improvement

You have now been in your first job for two years and are itching to get promoted as quickly as possible. In your last performance review, however, your boss identified time management as a weakness. You have never felt that your time management was superb, but you did not know that weakness might affect your career advancement. In any case, you are now committed to improving your management of time. However, realizing that old habits die hard and that accomplishing personal change is very difficult, you know you will have to do more than just "hope" to change.

So how would you most intelligently proceed to improve yourself? What would you do first? What strategies would give you the best chance of actually improving your time management skills significantly?

2. Describing Yourself and Your Style: Expanding Your Self-Awareness

"Tell us about yourself" is the first question asked in your introductory meeting with the four people who will be reporting to you in your new managerial job. You naturally struggle with where to start. You have been a great individual contributor for four years, but everyone has told you that managing people is a very different responsibility. And the thing that really scares you is you have heard sarcastic joking around the firm about a colleague who got promoted to manager and how with that promotion the firm "lost a great analyst and found a terrible manager."

So what should you tell the group about who you are and how you will manage? What would be most relevant and useful? Based on your own self-assessment, what particular characteristics would you highlight? What should you be doing to know yourself even better so you can answer this question more confidently in the future? What would it be like to be managed by you?

Written to be **learner centered**

Along with examples sprinkled liberally within the text, Management Live boxes highlight the most vivid and engaging illustrations, stories, and short cases to enliven the text and bring to life the concepts in ways meaningful and memorable to learners.

Management Live 1.1

Where Does Talent Really Come From?

Some fascinating findings are emerging from a group of researchers trying to answer an important and age-old question: When someone is very good at doing something, what is it that actually makes him or her good? This stream of research work, led by Anders Ericsson, Conradi Eminent Scholar and Professor of Psychology at Florida State University is collectively known as the Expert Performance Movement. Ericsson's first experiment, nearly 30 years ago, involved memory—training a person to hear and then repeat a random series of numbers.

Ericsson's study refuted the commonly held notion that cognitive skills, particularly those like memory, are mostly genetically determined (for example, "he was born with a photographic memory"). As he notes, "With the first subject, after about 20 hours of training, his digit span had risen from 7 to 20. He just kept improving, and after about 200 hours of training he had risen to over 80 numbers."

Based on that and later research showing memory is *not* genetically determined, Ericsson concludes that the act of memorizing is more a function of dedicated commitment and practice than a genetic gift. In other words, whatever innate differences two people may exhibit in their abilities, those differences are overwhelmed by how well each person has engaged in *deliberate practice*. Deliberate practice is not just simply repeating a task—playing a C-minor scale 100 times, for instance, or hitting tennis serves until your shoulder pops out of its socket. Rather, it involves setting specific goals, obtaining immediate feedback, and concentrating as much on technique as on outcome.

Ericsson and his colleagues have since taken to studying expert performers in a wide range of pursuits, including soccer, golf, surgery, piano playing, Scrabble, writing, chess, software design, stock picking, and darts. Based on that work they make the startling assertion that the trait we commonly call talent is important but generally *overrated*.

Ericsson's research further suggests that when it comes to choosing a life path, you should do what you love—because if you don't love it, you are unlikely to work hard enough to get very good. Most people naturally don't like to do things they aren't "good" at. So they often give up, telling themselves they simply don't possess the talent for math or skiing or the violin. But what they really lack is the desire to be good and to undertake the deliberate practice that would make them better.

Source: Adapted from Dubner, S.J., & S.D. Levitt. (2006, May 7). "A Star is Made." *New York Times Magazine*, p. 24.

TABLE 1.2	Five Behavior-Focused Strategies to Improve Self-Management[9]

1. **Self-Observation/Exploration**: Observe and collect information about the specific behaviors you have targeted for change.
2. **Self-Set Goals**: Determine what more effective behavior is (often by observing effective models) and set specific goals for your own behaviors.
3. **Management of Cues**: Organize your work environment to assist you in performing the behaviors you want to change.
4. **Positive Self-Talk and Rehearsal**: Go over the behavior in your head and imagine successful application. Actually practice the new behavior at available opportunities and seek feedback.
5. **Self-Reward and Punishment**: Provide yourself with personally valued rewards that are linked to performing desirable behaviors or with punishments linked to undesirable behaviors.

Tables and Figures succinctly and effectively illustrate key chapter concepts.

Took Kits, available at the end of each chapter, offer "takeaways" for students - self-assessments, forms, and quick checklists.

[This text provides an] *Even mix of concept, examples and application/action. —In academic circles from years past, authors seemed to believe the more theory and cases the better. But, today, it is about tell them what they need to know, show them how to do it and then let them experience the material. Students will like the text. This text, as indicated, covers everything, but it is application based. Enough theory and concept to move you forward, but clear application so that you can move forward sooner.*

—Stephen Peters,
Clarkson College

Personal Effectivness Tool Kits

Tool Kit 1.1   Action Planning

Goals are not enough. You must create a plan of action that details exactly how you accomplish your goals. The action planning process, although relatively simple, is an essential step in personally achieving your goals. Every goal you set should have a corresponding action plan. The critical elements of that plan include the following:

- **A goal statement.** This is your SMART goal. Consistent with that acronym it needs to be specific, measurable, attainable, realtisic, and time-bound.
- **Action steps.** How will you accomplish your goal?
- **Deadlines.** For each action step listed, set a corresponding deadline or target date.
- **Required resources.** For each action step, list the required resources needed.
- **People involved.** For each action step, list people who should be involved and indicate their type of involvement.
- **Evaluation plan.** A plan for determining how you will know you are on track toward your goal and whether or not your goal has been achieved.

This text is based on the best models and frameworks generated by researchers over the last fifty years. These evidence-based frameworks can help you diagnose situations and proceed more thoughtfully.

TABLE 5.2	Selection Method Effectiveness			
Selection Method (Ranked from Best to Worst for Validity)		**Fairness**	**Feasibility**	**Face Validity**
1. Work Sample		High	Medium	High
2. Cognitive Ability Test		Low	High	Medium
3. Structured Interview		Medium	High	High
4. Job Knowledge Test		High	High	High
5. Assessment Center Evaluation		Medium	Low	High
6. Biographical Data*		Medium	Medium	Low
6. Personality Assessments*		Medium	High	Low
8. Reference Checks		High	High	High
9. Training and Experience Points		High	High	High
10. Years of Education		High	High	High
11. Graphology (Handwriting Analysis)		Low	Medium	Low
12. Flip of a Coin		Low	High	Low

* Tied for sixth place in rank order.

How Do I Think Critically and Analytically?

Cognitive ability is the capacity to learn and process cognitive information such as reading comprehension, mathematical patterns, and spatial patterns. SATs, ACTs, LSATs, GMATs, and similar aptitude tests are designed to test your cognitive abilities. While there is contention about the nature and role of cognitive ability, the evidence is compelling that it does predict a variety of important outcomes, and a number of studies have linked it positively to managerial job performance.[18] Even the National Football League requires a measure of cognitive ability (Wonderlic Personnel Test) from all players eligible for the annual draft.

The focus of this text is exactly what I've been looking for . . . It is more comprehensive, includes relevant research evidence for its propositions and the theories explained, and includes a truly relevant set of experiential exercises and examples.

—Deborah Erdos Knapp, Ph.D., Kent State University

Instructor and Student Supplements

Instructor's Manual (in print, ISBN: 0072920157)

The Instructor's Manual (prepared by Carol F. Moore, California State University-East Bay) is a comprehensive resource for the instructor. For each chapter in the text, you will find a chapter overview, learning objectives, a chapter/class outline, key student questions and answers, and answers to the "Manage What" cases found in the text. Additional exercises not found in the text are also included, along with instructions for facilitating them, and suggestions on where they most effectively fall in the class outline.

Testbank (in print, ISBN: 0072920157)

The Testbank (prepared by Trudy Somers, Pfeifer University) includes true/false, multiple choice, and essay questions, with a portion of the multiple choice as "scenario-based" questions. We've also aligned our Testbank with new AACSB guidelines, tagging each question according to its knowledge and skills areas. Designations aligning questions with Learning Objectives, boxes and features also exist, with over 1,000 questions to choose from.

PowerPoint® Presentation Slides

The PowerPoint® Presentation slides (prepared by Brad Cox, Midlands Technical College) consist of two types of presentations – **Basic** and **Premium**—to give instructors the flexibility to tailor their presentations to their class needs. The **Basic** set follows in outline format the major topics and points of the chapter. The **Premium** set has an expanded outline, including photos and figures from the text, links to additional information on the web, and multiple-choice like discussion questions that can be used in a Classroom Performance System.

All three Instructor Supplements above can be found on the Instructor's Resource CD-Rom ISBN: 0072920122

Video Forum

A wealth of video information is available in both the Instructor's Manual and on the Online Learning Center at www.mhhe.com/baldwin1e. Suggestions for clips from popular video and TV shows which can be obtained by the professor/student from iTunes or DVD are offered in the Instructor's Manual, along with hints on how to incorporate them into the classroom. A selection from news venues like NBC, PBS, and BusinessWeek TV is also available on DVD (ISBN: 0072920130), along with a streaming collection that can be found on the Online

Learning Center. Check our Information Center at www.mhhe.com/baldwin1e for continual updates to programs available.

Online Learning Center www.mhhe.com/baldwin1e

With all of the possibilities that technology can offer, we've organized our Online Learning Center for ease of use for both Instructor and Student. Password-protected instructor materials can be found in the **Instructor Center,** including additional resources for classroom exercises, additional videos, and notes on how to incorporate all into the classroom. The **Group and Video Resource Manual** and the **Manager's HotSeat Online** (detailed below) are both linked for accessibility and convenience. The **Student Center** has chapter quizzes, interactive self-assessment exercises, additional video, podcasts, and much more. Find out more information by going to www.mhhe.com/baldwin1e and clicking on the **Information Center.**

The Manager's HotSeat Online www.mhhe.com/MHS

In today's workplace, managers are confronted daily with issues like ethics, diversity, working in teams, and the virtual workplace. The Manager's HotSeat videos allow students to watch as 15 real managers apply their years of experience to confront these issues.

Students assume the role of the manager as they watch the video and answer multiple choice questions that pop up forcing them to make decisions on the spot. They learn from the manager's mistakes and successes, and then do a report critiquing the manager's approach by defending their reasoning. Reports can be emailed or printed out for credit. These video 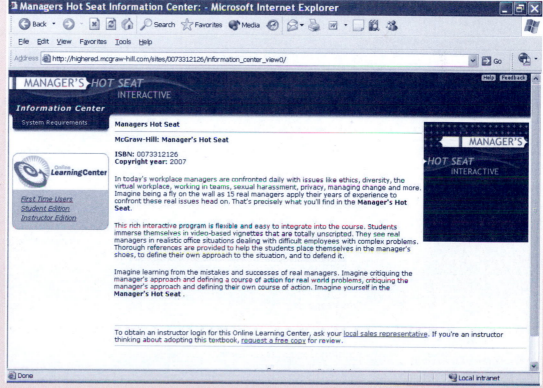 segments are a powerful tool for your course that truly immerses your students in the learning experience. **Ask your local McGraw-Hill sales representative how to gain access to the Manager's HotSeat Online for your course.**

Group and Video Resource Manual: An Instructor's Guide to an Active Classroom (in print 0073044342 or online at www.mhhe.com/mobmanual)

Created for instructors, this manual contains everything needed to successfully integrate activities into the classroom. It includes a menu of items to use as teaching tools in class. All of our self-assessment exercises, Test Your Knowledge quizzes, group exercises, and Manager's Hot Seat exercises are located in this one manual along with teaching notes and Power-Point slides to use in class. Group exercises include everything you would need to use the exercise in class—handouts, figures, etc.

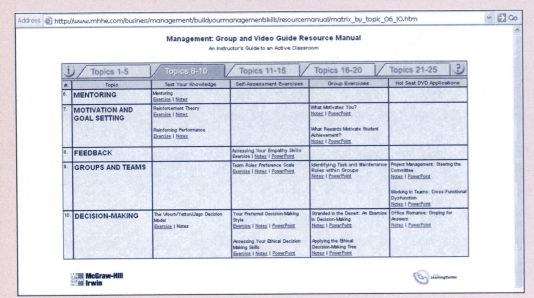

This manual is organized into 25 topics like ethics, decision-making, change, and leadership for easy inclusion in your lecture. A matrix is included at the front of the manual that references each resource by topic. Students access all of the exercises and self-assessments on their textbook's Web site. The Manager's Hot Seat exercises are located online at www.mhhe.com/MHS.

Brief Contents

Contents

CHAPTER 2 Communication

CHAPTER 3 Problem Solving and Ethics

PART TWO   Interpersonal Skills

CHAPTER 4 Motivation

CHAPTER 5 Performance Management

CHAPTER 6 Power and Influence

CHAPTER 7 Leadership

PART THREE Group and Organizational Skills

CHAPTER 8 Team Effectiveness and Diversity

CHAPTER 9 Conflict and Negotiation

CHAPTER 10 Making Change

CONCLUSION Building High Performance Organizatons and Great Places to Work

Intro
The Importance and Challenge of Learning Management Skills

The idea for this book was born out of three observations we shared from our collective experience of teaching management courses to college students and practicing managers. First, from John D. Rockefeller and Andrew Carnegie a century ago, to Herb Kelleher and John Chambers today, our most influential business leaders have always recognized that management *skills*—not just knowledge—are critically important to the success of people and organizations. Yet such skills still often do not get the educational attention they deserve. Second, the reason that management skills create a competitive advantage for people and organizations is that, though they may seem relatively straightforward, they remain in short supply. Third, most existing books and courses on management are not well suited to helping students—particularly those with little work experience or organizational context—develop and refine the skills they really need to become great managers. We elaborate on these observations below.

The Hard Case for "Soft" Skills

In recent years, a number of different labels have emerged to categorize the skills of great managers.[1] Among the more popular are emotional intelligence, interpersonal competence, social intelligence, or just plain "people skills." We like all of those, and although distinctions have been suggested, we see them as largely interchangeable. In this book, we use the broader label of *management skills*. While clearly inclusive of people skills, that label also encompasses a fuller range of personal, interpersonal, and organizational knowledge and competence.

Although such skills are essential for those wanting to be great managers, our experience is that these skills are also critical to those wanting virtually any type of career that involves substantial interaction with people (e.g., nurse, sales representative, engineer). Moreover, while such skills are certainly necessary for *future* success, we would also contend they should have an impact on your performance *right now*. Indeed, this book is written primarily for the person with limited, if any, managerial experience.

By whatever name, the research evidence is now overwhelming that management skills matter, and they matter in several important ways. First, management skills matter to career success. A variety of studies have shown that management or interpersonal competencies are the key determinant of organizational advancement and achievement. In his popular books on emotional intelligence, Daniel Goleman reports the results of research that suggest as much as 90 percent of the difference between outstanding performers and average performers is

"Take away my people, but leave my factory, and soon grass will grow on the factory floor. Take away my factory, but leave my people, and soon we will have a new and better factory."

—Andrew Carnegie

"I will pay more for the ability to handle people than for any other talent under the sun."

—John D. Rockefeller

"We have the most technical of companies, but one key to success here is still people skills."

—John Chambers, president and CEO, Cisco Systems

"The most important single ingredient in the formula for success at Southwest Airlines is knowing how to get along with people."

—Herb Kelleher, former CEO, Southwest Airlines

their application of the skills that comprise emotional intelligence.[2] One compelling study at PepsiCo found that sales managers with well-developed people skills outperformed yearly revenue targets by 15 to 20 percent while those with underdeveloped skills underperformed their targets by about the same amount.[3]

Even in situations where technical ability and IQ would seem naturally predominant, such as the science labs at University of California Berkeley and formerly Bell Labs (now known as Lucent Technologies), intriguing studies have found that it is still the "softer" managerial skills that distinguish star scientists from average performers.[4] Do not misunderstand; technical, financial, strategic and operational competencies are, of course, important elements in job success and career advancement. But a steadily increasing body of research is showing that what ultimately distinguishes the good from the great achievers is the development and refinement of their *management* skills.

Management skills are also the key elements in what makes for healthy and desirable workplaces. Indeed, the Great Place To Work Institute (GPTWI), which

Management Live

The Best Places to Work Are Also the Best Performing Companies

Independent financial analysts have studied the financial performance of the "100 Best" companies beginning with the publication of the book, *The 100 Best Companies to Work For in America* (by Robert Levering and Milton Moskowitz, 1994), and on an ongoing basis to accompany each of the "100 Best Companies" lists with *Fortune* since that list's inception in 1998. Using various profitability indicators, these data illustrate the extent to which the publicly traded 100 Best Companies consistently outperform major stock indices over the 10-year periods preceding the publication of the 100 Best lists. It is notable that those companies selected for the 100 Best list generally spend far more on employee benefits and services than their counterparts—that is, it is often *expensive* to be a best place to work. However, the data clearly support that the expense is worthwhile because people ultimately engage, work productively, and lift company performance.

100 Best Companies to Work For vs. Overall Stock Market 1998–2005

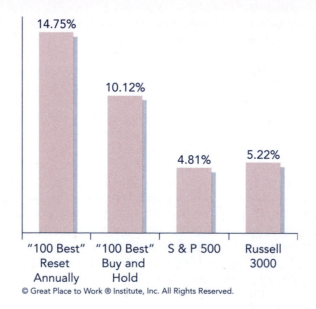

conducts the research on the nation's best employers for *Fortune* magazine's "100 Best Companies to Work for in America" annual article, has found that the single most important element of every great workplace is the trust between employees and management.[5] Such trust stems from the managers' skill level in those organizations. GPTWI research has found that workplaces with great managers receive more qualified job applications for open positions, experience a lower level of turnover, have reduced health care costs, enjoy higher levels of customer satisfaction, and induce greater customer loyalty. Evidence from the GPTWI studies and elsewhere is helping us fully appreciate realities such as: (1) people do not leave companies, they leave managers, (2) people generally manage the way they were managed, and (3) people's work performance and satisfaction is more heavily influenced by their immediate manager than any other factor.

Perhaps most intriguingly, management skills matter significantly to the financial success of organizations. Indeed, a growing collection of studies, including hundreds of different firms from every major industry in the United States, supports the notion that the effectiveness of people management in a firm is a major determinant of organizational performance. For example, studies by Jeffrey Pfeffer, Mark Huselid, and their colleagues have found that firms with effective people management have lower employee turnover, higher profitability, and higher shareholder value.[6] In a comprehensive meta-analytic study (that is, a statistical summary of other studies) of 198,514 employees across 7,939 business units, Joseph Harter and his colleagues found strong correlations between employee engagement and satisfaction, at the business unit level, and a composite index of business-unit performance that included turnover, customer loyalty, and financial success.[7] Similarly, other extensive research projects by Gallup Company and GPTWI have found strong relationships between people management effectiveness and measures of employee satisfaction, employee retention, productivity, and profitability.[8]

While you may not be familiar with the research evidence, we hope none of this comes as a huge shock to you. Anyone would rather have a good manager than an incompetent one. You probably know of someone who is technically or analytically skilled but has few "people skills," or is de-motivating, or cannot "get along well with others." Few of us would refute that it takes a competent manager to lead groups who go the extra mile required to achieve highly satisfied customers, and so on.

But, having taught management courses for many years, what we find is not typically intuitive to most aspiring managers is that good management is so essential to good business. The same skills that will advance your career also happen to be the skills that make an organization a great place to work. And the best places to work also happen to be the highest performing firms. That's the good news. The bad news is that the reason management skills create a competitive advantage for people and organizations is because they are hard to master and are therefore still rare.

Management Skills Are Hard To Do

Unfortunately, as important as they may be, management skills have proven stubbornly and curiously hard to develop. Thus, great managers are still the exception, not the rule. For example, studies by the Center for Creative Leadership and others have found the single most common cause of career derailment is a lack of management skills.[9] Similarly, some estimates indicate that nearly 50 percent of people moved into management roles essentially fail.[10] In other rather depressing surveys, over half of employees have reported they were less than satisfied with

"If people are our most valuable asset, I say we sell them."
— Jerry Seinfeld

their current manager and many report that the worst aspect of their job is their immediate boss.[11] Some even rated their manager as "remarkably bad." Other studies have found that less than 25 percent of managers regularly engage in the basics of good management (such as providing clear expectations and goals, and giving regular feedback).[12] Given the clear importance of management skills, how can that be?

"Then I made the leap from skilled labor to unskilled management."

© *The New Yorker* Collection 2001 Lee Cullum from cartoonbank.com. All Rights Reserved.

The answer lies in the disconnect between *knowing* and *doing*. For most management skills, the conceptual rules are relatively easy to know and understand. Most twelve-year olds could be taught to pass a test on the general rules or guidelines of the skills that comprise great management. The real challenge is to actually execute them. For example, listing the rules of effective behavior in a team is relatively easy. However, actually joining a team in a competitive business situation and contributing in a way that adds real value to that team is an entirely different matter. Similarly, the fundamental elements of models of motivation are elementary. But trying to create a culture that motivates peoples' best efforts is extraordinarily complex.

We chose the subtitle of this book—"What Great Managers Know and Do"—because it takes both knowledge ("know *that*") and application practice ("know *how*") to master a skill. Successful application of management skills is more than just following a cookbook list of sequential behaviors and is much more complicated than developing skills such as those associated with a trade (say, welding) or a sport (hitting a golf ball). That is because management skills are (1) linked to a more complex knowledge base than other types of skills and (2) inherently connected to interaction with other (frequently unpredictable) people. A standardized approach to welding or hitting golf balls or baking a cake may be feasible, but no standardized approach to managing human beings is possible.[13]

Nonetheless, one of the most encouraging elements of management skills is that they *can* be improved—we have seen it happen countless times. But you do not master the skills simply via hope, intuition, or common sense. Rather, it requires conscious, persistent effort and practice. At the same time, practice without the necessary conceptual foundation is sterile and ignores the need for flexibility and adaptation to different situations. In short, any serious attempt to develop management skills must involve a dose of both conceptual learning and behavioral practice. It requires intentional study and a skill-oriented and problem-based approach.[14]

The Keys to Learning Skills

The goal of purely cognitive or content-oriented learning is understanding. In contrast, the goal of skill development is application. To make the shift to application, however, you must focus on the actual problems and challenges people face and decide which different skills would be appropriate in specific situations. Moreover, it requires you have a conceptual foundation or set of frameworks based on research evidence and not just opinion, anecdote, or management war stories from one particular company or situation. In that vein, to become a great manager you will have to learn to become something of a "bullfighter," able to sort out the many myths and misconceptions frequently espoused about what is and is not effective management. Finally, managerial skill learning absolutely requires you get beyond just reading and study. To really learn and master skills you will have to actively engage in practice and actually *experience* those skills in your life and work. Below we briefly highlight each of those keys to skill learning.

"It is often not what we don't know that gets us into trouble. It is what we know that just ain't so."

— Will Rogers

Start Your Learning with a Problem

This skill-learning essential comes from a compelling approach known as problem-based learning. Simply put, problem-based learning is based on the assumption that we are most inclined to learn when we really need to know something. Thus, the best educational experiences generally happen when we are "hungry at the buffet of learning." Countless examples from our lives confirm this assumption. We tend to be more attentive in our golf lessons if we are preparing for a big match, we carefully read the manual right before our driving test, or we keep our accounting notes because we know we will be taking the CPA exam shortly.

So, one key to learning management skills is to focus primarily on the most important "need to know" questions related to different skill dimensions. For example, with respect to effective teamwork, our experience is that managers struggle with whether or not to use a team in certain situations, how to deal with problem team members, how to more effectively brainstorm and make good team decisions, and so on. In contrast, they do *not* wonder about the different types of teams or the chronological history of teams. Those are topics for understanding, without an associated skill application, and so not critical to skill learning.

Another key is to be intently on the lookout for what is *not* true or *not really* a characteristic of great management. Indeed, we often refer to the need for good students of management to become bullfighters because there is so much unsupported and unsubstantiated "bull" put forth. Indeed, research has shown that, in practice, great management is not just masterfully doing the right things, but often just *deftly avoiding what "not to do."*[15] In every chapter this book contains tables and examples of myths or common mistakes to help students recognize some of the more common and insidious "bull" that is out there.

"Education is not filling a bucket, but lighting a fire."

— William Butler Yeats

"People learn what they need to know."

—Linda Hill, author of *Becoming a Manager*

Seek Evidence-Based Frameworks

It may strike you as unusual that, in a skills-oriented book, we do not avoid discussions of research evidence and theories. In fact, we *sought out* every good research study we could find. That may seem like a direct contradiction of a problem-based approach described above, but actually it is central to it. Many students these days are unfortunately led to believe that theoretical means irrelevant or not practical or just simply boring. But in reality, to paraphrase the great sociologist Kurt Lewin, nothing is as practical as a good theory. Our goal is to have a practical skills development text based in the best and most recent theory and research. Short of that, any material becomes just someone's opinion or cannot rightly be generalized to other situations.

"There is no one best way, but all ways are not equally effective."

—Jay Galbraith, *on the essence of contingency theory*

Studies in many fields have explored how experts go about attacking particular challenges or problems in practice. What those studies have generally found is that such experts internalize their own "theories in use" or what we term frameworks. That is, they do not have a rote way to act in every situation. However, they do habitually evoke ways of framing problems and considering options. So a great deal of our focus in designing this book was to include frameworks that are conceptually sound but also practical in application.

Management and interpersonal situations are too complex and unpredictable to ever try to specify the single best way to act. But over the last 50 years researchers have generated terrific sets of frameworks for managing time, communicating persuasively, setting goals, motivating others, giving effective feedback, leading change efforts, and so on. Those frameworks can help you diagnose situations and proceed more thoughtfully. Hopefully, the frameworks will stick with you and help you know where to start, what information to get, and what not to do as you face new and different situations.

Getting Beyond a Book

"Management skills are part taught and part 'caught.'"

—Unknown

A good book can give you the conceptual background and frameworks essential to lasting skill development. At the same time, skills simply cannot be learned and mastered with book learning and classroom study alone. With that in mind, you will need to seek opportunities to practice and apply the skills wherever such opportunities present themselves. Studies by the Center for Creative Leadership and others have made a compelling case that some significant elements of effective management are "lessons from experience" and cannot really be taught; that is, they have to be learned in the context of actual interpersonal situations or a leadership role.[16]

"I never let my schooling interfere with my education."

— Mark Twain

One recent study we conducted found corporate recruiters rightly value college-student extracurricular experience because it leads to skill development beyond conceptual knowledge.[17] Simply put, if the lessons in the book are not applied outside the classroom, little or no progress can be achieved. Our hope is the lessons of this book will even carry over into your life activities. Now let's get on with the journey toward management skill development!

CHAPTER

1

Personal Effectiveness

"If you want to be a great manager, there is a lot to learn. But the most fundamental lesson is that it starts with your own personal effectiveness. Know yourself. Listen to feedback. Build on your strengths. Do what you say you will do. Manage your time. If we can just find managers who do those things well, the rest tends to take care of itself."

— Beth Bledsoe, Director of Strategic Initiatives, Ingersoll Rand University

Manage *What*?

1. Making a Personal Improvement

You have been in your first job for two years and are itching to get promoted as quickly as possible. In your last performance review, however, your boss identified time management as a weakness. You have never felt that your time management was superb, but you did not know that weakness might affect your career advancement. In any case, you are now committed to improving your management of time. However, realizing that old habits die hard and that accomplishing personal change is very difficult, you know you will have to do more than just "hope" to change.

So how would you most intelligently proceed to improve yourself? What would you do first? What strategies would give you the best chance of actually improving your time management skills significantly?

2. Describing Yourself and Your Style: Expanding Your Self-Awareness

"Tell us about yourself" is the first question asked in your introductory meeting with the four people who will be reporting to you in your new managerial job. You naturally struggle with where to start. You have been a great individual contributor for four years, but everyone has told you that managing people is a very different responsibility. And the thing that really scares you is you have heard sarcastic joking around the firm about a colleague who got promoted to manager and how with that promotion the firm "lost a great analyst and found a terrible manager."

So what should you tell the group about who you are and how you will manage? What would be most relevant and useful? Based on your own self-assessment, what particular characteristics would you highlight? What should you be doing to know yourself even better so you can answer this question more confidently in the future? What would it be like to be managed by you?

3. Getting a Priority Done under Stress

You have been in a management role for two years and find yourself absolutely overwhelmed. While you feel as if you are working hard most every hour of the day, you are frustrated with your inability to get all your priority work done. You have begun to work much longer hours and are experiencing a great deal of stress and a loss of balance in your life. There are so many distractions during the day that you generally find it difficult to get started on bigger projects. Now you have a really important project due and have already missed one deadline. You feel guilty about missing that deadline, but you feel so tired and stressed you aren't sure how you're going to keep from slipping further behind in your most important work.

How would you define the problem here? How might you deal with the many time robbers and distractions that keep you from working on the big project? What specific strategies might you use? Are there common traps to avoid? What should you do right away?

LEARNING OBJECTIVES

1. Use behavior-focused strategies to improve self-management.
2. Assess your managerial profile on seven dimensions: cognitive ability, emotional intelligence, cultural intelligence, personality traits, personality preferences, personal values, and career orientation.
3. Analyze self-assessments, looking for patterns and consistency, to identify managerial strengths and weaknesses.
4. Manage stress by improving physical and psychological hardiness.
5. Apply time management techniques to get priorities done under stress.

Learning and Personal Improvement

Personal Effectiveness: The Foundation of Great Management

Effective management starts from the inside. Indeed, when people are asked to describe great managers, it is remarkable how often they give personal, rather than interpersonal, or organizational, descriptions. Put simply, only those who can first manage themselves will ultimately be able to effectively manage others. Personal effectiveness is the foundation of great management, and the skills presented in the chapters that follow this one all stem from a base of personal excellence.

Although many elements comprise personal effectiveness, our focus is on *actionable* knowledge and behaviors—things you can actively learn and do to improve your personal competence. No one is born a great manager, nor becomes one overnight. So the most fundamental aspect of personal competence is to know yourself and to have a clear understanding of how you learn new skills and motivate yourself to improve your capability.

"Hope is not a personal improvement strategy."
—Anonymous

We start with models of learning and self-management. The remaining sections of the chapter are devoted to self-awareness and stress and time management. Note that these very skill sets are the ones most likely to challenge young managers and are often where the greatest deficiencies are observed.[1] Great management is often as much about not acting on misconceptions, and avoiding what not to do, as it is about expertly pursuing a course of action.[2] With that in mind, Myths 1.1 contains five of the more persistent myths of personal effectiveness.

"Success is not the result of spontaneous combustion. You have to set yourself on fire."
—Unknown

Learning How to Learn

Much has been written about the high failure rates of people trying to learn and change. For example, a tiny percentage of people actually keep their New Year's resolutions. The vast majority of people who set out to "get in shape" are back to being overweight in a couple of months. Most of those who say, "this is the year I am going to get organized," find that it ultimately was, in fact, not the year. The problem with most personal improvement attempts is they are mostly wishful thinking with far too little understanding of how personal improvement really happens. That is, most everyone *hopes* to improve, or *wishes* they could enhance

"The will to win is vastly overrated as a means of doing so. What is more important is the will to practice and the means to execute."
—Bob Knight, Basketball Hall of Fame Coach

MYTHS 1.1 | **Myths of Personal Effectiveness**

Management learning comes with age and experience. Unfortunately, that simply is not true. Learning is hard work and comes from a conscious and persistent desire to attend to effective models, learn and retain what they do, and practice new behaviors consistently.

We know ourselves. In fact, a number of revealing research studies have shown that the gap between how we perceive ourselves and how others perceive us is often significant. These gaps, many of which we are blind to, frequently lead to management problems or failure.[3] True self-awareness is the foundation of personal effectiveness.

Growth opportunities lie solely in our weaknesses. We succeed because of what we do well. However, it is common to become so focused on improving our weak areas and gaps that we neglect our strengths. Personal development of new skills is important, but you should also spend time clarifying what it is you do well and then try to position yourself in situations where you can leverage your strengths to excel.

It's not me, it's them! If you learn one management "truth" it should be this: You can never fully control the behavior of others, but you *do* have control over your own behavior. The best way to change others is to first change *yourself*.

The best managers are hyper-organized and workaholics. Effective time management is *not* primarily about efficiency or being a time nut, but rather enabling us to reduce stress, achieve balance, and do the things we really want to do. The goal is to work smarter not harder.

FIGURE 1.1

Social Learning Theory

Personal factors include a person's internal mental processes such as motivation, attention, self-regulation, and self-efficacy. *Behavior* is the person's response or action. *Environment* includes the physical and social environment surrounding an individual. It includes reinforcement and punishment contingencies and models.

their effectiveness. However, far too few actually know and discipline themselves to do what is necessary to learn new skills.

The most powerful and useful framework for thinking about personal improvement in management skills comes from the work of Albert Bandura, and his **social learning theory.**[4] Bandura's theory suggests that learning of any new behavior is the result of three main factors—the person, the environment, and the behavior—and they all influence each other. Behavior is not simply the result of the environment and the person, just as the environment is not simply the result of the person and the behavior. This mutual influence is referred to as **reciprocal determinism** and is at the root of social learning theory. This is because the environment provides important models of behavior from which we learn. A model of social learning theory can be seen in Figure 1.1.

Although this concept may sound a little abstract, the principles of social learning theory are exceptionally practical and have been applied to help foster personal change in a wide variety of settings including counseling, acting, addictive behaviors, and athletics. One reason social learning has been so influential is it refutes widely held notions that people only learn through their own personal experience of rewards and consequences. For example, traditional conceptions of learning suggest you would learn that a stove burns you only by *actually touching* that stove yourself. Bandura suggests that, in fact, most learning is actually done

Management Live 1.1

Where Does Talent Really Come From?

Some fascinating findings are emerging from a group of researchers trying to answer an important and age-old question: When someone is very good at doing something, what is it that actually makes him or her good? This stream of research work, led by Anders Ericsson, Conradi Eminent Scholar and Professor of Psychology at Florida State University is collectively known as the Expert Performance Movement. Ericsson's first experiment, nearly 30 years ago, involved memory—training a person to hear and then repeat a random series of numbers.

Ericsson's study refuted the commonly held notion that cognitive skills, particularly those like memory, are mostly genetically determined (for example, "he was born with a photographic memory"). As he notes, "With the first subject, after about 20 hours of training, his digit span had risen from 7 to 20. He just kept improving, and after about 200 hours of training he had risen to over 80 numbers."

Based on that and later research showing memory is *not* genetically determined, Ericsson concludes that the act of memorizing is more a function of dedicated commitment and practice than a genetic gift. In other words, whatever innate differences two people may exhibit in their abilities, those differences are overwhelmed by how well each person has engaged in *deliberate practice*. Deliberate practice is not just simply repeating a task—playing a C-minor scale 100 times, for instance, or hitting tennis serves until your shoulder pops out of its socket. Rather, it involves setting specific goals, obtaining immediate feedback, and concentrating as much on technique as on outcome.

Ericsson and his colleagues have since taken to studying expert performers in a wide range of pursuits, including soccer, golf, surgery, piano playing, Scrabble, writing, chess, software design, stock picking, and darts. Based on that work they make the startling assertion that the trait we commonly call talent is important but generally *overrated*.

Ericsson's research further suggests that when it comes to choosing a life path, you should do what you love—because if you don't love it, you are unlikely to work hard enough to get very good. Most people naturally don't like to do things they aren't "good" at. So they often give up, telling themselves they simply don't possess the talent for math or skiing or the violin. But what they really lack is the desire to be good and to undertake the deliberate practice that would make them better.

Source: Adapted from Dubner, S.J., & S.D. Levitt. (2006, May 7). "A Star is Made." *New York Times Magazine,* p. 24.

through observation and **modeling** of the behaviors of others. That is, most people learn the stove burns by watching the behavior of others (perhaps seeing them burned or actively avoiding it). This simple phenomenon helps explains why so many people who work for ineffective managers often become poor managers themselves; we often manage the way in which we were managed.

A second reason social learning notions are particularly appropriate for management skills is because there is such a big disconnect between knowing and doing. For most management skills, the conceptual rules are relatively easy to know and understand. Most teenagers could be taught to pass a test on the general rules or guidelines of the skills that comprise great management. But the real challenge is to actually execute them.

Fortunately, one of the most encouraging elements of management skills is that it is possible to improve your execution of such skills—but not simply via intuition or common sense. Rather, improvement requires conscious, persistent effort and practice. Bandura outlines four critical components required to learn through observation, and these are the key building blocks of the most successful management training methods used in organizations today.[5] These components are attention, retention, reproduction, and motivation.

> *"In theory, there is no difference between theory and practice. But, in practice, there is."*
> —Jan L.A. van de Snepscheut

Attention

If you want to learn anything, you have to pay specific attention. Thus, the first challenge of learning is to focus. Anything that puts a damper on attention will decrease your learning comprehension. If you are unfocused, nervous, or distracted by other things, you will learn less well. Thus, a critical step in learning new skills is to find the right models and devote undivided attention to them. If you do not make what you want to learn a top priority and give the subject ample attention, you are unlikely to succeed.

In addition, it is critical you isolate as specifically as possible the behaviors you hope to learn. This approach may seem like common sense, but it is frequently violated. Many try to learn too much or change too many things at once.

Retention

You must be able to understand and remember what you have observed. Coding what we observe into words, labels, or images results in better retention than simply observing. If you can relate your observations to a theory or framework, and understand *why* what you observed was effective or ineffective, you have a better chance of retrieving it when you need it. This is where the study of written models and frameworks can be most useful. That is, just observing an effective speech, decision process, or team meeting is a good start. But real learning—the kind you can ultimately transfer to your own situations—comes from understanding the underlying principles that made the behaviors effective and being able to recall and translate those principles when appropriate.

Reproduction

Perhaps the most critical contribution of social learning theory to developing management skills is it highlights the importance of practice, or actual demonstration, of a skill. That is, you cannot learn management by just observing, reading, or understanding the concept. Rather, you have to translate the images or descriptions into actual behavior. Research shows that our abilities improve even when we just imagine ourselves performing![6] Many athletes, for example, imagine their performance in their mind's eye prior to actually competing. However, the more we can actually reproduce the skill we aim to learn, in the actual context where the skill will be applied, the more likely we are to add that skill to our repertoire.

> *"You play like you practice."*
> —Vince Lombardi, Football Hall of Fame Coach

Another critical point with respect to reproduction is that the saying "practice makes perfect" is only a half-truth. "Practice with *feedback* makes perfect" or at least enables people to learn. Feedback is essential for learning or developing any kind of skill.

Motivation

Finally, even with careful attention, retention, reproduction, and feedback, you still won't successfully acquire a new skill unless you are motivated to persist and stay with it. Without some conscious reason to keep up the effort required to learn a new skill, or change a habit, you are doomed to fail. Your motivation may derive from past reinforcement, promised reinforcements (incentives) that you can imagine, or vicarious reinforcement—seeing and recalling the models you observe being reinforced. Of course, you may also use punishments for *failure* to achieve your learning goals. However, Bandura has found that punishment does not work as well as reinforcement and, in fact, has a tendency to backfire on us.

"The way to get started is to quit talking and begin doing."
—Walt Disney

Bandura's principles may seem intuitive to most of us, but observational learning is neither easy nor self-evident. If it were easy to just observe and mimic the effective behavior of others, many more people would be successful in improving themselves. Rather, it takes disciplined self-management to apply the principles Bandura has proposed. In Table 1.1, we present a common example of breakdowns in learning, using the example of improving interviewing skills.

TABLE 1.1   **What's Keeping Max from Learning to Interview Better?**

Max, who is soon graduating from college, has a strong record of achievement (high grades and a good extracurricular profile) but is struggling with the recruiting process. After several interviews, he has failed to make it to the next round a single time, and, feeling discouraged, he has asked some of his interviewers for comments. The three who were willing to respond all essentially said he did not "interview well." So Max hopes to improve his interviewing skills. Overlaying the principles of social learning and self-management can help illuminate Max's challenge and common traps that occur.

Attention. Max needs to address at least two issues to be consistent with effective social learning. First, he needs to set aside time to practice his interviewing skills in the midst of many competing time demands. He is likely to feel his classes, part-time job, and social life take precedence and thus may well not devote enough time to improve his interviewing skills—a classic case where hoping will supercede a real learning strategy.

Second, Max needs to understand more specifically what he is doing or *not doing* in his interviews that is leading to poor outcomes. Without some specific understanding of his weaknesses (and relative strengths), he is destined to flounder in trying to determine how to improve. Unfortunately, that information may well be hard to come by in this case and he may need some mock interviews to tease it out.

Retention. Max needs to build an understanding of what makes for an impressive interview performance. Learning how to illustrate his background and accomplishments using the STAR model outlined in Chapter 5 would likely be a good step.

Max would also benefit from observing models with *recognizable excellence* in what he is trying to improve. In these cases, we often see people make the mistake of attempting to learn from friends or relying on anecdotal evidence from well-intentioned, but non-expert, sources.

Reproduction. Max needs practice accompanied by feedback on that practice. Practice should be treated like an actual interview. The more elements Max can re-create, the better his learning will be. A great deal of time needs to be spent dedicated to rehearsal, feedback, and more rehearsal. Mock interviews would seem to be essential here but are often awkward or difficult to arrange and therefore not utilized.

Motivation. Max needs to decide how important improving his interview skills are to him and if he is willing to dedicate the time to changing. He needs the discipline to avoid taking shortcuts and saying "good enough" to really make a long-term, lasting change. He should find ways to reinforce himself for devoting the time and should certainly celebrate any success on the interview front.

A Model of Self-Management

Using Bandura's work as a base, Charles Manz and his colleagues have created a simple and practical framework for self-management.[7] They define **self-management** as a process of modifying one's own behavior by systematically altering how we arrange different cues in our world, how we think about what we hope to change, and how we attach behavioral consequences to our actions. The framework takes into account that personal change is rarely a discrete, single event but rather a process with multiple influences. The underlying theme is we all have the ability to change our immediate worlds in ways that will help us learn new things and behave in desirable ways.

The framework provides a means of avoiding some of the most common "hope vs. action" traps and of putting Bandura's principles in practice. It includes strategies we directly impose on ourselves to influence our own behavior and those whereby we attempt to alter our external world to help affect our behavioral change. While Manz and colleagues have presented their model in a variety of ways and with different labels (for example, self-management, self-leadership, super leadership),[8] we have condensed it here to the five essential elements most effective in facilitating personal improvement (see Table 1.2).

Note that this self-management framework has been successfully applied in many different contexts including drug therapy, weight loss, health care, theater, and athletics. For example, all successful golf training is based on the elements of this framework. As you progress further in this book, you will see that the effective behaviors of self-management are also entirely consistent with what great managers do when it comes to coaching and motivating *others*. This should not be surprising because, as we note above, effective people managers are first successful in managing themselves.

"Nothing will work unless you do."

—Maya Angelou

"Quality improvement is not just an institutional assignment; it is a daily personal priority obligation."

—Bob Galvin, Motorola

Self-Observation/Exploration

You can't induce or recognize a change in behavior until you have some information about what you currently are doing. **Self-observation** involves determining when, why, and under what conditions you currently use certain behaviors. For example, if your personal improvement challenge is to improve your grades via more focused study time, it is important to ask when and where you find you study best now? How many hours are you currently devoting to each subject? Which courses are you doing the best in? And so on.

"Not everything that is faced can be changed, but nothing can be changed until it is faced."

—James Baldwin

TABLE 1.2	Five Behavior-Focused Strategies to Improve Self-Management[9]

1. **Self-Observation/Exploration**: Observe and collect information about the specific behaviors you have targeted for change.

2. **Self-Set Goals**: Determine what more effective behavior is (often by observing effective models) and set specific goals for your own behaviors.

3. **Management of Cues**: Organize your work environment to assist you in performing the behaviors you want to change.

4. **Positive Self-Talk and Rehearsal**: Go over the behavior in your head and imagine successful application. Actually practice the new behavior at available opportunities and seek feedback.

5. **Self-Reward and Punishment**: Provide yourself with personally valued rewards that are linked to performing desirable behaviors or with punishments linked to undesirable behaviors.

Self-observations provide the building blocks for managing ourselves. The best self-observation strategies involve actually recording your observations and keeping close tabs on your behavior, both before you begin changes and after. This recording can be as simple as counting how many minutes you are late to meetings to more complex diaries of your behavior. Learning a new skill or habit often requires we also change or *unlearn* other dysfunctional habits, adding significantly to the challenge.

In that vein, a critical aspect of self-observation is to learn from mistakes or failed efforts. While we all have a tendency to be defensive, look to blame others, or ignore failure, viewing mistakes as learning opportunities builds a foundation for further learning. Mistakes can prompt us to look inward and evaluate our limitations and shortcomings. Mistakes are only problems if you repeat them or do not learn from them. Indeed, if you are not making mistakes, it is worth asking whether you are stretching yourself in your job and taking any developmental risks. Great managers make a lot of mistakes, but those mistakes are seen as "productive failures" and are rarely made twice.[10]

"Success consists of going from failure to failure without loss of enthusiasm."

—Winston Churchill

Self-Set Improvement Goals

The first task of setting goals is to determine what your desired outcome or effective behaviors look like. The best goals often derive from attention to effective models. Some of the things that influence our attention involve characteristics of the model or learning stimuli. We are more likely to adopt a modeled behavior if the model is similar to the observer (more like us) and has admired status and if the behavior has functional value (gets us something we want). If the model is attractive or prestigious or appears to be particularly competent, we pay more attention.

So one tactic for the studying challenge would be to observe the study habits of highly successful students to see if you might emulate some of their behaviors. Self-set goals need to address long-range pursuits and short-run objectives along the way. The shorter-range goals should be consistent with the long-range goals for maximum consistency. The process takes effort, and although our goals are likely to change, it is important we try to have current goals for our immediate efforts. Goal setting is so fundamental to great management that we reinforce it throughout this book.

"The people who succeed are the efficient few. They are the few who have the ambition and the willpower to develop themselves."

—Herbert Casson

Studies have shown that setting goals works because:

1. In committing to a goal, a person devotes attention toward goal-relevant activities and away from goal-irrelevant activities.
2. Goals energize people. Challenging goals lead to higher effort than easy goals.
3. Goals affect persistence. High goals prolong effort, and tight deadlines lead to more rapid work pace than loose deadlines.
4. Goals motivate people to use their knowledge to help them attain the goal and to discover the knowledge needed to obtain it.[11]

The best goals are characterized by the acronym **SMART,** which represents specific, measurable, attainable, relevant, and time-bound. SMART goals make for smarter learners.[12]

Management of Cues

Taking your lead from your self-observations and goals, you can begin to modify your environment. The objective is to organize your world to assist you in performing the behaviors you want to change. For example, if you are trying to quit smoking and improve your health, put away the ashtrays, drink tea instead of coffee, and take the ice cream out of the freezer and replace it with low-fat substitutes. If you are trying to study more on Thursday nights, get out of the apartment when everyone is heading to social engagements (and enticing you to come along), and go to the library or some quiet spot.

A related strategy is to create reminders and attention focusers you will notice and act on. A sticky note on the refrigerator reminding you of your weight loss goal, or a screen saver or text message to yourself about a forthcoming test, can provide a cue that will help you focus on an important improvement objective.

Positive Self-Talk and Rehearsal

Positive self-talk and rehearsal are applications of the social learning principle of *reproduction*. Search for opportunities to practice new behavior in the most realistic situations you can find. Basketball players know that just shooting 100 free throws will not simulate the pressure of shooting one at the end of a close game. So the best shooters find ways to practice under conditions that mirror those pressurized conditions (for example, team running for missed free throws, everyone lined up around the key trying to distract the shooter, simulated crowd noise). Some people treat their jobs as games (like salespeople) by trying out new techniques and seeing how well they work. Whatever the context, you must practice and rehearse any new skill for it to ultimately become part of your repertoire.

"One must learn by doing the thing, for though you think you know it, you have no certainty until you try."
—Sophocles

Further, the use of **positive self-talk** is extremely important. If you have ever repeatedly said to yourself, "I know I can do this," before attempting a difficult task, you were practicing a proven technique of self-management. The idea is to create a frame of mind that energizes your self-confidence and gets you beyond self-defeating and negative feelings that can accompany learning difficult tasks. Just as managers and coaches work on team morale and motivation, individuals can affect their behavior by getting "pumped up" and self-motivated.

"Whether you think you can or you think you can't, you are right."
—Henry Ford

Self-Reward and Punishment

Although no manager would deny the importance of **reward** and **punishment** for influencing employee behavior, the concept is strangely neglected when we think of ourselves. The truth is we can profoundly induce our actions by rewarding ourselves for desirable behavior. For example, "I will go out to dinner on Saturday night if I accomplish my goal. I will do paperwork instead if I do not." You simply arrange to reward yourself when you adhere to your plan and possibly punish yourself when you do not.

Generally speaking, it is better to use self-reward, than self-punishment. Celebrate your victories and don't dwell on your failures. A great deal of learning research has found that punishment does not work as well as reinforcement.[13] However, there may be times when the most powerful or immediate incentive for you may be a punishment, and in such cases it may make an appropriate disincentive. Do not, however, punish yourself for slips or lapses. Changing habits and learning new things is never a straight path, and, as the tool-kit on relapse prevention at the end of this chapter illustrates, expecting and preparing for those inevitable lapses will be more fruitful.[14]

Putting It All into Practice

The self-management model represents the best methodology currently available for facilitating personal improvement. The basic notions are simple. To really get beyond mere hope and make a sustainable personal improvement requires you to:

1. Know where you are currently.
2. Set SMART goals for your change.

3. Arrange your world so it focuses your attention and reminds you of your improvement plan and goals.

4. Stay positive and rehearse the desired behaviors at every opportunity.

5. Create your own rewards for accomplishing your targets.

Since many of us already use some of these strategies, and they seem simple enough, why are most people not more effective at self-management? It is mostly because we often use them either ineffectively, or inconsistently. That is, the piecemeal use of these strategies tends to make them relatively ineffective. Thinking through your own experiences, consider how often you see (or practice) one of these strategies in isolation, but how rarely you see them together.

For instance, many people have started down a path of weight loss by setting a goal and monitoring their eating behavior—a good start. But more often than not, they do not consistently manage their cues, practice new habits of grocery shopping and ordering while dining out, or create reinforcements powerful enough to sustain their efforts. So they start well, with much hope, but do not have the strategies in place to persist until they have succeeded. Engaging in one strategy, while not engaging in the others, is much like ordering a Diet Coke to go with a big greasy cheeseburger and super-sized fries.

We suspect that much here has validated what you already knew and are doing to some extent. Hopefully, though, it can make it easier to more systematically go about learning and managing yourself in an increasingly turbulent and hostile world.

"We all have dreams. But in order to make dreams into reality, it takes an awful lot of determination, dedication, self-discipline, and effort."

—Jesse Owens, Olympic Gold Medalist

Building Self-Awareness

Self-Awareness: The Key to Successful Learning and Growth

The models of learning and self-management described above point to the critical importance of self-awareness for those attempting to accelerate their managerial learning and to become more personally effective. The best managers are not only consistently seeking feedback to know themselves better and what areas they need to improve, but also to isolate their personal strengths and preferences so they can best position themselves for success. Self-awareness is essential to learning and growth in a management role because it forms the basis by which we learn about ourselves and how we differ from others.

Individual Differences and Their Importance

"Success in the new economy comes to those who know themselves—their strengths, their values, and how they best perform."

—Peter Drucker

There is perhaps no more obvious, yet curiously neglected, truth than "people are different." Recognizing our own differences is important because they impact how we react and behave in different situations.

Every popular magazine these days seems to include some sort of self-assessment of an intriguing individual difference. Headlines claim you can learn some hidden truth about yourself by answering a few questions and then scoring yourself with the provided scoring guide. But since your "cool quotient", "hottie index" or "marriage potential" are not of great concern in managerial environments (at least hopefully not), what, specifically, should the self-aware manager know?

Of course, people differ in an infinite number of ways. From a managerial performance perspective, however, the two important categories of difference are: (1) ability and (2) personality (which includes values and motives).[15] **Ability** can be simply defined as what a person is capable of doing.[16] This "capacity to do" leads some people to be able to dunk a basketball, calculate complex math in their heads, or interpret abstract patterns very quickly. Abilities come in many dimensions and include cognitive ability, physical ability, and emotional ability (now often referred to as emotional intelligence and an area of study in which there's been a recent explosion of interest).

Personality represents the pattern of relatively enduring ways in which a person thinks, acts, and behaves.[17] Personality is determined both by nature (genetics) and nurture (situational factors) and tends to represent our "dominant" or "natural" behavior. There is not a good or bad personality profile. Although some personality characteristics have been associated more frequently with some occupations and interests, no personality combination limits you from types of occupations you might enjoy or determines your destiny.

How you behave at any given time is an interaction of your personality and your environment. This interaction accounts for why we often behave differently at home than we might at work or school. For example, your dominant personality trait may be one of **introversion,** yet in order to perform well on your job you have to "turn it on" to talk with clients and customers, that is, demonstrate **extraversion.** Sometimes the situation or environment has much more to do with how we behave than does our personality. It is a fundamental error to assume that behavior is solely a function of one's personality since the environment will always play a role as well.

Assessment of managerial ability and personality has become increasingly popular in both organizational and educational contexts. It can be intriguing, even fun, to see where we stand on different scales (for example, who would not be curious about your own love quotient?), and some form of assessment is essential if we are to clarify our own abilities and personality traits, values, and preferences. However, our experience suggests assessments are most useful when an individual has a defined *need to know*. Put another way, the most fruitful assessment process is ideally a research project where you are the focus of the research.

With that in mind, we sought to identify the set of fundamental personal questions most important to managerial and interpersonal self-awareness, and to identify assessment tools that can help you begin your personal inquiry into those questions. We boldly call our seven elements of self-awareness the Essential Managerial Assessment Profile. Other aspects of self-awareness (e.g., learning style, tolerance of ambiguity, conflict style, leadership behavior) are relevant and important, and we include measures of some in your instructor's supplemental materials and on the Internet. If you become more self-aware on these seven aspects in an informed and thoughtful way, you will have a firm baseline of self-knowledge.

Ultimately, we want you to be able to answer the question "Tell me about yourself" in a way that will have meaning and relevance to those you might work with or manage. The goal is not simply to describe your favorite characteristics, but to know how your abilities and personality may impact your behavior and performance. Table 1.3 categorizes and defines the seven dimensions, identifies leading assessment tools associated with each dimension, and briefly highlights the positive implications of higher self-knowledge on each dimension.

How Do I Think Critically and Analytically?

Cognitive ability is the capacity to learn and process cognitive information such as reading comprehension, mathematical patterns, and spatial patterns. SATs, ACTs, LSATs, GMATs, and similar aptitude tests are designed to test your cognitive abilities. While there is contention about the nature and role of cognitive ability, the evidence is compelling that it does predict a variety of important

"All facts are friendly."
—Unknown

TABLE 1.3 | **The Essential Managerial Assessment Profile**

Self-Awareness Dimension	Ability, Personality, or Preference?	Examples of Commonly Used Assessment Tools	Implication
Cognitive Ability (critical and analytical thinking)	**Ability** to recognize quantitative and verbal patterns quickly and accurately. Includes the ability to acquire knowledge.	• Watson-Glaser Critical Thinking Test • Wonderlic Personnel Test	Is cognitive ability a strength or an area to supplement with the help of others? What types of jobs and industries suit my analytical ability?
Emotional Intelligence	**Ability** to accurately recognize and understand emotions in others and self and to use emotional information productively.	• MSCEIT	Do I understand and use emotion to make effective decisions? Can I relate to people well because I appropriately read their emotional states?
Cultural Intelligence	**Ability** to function effectively in the context of differences.	• Cultural Quotient Scale (CQS)	Am I aware of important cultural differences? Do I understand and act in ways that will value those differences and create stronger relationships?
Personality Traits	Primary **personality** characteristics that remain relatively stable over one's life.	• Big Five Inventory	What are my dominant personality traits? How do I maximize my fit to best utilize my personality?
Personality Preferences (temperament)	**Preference** for direction of energy, decision-making, information acquisition, and orientation to the outer world	• Myers-Briggs Type Indicator	How do I like to work with others and process information? What do I look for in others to complement my preferences? How will I best interact in different team combinations?
Personal Values	**Preference** for desirable ends or goals and the process for attaining them.	• Rokeach Values Checklist • Hogan MPV Scale	What do I value most and seek in others? What will I not bend or compromise on? What to me is non-negotiable?
Career Orientation	**Preference** for particular types of work environment and occupations.	• Holland Occupational Preference Scale	What occupational elements are most important to me? With what types of people will I thrive?

outcomes, and a number of studies have linked it positively to managerial job performance.[18] Even the National Football League requires a measure of cognitive ability (Wonderlic Personnel Test) from all players eligible for the annual draft.

A key attribute of cognitive ability assessments is they are timed. Many of us may be able to solve that pesky word problem if given all day, but fewer can solve it in 30 seconds or less. It is partly this "speed" in cognitive processing that sets people apart in their cognitive abilities. As you might expect, that speed is extremely useful for complex jobs such as NASA engineers who must make difficult decisions quickly using less than perfect data.

How Well Do I Understand and Use Emotion?

Emotional abilities, often called **emotional intelligence,** refer to the ability to accurately identify emotions (in self and others) as well as understand and manage those emotions successfully. For example, how many times have you been upset with someone but couldn't figure out why? Have you have ever misinterpreted someone's gestures, facial expressions, or tone of voice? Have you ever been moved by an effective speaker who seemed to capture your emotions?

People differ significantly in their ability to deal effectively with their emotional states, and researchers have shown that this ability is important to job success.[19] Unlike cognitive ability, many emotional abilities can be learned. For example, with some training you can learn to more accurately recognize emotions from others' facial expressions or learn to more quickly and accurately identify the emotions you personally are experiencing. Thus, learning about your ability to manage your own and others' emotions can benefit you.

According to researchers David Caruso and Peter Salovey, the aspects presented in Table 1.4 can be used as a blueprint for becoming more emotionally intelligent. Research has demonstrated that individuals who are better able to manage their own and others' emotions are more likely to be perceived as leaders, show higher job performance, and cope with emotional stress on the job (for example, customer complaints).[20]

TABLE 1.4 | **Key Aspects of Emotional Intelligence[21]**

- **Be able to accurately identify and express yours and others feelings**. This is critical if you expect to maintain strong relationships at work.

- **Get in the right mood.** Believe it or not, your mood has a large impact on your effectiveness. Managers who are better able to maintain positive moods are often perceived by their employees as leaders and are more optimistic about the future. Knowing what puts you in a positive mood and seeking out those opportunities is important.

- **Predict the emotional future.** When you use emotional information ("I'm experiencing fear right now"), you can then decide what to do with it in the future. If, however, you're angry, for example, and you don't know why, then you can't figure out how to get past the anger in the future.

- **Do it with feeling.** When you use your emotions productively, you'll be better able to make the right decision about your behavior. For example, if you know a certain action will bring remorse and sadness when others find out, you may reconsider that decision.[22]

Cultural Intelligence

Cultural intelligence represents a person's capability to function effectively in situations characterized by cultural diversity.[23] Cultural intelligence has been positively associated with certain types of job performance and a person's ability to perform well in culturally diverse work groups, navigate cross-cultural interactions, and adapt successfully to multi-cultural situations (e.g., overseas assignments).

For example, if someone from a culture in which a limp hand is offered as a symbol of humility and respect (as with some Native American groups) is introduced to a group of American males who judge another male's character by the firmness of the handshake, each will walk away with an invalid impression of the other. Similarly, in some Asian cultures, silence is a way of showing respect and being polite. In American contexts, however, people can be deemed unassertive or otherwise misjudged based on their silence.[24]

Linn Van Dyne and Soon Ang have identified cultural intelligence (or CQ for Cultural Quotient) as consisting of four different sub-skills, which we briefly describe below.[25]

- **CQ-Strategy** is how a person interprets and understands intercultural experiences. This includes strategizing before an intercultural encounter, checking assumptions during an encounter, and adjusting perceptions when actual experiences differ from expectations.

- **CQ-Knowledge** is a person's understanding of how cultures are similar and different. It includes knowledge about economic and legal systems, norms for social interaction, religious beliefs, aesthetic values, and language in different cultures. Often, this type of knowledge is best gained through a combination of formal study and travel (with the best examples being the ability to actually live in different cultures for some period of time).

- **CQ-Motivation** is a person's interest in experiencing other cultures and interacting with people from different cultures. CQ-Motivation can be considered the amount of energy applied toward learning about and functioning in cross-cultural situations. It includes the intrinsic value people place on culturally diverse interactions as well as their sense of confidence that they can function effectively in settings characterized by cultural diversity.

- **CQ-Behavior** is a person's capability to modify their own verbal and nonverbal behavior so it is appropriate for different cultures. It includes having a flexible set of responses that are appropriate in a variety of situations and having the ability to alter verbal and nonverbal behavior based on the people and characteristics of a particular setting. A great example of low CQ-Behavior was observed firsthand in an airport shuttle at Paris' Charles de Gaulle International Airport. An American was complaining very loudly to anyone in earshot, "How are we supposed to find anything? The signs are in French."

Working effectively with those who are different is a core competency that will be in demand more in the coming years than ever before. Self-awareness of your own cultural intelligence can be useful in several ways. If you are already relatively strong in CQ, you may wish to actively pursue international opportunities or organizational initiatives that include diverse cultural representatives. However, if you know your CQ is not particularly strong, you can set a goal to plan more carefully before intercultural interactions. You can remind yourself to look for ways in which multicultural interactions differ from what you expect. You can read about other cultures, attend events that highlight other cultures, ask questions, and travel with a curious and open mind.

What Are My Dominant Personality Traits?

For the past 50 years, personality researchers have been looking to answer the following question: Is there a relatively simple yet meaningful way to compare different people on their personality characteristics? Fortunately, after decades of research examining nearly 18,000 descriptors of personality, researchers have synthesized a clear and straightforward definition of personality called the Big Five (because there are only five key factors in the model). More specifically, a person's personality can be organized in a hierarchy with five basic and universal dimensions or factors at the top of that hierarchy. The **Big Five** dimensions are (1) extraversion, (2) emotional stability, (3) agreeableness, (4) conscientiousness, and (5) openness to experience (Table 1.5). All five dimensions have been shown to be consistent across cultures and nationalities.

"I always wanted to be somebody. Now I realize I should have been a little more specific."

—Lily Tomlin

Each of the Big Five factors is composed of various specific traits, and all general and specific traits represent a continuum along which a certain aspect or dimension of personality can be placed. For example, a person can be high, low, average, or anywhere in between on the continuum for each trait.

Recent research has shown some traits may be more or less important for certain jobs. For example, conscientiousness seems to be important for most all jobs. Emotional stability and extraversion play an important role in salesperson success. Agreeableness is connected with successful customer service performance, and openness to experience is related to success in managerial training positions.[26] Personality traits are only one influence on performance, however. For example, although being introverted may put a sales rep at some initial disadvantage, that characteristic by no means guarantees failure. Other behaviors (product knowledge, follow-through, and professionalism) also play a strong role in that person's job success.

In this vein, many wonder to what degree you can change your personality traits. Generally speaking, a person's personality assessment on the Big Five continuum will not change much over time. However, human beings are adaptive and, with some effort, can learn to mimic the behaviors associated with a particular trait. For example, if you are less agreeable and want to be more agreeable (because, say, you want to project warmth to potential customers), you can learn to behave in a warm way to customers (smiling, speaking in a soothing voice). This doesn't mean you've come to possess a high degree of agreeableness, but have learned to use more energy and conscious thought to act agreeably relative to those for whom agreeableness comes naturally.

TABLE 1.5 **Hierarchy of Personality: Big Five Description**

The Big Five Factors of Personality	Extraversion	Emotional stability	Agreeableness	Conscientiousness	Openness to experience
Specific Traits Related to the Big Five	• Positive emotions • Gregariousness • Warmth	• Anxiety • Self-consciousness • Vulnerability	• Trust • Straight-forwardness • Tender-mindedness	• Competence • Order • Self-Discipline	• Fantasy • Actions • Ideas

What Are My Personality Preferences?

German psychologist Carl Jung noted that if carefully observed, people's behavior is rarely random but reflects a stable pattern of personal preferences. That is, our behavior is a function of how we *prefer* to navigate our world. Our **preferences** are not traits—deeply rooted dominant characteristics—but rather choices we make (mostly unconsciously) to navigate the world. In that sense, preference is much like handedness: you can certainly write with your opposite, less preferred hand, but it takes a lot more energy and concentration to do so![27]

Jung's work is frequently applied to career management and development. One of the most interesting findings related to his work is that large percentages of people in certain occupations tend to share similar preferences. For example, roughly 80 percent of professors prefer introversion over extraversion. That is most likely because academic professions require a great deal of solitary work such as writing research papers, preparing lectures, and grading student work, thereby attracting those with such preferences. Ministers and salespeople and attorneys largely cluster into certain preference sets as well. That doesn't mean a person can't succeed in a career where she is not in the mainstream preference category, but rather she would likely have to commit more energy to the daily tasks where others might handle those same tasks more naturally.

Jung found people's preferences varied according to four major preference areas:[28]

1. **Extraversion (E) or Introversion (I)** Jung describes this as one's preferred direction of energy and attention. People with a preference for extraversion prefer to direct their attention and energy toward people and things, whereas introversion preferences usually involve directing energy inwards toward ideas and concepts. If after a hard day's work, you'd prefer to go out with friends versus a quiet spot away from others, you likely have a strong preference for extraversion.

2. **Sensing (S) or Intuition (N)** These preferences vary according to one's preferred method of taking in or seeking information. Sensing preferences lead people to desire actual data and well-documented experience and to pay attention to detail. Intuition preferences lead individuals to seek out the "big picture" and complex patterns rather than minute details.

3. **Thinking (T) or Feeling (F)** Thinking preferences lead individuals toward the use of logic, impartiality, and utility to make decisions. People with a preference for feeling often base decisions on human values and needs and personalize decisions. If you're ever in a meeting and a team member says, "I understand the cost-benefit analysis, but it doesn't seem to take into account the impact on people," you are likely dealing with an individual who has a preference for feeling.

4. **Judgment (J) or Perception (P)** This area represents an individual's preferred orientation to the external world. Those preferring judgment orientation tend to deal with their outside world in planned ways, focusing on task completion and goal attainment. Perception preferences often lead individuals toward spontaneity and curiosity. If you are drawn to your planner or PDA, you likely have a preference for judgment. If you live by the mantra, "it'll get done when it gets done," you probably prefer perception.

Jung's theory has been immensely popular, thanks mostly to the work of Katherine Briggs and Isabel Briggs Myers (mother-daughter team) that created the most widely adopted self-assessment for measuring preferences, the Myers-Briggs Type Indicator (MBTI). The MBTI and similar measures provides an individual with a series of "forced-choice" questions about their preferences, which produce a four-letter designation to describe the individual's preferences.

Certainly no one preference type is ideal or optimal. Each preference type describes a unique profile in which a person's preferences may help or hinder their ability to interact with others or fit in to a particular work environment. Unfortunately, the MBTI is often used inappropriately. Keep in mind that the MBTI measures *preferences,* and we know of no research that has demonstrated that any certain MBTI profile is positively related to job performance. While it may not be someone's preference to make decisions via "thinking," he or she may well be able to do it skillfully if the job demands. Thus, the MBTI should never be used to (1) hire an individual for a job or (2) indicate intelligence or competence. The MBTI is best used for self-awareness and awareness of others' preferences at work. When used for those purposes, the MBTI can provide useful information and particularly help individuals find good career fits and in team development (see Chapter 8).

What Are My Core Values?

Just as with styles of learning and personality preferences, people vary with respect to what they *value* most in their world and work. Such differences can affect working relationships and team compatibility. Milton Rokeach, the most recognized writer in the area of values, describes an individual's **value system** (that is, a rank ordering of one's values) as enduring beliefs about what's most important in the world.[29] Put another way, values are non-negotiable, deeply held beliefs.

Rokeach suggests the total number of values is relatively small and that we all possess the same values, just in different degrees. For example, everyone values security and peace and social recognition, but different people give higher priorities to those values than others. One of the most important ways in which values awareness operates is attempting to determine compatibility and your fit with others in jobs, occupations, organizations, and even marriages.[30]

Occupational fit is a condition that exists when there is relative agreement among the parties (for example, between an organization's values and individual's values) about what is most important. Think about a time when you felt like you didn't fit in, where those around you simply didn't share your values. Poor fit can result in frustration, low commitment, and anxiety. Recent research has demonstrated that a strong fit of your values with your co-workers can result in decreased turnover, increased job and career satisfaction, and increased willingness to help out co-workers.[31] Thus, clarifying your values is a key step in understanding the types of environments in which you will be most productive and comfortable, as well as the type of individuals with whom you'd like to surround yourself.

What Is My Preferred Career Orientation?

Nothing is worse than feeling like your talents aren't being used well or that you simply are in the wrong career. Fundamental to managerial self-awareness is having a good understanding of your occupational interests or career orientation. You may have already thought about this while selecting a college major, searching for internships, or choosing a career. **Career orientation** is a preference for a specific type of occupation and work context. Not surprisingly, people differ greatly in their preference for specific jobs and work environments. Like values, career preferences are most useful with regard to seeking fit with a job, environment, and group of colleagues.

When you match your preference to the right occupations and environments you're more likely to feel energized, committed, and satisfied with your work. If you find yourself working in an occupation outside your preferences, you're more likely to burn out and be dissatisfied. Further, some research now shows that, when people make career choices consistent with their occupational preferences, they are more likely to outperform those without such a match.[32] Given the time and energy most people invest in finding the right job and working hard to perform, knowing your preferences can only serve to bolster your ability to put yourself in the right place and right job.

The seventh and final measure in your essentials profile is an assessment built on the work of John Holland and his colleagues—the most widely accepted research on careers in existence. Based on several decades of research and assessment, Holland has identified six general types of career preferences (Table 1.6).[33]

According to Holland, it is common for people to have strong preferences for *multiple* occupational types, but most usually favor one predominant type. The types are organized on a hexagon. Orientations closer together are more likely to coexist than ones farther apart (see Figure 1.2). So, for example, if you find that you prefer realistic work environments, you are more likely to also prefer conventional and investigative than enterprising, artistic, and social environments.

Important Self-Awareness Issues

As you embark on a journey toward greater self-awareness, you should also take into account several important points regarding the interpretation of assessments. First, assessment results are simply feedback. As we've stated before,

| TABLE 1.6 | Holland's Career Preferences |

Preference	Preferred Type of Work	Example Occupations	
Realistic	Work with animals, tools, or machines. Manual and mechanical activities.	• Farmer • Police Officer • Pilot	• Electrician • Mechanic • Carpenter
Investigative	Work involving problem solving, troubleshooting, or creation of knowledge.	• Chemist • Architect • Pharmacist	• Medical Technician • Physician • Meteorologist
Artistic	Work involving innovations, creativity, and unstructured intellectual activities.	• Dancer • Book Editor • Musician	• Art Teacher • Graphic Designer • Comedian
Social	Work that involves helping others learn or solve social problems.	• Counselor • Teacher • Librarian	• Nurse • Social Worker • Physical Therapist
Enterprising	Work involving persuasion, social interaction, and energy.	• Salesperson • Lawyer • TV Newscaster	• Camp Director • Customs Inspector • School Principal
Conventional	Work that involves meeting precise standards, and using numbers in a structured way.	• Accountant • Bank Teller • Title Examiner	• Mail Carrier • Secretary • Court Clerk

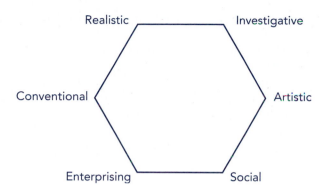

FIGURE 1.2

Career Orientations

these results are not the absolute or final truth, nor do they indicate your destiny. Abilities (sometimes called talents) are only valuable when they are applied and manifested as skills or behaviors. The world is full of high-ability folks who do not succeed; athletic coaches often refer to such people as "wasted talent." Similarly, just *having* certain personality characteristics is less important than how you attempt to put yourself in positions where those traits are most valued and rewarded.

Second, as we note above, literally thousands of self-assessments exist but many have questionable legitimacy. So look for measures that have an established norm base (significant data reporting from prior assessments) and have stood the test of time. The example assessments included in your essentials profile are all well established with a base of research evidence related to their outcomes and relevance for managerial contexts.

Third, preferences are choices we make about how we perceive the world and function best in it. Some of these "choices" are not necessarily conscious ones but rather modes of behaving that seem most natural for us. If you've ever done any acting, you know that attempting to "be someone you're not" is not easy and requires a great degree of attention, direction, and energy. Our personal characteristics such as core values, interpersonal preferences, and career orientations are those with which we feel most comfortable and natural. You can choose to behave outside your preferences, but it will require a significantly higher level of your conscious energy to do so.

Finally, we always recommend you look for patterns and consistency across your assessments. When you find consistency, it is evidence of a more dominant trait or preference. Inconsistency suggests a less-defined characteristic. Perhaps most importantly, you should always interpret your self-assessments in the context of other feedback you've received and not dwell on assessed weaknesses or limitations. We elaborate on those two issues below.

Involve Others: Seek Regular Feedback

Although the evidence is compelling that feedback-seeking behavior and increases in self-awareness are associated with positive outcomes like follower job satisfaction and performance,[34] many young managers do not actively pursue greater self-awareness. Why is that so?

A useful analogy for this curious reluctance can be found in the field of medicine. Many illnesses could be cured and diseases halted, if only people were not afraid to get a checkup—but they are often too scared to find out if anything is wrong. The same holds for seeking interpersonal and management feedback. We all want to protect, maintain, and enhance our self-concepts and the impressions we think others hold of us. And we often have fears and inadequacies (for example, I am bad at math; I hate speaking to groups; I freeze up when people in a group start to get mad) that we would prefer not to focus on or reveal even to ourselves.

Reliable knowledge about ourselves can help us gain insights into what areas we want to change and improve and, even more importantly, the strengths we should aim to utilize more in our work and relationships. Always keep in mind your perception of yourself is likely to differ from others,[35] and some folks we typically turn to (for instance, our mothers) are not always likely to be entirely truthful with us.

Simply put, the major obstacle to seeking feedback is fear. So the first and most important step toward developing self-awareness is a willingness to put aside that natural fear and push beyond our comfort zone in learning things about ourselves. However, a critically important point is it is virtually impossible to dramatically increase self-awareness unless we interact with and disclose ourselves to others. That is, while self-assessments are a good first step, no amount of introspection or self-examination is enough to really know yourself. You can analyze yourself for weeks, or meditate for months, and you will not fully know yourself, any more than you can tickle yourself or smell your own breath.

The reason it is so important to get beyond yourself is that we are just not very good judges of our own behavior and ability. There are many ways in which other people know us better than we know ourselves, particularly when it comes to how adept we are in our relationships. **Multi-source feedback** (that is, feedback provided by many sources other than yourself, such as a boss, co worker, customer, and subordinate) enhances self-knowledge and consequently improves managerial behavior.[36] In fact, research has found that higher levels of agreement between managerial "self" and "other" behavioral ratings are associated with managerial effectiveness and performance.[37]

In short, the ideal evaluation relies not on any one source but on multiple perspectives. These may include self-reports as well as peer, boss, and subordinate feedback. Feedback from multiple sources can be a powerful source of data for highlighting your strengths and targeting the competencies that need to improve. Multiple perspectives on yourself are extremely powerful ways to build self-awareness and get you ready to embark on personal improvement.

Focus on Strengths, Not Just Weaknesses

Getting assessment feedback can be humbling, and sometimes even discouraging, so it is particularly important to not be overwhelmed with focusing on just the gaps or weaknesses in your profile. Of course, some focus on weak areas needing improvement is often appropriate, but it is all too easy to become obsessed with just the negative feedback. Indeed, some recent authors have made the case that a "deficit reduction" or problem fixing approach may actually hinder personal effectiveness.[38] Rather, they contend individuals are far better served by recognizing and building on their strengths and *managing*, rather than obsessively trying to improve, their weaknesses.

Managing a weakness means taking ownership of it and acknowledging it both as a weakness and as part of you. Rather than trying to make it a strength, aim to find ways to minimize its impact on you. Such strategies can include doing it as little as possible, engaging others for whom the characteristic is a strength, and developing and using support systems and tools to compensate (for example, become a zealot for a practical time management system if managing time is a weakness for you). The key point is placing your focus on your strengths and those things you can realistically change is often the most productive.

Appropriately Managing a Strength

"And *you*, Johnson! You stick with your
man and *keep that hand in his face!*"

Managing Stress

The Prevalence and Dangers of Stress

The demands of work are ever increasing, and organizations are expecting managers will do more and more with less and less. A recent survey of American workers found almost 80 percent of employees felt the previous year was their most stressful year ever at work.[39] **Stress** is a pattern of mental and physical responses to conditions of uncertainty and perceived threat. Think about a time you have experienced stress. Almost always, it was because you were uncertain about something you really cared about: You weren't sure you could finish an important project on time, you worried whether you had the ability to handle an assignment, or perhaps you were overwhelmed with the prospect of competing with someone you perceived as more skilled or competent.

Stress has many detrimental consequences for managers and can inhibit effective listening, decision-making, planning, and the generation of new ideas. For example, several research studies have shown that managers experiencing

"No, not there, please. That's where I'm going to put my head."

high stress are more likely to selectively perceive information, fixate on single solutions to problems, revert to old habits to cope with current situations, show less creativity, and overestimate how fast time is passing.[40]

In addition to the direct effects on managerial performance, people who incur long-term stress are also much more likely to develop physical and mental problems. Medical researchers estimate that between 50 and 70 percent of disease and illness are in part due to long-term stress. Common stress-related physical problems include heart disease, stroke, cancer, diabetes, and lung disease. Common stress-related psychological problems include sleep dysfunction, sexual dysfunction, depression, and problems with interpersonal relationships. The evidence is clear that a high degree of sustained stress makes our immune systems less effective at fighting illness.

At the same time, some level of stress is essential to high performance. The father of stress research, Hans Selye, called this **eustress,** which he defined as a controlled or productive stress.[41] It is eustress (pronounced "u-stress") that gives us our competitive edge. So, the paradox of stress is too much will kill performance, but so will too little! Each person has an optimal point at which stress helps improve performance by motivating and grabbing attention as if to say, "Don't take this for granted, it's important." The challenge is not to eliminate stress, but to understand how it arises and to manage it in a way that does not derail your life and work. Great managers are aware of different sources of stress and seek ways to proactively manage it to avoid its damaging and harmful effects.

Sources of Stress: Big Events and Daily Hassles

"Stress primarily comes from not taking action over something that you can have some control over. So if I find that some particular thing is causing me to have stress, that's a warning flag for me. What it means is there's something that I haven't completely identified that is bothering me, and I haven't yet taken any action on it."

—Jeff Bezos, CEO, Amazon

Everyone encounters a variety of stressors, and they can derive from many sources. Stress may stem from interpersonal relationships such as conflict with co-workers or subordinates, ambiguity regarding one's role, or feelings of inequity or poor communication with others. It may also stem from conditions in the working environment such as changes in responsibility, reduction in company resources, or pay cuts. It might come from personal issues such as a divorce, potential lawsuit, or death of a family member. And it may emerge from the pressure of too little time to handle the workload, scheduling conflicts, and deadlines.

One important research finding related to the sources of stress is people tend to overestimate how much large events in their lives contribute to their stress level and grossly underestimate the effects of "daily hassles."[42] Certainly, major life event stressors such as moving, a new job, or the death of a loved one can take a toll on an individual. Yet, these stressors are often accepted as traumatic in people's lives and thus organizations often make accommodations for them.

On the other hand, the stressful effects of daily hassles are typically discounted. **Daily hassles** are annoying events that occur during the workday that make accomplishing work more difficult. Take, for example, the all-too-common event of a computer crash, and losing all access to e-mail and work files. For many of us, daily hassles also include unexpected walk-ins who want to "shoot the bull," phone calls or e-mails from bosses or colleagues who need immediate responses, and other urgent meetings or requests.

Research has shown that these daily hassles are more likely associated with reported stress than more major life events. Indeed, some research has found that daily hassles are the most significant influence on mood, fatigue, and perceived workload.[43] Put simply, the more you must deal with daily hassles, the more stressed out you are likely to be. Trying to overcome the unexpected, unplanned obstacles of daily hassles is often what really wears you down. Conversely, **daily uplifts** or unexpected positive outcomes can have the opposite impact and can recharge a manager.

Strategies for Managing Stress

Why is it that some people under stress can still function and move forward while others sit depressed, withdraw, or become physically sick? Given that so many stressors are inevitable and beyond our control, the most critical lesson of stress management is not to aim to eliminate all stresses in your life, but rather to build your resiliency and personal systems (for example, time management) to cope with the stress you will face. The fact is events do not cause stress, we do. It is how we experience events, and how resilient we are, that determines how stress affects us.

It is not falling in the water that makes you drown. It is what you do once you're in there.
—Anonymous

Building resiliency to stress can involve a variety of skills, many of which are connected to topics covered in this text, such as communication, managing conflict, and decision-making. At the most fundamental level, however, effective stress control is largely a function of your physical hardiness, your psychological hardiness, and your management of time. Learning the behaviors that contribute to each of those three can yield big payoffs in your productivity and health.

Physical Hardiness

It may seem a bit far afield for a management book to discuss physical fitness, but various studies show fitness boosts mental performance and is critical to coping with stress.[44] For example, one study of college professors found that those most physically active processed data faster and experienced slower age-related decline in information processing.[45] In another study, commercial real estate brokers who participated in an aerobics training program (walking or running once a day, three times a week, for 12 weeks) earned larger commissions than brokers who did not participate.[46]

"Physical fitness is the basis for all other forms of excellence."
—John F. Kennedy

People who are fit are also less likely to suffer from illnesses exacerbated by obesity and more likely to possess higher levels of energy and become more resilient to depression tension and stress. The resiliency allows you to fend off those uncontrollable stressors and deal more productively with daily hassles. In an aptly named book, *Fit to Lead*, Christopher Neck and his colleagues outline three essential elements of fitness: body fitness, nutritional fitness, and mental fitness (that is, psychological hardiness).[47] While it is beyond our scope to go into specifics of fitness and nutritional programs, we would simply underscore their importance to stress management because they are directly related to psychological hardiness.

For example, in a study of managers in an extremely stressful transition, it was found that those with the highest psychological hardiness engaged in significantly more regular physical exercise.[48] Unfortunately, a common stress-induced trap is to believe we are too busy to exercise and maintain our physical condition. That thinking produces a negative cycle that further reduces our physical capacity to deal with stress at the very times we need it most. The importance of physical hardiness is further underscored in Management Live 1.2.

Psychological Hardiness

The fact is people who have their stress levels under control still experience an equal share of bad events and daily hassles in their lives. They face the same pressures and adversities as everyone else. Yet some people do have a mental resiliency or hardiness that helps them cope with stress. During the breakup of AT&T in the 1980s, researchers explored what distinguished those managers who were most susceptible to physical and emotional illness from those who demonstrated **psychological hardiness,**[49] the ability to remain psychologically stable and healthy in the face of significant stress. Other studies of successful coping have been conducted in a variety of demanding settings including businesses, battlefields, schools, and medical clinics.[50] That research has helped identify three recurring factors that distinguish those with psychological hardiness: commitment, control, and challenge.

Commitment   Commitment refers to persevering or sticking it out through a hard time. Being committed to an outcome keeps us going even in the midst of setbacks, obstacles, and discouraging news. Being committed to a goal helps us overcome occasional losses of motivation and remain steadfast in our efforts. Commitment can also refer to a sense of connection beyond a single domain.

Management Live 1.2

Executive Fitness and Performance[51]

Research has demonstrated that physical fitness is associated with performance. Fit managers have more energy and experience more positive moods and well-being. In addition, fit managers are more likely than unfit managers to have lower anxiety, tension, and, of course, stress. A large percentage of disease in the United States stems from or is exacerbated by stress. Obviously, the sicker one is, the less likely he or she is able to perform at peak. A survey of 3,000 companies revealed many leading executives understand the role diet and exercise play in their performance, including:

- Charles Rossotti, commissioner of the IRS, who jogs five miles a day.
- Julian Day, CFO of Sears, who runs half-marathons and surfs.
- Tom Monaghan, founder of Domino's Pizza, who runs four miles every day and lifts weights for 30 minutes.
- Thomas Frist, Jr., chairman of Columbia/HCA Healthcare, who uses time between flights to jog along airport roads or neighboring streets.

Managers serious about their performance know exercise and diet are key to enhancing their ability to stave off work stress and stay productive under pressure.

For example, in the AT&T study, while the hardy managers were clearly invested in the company's reorganization, they were not restricted to interest in their work life. They had a broader life and were nurtured by their commitment to family, friends, religious practice, recreation, and hobbies. In fact, research has shown that social support (friends, family, and others who will say to you, "You can do this" or "We believe in you") is important in buffering the effects of stress. Social support can help you put your stressors in perspective.

When under intense stress, we naturally withdraw from the world and concentrate exclusively on solving the problem causing the stress. Sometimes that reaction is useful and appropriate, but, more often, asking for help from our network of family and friends is crucially important to coping with stress. Commitments that extend beyond our work world are an especially good antibody for stress.

Control The second element of hardiness is control. In a tough situation hardy individuals do not become overwhelmed or helpless. Instead, they strive to gain control of what they can by going into action. While acknowledging that many aspects of a crisis situation cannot be controlled, they also understand that, by intentionally holding onto a positive, optimistic, hopeful outlook, they can determine their reaction to any predicament. The greater our capacity to choose our best attitude, the greater our sense of being in charge of our circumstances.

> *"Only optimists get things done."*
> —Ralph Waldo Emerson

One stress-management strategy closely aligned with control is that of seeking **small wins**. Large projects can be inordinately stressful, and many people facing a daunting task will avoid it as long as possible, thereby only increasing their stress. However, if you break a large task into smaller chunks, with action steps, you'll find you can get early wins. Small but meaningful milestones can give us confidence and insight to know "we can do it." So celebrate and reward yourself each time you get a small win in whatever way reinforces your behavior best.

> *"Celebrate any progress. Don't wait to get perfect."*
> —Ann McGee Cooper

Challenge Psychologically hardy individuals see problems as challenges rather than threats. This difference is important because, rather than being overwhelmed and seeking to retreat, these individuals get busy looking for solutions. Seeing a problem as a challenge mobilizes our resources to deal with it and encourages us to pursue the possibilities of a successful outcome. Quickly dealing with feelings of loss, while not harboring false hopes and illusions about the future, enables us to explore new options. Hardy players view change as a stepping stone, not a stumbling block.

Dealing with Stress in the Moment

Psychologically hardy managers are also able to deal with stress in the moment. They do not panic, withdraw, or flounder, but rather rely on several techniques for dealing with their stressors. That is, they are more skilled in relaxing their mind and body, taking a time-out, and knowing how to "repair" their mood. The following are examples of techniques you can use to deal with stress in the moment:

> **Muscle relaxation.** Sometimes stress is so great a time-out is needed. Muscle relaxation only takes a few minutes, but can help relieve the stress you feel immediately. Simply tense then release muscle groups, starting with your feet and working your way up your body (legs, torso, arms, neck). Roll your head and shrug your shoulders.

> **Deep breathing.** This simple exercise can make a difference in short-term stress relief. First, take in a deep breath and hold it for about 5 seconds.

Then breathe out slowly (that's important) until you have completely exhaled, trying to extend the length of the out-breath a little bit longer each time. Repeat this about 5-10 times.

Mood repair. Much research demonstrates that people in positive mood states are more resilient to stress.[52] Moreover, it has been found that you can curb or "repair" your negative moods by understanding what triggers your positive moods.[53] For some it's a piece of chocolate or a latte, for others it may be listening to a piece of music, talking on the phone with a friend, or visualizing a scenario that gives them pleasure (their "happy place"). Learn what puts you in a positive mood and use it when you're in a stressed or negative frame of mind.

Managing Time

One of the most important ways of handling stress is through effective time management. By managing time better, most of us can prevent many of the problems that stress causes by not putting ourselves in stressful situations in the first place.

The inability to manage time is among the greatest sources of stress and can doom the most talented, motivated, and conscientious of managers. While most everyone would agree that time management and organization are among the most critical elements of personal effectiveness, a person trying to enhance his or her time management is often told to exercise willpower, try harder, resist temptation, or seek divine guidance. Although well intentioned, this advice offers little in terms of actionable strategies or skills to help an individual undertake the process of development. Remember, it's the execution of personal effectiveness skills that remains your biggest challenge. So learn the fundamentals of time management, but remember that it is the discipline to apply them that is your ultimate objective.

Today there are thousands of books on time management and a staggering number of training programs and "systems" on the market. Close inspection of this bewildering volume of material, however, reveals a few simple but powerful principles. Below we discuss and illustrate four principles that, although called by various names and labels, are consistently present in the research and writing of time management experts.

"If you are not sure why you are doing something, you can never do enough of it."
—David Allen

First Be Effective, Then Be Efficient

Managing time with an effectiveness approach means you actually pay attention to your goals and regularly revisit what is important to you—and avoid just diligently working on whatever comes up or is urgent or in front of you. As management guru Peter Drucker has famously noted, *doing the right things* should come before *doing things right*.

Start with Written Goals

Most people have an intuitive sense that goals are an important organizing mechanism. Stephen Covey, author of *The 7 Habits of Highly Effective People*, calls this "starting with the end in mind." The notion is simple. A set of long-term, lifetime goals can help you discover what you really want to do, help motivate you to do it, and give meaning to the way you spend your time. It can help you feel in control of your destiny and provide a measuring stick to gauge your success. It can help you choose and decide among many different aspects of your life.

"A goal unwritten is only a dream."
—Anonymous

For some reason, however, a surprisingly small percentage of people actually write down and frequently review and update their goals, both long and short term. This is unfortunate because studies have shown that those with written goals have actually achieved higher levels of life success. There is nothing cosmic or mystical about writing personal goals, and though perhaps not explicitly aware of it, you have probably been thinking about your lifetime goals almost as long as you have been alive. However, thinking about your goals is quite different from writing them down. Unwritten goals often remain vague or utopian dreams such as "get a great job" or "become wealthy." Writing down goals tends to make them more concrete and specific and helps you probe beneath the surface. So always start with goals and revisit them regularly. And don't limit them to financial or career progression goals. What personal, social, or spiritual aspirations do you have?

Follow the 80/20 Rule

Often referred to as Pareto's Law, the **80/20 rule** holds that only 20 percent of the work produces 80 percent of the value, 80 percent of sales come from 20 percent of customers, 80 percent of file usage is in 20 percent of the files, and so on. Sometimes that ratio may be a little more, and sometimes a little less, but the rule generally holds true. In the context of time management, then, if all tasks on a list were arranged in order of value, 80 percent of the value would come from 20 percent of the items, while the remaining 20 percent of the value would come from 80 percent of the items. Therefore, it is important to analyze which tasks make up the most important 20 percent and spend the bulk of your time on those.

Use the Time Management Matrix

Expanding on the 80/20 principle, several time management experts have pointed out the usefulness of a "time management matrix," in which your activities can be categorized in terms of their relative importance and urgency (Table 1.7).[54]

Important activities are those that are tied to your goals and produce a desired result. They accomplish a valued end or achieve a meaningful purpose.

TABLE 1.7 Time Management Matrix

	Urgent	Not Urgent
Important	**QUADRANT I** • Crises • Pressing problems • Deadline-driven projects	**QUADRANT II** • Prevention • Relationship building • Recognizing new opportunities • Planning • Recreation
Not Important	**QUADRANT III** • Interruptions • Some calls • Some mail • Some reports • Some meetings • Popular activities	**QUADRANT IV** • Trivia • Busy work • Some mail • Some phone calls • Time wasters • Pleasant activities

Urgent activities are those that demand immediate attention. They are associated with a need expressed by someone else or relate to an uncomfortable problem or situation that requires a solution as soon as possible.

Of course, one of the most difficult decisions you must make is determining what is important and what is urgent. There are no easy rules, and life's events and demands do not come with important or urgent tags. In fact, every problem or time demand is likely important to someone. However, if you let others determine what is and is not important, then you certainly will never effectively manage your time. Perhaps the most important objective is to manage your time in a way that reduces the number of things you do on an urgent basis and allows you to devote your attention to those things of true importance to your life and work.

Just DON'T Do It: Learn to Say No

One of the most powerful words in your time management vocabulary should be the word *no*. In fact, a good axiom for your time management improvement might well be a reversal of Nike's popular *Just do it!* slogan to *Just don't do it!* Of course, that approach is a lot easier to talk about than to actually use when we are confronted with demands or attractive offers from others. Many of us have an inherent desire to please and to accommodate or fear we may miss out on some apparent opportunity. However, as noted above, effective time management is largely learning to devote yourself fully to your most important tasks. That means what you choose *not* to do can be as important as what you do. So learn how to say no. Three effective ways to say no are:

1. "I'm sorry. That's not a priority for me right now."
2. "I have made so many commitments to others, it would be unfair to them and you if I took on anything more at this point."
3. "No."

"No, Thursday's out. How about never—is never good for you?"

Plan the Work, Then Work the Plan

Make Good Lists for Effective Prioritization

The time management matrix is essentially about prioritization, and virtually every time management expert focuses on the importance of prioritizing and scheduling, usually in the form of a daily or weekly "to-do" list, a "next-action" listing, or a defect tally checklist (see the Tool Kits at the end of the chapter). The basics of good lists are simple: create and review them every day, ideally at the same consistent time; keep them visible; and use them as a guide to action. One of the important rules is to write all your to-do items on a master list or lists kept together, rather than jotting them down on miscellaneous scraps of paper. You may want to keep your list in a separate planner or electronically in your PDA (personal digital assistant) or laptop computer.

Perhaps the more difficult challenge is to determine what goes on the list and how to prioritize it. David Allen, author of the best seller, *Getting Things Done*, argues that what he calls "collection" is the foundation of productive time management.[55] He suggests you need to collect everything that commands your attention and do so in some place other than in your head. Contrary to some traditional time management advice, you do not want things on the top of your mind, unless you are working on them. Some people, students in particular, often try to just keep their to-do list in their heads. That rarely works well. Effective time managers collect and organize their tasks where they can be reviewed and serve as a reminder, but then do not have to be stored in their minds.

Once you've collected your to-do list, most experts recommend you review not just routine items but everything that has high priority today or might not get done without special attention. Alan Lakein further suggests you use what he calls the **ABC method**: assigning an A to a high-priority item, a B to an item of medium priority, and a C to low-priority items. To use the ABC system effectively, you should ensure you are incorporating not just short-term but long-term items, derived from your lifetime goals. Most importantly, always start with As, not with Cs, even when you have just a few minutes of free time. The essence of effective time management is to direct your efforts to high priorities. That is easily stated but exceedingly hard to do.[56]

Ask "What's The Next Action?"

The most critical question for any to-do item you have collected is: What is the next action? Consideration of that step is one of the most powerful mind-sets of effective time management. Many people think they have determined the next action when they write it down or note something like "set meeting." But in this instance, "set meeting" is not the next action because it does not describe a physical behavior. What is the first step to actually setting a meeting? It could be making a phone call or sending an e-mail, but to whom? Decide. If you don't, you simply postpone the decision and create inefficiency in your process because you will have to revisit the issue and will have it hanging over you. The next action is truly the next physical visible activity that needs to be engaged in to move toward completion. This is not just a listing of the item or demand but specifically the next action step.

Know Yourself and Your Time Use

Consistent with the section above on self-awareness, a principle that is included in almost every good time management discussion is that you have to know yourself and your style. While we would not recommend you monitor *every* minute of your time, some documented record of how you currently spend your time is certainly a useful exercise. One good strategy is to record your time selectively, keeping track of particular problem items you feel are consuming an inordinate amount of time.

Each of us has both external and internal prime time. Internal prime time is that time of the day when we typically work best—morning, afternoon, or evening. External prime time is the best time to attend to other people—those you have to deal with in classes, at work, or at home.

Internal prime time is the time when you concentrate best. If you had to pick the two hours of the day when you think most clearly, which would you pick? The two hours you select are probably your internal prime time and you should aim to save all your internal prime time for prime high-priority projects.

Interestingly, studies have shown that most business people pick the first couple hours at work as their internal prime time, yet this is usually the time they read the newspaper, answer routine mail, get yesterday's unanswered e-mails and voice mails, and talk to colleagues and employees. It would be much better to save such routine tasks for non-prime hours.

Fight Procrastination

"The secret of getting ahead is getting started. The secret of getting started is breaking your complex overwhelming tasks into small manageable tasks, and then starting on the first one."

—Mark Twain

It is hardly provocative to point out that procrastination is a major stumbling block everyone faces in trying to achieve both long- and short-term goals. Procrastination is that familiar situation when you have written down and prioritized a critical A task and just can't seem to get started on it. Instead, we may resort to doing a bunch of C priority tasks, like straightening the desk, checking our e-mail, or reading a magazine, to avoid focusing on the A task.

One strategy to address this common human scenario is what Alan Lakein calls the **Swiss Cheese Method.**[58] The Swiss Cheese Method refers to poking small holes in the A project and those holes are what Lakein calls instant tasks. An instant task requires 5 minutes or less of your time and makes some sort of hole in your high-priority task. So in the 10 minutes before you head off to class, you have time for two instant tasks. To find out what they should be, (1) make a list of possible instant tasks and (2) set priorities. The only rule for generating instant tasks is that they can be started quickly and easily and are in some way

Management Live 1.3

Is This Advice Worth $250,000.00?[57]

Charles Schwab was appointed in 1903 to run Bethlehem Steel, which became the largest independent steel producer in the field. Schwab was, one day, approached by a man named Ivy Lee, an efficiency consultant. Unlike most modern consultants, Lee agreed to work for nothing if his techniques did not pay off. After a few days, Lee left without payment. He asked Schwab to give his technique 90 days and send whatever amount his advice had been worth. In three months, Schwab generously sent $35,000.00—or the modern-day equivalent of roughly $250,000.00.

What was the advice Schwab felt was so valuable? Lee said,

For each day, write down six things you must accomplish. Then do those six things in order of priority. Work on the first until it's finished, then the second, and so on. If you don't complete the list, don't worry; you finished the most important tasks. Make a list, prioritize, and do it. That's $250,000.00 worth of advice.

connected to your overwhelming A project. Perhaps the nicest thing about the Swiss Cheese Method is it does not really matter what instant tasks you ultimately select. How much of a contribution a particular instant task will make to getting your A project done is far less important than to do something, anything, on that project. Whatever you choose, at least you will have begun.

The 2-Minute Rule

One of the great shared traditions of many families with young children is the "5-second rule." The 5-second rule holds that if a piece of food accidentally ends up on the ground it can still be eaten safely, provided it was retrieved in less than 5 seconds. While the 5-second rule is actually nonsense,[59] the 2-minute rule is a functional and rational approach to time management. The 2-minute rule suggests that any time demand that will take less than 2 minutes should be done *now*. The logic is it will take more time to categorize and return to it than it will to simply do it immediately. In other words, it is right at the efficiency cutoff. If the thing to be done is not important, throw it away. If you are going to do it sometime, do it now. Getting in the habit of following the 2-minute rule can be magic in helping you avoid procrastination. Do it now if you are ever going to do it at all.

Concluding Note

Much of management deals with managing other people, but the subject of this opening chapter is about managing oneself. The most personally effective managers are those who are active learners, know themselves and their strengths and weaknesses, and manage their time well. Of course, self-improvement, self-awareness, stress management, and time management are skill sets that challenge us all. You will undoubtedly find it difficult to apply these principles all the time. But a large part of management is by example; managers who are not personally effective set the wrong example. Personal effectiveness is perhaps more a self-discipline than a complex learning task and is a lifetime endeavor. Great management starts with your personal effectiveness—make it your first priority!

"It is easier to act yourself into a better way of feeling that to feel yourself into a better way of acting."

—O.H. Mowrer

Key Terms

ABC method	extraversion	self-management
ability	introversion	self-observation
Big Five	modeling	small wins
career orientation	multi-source feedback	SMART goals
cognitive ability	occupational fit	social learning theory
daily hassles	personality	stress
daily uplifts	positive self-talk	Swiss Cheese Method
80/20 rule	preferences	value system
emotional intelligence	psychological hardiness	
eustress	reciprocal determinism	

Personal Effectivness Tool Kits

Tool Kit 1.1   Action Planning

Goals are not enough. You must create a plan of action that details exactly how you accomplish your goals. The action planning process, although relatively simple, is an essential step in personally achieving your goals. Every goal you set should have a corresponding action plan. The critical elements of that plan include the following:

- **A goal statement.** This is your SMART goal. Consistent with that acronym it needs to be specific, measurable, attainable, realtisic, and time-bound.
- **Action steps.** How will you accomplish your goal?
  - **Deadlines.** For each action step listed, set a corresponding deadline or target date.
  - **Required resources.** For each action step, list the required resources needed.
  - **People involved.** For each action step, list people who should be involved and indicate their type of involvement.
- **Evaluation plan.** A plan for determining how you will know you are on track toward your goal and whether or not your goal has been achieved.

Example

SMART Goal: To improve my preparation for the Management Course's final exam by December 7, resulting in a 20 percent increase in my midterm score. Starting immediately (October 15).

Action Step 1: See professor and ask to go over midterm to determine weak areas in testing and studying preparation. Make goal public to professor and two classmates.

- **Deadline:** October 18
- **Resources:** Test materials, notes
- **People involved:** Professor, me, two classmates

Action Step 2: Begin new pre- and post-class studying patterns: Preclass (1–3 hours)—read text, take notes on all chapters, record any area of confusion for clarification in class. Post-class (1 hour)—reconcile text notes with lecture notes, record areas of confusion, seek professor's help during office hours or speak with colleagues. Reward self with 1/2 hour of video games for every 3 hours of studying.

- **Deadline:** Weekly
- **Resources:** Course materials, quiet study environment, dedicated time
- **People involved:** Professor, me, Jim, Sherry

Action Step 3: One week prior to the exam, increase study time to 2–4 hours and begin to synthesize information. Perform analysis of gap between text and lecture. Arrange study group to meet twice prior to exam. Take day off of studying if can answer all practice test questions.

- **Deadline:** Week before exam
- **Resources:** Course materials, quiet study environment, dedicated time
- **People involved:** Professor, me, Jim, Sherry, and others

Action Step 4: The day before the exam, review notes, write out answers to potential questions, exercise to reduce stress, eat a good meal, and get a full night's sleep.

- **Deadline:** Day before exam
- **Resources:** Course materials, quiet study environment, dedicated time
- **People involved:** Me

Tool Kit 1.2   Getting Organized: The TRAF System

Like other aspects of time management, the keys to good organization are straightforward. The best skills framework for organizing paper and e-mail, popularized by Stephanie Winston, is known by the acronym TRAF: toss, refer, act, and file.[60]

- **Toss:** Open your mail over the wastebasket, tossing as you go. This goes symbolically for your e-mail as well: Use the delete button in the same way you would dispose of paper. For those items you are unsure about, it is generally preferable to bite the bullet and throw them away or delete.
- **Refer:** Create individual "referral folders" for the handful of classes or projects you deal with most frequently. Make those folders especially accessible. For your personal affairs, create a Personal file.
- **Act:** A key obstacle to good organization is to push aside a piece of paper or quickly blow by an e-mail thinking, this isn't pressing, I will just look at it tomorrow. A good rule is to take some action, however small, on every paper or e-mail touched. Remember the 2-minute rule – it is worth doing and can be done in two minutes or less go ahead and do it now.
- **File:** A good filing system can be a gift to yourself and your future. Start now and get in the habit of maintaining such a system. Three important rules are (1) opt for a few big files instead of many little ones, (2) name your files using general recognizable labels (e.g., job search) and store them alphabetically, and (3) make a point to mark the files you use. After a year, throw out or store in a remote place any file you did not use in that year. This is hard to do but key to good organization.

Tool Kit 1.3   Personal Quality Checklist[61]

Building on the principles of organizational quality improvement efforts, Bernie Sergesteketter and Harry Roberts have devised a tool for self-management called the personal quality checklist (PQC). Using their approach, you define desirable standards of personal behavior and performance and then keep track of failures or "defects" to meet those standards. The specific steps to the approach are:

1. **Draw up a checklist of standards.** This is the hardest part. Two samples are included at the end of this tool kit as illustrations (one by a practicing manager and one from a college student). Each standard should have a clear relationship to a "customer" either in the workplace or in your family or circle of friends. Anybody in an organization that depends on your work is a customer. Beyond organizational customers, we all have customers such as family, friends, neighbors, and community. Each standard has to be unambiguously defined so you can recognize and tally a defect when it occurs. Thus, "get in shape" is not a good standard. Better would be "break a sweat every day."

   There are two broad types of standards: (1) waste reducers/time savers (e.g., be on time to class or group meetings) and (2) activity expanders (call parents at least once a week, get resume completed). If you include all activity expanders on your list, be sure you will have enough waste reducers and time savers to open up free time for them.

2. **Tally your daily defects.** Defects should be tallied by days but can ultimately be aggregated by weeks or months. One intriguing strategy is to let others help you keep score. For example, if a checklist standard is to talk to your spouse only in respectful tones, or spend at least a half hour with your daughter each day, then your spouse or daughter may well be the best tally keeper for those standards.

3. **Review your tallies and action plan.** Some people find the word "defect" objectionable, but it is key to the system. First, it is easy to recognize and tally. Moreover, defects can become your friends because they suggest opportunities for improvement. Why did it occur? How can it be prevented? The whys lead to hows and suggest possible routes toward improvement.

   Do not put faith in trying harder; you probably already are trying hard. Rather, figure out a different way to reach your objective. As the adage goes, rather than try to be a better caterpillar, become a butterfly.

   As a general rule you should stick with 10 or fewer standards, or the process becomes unwieldy and unfocused. Of course, your checklist standards will be only a small fraction of your activities. Your first PQC should focus on a few things you currently do that, if improved, could increase your customer satisfaction. Once you determine that you have those standards under control and customer satisfaction is high, then you can ask your colleagues and family for help in raising the bar and adding new standards. The approach is deceptively simple but powerful. Sergesteketter and Roberts report on a wide variety of successes by managers and executives from leading firms who have enjoyed success with the personal quality checklist approach. Draw up your own checklist and give it a try!

Sample Manager PQC

- On time for meetings
- Never need a haircut
- Answer phone in two rings
- No more than one project on desk at time
- Shoes always shined
- Weight below 190 pounds
- Exercise at least 3 times a week

Sample College Student PQC

- No more than 10 hours of TV viewing a week
- Use stairs instead of elevator for 4 floors or less
- Follow up job contacts within 24 hours
- Stick to one subject when studying, do not hop around
- In bed before midnight on all school nights
- Pay bills on time
- Make a to-do list for the next day before turning in

Tool Kit 1.4   Preventing Relapse in Personal Improvement

It is quite common for those who want to apply new learning to real life to run into formidable obstacles. These obstacles may come from the environment itself or personal doubts about the usefulness of your new learning. Relapse prevention (RP) is a self-management technique originally created for treating addictive behaviors such as alcohol and drug use, smoking cessation, and weight loss. A lapse is a slight error or slip—a re-emergence of a previous habit or behavior such as an alcoholic's "first drink" after treatment. It is how we respond to a lapse that determines whether a relapse will occur.

A creative approach to handling relapses in managerial skill learning has been developed by Robert Marx of the University of Massachusetts. His model of preventing relapses helps individuals become aware of the threats to skill maintenance, referred to as high-risk situations, so they can anticipate and recover from lapses and ultimately prevent a full relapse.

The foundation of relapse prevention is to recognize that lapses are inevitable. If you come away from any learning experience with a strong vow to put your learnings to use, and then fail to follow through, you may feel like a failure. You may be critical of yourself for being weak or begin to question the value or appropriateness of the learning itself. However, a lapse is no crime. In fact, it is inevitable and happens to everyone, particularly for those trying to make significant changes in their habits and work behaviors. With that in mind, it can be useful to predict your most likely first slips and to strategize how you will respond. There are also a variety of coping strategies such as finding a learning partner and quickly asking for support and feedback at the first lapse.

Several studies have supported the value of RP training in helping people maintain their skill use and avoid relapse. Do not embark on personal improvement with a naïve euphoria that it will all be easy and go well. Use ideas from relapse prevention to enhance your chance of making and sustaining a personal improvement.

Tool Kit 1.5   Advancing Your Self-Awareness

In this chapter we discuss seven areas of self-awareness essential to great managers. Though there are many more types of individual differences we do not cover, these seven represent the foundation of personal effectiveness and should provide you ample opportunity to sharpen your awareness. This exercise is designed to help you enhance and advance your self-awareness as it relates to your personal, career, and managerial effectiveness. There are two steps involved: (1) Take the self-assessments and understand your results, and (2) make sense of your results and decide what to do.

Step 1: Complete the Online Assessments

Go to www.mhhe.com/baldwin1e to complete all seven assessments. The password has been provided for you on the inside cover of your text. Though your instructor will be able to see results for the entire class, he or she will not be able to see your specific scores; that is, your assessment is confidential and anonymous. Each assessment comes with a brief explanation of your results. Once you have completed the assessments, return to this exercise and begin step 2.

Step 2: Make Sense of Your Results

Let's step through each of your results to help you dig deeper into your awareness by answering the question, "So what?" In other words, your results don't matter much until you figure out *why* they should matter. Answer the following questions for each of the seven assessment areas.

1. Critical Thinking

- What are your scores for the various facets of critical thinking? Can you see any holes in your ability to think critically? What strengths can you leverage?
- What type of work situation might be particularly advantageous given your scores?

2. Emotional Intelligence

- Were you surprised at your ability to recognize emotions? Are there particular emotions you recognize more accurately than others?
- How might your level of ability to understand your own emotions factor into success on the job?
- Do your results confirm or disconfirm what you already knew about how you deal with others' emotions at work or school?

3. Cultural Intelligence

- In general, how would you describe your cultural IQ?
- What areas were particular weaknesses and/or strengths?
- Do your results point to any strategies for developing a higher Cultural IQ?

4. Personality Traits: The Big 5

- Which trait(s) seem to stand out most?
- Given what you know about the Big 5 and job performance, which traits may be most important to your personal development and success?
- Conscientiousness is said to be important for job performance in almost all jobs. Are you conscientious? If not, what can you do to be more conscientious?

5. Personality Preferences: The MBTI

- What are your primary personality preferences?
- Given your "type," what about your preferences is likely to make you personally effective? When might your preferences make you less personally effective?
- In working with other team members, how might your preferences get in the way or block the success of the team?

6. Personal Values: Rokeach Values Ranking

- True personal values are said to be "non-negotiable." What are your three most non-negotiable values?
- What types of people will you be most attracted to working with, given your values?

- What do your values say about what type of work you will or will not do? For example, given your primary values, would you be willing to work for a tobacco company? How about on Wall Street?

7. Career Orientation: The Career Key

- What are your RAISEC scores? What are your two highest scores?

- What jobs are your primary preferences most often associated with? Do your results confirm your career aspirations or are they at odds with it?

- Regardless of the job, what type of work activities will you likely find most enjoyable and require less energy from you to perform?

What's Your Essential Profile?

Although understanding each assessment separately is important, great managers know a complex combination of these assessments provides the best insight to a person's personal effectiveness. So, considering all the results at once, do you see any trends or consistencies? How about any inconsistencies? Trends and consistencies likely indicate an area of strength for your personal effectiveness. You can really count on these differences to help you succeed. Inconsistencies may indicate you haven't fully developed preferences or abilities or that your preferences change from situation to situation. In any case, examining your results at this level is very helpful. For example, let's say Sally's results generally show that:

> *Sally is highly extraverted, considers others in decisions (feeler), values social recognition and helpfulness, and has a career orientation that is social and enterprising.*

What can Sally say about her "profile?" Well, it would seem her strengths lie in her abilities and preferences of connecting with or relating to other people. She is likely to be most successful in environments that allow for teamwork and expression and where rewards are given publicly and she has a feeling of making a contribution to other people's efforts. In other words, although Sally may want to be an engineer, her personal effectiveness profile might suggest she steer her career toward more social occupations.

Try to distill your results to highlights. What can you say about yourself in general, like Sally above, which would synthesize your results? If you had to communicate the most essential aspects of these results, what would you say? Try putting together a short statement that communicates your results quickly and accurately.

Here are some questions to get you started:

1. Overall, does the information presented accurately describe you? What stands out as particularly accurate or inaccurate?

Most Accurate	Least Accurate

2. Is this information important *to you* for your professional (or personal) future? What's most important? What's least important?

Most Important	Least Important

3. Looking across all your results, how would you describe your strengths?

```

```

4. Do you want to focus on anything in particular? Are you ready to make changes that might require you to be uncomfortable or act outside your preferences? What are the potential consequences (positive and negative) to making certain changes?

```

```

C H A P T E R

2

Communication

"People five or six levels down in the organization present to the CEO today. Most of them are terrified. The typical scenario is an up-and-comer, someone in their 20s or 30s, who gets in front of top management and gets beaten up. Be prepared."

—Rae Gorin Cook,
Trainer for Hewlett-Packard,
SmithKline Beacham, and
ExxonMobil[1]

Manage *What*?

1. Making a Persuasive Last-Minute Presentation

You manage a team of writers for the local newspaper. Your staff is hard working and very willing to put in long hours to make deadlines, but they have to work with electronic equipment (computers, laptops, PDAs) that is outdated and commonly crashes. While you recognize that other departments at the paper do similar work and have similar needs, you feel your team needs a little more than their standard allocation for computer upgrades in this year's budget. You mention this problem in a meeting with your boss, and she replies, "Well, your timing is perfect. I'm on my way to a budget meeting in about 10 minutes. Why don't you come with me and make a quick presentation to the budget committee and see if you can convince them to increase your allocation?"

What strategy should you follow in creating and delivering your pitch? Are there any "must dos" you should consider if you want to persuade this group? Any common mistakes you should try to avoid?

2. Responding Assertively to a Customer Complaint

You are the assistant manager of a paint store. Your store manager and all the service technicians have already gone home for the day. The phone rings and you find yourself talking to Mrs. Johnson, a customer who says (in an angry tone of voice), "You sold me a basement floor sealer and it did not work. My basement flooded with the last rain and ruined my new flooring and drywall. I am coming in right now and expect a full refund and a check for the damages". When you ask whether she fully prepared the floor with acid etching to insure adhesion, she says "No, but you shouldn't have to do all that. I am really mad. When I bought the sealer from you guys you promised it would seal out the water. So I expect you to fix it, right now. If not, you will be talking to my lawyer." You know that your boss might refund her money but will never go for paying any damages.

Given that you want to preserve the firm's reputation and the customer's goodwill, how would you respond? What would be your ultimate goal in this exchange and what assertive behaviors could you invoke to help you achieve your goal? Is there anything you absolutely would not want to say or do?

3. Actively Listening to Understand a Problem

You work in the customer service department of a software manufacturer. You have already received a number of complaints regarding a product designed to help young people make their own home video productions. Now you are about to meet with a waiting customer who has had problems trying to use the product with his son. You are a bit annoyed in that you suspect that this guy either does not have sufficient hardware capacity or is not using the product correctly, which is usually the case.

What traps or barriers could get in the way of really listening to this customer? What type of active listening would be warranted here—what strategies would you use? This could be a good chance to gather information that would be very useful to your marketing group. How do you make sure you engage this customer and truly listen and consider his perspective?

Introduction

Abraham Lincoln was criticized, usually by opponents he defeated in debates, as lacking a sophisticated style of speaking and writing—"a crude backwoods orator." But could he ever communicate! That's because he listened to people, understood them, and used simple, clear words that made sense. He told stories that illustrated his points and energized people to agree with him.

We should all be so lucky as to possess some of the charm that enabled Honest Abe to reach people and motivate them. However, regardless of your level of personal charisma or charm, communicating clearly and persuasively is a skill everyone can learn and refine. Indeed, communication skills are central to success in today's corporations. Those who become managers—and successful leaders—are the people who can best transmit their views, ideas, and enthusiasm to others.

Simply put, communication matters to managerial success. People who can communicate well are often promoted faster and given more and better work opportunities than those without strong communication skills. This is because good communicators inspire confidence in others and are perceived as having more credible ideas than are those with weaker communication skills, whether or not their ideas are actually better.[2] Study after study confirms that people who make articulate and complete arguments, use proper grammar and language, speak confidently, and present their ideas clearly and persuasively are more successful in business than those who do not.[3]

So what is communication? Figure 2.1 presents a traditional model of the communication process. While straightforward in appearance, a model of the process is useful in that it highlights that communication success and failure is multidimensional (not just one event or element) and thus dependent on several links in a chain. For example, an intended communication from a source may not be what is ultimately heard by the receiver because of an ill-conceived message, faulty transmission, noise (distractions) in the system, or selective perception on the part of the receiver. The model can be a good starting point in designing a communication strategy or diagnosing the specific cause(s) of a communication breakdown.

Perhaps the most defining feature of communication is *sharing information with other people*. We tell our supervisor how a project is progressing, our partner the highlights of our day at work, or a supplier there is a flaw in their product.

FIGURE 2.1 Model of the Communication Process

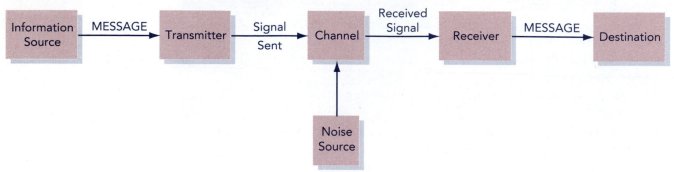

Adapted from Berlo, D.K. (1960). *The Process of Communication.* New York; Holt, Rinehart and Winston.

"At its heart, communication is speaking so other people will listen, and listening so other people will speak."

—Anonymous

However, merely sharing words is not enough. To be effective, communication also requires that people *reach a common understanding.* That is the tricky part. It doesn't imply that people need to be in agreement or share the same perspective. For communication to work, listeners need to understand what is being said to them and interpret that information in a similar way to the person making the original statement.

Communication is included in the personal or core skills section of this text because it affects almost every aspect of managerial behavior. To motivate, give feedback, work in teams, negotiate, or lead change all require effective communication skills. Research also indicates a strong positive link between a leader's communication ability and worker innovativeness.[4] That is, the better a manager communicates with employees, the more likely those people are to come up with new and creative ideas to help the organization. In short, to be an effective manager, you must be an effective communicator.

In this chapter, we focus on key communication skills from the perspective of both sender and receiver. How do you craft and deliver a persuasive message? What are the elements of a successful presentation? How do you respond assertively to requests and demands, even in crisis or emergency situations? How can you more actively listen and overcome the traps and barriers that get in the way of understanding?

As with many management skills, communication is an area associated with a number of misperceptions or myths and we identify a few of the most common of those below.

MYTHS 2.1 Communication Myths

"Be a good listener. Your ears will never get you in trouble."

—Frank Tyger

If you have a strong case, everyone will be convinced. Many attorneys often wish this were true, but they quickly realize people are moved not just by evidence, but by *who* presents that evidence and *how* it is presented. Moreover, a single well-told story or anecdote can often be as effective as a pile of hard evidence.

Words mean what they mean. I *love* French toast. I also *love* my spouse. Clearly, words carry different meanings. Ensuring mutual understanding is the primary challenge of communication. Words that mean one thing to you may mean something else to your listener.

(Continued)

> ***PowerPoint presentations are always the best way to persuade.*** Slides do provide continuity and structure to a message, can be changed easily, and can reflect creativity. However, with the now widespread use of PowerPoint, too many slide shows become one-way information dumps, are too scripted and inflexible, and have too little connection with the needs of the audience. Before opting for PowerPoint, be sure it is the best medium for accomplishing your objectives.
>
> ***Assertive communication means being a jerk.*** True assertive communication is not being hostile or aggressive. When you are assertive, you stand up for your (or someone else's) rights without hurting or diminishing anyone else.
>
> ***Listening is a passive activity.*** *Hearing* is a passive activity, but research shows we ultimately fail to listen to the majority of what we hear. Good listening is hard work and an *active*, not a passive skill.

Creating Persuasive Messages

Audience Analysis

The first rule of effective communication is to analyze your audience. What will your audience care most about? What can you learn about the people with whom you will be communicating? What kinds of goals and objectives do they have? The key to persuasion is to develop an argument that speaks to your listeners. They probably don't want to hear about *your* issues or frustrations or problems—remember, this is not to persuade you. Your audience will always be more persuaded by issues that directly affect *them*. So, regardless of the situation or limited time you may have to prepare, your first task is to analyze your audience. Sometimes it can even be useful to do some audience analysis at the beginning of a presentation by directly asking your audience about their expectations and preferences for your talk. However you choose to conduct your analysis, the fundamental lesson is to align your appeals with the values and beliefs of your audience, to "hit them where they live."

Adam Hanft, a Manhattan-based consultant to small businesses, emphasizes the importance of audience analysis when helping his customers pitch new products. He says:

> I once had a client who had spent many years—and many millions of dollars—creating a powerful database of historical financial data. It was a significant achievement, and the company, rightfully proud of having pulled it off, was eager to cast itself as the leading provider of historical data. I reminded the company of an important fact that had gotten lost in the process: Customers do not want data because they are historians. They use it to help predict what's going to happen next. Armed with that insight, the client switched from selling the past to offering the future. Guess which one commands a higher price?[5]

People are convinced to align their attitudes and behaviors with those of someone else for three main reasons. Aristotle first articulated these three elements of persuasion, which have changed little since his time in ancient Greece. First, we are persuaded by the personal credibility, or *ethos*, of a speaker. Second, we respond to emotional appeals, or *pathos*, in a message. Finally, we are moved by the logical arguments, or *logos*, supporting a position.

Bad Audience Analysis

*"Good God! He's giving the
white-collar voters' speech to the blue collars."*

Ethos: Personal Credibility

Sometimes, we accept what people say simply because we believe they know what they are talking about. The Greeks referred to this as **ethos,** and you might think of it as belief in someone's ethical and professional character or the belief that the speaker shares your values. You respond to this kind of persuasion when you rely on the expertise of your professors or believe your best friend has your best interests in mind. This is persuasion based on personal credibility. If you ever wondered why it was important to gain and maintain a trustworthy reputation, now you know the answer: so that you have the kind of character that inspires *ethos*. In fact, research indicates that, as the requests you make require others to do more and more, your personal credibility becomes more and more important.[6]

"When the character of a man is not clear to you, look at his friends."
—Japanese Proverb

Research investigations have discovered some specific ways in which you can enhance your *ethos* for an audience. First, people find your message most appealing when it is clear that you truly understand them. This means that you can develop *ethos* by emphasizing ways you are similar to your audience. While studies have shown people respond most positively to others like them in age, politics, and so on, it is not necessary for you to share these characteristics with your listeners. Through small talk, you can often find things you have in common with your audience: a love of sports, growing up in a similar area, or perhaps even identification with a specific type of music. The important thing is to find a bond and reinforce it early in the relationship, to remind people that some of your credibility comes from being similar to them.

Another way to enhance your *ethos* is by establishing your authority or expertise. Significant research supports the argument that people believe, and are persuaded by, testimony from someone perceived to be an expert. People defer to others' expertise in matters where they either lack sufficient knowledge or background to make an informed decision or when the issue is simply too complex for them to properly analyze.[7] To capitalize on this, you need to ensure you establish yourself as an expert on your topic of choice. People will not recognize you as an expert simply because you are the one chosen to speak on a particular

"What you do speaks so loudly that I can not hear what you say."
—Ralph Waldo Emerson

topic, so you need to go an extra step to prove your knowledge and skills. You don't need to go overboard, toting diplomas and other credentials wherever you go. Instead, you can tell stories about your role in solving previous problems or explain research you have done that led to your chosen conclusion. These personal disclosures should be made early in a presentation so your audience is primed to listen to your ultimate recommendations.[8]

"Personality can open doors, but only character can keep them open."

—Elmer G. Letterman

In short, ethos boils down to expertise and relationships. Expertise involves knowledge and a history of sound judgment. Relationships stem from demonstrating you can be trusted to listen and to work in the best interests of others. While that may seem relatively straightforward, research has shown most presenters overestimate their own credibility.[9] As a result, many speakers ignore these straightforward strategies to build *ethos*.

One final note: When your audience has no prior knowledge of you or your reputation, they are likely to determine your credibility partly on the basis of the quality of your presentation. They will also use cues such as how you are dressed, how confident you appear, or how professional your visual aids appear to be.[10] To be sure you have the maximum possible credibility, you need to make certain the quality of your presentation reflects your expertise.

Pathos: Arousing Others' Emotions

Persuasive appeals that tug at your heartstrings, make you laugh, or even scare you are using **pathos** to arouse your emotions. This form of persuasion is most effective when speakers use stories and examples that are highly relevant to their listeners, or when listeners' emotions are aroused in a way that prompts their compliance with the message. For example, Robert Cialdini, Regents' Professor of Psychology at Arizona State University, has noted multiple techniques speakers can use when trying to move their audience to action. Two of these are the use of fairness and storytelling.[11]

"When dealing with people, let us remember we are not dealing with creatures of logic. We are dealing with creatures of emotion, creatures bustling with prejudices and motivated by pride and vanity."

—Dale Carnegie

The first technique is one of fairness. This technique relies on the universal human tendency for people to treat others as they are themselves treated. Think about how automatic this is: We smile at others when they smile at us; if someone holds a door for us, we hold the next door for them; or if someone gives us a gift, we seek to offer something in return. A classic example

Management Live 2.1

Storytelling at Nike

One of the most effective ways to arouse pathos in an audience is to tell a story they can relate to or learn from. Corporate executives at Nike know this, and use storytelling to fully engage their workers in the company's culture. "Our stories are not about extraordinary business plans or financial manipulations," says Nelson Farris, Nike's director of corporate education and the company's chief storyteller. "They're about getting things done."

Like all great stories, those at Nike offer lessons people can learn from. For example, employees hear how Bill Bowerman, cofounder of Nike, decided the running team he coached needed better running shoes. So he went out to his workshop and poured rubber into the family waffle iron, and Nike's famous "waffle soled shoe" was born. From this, listeners learn about Nike's support for innovation. Similarly, when they hear about Steve Prefontaine, one of Bowerman's students who fought to make running a professional sport, they remember Nike's commitment to helping athletes. The company's success in each of these areas is testimony to the power these stories have in shaping employee behavior at Nike.

Source: Randsell, E. (2000, January). The Nike Story? Just Tell It. *Fast Company*, 31, pp. 44–45.

of this behavior comes from Hari Krishnas. For years, members of this sect solicited funds in and around airports, with very limited success. Then they developed the strategy of handing small, hand-made paper flowers to people before asking them for a donation. The rate of donations increased dramatically—largely because people felt compelled to pay for the gift they had just been given.

To use this principle to your advantage, remember that people will treat you as you have treated them. Being trusting, cooperative, pleasant, or responsive to others' needs will encourage others to act similarly toward you. It may be necessary to gently remind an audience of their obligation for fairness, but you can do this by remarking on the history of your relationship with them and subtly recalling times when you provided favors.

Another technique is **storytelling,** one of the oldest, most powerful modes of communication. Research has found that stories are more convincing to an audience than rational arguments, statistics, or facts.[12] Well-told stories can illustrate almost any business concept: customer service, culture, teamwork, decision-making, or leadership. Stories make information more relevant and "richer" to the listener. Those on the receiving end can see themselves in the story and become emotionally charged as the narrative continues. When listeners begin to ask themselves, "Who do I know like that?" or "When did something like that happen to me?", they're hooked.[13] An example of storytelling at Nike is presented in Management Live 2.1.

> "Men decide far more problems by hate, love, lust, rage, sorrow, joy, hope, fear, illusion, or some other inward emotion, than by reality, authority, any legal standard, judicial precedent, or statute."
>
> —Cicero

Logos: Using Evidence

Logos, the logical arguments presented by speakers, can also be compelling. These facts, figures, and other forms of persuasion help listeners believe they are making an informed, rational choice. As a speaker, you have two obligations. The first is to construct logically sound arguments in support of your position, and the second is to find evidence in support of those claims. We'll discuss each in turn.

While you may not know them by name, most of us are intuitively familiar with the two basic kinds of arguments: **deductive,** which moves from the general to the specific, and **inductive,** which moves from talking about specific things to generalizing. For deductive arguments, we make an assertion, and then provide evidence in support of that assertion. For inductive arguments, we

Management Live 2.2

Should I Tell Them the Downside?

Research in advertising demonstrates that, in some cases, it is beneficial to tell your listeners the disadvantage of your proposal.[14] These two-sided messages tend to attract attention and encourage listeners to consider them carefully because they are perceived as novel, interesting, and credible. Additionally, listeners are more likely to believe everything that is said (both positive and negative) when they hear a two-sided message.[15] However, this same research provides some guidelines for using two-sided messages most effectively.

- Use a moderate amount of negative information. No more than forty percent of your presentation should focus on the disadvantages of your proposal.
- Negative information should come early in the presentation, but should not come first. The last thing your audience should hear is the list of benefits of your proposal.
- Be sure you clearly show that the benefits of your proposal outweigh the costs you highlight with your negative information.

present the evidence and then draw conclusions from it. The deductive method relies on a major premise that, on its own, is widely accepted (such as harassment-free workplaces are good). This is followed by a minor, but more concrete, premise that is logically linked to the major premise (that is, we need harassment training to ensure no one is harassed in our workplace). Speakers using the inductive method assemble the evidence and then seek to provide the simplest explanation or recommendation. This approach would lay out a series of problems (for example, listing harassment complaints the company has endured) and then propose a general solution (we need diversity training to ensure no one is harassed in our workplace). Each of these approaches works only if listeners accept each piece of the argument.[16]

> *"If any man wish to write in a clear style, let him be first clear in his thoughts."*
>
> —Johann Wolfgang von Goethe

In addition to these basic inductive and deductive logical strategies, other logically sound arguments can be made. You likely use these all the time, but don't think of them as *logos* strategies. First, you might argue from experience that what has been done in the past should continue, as similar actions will produce similar results in the current situation. You can also persuade from a shared identity, arguing that an action is consistent with currently stated values. Another strategy is arguing from cause and effect. Here, you note a problem and, rather than proposing a direct solution as in inductive reasoning, look to the root cause and attempt to remedy things there.

Still, all of these strategies require evidence. In most business settings, the types of evidence available to you include:

1. **Statistics.** Facts and figures are the most used evidence in business presentations. Given the for-profit nature of most businesses, decisions are made based on the action's likely effect on the company's bottom line. The most important considerations when using data are the accuracy of your information and its relevance.

2. **Appeal to authority.** This appeal works if the group shares a common authority to whom they are accountable. Consider a company's safety officer arguing that the Occupational Safety and Health Administration's regulations are being violated by current practice. To persuade successfully, she needs to explain how her recommendation brings the company into compliance and why the action fits into the larger goal of organizational success.

Remember, you don't want to overwhelm your audience with evidence. While it is important, it is not the only component of a successful message. What an audience is looking for in a speaker is **prudence,** the practical wisdom to make the right choice at the right time. You show prudence by demonstrating your mastery over the subject matter, not by proving yourself to be the smartest or best-informed person in the room.[17]

A typically asked question concerns which approach is the *most* important among *ethos, pathos,* or *logos.* The answer is twofold: (1) it depends on the audience—so analyze your audience and know the type of appeals likely to persuade them; and (2) since all three elements have persuasive potential, a good general presentation strategy is to always aim to use all three elements as part of your message. Using all three is not always possible or appropriate but is certainly a good starting point for planning persuasive appeals.

Research also tells us listeners get information on two levels. One is from the message itself, when they carefully scrutinize the content to determine if they agree or disagree with what is being said. However, that takes a lot of mental work, and people don't often expend the energy required for this kind of processing. Instead, they allow themselves to be persuaded by things that aren't central to the message itself. These might include the attractiveness of the speaker, the length of the message, or the number of arguments presented. The reality is that, while having a strong, well-supported message is naturally important, the "little things" such as delivery, speaker credibility, and polished visual aids on their own can persuade some members of your audience.[18] Recognizing this, we'll focus next on the delivery and style of effective presentations.

"I've told you why I need a dog. Now suppose you tell me what makes you think you might be that dog."

Delivering Powerful Messages

A simple, five-step process can guide you when preparing any persuasive presentation. For simplicity, they are known as the **Five S's,** and are shown in Figure 2.2. The S's are sequential, in that each step builds on the preceding one. The most important key to persuasive communication is good planning. So, as you see below, the first three steps involve preparation, while the fourth and fifth focus on the actual presentation. We'll discuss each of the steps in more detail beginning on the next page.

The Five S's of Effective Presentations

Strategy

Think about this scenario for a moment. You need $50 for the upcoming weekend's social festivities. You have two possible sources for the money: your parent/guardian, and your best friend. Both have the money, but need to be persuaded to lend it to you. What will you do?

If you are an effective persuader, you will not likely use the same approach for both sources. Instead, you may focus on the personal development and social growth your plans will allow you to achieve when you develop your persuasive message for your parent/guardian. On the other hand, you will likely draw on shared experiences when making the pitch to your best friend. You would choose different approaches and arguments because you know each of these audiences well, and you are aware of the kinds of messages that would motivate them.

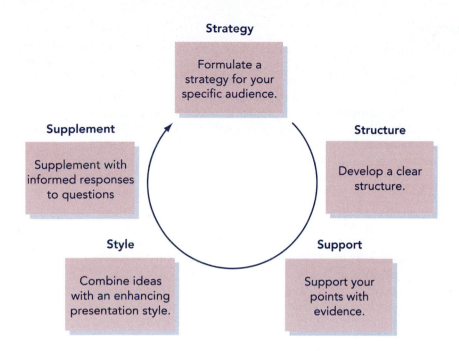

FIGURE 2.2

The 5 S's of Persuasive Presentations

Similarly, you might even use different language and presentation styles when you interact with your friends versus when you talk with your parents.

Consistent with our prior discussion of audience analysis and the elements of persuasion, good strategizing for a presentation would include considering the following questions:

- **Who is my audience?** List everything you know about the person or people who need to be influenced by your presentation. What do they care about? What shared experiences do they have that you can draw on? What is important to them, and what is unimportant? Also, list the things about your goal that will be most meaningful to your audience. How will your proposal help them accomplish things they deem important, or how will it relate to experiences they have had? If you were in your audience members' shoes, what might motivate *you* to endorse this goal?

- **What is my goal?** Work until you have a one-sentence explanation of what you want to accomplish. It helps to begin with the statement, "After my presentation, I want my listeners to. . . ." Be succinct and clear.

- **Ethos, pathos, logos.** First, think about the common ground you might have with this audience. They need to believe you are on their side. Why should they believe you or endorse your goal? Why should they trust you? Managers' credibility is usually established through two sources—expertise and relationships. What expertise should your audience know about? Is there someone who knows the audience better than you do and can vouch for your character? You may have wondered why most speakers ask for a member of the group they are addressing to introduce them. The answer is simple: By acknowledging a relationship with a person in the audience, speakers hope to impress other listeners with their trustworthiness. Pick the single most impressive credential you have to establish your credibility with this particular audience. Similarly, what arguments will be most compelling to this group, both logically and emotionally? What do they care about, and what values can you use to appeal to them? Use what you have learned about these three elements earlier in this chapter to prepare your talk.

"If there are twelve clowns in a ring, you can jump in the middle and start reciting Shakespeare, but to the audience, you'll just be the thirteenth clown."

—Adam Walinsky

Structure

Now that you know the arguments most persuasive to your audience, the next step is to determine the order in which you will present them. Research has shown audiences remember material better and respond to it more positively when it is arranged in a logical sequence or tells a story. You can create a story by organizing the elements of your presentation in a compelling way.

Former McKinsey & Company consultant Barbara Minto has developed a winning strategy for beginning effective presentations in a manner that tells the audience a story.[19] She recommends beginning "with the end in mind" and easing your listeners into the message. Using this strategy, you state your recommendation up front, rather than building up to it. You begin with a statement you know your audience agrees with, such as, "We all know that our company needs to remain profitable." Second is a statement of complication: "However, our profits are higher at some times of the year, then bottom out at other times, making it hard for us to project budgets from quarter to quarter." Then, you state your recommendation: "I want to tell you about a diversification in our product line that can protect our profits from cyclical downturns. Adding X to our product line will alleviate our problem." The rest of the speech then explains why X (your recommendation) is going to resolve the problem you stated (and have other benefits too!).

Of course, you should also organize the remainder of your presentation in such a way that the audience feels it is listening to a story. Evidence suggests that people remember material better and respond to it more positively when it is arranged in a logical sequence. Table 2.1 shows several ways you can organize a persuasive message. There are literally hundreds of other ways speeches can be organized, but these are the most common.

Management Live   2.3

Presentation War Stories

Peter Shea, a controller for Imperial Chemical Industries, was summoned to his company's headquarters to give a five-minute presentation on his value to the company. He wanted the 18 senior managers to remember him, so he devised a metaphor comparing his factory to a racecar, where his job was to keep it running fast. Bad idea. The executives cut him off after four sentences and asked him to leave the room. "I lost it," he cringed. "I wilted and died."

Dave Jensen of Search Masters International is an executive recruiter in the biotechnology industry. Wanting a memorable beginning for a presentation, he took a joke from a book of speaking tips. Bad idea. "It just died," he reported. "It wasn't very funny. And industrial microbiologists aren't a funny group to begin with. When you lose something in the first two minutes of a talk, you just can't get it back."

Darryl Gordon, from an advertising agency in La Jolla, California, was invited to demonstrate the power of digital technology to 60 ad agency presidents. He devised a creative computer-based presentation with colorful slides, bright graphics, and lots of sound. Bad idea. He flipped on the power button and nothing happened. It took 15 minutes to load the presentation onto another machine; the first one was ill-equipped to handle a presentation of this size. "Every second of that 15 minutes felt like a lifetime," he recalled. "I'll never forget it."[20]

So what can we learn from these blunders? First, know your audience, and consider their need for information first—and judge your creative ideas using that criteria. Second, unless you are sure a joke is funny to the type of people in your audience, it is not advisable to use it in your presentation. Third, know your available technology and plan accordingly.

TABLE 2.1 **Organizing Strategies for Persuasive Messages**

Strategy	Explanation
Chronological	Traces the order of events in a time sequence (such as past, present, future or first step, second step, third step).
Problem–Solution	Describes a problem, then explains how your proposal solves that problem.
Causal	Develops ideas from cause to effect, or from effect to cause.
Familiarity–Acceptance	Begins with ideas the listener knows or believes, and moves on to new ideas, relating them to the "old" ones.
Inquiry Order	Develops the topic in steps, the same way you acquire information to solve a problem.
Question–Answer	Raises and answers a series of listeners' likely questions.
Elimination	Surveys all available solutions and systematically eliminates each possibility until one remains.

Support

No matter how credible you are, you need to provide some evidence other than your own opinion if you wish to change the "hearts and minds" of an audience. Based on research exploring the use of supporting materials or evidence in speeches, the following patterns emerge as general guidelines:

"Make sure you have finished speaking before your audience has finished listening."

—Dorothy Sarnoff

- If you have moderate credibility, evidence will probably increase your persuasive effectiveness. Speakers with low credibility are almost always seen as more credible when they cite evidence.
- Using evidence is usually better than not using it.
- Evidence can reinforce the long-term effectiveness of persuasion.
- Evidence produces more attitude change when the source and source's qualifications are provided.
- Using irrelevant evidence or poorly qualified sources may provide an effect opposite to what the speaker intends.

There are a wide variety of supporting materials you can use in a persuasive appeal. Some of the most common types are listed in Table 2.2.

TABLE 2.2 **Types of Supporting Materials**

Type	Explanation
Examples	Specific instances that illustrate the point or clarify the idea.
Statistics	Numbers that express relationships of magnitude, segments, or trends.
Testimony	The opinions or conclusions of others, particularly subject-matter experts.
Stories	Narratives that illustrate a key principle or point, or establish common ground with the audience.

Style

The next step is to deliver your speech in a compelling way. Public speaking is more formal than an extended conversation. While listeners prefer a conversational style of public speaking, there are at least three noteworthy differences between giving speeches and holding conversations.

First, public speaking is more structured. It requires more detailed planning and development. Specific time limits may be imposed, and the speaker does not have the advantage of being able to respond individually to listeners.

Second, public speaking is also more formal. It requires more formal language. Slang, **jargon,** profanity, and poor grammar all lower speakers' credibility, even in the most informal of speech situations. Listeners usually react negatively to poor language choices. In fact, many studies have shown that overuse of slang or any use of obscene language dramatically lowers a speaker's credibility, unless it is used only for special emphasis and only once during the presentation. Additionally, speakers' posture should be more correct, and distracting mannerisms and verbal habits (such as excessive use of "like" or "um") should be avoided.

Management Live 2.4

Too Much Buzzspeak?

Frank Lingua, president and CEO of Dissembling Associates, is the nation's leading purveyor of buzzwords, catchphrases, and clichés for people too busy to speak in plain English. Business Finance contributing editor Dan Danbom interviewed Lingua in his New York City office.

Danbom: Is being a cliché expert a full-time job?

Lingua: Bottom line is I have a full plate 24/7.

D: Is it hard to keep up with the seemingly endless supply of clichés that spew from business?

L: Some days, I don't have the bandwidth. It's like drinking from a fire hydrant. Harder than nailing Jell-O to the wall.

D: How do you track clichés once they've been coined?

L: It's like herding cats.

D: Can you predict whether a phrase is going to become a cliché?

L: Yes, I skate to where the puck is going to be. Because if you aren't the lead dog, you're not providing a customer-centric proactive solution.

D: Do people understand your role as a cliché expert?

L: No, they can't get their arms around that. But they aren't incented to.

D: What did you do to develop this talent?

L: It's not rocket science. It's not brain surgery. When you drill down to the granular level, it's just basic blocking and tackling.

D: How do you know if you're successful in your work?

L: At the end of the day, it's all about robust, world-class language solutions.

D: Does everyone in business eventually devolve into the sort of mindless drivel you spout?

L: If you walk like a duck and talk like a duck, you're a duck. They all drank the Kool-Aid.

Source: Excerpted from Danbom, D. (2002 July). Laughing matters: Cliché expert opens the kimono. *Business Finance,* 64.

The third difference, as a result of the above, is that public speaking requires a different kind of talking. The speaker's volume must be sufficient for everyone in the room to hear clearly. Nothing damages credibility like a soft-spoken voice, for two reasons: Pragmatically, if I can't hear you, how can I decide whether or not to support your arguments? And speaking with appropriate volume shows confidence in your position. That confidence can—and will—translate into *ethos* for your argument.

Supplement

Finally, you will need to be prepared to handle questions after your presentation. Don't make the mistake of thinking your attempt at persuasion ends when your speech is done. How you handle the questions and concerns raised by your audience can make or break your persuasive appeal. This is a vulnerable moment, since you are outside the realm of your carefully planned presentation. Still, there are effective ways to prepare for and handle the question-and-answer (Q&A) component of a presentation.

Gather additional evidence to support your claims. Ideally, you will have chosen compelling evidence to present in your speech. However, keep back some statistics, testimony, and other forms of evidence you considered, but did not add to your presentation. These provide additional justification during Q&As, should you need it. Also, be sure to have the "obvious" questions answered beforehand. Covering the journalistic basics is a good idea: who, what, when, where, why, and how. Similarly, you want to be able to talk about the costs of your proposal, in both time and other resources.

When answering questions paraphrase difficult questions to be sure you understand what the audience member wants to know. Not only does this give you time to think through your response, but it also helps to ensure you really understand the listener's concerns and are prioritizing them appropriately. After you paraphrase, ask the listener if you have interpreted the question correctly. The added bonus to this technique is that, if you have it right, you have the listener agreeing with you from the start.

Listen—carefully. It is easy to forget about practicing good listening habits when you are nervous or basking in the wonderful "I'm DONE!" glow that follows a really excellent presentation. We'll talk more about listening later in this chapter.

Finally, specify when you want the Q&A session. In your introduction, you should state that you'll entertain questions at any time, after each section of the talk, or at the end of the talk. Although taking questions during your presentation can make it longer (and possibly disturb your focus), doing so can also make your talk interactive and more engaging.[21]

Using Visual Aids

Whether you are presenting an operations budget to the board of directors or doing a sales presentation for an important client, visual support of your message is often essential for success. Certainly some speakers can hold an audience's attention without visual aids, but they are exceptions to the rule (see Table 2.3, page 60). In today's digital world, listeners are more visually oriented than ever before. If the audience can't visually relate to what you're saying, they'll tend to shut you out. Visual aids also help your audience track where you are going and feel more comfortable that they understand. They know your presentation has a plan and that you are following it. Graphics also keep people more alert and focused by stimulating their senses.

More pragmatically, visual aids help your audience remember what you said. Of all the information we absorb in a day, only 13 percent comes from hearing

"A good question is never answered. It is not a bolt to be tightened into place but a seed to be planted and bear more seed toward the hope of greening the landscape of ideas."

—John Ciardi

"Effective management always means asking the right question."

—Robert Heller

alone.[22] The ability to retain your message has another benefit: Research has shown presentations that use visual aids are significantly more persuasive than those without them.[23] Visual support helps listeners understand abstract concepts, organize complex data, and see connections between topics. Effective visual support also increases audience retention of the material.

With that in mind, some key points to remember when designing your visuals are:[24]

"Color in a picture is like enthusiasm in life."

—Vincent van Gogh

1. **Color.** Whenever possible, use color in your visuals. Color attracts attention, adds vitality, and increases people's willingness to pay attention. Using the right colors is important, however. Never sacrifice legibility for color. Black text on a blue background is problematic, for example, since the letters tend to look fuzzy to the audience. Similarly, avoid using colors that are opposite each other on the color wheel near each other; red and green, particularly, will—appear to vibrate if placed side by side. Finally, choose colors that evoke emotions consistent with your presentation. People tend to respond to red with increased pulses and breathing rates, whereas blue is calming.

2. **Consistency.** Keep your general color scheme and design consistent throughout your presentation. The background color, font style and size, and so on should be the same on each visual aid you present.

3. **Simplicity.** Visuals should be easy to read and absorb. Follow the "one main concept per visual" rule, and consider your visual aid as a billboard. Do not write out your comments on a slide. Use slides as an outline and illustration for your talk, not as a script.

4. **Balance.** Design visuals in the way people naturally think. Words and phrases should be left to right, or top to bottom, the way people are used to reading. Don't put the title anywhere but on the top. If necessary, use arrows and other visual clues to guide listeners through the visual.

5. **Visibility.** Everything on your visual aid should be easily seen from every point in the room.

6. **Evaluation.** Slip into an audience member's shoes, and evaluate your visuals before your presentation. Is each one easy to absorb within five to eight seconds? Is it clear where the eye should travel, and what the listener should look at first? Does the visual hold your attention and support a key point in your overall message?

TABLE 2.3   **Visual Aid Misconceptions[25]**

Presentations require a magic number of visual aids. Some talks benefit from extensive visual illustrations, while others may require very little. Let content be your guide. Ask yourself, "Is there something visual I could use to make my point?"
The audience cannot read. Many, perhaps most, speakers are guilty of reading their visual aids to the audience. Sure, having the script on your visual aids provides a sense of security, but this method of presentation is boring and somewhat insulting. If you need a more detailed script, stick to note cards or an outline.
Graphical displays are obvious. They may be to those who created them but sadly are often not as clear to the receivers. When you display a numerical, graphical, or other similar message during your presentation, it is always a good idea to cover the highlights and take a few moments to explain its key components. Like everything else on your visual aids, graphs need to be readable from the back of the room.

Special Communication Skills and Contexts

Persuasive messages are important not just in formal speeches or presentations but in everyday interactions as well. Choosing which communication medium to use, and refining your ability to be effective, in situations that demand assertiveness or a response to an emergency or crisis are special skills.

Choosing Your Communication Medium

There are many ways you could choose to communicate with someone. Research is clear, however, that some ways clearly are not as effective as others. So when should you rely on face-to-face communication, and when is an e-mail more effective? Will a phone call do, or should you arrange a personal meeting? You should consider two important variables when making such decisions: (1) the information richness of the available communication channels, and (2) the topic's complexity.

Information richness is the potential information-carrying capacity of a communication channel, and the extent to which it facilitates developing a common understanding between people.[26] Media high in information richness can translate more information. In this context, we define information in three ways:

1. **Feedback.** Some ways of communicating offer immediate feedback, while for other channels the rate and amount of available feedback is very low.

2. **Audio/visual.** With visual communication, you have the added benefit of being able to read someone's body language and nonverbal communication. With only audio interaction, you lose this ability.

3. **Personal/impersonal.** Some forms of communication help build relationships between people by encouraging and facilitating personal contact. Other modes are more formal, and the ability to develop relationships outside the topic at hand may be more easily lost.

Naturally, face-to-face communication is highest in information richness. First, the participants get the benefit of both visual and audio stimuli. They can read facial expressions, body language, tone of voice, and other nonverbal clues as well as hear the words being spoken. Second, feedback in face-to-face conversations is immediate, both verbally and nonverbally. How many times have you changed tactics in a conversation simply because of the other person's changed facial expression, when they haven't said a word? Face-to-face interaction allows you to clarify things you don't understand immediately and to provide additional support or insight if needed. Finally, conversations are the most intimate type of verbal communication available, and they facilitate relationship development. We learn about someone's sense of humor, interests, and values when we converse, and these allow us to develop trust.

While telephone conversations do allow instant access to additional information, they are less information rich than face-to-face conversations. Some nonverbal clues can be gleaned from the tone of the other person's voice, but the person's facial expressions and body language are unclear. Though some information richness is lost, telephone communication has the benefit of being personal and provides the ability to access additional thoughts or information quickly.

"This 'telephone' has too many shortcomings to be seriously considered as a means of communication. The device is inherently of no value to us."

—Western Union Internal Memo, 1876

"The real problem is not whether machines think, but whether men do."

—B.F. Skinner

Written communication addressed to a specific person is next on the continuum. There is, however, a large drop in information richness between a phone call and an e-mail or note. First, the feedback time is significantly longer with written communication. Since misconceptions often cannot be cleared up as they occur, additional communication is often necessary to clarify intentions and glean additional information. Nonverbal communication is also eliminated from the equation. Although some e-mail users are adept at using **emoticons,** or typewritten faces such as :-), these are not universally accepted. Still, because the message is being sent directly and clearly from one person to another, the communication does have a personal component and can help develop relationships. In fact, the number of people developing friendships online continues to grow.

Finally, formal written communication is essentially one-way. When a memo is sent to a large group of people, usually to outline a new policy or serve as a reminder, there is little opportunity to receive feedback. No audio cues are available, nor is it usually possible for someone to get additional information in a timely way. Because it is not personally addressed, no sense of relationship exists between sender and receiver. As we'll see below, this method of communication may be fine for routine information, but is inappropriate for more complex or personal topics. Table 2.4 provides a quick summary of the varying levels of information richness for different communication channels.

"A memorandum is written not to inform the reader but to protect the writer."

—Dean Acheson

The second aspect to consider when choosing a medium is the complexity of the topic you will be discussing. Low-complexity situations are routine, minor matters where each party has its own ready access to information. On the other hand, high-complexity issues don't happen every day and usually involve several

Management Live 2.5

What Corporate America Cannot Build: A Sentence

A 2004 survey of 120 U.S. corporations found startling news: One-third of employees in the nation's largest and most successful companies write poorly. Consequently, businesses have spent as much as $3.1 billion annually on remedial writing training. While most of the money is spent on existing employees, millions are spent on new hires, many of whom are college educated. "It's not that companies want to hire Tolstoy," says Susan Traiman, one of the study's coordinators. "But they need people who can write clearly, and many employees and applicants fall short of that standard."

The problem shows up routinely in e-mail, where poorly written messages set off requests for clarification, many of which are similarly poorly written, resulting in cycles of confusion. Here's one from a systems analyst to her supervisor at a high-tech corporation based in Palo Alto, California:

I updated the Status report for the four discrepancies Lennie forwarded to use via e-mail (they in Barry file). . . to make sure my logic was correct. It seems we provide Murray with incorrect information . . . However after verifying controls on JBL—JBL has the indicator as B????—I wanted to make sure with the recent changes—I processed today – before Murray make the changes again on the mainframe to "C".

No, this isn't written in code—her supervisor didn't understand it either. But this kind of communication is unfortunately too common in e-mail. R. Craig Hogan, director of the online Business Writing Center, comments, "E-mail has just erupted like a weed, and instead of considering what to say when they write, people now just let thoughts drool out onto the screen. It has companies at their wits' end."

Dillon, S. (2004, December 7). What Corporate America Cannot Build: A Sentence. *New York Times.*

TABLE 2.4 | **Information Richness of Communication Channels**[27]

Channel	Feedback Rate	Audio/Visual	Personal/Impersonal	Information Richness
Face-to-face communication	Immediate	Both	Personal	High
Telephone	Fast	Audio	Personal	Moderately high
Personally written missive (i.e., e-mail)	Moderate	No audio or visual	Can be both	Moderately low
Formal letter	Slow	No audio or visual	Impersonal	Low

people to adequately address the problem or opportunity. Ideally, the problem's complexity should dictate which communication channel to use. More complex problems need channels that allow for high information richness so that ideas can be more readily exchanged. Routine problems can, on the other hand, be handled through communication channels low in information richness.

Research supports the idea that more complex problems need to be handled in face-to-face meetings. This may explain why, on average, senior level executives spend significantly more time in meetings than do middle managers, since senior execs typically deal with the most complex issues in the organization.

There are a couple of other aspects to consider when choosing a communication channel. First, you should know how comfortable your intended recipient is with the channel you're planning to use. People who are very familiar with e-mail and have been using it for a long time perceive it as a richer communication channel than do those who lack this experience.[28]

Similarly, your relationship with the receiver influences the richness of the communication channel. When people have had significant interaction face-to-face, they are often able to overcome the limitations of less rich media. In one study, people who had a history of interaction actually did better on a complex decision-making project they completed over e-mail than teams meeting face-to-face who had not met before.[29] Again, this makes the value of face-to-face meetings more clear: When people have a chance to get to know one another, they are able to use less rich communication channels more effectively. Table 2.5 summarizes which medium to choose depending on the situation and results you want.

"It has become appallingly obvious that our technology has exceeded our humanity."

—Albert Einstein

TABLE 2.5 | **Choosing Your Medium: Written vs. Verbal**

Put it in writing when. . .	Communicate verbally when. . .
A number of people must receive consistent instructions or information.	You want immediate and direct feedback and input.
You are concerned about legal, regulatory, or other documentation requirements.	You don't want or need a written record of the communication.
You want your position on something to be perceived as formal.	Delivering the message in person will enhance its sense of urgency.
Your recipient has a history of problems with verbal instructions.	Your message may spark an emotional reaction that you need to acknowledge.

About E-mail

First, some legal issues. The e-mail you write on any computer owned by your employer can be monitored by your employer, and likely is. Most large companies have some sort of monitoring system in place. It is a good idea to keep your personal e-mail communication on your personal computer at home, rather than dealing with personal issues at work. Second, the messages you send and some of those you receive are routinely saved and stored whenever your employer backs up data. These messages are official documents of the organization, just like memos and other written materials. For example, in the government's antitrust case against Microsoft, e-mail messages sent between the company's executives were subpoenaed and used against the company during the trial.

Third, some pragmatic advice. Even though e-mail communication has become less formal as the medium has become more common, electronic communication still takes place between people who are not physically near one another. Messages can be misinterpreted, jokes taken literally, and succinct and direct messages viewed as abrupt and rude. Before you dash off a quick e-mail, make sure it is complete, clear, and not easily misinterpreted. Above all, be sure it is professional. It's always better to error on the side of professionalism than on the side of casualness.

Assertive Communication

Assertive communication means being clear about your needs and expressing them respectfully to others. It seeks to achieve objectives through direct, clear, specific statements. Such communication is not passive because you are actively stating your wishes. It is not aggression because it does not rely on fear, threats, hostility, or intimidation to get your wishes across. It is not manipulative, because it does not rely on emotional appeals or guilt to get someone else to do what you want. Communicating assertively means acting with confidence, assurance, and a positive attitude. When you are assertive, you stand up for your or someone else's position without hurting or diminishing anyone else. Assertiveness is a valuable communication skill in managerial situations and in life.

For example, think of different ways to respond to an unwanted dinner invitation. A passive person would accept the invitation, but inwardly resent having to go. An aggressive person would laugh in the inviter's face: "I wouldn't go if you paid me!" An assertive person would simply say, "I appreciate the invitation, but I have to pass."

Being assertive does not mean you will always get what you want. Indeed, assertive communication is often mischaracterized as being pushy, aggressive, and disrespectful. Aggressive communicators may get more of what they say they want in the short term but often at the price of the quality of their relationships. On the other hand, being assertive builds stronger relationships because you are clear, respectful, and honest in your communications.

In work contexts, assertive managers can make their employees more productive, while a lack of assertiveness can thwart both productivity and morale. Assertive managers encourage associates to be straightforward by using candid language and requesting the same. Being assertive can reduce stress because you are being true to yourself and have no apologies to make. Moreover, assertive professionals speak up for themselves, defend those who work for them, speak up in meetings, and make their ideas known.

While a variety of specific assertive behaviors have been put forth (see Management Live 2.6) there are two recurring lessons for positive, assertive exchanges. The first is empathy/validation, whereby you say something that conveys to the other person you understand his position. This message serves to demonstrate you are not entirely self-focused and are sincere in trying to understand his perspective. Try, "So what you are trying to tell me is. . .."

The second is an unambiguous statement of the problem and of what you want. Here, you describe your difficulty or dissatisfaction, giving a reason why

Management Live 2.6

When I Say No, I Feel Guilty: Fundamental Assertive Rights and Skills

Maneal J. Smith, author of the best-selling book *When I Say No, I Feel Guilty*, has done the most widely known and evidence-based work on assertive communication skills. The beauty of Smith's work is he gets beyond simple platitudes about "standing up for yourself" and identifies the specific assertive behaviors that will lead to desired outcomes. That is, he explains assertiveness in terms of the appropriate mind-set or "rights" you bring to any situation, and what you can actually *do* to communicate assertively. Smith's Bill of Assertive Rights and a synthesis of his most applicable assertive skills are summarized below.

Bill of Assertive Rights

- You have the right to judge your own behavior, thoughts, and emotions, and to take the responsibility for their initiation and consequences upon yourself.
- You have the right to offer no reasons or excuses for justifying your behavior.
- You have the right to judge if you are responsible for finding solutions to other people's problems.
- You have the right to change your mind.
- You have the right to make mistakes—and be responsible for them.
- You have the right to say, "I don't know."
- You have the right to be independent of the goodwill of others before coping with them.
- You have the right to be illogical in making decisions.
- You have the right to say, "I don't understand."
- You have the right to say, "I don't care."

Source: Smith, M.J. (1975). *When I Say No, I Feel Guilty*. New York: Bantam Books.

The Fundamental Assertive Skills

Skill	Example	How It Helps You
Broken Record: Use calm repetition to say what you want over and over again.	"I understand that you usually don't give refunds, but as I've said, I want my money back."	Keeps you focused on your message, and not sidetracked by others' manipulation.
Fogging: Agree with part of your critic's statement, without giving in.	"You are right that this will cause some extra paperwork, but I still want my money back."	Helps you receive criticism from others without becoming anxious or defensive; keeps others from becoming defensive.
Self-Disclosure: Tell the other person something about yourself to keep communication flowing both ways.	"I used to work in a hardware store myself so I understand how tough requests that are 'non-mainstream' can be."	Develops rapport and empathy with the other party; can keep the other from becoming defensive.
Negative Assertion: Accept criticism when you have made an error.	"I recognize that I should have brought the item in for a refund last week. That was shortsighted of me."	Discussion of your error is over more quickly so you can focus on other things.

you need something to change. Then be very specific about what you want the other person to do. For example, you might tell an associate who has been sleeping on the job, "When you fall asleep at your desk, your phone doesn't get answered and customers can't get the technical assistance they need. I need you to stay awake during work hours." Other good techniques for using assertive communication include:

- **Use "I" statements.** Keep the focus on the problem you're having, not on accusing or blaming the other person. *Example:* "I'd like to be able to run with my idea without interference," instead of "You're always interfering with my ideas and projects."

- **Use facts, not judgments.** *Example:* "Your punctuation needs work and your formatting is inconsistent," instead of "This is sloppy work," or "Did you know that shirt has some stains?" instead of "You're not going out looking like *that,* are you?"

- **Take ownership of your thoughts, feelings, and opinions.** *Example:* "I get angry when you break your promises," instead of "You make me angry," or "I believe the best policy is to. . ." instead of "The only sensible thing is to. . . ."

- **Make clear, direct, requests.** Don't invite the person to say no. *Example:* "Will you please. . . ?" instead of "Would you mind. . . ?" or "Why don't you. . . ?"

Crisis Communication

Perhaps the only thing certain in today's business environment is that managers must prepare for uncertainty. Crises are negative incidents that can harm or even cause the demise of an organization. Crisis situations could include product failure—as when Firestone tires began causing accidents in Ford Explorers—inappropriate management behavior, or high-visibility labor relations issues. Crisis situations can thrust us into situations where our communication is critical and can have lasting and significant consequences for people and organizations. Indeed, one of the most difficult managerial challenges is knowing what and how to communicate when a crisis hits. While the varied nature of business crises make it impossible to prescribe specific recommendations, some general guidelines should be followed.

1. **Choose language that is clear and accurate.** This is not the time to hide behind euphemisms. In fact, doing so can aggravate an already difficult situation by conveying coldness or insincerity to listeners. A company declaring bankruptcy does not have a "minor financial setback." Laying off 200 people is not a "small personnel matter." When you acknowledge the magnitude of the problem accurately and completely, you engender confidence in your listeners: They know things won't be worse than you actually told them. Be as up front and honest as you can.

2. **Know your audience.** The target audience will change based on the nature of the crisis. Their circumstances dictate the language and messages you incorporate into your communication. If employees' jobs are at risk, you need to address that issue clearly, ideally with a timeline for announcing which jobs are affected. If one of your products has been recalled, you need to stress the safety of your other products and what you are doing to ensure future product risks are minimized. Customers need this information to feel secure with your products. Imagine you're a doctor giving a patient bad news about some medical test results. Erica

Friedman of the Mount Sinai School of Medicine gives great advice: "It's important to understand who the patient is to put it in the context of their life."[30]

3. **Be prepared to talk about emotions.** Many people are uncomfortable with the idea of talking openly about emotions in the workplace, but in a crisis people need to feel comfortable expressing what they feel. Managers need to recognize that relationships with subordinates are based in emotion, and so be willing to talk about anger, guilt, or fear when those emotions are brought to the forefront. A crisis may require you to set work goals aside for a while and give people time to vent. It isn't a bad idea to talk about your own emotions of grief or frustration, particularly when you know others will be feeling the same way.

4. **Communicate consistently.** In times of stress, people are nervous, not sure what to think or who to listen to, and unsure of how changes might affect them. Consistent communication—even if to you it feels a bit repetitive—will help diffuse anxiety and ultimately allow your employees to get back to productive work sooner. Even if you have nothing new to report, your audience will be reassured by learning that nothing has changed without their knowledge.

> "A leader in a crisis almost always acts subconsciously and then thinks of the reasons for his action."
>
> —Jawaharlal Nehru

Berkshire Hathaway CEO Warren Buffett provides this advice for effective crisis communication:

> First, state clearly that you do not know all the facts. Then promptly state the facts you do know. One's objective should be to get it right, get it quick, get it out, and get it over. You see, your problem won't improve with age.[31]

Active Listening

The Paradox and Importance of Active Listening

The paradox is that, despite that we spend more waking hours listening than in any other activity, we are typically not very good at it. Listening is a very different process from hearing. **Hearing** refers to the physical reality of receiving sounds; it is a passive act that happens even when we are asleep. **Listening**, on the other hand, is an active process that means a conscious effort to hear and understand. To listen we must not only hear but also pay attention, understand, and assimilate. **Active listening** involves interaction and good questioning.

Listening is a vital yet underestimated part of the communication process. Listening skills can greatly influence the quality of your friendships, the cohesion of your family relationships, and your success as a student and manager. Unfortunately, few people are naturally good listeners. Even at the level of simple information, many people do not listen well. Studies show 75 percent of oral communication is ignored or misunderstood and that very few of us are skilled at listening for the deepest meaning in what people say.

> "My friends listen to what I say, but my parents only hear me talk."
>
> —A teenager's lament

Listening involves caring, hearing, interpreting, evaluating, and responding to oral messages to gain a shared understanding.[32] For managers, listening is how we learn what motivates our associates and what their values and expectations are. Even when managers cannot give employees what they want, employees feel better when they believe their point of view has been heard. Listening to employees is a way of showing support and acceptance, which makes for a more open work climate and higher satisfaction and productivity.[33]

Moreover, managers who listen to employees can learn new ways to approach company problems. Harvard professor Rosabeth Moss Kanter tells of a textile company that for years had a high frequency of yarn breakage. Management considered the breakage as an unavoidable business expense until a new manager who listened to his employees discovered a worker with an idea on how to modify the machines to greatly reduce the breakage. The new manager was shocked to learn that the man had wondered about the machine modification for *thirty-two years*. "Why didn't you say something before?" the manager asked. The reply: "My supervisor wasn't interested, and I had no one else to tell it to."[34]

On a more personal note, listening is an essential skill for making and keeping good relationships. If you're a good listener, you'll notice others are drawn to you. Friends confide in you and your friendships deepen. Success comes easier because you hear and understand people. You know what they want and what hurts or irritates them, and you can act accordingly. People appreciate you and want you around.

Finally, the success of many leading companies in the Unites States has been attributed to the way in which they listen to their customers. These companies learn valuable information about their products and services, and get suggestions for future offerings. Listening to customers can also increase sales and customer satisfaction. Consider the following example from the training manager at Macy's department store in New York:

> One big difficulty with new, inexperienced sales clerks is that they don't listen. Here's what an inexperienced clerk often does: A customer steps to the counter and says, "I want that blouse on display there. I'd like size 14 with short sleeves." [The clerk] rushes away and brings back a blouse, size 14, but with long sleeves. The customer again explains, "Short sleeves." Back goes the clerk, and again the customer waits. In a store the size of ours, such incidents can run into money. There's useless work for the clerk, unnecessary handling of merchandise and, most important, possibly an irritated customer. That's why in our training we stress, "Listen before you act."[35]

Traps and Barriers to Active Listening

Active listening is a skill that is part what you do right and part what you avoid doing *wrong*. Most people have all the right stuff to listen well and are well-intentioned, but have simply acquired bad habits. If you can overcome just some of these habits, you will be a long way toward being a more effective listener.

The Tendency to Evaluate

Humans have a natural urge to evaluate what other people say. If you express confidence that the Chicago Cubs will win baseball's World Series, I will likely respond by agreeing or disagreeing with you, basing my evaluation on my own frame of reference. This tendency to evaluate gets stronger as my emotional stake in the conversation rises. So, if I don't care much about the game of baseball, I may think something like, "Oh, she must be from Chicago." On the other hand, if I am an avid fan of Chicago's other baseball team, the White Sox, I will respond more viscerally—"Are you nuts?" Because I have such a strong emotional stake in my own position, I am less likely to listen to the content of your position. This impulse to use our own perspective to evaluate others' statements effectively blocks good listening.

The key to stopping our tendency to evaluate is to be aware of it. For communication to be most effective, we need to hear other people's statements *from their point of view*. Seeking understanding, rather than evaluating, can lead to fewer emotional and irrational conversations. The next time you find yourself in an argument with someone, try this rule: Before each person talks about their perspective, they have to accurately rephrase what the other person has just said,

"A good listener is not only popular everywhere, but after a while he gets to know something."

—Wilson Mizner

"Let go of your attachment to being right, and suddenly your mind is more open. You're able to benefit from the unique viewpoints of others, without being crippled by your own judgment."

—Ralph Marston

in a manner that shows they comprehend. This is communication, or coordination of meaning, at its finest.

Misreading Nonverbal Cues

Nonverbal communication happens all around you. Sometimes it is conscious, as when one person smiles at another in a friendly greeting. Other times it is unconscious, as when someone absentmindedly drums his fingers on a desk. To accurately determine the meaning of a nonverbal message in a business or professional setting, you need to know the sender's personal frame of reference, her cultural background, and the specifics of the situation from her perspective.

Cultural differences can be a big source of misinterpretation (see Figure 2.3). Although research supports the idea that some facial expressions such as laughing, smiling, frowning, and crying are fairly universal,[36] the meaning of most nonverbal messages depends on the culture in which they occur. For example, in the United States embarrassment is normally shown by lowering the head or blushing; in Japan embarrassment is shown by laughter and giggling. Arabs show embarrassment by sticking out their tongues slightly.[37]

Not surprisingly, many managers use only American norms when interpreting nonverbal communication. For example, in American culture, eye contact performs several functions: It shows interest and attention in a speaker, signals someone's willingness to participate and be recognized, and controls the flow of conversation by signaling others that it's OK to talk. However, in some Latin and Asian cultures, eye contact with a superior indicates disrespect.[38]

Here again, awareness is the first step toward improving your ability to understand nonverbal communication. Do not rely solely on your personal lens to

"The most important thing in communication is to hear what isn't being said."

—Peter Drucker, Management Theorist and Presidential Medal of Freedom winner

The A-OK Sign

In the United States, this is just a friendly sign for "All right!" or "Good going." In Australia and Islamic countries, it is equivalent to what generations of high school students know as "flipping the bird."

The "Hook'em Horns" Sign

This sign encourages University of Texas athletes, and it's a good luck gesture in Brazil and Venezuela. In parts of Africa, it is a curse. In Italy, it is signaling to another that "your spouse is being unfaithful."

"V" for Victory Sign

In many parts of the world, this means "victory" or "peace." In England, if the palm and fingers face inward, it means "Up yours!" especially if executed with an upward jerk of the fingers.

Finger-Beckoning Sign

This sign means "come here" in the United States. In Malaysia, it is used only for calling animals. In Indonesia and Australia, it is used for beckoning "ladies of the night."

FIGURE 2.3

Cultural Misunderstandings in Nonverbal Communication

view nonverbal behaviors, but instead inquire about the situational and cultural norms that influence others. When you observe nonverbal behaviors, don't jump to conclusions or assume you know what a particular behavior means.

Personal Focus

Many of us either overtly or covertly like to hear ourselves talk and be a significant part of any conversation. This often leads us to focus on what *we* are going to say, rather than paying attention to what others are saying. Several studies have revealed this barrier is particularly common in that most people can remember nearly everything they said in a conversation, but hardly anything about what the other person said. A simple maxim is it is hard to listen to someone else when you are doing the talking.

Thinking is Faster than Speaking

"No man ever listened himself out of a job."

—Calvin Coolidge

The human mind is capable of thinking from 400 to 600 words per minute, but the average conversation proceeds at only about 125 words per minute, sometimes slowing to 100 words per minute (particularly if the information is complex).[39] This discrepancy means that the listener's brain has quite a bit of leisure time available while listening. Consequently, listeners often take "side trips" that reduce the amount of things they actually hear. One strategy to help with the thinking versus speaking rate disparity is to try and guess where the speaker is going—either confirming or disconfirming as he gets there. This at least keeps you focused on the conversation at hand and not daydreaming or having your thoughts wander to other concerns.

Selective Perception/Filtering

When you **filter,** you listen to some things and not to others. You pay attention only long enough to discern what you predetermined is of interest or what you need. Another way people filter is simply by avoiding hearing certain things—particularly anything threatening, negative, critical, or unpleasant. It's as if the words were never said; you have no memory of them.

Tendency to Advise

Many of us, often substitute advice for listening. That is, we don't have to hear more than a few sentences before we begin searching for the right advice. However, while we are cooking up suggestions and convincing someone to "just try it," we

Management Live 2.7

Gorillas in Our Midst?

One powerful and humorous study related to filtering and selective perception was conducted by Dan Simons of the University of Minnesota. Participants were asked to watch a tape of a basketball game and count the number of passes made by the team in white uniforms. Roughly halfway through the video a man dressed in a gorilla suit runs out on the court, pounds his chest, and stalks off. Approximately one-half of those who watched the video in the study didn't even see the gorilla. Indeed, they express shock and surprise when the tape is rerun for them. Apparently, when we are paying very close attention to something in an active way, we can be completely blind to anything else, no matter how odd or exciting it may be. The key to listening is attention, and this study highlights just how dramatic our unintentional blindness can be.

Source: Simons, D.J. & Chabris, C.F. (1999). Gorillas in our midst. *Perception, 28,* 1059–1074.

may miss what's most important. That is, we often don't hear the feelings being expressed or recognize that the person may not have been looking for advice. Sometimes people just want to know they've been heard.

Selective Perception

Principles of Good Listening

Of course, just avoiding biases does not constitute truly great active listening. Great listening skill comes from wanting and intending to do so and a mastery of a short set of fundamental behaviors.

Know Your Objective

Not all listening contexts are similar, and thus it is important to first know what your objective is. In some cases, you are trying to empathize with someone, in others you are trying to analyze data or solve problems. How you listen should always be based on what you are trying to achieve. The three types of active listening and associated strategies are summarized in Table 2.6.

Actively Interact

Just being quiet while someone talks is not good listening. Active listening requires a conscious effort to interact. Reporters often say their jobs require them to be experts for a day depending on their story—one day an expert on public schools and the next an expert in military policy. The truth is the main expertise of great journalists is asking informed and insightful questions. It's the same for

"We have two ears and one mouth so that we can listen twice as much as we speak."
—Epictetus

TABLE 2.6	Types of Active Listening[40]
Type of Listening	**How to Do It**
Empathizing Drawing out the speaker and getting information in a helpful, supportive way.	Empathize with the other person, try to understand not just what they are saying, but the feelings behind the words. You can make the other person feel comfortable by maintaining eye contact and minimizing the physical distance between you. Pay close attention to what the person is saying, talk very little, and use encouraging nods and words to keep the person talking (such as "go on" or "I see").
Analyzing Seeking concrete information and trying to disentangle fact from emotion.	Use analytical questions to discover the reasons behind the speaker's statements, especially if you need to understand a sequence of facts or thoughts. Ask questions carefully, and use the person's responses to help you form your next set of questions. Once you are clear on a key point, write it down and then turn to the next one.
Synthesizing Guiding the conversation toward a desired objective.	Solicit others' ideas so that you understand potential advantages and disadvantages to your proposal. Keep your mind open and your thoughts unselfish. Focus on the idea and the objective, rather than the personalities involved (including your own).

successful listeners. Like a reporter, you can learn to put people at ease and ask questions that engage them and prompt thoughtful responses.

When asking questions it is useful to ask "how" and "why" questions that require a certain amount of elaboration as opposed to questions that can be answered with a simple yes or no. It also can help if you share a little bit about yourself while asking questions. For example, "I have been having a hard time getting customers to buy the extended warranty product. How do you recommend I deal with it?"

Other good interactive listening tips include:

"I like to listen. I have learned a great deal from listening carefully. Most people never listen."

—Ernest Hemingway

- Paraphrase their comments in your own words. This lets the other person know you're really understanding what's being said.
- Frequently mirror back to them what they've said and your empathy for their position. Let them know you recognize their feelings.
- Make supportive comments. Well-placed phrases such as, "That's interesting" or "Why do you think that?" not only show the talker that you're focused on the conversation, but encourage him to elaborate on the topics you find personally most interesting or helpful.[41]

Stay Focused

Focus is probably both the most important and most difficult of all listening skills. Listening well requires self-control and to not allow your mind to drift into random thoughts. Consider the case of a college lecture. Most students accurately comprehend and retain only about half of what they hear in a 10-minute period.[42] Therefore, students who can stay mentally engaged and focused on listening to their instructors during class stand a much better chance of learning the material presented and accurately applying it in assignments and examinations. One way to increase your focus is to tell yourself at the beginning of a lecture that you're going to find some nugget of valuable information or thought stimulator in what you're about to hear. Think of it as a treasure hunt, a game, or challenge. That's much more fun than being bored, and a better route to good listening.

Concluding Note

Communication is central to great management. Research has uncovered and verified sound principles regarding what makes messages persuasive, as well as how best to structure visuals, deal effectively with superiors and crises, and overcome barriers to poor listening and understanding. The challenge is to resist our human tendency to "wing it" and rather consciously plan and execute those principles in our various communications. Few areas can have as much impact on your future success as a refined skill in persuasive communication.

Key Terms

active listening	filter	jargon
assertive communication	Five S's	listening
deductive	hearing	logos
emoticons	inductive	pathos
ethos	information richness	prudence

Communication Tool Kits

Tool Kit 2.1   The Basic Presentation Checklist[43]

- ❑ **Answer the question, "Who is this audience and why are they here?"** What information have you come to share? What do you uniquely contribute to this audience? This helps clarify your mission and focus.

- ❑ **Prepare an "elevator pitch?"** This step is critical, but often ignored. Imagine you're in an elevator, on the way to give a speech. Someone sees your nametag, recognizes you as the impending speaker, and asks, "What's your talk about?" You've got about 15 seconds to tell her. What will you say? In other words, you should develop a one- to two-sentence statement that clearly describes the benefits listeners will derive from your speech.

- ❑ **Craft the opening and ending.** Find something that will make a strong first impression and leave the audience with a memorable, meaningful final statement.

- ❑ **Seek multiple persuasive elements, targeting logos, pathos, and ethos.** Do you have some evidence, a compelling story, and a means to convey your expertise and credibility?

- ❑ **Eliminate the extraneous.** Most speakers try to cover too much material. Make sure you stick to the topic and that everything included in your presentation is relevant to that topic. Remember: Few people protest when a presentation ends a little early.

- ❑ **Rehearse, preferably in the room.** If you can invite a "preview audience" to listen to you, do so. Presentations often run longer when we give them than they did in our minds so timing your talk is also a good idea.

- ❑ **Double-check the technology.** Not only does this avoid technical glitches, but it makes you more confident in the room.

- ❑ **When the time comes, be ready.** Put your game face on, smile, and remind yourself the material you have prepared is valuable and that people will benefit from listening to you. Then take a deep breath, smile again, and have fun.

Tool Kit 2.2   Writing an Effective Memo[44]

- **Organization.** The secret to writing a good memo is the same for effective writing in any form—organization. If you take the time to organize your thoughts and information first, the process will be easier and your memo will be clearer.

- **Know your audience.** Next, understand what kind of information your reader wants. Some people want a broad and deep understanding of every topic, while others want bare-bones facts. For clues, look at the kind of information your reader sends to others and mirror that as best you can.

- **Don't assume.** Other people don't know what you are thinking. For example, you might write a memo to your boss telling her a meeting is scheduled for 3 o'clock tomorrow afternoon at a hotel on Main Street. Even though the memo has a date on it, you should clarify "tomorrow" as "Thursday, May 4." In other words, leave nothing to chance.

- **Remember the 5 W's.** The first sentence or two should sum up what journalists call the 5 W's: who, what, why, where, and when. This keeps you on track and helps avoid extraneous verbiage.

- **Keep it simple.** Use simple words. Write in short, declarative sentences. If action is required, state clearly what it is.

Tool Kit 2.3   Nonverbal Ways to Communicative Assertiveness

Among the many behaviors and gestures you might exhibit, following are some that convey physically that you are an assertive person. Remember, these are relevant for North American contexts. Other situations may vary significantly.

- Look the other party right in the eye.
- Enter a room with confidence, and take the seat of your choice.
- Maintain good posture.
- Dress well.
- Take the initiative to greet the other party, and shake hands firmly.
- Smile.

Tool Kit 2.4   Tips for Good Listening

1. **Focus and commit to overcoming bad habits.** Awareness of your own listening deficits is the greatest contributor to improved listening. Some experts claim that 50 percent or more of an average adult's potential improvement in listening can come from realizing he or she has bad listening habits and is capable of listening more effectively.

2. **Look at the person talking.** Looking at the speaker affirms you are interested in what that person is saying. Other good nonverbal behaviors of listeners include unfolding your arms and turning toward the person who is speaking.

3. **Control random thoughts.** Daydreaming and preoccupation with other matters often preclude people from hearing what is being said.

4. **Make supportive comments.** In informal conversations, well-placed exclamations or questions (such as "That's interesting!" or "Why do you think that?") not only show the speaker you're focused on the conversation, but encourage that person to elaborate on the topics you personally find most interesting or helpful.

5. **Find something to get interested in.** Make up your mind at the outset that you're going to find some nugget of valuable information or thought stimulator in what you're about to hear.

6. **Put yourself in the speaker's shoes.** There's nothing like a little empathy to enhance listening. It is often hard to really understand what someone is saying unless you try to see the world from his or her perspective.

7. **Sift and sort.** Mentally consider the words being presented to pull out ideas and feelings that are central to the message. Be sure you're following the main, central ideas rather than merely hearing every word. Don't get sidetracked on irrelevant material.

8. **Rephrase what you're hearing.** In large groups you can do this in your mind, but in conversations it can be very effective to verbally take "reality checks" every once in awhile to be sure you're on the same page with the speaker.

9. **Conquer your fear of silence.** For many people, the urge to fill silence with talk is irresistible. Take time to think before answering questions, and make sure you're allowing the other person ample time to do the same.

Tool Kit 2.5 Making E-mails Reader-Friendly[45]

1. **Beware of confidential subjects.** You can never be sure where your messages will be forwarded, how long they will be kept, or by whom.

2. **Assume high standards.** Many readers are put off by bad writing in any form, e-mail or hard copy. Write as well as you can, whenever you can.

3. **Select your readers.** When messaging many people, be selective. Send copies only to those who absolutely need to see it.

4. **Don't assume what you see is what they get.** If your readers' systems are different from yours, your line lengths may spill over and cause an annoying text-wrap effect on their screens. To be safe, keep your line lengths to 55 or 60 characters, including spaces. Exaggerate any indentation you use to make sure it "catches" on your readers' screens.

5. **Avoid typing in all capitals.** It's easier to type, but IT SURE SOUNDS LIKE SHOUTING, DOESN'T IT? Also, "all cap" writing slows reading by inhibiting recognition of acronyms, proper names, and sentence starts, which all depend on upper/lowercase contrasts.

6. **Use informative subject lines.** Readers may screen their e-mails by scanning subject lines, discarding messages that don't seem relevant or clear without reading them. To get your e-mails read, don't use subjects like "Management meeting" or "Project XYZ" if you can use "Request to reschedule meeting" or "How Project XYZ will save $500K this year."

7. **Keep it short.** Try to get your whole message on one screen.

8. **Use emphasis devices.** Even though some e-mail systems don't allow many word processing options, you can still facilitate reading by using headings, white space, occasional all caps, indents, lists, simulated underlines, and other devices.

9. **Change the subject line of your reply.** Your reply is not the same message as the original e-mail you were sent, is it? So if you can, change the subject line. Reply to "Request to reschedule meeting" with "Meeting rescheduled to May 31," or reply to "How Project XYZ will save $500K this year" with "I'm sold, let's do Project XYZ."

Tool Kit 2.6 Right-Hand/Left-Hand Column

Perhaps no other tool is more effective for analyzing communication problems than Harvard Professor Chris Argyris' "Right-Hand/Left-Hand" Column exercise. Argyris' main premise is that authentic communication cannot occur until people find ways to reveal their suspicions and skepticism about their partner(s) in communication. The problem is that most of our work environments do not afford us or encourage such authenticity, but rather encourage the withholding of such openness in the name of being positive. Argyris notes that most managers place a high premium on positivity in order to avoid feelings of embarrassment or failure as the key road block to truly productive communication. Yet it is precisely this "negative" information that is critical for helping people work together to solve problems. Argyris uses the term "undiscussables" to describe this critical, though rarely shared information. Use this tool to help make sense of the undiscussables playing out in your communication behavior and to learn how to more effectively express them.

Step 1   In one paragraph, describe a key professional or personal problem you've recently encountered. Describe a particularly frustrating conversation you've had with another person (or one that you would anticipate having) regarding this problem.

Step 2   Using the following format, describe the actual dialog that transpired in the right hand column, using a new box for each exchange of dialog (i.e., what you said, what she/he said, then what you said and so on). Then, in the left-hand column write any of your thoughts or feelings that you experienced while talking or listening but did not communicate for any reason.

What I was thinking/feeling but didn't say. . .	What was actually said. . .

Step 3   Reflect on your case. Think about the following questions:

- What did I hope to achieve from this conversation? Was I successful? How do I know?
- Did what I say facilitate or hinder my success?
- Why didn't I communicate what was in my left-hand column?
- What assumptions was I making about the other person?

CHAPTER

3

Problem Solving and Ethics

"The great thing about fact-based decisions is that they overrule the hierarchy. The most junior person in the company can win an argument with the most senior person with regard to a fact-based decision. For intuitive decisions, on the other hand, you have to rely on experienced executives who've honed their instincts."

—Jeff Bezos,
CEO, Amazon

Manage **What**?

1. Defining and Structuring a Vague Problem

The third-quarter quality figures for the customer call center you manage have been posted. Although your numbers look good, you quickly notice that, compared to other call centers in the company, your ratings for customer service are below average. Given that part of your bonus is tied to these figures, you are obviously concerned and very motivated to fix the problem. You call your counterparts in other call centers to see what they've been doing recently and to generate some ideas that might influence customer service. One manager said she instituted a new game called "Answer the Call for Baseball," where the top 10 customer service representatives get to take off work for a midday baseball game. Another manager in a successful call center has increased his monitoring of reps on the phone and is intervening immediately when a rep doesn't perform well. A third manager hasn't done much of anything innovative and said, "I guess my customers are much easier to handle than yours." You sit back in your chair, perplexed to say the least.

What is the problem here? What other information would be useful? How would you begin to improve your customer service quality rating? Is the problem definitely with your reps, or could it be something else?

2. Avoiding Common Decision Errors

Putting your answers in the grid below, respond with your *first instinct* to each of the following six items. Also include your level of confidence in each of the responses you provide.

A. Take just 5 seconds for each and estimate the multiplicative product of $8 \times 7 \times 6 \times 5 \times 4 \times 3 \times 2 \times 1$, then $1 \times 2 \times 3 \times 4 \times 5 \times 6 \times 7 \times 8$.

B. You have been carefully monitoring two slot machines in a Las Vegas casino. One has paid off twice in the last hour. The other has not paid off. You are now ready to play yourself. Which one of those machines would give you the best chance of winning?

C. Suppose each of the cards below has a number on one side and letter on the other, and someone tells you: "If a card has a vowel on one side, then it has an even number on the other side." Which card(s) would you need to turn over in order to decide whether the person is lying?

- Card 1: E

- Card 2: K

- Card 3: 4

- Card 4: 7

D. Which city is located farther north, New York or Rome?

E. Which of the following is a more likely cause of death in the United States: being killed by falling airplane parts or attacked by a shark?

F. Six months ago you sank the last $5,000 of your student loan money into the purchase of a stock that was highly recommended to you by a trusted family friend. As of today the stock has already dropped 20 percent and is now worth just $4,000. You are nervously ready to sell, but you simply cannot afford to lose that $1,000 (plus commission costs) and still pay for school next year. Would you sell?

How confident are you in each of your decisions to these problems? Do you suspect there might be inaccurate biases or judgment errors in any of your decisions? Are there any keys or cues you can look for to avoid falling prey to the most common and insidious judgment errors and decision traps?

Problem	Record Your Answer	Confidence Level How confident are you that your answer is correct, on a scale from 1 (not at all) to 100 (totally)?
A		
B		
C		
D		
E		
F		

3. Excelling in a Case Interview

Recognizing the importance of problem solving skills, many progressive organizations now use short brain teasers or more extensive case interviews to evaluate candidates for jobs. Assume you are in an interview and are first asked the question: "How many gas stations are there in the United States?" How would you respond? How might you demonstrate your problem solving skills? How many stations would you estimate there are?

Next, assume that you have been presented with the following case problem: "Your firm is a United States-based manufacturer of natural, health food products and is considering growing the business by entering the huge and expanding Chinese market. Should they?" How would you respond? How would you go about analyzing the opportunity? What questions would you ask? How might you structure your answer to best demonstrate problem solving skills?

4. Making a Tough Ethical Choice

You have worked for your boss for five years, and he has become a trusted mentor and champion for you in the firm. Indeed, there is no one in the firm toward whom you feel more respect or loyalty. You just met with him and, due to an unforeseen market downturn, he let you know of a proposed layoff that will affect one of the three people who report to you (Joe). Because the decision has not been announced, and it will surely send shockwaves through the firm, he asked that you absolutely not tell any of your subordinates. In fact, concerned the information might get prematurely leaked, he even says, "It is critically important that no one know. Can I count on you?" You agreed emphatically that he could. Unfortunately, that evening you see Joe, who coaches a little league team with you. He tells you he and his wife have been accepted into an adoption process for a new child and he wanted to share his joy with you. He also has heard rumors of a layoff and says, sort of jokingly, "I am not going to be laid off, am I? We could never afford to take care of a new child without my income."

What should you do? Is this an ethical issue? You are forced to choose between loyalty and your expressed promise on one hand, and your sense of caring and honesty toward Joe (and his potential new child) on the other. What factors will you consider in your decision? On what basis would you justify the ethics of your decision?

LEARNING OBJECTIVES

1. Define and structure a vague problem.
2. Recognize judgment traps that hinder the decision making process.
3. Implement defenses to minimize or avoid decision making biases.
4. Solve problems using the PADIL framework.
5. Recognize the ethical implications of a given problem.
6. Use moral imagination and "quick tests" to make tough choices ethically.

Introduction

"Somewhere out there, Patrick, is the key to increased sales. I want you to find that key, Patrick, and bring it to me."

If you are like most people, you make about 100 decisions a day. Some are easy decisions (for example, what to eat for breakfast), while others are more difficult (how to allocate your work time). Every day, management life brings new decisions to be made and problems to be solved. Many managers report truly loving the problem-solving aspect of the job—ever changing, always interesting— while others frequently cite problem solving as among the most challenging and difficult aspects of management life. Deciding courses of action, especially when other people and ethical issues are involved, is what keeps managers awake at night. Unfortunately, examples in today's organizations of *poor problem solving and unethical decisions* are all too common. The good news is much is known about solving problems, avoiding decision traps, and making ethical choices. This chapter is devoted to those skills.

The Challenge of Problem Solving

Of the skills covered in this book, problem solving may well be the most complex. By definition, a "problem" does not have a clear solution; otherwise it wouldn't be seen as a problem. Given the complexity inherent in most problems, it is probably not surprising that problem solving is typically found to be among the most deficient skills in assessments of young managers. Some research even suggests as high as 50 percent of managerial decisions made in organizations either fail or are suboptimal.[1] With odds like that, it might seem that flipping a coin would save the time and effort involved. The reality, however, is we can achieve a much higher decision success rate—but only if we consistently adhere to methods of solving problems that have a demonstrated record of success.

"When you confront a problem, you begin to solve it."

—Rudy Giuliani

Most problem solving frameworks are simple in form and concept, but the trap is assuming simple understanding can substitute for the discipline of execution. Moreover, perhaps more than any other skill, good problem solving and decision making are in large part a function of what traps to avoid and what *not* to do. The following section outlines some of the most common traps to

MYTHS 3.1 Problem Solving Myths

- *Taking action is better than standing by.* When faced with a problem, we want to act; it makes us feel like we're accomplishing something. But taking action isn't always better. Sometimes a poorly conceived cure can be much worse than the disease. Many problems managers face *today* come directly from *yesterday's* solutions. The "do nothing" option is too often ignored or neglected and should be at least recognized as an option in almost all problem solving situations.

- *Trust your gut.* Of course, sometimes your "gut" is right. But unless you've tracked your gut decisions to know your success rate, your gut probably won't be very helpful. Experience can play an important role in problem solving, but requires knowledge of previous results to evaluate its effectiveness. In organizational situations, intuition is vastly overrated as a source of decision success.

- *I know when I'm making a poor decision.* In truth, few people can know this without training and practice. Researchers have discovered a phenomenon known as the bias blind spot. Even when people are good at spotting decision traps and logical fallacies in the decisions of *others*, they often fail miserably in spotting the same fallacies in their *own* decisions.

- *Dividing an elephant in half produces two small elephants.* In reality few complex problems lend themselves to easy solutions or effective knee-jerk compromises. Effective problem solving is focused on facts and recognizes that problems are rarely as they appear. Most are symptomatic of more complex issues and require a holistic approach to solve effectively.

- *Ethics is not my problem.* Like it or not, ethical issues are with us every day and each decision you make as a manager holds the potential for ethical issues to arise.

- *Ethical abuses are due to unethical people.* Some are, of course, but even people that most of us would judge as having strong ethical values make unethical decisions. The challenge in ethics is not so much choosing between right and wrong, but between two *right* choices. That is, the hardest cases are when a person could justify either of two choices with strong ethical consciousness. It is not enough to be an ethical person; you need to know how to weigh decisions using sound ethical frameworks.

good decisions and why smart people can often make such bad choices. We then describe a framework to help overcome biases and approach problem solving in an effective and ethical way.

Why Smart People Make Bad Decisions

"I'm guilty of doing too much, and I'm guilty of not seeing my mistakes coming. What I'm not guilty of is making the same mistake twice."

—Michael Dell

As we noted in the introduction, research on decision making suggests bad decisions happen about as frequently as good ones. Very smart, well-intentioned managers make many of these flawed decisions. In fact, very smart people often make very bad decisions because several insidious judgment traps exist that have been found to hamper the decision making of the best of us. Decision making is another area where true expertise involves knowing the traps that so frequently hinder sound judgment.

Management Live 3.1

The "First Instinct" Fallacy

One great example of how conventional intuitive wisdom can be wrong involves the question of whether to change answers in the course of taking a test. Most of us have probably been told something on the order of "When taking a multiple-choice test, always trust your first instinct." It usually includes a rationale such as "If you are not fully certain of an answer, do not change it because your first instinct was probably right."

While that may sound reasonable enough, a recent meta-analysis (33 studies in all, representing over 70 years of research) found that going with your first instinct is actually likely to be a *poor* choice. In one study, researchers examined midterm exam answer sheets (or Scantrons) of over 1,500 students taking the same course. They noted each instance in which students changed an initial response to an alternative response by examining erasure marks made on the Scantron sheets. If the saying about trusting your first instinct is true, then students hoping for the right answer should stick with their first response. Yet, the results showed that over *half the time* a student changed an initial response, they benefited!

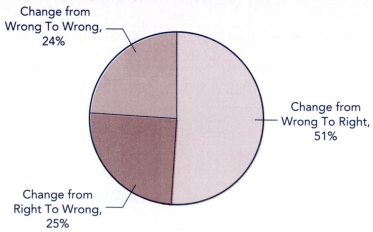

Student Response Changes and Results

Change from Wrong To Wrong, 24%

Change from Wrong To Right, 51%

Change from Right To Wrong, 25%

The researchers found that students dread the notion of potentially changing a right answer to a wrong one. Thus, they become paralyzed and place more stock in their first instinct than they should. This first instinct, which is hard to detect in ourselves, drives our behavior and leads to poorer decisions.

Intuition

Talking glowingly about the importance and value of "going with your gut" or of using your intuition to guide decisions is popular these days. However, evidence is mixed regarding how useful intuition is in solving problems. Despite the courageous tone often characterizing descriptions of making decisions from the gut, we can't comfortably recommend relying solely on your intuition in problem solving. That doesn't mean you should totally discount intuition, just that you should bear in mind most people have a difficult time applying their intuition *systematically* to solve problems.

Intuition represents a collection of what we've learned about the world, *without knowing we actually learned it.*[2] Intuition can be useful if we track what we have learned and under what circumstances that learning led to success so we can replicate it in the future. Moreover, some research shows intuition is important in automatic processes such as social interactions or driving a car—things we do without thinking about them.

However, knowing without understanding becomes problematic in decision making. For example, unconscious biases we bring to bear on situations commonly influence our intuition. Such biases help explain the long-standing phenomenon of a disproportionately large number of men being selected to professional orchestras. Orchestra directors traditionally held auditions face-to-face and apparently held an unconscious bias in favor of men.[3] When the auditions were held blindly (with a screen separating the director and the musician), women were selected at a much higher rate than before.

"My life is the complete opposite of everything I want it to be. Every instinct I have in every aspect of life, be it something to wear, something to eat. . . It's all been wrong."

—George Costanza, character from TV sitcom "Seinfeld"

The Ladder of Inference

A Type of Inference Error

THE FAR SIDE®   By GARY LARSON

Where "minute" steaks come from

FIGURE 3.1

The Ladder of Inference

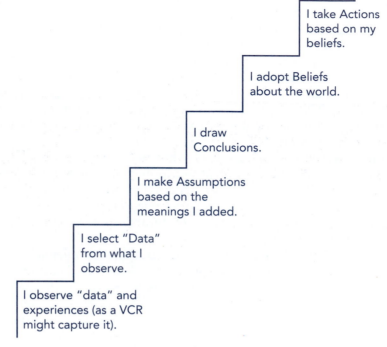

Source: Senge, P.M.; Kleiner, A; Roberts, C.; Ross, R.B.; and Smith, B.J. (1994). The fifth discipline fieldbook. New York, Doubleday.

To show how our intuition operates and can lead to mistakes, it's useful to consider what has been termed the **ladder of inference.**[4] Inference is drawing a conclusion about something we don't know based on things we do know. We make inferences multiple times a day to try to make sense of our world. The problem is we don't realize we're making such inferences. Why? The process happens so quickly and effortlessly we almost never devote cognitive energy to it. The ladder of inference (Figure 3.1) is an analogy that illustrates just how this process of making inferences occurs.

At the very bottom of the ladder, we observe or experience what people say and do. This information is objective in the sense that the behavior doesn't change from person to person. For example, say your teammate Bob is 45 minutes late for a team meeting. You would all observe that fact—that he is indeed 45 minutes late. There is no disputing that.

Yet people have a hard time observing every possible aspect of situations so they select certain aspects of the behavior to pay attention to. You may have noticed that the content of a meeting was particularly controversial; others may have noted it was a nice day out, perfect for golf. You probably didn't pay attention to everything either, however. Next, you make some assumptions about what you've observed based upon your own cultural and personal experiences with the observed behavior. You might assume people who don't show up for meetings have something to hide. Or perhaps your experience tells you traffic is particularly bad at this time of day. Either way, you draw conclusions about the behavior—for example, "Bob knew it would be a difficult meeting and opted out."

At this point, you have adopted a belief about how the world works: "Some people skip meetings when they anticipate controversy." Those adopted beliefs then influence how you see future events and the actions you take. You might then believe, "Bob can't deal with tough issues," and take action that says, "We shouldn't include Bob in our meetings going forward" (see Figure 3.2).

Well, the truth is Bob was just at the wrong location. Let's not let Bob off the hook for that move, but should we take the action of not including him on the

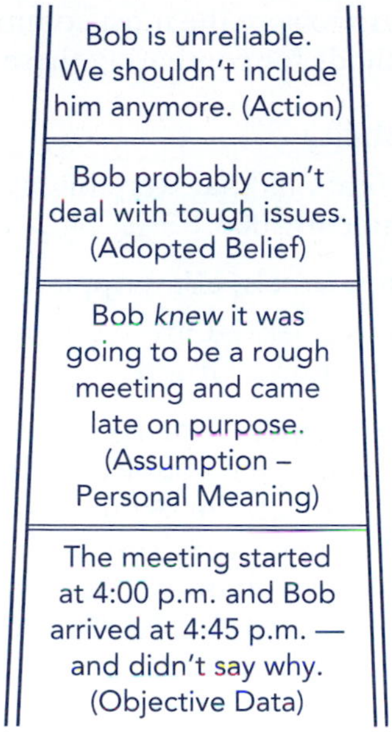

FIGURE 3.2

Ladder of Inference Example

team? Solving problems requires heightened awareness to our limited human abilities to consider all alternatives simultaneously. Solving problems also requires we not jump to inappropriate conclusions and that we keep an open mind about people, problems, and situations.

When we analyze people's ladders of inference, a highly destructive error becomes readily apparent. The error deals with the process of attributing cause to events—that is, explaining why things occurred. This error is so important to understanding human behavior it has been termed **fundamental attribution error.** The essence of the fundamental attribution error is people tend to over-attribute behavior to internal rather than external causes. Thus, when determining the cause of another person's behavior, you are more likely to consider factors related to the person's disposition (personality, ethnicity, gender, and so on) than to her particular situation (weather, lighting, traffic, and so on).

Perhaps more insidious is the **self-serving bias,** where we attribute personal *successes* to internal causes and personal *failures* to external causes. For example, let's say you got an A on your last test. To what would you likely attribute your success? Hard work, excellent study habits, natural intellect? But what if you failed the test miserably? To what would you likely attribute your failure? Tricky questions. Perhaps a confusing professor or the sniffling of students with colds during the test. The self-serving bias helps us maintain a comfortable positive image about ourselves; unfortunately, that image is often built on false information.

This process plays out in problem solving every day. "Why is our customer service so poor? Must be those customer service agents; they're incompetent." Or "How are we ever going to compete in this market? Get more talented people in the organization." If you are going to solve problems well, you need to expand your thinking about the causes of events and others' behaviors.

"If there is such a thing as a basic human quality, self-deception is it."

—Colin Turnbull

"Informed decision-making comes from a long tradition of guessing and then blaming others for inadequate results."

—Scott Adams, creator of "Dilbert" cartoon strip

Six Ways People Exercise Poor Judgment Without Knowing It[5]

We've tried to show that people are just not very good at consistently drawing appropriate or accurate conclusions from intuition.[6] We now discuss ways in which people, using their gut instinct and "experience," exercise poor judgment. Our hope is you will: (1) recognize quickly how easy it is to make simple mistakes by using intuition alone, (2) learn to spot the most common decision making biases, and (3) discover simple methods for combating these biases in judgment.

Judgment Error 1: Availability

Listed below are eight corporations that were highly ranked in the Fortune 500 according to total sales volume in 2006.

> **Group A includes:** Hilton Hotels, eBay, Apple Computer, Gap
>
> **Group B includes:** Valero Energy, Cardinal Health, Albertson's, American International Group.

Which group of four companies (A or B) had the larger total sales volume in 2006? If you answered Group A, pat yourself on the back, as you're not alone. You're wrong, but not alone! In fact, the Group B sales were approximately five times that of Group A. Further, every company in Group B had sales higher than all of Group A combined. Let's try another one. Which of the following causes more deaths per year in the United States, stomach cancer or car accidents? Most people believe car accidents cause more deaths, but in fact stomach cancers lead to more deaths by a ratio of 2 to 1.

These two simple problems represent what's known as the **availability bias.** This bias clouds our judgment because things more readily available to us (that is, they can be more easily brought to mind) are likely to be interpreted as more frequent or important. There are many stories in the news about car crashes, few about stomach cancer. The companies in Group A are household names, but not as large as the lesser known companies in Group B. When solving a problem, we often choose solutions we've heard about; we feel more comfortable with them and assume that if we've heard about them, they'll work. Marketing firms know this well, which explains why they want their products on the tip of your tongue.

Judgment Error 2: Representativeness

Let's say we told you the best student in our MBA class this past term writes poetry and is rather shy and quite introspective. What was the student's undergraduate major—fine arts or business? Which type of job is the student likely to accept—management of the arts or management consulting? When asked these questions, most students suggest the student's major must have been fine arts and that the student will likely take a job in managing the arts. These conclusions completely ignore, however, that the majority of MBA students hold undergraduate degrees in business and that many more MBAs take jobs in management consulting firms than they do in arts management. In other words, people ignore the "base rate" or the frequency of which people belong to certain groups or categories. The easily made mistake— **representative bias**—is that people pay more attention to descriptors they believe to be more *representative* of the person's career choice than the key base rate information that leads to the better choice.

Another classic example of the representative bias comes in the form of people's misconceptions about chance. For example, people assume that, when a sequence appears nonrandom, it must be nonrandom.[7] If you won the lottery, would you play different numbers? If you flipped a coin and it was heads 9 times in a row, are you due for a tails on the 10th toss? Of course not, but this bias is applied with great regularity. So much so, it has been termed the "gambler's fallacy," in which people truly believe that each coin flip or pull of the slot machine, are somehow connected to previous actions. The coin, the slot machine, and so on, have no memory, yet it is common to assume the probabilities of future outcomes must somehow increase or decrease to offset or "compensate for" earlier outcomes. If you have ever played roulette, the posting of previous winning numbers is designed to trick you into making this error. Another great example of this is the "hot hand" in basketball we discuss in Management Live 3.2. Even highly paid, experienced coaches make some very poor decisions based on this very seductive fallacy.

Another special case of the representative bias is what is known as the **hasty generalization fallacy.** For a variety of reasons, people often draw inappropriate general conclusions from specific cases because they do not realize (or they think *you* don't realize) their specific example is not necessarily so in all, or even most, cases. Consider the guy who argues against motorcycle helmet legislation because he has ridden for 25 years without a helmet and has never been hurt. That may well be true, but so what? One helmet-less rider's personal experience in no way refutes the notion that it is safer to ride with a helmet. Similarly, it is not uncommon to hear someone assert, "I do not agree with all the fuss over cholesterol. My grandfather lived to 95, and he ate bacon and eggs every morning."

The hasty generalization fallacy occurs because we tend to operate by what has been called the law of small numbers—that is, we are willing to leap to general conclusions after seeing only one or two examples. In fact, we are particularly prone to make this thinking error because we tend to personalize all experience (we assume our experience is everyone else's) or even misinterpret our experience ("That's the way the world is, I have seen it with my own two eyes").

Management Live 3.2

The Hot Hand

Imagine that your favorite team is in the NCAA championship basketball game. There are 3 seconds left on the clock and your team is down by one. The coach is huddled with his players designing the final play. But everyone knows who's getting the ball—the player with the "hot hand," the one who has made his last six shots. He's on fire! Anyone who has played sports long enough believes in the phenomenon of the streak and the hot hand. Unfortunately, it simply isn't true.

Researchers did an analysis of the shooting patterns of the Boston Celtics and Philadelphia 76ers in the mid-1980s.[8] They found prior shot performance did not influence or change the likelihood of success on later shot performance. That is, if you make your first three shots, you're no more likely to make the fourth than you were the first three. This is a classic representative bias regarding chance and doesn't only occur in sports but biases decisions in many contexts including where and when to invest money.

Philadelphia 76ers[9]

Probability of Next Shot Being a Hit After. . .	
Three Straight Hits	.46
Two Straight Hits	.50
One Hit	.51
One Miss	.54
Two Misses	.53
Three Misses	.56

Source: Reprinted from *Cognitive Psychology*, Vol. 17, no. 3, by Gilovich, Vallone, and Tuersky, "The Hot Hand in Basketball," pp. 295–314. Copyright © 1985, with permission from Elsevier.

Judgment Error 3: Anchoring and Adjustment

Consider an experiment in which students were asked to add 400 to the last three numbers of their student ID and write it down. Then they were asked to use this number to estimate when Attila the Hun invaded Europe into regions of France—that is, whether that event happened before or after the date created by ID number). The results showed the following:

If ID number "date" was between:	Average response was:
400-700	676 CE
701-1000	738 CE
1001-1200	848 CE
1201-1400	759 CE

Students tended to use their initial value as a starting point and adjusted their estimates around that starting value. But remember, this initial value was based on their ID numbers, not any historically relevant data! (By the way, the correct answer is 451 CE.) Research shows we often provide estimates based on the initial starting estimate. Even when people are told the initial estimate is random, their adjusted estimates remain close to the initial estimate or *anchor*.[10] This pattern of **anchoring and adjustment** is quite prevalent. That is, different starting points lead to different end results. Consider the following scenario:

> A newly hired teacher for a large private high school has five years of experience and solid qualifications. When asked to estimate the starting salary for this employee, one author's acquaintance (who knows very little about the profession) guessed an annual salary of $31,000. What is your estimate?

If you're like most people, your answer will be affected by the acquaintance's initial estimate. In studies using similar scenarios, when the acquaintance's estimate was much higher, say $70,000, subsequent estimates were much higher. This is the case even when the scenario states that the acquaintance knows very little about the profession!

The common mishaps resulting from this bias abound. Think about the last time you negotiated for anything. Who threw out the first number? That figure served as a starting point for the negotiation, regardless of whether it was a reasonable figure or based on anything objective.

Judgment Error 4: Confirmation

Students were asked in a research study to think about this series of numbers: 2, 4, 6. This series conforms to some rule. Students were asked to identify the rule and, to do so, were allowed to propose a new sequence of numbers they believed conformed to the rule to test whether their rule was correct. After this period of experimentation, the students were asked to identify the rule. Common responses were:

- Numbers that increase by two.
- The difference between the first two numbers is equivalent to the difference between the last two.

The rule used in the experiment was actually *any three ascending numbers*. Few students actually identified this rule because the solution requires students to collect disconfirming, rather than confirming information. In other words, the **confirmation bias** represents people's tendency to collect evidence that supports rather than negates our intuition before deciding. When students found a rule that seemed to work, they were done searching. In solving problems, one of the most insidious traps is gathering data that seeks to confirm our ideas and exclude data that might disconfirm them.

Judgment Error 5: Overconfidence

Consider the following quotes:

> Heavier-than-air flying machines are impossible.—Lord Kelvin, president of the British Royal Society, 1895.
> I think there is a world market for about five computers.—Thomas J. Watson, chairman of IBM, 1943.
> We don't like their sound, and guitar music is on the way out.—Decca Recording Co. rejecting The Beatles.

Now consider these facts:[11]

- 81 percent of surveyed new business owners thought their business had at least a 70 percent chance of success, but only 39 percent thought that most businesses like theirs would succeed.

- 80 percent of students believed they were in the top 30 percent of safe drivers.

- A survey asked 829,000 high school students to rate their own ability to "get along with others," and less than 1 percent rated themselves as below average. Further, 60 percent rated themselves in the top 10 percent, and 25 percent rated themselves in the top 1 percent.

What do all of these things have in common? They are indicative of people's overconfidence in their abilities and underconfidence in others'. Often termed the Lake Wobegon Effect (after the radio show in which the imaginary town boasts all of its children are above average), this **overconfidence bias** leads us to believe we posses some unique trait or ability that allows us to defy odds, whereas others simply don't have such a trait. An example of the overconfidence bias in action can be seen in investor behavior in the late 1990s. Because of a boom in technology stocks, even novice investors experienced huge growth in their portfolios. As technology stocks kept going up, many investors believed that their success was due to their stock-picking ability rather than unsustainable growth in one sector of the economy. The result for many was huge losses.

Being confident is a great thing: It allows people to approach difficult situations with courage and determination. Unfortunately, most of us are overconfident and we greatly overestimate the true probability of success. Research has shown there is virtually no relationship between one's confidence level about being right and actually being right. That is, people (think consultants, experts, advisers) often exude confidence about their opinions, but confidence doesn't make them any more accurate. The good news is some research shows that, when given feedback about being overconfident or asking people to explain their estimates, people reduce their subsequent estimates to be more realistic.

Judgment Error 6: Escalation of Commitment

You just replaced the entire exhaust system on your somewhat rusty 1996 Volvo sedan, for $850. Two days later, you hear a clanking sound and take your Volvo

"When you discover you are riding a dead horse, the best strategy is to dismount . . . do not buy a stronger whip, declare that the horse is better, faster or cheaper dead, or harness several other dead horses together for increased speed."

—Judge Thomas Penfield Jackson

directly to the mechanic. She tells you your Volvo will need a new clutch and major engine overhaul—at a cost of $1,400. Most people in this situation would spring for the repairs on the car, believing they have already spent $850 on the car, despite that the money already spent is irrelevant to the cost of the new repairs. This phenomenon is known as **escalation of commitment.** The idea is simple: People are likely to continue to invest additional resources (time, money, and so on) in failing courses of action even though no foreseeable payoff is evident. The phrase, "throwing good money after bad," is the essence of escalation of commitment.

Escalation is prevalent for several reasons. First, we don't want to admit that our solution may not have been the right one so we stay the course. Second, we don't want to appear inconsistent or irrational so we continue to hope for the best even though data simply don't justify such a response. Third, in organizations, not continuing could be seen as giving up rather than fighting onward—and nobody likes a quitter.

Overcoming Judgment Biases

Unfortunately, there are no simple or surefire ways to always avoid common decision biases. Such biases remain exceedingly hard to avoid even when we are acutely aware of what they are and how often they occur. Consider the case of Jeffrey Z. Rubin, who was among the most notable scholars in the study of escalation before his death in 1995. Professor Rubin was killed in a climbing accident when he continued to climb after his climbing partner turned back due to adverse weather conditions. Make no mistake, the biases are insidious and hardest to detect in our *own* decision making. Nonetheless, useful tactics, perhaps more aptly called *defenses*, exist: (1) confidence estimates, (2) trial and error calibration, and (3) healthy skepticism.

Confidence Estimates

Since we tend toward overconfidence in our decision making, one way to curb that bias is to attach an estimate of confidence to beliefs held by ourselves and others. For example, say you want to improve the on-time delivery problem of your pizza delivery drivers. You ask one driver, "How many deliveries per week can you make on-time?" Your driver says 18. Okay, fair enough. But how confident is your driver? When asked, she (You were thinking it was a man, weren't you? Pesky biases!) claims about an 80 percent confidence level. Well, now it seems 18 isn't really a good estimate after all. In fact, a more accurate and useable estimate would be 15 to 22 on-time deliveries per week. Now, you have a more realistic estimate of what your driver can reasonably accomplish.

Most experts agree reliance on "single point" estimates is dangerous—they just don't provide enough information. So using confidence estimations to build "confidence ranges" can move you away from single-point estimations. As psychologist Scott Plous notes, the best method is simply to stop yourself or others and ask, "What is the chance that this judgment is wrong?"[12]

Trial and Error Calibration

One familiar, but underutilized, method for improving problem solving is through trial and error. That is, if you want to improve your success rate and reduce failure *tomorrow,* you must learn from your successes and failures *today.* To illustrate, most people are surprised to learn weather forecasters are

"If at first you don't succeed, try again. Then quit. There's no use being a damn fool about it."

—W.C. Fields

"Good judgment comes from experience. Experience comes from bad judgment."

—Walter Wriston

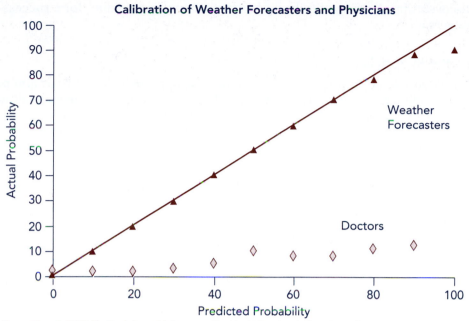

Calibration of Weather Forecasters and Physicians

Source: Plous, S. (1993). *The Psychology of Judgment and Decision Making*. New York: McGraw Hill.

FIGURE 3.3

Accuracy of Weather Forecasters versus Physicians

incredibly accurate. In fact, when an experienced weather person predicts a 40 percent chance of rain, it rains 39 percent of the time!

Compare that accuracy rate to that of physicians. One study in a clinical setting asked physicians to review patients' medical history and conduct a physical examination and then predict the likelihood that a patient had pneumonia.[13] The results make you wish that physicians were more like weather forecasters. That is, when physicians said there was a 65 percent chance of pneumonia, they were accurate only 10 percent of the time. It didn't improve with confidence either. When they predicted an 89 percent chance of pneumonia, they were right just 12 percent of the time (see Figure 3.3). Why are weather forecasters so accurate and physicians less accurate? The answer lies in a key aspect of trial and error, namely regular feedback and knowledge of results.

Weather forecasters predict rain and in a few hours get the results of their prediction; they get to see immediately weather that confirms or disconfirms their meteorological model. If the model was right, they note what they did; if it was wrong, they examine the data and note the aspects that led to the wrong prediction. This process repeats itself everyday as forecasters *calibrate* their predictions with the results. Research supports this calibration process as a way to avoid biases and make better decisions.

Training yourself to use trial and error calibration involves a few simple steps. First, with every prediction, record the reasons why you've established the prediction. In several studies, researchers have found that when they make note of the reasons for their decision they do a better job of tracking and learning.[14]

Second, track the results. Consequences are often separated greatly by time; not all of us get the luxury of seeing the immediate results of our forecasts each day. So keep good records of what happened so you have the ability to defend decisions. When others say, "We always lose business when we release a product too soon," you'll be ready with data that might poke holes in such thinking.

Third, study the success *and* failures—you need *both* confirming and disconfirming evidence to truly know. Fourth, remember that chance is not

"I've learned that mistakes can often be as good a teacher as success."

—Jack Welch

self-correcting. A string of failures does not mean you are "due" for a success or vice versa.

Healthy Skepticism

Another simple but powerful rule of thumb is to approach all decisions and presented evidence with healthy skepticism. Be prepared to challenge yourself and other "experts" and seek out negative or disconfirming evidence. Here are a few specific questions that reflect a healthy skepticism and can ultimately lead to better decisions:

- What are the strongest arguments against my position? On what basis am I rejecting them? (You may want to write these down.)
- What are the weakest parts of my position? On what basis am I accepting them? Would I find this reasoning convincing if an opponent used it to justify her arguments?
- How will I know if I am wrong? Given that we have a strong tendency toward escalation of commitment and denial, if we can construct in advance a personal definition of failure/error, then we may know when it's time for plan B. Sharing that with someone else is a good way to keep you honest.
- In considering facts, ask questions like: How do we know this? What is the base rate (could something just be random and we mistakenly presume cause)? Percentage of what? What are the available facts?
- Are there more alternatives?

In short, the best defenses for decision biases are:

1. Do not jump to conclusions.
2. Do not assume a relationship is a cause; record and test your decision outcomes.
3. Do not base your conclusion only on your own experience.
4. Do not just look to support your case; look for the nonsupporting evidence too.
5. Do not fall prey to overconfidence; get confidence estimates and ranges.

These defenses are simple to know but hard to do. If you find yourself thinking how commonsensical these defenses may seem, you would be wise to recall the remarkable frequency of decision biases even among the brightest of people. Challenge yourself to recognize and steer clear of those biases in your own thinking.

Solving Problems Ethically and Effectively

"A good decision cannot guarantee a good outcome. All real decisions are made under uncertainty. A decision is therefore a bet, and evaluating it as good or not must depend on the stakes and the odds, not on the outcome."

—W. Edwards Deming

In thinking about an effective model for attacking problems, two notes are important to make at the outset. First, as the quote from W. Edwards Deming insightfully conveys, there truly is a difference between good *decisions* and good *outcomes*. That is, you can never fully control the outcomes of your decisions. What you can control is *how* you will decide—and that is the importance of understanding a framework and having the discipline to use it.

Second, there is no such thing as a perfect decision or a perfect decision process. As humans, we will always be subject to **bounded rationality.**[15] Our brains' limitations constrain our thinking and reasoning ability, and, thus, it is impossible to consider simultaneously all information relevant to any decision or problem. Bounded rationality leads managers to engage in what is known as **satisficing** or determining the most acceptable solution to a problem, rather than an optimal one. Nonetheless, adhering to a problem solving model has been shown to improve decision quality, and a number of proven tools and techniques are worth utilizing in different situations. Below we outline a popular model as well as some of the better tools for employing each element of that model. The model consists of five major steps that we abbreviate into the acronym **PADIL** (pronounced "paddle"), or problem, alternatives, decide, implement, learn.

A Problem Solving Framework: PADIL

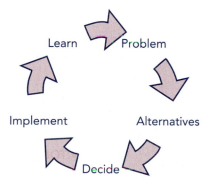

FIGURE 3.4

The PADIL Problem Solving Framework

Define and Structure the Problem

The first step in any good problem solving process is to define and structure the problem. Put another way, you want to be sure you are working on the *correct* problem. One common way this seemingly obvious starting point is mishandled is to begin with a *solution*, not the problem. For example, take the common managerial lament: "In my company, there is a serious lack of training." That may potentially be true, but a more appropriate problem framing process would bring forth the question, "What's the problem that more training would address?" Training is one potential solution to a problem of skill deficiency, but we first need to clarify that skill deficiency is a problem rather than, say, motivation or availability of resources. Moreover, even if skill deficiency is the problem, training is only one possible solution. People can acquire skills through several other means, such as on-the-job practice, experience, and mentoring.

A problem well stated is a problem half solved.

–John Dewey

The temptation to jump to a solution is very powerful and leads to what problem solving expert Ian Mitroff calls "solving the wrong problem precisely."[16] There are several ways in which people solve the wrong problem precisely.

- **Picking the wrong stakeholders.** Solving the wrong problem often occurs because the problem solver fails to include key players. For example, in order to solve a problem on a manufacturing line, including people who actually work on the line to help define the problem would be helpful.

- **Framing the problem too narrowly.** Problems are often larger than they may at first appear. Managers can mistakenly limit that scope early by assuming the problem is narrow. For example, a manager might deal with theft in his department by assuming the problem is unique to his department rather than throughout the organization. Starting with a particular solution in mind is not an effective strategy.

- **Failure to think systemically.** Individuals focus on a particular aspect of the problem, rather than the entire system or interrelated aspects of the problem. Focusing on the system allows for the examination of the real problem or "root cause."

- **Failure to find the facts.** The old adage "first seek to understand" is critical if you are to solve the right problem. There are good and efficient tools for uncovering the facts in any problem situation, rather than making hasty generalizations with untested assumptions and anecdotes.

Assess Key Stakeholders

Few problems in organizations are unique to one person. That is, problems and their proposed solutions likely have far-reaching implications beyond those in your immediate surroundings. For this reason, no problem solving effort is complete without an understanding of the key stakeholders. A **stakeholder** is literally anyone who has a stake in the problem or solution. Any problem you're trying to solve usually impacts more people than you might initially think. Therefore, one critical piece of problem definition is to conduct a stakeholder analysis, which will help you uncover the various parties involved in a problem and its potential solution. Tool Kit 3.1 at the end of the chapter describes the specific steps involved in completing such an analysis.

Management Live 3.3

Solving the Wrong Problem Precisely

Examples abound of solving the wrong problem precisely. One compelling example is the story of the Make-A-Wish Foundation, a first-rate non-profit with passion. Its sole mission is to find ways to grant dreams and wishes to terminally ill children. In 1996, the organization made headlines as it attempted to fulfill the wish of a 17-year-old boy named Erik. Erik's dream was to kill a Kodiak bear in the wild and display the skin in front of the fireplace. To fulfill the wish, the foundation enlisted the Safari Club International to purchase all the hunting equipment and make the dream happen. With outstanding coordination, the Safari Club and Make-A-Wish fulfilled Erik's wish. Unfortunately, the decision to grant this wish had some unforeseen consequences, namely, outraging every animal activist group in the country. Newspapers were flooded with bad press about the foundation's inability to make good decisions, tarnishing the group's reputation. The foundation solved the problem of "finding a way to make Erik's wish come true" quite precisely because they viewed the problem simply as "granting the wish." In reality, the problem was much more complex and required a full examination of all those potentially affected by this solution, namely the key stakeholders.

Determining Whom to Involve

One of the more challenging issues you will face in problem solving is determining who owns a particular problem; that is, who should be primarily accountable for solving the problem. For example, it is common for a manager to mistakenly delegate problems to an employee or team when the manager is actually the most appropriate person to solve the problem. Equally common, managers often attempt to solve a problem on their own when employee input or actual delegation is required.

Although research shows getting others involved in problem solving usually results in better decisions, it does not mean others should always make the final decision. In other words, sometimes a manager just needs input from employees (a voice not a vote) and that is the extent of their involvement. In other cases, delegating the decision to those most closely involved is appropriate. As noted above, a common trap is to make a habit of solving employee problems in isolation.

One useful tool for helping gauge the appropriate level of involvement in problem solving is that developed by Victor Vroom and Phillip Yetton.[17] Those authors note that a decision-maker could involve others on a broad continuum ranging from no involvement to full employee delegation. As seen in Figure 3.5, this continuum represents five key participation approaches: decide, consult individually, consult group, facilitate group, delegate to group.

Thus, you have five approaches for engaging (or disengaging) in the problem solving process. The model goes one step further, however, in helping you decide which of the five approaches will be most useful given the problem you are facing. The framework identifies seven factors that must be addressed before you decide which approach is best. These factors can be framed as

| FIGURE 3.5 | **Vroom and Yetton's Problem Solving Approaches[18]** |

Decide	Consult Individually	Consult Group	Facilitate Group	Delegate to Group
Manager makes the decision alone and announces it to employees.	Manager presents the problem to individual employees and uses input to make the decision.	Manager presents the problem to all employees in manager's group and uses group's input to make the decision.	Manager presents the problem to group and acts as a facilitator to help define the problem. Manager acts as a peer on the problem solving team.	Manager gives problem to employees and permits employees to decide using an appropriate decision making model. Manager provides necessary resources to ensure the group's success.

Manager-Driven Problem Solving → Employee-Driven Problem Solving

Source: Reprinted from *Organizational Dynamics*, vol. 28, no.4, by V.H. Vroom, "Leadership and the Decision Making Process," pp. 82–94. Copyright © 2000, with permission from Elsevier.

questions to be answered, though not all factors will be present in every problem situation.[19]

1. Decision Significance—the significance of the decision to the success of the unit/organization.

2. Importance of Commitment—importance of employee commitment to the decision.

3. Leader's Expertise—manager's knowledge or expertise regarding the problem.

4. Likelihood of Commitment—the likelihood that employees would commit themselves to a decision made by the manager alone.

5. Group Support—the degree to which employees support the unit or organization's stake in the problem.

6. Group Expertise—the degree to which the group of employees has knowledge or expertise regarding the problem.

7. Group Competence—the employees' abilities to work together in solving the problem.

Using your evaluation of the seven factors in simple high(H) or low(L) terms, you can create a flow chart (see Figure 3.6) that will yield the most effective participation approach. Keep in mind this is a highly prescriptive approach and certainly cannot take into account every possible scenario. However, Vroom and his colleagues have demonstrated in multiple studies that managers using this method had a success rate of 62 percent versus a 37 percent success rate for

FIGURE 3.6

Vroom Participation Decision Tree

Source: Reprinted from *Organizational Dynamics*, vol. 28, no. 4, by V.H. Vroom, "Leadership and the Decision-Making Process," pp. 82–94. Copyright © 2000, with permission from Elserier.

Time-Driven Model

Decision Significance	Importance of Commitment	Leader's Expertise	Likelihood of Commitment	Group Support	Group Expertise	Team Competence	
H	H	H	H	-	-	-	Decide
			L	H	H	H	Delegate
						L	Consult (Group)
					L	-	Consult (Group)
				L	-	-	Consult (Group)
		L	H	H	H	H	Facilitate
						L	Consult (Individually)
					L	-	Consult (Individually)
				L	-	-	Consult (Individually)
			L	H	H	H	Facilitate
						L	Consult (Group)
					L	-	Consult (Group)
				L	-	-	Consult (Group)
	L	H	-	-	-	-	Decide
		L		H	H	H	Facilitate
						L	Consult (Individually)
					L	-	Consult (Individually)
				L	-	-	Consult (Individually)
L	H	-	H	-	-	-	Decide
			L	-	-	H	Delegate
						L	Facilitate
	L	-	-	-	-	-	Decide

(Left margin vertical label: PROBLEM STATEMENT)

managers who did not use the method.[20] Thus, even though it may not take into account every possible factor, it seems to do a good job at capturing the most *important* factors.

Framing the Problem Correctly

Before you begin to solve any problem, you must learn to frame the problem correctly. This is the essence of solving the right problem precisely. Strong evidence suggests the way in which a problem is stated determines the quantity and quality of solutions generated.[21] Consider the following problem:

> The parking lot outside an office building is jammed with workers' cars. Management decides to tackle the problem so they convene a committee with instructions to devise different ways to redesign the parking lot to hold more cars. The work group does its job, coming up with six different methods for increasing the lot's capacity.[22]

The problem defined by management in this case is "to redesign the parking lot to hold more cars." Has the real problem been framed correctly? No! Management didn't charge the work group with solving the problem (the jammed parking lot), but rather gave them a solution (redesign the lot) and asked for different methods to implement that solution. Further, the real problem as framed correctly would be, "The parking lot is jammed with cars," and a statement of *why* this is a problem, perhaps "Thus, it can't accommodate all of our employees who drive to work." Framed this way, the work group is free to consider all sorts of potential solutions, which may include expanding the parking lot, but could also include providing benefits for taking public transportation or carpool programs.

Framing problems correctly is difficult since our immediate need is to begin solving the problem. But the way in which a problem is framed can lead to drastically different actions with varied consequences.[23] Consider some research that asked participants either "Do you get headaches *frequently*, and if so, how often?" or "Do you get headaches *occasionally*, and if so, how often?" The words "frequently" versus "occasionally" are the only difference in these statements. In this study, participants asked the first question responded with an average of 2.2 headaches per week (*frequently*), whereas participants asked the second question reported 0.7 headaches per week (*occasionally*). A simple word change in how a problem statement is phrased can lead people to arrive at very different conclusions about the nature of the problem.

When you start to examine problem framing, you will notice the tendency for people to generally frame problems in "either–or" terms. This tendency has been termed the **black or white fallacy,** which assumes our choices are clear and limited to two (it's either black or white), when in reality there may be many other choices (shades of gray). Sometimes people make this mistake unconsciously because it does not occur to them that they have other choices. Other times they do it consciously for manipulative purposes—for example, "If I want you to do A, I can increase your odds of doing it by convincing you your only other alternative is B, which is clearly unacceptable."

Let's look at another example of how framing problems is tricky. In a research study, one group of participants read the following first scenario and another group read the second:

1. The government is preparing to combat a rare disease expected to take 600 lives. Two alternative programs to combat the disease have been proposed, each of which, scientists believe, will have certain consequences. Program A will save 200 people if adopted. Program B has a one-third chance of saving all 600, but a two-thirds chance of saving no one. Which program do you prefer?

"If you're seeking a creative answer to your problem, you must first give sufficient attention to understanding what the problem is."

—Gerard Nierenberg

2. The government is preparing to combat a rare disease expected to take 600 lives. Two alternative programs to combat the disease have been proposed, each of which, scientists believe, will have certain consequences. Through Program A, 400 people would die if adopted. For Program B, there is a one-third chance that no one would die, but a two-thirds chance that all 600 would die. Which program do you prefer?

Both scenarios are exactly the same, that is, they are logically equivalent. In scenario 1, the problem is framed in terms of *lives saved*, whereas in scenario 2 the problem is framed in terms of *lives lost*. This simple change leads participants to avoid risk and heavily endorse program A (72 percent) in the "lives saved" frame and largely seek risk by selecting program B (78 percent) in the "lives lost" frame (see Figure 3.7).

FIGURE 3.7

Framing Effects and Risk

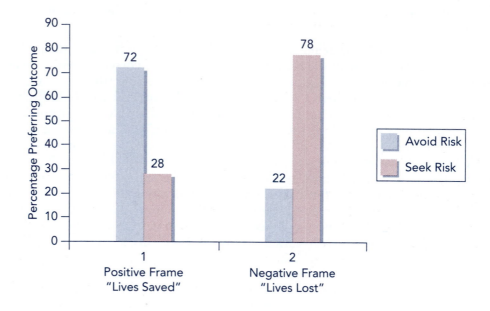

Thinking Systemically

No discussion of solving the right problem is complete without a basic understanding of systems and systems thinking. A **system** is a perceived whole whose elements "hang together" because they continually affect each other over time and operate toward a common purpose.[24] The human body is a great example of a system. When you see the doctor because your stomach hurts, the doctor examine other areas of your body and takes your temperature, blood pressure, and pulse. Why is that?

It is because the stomach is part of a larger bodily system. Thus, your doctor is attempting to find the root cause of your stomach problem, which may have nothing to do with your stomach at all, but rather be a problem with your pancreas that contributes to stomach pain or sore back muscles creating pain that feels like it's coming from your stomach. Effective problem solving almost always demands attention to a larger system and uncovering the root cause(s) (for example, pancreas) whereas simply treating the symptoms (stomach pain) will not solve the problem adequately.

Organizations are elaborate systems and contain thousands of interrelated parts, some of which are more obvious than others. All systems express what is known as **systemic structure** or a pattern of interrelationships among the system components. The challenge is symptoms are always much more visible than their underlying systemic structure. Yet this underlying structure is what holds the promise for real problem solving.

"As soon as one problem is solved, another rears its ugly head."

So a systems approach—"How will this change affect other things?"—is critical to being effective. A helpful visual is to think of system structure as being part of an iceberg. Icebergs exist above and below the water, meaning part of the iceberg is quite visible while another part is completely concealed (see Figure 3.8).

At the tip of the iceberg are events in the system. Turnover has increased, sales are down, or orders are delayed are all examples of events that take place in an organizational system. Problems solved at the event level tend to be short-lived and do nothing to actually address the real problem. For example, if turnover is high, we might institute a new bonus system, hoping to retain employees. But if the real reason turnover is high has nothing to do with the pay system, it is unlikely to work.

"The significant problems we face cannot be solved at the same level of thinking we were at when we created them."

—Albert Einstein

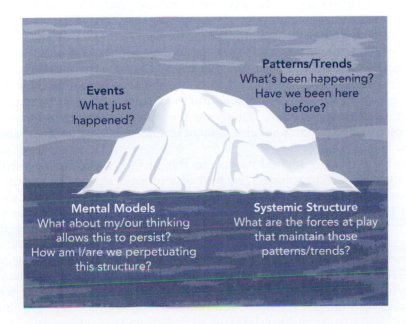

FIGURE 3.8

The Systems Approach Iceberg

Working our way toward the water are patterns of behavior or trends. That means examining the problem by seeking to understand the overall pattern that has persisted over time. For example, as we plot data for turnover, we might find turnover is always highest in one particular month out of the year when the competition tends to seek new talent. Thinking at the trend level, as opposed to the event level, helps us to put the most recent events in context.

Finally, under the water is the systemic structure. The systemic structure represents the most powerful information because it focuses on the actual cause of the patterns of behavior, which then explain the events. If you really want to solve a problem, you must solve the right problem by getting to the systemic structure.

One reason people have trouble thinking systemically is we are taught to view the world in linear, rather than nonlinear terms. Purely linear thinking is a bit of a fallacy in that it rests on the assumption that present trends will continue in the same direction and pace (for example, when you retire, a Toyota Prius will cost $209,000 and a Big Mac $25). Strategy plans often fail because strategists assume the world as we know it will not change much and that current trends are permanent. Perhaps the most common example of linear management thinking is that companies with a hot new product overexpand their capacity only to find themselves out of luck when demand softens.

Let's view another example using the iceberg approach. Suppose a fire breaks out in your area. This is an *event*. If you respond by putting the fire out, you are simply reacting. In other words, you've not doing anything that would prevent new fires. If however you not only extinguish the fire but study the location of fires in your area, you are paying attention to *patterns*. For example, you might notice certain neighborhoods incur more fires than others. One response would be to adapt to this pattern by adding more fire houses in those areas. What if, however, you examined the *systems*—which might include smoke detector distribution and building material used—that sustain the patterns fires? That might lead you to build new fire alarm systems and establish new safety codes. Using this approach, you are getting to the bottom of preventing new fires.[25]

Why do most communities respond to an increase of fires by hiring more fire personnel? The answer is people often solve problems based on faulty thinking and rarely identify the systemic structures at work. To identify these systemic structures requires uncovering one's assumptions (discovering what's below the surface) or our mental models about the systemic structure. **Mental models** are the prevailing assumptions, beliefs, and values that sustain current systems. These habits of thought enable us to ignore valid data, despite the fact that those data are essential to solving the problem. In addition, we protect and preserve these mental models by making them "undiscussable." That is, they become ways of being in organizations. So even if our thinking is faulty, we don't question it or examine it. If you've ever heard, "That's just the way its done," or "We have an understanding about that," that's a clue a mental model may be contributing to the problem.

Learning how to bring mental models to the surface or challenge them is important to good problem solving. The best way to learn this skill is by understanding how to ask the right questions about a problem, that is, developing **inquiry skills.** Inquiry skills allow you to examine your own mental models as well as others. For example, let's say you're trying to solve the problem of dropped calls in your customer service center. You seek your employees' opinion by asking the following question: "Why are there so many dropped calls in the service center?" You're likely to get great responses, but how will you know what the real problem is? You won't unless you attempt to find the root cause. That is, when your employees respond with reasons, your response should not be, "OK, thank

"He who asks a question may be a fool for five minutes, but he who never asks a question remains a fool forever."

—Tom Connelly

you," but to dig deeper. These question stems can help you dig deeper toward the root cause:

- What leads you to believe that is the case?
- What conditions exist that allow this to occur?
- Can you tell me more?
- What have you seen that may contribute to this problem?
- Can you help me understand your thinking?
- What do we assume to be true?

Inquiry skills are aimed at understanding people's mental models. This includes examining your own mental models, including asking "What is my role in this problem?" and "What about my behavior allows this problem to persist?" You can easily delude yourself into thinking the problem is out there when in fact it may be closer to home than you think! One good way to examine mental models is through the right-hand/left-hand exercise described in Chapter 2—it is truly an outstanding tool.

Tools for Understanding the Problem Scope

Some problems have a very well defined scope while others are quite broad. Your job is to determine the boundaries of your problem—that is, determining what is truly germane to your problem and what falls outside the realm of the problem. With most problems, potential causes and solutions are infinite. Your job is to narrow the potential causes down and move on to the next step in the PADIL process—*alternatives*. We discuss various tools for helping you understand the problem scope. You can use these tools on your own, but they work best when you have a few key stakeholders working with you. If you engage in these exercises with a team, keep in mind your team members are likely to censor their comments about problems if they think you won't want to hear them. Don't kick off the exercises by offering your opinion first; the group will likely conform to it. Let others go first.

"It's not that I'm so smart; it's just that I stay with problems longer."

—Albert Einstein

Affinity Diagram. The affinity (similarity) diagram is an idea generation method that allows you to sort the major aspects of the problem into themes or categories. The categories will help when you begin to gather data about the problem and research alternatives. The following steps outline how to create an affinity diagram.

1. Write the problem statement (one you've framed well) on a flip chart or board. Underneath the problem, write the phrase, "What are the possible causes of it?"
2. Using sticky notes, allow each person to write as many potential causes of the problem as possible, one per sticky note, and place them on the board or flip chart. Do not evaluate the merit of each person's idea.
3. Once all the ideas are posted, begin to look for similarities in the ideas. Group the similar notes and label them by the category they represent. For example, "These five seem to deal with our 'Delivery Process' and these three with our 'Customer Service Structure'." You now have some ideas for where to begin your data collection.

Is/Is Not. This simple method determines your problem's boundaries by describing aspects that are part of the problem and those that are not. Use the following steps as a guideline.

1. On a piece of paper or flip chart, write the problem statement.

2. Draw a line down the middle. On one side put the word "Is" and on the other the words "Is Not." Down the left-hand side of the paper, write the words "what," "who," "when," and "where."

3. Answer the questions. What *is* the crux of the problem, what *is not* the crux of the problem? Who *is* involved with this problem, who *is not* involved? When *is* the problem a problem, when *is it not* a problem? Where *is* the problem appearing most, where *is it not* appearing most?

Graphic Displays.   Sometimes, a picture is worth a thousand words. Taking what you know about the problem so far and graphing it in some meaningful way can be incredibly helpful. A **histogram** or bar chart allows for the display of data categories (on the X axis) tracked against some important standard (on the Y axis). For example, type of part manufactured (X axis) and the number of parts per type made each hour (Y axis). A scatter plot can also be useful. The scatter plot demonstrates the relationship between two variables. For instance, you might track students' test grades on one axis (Y) and student absences on the other axis (X) to see if there is some type of relationship between test grades and class attendance. For instance, we might expect to find that, as absences decrease, test grades increase.

One of the most powerful graphic displays is known as a behavior over time chart, or BOT. In order to create a BOT, you need to have been collecting data for some given time period. Let's say you regularly track customer service behaviors (for example, problems solved in first call, number of calls handled per hour, and so on). As you plot these behaviors over time, you may start to see patterns emerge. For example, you may notice that during two months in the year the call volume skyrockets. As you piece this information together with other data you routinely collect, you also note an increase in employee absenteeism that corresponds with those spikes. Problem solving experts agree certain patterns that appear in BOTs can help to identify a *systematic* problem, one not likely to respond to a quick fix[26]. These include:

- Increases that level off.
- Steeply rising increases.
- Steeply falling decreases.
- "Boom and bust" cycles (such as up- and downswings).

Generate Creative Alternatives

Hopefully, the process of framing the problem will lead you to think about many potential solutions to the problem. Research shows that generating multiple alternatives to problems results in higher quality solutions. And the key to doing so is finding ways to generate as many creative alternatives as possible. Let's examine the following scenario:

> A building manager receives several complaints about the long wait times for the building's elevator. He calls a consultant who recommends three alternatives: (1) build new elevators, (2) space out the elevators between floors or (3) make the elevators faster. The manager thinks these solutions are good, but costly. The manager then consults a psychologist, who recommends giving people something to do while they wait. The manager installs mirrors by the elevators and the complaints stop.

The alternative proposed by the psychologist was not only cheap, it was incredibly effective; people simply occupied their time looking at themselves. Would you have thought of that? We certainly didn't and herein lies the quandary: Left

"The key to having a good idea is to have lots of ideas."
—Linus Pauling

to our own thinking, we rarely arrive at truly creative and unique alternatives to problems. Most of the time, our alternative solutions look awfully familiar and offer only slight improvements. (What should we do this weekend? Well, what did we do last weekend?) Moreover, we often trust the first solution out of the box.[27] We don't question whether other, perhaps better solutions exist. Say that a recruiter calls you and offers you a job more attractive than your current one. Would you take the job? Most people will compare their current job with the new offer and arrive at an emphatic, "Yes! Where do I sign up?" Yet, if you're going to take the step of leaving your current job, why limit yourself to one alternative, the one presented by the recruiter? Wouldn't you want to explore other possible job opportunities that could be even more attractive?[28]

Brainstorming

Another key process issue is idea generation. While it may seem contradictory, good brainstorming sessions are more likely to result from a disciplined protocol (see Management Live 3.4 on IDEO's brainstorming rules). In an effective

Management Live 3.4

Brainstorming at IDEO

Below is a list of brainstorming techniques used by IDEO, a consulting firm noted for its creative ideas and client list of major companies. IDEO staff recommends setting a 20- to 30-minute time limit on your brainstorming and appointing one team member to make sure the team honors these rules.

1. **Defer Judgment.** Don't dismiss any ideas. This will be difficult for a group of analytical types who will instantly want to talk about what is wrong with the idea and why it wouldn't work. But nothing shuts down a brainstorming session like criticism.

2. **Build on the Ideas of Others.** No "buts," only "ands."

3. **Encourage Wild Ideas.** Embrace the most out-of–the-box notions because they can be the key to solutions. Every idea is a good idea. These ideas may not ultimately be adopted, but might trigger other ideas.

4. **Go for Quantity.** Aim for as many new ideas as possible. In a good session, up to 50 ideas are generated in 30 minutes.

5. **Be Visual and Auditory.** Use yellow, red, and blue markers to write on big 30-inch by 25-inch sticky notes that are put on the wall. This is important because reading others' ideas will spur your thinking. As you write your idea, say it out loud for everyone to hear.

6. **Stay Focused on the Topic.** Always keep the discussion on target. Your facilitator will help with this. If there is a question about whether something should be included on the wall, put it up there.

7. **One Conversation at a Time.** No interrupting, no dismissing, no disrespect, and no rudeness.

After the 30-minute brainstorming session, go to the wall and have the team attempt to group the ideas. Precision isn't as important as establishing general categories. Discard identical ideas and pair up ideas that are similar. Next, discuss the ideas the team has come up with, and be sure to discuss what might be interesting about an idea before the team goes into a criticism mode. New ideas may still be popping up. Write down these additional ideas and get them up on the wall. Consider how ideas may be combined to create an even better solution.

The team may then have a long list of ideas and need to narrow them down to a more manageable number for further development. Use a multivote system to narrow the list to three to five items.

Source: *BusinessWeek,* May 17, 2004, 89.

brainstorming session, the group sits around a table with a flip chart or some way to visibly present the input. The brainstorming facilitator states the problem in a clear manner so all participants understand it. Members then "free-wheel" (without limiting themselves) as many alternatives as they can in a given length of time. No criticism is allowed, and all alternatives are recorded for later discussion and analysis. Judgments of even the most bizarre suggestions are withheld until later because one idea can stimulate others. Disallowing criticism thus encourages group members to "think the unusual."

Brainwriting

Organizations now love brainstorming, and the prevailing assumption is it works in generating many creative ideas. So companies all across the country place people in conference rooms and tell them, "Be creative, solve our problems." Unfortunately, recent syntheses of research on brainstorming suggest in some cases brainstorming sessions are rendered ineffective because of problems related to group dynamics in which people aren't able to defer judgment, can be critical of others, and usually don't "let it all hang out" toward solving the problem.[29] Indeed, one meta-analytic study found that involving a team or group of people actually produced far fewer ideas than the same number of individuals generating ideas on their own.

"All it takes is one idea to solve an impossible problem."

—Robert H. Schuller

With that in mind, a modest variant of brainstorming called **brainwriting** has emerged as the superior method for generating the highest volume of creative ideas.[30] Using the same rules as brainstorming, brainwriting allows participants time to generate ideas on their own, recording them but not sharing them with the group initially. Then participants in a round-robin format read off their ideas until all alternatives have been presented and people can then build upon them. There are several ways to improve the quantity and quality of the alternatives presented:[31]

- **Diversify Participants.** Make sure the people involved in brainstorming represent diverse perspectives on the topic—your key stakeholders and even some outsiders (customers, suppliers) who aren't familiar with your particular problems. Research shows diverse groups perform better than nondiverse groups on creative problem-solving tasks.[32]

- **Use Metaphors and Analogies.** When a car dealership wanted to increase the number of people walking in the door by creating a more pleasurable shopping experience, they focused on pleasurable things such as food. Using food as a metaphor they agreed that chocolate (smooth, sweet, comforting) made for a good metaphor to focus on delivering services that went smoothly and were sweet and comforting, as opposed to aggressive.[33] The popular potato chips, Pringles, were the result of an analogical process. The problem was potato chips required too much shelf space, but packing them tightly destroyed them. The manufacturer used the analogy of dried leaves (noting similar properties to potato chips) and showed that when leaves were slightly damp, they could be stacked without losing their shapes, hence Pringles.

- **Performance Standards and Feedback.** Research shows a group of problem solvers can increase the number of ideas generated by setting high performance standards, as long as they are not impossible. In addition, providing feedback on how the brainwriting is going is central. Simply stop every now and then and gauge the number of ideas generated and let people know whether they are ahead or behind the curve.

- **Assume a "Perfect World."** Key to generating really creative alternatives is to encourage people to simply assume there are no constraints to solving a problem. What would you wish for if you could get it? What would a perfect world look like?[34]

Benchmarking

A popular form of generating alternatives known as benchmarking is used in approximately one-quarter of organizational problem solving scenarios.[35] In **benchmarking,** organizational representatives trying to solve a problem go to visit (either literally or figuratively) other organizations thought to have successfully solved the problem or a similar one. During the visit, problem solvers generate ideas that might work in their own organization. The knee-jerk reaction of most managers is to try to visit others in the same industry that might have some great practices to share. However, benchmarking seems to be most effective for generating ideas when managers visit organizations that specialize in the particular problem area, regardless of the industry. For example, a bank that wants to improve customer service would often benefit more by visiting the Ritz-Carlton or Nordstrom to generate new ideas rather than visiting another financial services organization.

"You don't need to necessarily have any good ideas; you just need to be able to recognize them."

—Unknown

Although benchmarking can be a good starting point and impetus for change, it is hardly a foolproof means of generating alternatives and sometimes even leads to decision failures. For example, problem solvers can be inclined to rush to implement the exact process of the benchmarked company assuming it will work similarly in their organization. It falls short when problem solvers fail to realize their problem is truly different than the one addressed by the benchmark company and that the new solution doesn't quite work in their culture. In addition, people often have strong negative reactions to, and are inclined to resist, ideas not invented in or derived from their own organizations.

Once alternatives have been generated, how will you know you've got good ones to choose from? Good alternatives will have the following characteristics:[36]

- **Postponed Evaluation.** The alternatives proposed were all offered without any evaluative components. No one qualified them as "good" or "feasible," they were simply offered as potential alternatives.
- **Stakeholder Involvement.** The right mix of people had opportunities to look at the problem and offer their take. A well-executed decision will fail if important others don't have input.
- **Organizational Focus.** Great alternatives are consistent with the goals of the organization. Many alternatives may be proposed to fix a problem, but if they violate the organization's values or are inconsistent with its strategic direction, they will likely lead to failure.
- **Time Implications.** The alternatives are not quick fixes but real solutions, not Band-Aids. They focus on short- and long-term solutions.
- **Effective.** The key litmus test of a good alternative is it addresses the actual problem, not something else or even a tangentially related problem.

Decide on a Solution

After the problem has been defined and the alternatives generated, you'll probably want to collect more information about the alternatives. In fact, no manager worth her salt would ever make a decision without knowing a few key factors, such as 1) How much would implementing the solution cost? 2) Who would be involved? 3) Who would be affected? 4) How much time would it take to implement? Put simply, is the alternative feasible and effective, or can it be done given our resources (or with a reasonable resource stretch) and will it actually solve the problem?

Invariably, managers will use one of two approaches to collect this type of information about their alternatives. Managers under time constraints and pressure to solve a problem will seek out very little information and seek only to confirm what they think they already know about the problem. Other managers, in their desire to reduce the uncertainty associated with a problem, will conduct an endless search for information about each potential alternative, so much so they become paralyzed by the mass of data they accumulate. Neither case is ideal. Some research now shows great problem solvers know when to say when. One such study found that, as the amount of information available increases, so does one's confidence about one's ability to make the right decision. Unfortunately, decision accuracy does not increase proportional to increases in information or one's confidence (as seen in Figure 3.9).[37]

We've said we'd present a "management truth" when it exists and here is one: *You will always feel like you don't have enough information.* "If only I knew *X*, I would feel better." You can find some comfort in the fact that having "more" information won't improve your chances of making the right decision. Seek out a handful of critically relevant items and then go with them. Otherwise you will simply delude yourself into thinking that more data will make the decision easier. You will be more familiar with the problem, which makes the problem appear less ambiguous, but in reality the nature of the problem and its potential solutions won't change.

Narrowing Alternatives Tools

One of the most difficult things to do in evaluating alternatives is to narrow your choices. Furtunately, various tools are at your disposal that can help you evaluate the potential of each alternative and quickly narrow them to the few best

> *"I am quick to admit that I do not have all of the answers. So I am going to listen. But shortly after I listen, the second piece is to pull the trigger. I have all the input, and here is what we are going to do. People need closure on a decision. If you listen and then noodle on it, people get confused, and that's not effective leadership."*
>
> —Terry Lundgren, CEO, Federated

FIGURE 3.9   **Accuracy, Confidence, and Amount of Information**

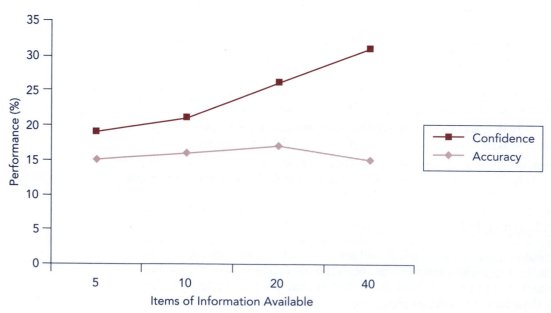

TABLE 3.1 | **Alternatives Table**

Criteria	Alternatives			
	Job 1	Job 2	Job 3	Job 4
Annual Salary	$38,000	$42,000	$41,000	$46,000
Work Schedule	38 hours/week	40 hours/week	50 + hours/week	60 + hours/week
Benefits	Medical, dental, 401(k)	Medical, dental	Medical, company car	Medical, dental, 401(k), concierge service
Work Environment	Cubicle, relaxed	Office, relaxed	Travel, flexible, relaxed	Travel, intense

alternatives. Key to almost all narrowing tools is choosing your criteria carefully. On what basis will you decide which alternative is most attractive? You don't have to identify every single criterion for making the choice, just the big ones.

For example, if you were considering two different job offers, what criteria would be most important? Perhaps salary, work schedule, benefits, and work environment would be the most important. You might deem other criteria like commute time, while important, less critical. Know what criteria are most critical, and then use them to help you narrow the alternatives.

Alternatives Table. The most basic decision tool then is to explicitly state the consequences in one table where comparisons can be made easily. Let's continue with our job example.

As can be seen in Table 3.1, we have simply listed our most important decision criteria on the left side of the table and the job alternatives across the top. Then, in simple terms we have listed all the information about each alternative. The beauty of this table is you can quickly see the tradeoffs. Job 1 pays less, but it has good benefits and offers a great lifestyle, whereas Job 4 pays more, has good benefits, but work will be your life. You might be inclined to ask, "Why do I need this hokey table, can't I simply do these comparisons in my head?" Here again is where the non-obvious traps of problem solving cause problems. According to research, few people can compare even a short list of alternatives in their head effectively[38] and end up focusing or giving too much weight to one particular alternative.

Weighted Ranking. If you've done a great job at generating alternatives and you're facing 25 interesting ideas, you'll probably want to narrow this list rather quickly. Weighted ranking allows you to do this quite nicely. First, in a table, list the criteria down the left side of the first column. Next, compare each criterion to the next and make a tick mark next to the criterion in each pairing you believe to be more important. That is, compare all criteria against each other so that you end up with a rank ordering of the most to least important criteria. In other words, count the tick marks next to each criterion and you've got your ranking for your criteria (high numbers are ranked as most important). This captures reality as some criteria will naturally carry more weight (be more important) than others.

Second, list your alternatives across the top row of the table. Third, on each of your criteria, rate every alternative on some scale, such as 1 through 10 where 1 is very poor and 10 is outstanding. It doesn't matter what scale you use, just be

TABLE 3.2	Weighted Ranking Example					
Criteria	Rank Ordering	Train	Car	Plane	Bicycle	Teleportation
Speed	2	$2 \times 6 = 12$	$2 \times 5 = 10$	$2 \times 10 = 20$	$3 \times 2 = 6$	$2 \times 10 = 20$
Safety	2	$2 \times 5 = 10$	$2 \times 3 = 6$	$2 \times 9 = 18$	$2 \times 1 = 2$	$2 \times 1 = 2$
Cost	1	$1 \times 7 = 7$	$1 \times 9 = 9$	$1 \times 5 = 5$	$1 \times 2 = 2$	$1 \times 1 = 1$
Reliability	1	$1 \times 6 = 6$	$1 \times 7 = 7$	$1 \times 6 = 6$	$1 \times 1 = 1$	$1 \times 1 = 1$
	Totals	35	32	49	11	24

consistent. Finally, multiply your rank ordering by your rating of each alternative. Let's look at an example in which you're determining the best mode of transportation for your vacation (Table 3.2).

As can be seen in Table 3.2, the "plane" satisfies our decision criteria the best. Interestingly, teleportation is better than riding a bike—at least once it's invented (Beam me to South Beach, Scottie).

Paralyzed by Choices

Organizational systems display what is known as **equifinality,** a condition in which *different* initial conditions lead to *similar* effects. In other words, not all roads lead to Rome, but many do. Sometimes the best way to solve a problem is to select *any one* of your final solutions. It may not be the perfect solution or even the optimal one, but it is likely to jump-start your problem solving. Using this logic, attempt to choose the solution that will provide the greatest payoff (not always financial) or leverage. Remember, systems are comprised of thousands of interrelated parts. Your final solution likely will trigger reactions in the system that provide feedback about whether you're on the right track. That doesn't mean you should just start with any old solution; rather, you can breathe easier knowing that, when you've narrowed your choices to a few strong, well-crafted solutions, you are likely to make an impact.

One important technique to help illuminate tradeoffs is known as the **devil's advocate** method, which increases debate and explores a problem from all angles.[39] This method can be accomplished with a group of people or with individuals. Either way, you start by clearly articulating the problem and your favored alternative solution (the one you're "leaning" toward). Assign someone (co-worker, key customer, experienced employee) to play the role of devil's advocate. Your instructions to this person are simple: to challenge the idea, provide a scathing critique of the proposal, poke holes in the logic, and question the assumptions behind it. The devil's advocate will not only help you think through previous blind spots in your solution, he will also help you anticipate consequences. Again, no decision will be perfect, but the more you can anticipate up front, the better you can prepare as you go forward and implement the decision.

Once you've made your decision, state the solution plainly and succinctly. You should be able to explain the problem and the solution in less than 30 seconds. If you can't, others probably won't understand it either. A simple method for doing this is to follow this template: (1) state the problem, (2) state the assumed reason or cause, (3) state the proposed solution, and (4) describe what the solution will do and for whom. For example:

- **Problem:** Customers are complaining about a long wait time at the elevators.

"Be willing to make decisions. That's the most important quality in a good leader. Don't fall victim to what I call the 'ready-aim-aim-aim-aim syndrome.' You must be willing to fire."

—George S. Patton

- **Reason:** The elevators are not significantly slow; customers are just bored waiting.
- **Solution:** Install video screens with CNN and other news channels by elevators.
- **Outcome:** Video screens will preoccupy customers with something other than the elevator, lessen complaints, and increase management's time to devote to other problems and has the additional benefit of keeping customers informed about world events!

Make the Decision

The reality is that all decisions require trade-offs. By definition, when you decide on one course of action, you will eliminate others. You can't do everything. You'll likely find that, when you narrow your alternatives down to only a few, each will have pros and cons. One might cost less, but take much longer to implement than another, whereas another alternative may maximize use of funding and time, but is in direct opposition to top management's wishes. Nothing is perfect, but don't panic.

Inherent to all decisions is the issue of risk and perceptions of fairness. Although you can produce elegant mathematical calculations, algorithms, and probability charts for any decision to represent how much risk is involved, there is always an element of personal perception and judgment.[40] Risk usually presents itself in a few different forms, leading people to make different judgments about how much risk is involved.

First, risk presents itself in terms of *dread*, or circumstances in which people feel they have no control or influence. Terrorism is a prime example of such forms of risk. Second, risk often appears as *unknown*, whereby people assume consequences truly are unknown. The risks involved in mapping the human genome, for instance, remain largely unknown at this time. Third, risk presents itself differently depending on the sheer number of people exposed to a given risk. For example, if a single case of a rare disease is found in your town, you are less likely to see it as a high risk compared to an outbreak where 1 in 3 have contracted the disease. Thus, the manner in which risk presents itself leads people to assess their risk exposure quite differently.

In addition, there are a number of traps involved in people's assessment of risk. For example, research shows that, all things being equal, people are more likely to view positive outcomes as more probable then negative outcomes. In one study, students on average stated that, compared to their peers, they were 15 percent more likely to have positive life events and 20 percent less likely to experience negative life events. That is, although the "objective" risk generally does not change, we believe that for us nature, risk, or chance behaves differently. What does this mean for you? You should attempt to calculate risks objectively but also recognize others will likely view the numbers and the meaning of the risk differently than you.

Implement

As if making the decision were not difficult enough, you must then implement the solution. This chapter is primarily about solving the problem, meaning determining the most appropriate solution. Executing any change in an organization is itself a complex process, one you will read about more fully in Chapter 10 on implementing change. However, a few points deserve mention here.

First, implementing a solution invariably involves others—your stakeholders. That means before you "just do it" you should revisit your stakeholder analysis and discuss with your key stakeholders the best way to roll out your solution. Second, implementation doesn't have to happen all at once. Sometimes the best way to execute a decision is to attain **small wins.** The concept of small wins is a simple but powerful notion of splitting an implementation plan into many steps. Each step is considered a mini-project, and momentum is gained. In this way, you can demonstrate to others your solution has merit, without dumping the whole solution in their lap at one time.

Third, while implementing a solution, many problem solvers unfortunately find they underestimated the problem's scope or defined the problem incorrectly. Although underestimating is discouraging, nothing is gained by staying the course simply to be perceived as consistent or confident in the solution. In the course of implementation, if you uncover significant information indicating you've solved the wrong problem, stop the implementation. Many managers have been burned by implementing solutions they knew were incorrect but forging ahead even with this knowledge. Retreating so far along in the process will cause pain in the short term, but in the long term you will have acted appropriately.

Learn and Seek Feedback

"Punishing honest mistakes stifles creativity. I want people moving and shaking the earth and they're going to make mistakes."

—Ross Perot

Have you ever made the same mistake twice? Do you remember saying to yourself, "I'll never do that again," and lo and behold, you do it again? Harvard's Chris Argyris observes that everyone fails, but truly successful people view the failure as an opportunity to learn or to have a "productive failure."[41] In addition, he notes that most professionals are defensive of their failures and rarely examine their successes. In that sense, very little learning takes place after implementing a decision that will help a manager repeat the success or avoid the failure of the problem solving process.

So the first step in the post-implementation phase of problem solving is to attempt to determine whether the decision was truly successful and continues to be the right solution. That is, the problem should be solved in the way you have defined it. Luckily, because you presumably have already defined success in the early stages of the problem solving process, you have the basics of what's needed.

Management Live 3.5

After Action Review (AAR)

One business buzzword—*knowledge management*—has received a lot of recent attention. The basic idea is that organizations and managers tend to repeat poor decisions. Using knowledge management, managers can attempt to build a database of these poor decisions and learn from them so as to not make the same mistakes in the future. This is much easier said than done as politics and turf battles take precedent and managers feel reluctant to take accountability for poor decisions. An outstanding tool known as **after action review** (AAR) has been developed, however, in which the sole purpose is to learn from mistakes and dilute the political atmosphere.

The AAR was created in the military to review the results of a military exercise immediately after the exercise was completed. To do so, the military exposes every aspect of the exercise to a thorough review of what went well and what did not. This includes an examination of everyone's role in the exercises, including the unit's highest leaders. When a private feels his commanding officer failed to provide information in time, for example, the private reports this information as part of the AAR—a rare opportunity to question commanding officers. Tool Kit 3.5 describes a basic AAR plan.

In the elevator problem, for example, we stated we had hoped our solution would lower customer complaints and increase management's time. Clearly, these measurements are easy to take and should be done periodically to ensure your decision continues to be the right one.

Beyond these primary points of learning, you should also return to your stakeholders once again and collect information about their perceptions of the problem and the solution. We want to know whether or not the final implementation has satisfied stakeholders, but also whether or not the stakeholders were pleased with the process. Did they feel included in the process? Were their voices heard throughout? Completing another brief stockholder analysis is helpful as you look forward to solving other problems in the future. You will know what people like and dislike and the degree to which they wish to be included.

> *"A man who has committed a mistake and doesn't correct it is committing another mistake."*
> —Confucius

Ethics: Making The Tough Choices

"Miss Dugan, will you send someone in here who can distinguish right from wrong?"

Most discussions of ethics, particularly directed at young people, have an idealistic tone. For example, it is common to hear platitudes like "good ethics pay" and "ethics is good business." Unfortunately (and disturbingly), any casual observer of business these days knows behaving unethically can "pay off" as well, and ethical behavior can often result in a loss of business or desired outcomes. Further, traditional conceptions of right and wrong are often blurred in today's workplace. Consider that a recent survey of 111 executives found 52 to 90 percent of executives agreed behaving unethically was appropriate when: (1) performance contingencies demand otherwise, (2) it is necessary to get the job done, (3) unfair or overly restrictive performance standards exist, and (4) it would be necessary to avoid negatively affecting the organization.[42] Most frightening was that 56 percent of those surveyed indicated managers who bend rules are more effective than managers who do not.

> *"The first of all moral obligations is to think clearly."*
> —Michael Novak

FIGURE 3.10 | **College Student Actions**

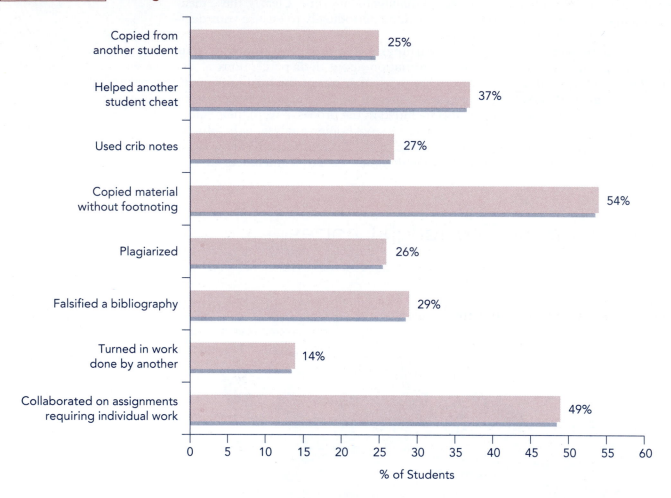

A few other statistics may hit closer to home. In a major study of 6,000 students on 31 campuses in the United States, researchers found the data presented in Figure 3.10.[43]

Roughly two-thirds of students in this research admitted to cheating at least once as an undergraduate. When asked why, students cited pressures and competition related to graduate school admissions. Researchers also collected information about the students' future career choices. The lowest number of admitted cheaters (57 percent) was found in students planning on pursing education-related professions. The numbers rise from there, including medicine (68 percent admitted cheating), government (66 percent), engineers (71 percent) and future MBAs (76 percent). Students also indicated cheating was a relatively harmless crime.

Of course, as ethics author Rushworth Kidder points out, cheating really isn't so harmless:[44]

> You have only to ask who engineered the bridge you are about to cross, or where your doctor got his or her training, to begin questioning whether a widespread propensity for cheating among professionals—and the consequent danger of unleashing into the world a cadre of individuals who don't know what they are doing—is in fact a "victimless crime."

While it may seem that one small act of cheating may not be such a big deal, when you consider the ramifications of a professional culture based on cheating, the act becomes abhorrent. If you knew your heart surgeon cheated her way through medical school, would you be eager to let her perform a triple bypass?

At the same time, ethical behavior is almost never simple or easy, and it is often not self-evident (and no shared consensus exists) what the most ethical action is in any given situation. There are no ethical switches that we can turn on or off, and simply stating that "I am an ethical person" provides nothing to substantiate that claim. According to the Josephson Institute, a center dedicated to the study and practice of ethics, ethical behavior is multidimensional, and the most ethical people act in ways that reflect ethical commitment, consciousness, and competency.

If you choose to strive toward ethical decisions and behavior, it will require your **ethical commitment.** Ethical commitment refers to your level of dedication or desire to do what is right even in the face of potentially harmful personal repercussions. This requires a healthy dose of courage and integrity to make decisions that may be unpopular or go against the prevailing culture. How do you want to live your life? What do you want to be remembered for? What values are worth fighting for? What kind of relationships do you want to have? Do you want to be known as someone who will take a stance for what they believe is right? It has been and always will be quite challenging to be an ethical person. Ethical commitment is about accepting that challenge.

Solving problems ethically also requires an **ethical consciousness** in which you develop an ability to understand the ramifications of choosing less ethical courses of action. Unlike the student who believes that cheating doesn't hurt anyone else, students with an ethical consciousness understand the far-reaching implications of such behavior. Those who are ethically conscious make themselves aware of the implications of their actions and are not oblivious to the many ethical concerns around us.

Finally, a third dimension of ethical behavior is **ethical competency,** which involves a thoughtful consideration of ethics in each stage of the problem solving process. There are no easy ways to ascertain the most ethical choice in a given situation, but there are very useful models for framing and dissecting ethical dilemmas. Whether defining a problem, generating alternatives, or making a decision, ethically competent people consider such models in their choices.

> *"Obviously everyone wants to be successful, but I want to be looked back on as being very innovative, very trusted and ethical and ultimately making a big difference in the world."*
>
> —Sergey Brin, Google founder

Recognizing Ethical Issues

Perhaps the most difficult challenge in solving problems ethically is recognizing what ethical implications exist relating to a given problem. Most problems have ethical implications. Some problems, however, seem to be more easily identifiable as having ethical implications; that is we sense the tension or dilemma immediately. In fact, most dilemmas present themselves not as "right versus wrong" but as "right versus right."[45] That is, ethical dilemmas, the really tough choices, often don't involve clearly right and wrong alternatives, but rather two alternatives that may both have merit. Consider tough issues like:

- It is right to give all little league players equal playing time, and it is also right to field the best team possible.
- It is right to help out a struggling fellow student by letting him see your homework, and it is right to keep your homework proprietary.
- It is right to give money to those living in poverty, and it is right to save money for your family.

Right versus Right Scenarios

"Right versus right" scenarios are the most perplexing of ethical dilemmas. According to Kidder, these dilemmas can be boiled down to a few major themes. With *truth versus loyalty dilemmas,* the struggle is between providing information about some objective truth versus compromising one's loyalty to others. For example, doctors know when a patient discloses a likelihood to commit suicide, the doctor is ethically obligated to breach patient confidentiality, compromising loyalty to the patient. Not all truth versus loyalty situations are so clear. Managers often face such dilemmas when caught between the confidence of a senior manager ("Don't announce the pay cuts.") and an employee who wants to know particular information ("Will our pay be cut?").

A second major theme is *individual versus community.* The needs of individuals such as confidentiality or privacy often clash with those of the community. Terrorism has brought this dilemma clearly to the forefront with governments attempting to preserve individual rights and needs while also understanding the greater good of the community. Much of the conflict regarding the Patriot Act is based on this very issue.

A third category of dilemmas are *short-term versus long-term,* which involve the clash between living in the present versus thinking about the future. Investing financially for the future, for example, often clashes with enjoying the present.

Finally, a fourth theme has to do with *justice versus mercy.* Professors who catch a student cheating face this very problem. On one hand, students who cheat deserve a punishment commensurate with their behavior. On the other hand, students are human and sometimes make bad choices and deserve our compassion to help avoid such mistakes in the future. These themes play out every day. As you explore ethical dilemmas, try to identify the theme at play; it will help you understand the issues more clearly.

Fairness in Decision-Making

When judging the ethical nature of decisions, three factors often come into play: economics, equality, and justice.

Economics

Perhaps the most common ethical issues that arises in the economic domain relate to supply and demand. To illustrate, imagine you're in downtown Seattle and it begins to rain heavily. You stop in a store and ask, "How much for that umbrella over there?" The clerk tells you $18. You look at the price tag that says $13 and immediately rebuke the clerk, but he doesn't budge on the price and says take it or leave it. Is it ethical for the clerk to change the price? Economically speaking, the clerk made the right call. The quality demanded is obviously higher for umbrellas when it's raining and, thus, the market will support a higher price—great decision. Yet this practice violates most people's sense of basic fairness. A research study asked participants whether they believed raising the price in such a situation was fair or unfair; 82 percent responded it was unfair.

In this same vein, consider the following two scenarios from a research study:

1. A company is making a small profit. It is located in a community experiencing a recession with substantial unemployment but no inflation. Many workers are anxious to work at the company. The company decides to decrease wages and salaries 7 percent this year.

2. A company is making a small profit. It is located in a community experiencing a recession with substantial unemployment and inflation of 12 percent. Many workers are anxious to work at the company. The company decides to increase wages and salaries 5 percent this year.

In case one, 62 percent of the study's participants believed the organization's behavior was unfair compared to only 22 percent of participants in case two. Factoring in inflation, the two scenarios provide a net wage and salary of the exact same amount. Yet most people perceive any form of pay cut as unfair, while pay increases are seen as fair, despite the fact the increase is being outpaced by inflation. These studies make clear that even the most rational, economically based decisions will not be seen universally as fair by stakeholders.

Equality

Consider the following scenario. You go out to buy a mattress. You lie on a number of them and decide on the one you want. The price tag says $1,200. You approach the salesperson and say, "I'd like to buy that mattress, I'll give you $800 for it." He counters with $1,150, and you counter with $900. He counters again with $1,100 and you counter with $950. He pauses and says, "Look, it seems to me you want to buy this mattress, and I want to provide you with the best service possible. I assume we're both reasonable people, so why don't we just split the difference with $1,025." Most people see this logic as fair, disregarding the fact that the split agreed upon is totally arbitrary. Had you started with a lower number or countered with lower numbers, and then split, you may have saved yourself a few hundred bucks.

People inherently see anything that seems like a 50-50 split as fair and ethical. Many people have been exploited on these seemingly equality-driven splits. Decisions framed in terms of compromise and "middle ground" usually appeal to people's need for equality, that is, to treat everything and everyone as equal. Just remember that equality doesn't necessarily make a decision fair or ethical.

Justice

Finally, consider this situation. Two of your employees are up for a promotion. Ted has been with you 5 years and is seen by all as your second in command. Jim has been with you for about 3 years but is considered by many employees to be the most talented employee in your group. After an exhaustive process, you end up selecting Ted for the job. Your employees are outraged and confront you. "How could you hire Ted over Jim?" You respond, "He's the right person for the job." They say, "Well how do you know? Ted didn't have to take the tests you gave Jim nor interview with you." Stunned, you respond, "well, I know Ted very well, I don't know Jim as well."

In your eyes, the decision was very easy. Ted's demonstrated track record and loyalty to you won the day. In employees' eyes, Ted was given preferential treatment. At the heart of many issues that concern ethics and fairness are perceptions of justice. Justice judgments can be categorized into three forms: **distributive justice** (outcomes), **procedural justice** (process), and **interactional justice** (personal treatment).

- **Distributive Justice** is perceived when people view fairness of a particular *outcome*. First, people examine the outcome of a decision's impact on *equity*. That is, were the resources distributed with respect to people's contributions rather than favoritism or other preferences? Second, in some situations, people desire *equality* where resources are distributed so each person gets the same outcome, regardless of their contributions, for example, in distributing medical benefits. Third, people evaluate distributive justice based on *need,* or examining whether resources are distributed to the person who needs them the most, as in distributing food to the disadvantaged.

- **Procedural Justice** is perceived when the *process* used to make the decision was fair. Several conditions lead people to perceive justice in a process. For example, people want to be able to have a say or voice in any decision that might affect them. People also want to be treated with consistency over time. Further, people want to know that managers and those with power in an organization are suspending their personal biases and relying on objective data to the best possible extent. Finally, procedural justice is perceived when people are presented with a mechanism for correcting perceived errors or poor decisions. For example, when a student is accused of plagiarizing, it is only procedurally fair he be able to appeal such a claim.

- **Interactional Justice** is perceived when people treat others respectfully and explain decisions adequately. This includes treating people with dignity and respect by refraining from improper remarks and establishing a collegial relationship. In addition, interactional justice is perceived when people believe they have been given the whole story, that managers are not purposely or strategically withholding information that might affect them.

"There are three kinds of lies: lies, damn lies, and statistics."
—Mark Twain

As can be seen, justice, economics, and equality play significant roles in how managers' and others' actions are perceived, regardless of some objective reality or truth. Great managers understand that even well-intentioned decisions based on seemingly flawless logic can be seen by others as unfair, unjust, and unethical.

Moral Intensity

"I think if you look at people, whether in business or government, who haven't had any moral compass, who've just changed to say whatever they thought the popular thing was, in the end they're losers."
—Michael Bloomberg

As you know by now, human bias often leads to poor judgment. Judging ethical dilemmas is not different. The framing of an ethical dilemma, for example, leads to very different judgments of what to do. For example, what if we stated the following problem: "People who download music from the Internet without paying for it are unethical." Do you agree? What if we state it slightly differently: "People who steal music from the Internet without paying for it are unethical." Is downloading without permission different from stealing without permission? Not really, but people see stealing as clearly wrong and downloading as more acceptable. The way in which we perceive ethical dilemmas depends heavily on the **moral intensity** the issue possesses. That is, something in the context or situation of how an ethical dilemma is perceived leads people to endorse the situation as unethical. Yet the same situation with less intensity would not lead people to see it as unethical. Researcher Thomas Jones identified six ways in which ethical issues are perceived as more or less intense and therefore as more ethical or unethical.[46]

1. **Magnitude of Consequences.** The sum of the cost-benefit to the object of the action in question. For example, an action that causes the death of a human being is of greater magnitude of consequence than

"Ok honesty is the best policy.
Let's call that option A."

an act that causes a person to suffer a minor injury. This is often how people will judge whether an act was "bad enough" to be considered unethical.

2. **Social Consensus of Evil/Good.** The amount of social agreement toward the action. For example, many believe it far more unethical to bribe a customs official in Texas than a customs official in Mexico. Both involve bribery, but what is considered unethical in one situation may be less so in others.

3. **Probability of Harm/Benefit.** The likelihood that the act in question will actually happen and produce the predicted harm/benefit. For example, selling a gun to a known armed robber has a greater probability of harm than selling a gun to a law-abiding citizen. We immediately underestimate the probability that a law-abiding citizen will do harm and overestimate the probability that the known armed robber won't.

4. **Temporal Immediacy.** The time between the act and the onset of the consequences. For example, reducing the retirement benefits of current retirees has a greater temporal immediacy than reducing the retirement benefits of current employees who are between the ages of 40 and 50. We tend to perceive decisions that affect us today as less ethical, whereas we view decisions in which the consequences are delayed in time as more acceptable since people might have time to recover from the decision.

5. **Proximity.** The feeling of nearness (psychologically or physically) people have to the object of the action. For example, layoffs in your own work unit have greater issue intensity than layoffs in another part of the company. Layoffs are never easy, but we have less trouble endorsing a layoff as ethical when it doesn't hit as close to home.

6. **Concentration of Effect.** The magnitude of the action on those involved. For example, denying coverage to 10 people with claims of $100,000 each has a greater concentration of effect than denying

coverage of 100,000 people with claims of $10 each. No one wants to lose $10, but it's not likely to change your life significantly. On the other hand, losing $100,000 would force many people to make some very tough financial choices. People perceive a highly concentrated effect like this as unethical.

As can be seen from the six issue intensity types above, the very nature of a situation can easily change your perspective on what you judge to be ethical versus unethical.

Making the Tough Choices

Overall, research has found that **downsizing**—terminating large numbers of employees to recapture losses or gain some form of competitive advantage—does not work[47]. That is, it doesn't accomplish what people say it's supposed to accomplish. Companies downsize as the result of a simple economic formula that says there are two ways to profit, one through costs and one through revenues. For most companies, cutting costs seems a heck of a lot easier than increasing revenues, and payroll expenses tend to be a very large expense. So when companies feel the pinch they start shaving the biggest expense—people. Yet significant research has shown organizations rarely achieve the level of profitability they once had prior to downsizing. In fact, successful companies don't cut their way to success but grow their way to financial performance. Further, the research shows many companies aren't downsizing because they are in real financial straits, but rather are looking for a quick boost in their quarterly earnings and stock price. Armed with this knowledge, would you say downsizing is an ethical choice? Consultants often frame downsizing as a necessary evil or a tough business decision—that is, it is entirely removed from ethics.

Management Live 3.6

Moral Imagination at American Airlines[48]

After 9/11, like most airlines, American Airlines was in deep financial troubles. American's union agreed to cut $1.8 billion in salary, benefits, and vacation. At the same time, CEO Don Carty secretly arranged for top executives to receive millions of dollars in retention bonuses. As you can imagine, that didn't fly with employees, so exit Don Carty. Enter CEO Gerard Arpey who thought slashing the way back to profitability wouldn't work. Arpey believed American could save millions by asking employees for creative alternatives. In monthly meetings with executives, employees began the process of describing ways to reduce expenses, and the executives listened. For example, engine overhaul mechanics used to have to be strapped in a harness to repair the 11-foot engines, a time-consuming and difficult process. One employee suggested the engines be turned vertical and lowered into the shop floor. They did it. Savings: 140/hours per employee per year and millions of dollars. One employee figured out that seating passengers in the rear of a non-full plane changes the center of gravity and improves fuel consumption, again saving millions. A pilot figured out that, because of the 42 cents or more per gallon difference in gas prices between Los Angeles and Dallas, planes going to Los Angeles should carry enough fuel to get back to Dallas, an idea that saved the airline $50,000 a day. Total savings for American: $4 billion annually.

When it comes down to making the tough choice involved in ethical dilemmas, you must learn to improve your **moral imagination.** Moral imagination is the ability to: (1) step out of your situation and see the possible ethical problems present, (2) imagine other possibilities and alternatives, and (3) evaluate from an ethical standpoint the new possibilities you have envisioned. In other words, making the tough ethical decision is the same thing as solving a difficult problem. At some point you must flex your ability to generate truly unique alternatives and offer possibilities beyond a single course of action. Moral imagination is this process as it is applied to solving problems ethically.

Let's return to our downsizing example. If managers making downsizing decisions would use their moral imagination, they would first frame the problem differently. If the problem is framed as "Should we or shouldn't we downsize?" then it will necessarily lead to one of two conclusions. But if the question is "How can we revitalize our financial performance?" then moral imagination is free to run. Sometimes it is truly necessary to reduce the number of people on the payroll, but even then, morally imaginative managers understand there are some creative alternatives, including asking people to make sacrifices in pay and benefits, designing new ways to cut costs, and so on. In other words, there are creative ways to get to the bottom line that don't involve purging an organization of its people. (See Management Live 3.6)

Rationalizations and Ethical Traps

Unfortunately, as with most problem solving, people begin the process with a solution in mind and spend time rationalizing why that solution is ethical and effective. In fact, people go to great lengths to justify their predetermined solution to an ethical problem. Here is just a partial list of the most common rationalizations used to justify unethical behavior:

- **If it's legal, it's ethical.** The law stipulates what is minimally acceptable. Thus, the law is the floor for any ethical decision, not the ceiling. The law cannot take into account all the various potential impacts of any decision, ethics does. As a general guideline, we always tell our students that just because it's legal doesn't mean it's ethical.

- **I was only trying to help.** We can rationalize very easily that our behavior was for the good of someone else. So we withhold the truth from people and act as vigilantes protecting others from information. This type of behavior generally is not helpful to others but really is a means of avoiding difficult or uncomfortable situations.

- **Everyone else does it.** Just because you perceive that others behave unethically in no way transforms it into ethical behavior. Behaving ethically takes courage, and bucking norms is often part of it.

- **It's owed to me.** People often feel like due to their hard work or frequent patronage or the like that certain rewards are owed them. This may be why office supply theft, personal copies at work, or long-distance phone calls on the job are so commonplace—people see it as a right owed them.

- **As long as I don't gain.** Behaving unethically for the greater good of the organization is no more ethical than stealing food for your family is legal. Personal gain is not the sole metric for determining ethical behavior; the impact of your behavior, regardless of who benefits, has far-reaching implications.

"Quick Tests" of Your Actions

Something Short of a Good Ethical Test

"Don't get caught."

At a very minimum, you may want to subject your decision to gut checks that will help put your choice in perspective. In Tool Kit 3.5, we provide a checklist of questions to use in identifying and dealing with an ethical dilemma. In addition, all great problem solvers ask themselves the following questions before making the tough choice:

1. Is my action legal?
2. Am I behaving fairly?
3. Is my decision in line with my own values?
4. Will others be negatively impacted?

Beyond these key questions, we think some other checks are in order and will put your decision into perspective.

- **The Wall Street Journal Test.** Would I stand by my decision if it made the front page of *The Wall Street Journal?* Would I be embarrassed if others knew of the choice I had made?
- **Platinum Rule Test.** Am I treating others in a way in which they would want to be treated?
- **Mom Test.** Would I be proud to tell my mother of my decision?
- **Personal Gain Test.** Is the opportunity to gain personally standing in the way of my thinking? Have I given my personal gain too much weight?
- **Cost-Benefit Test.** Does my decision benefit some to the detriment of others? Have I considered the true impact on others?

Concluding Note

Problem solving is tough, and good decisions never guarantee good outcomes. However, as we have attempted to show throughout this chapter, being conscious of common biases, coupled with careful consideration of how you go about solving a problem, can greatly increase your odds of good outcomes. Similarly, being ethical is never easy, and the most critical element will always be your personal dedication and the commitment to do what is right. However, because what is right is not always crystal clear, it is important to have a toolbox of frameworks or ways of thinking about ethical dilemmas that can facilitate clear thinking and ultimately ethical choices.

Key Terms

after action review

anchoring and adjustment

availability bias

benchmarking

black or white fallacy

bounded rationality

brainwriting

confirmation bias

devil's advocate

distributive justice

downsizing

equifinality

escalation of commitment

ethical commitment

ethical competency

ethical consciousness

fundamental attribution error

hasty generalization fallacy

histogram

inquiry skills

interactional justice

intuition

ladder of inference

mental models

moral imagination

moral intensity

overconfidence bias

PADIL

procedural justice

representative bias

satisficing

self-serving bias

small wins

stakeholder

system

systemic structure

Problem Solving Tool Kits

Tool Kit 3.1   Stakeholder Analysis

Stakeholder analysis is an essential tool for any problem solving endeavor. It is also a "living" document, meaning that stakeholders require constant attention while solving a problem. Thus, a careful analysis will help you get an understanding on how the decision impacts different groups of people, who have the biggest stake and most power, and which stakeholders are likely to support or resist potential solutions to the problem.

1. **Identify Key Stakeholders.** Create a chart of *primary stakeholders*—individuals or groups that have direct authority or economic influence over the problem—and *secondary stakeholders*—individuals or groups that might be affected indirectly by the problem.

2. **Prioritize Your Stakeholders.** Using a simple 2 × 2 matrix, with the dimensions of Stake and Power, classify (plot) each stakeholder to get a graphic representation of who your most important stakeholders to involve in the process are. For example, those stakeholders who have a high stake and a lot of power or influence should be your top priority. They should be involved in every step of the PADIL process.

3. **Examine Support/Resistance.** Once you've begun defining the problem and generating solutions, it's helpful to determine the degree of support or resistance. Talk to you stakeholders, describe the problem

as it has been framed, and talk about potential solutions. Gauge their relative support or resistance for how the problem has been defined and framed.

Stakeholder Analysis

Names	Strongly Against	Moderately Against	Neutral	Moderately Supportive	Strongly Supportive

Tool Kit 3.2   Methods for Reframing Problems

Here are four simple methods that will help you to view problems differently.

1. Paraphrase: Restate in your own words what someone else has stated.
   Initial: How can we reduce our shipping delays?
   Reframe: How can we keep shipping delays from increasing?

2. 180° Turnaround: Simply turn the problem around.
   Initial: How can we encourage students to study for exams?
   Reframe: How can we discourage students to study for exams?

3. Broaden It: Reframe the problem with a broader frame of reference.
   Initial: Should we expand our product line in China?
   Reframe: How can we achieve increased financial success in China?

4. Redirect the Problem: Change the actual focus of the problem.
   Initial: How can we increase our revenue?
   Reframe: How can we decrease our costs?

Tool Kit 3.3   Pareto Graphing

Sometimes, in attempting to solve a problem, you can't solve the whole thing, yet solving one component still would make a significant improvement. Applying the Pareto principle, 80 percent of the value to be gained is likely to be accomplished by solving 20 percent of the problem. In other words, some things are just much more important than others. If you could fix the one or two major problem areas, you'd be likely to eradicate over three-quarters of the problem. For that reason, the Pareto principle has become known as the 80/20 rule. Using this principle can help you quickly isolate where you'd like to spend your problem solving efforts.

For example, professors often get poorly written papers. Yet it's sometimes difficult to determine where to spend time helping students improve their writing, particularly when the course is not an English course. Using the Pareto principle, a professor could quickly isolate the major source of her students' writing problems. While grading an assignment, she could track the following information in all 40 papers she receives: grammar, punctuation, spelling, and typing/computer errors. After compiling the data, she could then create a chart like the following:

Problem	# of Errors	% of Total	Cumulative %
Grammar	47	44	44
Punctuation	28	26	70
Spelling	21	19	89
Typing/Computer	12	11	100
Total	108	100	

Looking at the chart, she would easily see the largest problem by far is grammar. In addition, punctuation causes problems as well. Even if the professor chose only to deal with the grammatical errors of her students, she would drastically improve their writing skills. This is only evident after charting the data.

Tool Kit 3.4   After Action Review

The basic premise of the after action review (AAR) is simple. Each problem solving effort should be thoroughly reviewed on several factors including answering these key questions:

- What did we intend to accomplish in solving this problem?
- What was actually realized?
- Is there a gap between what we intended and what actually happened?
- If so, what is causing that gap? Why didn't the solution solve the problem?
- What were the strengths involved in this process, and how can they be repeated in the future?
- What were the weaknesses involved in this process, and how can they be improved or avoided in the future?

The AAR is not simply a post-mortem in which positives and negatives are listed; rather, it involves serious conversations with stakeholders about the impact of the solution and an examination of what to do to improve the problem solving process in the future.

Tool Kit 3.5   Ethical Decision Making Checklist

1. **Recognize that an ethical issue exists.**
   - What is the nature of the problem?
   - Is there a conflict that may exist when solving this problem?
   - What are the likely benefits and costs associated with this problem?
   - What might be particularly unethical?

2. Determine your responsibilities.

- To whom am I ultimately responsible?
- Do I have obligations to get involved or solve the problem, and if so, what are those obligations?
- Who would likely be affected, negatively or positively, by this problem?

3. Collect information about your options.

- What scenarios produce the most ethical outcome?
- What could happen in the future, or what are the potential unintended consequences?

4. Examine the type of dilemma being faced.

- Is it legal?
- Is this a right-versus-right dilemma?

5. Determine the right approach via PADIL.

- Which approach makes the most sense?

C H A P T E R

4

Motivation

"The one factor that distinguishes a high-performing individual is motivation. Those with high motivation consistently excel and outperform. I will always take a modestly talented person with a driving motivation to succeed over a brilliant person with little hunger in his eye."

—Bill Carpenter,
Vice President of
Human Resources and
Safety, Rogers Group, Inc.

Manage *What*?

1. Taking Over as Manager: Building a More Motivational Workplace

You have worked as a sales representative for the last three years, and your boss has just quit. You have been asked to take over as manager of your region, and you are going to accept for two reasons. First, you are at a career stage where you would like to move up and try something a bit different and more challenging. Second, you have personally been very disappointed with the way your prior manager ran your sales group. He was not a good people manager and he did very little to motivate the sales representatives in your group. More specifically, he let the low performers slide by, while the top performers (you feel like you are one of those) did not seem to be recognized for their contributions. The situation was not horrible, he was not abusive or hostile in any way. But you know the group has some talented people and could do much better—if only they had a motivational spark.

So how would you proceed in this situation? Where would you start? What types of things would you do to enhance motivation? What would be the biggest obstacles to getting this group energized? Would there be any predictable traps to avoid?

2. Dealing with the Unmotivated Person

As a new employee in the accounting department, you are surprised at how few people seem willing to do more than their most basic job duties. To you, it appears ridiculous; you know all of your co-workers have college degrees and several are CPAs. Clearly, they are well paid and have excellent working conditions. When you ask a more senior employee about his apparent lack of motivation, he answers, "Well, the only reward around here for working hard is more work so if you're smart, you are better off just doing what you are told and flying under the boss's radar. Moreover, all management tries to do is keep us from socializing and being together. I guess they feel like we cannot be trusted to give the company a fair day's work. Just try to have a game of cards at lunch with some buddies and see what management does." How would you diagnose this lack of motivation: Is it the people or the situation? What might be done to increase motivation in this situation?

3. Enriching the Boring Job

You share an office suite with four others. The five of you are blessed to work with a secretary who is exceptional at what she does. She handles all clerical requests in the office in a timely manner and with a high level of quality and presents a professional image to all who visit or call in to the office. The only problem is she has just come to you and said her job is boring. As she accurately points out, she is relatively isolated in her work and does the same tasks repeatedly. In addition, she rarely knows whether she is doing a really good job or how she can improve.

What makes a job enriched? What general strategies might make this job more interesting and fulfilling? Are there relatively simple things you could do that might help? What personal and organizational factors need to be considered in deciding whether to significantly change a job description and expectations? What is likely to happen if you do nothing?

LEARNING OBJECTIVES

1. Use expectancy theory to diagnose and understand motivational issues.
2. Increase personal motivation by using Maslow's hierarchy of needs, equity theory, and McClelland's learned needs theory.
3. Create a motivational work environment using goal setting and reinforcement theory.
4. Recognize that creative positive reinforcements are beyond just money.
5. Design motivational jobs using the job characteristics model.

Introduction

There is no more frequent lament of managers worldwide than "my employees are just not motivated." Undoubtedly, **motivation** is a mission-critical issue for all managers and can be one of the most perplexing, but potentially rewarding aspects of the management role. Skill in energizing and motivating others is a key area where great managers distinguish themselves. Indeed, creating an environment where people are highly motivated to do their best is a hallmark of great management. Unfortunately, myths and mistaken notions abound in this arena; a few of the more common ones are described in Myths 4.1.

> *"I consider my ability to arouse enthusiasm among men the greatest asset I possess. The way to develop the best that is in a man is by appreciation and encouragement."*
>
> —Charles Schwab

MYTHS 4.1 Myths of Motivation

Money is not the only effective motivator. In some situations, money is one of the best methods to motivate people. In others, it is entirely *ineffective*. Most importantly, it is certainly not the *only* motivator. What will motivate always depends on the people and the situation.

Everyone is motivated by the same things I am. Although many people share common needs and desires, different people in different situations are motivated by an extraordinary range of factors, including financial gain, recognition, esteem, personal achievement, desire for equity, need to belong, fear, freedom, involvement, interesting work, and so on. What motivates one may not motivate another, and the same factor that motivates a person in one situation may not motivate that same person in a different situation.

Punishment does not motivate. Although rarely the first choice to influence behavior, punishment, or the threat of it, can be an effective motivator. Here again, its appropriateness will depend on the situation. In some cases, it may be the only or most effective consequence available, and thus, it is important to learn how to most fairly administer punishment.

Low performance is always attributable to low motivation. Any performance is a function of motivation, ability, and the opportunity to perform. So, though low motivation is a common cause of low performance, it is certainly not the sole cause. Low performers may well lack the ability or the opportunity to achieve high performance.

Lack of motivation stems largely from lazy and apathetic people. That is sometimes the case, of course, but more often it is the *situation* that lacks sufficient incentives to energize people. People labeled as unmotivated in one situation (say their job) are sometimes highly engaged and committed in another case (for example, as a Little League coach). The managerial challenge is to discover what brings out the effort in your people and to influence what you can.

A good place to start in our understanding of motivation is with a formula first presented in the 1960s[1] that captures the relationship between motivation, ability, and performance.[2]

$$\text{Performance} = f(\textbf{Motivation} \times \textbf{Ability} \times \textbf{Opportunity})$$

According to this simple but useful equation, any performance (job, athletic, music, academic) is a multiplicative function of your ability ("can do"), motivation ("will do"), and opportunity ("get to do"). The multiplicative nature of the equation correctly captures that all three aspects are essential to performance and that one can only modestly compensate for the other.

For example, people who have high motivation and average ability to perform a task can perform at an above-average rate if given the opportunity. However, strong performance is unlikely to be present in the absence of some moderate level of all three factors. No amount of motivation can overcome a complete lack of ability, nor can great ability compensate for a dearth of motivation even when provided multiple opportunities. Thus, if someone is not performing well, a good starting point is to investigate whether the cause of the problem is an issue of motivation, ability, opportunity, or some combination of the three.

While ability tends to remain relatively stable over time, motivation and opportunity are more subject to managerial influence. That is the good news. The bad news is motivation derives from multiple sources and can be exceedingly complex to understand and manage. As a result, great managers devote much of their time to trying to discover what motivates their associates and to build work environments that engage those motives.

A recurring question in discussions of motivation is "How do you motivate people?" Although this may intuitively sound like the very question you *want* answered, it is overly simplistic. For example, drawing a parallel to the medical field, an analogous question for physicians would be "How do you heal patients?" Obviously, before doctors are able to make any informed judgment about appropriate medical treatment, they have to understand their patients' health and treatment history, apparent symptoms, and other specifics of the situation. There is certainly no one best way to heal patients.

Motivation of people is no different. As a result, the question "How do you motivate people?" should rightly be expanded to *"How do you motivate who, to do what, under what circumstances?"* That is, effective motivation strategies always depend on the people involved, their history, and context. While we can learn much from examples where supervisors succeeded using certain motivational tactics (e.g., parking spot of the month, frequent verbal feedback, spot bonuses), the recurring trap is to assume what worked in one context with one group of people will work similarly in another.

Never confuse will power with firepower.

—U.S. Marine axiom

". . . Nothing in the world can take the place of motivation. Talent will not; nothing is more common than unsuccessful people with talent. Genius will not; unrewarded genius is almost a proverb. Education will not; the world is full of educated derelicts. Motivation and determination are omnipotent."

—Calvin Coolidge

Framing Motivation Challenges and Ideas: The Expectancy Theory

It is because of the multidimensional and complex nature of motivation that a general theory is so important in framing and diagnosing motivational situations. The most encompassing and applicable theory of motivation for this type of practical diagnosis is the **expectancy theory.** Expectancy theory serves as both our starting point for diagnosing and framing motivational challenges, and our structure for integrating a variety of other motivational models and concepts. Expectancy theory is based on three beliefs: expectancy, instrumentality, and valence.

Expectancy is the understanding of what performance is desired and the person's belief that effort will lead to a desired level of performance. Put simply, do people know what they have to do and will they be able to accomplish the behavior desired? Motivation will decline any time we perceive a low probability of success. For example, few of us would be motivated to study hard for a test if we did not know what material was going to be covered or felt we had no chance of passing. Your resulting expectation would be "Regardless of how hard I study, I'm not likely to perform well." From a managerial perspective, then, expectancy beliefs point to the importance of clarifying goals and expectations, and ensuring that people have confidence that their effort can lead to good performance.

Instrumentality is the belief that a given level of performance will lead to specific outcomes. Instrumentality perceptions can range from zero—everyone gets the same pay no matter how hard they work and produce—to certain—every time I sell a unit I get a 7 percent commission. Motivation will be high only when people believe that there will be meaningful consequences, positive or negative, from their efforts (or lack thereof). From a managerial perspective, instrumentality beliefs point to the critical importance of *linking rewards directly* to desired performance.

A common example of instrumentality can be seen in the distribution of student grades. If you score a 97 percent on a test, you would normally believe your teacher would assign you an A on that test. However, what would happen if the teacher told you she was giving everyone Cs on the test, no matter what score they received? In this case, your instrumentality would be zero because you would not believe your performance (your test percentage) would lead to the expected reward (the A). Your resulting motivation to get a high score would therefore be low.

The final component of expectancy theory is **valence,** the value a person places on future outcomes. Valence is the most intuitive of expectancy theory elements and is another way of saying, "What's in it for me?" Any outcome could be either desirable (for example, a $10,000 bonus or a chance to get involved in a project you love) or undesirable (losing your job, being poked in the eye with a sharp stick). Much of what we know about motivating people is that different people will place different valences on the same outcome. So from a managerial perspective perhaps the greatest challenge is to find those outcomes that have high valences for your target individuals.

Imagine you worked hard and performed well only to be given the choice of choosing a trinket from a catalog or a small discount coupon. You were indeed rewarded for your performance, but not with something you really valued. It is important to keep in mind some outcomes will fail to motivate because they are insignificant relative to the effort expended. For example, a $50 bonus may be fine in some cases, but if the effort needed requires two extra weeks of work, then low valence is likely. By providing proportional outcomes, valences can be improved.

"Motivation is not something you do to people but something you discover about them."

—Unknown

Two important ideas of expectancy theory warrant special emphasis. First, like the ability, motivation, and opportunity equation introduced earlier, the three beliefs of expectancy theory—expectancy, instrumentality, and valence—combine multiplicatively to produce an individual's **motivating force**—symbolically represented as:[3]

$$MF = E \times I \times V.$$

Stated simply, high motivation will come only in the case of high levels of *all three* beliefs. Similarly, the absence of any of those three beliefs will render motivation low or zero. Second, always remember that expectancy theory is based on individual beliefs and perceptions, not necessarily on a manager's beliefs or some objective reality. It will not be enough that desirable outcomes are attainable and linked to appropriate behavior. Rather, an individual must *believe* that effort will lead to good performance, *believe* performance will be rewarded, and *believe* the reward will be personally valued. In matters of motivation, perception is reality. Contributing to a high level of each of these employee beliefs is a critical component in increasing motivation in the workplace. Some specific skills for effectively using the expectancy approach are provided in Tool Kit 4.1.

Why Capable People Are Not Motivated

Some discussions of motivation focus on "slackers," "deadwood," and other terms to categorize those who seem disinclined to work hard. Of course, some people are incapable or lazy and are special motivational challenges. However, far more common are cases where people have the ability to perform but are not inclined to do so. We have found one of the most useful ways to begin to diagnose motivational issues is to first think about why capable people might *not* be highly motivated.

To illustrate, consider the case of someone who is not motivated to attend or study hard in a particular college class. An expectancy theory diagnosis would tell us the causes of low motivation likely stem from one or more of three beliefs: (1) the student is unsure about what will lead to high grades or doesn't think his effort will lead to mastering the subject, (low expectancy), (2) he doesn't believe the professor will give him a good grade even if he performs well (low instrumentality), or (3) he doesn't value a high grade nor fear a low grade in the class (low valence).

The diagnosis concisely frames the potential belief pattern of low motivated students. The motivational challenge for an instructor is to find out which beliefs exist in any particular case and to focus intervention strategies accordingly. Perhaps the biggest trap is to create a motivational strategy geared to beliefs that do not exist. It is always critically important to test your assumptions and uncover the real causes of low motivation. To borrow a maxim from the medical world: "No treatment without diagnosis."

Although expectancy theory is exceptionally useful in framing motivation challenges, it hardly provides all the answers. That is, understanding that high-valence beliefs will be critical to motivate the students in the illustration above does not address just what might make different students value attending class if it is not grades. Similarly, recognizing that instrumentality is a key element in motivation does not specify the different types of consequences and how they might best be administered in different academic settings. Likewise, appreciating the importance of clear expectations and confidence does not provide specific guidance on how to enhance expectancy in various contexts.

Fortunately, there is a very good body of research, theorizing, and practical wisdom with respect to these issues. In this regard, we like to use a "bucket" analogy. (See Figure 4.1.) When a person's bucket is full, she is optimally motivated, and assuming sufficient ability, performance will follow. When a person's bucket is low, greater managerial effort will be required to fill that bucket. As depicted in Figure 4.1, there are three primary faucets or sources available to fill an employee's motivational bucket, each one helping to improve employees' expectancy, instrumentality, and valence beliefs: 1) personal drives, 2) managerial actions, and 3) the job or work itself. Obviously, turning on all of the faucets at once fills an employee's bucket more quickly. But in many cases, such a "flood" of motivation is not necessary. We review and synthesize these major sources of motivation in the following sections.

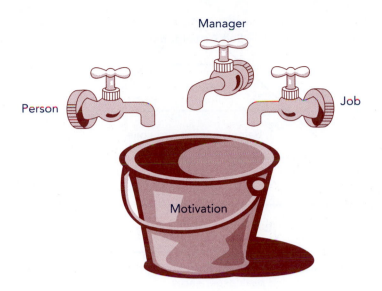

Person — Manager — Job

Motivation

FIGURE 4.1

Bucket Analogy of Motivation: Key Sources

The Person as a Source of Motivation

One source of motivation stems from a person's own motivational drives or needs. Influential theories of human needs include Maslow's hierarchy, equity theory, and David McClelland's model of learned needs.

Maslow's Hierarchy of Needs

Perhaps the most well-known person-centered theory of motivation is Abraham **Maslow's hierarchy of needs**[4] (Figure 4.2). Maslow's theory suggests each of us is motivated by five basic needs, which can be arranged in a hierarchy from lower order (physiological) to highest order (self-actualization). According to Maslow, only when the lower order needs of survival and physical and emotional well-being are satisfied will we be concerned with the higher order needs of esteem and self-actualization. Conversely, if the things that satisfy our lower order needs are taken away, we will no longer be concerned about the maintenance of our higher order needs.

Maslow's hierarchy is useful in highlighting that not only will different people be motivated by different needs but even the same people can have very different needs at various points in time. For example, it will likely be far more difficult to energize a sales representative to achieve his sales target (level 4) when he is having problems with his marriage (level 3). Similarly, it will be hard to get an employee to go the extra mile in customer service (level 4) when she feels underpaid and is struggling to meet her own family needs (level 2). Students low on discretionary money can be made to do most anything for free pizza while some more well-heeled populations would do most anything to *get out of* having cheap pizza.

Like any simple model, Maslow's theory has limitations and is certainly not a complete prescriptive guide to managing complex motivation issues. For example, while people move up or down the hierarchy depending on what's happening to them in their lives, their motivational "set" at any time comprises elements of all of the basic needs. In other words, people are concerned with all of the issues at a single point in time, not just one. Further, Maslow's model is not useful in explaining the phenomenon whereby people sacrifice lower order needs in favor of higher order motives like belonging, esteem, and self-actualization

"Money was never a big motivation for me, except as a way to keep score. The real excitement is playing the game."

—Donald Trump

FIGURE 4.2

Maslow's Hierarchy of Needs

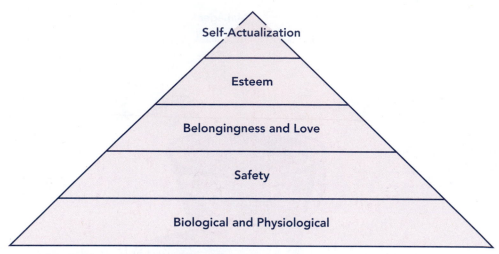

- **Level 5: Self-Actualization needs:** Realizing personal potential, self-fulfillment, seeking personal growth and peak experiences
- **Level 4: Esteem needs:** Self-esteem, achievement, mastery, independence, status, dominance, prestige, managerial responsibility
- **Level 3: Belongingness and Love needs:** Work group, family, affection, relationships
- **Level 2: Safety needs:** Protection from elements, security, order, law, limits, stability
- **Level 1: Biological and Physiological needs:** Air, food, drink, shelter, warmth, sex, sleep

(sometimes referred to as the "starving artist" syndrome). How well the theory transfers across cultures is also debated, particularly with respect to the placing of social needs—which, for example, is highly motivating in some cultures—in the hierarchy.

An Equity Approach to Motivation

Equity[5] refers to workers' perceptions of the fairness of outcomes they receive on the job. These personal equity judgments are based on a social comparison by which people compare what they are getting out of their job (their outcomes) to what they are putting into their job (inputs). Outcomes include pay, fringe benefits, increased responsibility, and prestige, while inputs may include hours worked and work quality, as well as education and experience. The ratio of outcomes to inputs is then compared to corresponding ratios of their comparison group. The outcome of this comparison is the basis for beliefs about fairness.[6] See Figure 4.3 for an overall representation of equity theory.

Potential Actions to Restore Equity

"Ethics and equity and the principles of justice do not change with the calendar."

—D.H. Lawrence

When people experience inequity, they will take some action to restore balance. Consider the case of a person who is paid $30,000 a year and then finds out his coworker is making $36,000 for doing the same job and their respective inputs (education, job tenure, skills, and so on) are the same. How will the lower paid person react? In all likelihood, the employee will take action to restore his sense of fairness. A person who wishes to restore a sense of equity on the job has multiple options, including both behavioral and perceptual actions.

Behaviorally, workers can increase their outcomes (by, say, requesting a pay raise) or decrease their efforts (take longer lunch breaks, or find ways to avoid work) to balance the equity equation. Perceptually, they may rationalize they weren't working as hard as they thought, thus reducing the perceived value of their own inputs. Further, they might convince themselves that coworkers are actually working harder than they thought. It is difficult to predict exactly how a person will react, but as you can see few of the choices are really great ones for

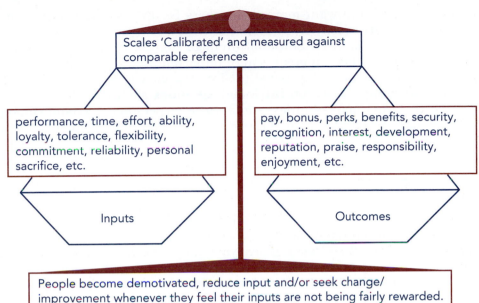

FIGURE 4.3

Equity Theory Diagram

Scales 'Calibrated' and measured against comparable references

performance, time, effort, ability, loyalty, tolerance, flexibility, commitment, reliability, personal sacrifice, etc.

pay, bonus, perks, benefits, security, recognition, interest, development, reputation, praise, responsibility, enjoyment, etc.

Inputs

Outcomes

People become demotivated, reduce input and/or seek change/improvement whenever they feel their inputs are not being fairly rewarded.

Adapted from Adams (1963).

the person or for the company. Equity perceptions can be surprisingly important in organizations and even nature. Equity is so central of an issue that it is even of substantial importance to brown capuchin monkeys! (See Management Live 4.1.)

Equity Sensitivity

While equity may seem like a relatively objective phenomenon, in truth what different people see as equitable can vary significantly. In fact, an emerging body of research is finding that people differ significantly in what is called **equity sensitivity**.[7] Research has found that those high in equity sensitivity are more

"Fairness is what justice really is."

—Potter Stewart

Management Live 4.1

Equity Is Also Monkey Business[8]

Even monkeys expect a fair day's pay for a fair day's work. Inspired by a history of work that humans inherently reject unfairness, Sarah Brosnan of Emory University wondered whether this was also true for capuchin monkeys. Brosnan designed an experiment that put two capuchin monkeys together where they were trained to exchange a small rock with human handlers to receive a reward—in most cases, a piece of cucumber. Brosnan points out that, while this may sound very simple, "not very many species are willing to relinquish things, especially intentionally."

Partners of monkeys who willingly exchanged received either the exact same reward (a cucumber slice) or a more desirable reward (a grape) for the same work or, in some instances, for doing no work at all. Brosnan observed that those monkeys who saw unfair treatment and failed to benefit from it were ultimately less likely to trade with the handlers in the future. Moreover, the monkeys who had been treated unfairly would often not eat the cucumbers they received and, in other cases, actually threw the cucumbers at the researchers!

While humorous at one level, the results are a powerful confirmation of the influence of equity perceptions. Not only did monkeys expect fair treatment and reject a desirable food item as a result of inequity, but the human desire for equity seems to have an evolutionary basis.

outcome-oriented and want more than others for the same level of inputs. Those low in equity sensitivity pay more attention to their inputs and are less sensitive to equity issues. Additional findings suggest people who are high in equity sensitivity place a great deal of importance on **extrinsic outcomes** such as pay, status, and fringe benefits.[9] Employees with low equity sensitivity place more importance on **intrinsic outcomes** such as feelings of personal worth, using one's abilities, and a sense of personal accomplishment. To better understand your own equity sensitivity and that of others, consult Tool Kit 4.2.

What Managers Need to Do to Maintain Equity

"These men ask for just the same thing—fairness, and fairness only. This, so far as in my power, they, and all others, shall have."

—Abraham Lincoln

Probably the most important and challenging thing to keep in mind about equity is we are dealing with both our own perceptions *and* the perceptions of other people, and those may not be the same. As a result, even if you perceive a serious injustice, others may not be aware of it or may consider the inequity trivial. Great managers monitor and constantly use reality checks to gauge associates' perceptions of equity. By asking others about equity issues—"Do you feel that promotion was fair? Why or why not?" or "What types of behaviors should be valued here?"—top managers realize they will be better able to manage equity perceptions and be more aware of treatment that may de-motivate workers.

An understanding of equity theory is why excellent managers *do not* treat or reward all workers exactly the same. That's right—great managers do not treat all people equally, but rather, fairly! Consder this for a minute. If managers provide the same treatment and rewards to everyone, then by definition the managers treat everyone as being "average." What workers would feel like they are being treated fairly under this system? The poor performer may prefer this system but would have little reason to improve his or her performance. The average performer would feel equitably treated and likely maintain his or her level of motivation. The high performer would see substantial inequity when everyone is treated equally. As a result, the high performers would be motivated to either reduce their inputs, seek more outcomes (which they will not be able to receive when everyone is rewarded the same), or leave to seek equity elsewhere. If we let a system of *equality* run to its logical conclusion, in a few years we would have all low and average performers. Treating everyone the same is not a prescription for great management. In fact, it is a formula for mediocrity or worse.

Management Live 4.2

What Equity Means for Drivers in Finland[10]

In Finland, fines for traffic offenses are based on the net income of the person being ticketed. That is, people who make more pay more, even for the identical offense. In an extreme case, Jaako Rytsola, a 27-year-old Finnish Internet multimillionaire and newspaper columnist, was ticketed for driving 43 miles per hour in a 25-mile-per-hour zone. The fine that resulted was $71,400.

While many Americans would likely find a system that exerts different levels of punishment for the exact same offense to be inherently unfair, many Finns view this as an equitable system. For example, Leena Harkimo, a member of the Finnish Parliament, attempted to introduce a bill that would have capped most speeding tickets at $7,825. The bill, however, only received support from about 15 percent of the parliament. Remember that equity perceptions depend on the person and the context and are not some objective reality.

The Platinum Rule

The lasting lesson is that even the best-intentioned managers often confuse the intuitive idea of equality with the real issue at hand—fairness. Therefore, we encourage you to follow this simple rule, often referred to as the **platinum rule** (a variation on the golden rule), which states "Treat others how *they* wish to be treated." That is, each employee may require a slightly different approach to ensure his or her perceptions of fairness are met, which in the end is entirely appropriate and highly effective to ensure motivation remains high. To further reinforce the idea that different people are motivated differently, a brief synthesis of the work of David McClelland follows.

McClelland's Learned Needs

We all have needs and wants, and it is easy to confuse the two. We may say we *need* nice clothes or a fast car, but the truth is we don't actually need these things; we *want* them! Food, shelter, love, social relationships, power, and achievement of our personal best are the true deeply held needs. David C. McClelland found that people would do well to learn the predominant needs in themselves and in others in order to find those roles and situations where success is most likely.[11] McClelland focused particularly on three needs or motives: achievement, affiliation, and power. Although we all have these needs to a greater or lesser extent, McClelland noted that people tend to have one need that is most dominant. McClelland's work generally focuses on **achievers**—people who perform tasks because of a compelling need for personal achievement—we can use McClelland's simple framework to provide some structure around the questions of "What do I need from work?" and "What motivates others?" Whether the focus is on you or others, the three basic needs remain the same: the **need for achievement, need for affiliation,** and **need for power** (Figure 4.4).

What Do I Need from Work?

McClelland's research suggests that motivational needs are an important predictor of who will be an effective manager.[12] For example, McClelland argues a high need for affiliation can often be problematic for managers. Since being *liked* is the dominant motive underlying the affiliation-oriented manager's actions, he may have difficulty resolving conflicts and be more likely to make exceptions to make people happy. A manager with a dominant need for affiliation may not be inclined to take decisive action when an unpopular course of action is warranted (for example, have people work late to finish an important project).

Further, McClelland argues that, while a high need for power will produce a strong work ethic and commitment to the organization, people possessing this drive may not possess the required flexibility and people-centered skills to be effective in leadership roles. Perhaps most importantly, McClelland argues that people with strong *achievement motivation* make the best leaders, although they

> ▸ **Need for Achievement (nAch)** - The drive to excel, to achieve in relation to a set of standards.
>
> ▸ **Need for Power (nPow)** - The need to make others behave in a way they would not have behaved otherwise.
>
> ▸ **Need for Affiliation (nAff)** - The desire for friendly and close interpersonal relationships.

FIGURE 4.4

McClelland's Theory of Needs

TABLE 4.1 | Typical Needs Profiles

Position	Achievement	Affiliation	Power
Sales	Very high	Low	Somewhat high
Entrepreneur	Very high	Very low	Somewhat low
Corporate Manager	Somewhat high	Somewhat low	Very high
Politician	High	Somewhat low	Very high
Support Staff	Somewhat low	Very high	Somewhat low
Information Systems	Very high	Very low	Low

can have a tendency to demand too much of their staff in the belief that they are all similarly and highly achievement-focused and results-driven. Maybe not too surprisingly, different personal profiles tend to gravitate toward different jobs. Some examples of these can be seen in Table 4.1.

What Motivates Others?

"The difference between a successful person and others is not a lack of strength, not a lack of knowledge, but rather in a lack of will."

—Vincent T. Lombardi

When it comes to addressing the question—"What motivates others?"— McClelland's model provides us with a nice framework for diagnosing basic motivational needs. Of course, the challenge in diagnosing needs is we can't see them. We can only infer them from a person's observable behavior. As a result, great managers pay very close attention to the behavior of people around them. Unfortunately, as Table 4.2 demonstrates, most of us are inaccurate judges of what other people want. The only real way to know is to pay attention and to ask people directly.

In explaining how different needs impact the way people behave, McClelland recounted a story about 450 workers who had been put out of work in Erie, Pennsylvania.[13] Most of the newly unemployed workers stayed at home for a while and then checked with the employment service to see if their old jobs or

TABLE 4.2 | What Do Employees Want?

What Employees Want	Items	What Employers Think Employees Want
1	Interesting work	5
2	Appreciation of work	8
3	Feeling "in on things"	10
4	Job security	2
5	Good wages	1
6	Promotion/growth	3
7	Good working conditions	4
8	Personal loyalty	6
9	Tactful discipline	7
10	Sympathetic help with problems	9

Source: Kovach, K. (1987). What Motivates Employees? Workers and Supervisors Give Different Answers. *Business Horizons*, Sept–Oct, 58–75.

similar ones were available. But a small minority behaved very differently; the day they were laid off, they started job hunting. They checked both national and local employment offices; they studied the Help Wanted sections of the papers; they checked through their union, their churches, and various fraternal organizations; they looked into training courses to learn a new skill; they even left town to look for work, while the majority when questioned said they would not under any circumstances move away to obtain a job. Obviously the members of the active minority were differently motivated.

Achievement-motivated people thrive on pursuing and attaining goals. They have a desire to do something better or more efficiently, solve problems, or master complex tasks. They like to be able to control situations. They take moderate, calculated risks. They like to get immediate feedback on how they have done and tend to be preoccupied with a task orientation toward the job to be done. McClelland describes the self-motivated achiever as a person with a tendency to think about ways to accomplish something difficult and significant when he is not being required to think about anything in particular—that is, when he is free to relax and let his or her mind just "idle." The self-motivated achiever tends to set goals and prefers tasks that provide feedback. Achievers strive to reach goals and measure success in terms of what those efforts have accomplished. They learn to set challenging but achievable goals for themselves and for their jobs and, when they achieve them, to set new goals.

Power-motivated individuals see most work situations as an opportunity to influence other people or to take control. Generally, people with strong power motives have the desire to control others, influence their behavior, and be responsible for them. Often these people will volunteer for leadership positions, recommend changes whether or not they are needed, and are very willing to assert themselves when a decision needs to be made. In an organizational sense, the need for power is the need to manage the behavior of others in order to achieve goals. A high need for power does not necessarily imply autocratic, tyrannical behavior, but rather a need to have impact, to be influential, and to be effective in achieving goals. People who spend their time thinking about how to influence others, how to mount arguments, and how to change other people's behavior toward organizational goals are exhibiting a high need for power.

Affiliation-motivated people have the desire to establish and maintain friendly and warm relations with others. Individuals who enjoy helping others, are concerned with the growth and development of subordinates, are fond of spending time in lengthy conversations, and are good listeners, tend to have a high need for affiliation. Some people with strong affiliation motives can be distracted from their work, as work can often take a backseat to the social environment. That is, the social environment may not just be viewed as a means of getting work done, it may be viewed as being *more important* than getting work done. They will usually respond to an appeal for cooperation and generally like to be part of a group. They prefer to share in accomplishments rather than to take individual initiative and sole responsibility. They are often presented with opportunities to capitalize on and take credit for ideas and actions they conceived and initiated, but generally do not have a high need for recognition for individual achievement and are often quite happy to have their group or department receive the credit.

Applying the Learned Needs in the Workplace

While the research is clear that different people have different needs, the skill challenge for you is how to apply that evidence in the workplace. The idea that people have a dominant need (achievement, affiliation, power) should provide you a starting place, with understanding what goes into each individual's "motivational bucket." For example, people with a high need for achievement are going to start off with their buckets being more full than other people. So your

"Achievement is largely the product of steadily raising one's levels of aspiration . . . and expectation."

—Jack Nicklaus

"Most people give up just when they're about to achieve success. They quit on the one-yard line. They give up at the last minute of the game, one foot from a winning touchdown."

—Ross Perot

"Power is the ultimate aphrodisiac."

—Henry Kissinger

first job with each employee is to get under the surface and determine how much of the bucket needs to be filled or to understand what sources of motivation you will need, because some employees will be starting with practically empty buckets while others will have a good head start on having their buckets full. McClelland, therefore, offers a helpful tool for understanding an important source of motivation, that is, the person as the source of motivation. See Management Live 4.3 for a detailed explanation.

The Manager as a Source of Motivation

Multiple models exist that offer ideas for managers to affect the expectancy and instrumentality beliefs of their people. Perhaps the two most universally recognized, evidence-based, and applicable theories are goal setting and behavior modification.

Management Live 4.3

McClelland's Ring Toss and the Need for Achievement[14]

David McClelland's main research focus was on achievement motivation, and the following experiment shows the power of achievement motivation and its relationship to personal goals.

Volunteers were asked to throw rings over pegs; no distance was specified, and most people seemed to throw from arbitrary, random distances, sometimes close, sometimes farther away. However, a small group of volunteers, whom McClelland suggested were strongly achievement-motivated, took some care to measure and test distances to produce an ideal challenge—not too easy and not impossible. Interestingly a parallel exists in biology, known as the overload principle. Commonly applied to fitness and exercising, the overload principle states that, to develop fitness or strength, the exercise must be sufficiently demanding to increase existing levels of ability or endurance, but not so demanding as to cause damage or strain. McClelland identified the same need for a balanced challenge in the approach of achievement-motivated people.

McClelland contrasted achievement-motivated people with gamblers and dispelled a common preconception that achievement-motivated (nAch) people are big risk takers. On the contrary, achievement-motivated individuals typically set goals they can influence with their effort and ability, and as such the goal is considered to be achievable. This determined results-driven approach is usually present in the character makeup of successful businesspeople and entrepreneurs.

McClelland suggested other characteristics and attitudes of achievement-motivated people:

- Achievement is more important than material or financial reward.
- Achieving the aim or task gives greater personal satisfaction than receiving praise or recognition.
- Financial reward is regarded as a measure of success, not an end in itself.
- Security is not a prime motivator, nor is status.
- Feedback is essential because it enables measurement of success, not for reasons of praise or recognition, the implication being that feedback must be reliable, quantifiable, and factual.
- Achievement-motivated people constantly seek improvements and ways of doing things better.
- Achievement-motivated people will logically favor jobs and responsibilities that naturally satisfy their needs, that is, offer flexibility and opportunity to set and achieve goals—for example, sales and business management and entrepreneurial roles.

McClelland firmly believed achievement-motivated people are normally the ones who make things happen and get results, and that this extends to getting results through organizing other people and resources. Although, as stated earlier, these same people often demand too much of their staff because they prioritize achieving the goal above the many varied interests and needs of their people.

Goal Setting

We might go so far as to say that if you learn only one thing about motivation, it should be the goal-setting effect. Simply stated, the goal-setting effect is that specific, difficult, but attainable goals lead to higher performance than no goals or "do your best" goals. In decades of research, scholars Ed Locke and Gary Latham[15] have convincingly argued and demonstrated with multiple studies that "the beneficial effect of goal setting on task performance is one of the most robust and replicable findings in the psychological literature." Goal setting is the most efficient and effective way to both clearly convey expectations and motivate people to achieve them.

The foundation of any effective motivation program is proper goal setting.[16] Managers should begin assessing the motivational climate of their work environment by asking themselves, "Do subordinates understand and accept my performance expectations?" Although goal setting works to improve motivation toward accomplishing objectives, great managers know that *not all goals are created equal.* A great deal of research has indicated that some goals are more likely to be accomplished than others; we call these "good goals" versus "bad goals." For some examples of ineffective goals, see Table 4.3. The characteristics of a good goal can be summarized by the acronym SMART, or specific, measurable, attainable, relevant, and time-bound.[17] See Chapter 1 for more detail on setting good goals.

Common Goal-Setting Traps

While a robust and powerful motivational technique, goal setting has several limitations and common traps involved in its implementation. For example, setting goals can create ceiling effects, whereby people can reach their goal and then abruptly stop, even though they might be capable of considerably higher performance levels. Thus, goals set too low can actually be harmful. In addition, goals can create the conditions for game-playing and **suboptimization.** That is, in the pursuit of goals, people may ignore other important objectives (not formally covered by goals) and may do things outside the spirit of the goals, even engaging in unethical behavior, to achieve them. This situation is illustrated in Management Live 4.4 about Sears Auto Centers.

Management Live 4.4

Sears Auto Centers and Aggressive Goals

In 1992, Sears Auto Centers were caught selling unnecessary repairs in the state of California. In the aftermath, many people were surprised to learn that the company actually had quotas, extra sales commissions, and special contests that encouraged the sale of additional repairs. Sears claimed that replacing good parts before they failed was "a common practice in the industry" and tried to pass it off as preventive maintenance. The company later admitted that mistakes occurred and agreed to pay $8 million to settle the California charges. As a result, Sears also agreed to make restitution to 900,000 customers nationwide, and they discontinued the use of quotas, commissions, and contests.

While Sear's incentive system led to recommendations of unnecessary repairs and costly retribution for the company, consider how their practices differed (or do not) from:

- Realtors recommending more expensive homes to home buyers (to make higher commisions)?
- Restaurants encouraging diners to eat the highest margin food and drink the most expensive beverages?
- Doctors recommending patient tests for which the doctor's office receives compensation?
- Stockbrokers encouraging stock purchases that enhance commisions?

Auto Repair Secrets, http://www.carinfo.com/autorepair.html. Technews Corp

TABLE 4.3 | **Examples of Ineffective Goals**

"Try your best."
"Give 110 percent."
"We need to increase our sales."
"Nothing short of a 300 percent improvement will do."
"Let's decrease copier use by 25 percent."
"You need to get 25 new accounts."
"If all goes well, you may be named Employee of the Month."

Further, in many situations, it can be hard to find quantitative metrics for goal setting. For example, consultants may find it quite difficult to derive SMART goals since their work is so often tied to helping or providing others service rather than easily quantifiable output. One good strategy in such cases is to identify the internal customers for the job and set goals tied to the satisfaction and needs of those customers. For instance, a secretary could potentially be held accountable for the customer satisfaction (and SMART goals set for the target level of overall satisfaction) of the people (customers) in his or her office suite.

Locke and his colleagues[18] have repeatedly found that setting vague goals, such as "do your best", is actually no better than having no goals at all and is of no real motivational importance. Remember this: Telling a person to "do their best" is equivalent motivationally to giving them no goals or instructions. Despite this, providing vague goals is exceedingly common in organizational contexts.

A truly specific goal can be seen in use at an Indiana machine shop. In this case, the goal for a lathe operator was to turn 100 feet of a 3/4-inch bar into 80 acceptable pieces per hour. That is a goal that certainly meets the standard of being specific!

In addition to setting SMART goals, you can increase your chances of success by getting people involved in the goal-setting process. This is because people are also unlikely to accept goals if they do not feel they were part of the goal-setting process.[19] So whenever you can have associates set their own goals or at least have a voice in the process, you are likely to benefit in terms of goal acceptance. Moreover, people are more likely to accept goals that have been declared in public. Those responsible for the treatment of addictive behaviors know this principle well; a tenet of treatment programs is a public statement of the affliction and a plan to treat it. A sense of outside pressure is increased when a goal has been made public, making people feel more bound by these public goals.

Reinforcement Theory and Behavior Modification

Another major approach for motivating employees that emanates from the supervisor is reinforcement theory. **Reinforcement theory,** or the notion that people are motivated to repeat behavior that gets rewarded, is perhaps one of the oldest and most well supported of all psychological principles.[20] Indeed, it is an undeniable reality of life that people do what is rewarded and avoid what is punished. Would you write a 10-page paper for a class if no grade were attached, but the professor said, "It will be great for your development?" When undesirable behaviors are rewarded and positive behaviors neglected (or sometimes even punished), dysfunctional results occur in organizations. Great managers tie desired behavior to positive behavior and are successful in communicating that linkage to their people.

For students, one close-to-home example of the folly described in Management Live 4.5 is right in our own university settings where learning and skill building are hoped to be the prized behaviors. However, it is hardly provocative

"If you don't know where you're going, you might not get there."

—Yogi Berra

"For the people who work for you or with you, you must lavish praise on them at all times. If a flower is watered, it flourishes. If not, it shrivels up and dies. It's much more fun looking for the best in people. People don't need to be told where they've slipped up or made a mess of something. They'll sort it out themselves."

—Richard Branson

"But there are advantages to being elected President. The day after I was elected, I had my high school grades classified Top Secret."

—Ronald Reagan

The Five Major Steps

to suggest the indicators we use for learning and knowledge gain—grades—have increasingly become more important than the goals that underlie them. It is now grades, independent of true knowledge or skill, that are most influential in job placement offices and graduate school admission departments. As a not very surprising result, fraternities and sororities are obsessive about keeping good test files, the Internet has emerged as a source of plagiarized term papers, and cheating is a greater problem than ever in U.S. universities. The point is that if we are going to avoid the folly, we first need to clearly identify the behaviors we want and then find ways to reward those behaviors and only those behaviors. This is exactly what the practice of behavior modification is designed to do.

Based on the basic tenets of reinforcement theory, the managerial practice known as **organizational behavior modification** commonly involves a five-step problem approach to increasing motivation and ultimately performance (Figure 4.5). The five major steps are that: (1) performance-related behaviors are identified; (2) the frequency of these behaviors is measured; (3) the contingencies supporting the current behaviors are identified; (4) a behaviorally based intervention strategy is developed and implemented; and (5) the resulting performance-related behaviors are measured.

Performance-related behaviors are identified

↓

The frequency of these behaviors is measured

↓

The contingencies supporting the current behaviors are identified

↓

A behaviorally based intervention strategy is developed and implemented

↓

The resulting performance-related behaviors are measured

"We reward top executives at the agency with a unique incentive program. Money."

FIGURE 4.5

Organizational Behavior Modification Model

Source: Adapted from Luthans, F. & Stajkovic, A.D. (1999). Reinforce for performance: The need to go beyond pay and even rewards, Academy of Management Executive, 13, 49–57.

Management Live 4.5

The Folly of Rewarding A, While Hoping for B[21]

One of the truly classic articles in all of the management literature is titled, "On the Folly of Rewarding A, While Hoping for B." The article was written by Steve Kerr, now chief learning officer for Goldman Sachs and formerly in the same position at General Electric. Kerr observed there are countless cases in organizations and society where the folly is present in that we sincerely hope for one thing, but reward another. Notable among his examples is the hope that doctors will make accurate diagnoses, but that the reward system in place disproportionately rewards treating well people as sick, because of more treatment revenue, reduced threat of malpractice, and appearance of prudent medicine. Another example is the hope that politicians will be open, frank, and honest; however, the existing reward system elects those who do not reveal any potentially divisive beliefs and who get money directed to their constituents. The lesson is to clarify what you really hope for and then dig into your culture to determine if that is truly what is perceived to be rewarded. Kerr has convincingly argued that it too often is not.

Examples of Behavior Modification in the Real World

Behavior modification has been used successfully in an extremely wide range of situations. In one of the most famous examples, Emery Air Freight Corp. used behavior modification to improve its customer service. Emery had a goal for its customer service department of responding to customer questions within 90 minutes. At first, the employees perceived that they met this goal about 9 times out of 10. In reality, however, Emery Air Freight was only meeting this goal 3 out of 10 times. Under any measure, 30 percent cannot be considered very good! As a result of this poor performance, a behavior modification system was established in which the employees physically recorded how quickly each customer request was answered. The supervisor then gave praise and recognition for high performance. Within one day, performance went from 30 percent to 90 percent goal attainment and stayed between 90 and 95 percent for over three years.[22] This example should give you an idea of just how powerful behaviour modification really is!

Some recent examples of the success of behavior modification in handling everyday work issues can be seen in the following examples. A food distribution company implemented a behavior modification program at one of its warehouses. The program reduced order errors by 10 percent, with a cost saving of about $10,000.[23] In the area of safety, recent research estimates suggest money spent on safety-related behavior modification programs can have payoffs of more than 10:1. In other words, for every $1 invested in these programs, more than $10 can be saved due to lower insurance costs, fewer accidents, and reduced worker compensation claims.[24]

To further make the case, behavior modification was recently used in a retail setting to modify the behavior of cashiers in keeping their register drawers balanced. Initially, daily cash shortages averaged $2.27. After the behavior modification program was implemented, average cash shortages were reduced to $0.06 per day.[25] An additional example of a success with pizza delivery drivers can be seen in Management Live 4.6.

Management Live 4.6

Behavior Modification and Pizza Delivery Drivers[26]

When most of us think of safe drivers, pizza delivery drivers aren't at the top of the list. In fact, reckless pizza delivery drivers have been the cause of numerous multimillion dollar lawsuits and been a serious concern to pizza makers all over the United States.

A study conducted by Timothy Ludwig, Jay Biggs, Sandra Wagner, and E. Scott Geller investigated the effects of a safe driving competition utilizing publicly posted individual feedback as the behavioral intervention. Their study looked at the safety behaviors (for example, turn-signal use, safety belt use, and complete stopping at intersections) of 82 pizza deliverers. After getting a baseline measure, pizza deliverers received posted weekly individual feedback on their turn-signal use (at Store A) or complete intersection stops (at Store B). The deliverers' safe driving scores were posted individually on a vertical scale along with their names. Each week the driver with the highest average performance was rewarded with a free vehicle-maintenance coupon. Turn-signal use among drivers at Store A increased 22 percent. Complete intersection stopping among drivers at Store B increased 17 percent. Although the winners of the weekly competitions had the greatest increase in performance, nonwinners also increased their instances of safe driving during the competition.

Developing and Implementing a Behavioral Strategy

While behavior modification is relatively straightforward, there are some important details specifically related to the fourth step of the process, developing and implementing a behavioral intervention strategy. To effectively develop and implement behavioral modification strategies, it is important to understand some fundamentals of learning and behavioral change.

The process of linking consequences with voluntary behaviors is referred to as **operant conditioning.** Operant conditioning employs strategies involving the addition or removal of pleasant or aversive consequences. Since there are two actions (addition and removal) and two types of consequences (pleasant and aversive), four different operant conditioning strategies are possible (see Table 4.4).

Positive Reinforcement

As indicated in Table 4.4, **positive reinforcement** occurs when a behavior is linked with a consequence an employee considers pleasant. Examples of positive reinforcement occur all around us every day. A child given a certificate for getting all As on his report card, an employee given a bonus for meeting a difficult performance goal, and a politician reelected after doing a good job for her constituents are all examples of positive reinforcement. Positive reinforcement should be used whenever the goal is to increase the frequency of a desirable behavior because it modifies behavior in a way that is not viewed as being controlling and because it does not bring about negative side effects. Basically, everybody wins with positive reinforcement. One of the challenges facing many managers, however, is what to provide as a reward. Remember that managers should seek rewards that have value to the employee. This ties back to the idea of strengthening valence from the beginning of the chapter.

A frequent lament of managers everywhere, public sector or private, is they have little discretionary power to reward their doers with more money. Since that is so often the case, an important management skill is to be creative in finding

TABLE 4.4 | **Four Operant Conditioning Strategies**

	Consequence Added	Consequence Removed
Pleasant Consequence	**Positive Reinforcement**	**Extinction**
	Increase frequency of a desired behavior.	Reduce frequency of an undesired behavior.
	Example: An athletics coach gives hard-working players more playing time to reward their effort.	*Example:* A club president withholds laughter because she is tired of her VP always making jokes.
Aversive Consequence	**Punishment**	**Negative Reinforcement**
	Decrease frequency of an undesired behavior.	Increase frequency of a desired behavior.
	Example: An Army sergeant has a private do 100 push-ups for being late for roll call.	*Example:* Your roommates tell you they will stop nagging you if you do the dishes.

reinforcements that are both motivating and cost-effective. As Management Live 4.7 illustrates, managers have had great success with showing appreciation using some surprisingly simple techniques.

Beyond showing appreciation for good work, it is also a good idea to recognize important milestones and be thoughtful regarding personal issues and crises people face. Purchase a large supply of note cards and get in the habit of sending them for birthdays and promotions or other events. Send flowers with a note for engagements, weddings, or family deaths. People will remember your kindness, probably much longer than you will!

Another good source for creative and cost-effective rewards is a collection of ideas put together by author Bob Nelson, in his book "1001 Ways to Reward Your Employees."[27] Nelson makes the point that rewards don't need to be expensive to have big impacts. The following list provides a flavor of the types of rewards he suggests:

"Simple observation suggests that most of us are trinket freaks – if they represent genuine thanks for a genuine assist."

—Tom Peters

- Write a letter to the employee's family about what his or her efforts mean.
- Arrange for a senior executive to have a recognition lunch with the employee.
- Find out what an employee's hobby is and purchase a small gift related to that hobby.
- Dedicate a prime parking space for the outstanding employee of the month.
- Wash an employee's car in the parking lot during business hours.
- Have a group of managers personally cook lunch for a group of top-performing employees.
- Use outstanding employees in the organization's advertisements.

"There are two things people want more than sex and money . . . recognition and praise."

—Mary Kay Ash

Management Live 4.7

Simple Rewards[28]

For some ideas of how simple rewards can demonstrate appreciation, take a look at the following successful programs from some top U.S. companies.

The Spirit of Fred Award. Walt Disney World in Orlando, Florida, uses this simple recognition program named for an employee named Fred (not too surprisingly!). When Fred got his first salaried position, a few key people taught him the values needed to be successful at Disney. The name Fred became an acronym for Friendly, Resourceful, Enthusiastic, and Dependable. The award has become highly valued within Disney.

Thanks a Bunch. Maritz Performance Improvement Co. in St. Louis, Missouri, has a Thanks a Bunch program in which employees receive a bouquet of flowers in appreciation for special favors or jobs well done. The employee receiving the award then passes the flowers on to someone else who has been helpful, with the idea of seeing how many people can be given the bouquet in a single day. With the flowers the employees get a written thank you card. At certain times through the year, the cards are entered into a drawing for prizes.

The Golden Banana Award. Years ago, a Hewlett-Packard Co. engineer burst into his manager's office in Palo Alto, California, to announce he had solved an important problem. In response, his manager looked around to find something to reward the employee with and ended up handing the employee a banana from his lunch with the words, "Well done. Congratulations!" The employee was somewhat confused at first, but over the years the Golden Banana Award became a prestigious honor given to inventive Hewlett-Packard employees.

We need to always remember, however, that different employees will have different valence scores for each of the examples listed. One person might view having lunch with a senior executive as a valued outcome while another might view it as being worse than a trip to the dentist. See Tool Kit 4.3 for a step-by-step approach to providing effective positive reinforcement and Tool Kit 4.5 for methods to deliver reinforces.

The work of Richard Easterlin[29] may provide some answers as to why monetary rewards may not always be the most effective reward. His research has to do with how people adapt to having increased amounts of money across their lives. Easterlin, an economist, has found that young adults start out with fairly similar material aspirations. As young adults, he finds that people with more money are happier because they are better able to fulfill their aspirations. In other words, when we all have similar material expectations, people with more money are better able to meet those expectations than people with less money.

As we age, however, getting more money does not cause well-being to increase (for people with low or high incomes) because it generates an equivalent growth in material aspirations. In other words, as you get more money you have an increased amount of wants. Since happiness is linked to the ratio of what we have versus what we want, this ratio will not tend to change for a person as their income goes up. So, the more we get, the more we want and we rarely can close the gap between what we have and what we want.

Extinction

As compared to the relatively straightforward application of positive reinforcement, **extinction** is the most difficult strategy to transfer from the laboratory to the work environment.[30] The technical definition of extinction is defined as a behavior followed by no response. The idea of extinction is that a behavior not followed by any consequence would not likely be repeated again (because it did not bring about any gain for the person performing the behavior). For instance, extinction is normally thought of as a strategy for modifying the behavior of a person who complains about petty issues at work. The idea is if the supervisor does not respond to petty complaints ("I don't like the colors of the walls in the office," "my desk chair has a stain on it," or "Tom's desk is newer than mine"), then the complainer will stop complaining because the complaints do not improve the situation.

However, in real-world situations, people hold expectations about what is likely to follow their actions based upon what they have observed in the past. As a result, what a supervisor intends as a nonresponse is usually interpreted either positively or negatively. Whatever the result, people clearly may interpret a great deal of meaning—quite possibly unintended meaning—from a nonresponse. One good example of extinction working as intended is as a response to a person who makes meetings longer because he's always making jokes. By not laughing at the jokes, co-workers can quickly make the joking stop.

Negative Reinforcement

Like positive reinforcement, **negative reinforcement** is an attempt to increase the frequency of a desirable behavior. Negative reinforcement, however, involves linking desired behaviors with the removal of undesirable consequences, rather than the addition of positive consequences associated with positive reinforcement. For instance, promising a sales representative she can delegate her 10 least favorite accounts if she can increase her sales by 30 percent would be a constructive form of negative reinforcement. It is important to remember the term negative reinforcement refers to the act of *removing* an aversive consequence. In general, positive reinforcement is the preferred method to increase

"I have found that you can get further with a smile, a kind word and a gun, than you can with a smile and kind word alone."

—Al Capone

the frequency of behavior, but negative reinforcement may serve as an additional tool when a manager is not able to control many desirable positive outcomes, but is able to remove negative ones.

When used improperly, negative reinforcement takes the form of "managing by threats." An example of this can be seen when a manager says, "if your numbers don't improve, you'll be fired." When the numbers improve, the person is not fired

Management Live 4.8

Show Me the Money!

In a large meta-analysis, researchers Alexander Stajkovic and Fred Luthans examined 72 studies that used behavior modification principles to increase employee performance. In each of these studies, a particular form of reinforcer was used, including money tied to performance (the employee receives money after reaching a previously set goal), social recognition (the employee receives public praise and honor), and feedback (the employee is told how well he or she is performing the job). The results tell an interesting and important story. As seen in the figure below, all three reinforcers were effective in improving employee performance: money, 21 percent increase; social recognition, 16 percent increase; and feedback, 11 percent increase.

The real lessons from this large study are twofold. First, the largest percentage increase (45 percent) occurred from a combination of providing money, social recognition, and feedback. If you have wondered how great managers use rewards to motivate performance, it seems to be rather straightforward: Frequently tell people how they're doing on the job, recognize their achievements in front of others and, when possible, reward performance with additional cash.

Second, one of managers' most frequent complaints is they have little power to provide financial rewards, making motivating people impossible. This study clearly demonstrates that by simply providing a little recognition or giving regular feedback, both of which require no financial commitment, managers can significantly increase overall employee performance. In the long run, such increases may ultimately allow a manager increased capacity to provide financial rewards.

Source: Stajkovic, A.D., & Luthans, F. (2003). Behavioral management and task performance in organizations: Conceptual background, meta-analysis, and test of alternative models. *Personnel Psychology*, 56, 155–194.

Effect of Reinforcers on Employee Performance Improvement

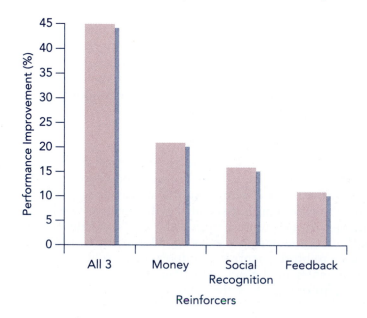

and the threat is removed. While this may work in the short term, it has harmful side effects and is not recommended as an effective management practice.

Punishment

The final behavioral strategy discussed here is **punishment,** which consists of adding an unpleasant consequence as a response to a person's behavior, with the goal of stopping the behavior from happening in the future. For example, if an employee disregards safety guidelines and acts recklessly on the job, a reprimand would be an appropriate means of trying to reduce this dangerous behavior. Most companies have punishment systems that increase in severity with the number of times the punishment has been administered. For instance, a first offense may be associated with a verbal warning, whereas a second offense will receive a written warning, and the employee is fired for a third offense.

Although punishment is relatively straightforward, it should be avoided unless it is really needed. Research has suggested that punishment, especially if it is viewed as being unfairly administered, can have negative, unintended side effects such as encouraging people to rebel because they feel they are being too tightly controlled.[31] Moreover, there is more useful motivational information in positive reinforcement because it essentially specifies what *to do*. By its very nature, punishment can only specify what *not to do*—of which there may be an infinite number of variations.

Since punishment normally provides people the most trouble, we wanted to provide more guidance on how to effectively discipline. A useful metaphor regarding the application of punishment is that of the "red hot stove." Specifically, that means punishment will be administered most effectively when it has the following four characteristics:

- **Clear Expectations.** The stove is *red hot*—anyone can see and feel that if they touch it they will be burned.

- **Consistent.** Any time anyone touches the stove (commits the behavior) they get burned.

- **Timely.** Anyone who touches the stove gets burned immediately.

- **Powerful.** The stove is *red* hot and leaves a severe and memorable burn. This makes the effect lasting.

> *"All in all, punishment hardens and renders people more insensible; it concentrates; it increases the feeling of estrangement; it strengthens the power of resistance."*
>
> —Friedrich Nietzsche

"Pretend to ask for a raise."

Another characteristic of effective punishment, in addition to the four described in the red hot stove example, is that it should focus exclusively on the specific behavioral problem. This is not the time to bring up old issues or to make general accusations. The focus of the punishment should be on eliminating a problem behavior, not on demoralizing or humiliating the other person. A behavioral focus increases the likelihood that the employee will associate the negative response with a specific act rather than viewing it as a generalized negative evaluation, which will reduce the hostility normally felt when being reprimanded. Please refer to Tool Kit 4.4 for more specific behavioral information about punishment.

The rules of the red hot stove apply equally as well to the administering of positive reinforcement. Try to catch people doing something right, be specific in telling them what they have done well, and present them with some type of recognition while the stove is hot in the positive sense. Although managers typically have more discomfort and even dread administering punishment, *ineffective positive reinforcement* is often a greater problem as managers are naturally inclined to assume people know they are doing well and to give only global, nonspecific feedback that has little motivating value (for example, "You are great, I wish I had five more like you.").

As is evident from the descriptions above, there is a time and place for all four of the behavioral strategies. These strategies can be used either to make unacceptable behaviors acceptable or to transform acceptable behaviors into exceptional ones. They are designed to avoid the harmful effects typically associated with the improper use of discipline as well as to assist with the appropriate use of rewards.

"Productivity is up nine per cent since I made everyone a vice-president."

The Job as a Source of Motivation

The Job Characteristics Model

"In a recent survey, 97 percent of Merck's employees said they were proud to work for the company and 86 percent said they thought their work had special meaning."

We have now seen that motivation can derive from the person to be motivated or the supervisor. Richard Hackman and Greg Oldham have presented an intuitive, practical, and evidence-based model of how motivation can stem from the job or work itself.[32] This addresses the third source for filling a person's motivational

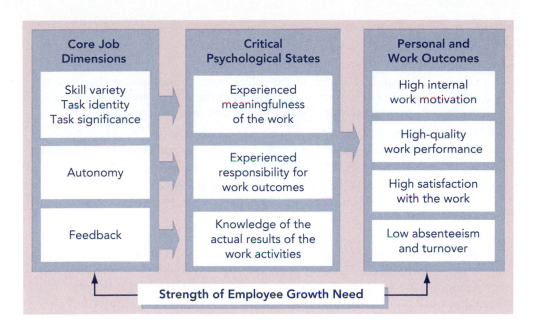

FIGURE 4.6

Job Characteristics Model

"bucket". Their **Job Characteristics Model (JCM)** provides a simple yet powerful explanation of why some jobs are more motivating than others and how the motivation potential of a job can be enriched. The model has proven so applicable it is among the most widely referenced frameworks in the management field.

The JCM identifies five **core job dimensions**—the vital characteristics of the work itself—and proposes a link between those and **psychological states** experienced by the worker. In Figure 4.6 the relationship between the core job dimensions, the psychological states they influence, and their subsequent outcomes are illustrated. As can be seen in Figure 4.6, well-designed work can lead to high-quality work performance, high levels of motivation, low absenteeism and turnover, and increased job satisfaction. See Table 4.5 for some examples of jobs with varying degrees of the core job dimensions.

To further understand the JCM and how it can help isolate desirable motivational perceptions to fill a portion of the motivation bucket, we need to further

"When they believe in the company and in what they are doing, employees tend to pitch in and do what it takes to succeed even when it means working longer and harder."

—Roger Ballou, President and CEO, CDI Corp.

TABLE 4.5 | **Examples of Jobs with Varying Degrees of the Core Job Dimensions**

Job Characteristics	"High" Examples	"Low" Examples
Skill Variety	Plant manager, elementary school teacher, astronaut	Data entry clerk, assembly worker, computer programmer
Task Identity	Sales account manager, attorney, artist, carpenter	Insurance underwriter, restaurant host or hostess
Task Significance	Medical doctor, nurse, social worker	Telemarketer, data entry clerk
Autonomy	Self-employed, salesperson, computer programmer	Auditor, police officer, military
Feedback	Telemarketer, medical professional, stand-up comic	Retail sales clerk

explain the model. People experience a job as more motivating when the job has a high degree of:

- **Skill variety,** or the range in number of skills used to complete the job tasks (conceptual, physical, technical, people skills). Astronauts have a high degree of skill variety stemming from their need to be technically proficient, in great physical shape, and good at problem solving.

- **Task identity,** or the degree to which the job requires completion of a whole or identifiable piece of work. Artists enjoy very high task identity as they see their work through from beginning to end.

- **Task significance,** or the degree to which the job has a direct effect on the work or lives of other people. For instance, surgeons perform a job with very high task significance.

- **Autonomy,** or the freedom to select how and when particular tasks are performed. As one of our colleagues likes to say, "If you have to ask permission to go to the bathroom, it's not likely you will experience high autonomy on the job." Professors, for example, have highly autonomous jobs, while manufacturing workers often have rather low autonomy.

- **Feedback,** or the degree to which individuals receive knowledge of their results from the job itself. Workers with jobs high in feedback normally receive feedback frequently and from multiple sources. Stand-up comics have a high degree of feedback on their job; they immediately know the results of their work.

Since these core job characteristics ultimately influence employee motivation and satisfaction on the job, enhancing core job dimensions will enhance employee motivation. When employee motivation is enhanced, both employees and managers are better off. Employees are better off because they have a job they find more interesting and satisfying. Managers and the organization are better off because high employee motivation is associated with reduced turnover and absenteeism, increased quantity of performance, and improved quality. In addition, maximizing employees' core job dimensions increases their intrinsic motivation and reduces the time a manager spends supervising their work. So, enhancing a job really does create a situation where everybody wins.

Using the JCM on the job

The JCM also provides direct implications for enriching poorly designed or boring jobs. When the JCM was developed in the 1970s it was primarily focused on repetitive assembly line work in manufacturing settings. A prime example of a typical setting where JCM was applied is the General Motors Assembly Division (GMAD) in Lordstown, Ohio. The history of the JCM at Lordstown is described in Management Live 4.9.

Although sometimes thought to be relevant only in manufacturing contexts, the JCM is applicable across the entire spectrum of jobs. For example, a recent study[33] used the JCM to redesign jobs of customer service representatives in a technical service call center. Findings indicated the call center workers responded quite well to the job redesign efforts. More specifically, after the intervention, the number of successfully solved problems significantly increased as did the overall customer service score. At the same time, the percentage of repeat calls needed and the percentage of calls escalated to a higher level decreased similarly.

An important part of that job redesign effort was a new process to facilitate learning called the "hot seat." The hot seat was devised to enable specialists to spend a portion of their time off the phones and working on problems on their own without interruption. The specialists worked three days on the phone (in the hot seat) and then two days off the phone working on problems they had been unable to solve. The result was a more in-depth understanding of the problems, problems being solved quicker, and problems being solved right the first time.

The MPS formula

One feature that makes the JCM so user friendly is its specification of the five core job dimensions and how they can be combined into an equation calculating the **motivation potential score (MPS)** for any job. The equation is provided in Figure 4.7.

Within this equation, the properties of multiplication are again very important (as they were in expectancy theory). That is, the absence of any of the core job dimensions is magnified in the model. To improve the motivating potential score of a job, then, it is important to consider each of the five elements since a lack of any can be detrimental to the motivating potential. Before we discuss how to increase the core job dimensions, there is an important caveat. If an employee does not have a need for growth, attempts to make a job more motivating will fail. The theory and use of the model is based on the assumption that people want their jobs to be more motivating. This may well be true for many people, but it is important to acknowledge that not all employees would look favorably on interventions to enrich their jobs. More specifically, employees with a low **growth need strength** may be very content to work in a relatively unenriched environment.

$$MPS = \left(\frac{Variety + Identity + Significance}{3} \right) \times Autonomy \times Feedback$$

FIGURE 4.7

The MPS Equation

Management Live 4.9

Job Design Comes Full Circle at GM's Lordstown Plant

A well-known case study regarding job redesign occurred in the General Motors Assembly Division plant in Lordstown, Ohio. The case essentially chronicles how to do job redesign the wrong way! In the early 1970s, General Motors substantially redesigned many jobs in the Lordstown plant so the firm could produce a small car (the Vega) intended to compete with Japanese cars.

To make the jobs "more efficient," industrial engineers with stopwatches were brought in to perform time and motion studies. As a result, the jobs were simplified so workers could do very simple tasks very quickly. The employees were not involved in this process, and the results were disastrous! Quality problems plagued the Vega throughout its existence, and there were multiple strikes at the Lordstown facility over the new working arrangements. To provide an idea of how strongly the employees resisted these changes, new Vegas would regularly come off the assembly line with broken windshields and slashed seats. The employees actually vandalized the cars as they were being built!

Today, however, the long history of problems in Lordstown seems to be mostly resolved. By working with the United Auto Workers to design more motivating work, General Motors made the decision to manufacture its newest small car, the Cobalt, in Lordstown.

Source: Jensen, C. (2004, August 22). New Life in an Old GM Plant. *The Plain Dealer*, p. G1.

JCM Interventions: How to Enrich Boring Work

The Unenriched Job

As noted, in addition to identifying the core dimensions themselves, Hackman and Oldham further outlined a set of interventions shown to influence the MPS. These five interventions provide a blueprint for designing more fulfilling work (see Table 4.6).

The first intervention is to *combine tasks*. A combination of tasks leads to a more challenging and complex work assignment because it requires people to use a wider variety of skills. Newport Corp., Irvine, California,[34] emphasizes its training and cross-training programs, which include combining tasks. Newport employees participate and are involved in both classroom and on-the-job training programs to stay current with the latest manufacturing and assembly techniques. The cross-training program adds to the workforce's adaptability and flexibility, allowing for smooth transitions between varied production volumes. A more flexible workforce simultaneously reduces costs and makes jobs more meaningful to the people performing them.

A related strategy is to *form natural work units*. Natural work units are implemented so that task identity and task significance can be increased. This is the basic idea behind the use of the manufacturing cell, instead of straight assembly lines. For years, Volvo has built cars in small groups of employees referred to as cells.[35] These cells are responsible for an entire component of the vehicle, for example, the interior or the engine.

| TABLE 4.6 | Implementing Concepts for the Job Characteristics Model |

Job-Enriching Technique	Enhances . . .
Combine Tasks	Skill variety, task identity, task significance
Form Natural Work Units	Task identity, task significance
Establish Client Relationships	Skill variety, task identity, autonomy, feedback
Vertically Load Jobs	Autonomy, task identity
Open Feedback Channels	Feedback

The third technique for enhancing jobs is to *establish client relationships*. A client relationship involves an ongoing personal relationship between an employee and the client or customer. This relationship can increase autonomy, task identity, skill variety, and feedback. Enhancing jobs in this way has been an important part of the success of Wainwright Industries, St. Peters, Missouri.[36] Wainwright employees serve as customer champions, interfacing with customers and solving problems for them. Any score below 95 percent on a customer satisfaction measure results in a customer champion assembling a cross-functional team, which then develops an action plan within 48 hours. This close personal relationship between employees and customers aids in fast and accurate problem resolution.

The fourth suggestion, vertically load jobs, refers to giving increased authority to workers for making job-related decisions. In reality, *vertical loading* can be thought of as being synonymous with employee empowerment. That is, workers and their boss share responsibility. As supervisors delegate more authority and responsibility, their subordinates perceive increases in autonomy, accountability, and task identity. At Phelps County Bank in Rolla, Missouri,[37] an extensive training program was set up to give employee owners the motivation and tools to take responsibility for the business. Management established classes in problem-solving and financial statement analysis, as well as tutorials where departments exchanged information with each other about their products and services. Employee-owners went through cross-training days where, for example, tellers would inform loan department staff about their roles and responsibilities. As a result of these efforts, employees became more empowered to deal with customer problems on the spot, without having to seek time-consuming approval from management or advice from colleagues.

The last intervention for improving job design is to *open feedback channels*. Feedback is important because workers need to know how well or how poorly they are performing their jobs if improvement is expected. Some jobs are blessed with immediate feedback, for example, a comedian knows within seconds whether or not her material was funny. For most jobs however, the problem is receiving too little feedback with few obvious mechanisms available to generate such feedback. When people receive timely and useful feedback, they are best able to adapt their behavior to achieve the highest performance. Karrie Jerman, human resources representative at Colorado Springs, Colorado-based Hamilton Standard Commercial Aircraft, says that 360-degree appraisals (a key tool used to open feedback channels) are imperative. "The thing we gain the most is input from so many people that know the employee's work. Now their peers and customers give feedback," says Jerman. "They feel it's more fair."[38]

Overall, job design interventions have achieved impressive results. Firms that have undergone job redesign efforts typically report higher productivity, higher work quality, improved worker satisfaction, and less absenteeism. Understanding how to create a motivating *job*, not just a motivated *person* is an important tool in the repertoire of any great manager.

> "Most employees have an opportunity to work a rally and do demo rides. They are encouraged to talk to the customers to get a better understanding of their needs and expectations, and how they feel about the product."
>
> —Ron Mundt, Director of Service Support Operations, Harley-Davidson

A recent Gallup survey found that only 26 percent of employees consider themselves "actively engaged" in their work. It is clear that job enrichment still has a long way to go.

Even though 360 feedback is a relatively new tool, virtually all Fortune 500 companies were using it by the year 2000.

Concluding Note

Putting It All Together to Increase Motivation

We have covered a lot of ground in our journey through motivation models and ideas, and it can be a little overwhelming. As you can see there are multiple ways to "fill up" an employee's motivational bucket. As managers, it is important to be aware of the dominant needs of our people and the various motivators available to us in rewards and the work itself. Motivation theories offer managers many applicable evidence-based tools for creating more energizing workplaces. The challenge is to put them to work in places that matter. Based on practical experience and the tools and techniques discussed in this chapter, we offer a few critical prescriptions for any manager in almost any situation to ensure high motivation:

1. **Recognize individual differences in motivation.** Few people are motivated by the same things. Use the platinum rule to find out what best motivates each individual, including what type of rewards each employee values most.

2. **Set good goals.** Always specifically define success. We can't emphasize enough that setting good goals is one of the most efficient ways to increase motivation.

3. **Strive for fairness, not equality, in rewards and punishments.** You do not have to give everyone the exact same reward. You *do* need to ensure the rewards you give out are proportional to the performance *and* are equitable.

4. **Link rewards and punishments directly to performance.** Make sure rewards people receive are based upon their performance.

5. **Give credit where credit is due.** Recognize people publicly for their achievements and don't take credit for your employees' work.

6. **Model the way.** Delegation is an important part of managing. However, nothing is more de-motivating than bosses who ask other people to do things they (the bosses) are not personally willing to do. Model the behavior you want from your people.

Key Terms

achievers	intrinsic outcomes	operant conditioning
core job dimensions	Job Characteristics Model (JCM)	organizational behavior modification
equity	Maslow's hierarchy of needs	platinum rule
equity sensitivity	motivating force	positive reinforcement
expectancy	motivation	psychological states
expectancy theory	motivation potential score (MPS)	punishment
extinction	need for achievement	reinforcement theory
extrinsic outcomes	need for affiliation	suboptimization
growth need strength	need for power	valence
instrumentality	negative reinforcement	

Motivation Tool Kits

Tool Kit 4.1   Equity Sensitivity Measure[39]

In Any Organization I Might Work For:

1. It would be more important for me to:
   _____ A. Get from the organization.
   _____ B. Give to the organization.

2. It would be more important for me to:
   _____ A. Help others.
   _____ B. Watch out for my own good.

3. I would be more concerned about:

_____ A. What I received from the organization.

_____ B. What I contributed to the organization.

4. The hard work I would do should:

_____ A. Benefit the organization.

_____ B. Benefit me.

5. My personal philosophy in dealing with the organization would be:

_____ A. If I don't look out for myself, nobody else will.

_____ B. It's better for me to give than to receive.

Scoring. Answering 1A, 2B, 3A, 4B, 5A all indicate being equity sensitive. 1B, 2A, 3B, 4A, and 5B indicate that you are not equity sensitive.

Tool Kit 4.2   Skills Needed to Improve Motivation Using Expectancy

The following actions are good ways to increase the components of the expectancy formula:

- Select capable and motivated people.
- Provide necessary training.
- Show successful examples.
- Be supportive and available.
- Make the link between performance and outcome extremely clear.
- Follow through quickly.
- Make rewards proportional to effort.
- Reward based on individual preferences.

Tool Kit 4.3   Steps to Rewarding Effectively

1. Describe the desirable behavior.
2. Explain the benefits that the desirable behavior is causing.
3. Explain consequences if the desirable behavior continues.
4. Provide examples and time for questions regarding desired behaviors.
5. Monitor behavior and reward desirable behavior.
6. Follow through with continued rewards should the positive behavior continue.

Tool Kit 4.4   Steps to Effective Punishment

1. Meet privately. Never punish in public.
2. Describe the undesirable behavior.
3. Explain the problems the undesirable behavior is causing.
4. Allow questions and opportunities for clarification.
5. Explain consequences if the undesirable behavior does not change.
6. Provide examples and time for questions regarding desired behaviors.
7. Monitor behavior, and reward desirable behavior.
8. Follow through with appropriate responses to behavior (aversive consequence if the behavior has not changed or positive outcomes if the behavior has changed).

Tool Kit 4.5 Methods to Deliver Reinforcers

Ways to Deliver Reinforcers	Description	When Applied	When Removed	Example
Continuous	Behavior is reinforced every time it occurs	Fastest method for establishing new behavior	Fastest method to cause extinction of new behavior	Praise, immediate recognition after every occurrence of behavior
Fixed Interval	Behavior is reinforced according to predetermined, constant schedule based on time	Some inconsistency in occurrence of behavior	Faster extinction of motivated behavior than with variable schedules	Weekly, bimonthly, monthly paycheck
Variable Interval	Behavior is reinforced after periods of time, but time span varies	Produces high rate of steady occurrences of behavior	Slower extinction of motivated behavior than with fixed schedules	Transfers, promotions, recognition
Fixed Ratio	Behavior is reinforced when certain number of occurrences of behavior is exhibited	Some inconsistency in occurrences of behavior	Faster extinction of motivated behavior than with variable schedules	Piece rate, commission on units sold
Variable Ratio	Behavior is reinforced according to number of occurrences of behavior, but number of occurrences needed varies	Can produce high rate of steady occurrences of behavior and resists extinction	Slower extinction of motivated behavior than with fixed schedules	Bonus, award, time off

Tool Kit 4.6 Diagnosing Motivational Problems

Given the complexity of motivational problems, here are some important questions that will help guide you through the diagnostic process.

- Are goals and performance expectations clearly communicated and understood?
- Does the person (or people) in question have the skills, training, and self-confidence needed to perform as asked?
- Is performance rewarded clearly and in a timely fashion? Does the person have strong reason to believe that if the work is performed, the outcome will be delivered?
- Is the outcome important to the person? Do I really know what that person values at this point in time and how do I know it? If I am offering something that person has told me he or she values, it is likely the valence is high.
- Are rewards proportional to effort and administered in a direct and timely way? Make sure the outcomes are proportional to the effort needed.
- Is the job designed to maximize the core job dimensions? What can be done to make the job more motivating?

Performance Management

"I never cease to be amazed at the power of the coaching process to draw out the skills or talent that was previously hidden within an individual, and which invariably finds a way to solve a problem previously thought unsolvable."

—John Russell,
Managing Director,
Harley-Davidson Europe Ltd.

Manage *What*?

1. Choosing the Best Person for a Role

You have just been promoted to the position of sales manager with a large salary increase, potential for a nice bonus, and responsibility for four sales representatives who will now report to you. As part of your new job, your boss asks you to hire a fifth sales representative in response to the rapid growth of the company. "In fact," he adds, "I've got a stack of resumes in my office for you, all you have to do is interview a few candidates and pick the best."

How would you go about filling the new sales position? Are there typical mistakes managers make in this type of situation which you should aim to avoid? What type of information would you hope to gather on these job applicants? How might you best determine who would be the highest performer?

2. Evaluating Someone's Job Performance

Last summer you were an intern at Techlo, a logistics company catering to the high-tech industry. The internships were extremely attractive with high pay and great perks. One reason the internships are so attractive is that of the three interns Techlo takes each summer, at least one is traditionally offered a job after graduation. In fact, you took a job offer and you've been working for Techlo for one year. Given your clear understanding of the intern role, your boss assigns you the responsibility of managing the new interns. Critical to this role will be to evaluate their performance over the four-month internship. Your boss will use your evaluation as the primary factor in determining which intern will be invited to join the firm full-time after graduation.

How should you determine the best performing intern? How can you ensure the process for evaluating the interns' performance is fair? Are there typical mistakes managers often make in these situations? The interns are all very talented, so what might help you distinguish good from great?

3. Managing the Problem Employee

Your assistant operations manager, Ken, is truly a great guy. Everybody loves him. He's funny, very social, and good-looking. He also seems to be a great source of support for other employees. Indeed, several fellow employees would claim Ken among their best friends. Ken seems to have everything going for him. There is only one problem—Ken doesn't get results. In the two years Ken has worked in your store, he has never once met a single goal. You've met with him on numerous occasions about his performance, and each time he tells you the same thing, "I'll work on it, boss. You don't have to worry about me." After these conversations, Ken puts in a few good weeks and sometimes shows improvement. Shortly thereafter, however, his performance slides again.

What steps should you take to deal with Ken's sub-par performance? What needs to be done first? How strict or harsh should you be? Should you be concerned about damaging the positive employee feelings toward Ken? One of Ken's peers, Armand, is very quiet and reserved but has had exceptional performance over the last year – in what ways should you manage Armand differently than you do Ken?

LEARNING OBJECTIVES

1. Differentiate between coaching and mentoring.
2. Choose the best person for a role.
3. Set clear performance expectations.
4. Evaluate job performance using multiple methods and multiple sources of data.
5. Avoid common errors in observing performance.
6. Provide consistent and constructive feedback.
7. Diagnose employee problems and manage them with performance improvement discussions and training.
8. Make a reassignment or termination decision.
9. Coach star employees with recognition and reinforcement.
10. Use consultative coaching to help employees grow.

Performance Management: The Day-to-Day Work of Great Managers

Coaching is truly fashionable these days. There are life coaches, romance coaches, executive coaches, and financial coaches, to name just a few. Discussions of coaching often conjure rich memories. Some people have had a great sports coach who taught them what it meant to work with others and challenged them to perform beyond their own expectations. Others may have had coaches they thought were unfair, played favorites, or only cared about outcomes and not personal development. Still others may realize they did not fully appreciate the impact and influence of a coach until years later, having at the time only seen their coaches as unfair or too demanding.

It is certainly popular to talk about managers as coaches and we very much like that analogy. It implies that managers support and encourage their people and treat them as part of a team with shared goals. The best coaches know that their success stems largely from their people and they clearly understand three fundamental principles about the manager as coach:[1]

Principle 1: Management is the intervention of getting things done through others.

Principle 2: Managers need their people more than those people need the manager.

Principle 3: Managers get rewarded for what their employees do, not for what the managers do.

Put simply, the job of managers is to make their people as successful as possible. Managers only succeed when their people succeed. While that may seem straightforward, it is often one of the most difficult realizations for successful individual contributors making the transition to a management role.

Helping employees succeed through coaching involves choosing the right people for the right job, assessing their job performance, and providing effective feedback. Coaching forms the basis of the relationship between employee and manager, and nothing is more important to a manager's success than that relationship. Employees rely on this relationship to understand their performance, obtain rewards, seek advancement, and gain social support. Managers rely on this relationship to effectively structure and delegate work, generate ideas, and solve problems. We use the term coach throughout this chapter to refer to managers who engage their employees day-to-day in the performance management process resulting in strong manager-employee relationships and results.

The Importance and Challenge of Performance Management

Recent work by Gallup Co. and others has found that a positive relationship between people and their immediate supervisor is among the most important predictors of organizational performance. More specifically, studies by Mark Huselid and colleagues, across 1,000 firms in different industries, has shown good coaching and performance management practices resulted in sales increases ranging from $27,000 to $44,000 per employee, cash flow increases of 16 percent, decreases in turnover of 7 percent, and increases in stock market value of $18,000 per employee.[2] Put simply, good coaching is good business, but it is neither self-evident nor easy to do well. Note that ample evidence also links *poor* performance management and coaching with decreases in productivity and lower perceptions of justice or fairness in firms.[3] Anyone who has experienced a "bad boss" can confirm that the cost of a poor manager is exceedingly high.

> "The things that make a good leader are being open-minded, having a willingness to really ask for and accept advice, showing a sense of humility, and putting the right people in the right seats."
>
> —Hank Paulson, CEO, Goldman Sachs

The challenge of becoming an effective coach lies in the inherent discomfort involved in judging others. Whether it's determining the right role for an employee, assessing an employee's performance, or delivering negative feedback, most people are not naturally comfortable playing such a role. There is a certain appeal to simply holding people accountable for results and ignoring the behaviors and processes they use to attain such results. However, that approach ignores the value of coaching, which, when done effectively, can dramatically improve individual performance.[4] Unfortunately, though we know a great deal about what makes for effective coaching, such information is often ignored in favor of intuition and common sense approaches. Indeed, the "common sense" of coaching often leads to dysfunctional practice and is one of several myths that contribute to misunderstandings.

Coaching versus Mentoring

Although great coaches help people develop, coaching should not be confused with mentoring. **Mentoring** is an intense, long-term relationship between a senior, more experienced person (**mentor**) and a more junior, less experienced person (**protégé**).[5] Mentoring differs from coaching in at least two significant ways. First, the goal of mentoring is focused on an employee's overall development, not necessarily focused on day-to-day performance. Second, mentors are typically *not* the employee's direct supervisor. As such, mentors and protégés (those being mentored) generally have a relationship quite different from that of employee and supervisor. Coaching, on the other hand, is about day-to-day work and focused directly on job performance.

MYTHS 5.1	**Myths of Performance Management**

People are naturally good observers of behavior. Although most people *think* they can make accurate judgments about others' behavior or intentions, the fact is that, without concerted discipline and utilization of some evidence-based methods, most human beings are miserable at accurately judging others' behavior. For example, interviewers often spend the majority of their interview time confirming what they assume to already know about the job candidate rather than trying to *disconfirm* their assumptions.[6] One study even showed that, the more the *interviewer* spent time talking during the interview, the more highly that interviewer rated the job candidate's potential![7]

Coaching is about personal style. While some famous sports coaches are charismatic and have distinctive styles, coaching for performance in organizations is less about personal style and more about using evidence-based methods that work.

Performance management is mostly common sense. While most everyone in organizations wishes that were true, the reality is that a majority of people are less than satisfied with the way they are managed. Recent studies have even identified an "under-management" phenomenon noting that as few as 10% of managers practice the most basic elements of effective performance management on a consistent basis (see Management Live 5.1).

Feedback is always effective. Conventional wisdom states that providing feedback to employees about their performance should generally lead to performance improvement. Yet recent research reveals that poorly administered feedback can even lead to *decreased* performance![8]

Coaching is only for low performers. All players can benefit from a coach—not just the struggling ones. Some people will need more time dedicated to them than others but a great coach can decipher when and what type of coaching each employee requires.

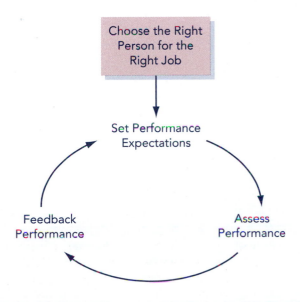

FIGURE 5.1

Performance Management Cycle (PMC)

The Performance Management Cycle

The essential elements of coaching can be concisely framed in a simple diagram (see Figure 5.1) of the **performance management cycle (PMC).** Generally stated, the primary role of a coach is to select, assess, and manage employee performance throughout the cycle. The best coaches help the right people perform the right job and fulfill their highest potential. This begins with choosing the right person for the right job. Great coaching starts with

Management Live 5.1

The "Under Management" Epidemic

According to Bruce Tulgan of RainmakerThinking Inc., all good managers should master five *management basics:*

1. Make clear performance statements.
2. Set measurable goals and hold people accountable for those goals.
3. Accurately monitor and evaluate work performance.
4. Provide clear feedback about performance and improvement.
5. Distribute rewards and punishments fairly.

> Following these management basics produces "engaged" employees who are motivated and productive. Yet Tulgan's research showed few managers actually do these management basics regularly.

Tulgan's Findings
Percentage of managers that provide every direct report with 5 management basics

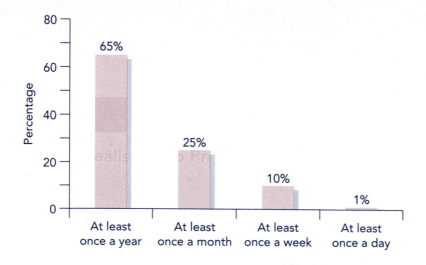

> The problem Tulgan uncovered is that, while good management boils down to a handful of critical behaviors, few managers are willing to do what is necessary to engage in those behaviors. Whether it is due to a lack of time, lack of skill, or the fear associated with judging people, "under management" is widespread.

selecting great people, whether internal applicants or external candidates for a job.

Yet for many managers hiring their own people is a luxury; most managers inherit a group of employees. There are of course no guarantees that the previous manager took careful steps to assess candidate potential in the selection process. Thus, great managers must learn to manage performance regardless of the circumstances they inherit. This includes evaluating performance as well as learning how to manage and develop employee performance. Through the PMC, managers set clear performance expectations early and often. In addition, they frequently assess performance and provide the feedback necessary to keep employees on track. When performance is achieved, great managers recognize and reward achievement. When expectations are not met, great managers diagnose the performance deficiency and repeat the PMC. Doing so sometimes may involve reassigning an employee to a job that more appropriately utilizes the employee's skills. In some cases, it could involve terminating the employment relationship.

Selecting People for Roles

Choosing the Right People for the Right Jobs

Making selection decisions remains one of the most misunderstood and poorly executed of all coaching endeavors. Managers are often bombarded by consultants who claim to hold the secrets of successfully choosing the right people for various roles. So how can you know who is telling the truth? First, keep in mind that, no matter what people may say, there are no mind-reading exams, no five-minute magic test, no one best personality, and no million-dollar interview questions that will help you successfully choose the right person for a role. Rather, a disciplined and systematic approach will move you toward success. Second, even the best selection tactics are subject to some error—that is, no method is foolproof. Our goal here is to help you improve your odds in selecting the right people by demystifying the process and demonstrating what works and what does not.

> "By and large, executives make poor promotion and staffing decisions. By all accounts, their batting average is no better than .333; at most, one-third of such decisions turn out right, a third are minimally effective, and one-third are outright failures."
>
> —Peter Drucker

"The bunny did not get the job because the bunny is cute.
The bunny got the job because the bunny knows WordPerfect."

Selection is Prediction

Before discussing selection methods, it's important to step back and look at what managers want to accomplish with respect to selection. Overall, managers are attempting to predict future employee success in the organization. Selection efforts target two important aspects of employee success:

- **Future Job Performance.** Selection methods allow managers to assess potential employees' fit with the overall job requirements. That is, managers must decide whether or not job candidates possess the right mix of knowledge, skill, and ability to successfully perform the job.

- **Future Person–Organization Fit.** Selection methods help both the candidate and the manager determine whether the candidate will fit within the culture of the organization. Even the most highly capable job candidates can fail within an organization when the culture of the organization (such as long-hour expectations) is not aligned with the candidates' work preferences.[9]

Thus, a good selection process involves a systematic approach of collecting data about job candidates' knowledge, skills, and abilities to assess these two aspects of fit. Achieving fit sounds simple, but managers typically have relatively little information at their disposal to help accurately predict the future. One of our colleagues is fond of saying that most employment decisions are made with less information than most people gather prior to buying a car. Actively collecting data will help form a more complete picture of the candidate and help predict success with more accuracy. Following a three-step selection process can greatly increase a manager's ability to collect the right data and use that information in a productive manner (Figure 5.2). We will now explain these three critical steps in more detail.

> *"If you get the right people on the bus, the right people in the right seats, and the wrong people off the bus, then you can figure out how to take it someplace great."*
>
> —Jim Collins

Clarify the Job Context

Before reviewing resumes, interviewing candidates, or giving any job-related test, you need to understand the context in which the job takes place. Remember, the goal of coaching in selection is to determine which job candidate is likely to succeed in the organization, both in terms of job performance and overall fit with the organization. Therefore, managers must be able to communicate key elements of the work environment and their own working style as outlined in Figure 5.2: knowing yourself, the job, and the law.

FIGURE 5.2

The Steps to a Great Hire

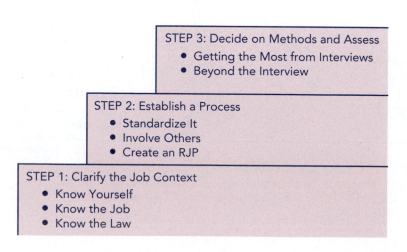

STEP 3: Decide on Methods and Assess
- Getting the Most from Interviews
- Beyond the Interview

STEP 2: Establish a Process
- Standardize It
- Involve Others
- Create an RJP

STEP 1: Clarify the Job Context
- Know Yourself
- Know the Job
- Know the Law

Know Yourself and What Kind of Boss You'll Be

Hall of fame basketball coach Bob Knight is well known for his firm and some-times controversial tactics. Over the years, people have certainly protested dif-ferent aspects of his approach, but one thing he does indisputably well is let players know what to expect prior to joining the team. Knight knows exactly what experience players will have playing for him and those players get exactly (for better or worse) what they are told in advance—no surprises. As a result, he has one of the highest retention (graduation) rates of all coaches.[10]

Potential employees need to know what it will be like to work for a man-ager. A simple exercise to start down the path of understanding what type of boss you'll be is to answer the following question: *Why should anyone want to work for you?* If you can successfully—honestly and with some objectivity—an-swer that question and understand the possible ramifications of the answer, the next step is to communicate it effectively to candidates. We'll come back to this point a bit later.

*"Remember, you weren't hired to think—you were
hired because you have opposable thumbs."*

Know the Job Well

While it seems self-evident selection decisions would be based on job descrip-tions, they often are not. Rather, managers commonly plunge right in looking for the "right person" without having defined what the "right person" actu-ally means. Great managers spend time describing and defining the job to be filled. Most often referred to as a **job analysis,** this process involves collect-ing information about what tasks (actual work) and knowledge, skills, and abilities (KSAs) are required for the job. The result of a job analysis is a job description that will help the hiring manager focus the recruitment and selec-tion efforts and provide a basis for communicating essential responsibilities to candidates.

To complete a job analysis and write a job description, managers should gather information about the job from many different sources, including job incumbents (people doing the job currently), customers, previous job descrip-tions, training materials, and performance appraisals. Unfortunately, those in positions of responsibility often do not have a good understanding of what em-ployees do "in the trenches" on a regular basis. The key then to completing a strong job analysis is to be thoughtful in the process and that almost always requires interviewing a few incumbents about what they do. A great aid in job analysis is the U.S. Department of Labor's online resource known as O*NET described in Management Live 5.2. Note that while O*Net descriptions are useful for those analyzing jobs they also can be helpful to job candidates who are trying to best present their credentials as fitting with the requirements of particular jobs.

After completing a job analysis, the job description almost writes itself. Job descriptions do not need to be exhaustive and probably shouldn't be. They should simply describe the most critical job tasks, KSAs, and other contextual information about the job. At minimum, a good job description should contain the following information:

- Critical or essential job duties and tasks.
- Knowledge, skills, and abilities (KSAs) required.
- Working conditions.
- Educational requirements.
- Physical demands.
- Legal or company policies or requirements.

The last bit of information—legalities—leads us to the third aspect of clarifying the job context.

Know the Law

The great myth about employment law is that it is overly restrictive and serves as a barrier to making the right coaching decisions. Managers fret over what

Management Live 5.2

O*NET

Writing a job description does not have to be an overly time-consuming process. The U.S. Department of Labor has created an extensive resource that can provide the basis of a manager's job analysis process. This online resource is known as O*NET, or the Occupational Information Network. It is described as "a comprehensive database of worker attributes and job characteristics. O*NET will be the nation's primary source of occupational information."

According to the O*NET Web site: the network offers a common language for communication across the economy and among workforce development efforts. It provides definitions and concepts for describing worker attributes and workplace requirements that can be broadly understood and easily accepted. Using comprehensive terms to describe the KSAs, interests, content, and context of work, O*NET provides a common frame of reference for understanding what is involved in effective job performance. The goal of O*NET's common language is straightforward: improve the quality of dialogue among people who communicate about jobs in the economy, generate employment statistics, and develop education and training programs. It provides the shared foundation of language upon which to build private- and public-sector workforce development efforts. Employer hiring requirements will have the same meaning for human resource practitioners, workers, education and training developers, program planners, and students.

A searchable keyword database at http://online.onetcenter.org helps individuals browse through the database of occupations.

Source: U.S. Department of Labor, National O*NET Consortium. O*NET OnLine [Interactive web application]. Available: http://online.onetcenter.org.

questions can be legally asked of job candidates and worry about potential discrimination suits tied to evaluating performance. Clearly, abiding by employment law has important implications for an organization's risk exposure, both financially and by reputation. However, less well understood is that the law also helps, not hinders, good coaching practice. The reason is that employment law requires managers to focus solely on information that is *job related*, which helps actively reduce natural biases by deterring the use of information not directly related to the job requirements. Table 5.1 discusses the basics of employment law.

Once you have clarified the context of the job, you're ready to move on to the next step in the selection process.

Establish a Process

The second step in selecting employees is establishing a process for making your decisions. Establishing a process *before* you decide to hire an employee is beneficial for several reasons. First, when a position becomes open or is newly created, there is usually a heightened sense of urgency to fill it *now*. This sense of urgency usually leads people to skip critical steps that would help avoid a poor selection decision. Second, in employment law cases, the courts typically want to see that an organization has a plan, that is, that the company has a process it uses uniformly and does not stray from.

Third, the best job candidates prefer a transparent (no hidden features) selection process. A manager who can articulate exactly what the process is and how it will transpire makes a good impression on candidates.[11]

Standardize It

Let's say you need to buy a new car. Based on price and features you narrow your choices down to two cars: a Honda Civic and a Toyota Corolla. You decide a

| TABLE 5.1 | Employment Law Basics |

Under employment law guidelines, discrimination is considered to be present regardless of intent. Intentional discrimination, or **disparate treatment,** is said to occur when a manager or organization intentionally discriminates. For example, a male manager decides to hire a male over a more qualified female because he "prefers to work with men." Sometimes unintentional discrimination, or **adverse impact,** can have equally negative affects. An example would be firefighters using a real fire simulation to test job candidates' physical abilities, which causes adverse impact for women. The test does not intentionally discriminate, but, because it's based on physical activity level, it does discriminate. Key guidelines to avoid disparate treatment and adverse impact follow:

Keep It Job Related. As mentioned, the best way to avoid legal problems is to ensure that all practices are truly job related. Avoid asking candidates about their personal lives and issues that have no relationship to the job (marital status, children, home location, and so on).

Treat All Candidates the Same. Discrimination occurs when one candidate gets a leg up on another because a manager gave preferential treatment.

Use Valid Predictors. Valid employment tests predict job performance (statistically speaking) consistently and with accuracy. Don't use predictors that do not have some supporting evidence of their reliability and validity in predicting job performance.

Don't Discriminate on Legally Protected Characteristics. Do not make decisions on the basis of race, age, nationality, sex, or disability—all classes protected by the federal government. To do so puts you and your organization at risk and takes your eye off what is really important.

test-drive is in order. When you test-drive the Honda, you drive down a long stretch of highway. A few hours later, you test-drive a Corolla down a backroad full of potholes. That night, you determine the Honda has a better ride and can't wait to buy it. Have you drawn the appropriate conclusion?

Of course not—and this is exactly the mistake many managers make when it comes to selection. They use an unstandardized selection process. If you want to be able to say one candidate is better than another, you must ensure your process is standardized. Of course the process may vary based on the type of job but should be consistent for all candidates for any one job. For instance, a selection process for a regional sales manager may differ greatly when compared with that of a staff accountant in the same organization. Tailoring the process to the job naturally makes the process that much more job related—a factor we have already emphasized as being important.

Taking time to hire selectively and getting it right the first time pays off.[12] Regardless of how long the process takes, however, applicants should always be kept informed about the process and where they stand at any given time. Research shows that highly qualified and marketable applicants often assume something is wrong with a company that does not provide this type of information in a timely manner.[13] Conversely, applicants often disproportionately favor a firm that promptly and professionally manages the critical contacts that the firm has with them in the selection process.

> *"We have learned the hard way that 'no hire' is ultimately better than a bad hire."*
>
> — HR Vice President

Involve Others

While an applicant may be targeted to work directly for the hiring manager, that applicant will also ultimately work with others in the firm. So involve those "others" in the process. They may be co-workers, subordinates, internal customers, or experienced employees who know the culture well. Involving others allows the candidate exposure to a variety of people and jobs in the organization and allows many people to help assess the candidate's future potential. But remember what was just discussed about standardization: Others should be involved in the same way for each candidate.

Create a Realistic Job Preview (RJP)

Recall the last product you bought from an actual salesperson. Did the individual tell you the product was the best on the market and that it had everything you'd want? If you're like us, more than once, we've purchased a product like that only to find it wasn't everything we wanted. Strictly "selling" a job to applicants rarely works out. At the same time, providing little to no information about the job doesn't work either. Great managers describe the job in detail to candidates. This process is more akin to arranging a good marriage than selling a product. In doing so, it is in the manager's best interest to present an accurate and realistic description of the job to the candidate, who, like the manager, is trying to determine fit and future potential. Evidence greatly supports the use of **realistic job previews (RJPs).**[14]

- Applicants receiving RJPs are less likely to drop out of the selection process.
- RJPs presented to applicants prior to hiring are associated with lower turnover *after* they have been hired.
- Though pre-hire RJPs are not associated with increased job performance post-hire, an RJP provided after an applicant is hired is associated with higher job performance.

- RJPs increase the job acceptance rate among applicants with no prior exposure to the job, and decrease the job acceptance rate among those with prior exposure.[15] Thus, RJPs can help to improve applicants' decisions about fit, especially when they are already familiar with the job.
- Providing an RJP verbally is generally more effective than handing an applicant a brochure with a job description or having the candidate view a videotaped presentation.

To help you with actually preparing a realistic job preview, Tool Kit 5.1 provides a worksheet.

Decide on Methods and Assess

Once you've done your homework on establishing your basic process, you can move to tailoring your methods for specific searches, and then on to the actual assessment. How much and what type of assessment method you choose depends greatly on the details of the job situation. Clearly, hiring extra staff for the holidays requires different assessment methods than selecting a district manager. That is not to say you should not assess your part-time holiday help; rather, the amount of time and number of methods you choose may be less. One thing is certain, however, it is imperative you collect data beyond the information readily available from resumes, prescreening processes, or basic job applications.

Great managers select multiple methods for collecting data about the applicant's suitability for the job. The process of selection should be both standardized and include methods such as interviews, work samples, and ability tests. Great managers attempt to select methods that reduce their own biases, are legally sound, are based on solid evidence, and make good business sense (that is, are cost effective and worth the time and effort). Here are a few guiding principles to follow for the most effective selection process:

- **First, define performance.** If you can't define what success looks like on the job, then you'll never be able to predict it.
- **Use different methods for different jobs.** Rarely is one method appropriate for all jobs.
- **Use reliable and valid methods** to predict future job success. Just remember, no method is perfect—some, however, are supported by a body of evidence while others are not.
- **Collect multiple pieces of data** before drawing conclusions. If an applicant seems like she will make a poor accountant in an interview, suspend judgment until she has completed other tests that might serve to disconfirm your judgment.
- **Defy conventional wisdom,** as it can often lead to wrong conclusions when assessing employees, though it often *feels* right. A number of studies have found a large gap between what methods people *think* are effective and those that evidence show are *actually* effective.[16]

To put the points above into practice requires some important knowledge about the relative usefulness of performance predictors. A great deal of research has been done on the relative value of the various types of methods or predictors. That is, some predictors are more useful than others along several dimensions, including:

- **Validity.** How well, statistically speaking, the method predicts future job performance. Usually the most important factor and one related most to legal defensibility.
- **Fairness.** The degree to which the method avoids adverse impact (unintentional discrimination).
- **Feasibility.** The degree to which the method can reasonably be employed in different situations and its overall cost.
- **Face Validity.** The degree to which applicants *believe* (whether it actually does or not) the selection method fairly measures requirements for the job.

In Table 5.2, we show the major employment testing methods and a rank order based on their validity[17] as well as information regarding fairness, feasibility, and face validity.

As can be seen in Table 5.2, validity evidence is strongest for work samples, cognitive ability tests, and structured interviews, while much less so for references and years of experience. The unfortunate irony, of course, is that the volume of usage in organizations today is *inversely* correlated with the evidence. That is, the least valid measures are often the most used. One reason for this can be seen in the chart. Tests such as reference checks, assignment of points to training and experience, and years of education are all easily collectable and face valid. The more valid predictors shown in the table can be difficult to administer and more costly and time intensive. A full examination of each predictor is beyond the scope of this chapter; however, we provide some detail on some of the best predictors: (1) interviews, (2) work samples, (3) cognitive ability, and (4) personality.

TABLE 5.2 | **Selection Method Effectiveness**

Selection Method (Ranked from Best to Worst for Validity)	Fairness	Feasibility	Face Validity
1. Work Sample	High	Medium	High
2. Cognitive Ability Test	Low	High	Medium
3. Structured Interview	Medium	High	High
4. Job Knowledge Test	High	High	High
5. Assessment Center Evaluation	Medium	Low	High
6. Biographical Data*	Medium	Medium	Low
6. Personality Assessments*	Medium	High	Low
8. Reference Checks	High	High	High
9. Training and Experience Points	High	High	High
10. Years of Education	High	High	High
11. Graphology (Handwriting Analysis)	Low	Medium	Low
12. Flip of a Coin	Low	High	Low

* Tied for sixth place in rank order.

Getting the Most from Interviews

Few managers would be willing to hire an applicant sight unseen, and thus almost all organizations use some form of employment interview.[18] Interviews can be effective tools for predicting future job success, but should not be used to measure all types of job requirements. In general, the interview is a highly effective method for measuring job knowledge and interpersonal skills.

When going about the interview process, it is important to distinguish between two general types of interviews:

- The **unstructured interview,** whereby the interviewer and applicant have a conversation that is unscripted. That is, the interviewer may have some general topics she wants covered, but it is unscripted.

- The **structured interview,** whereby the interviewer follows an interview script designed specifically to target certain KSAs required for the job, asking the same questions of all job applicants.

Recalling our car buying example, you probably won't be surprised to hear that structured interviews are much more valid predictors of performance than unstructured ones because they are standardized and maintain an interviewer's focus on job-related questions.[19] Though some research has shown that under very limited circumstances unstructured interviews can be effective, the evidence strongly supports structured interviews.[20] Despite the fact that structured interviews are much more valid than unstructured ones, too few managers employ such structure in their interview practice,[21] in effect trading off validity for the freedom of asking anything of anyone. This trade-off comes at a high price, namely, the ability to predict future success—your primary goal as a hiring manager!

Behavior, Behavior, Behavior

Though it may seem counterintuitive, when trying to predict future job performance the challenge is to pay less attention to how applicants describe themselves and rather focus on their behavior. For example, consider the following typical exchange in a selection interview:

Interviewer: Please describe your primary strengths as a sales representative.

Applicant: I'm a people person! Put me with people and I am at my best, I'm, golden. People love me and I love them.

Interviewer: OK, great. So, you love people. Why is that a particular strength in this case?

Applicant: Well, you see, sales reps must interact well with people: customers, managers, other reps, suppliers—so people skills are incredibly important. I can't stress that enough—no two ways about it.

Interviewer: Right, makes sense.

Aside from a pleasant conversation, what have we learned about this candidate's suitability for the job of sales representative? First, we learned how *he* describes himself. Second, we learned what *he* thinks is important for the job. Third, *he* is in control of the interview. In other words, we haven't really learned anything that will help us distinguish whether he is more or less capable of doing this job than are other candidates. Effective interviewing is all about *behavior.* Focus on what an applicant *can* or *did* do, rather than what she *says* or *said* she can do.

Great managers commonly use two types of structured interviews as valid predictors of job performance.[22] **Situational interviews** include hypothetical scenario questions that ask candidates to describe in detail how they would likely behave in such a situation. **Behavioral interviews** include questions that ask candidates to recount actual instances from their past work or relevant experiences relative to the job at hand. Both forms of structured interviews work well because they focus on behaviors or **behavioral intentions** (the motivation and thoughts that are immediate precursors of a person's actual behavior) and acknowledge the reality that past behavior is a strong predictor of future behavior.[23] Some recent research has found that for high-level positions behavioral interviews are more effective than situational while the reverse is true for lower level positions.[24]

One of the particular challenges of behavioral interviews is how best to evaluate the range of responses. One proven way is to use a number system from worst answer to best answer and jot down some potential responses that correspond to each of those categories of response. In general, the more detail an applicant provides, the better the response. If an applicant can't provide a detailed response after follow-up questions it's less likely he has actually done the behavior in question. Use the information from the job analysis to help match possible responses with level of quality. Tool Kit 5.3 demonstrates how

Management Live 5.3

Animals, Superheroes, and Other Themes

"What kind of animal would you be and why?"

For whatever reasons, many managers have a favorite interview question like that above which they believe helps them identify the strongest job candidates. While it is tempting to employ such novel or "out of the box" questions they often do not serve to differentiate candidates in desired ways. For example, one manager we have worked with likes to ask candidates for a marketing position, "Who is your favorite cartoon superhero and why?" He fully believes this question tests the creativity necessary for his marketing job. Before accepting his premise, however, we would encourage consideration of a few fundamental questions.

First, what is a strong response? When asked, the manager said there was no right answer; he wanted to see the applicant's creative thinking process. But notice that the question doesn't ask for applicants to detail how they arrive at their conclusion or what criteria they use. Second, this question is likely to be measuring something entirely different than creativity, that is, one's familiarity with cartoons and time spent contemplating those cartoons. Is that what this manager intended?

It is easy to fall into this trap. One way to avoid it is to ask yourself for every question, "What am I really measuring when I ask. . . ?" Stick to structured, job-related questions, and you will improve your ability to predict high performance. We like to say that interview questions are expensive; if you want to get the most return on your investment, spend questions wisely and precisely! And for the record, we like superhero Professor X for his ability to read minds.

Some Popular but Questionable Interview Questions

1. If you were to come back as an animal, what kind of animal would you be and why?

2. What's your favorite color and why?

3. If you could go back in time and meet anyone, who would you meet and why?

4. Describe your bedroom and what it tells me about you.

5. A plane crashes on the border between the United States and Canada. Where should they bury the survivors?

6. Give me two reasons why I should *not* hire you.

to construct and evaluate behavioral interview questions, including using the STAR (situation, task, action, result) method.

Important Interview Reminders Beyond using structured approaches, there are a few important reminders to highlight in regard to conducting interviews.

- **Avoid non-job-related questions.** Here again, keep it job related and focused. Your results will be better and you'll avoid possible legal recourse by applicants.

- **Use panel (group) interviews wisely.** The more people that crowd a room and "interrogate" applicants, the less likely the interview will be a valid predictor.[25] Involve other people with multiple small-group interviews, but avoid interview sessions with three or more. Applicants tend to prefer one-on-one, face-to-face interviews.[26] However, telephone interviews can often be just as effective as face-to-face meetings.[27]

- **Do not over-weight negative information.** Interviewers tend to give much more weight to negative information revealed by an applicant than positive. So much so that it often requires twice as much positive information to overcome a single piece of negative data.[28]

- **Be aware of subtle biases.** As we mentioned, interviewer ratings are too often influenced by things like applicant attractiveness, similarities in race and gender, and nonverbal behavior such as eye contact.[29] The more aware an interviewer is of these subtle influences, the less likely he is to fall prey to them.

Beyond the Interview: Other Effective Assessment Options

Interviewing generally reveals an applicant's job knowledge and interpersonal skills, but other tests are helpful in evaluating other skills the applicant needs to perform the job well, such as technical and managerial skills. These skills are specific job behaviors a person has learned to perform with consistent results. For example, an architect clearly needs to be able to read architectural drawings accurately. A flight attendant needs to know how to open the emergency exit door on an airplane. A teacher needs to be able to speak clearly in front of a group. Tests designed specifically to measure these "hands-on" skills are known generally as **performance tests** and are highly predictive of future job performance.

Performance Tests that Work. One type of performance test is known as a **work sample.** Work samples are, literally, samples of the work involved in the performance of a specific job. Underlying them is the assumption that performance obtained under realistic work conditions should be a strong predictor of work on the job. Athletic tryouts or musical auditions are good examples of work samples. Constructing a work sample does not need to be complicated—just follow these steps:

1. *Select the Sample.* Using the information from the job description, pick one or two essential job tasks.

2. *Define Performance.* Determine what results a candidate needs to obtain on these job tasks to be considered "excellent" through "poor."

3. *Create a Realistic Environment.* Provide the job candidate with the most realistic possible setting in which to perform the selected work sample.

To illustrate the construction of a performance test, let's take the example of an applicant for a sales representative job:

- **Step 1.** We select one of the key tasks of this job, which is to make a sales presentation to a prospective client.

- **Step 2.** We decide that to be considered excellent, the applicant must do all of the following: (a) establish a rapport with the customer, (b) determine the customer's product needs and requirements, (c) communicate the products available to meet the customer's needs, and (d) ask for questions or concerns from the client.

- **Step 3.** We design a short scenario to provide the applicant with information regarding the customer and the products, and a time limit of 30 minutes to prepare. The applicant would then "in character" make a sales presentation to our "customer." This takes a bit of preparation, but as can be seen, it doesn't require weeks and can be highly effective in predicting future success.

Other performance tests such as assessment centers measure more managerial-related skills such as delegating, planning/organizing, making decisions, and taking initiative. An **assessment center** (a method for evaluating managerial applicants, not a location) is a collection of work samples that mimic "a day in the life" of a manager (e.g., group discussions, employee feedback meetings, oral presentations, and in-basket exercises). Performance in the exercises is usually evaluated by trained raters who in some cases are more senior managers from the same firm as those being assessed. Although assessment centers are highly valid predictors, especially for managerial jobs, they are often quite expensive to develop and conduct. See Management Live 5.4 for more on assessment centers.

Tests that Work: Cognitive Ability and Personality

Perhaps the most widely discussed and misunderstood selection methods are paper and pencil tests of cognitive ability and personality. Misperceptions abound about the usefulness of these types of tests but both cognitive ability and personality measures can be valid predictors of performance when used appropriately. **Cognitive ability** tests measure a person's ability to learn and acquire cognitive skills, including verbal, mathematical, spatial, and reasoning.

"Talent wins games, but teamwork and intelligence wins championships"

—Michael Jordan

Let's say that you want to cause an uproar at your next family gathering. Simply tell your family members that cognitive ability is one of the best single predictors of job performance across most jobs, then look out for flying food. Despite the hot debate in the United States about intelligence, the evidence is clear: Cognitive ability is a valid predictor of job performance even when the applicant pool is already restricted to high intelligence[31] such as in the case of graduates from elite law schools or medical students applying for residency positions. Researcher Sara Rynes and her colleagues summarized the research stating, "deliberate attempts to assess and use GMA [general mental ability] as a basis for hiring should be made for *all* jobs. Failure to do so leaves money on the table." Cognitive ability can be quite efficiently assessed using short timed tests like the Wonderlic Personnel Test (WPT). The WPT takes 12 minutes to complete and is relatively unobtrusive from an applicant's perspective.[32]

So why doesn't everyone use cognitive ability tests? The answer is twofold. First, a great deal of misunderstanding regarding their usefulness permeates all levels of organizations. For example, in one survey, even high-level human resource executives demonstrated misperceptions about the validity of testing cognitive ability.[33] Second, cognitive ability tests may cause an adverse impact on hiring certain minority groups because of the way traditional tests are constructed. Thus, organizations hoping to increase their minority applicant pool will need to search for other ways to measure cognitive ability so as to not unintentionally discriminate. Here are a few recommendations to follow regarding the use of cognitive ability tests:

- **Job Complexity.** The more complex a job, the more important cognitive ability becomes. For most managerial positions, cognitive ability is an excellent predictor and should be used.

- **Diversity Goals.** If increasing minority representation in organizations is a top priority, use other predictors that are highly correlated with cognitive ability but cause less adverse impact, such as job knowledge tests, work samples, and simulations.

- **Experience.** Some research indicates significant experience can compensate for lower levels of cognitive ability. Thus, an experienced applicant with lower cognitive ability may perform as well as one with higher cognitive ability.

As with cognitive ability tests, uses of personality tests for selection are highly misunderstood and often inappropriately used. In Chapter 1, we discussed the major classifications of personality including what has become known as the Big Five personality factors. Recall that we never recommend using a single predictor to select an employee. Regardless of how strong or valid a predictor may be, multiple data points are always preferable. With that in mind, personality tests can often add some predictive value to a selection process. Of course, not all personality factors are

Management Live 5.4

Assessment Centers: Uncovering Managerial Talent

Assessment centers are not for everyone. But when it comes to predicting managerial talent early in employees' careers, assessment centers are hard to beat. The earliest uses of assessment centers can be traced to Germany during World War I, followed by the adoption of the technology for use in World War II by the United States and Great Britain. Specifically, the OSS (the precursor to the modern CIA) used assessment centers to select appropriate candidates for spying activities during World War II.

Basing their work on the earlier military applications, in 1956 AT&T conducted the best-known study of assessment centers (called the Management Progress Study) to investigate changes in managerial skills as managers moved through their careers. This led to the use of assessment centers as an aid in selecting first-line supervisors and higher level managers and other specialists. Subsequently, more than 1,100 U.S. organizations have utilized assessment centers for selecting and developing managerial talent.

More recently, assessment centers have been used in educational settings to provide critical feedback to business students regarding managerial skill strengths and weaknesses. Students receive objective, behavioral feedback about their managerial skills, which serves as a starting point for their development in college and beyond. Recent research has shown that students who perform well in collegiate assessment centers are offered higher starting salaries than those performing poorly. In addition, research shows students who demonstrate high skills in an assessment center receive promotions more quickly over a five-year postgraduation period and are more satisfied at work than their low-skill peers.[30] Thus, assessment center exercises can be powerful tools to help students identify their managerial strengths and weaknesses early in their career, providing focus to their business studies and preparing them for future success.

relevant for all jobs. In particular, the evidence shows that certain factors of the Big Five personality traits are more or less important depending on the type of job.

Based on that research, a measure of conscientiousness makes sense as part of a selection process for almost any job[35] In addition to conscientiousness, other personality dimensions can be valuable for select job classes such as:

- **Sales-oriented jobs** might also include a measure of extraversion and emotional stability.
- **Customer service jobs** might add a measure of agreeableness.
- **Management trainee jobs** might usefully assess agreeableness, extraversion, and openness to experience.

Setting Expectations and Evaluating Performance

Performance standards should never be a surprise as nothing frustrates employees more than not knowing what is expected of them. Expectations should never be set informally through hallway conversations or periodic e-mails;

Management Live 5.5

How Smart Is Your First-Round Draft Pick?[34]

Quarterback Eli Manning (Peyton Manning's brother) from Mississippi scored a 39 on the Wonderlic Personnel Test (WPT) before the 2004 draft. That's about 10 points higher than most other draft picks who take the 50-question, 12-minute test. The question is why do NFL players need to take an intelligence test? Team owners, it seems, place a great deal of stock in the test and believe in its validity in predicting the future performance of players. "Selecting a new quarterback is like hiring a president for a company," says Michael Callans, president of Wonderlic Consulting. "They need to lead, think on their feet, evaluate all of their options, and understand the impact their actions will have on the outcome of the game." Cognitive ability tests like the WPT help owners evaluate a player's cognitive and reasoning ability, which can help determine whether they have the skills to follow directions and react to their situation—all critical field skills.

Top 5 Quarterback Wonderlic Scores for 2004 Draft

Name	College	Wonderlic Score	2004 Draft Order
Manning, Eli	Mississippi	39	1
Krenzel, Craig	Ohio State	38	7
Losman, J.P.	Tulane	31	4
Rivers, Philip	NC State	30	2
Schaub, Matt	Virginia	30	5

Note: Average college graduate score is 25 with a standard deviation of 6.

rather, they should be established through a formal meeting with each person. Discussions should include expectations for the context of work (such as when the work day begins and ends), how work gets done (for example, telephone versus face-to-face sales calls), and actual work goals (complete 42 sales calls per month for existing customers). The goal should be to establish a *mutual performance contract*. This is not an employment contract, but a document that stipulates performance expectations. To create this contract, you will need to structure exactly what it is you want to communicate regarding performance. Topics to address in this contract discussion include:

- Critical job duties.
- Performance goals.
- Professional conduct.
- Resource requirements.
- Developmental goals.

Remember, this is a mutual process. Great managers make this conversation two-way by inviting employees to identify their expectations for the manager as well as their own personal performance.

"Give a man a 'why' and he will find a 'how'."

—Anonymous

Ensuring Goal Commitment

Recall from Chapter 1 and Chapter 4 the power of goal setting. This is one opportunity to put that technique into practice and tie it to performance standards and rewards. Setting SMART goals isn't enough; managers also need to gain employees' commitment to those goals. The mutual contract discussion is the perfect time to start enhancing employees' commitment to goals by engaging in the following behavior.[36]

- **Make it public.** Public goals increase goal commitment by creating an environment in which the employee is accountable to more than herself.
- **Be supportive.** When managers are supportive of employees' goals, they express confidence in the employee that he can attain the goal.
- **Tie to vision/mission.** Goals become more meaningful to employees when they are clearly relevant to the mission of the organization.
- **Set goals, not actions.** Sometimes employee work needs to be structured. In many cases, setting the goal is all that is required, and letting employees determine how to get there, and what actions to take, can increase commitment.
- **Track progress and give feedback.** Employees will be more committed to goals accompanied with regular feedback whereby they can assess their progress. More on feedback is provided later in the chapter.
- **Ensure resources.** Few employees will be committed to goals that require unattainable resources. The role of a coach is to ensure the proper resources (time, money, education, technology) are available or readily attainable.
- **Remove obstacles.** Managers must pave the way for employees by removing organizational obstacles. It is the role of a coach to advocate for employees and to deal with the political roadblocks that could keep them from meeting their goals.

Observing and Assessing Performance

According to a recent survey of Fortune 500 employees, both managers and employees alike have a particular disdain for performance evaluation.[37] People prefer not to be told about deficiencies, don't like vague performance standards, feel vulnerable without control, and fear evaluations will not be related to their actual performance but based more on their personal relationship with their managers. Managers dislike playing the role of judge, fear lawsuits, feel evaluation takes too much time, and that they have inadequate skills to differentiate performance. All of this is unfortunate as effective evaluation plays a central role in improving and sustaining employee performance.[38] To that end, overcoming these barriers and learning the basics of good performance evaluation is critically important.

Defining Performance Criteria: Behavior and Results

No matter what performance management assessment techniques you use, you must seek to capture employees' results and the process they used to get those results. Most jobs have some objective outcome or results and require certain behaviors to obtain those results. For example, litigation attorneys have some clear results such as number of cases won and settlements reached. Of course, some jobs might require a bit more ingenuity in finding the results to be measured. For example, customer service agents are primarily responsible for solving customer problems. Results might include the percentage of problems solved the first time versus those escalated to a specialist, or ratings from customer service surveys. To find the results for any job ask the following questions:

- *If this employee performs poorly, what would suffer?* For example, would customer service or repeat business suffer? How about revenue? What about employee satisfaction?
- *What will this employee's performance make possible and for whom?* For instance, will good performance lead to increased unit performance? What about lower turnover or increased receivables?

A common mistake in performance management occurs when managers *exclusively* pay attention to employee results. Although results are critical, great managers know there are many ways to get those results—and that achieving them in the right way should be rewarded. For example, customer service representatives should engage in behaviors like answering the telephone promptly, using professional language and asking questions that elicit the root of the problem. These are not actual results, but behaviors that lead to good outcomes. To identify the important *behaviors* associated with performance, ask these questions:

- What are the most critical steps involved in achieving results?
- If this employee doesn't do the most critical steps, will he still be able to succeed?

Using a results–behavior matrix is one way to visually classify and assess how an employee's performance behavior and results work together. Note that in Figure 5.3 the upper right-hand corner of the figure represents employee performance that achieved results through strong behavior. The lower left-hand corner represents the opposite: poor results and poor behavior. For most managers, these two boxes represent easy performance-related

FIGURE 5.3

The Results–Behavior Matrix

decisions. The upper right should clearly be rewarded with high performance assessments; the lower left certainly deserves lower performance marks.

More difficult, however, is what to do with employee performance that falls in the other two boxes of the figure. Take the lower right-hand corner, which represents good results attained, but through poor behavior. For example, Ted has the best sales numbers in his region. Unfortunately, Ted got those results by stealing contacts from other sales reps and making promises to customers the company couldn't deliver. Is Ted a good performer? Probably not. Few managers would endorse his behavior as worthy of praise and would likely view his process as detrimental to the organization. Looking at Ted's results, alone, however would have masked critical performance information.

Just as difficult is the upper left corner which represents the person who is achieving good behavior but not getting results. For instance, Sally has demonstrated she can build strong relationships with her clients, but can't seem to close the deal and make the sale. Is Sally a good performer? Here again, probably not. Results matter and achieving those results is part of performance. Unlike Ted, however, her behavior may lead her to results the right way, and she should certainly be recognized for her strong process.

Assessing Behavior, Not Traits

The appropriate performance management mantra remains the same; good assessment of future potential and current performance focuses on behavior and actual results, not traits or personal characteristics. Unfortunately, substantial research shows managers are highly influenced by traits or non-job-relevant information that reduces the accuracy of their assessment.[39] For example, many companies routinely ask managers to assess items such as dependability, initiative, and energy. But what does dependability mean? What would good dependability versus bad dependability look like? Instead of simply measuring the trait of dependability, the challenge is to determine what you mean when you say, "I want dependable employees." You might mean you want people who arrive on time, accomplish work without frequent reminders, and meet deadlines. These things are measurable! You can track timeliness, working without reminders, and meeting deadlines.

Using Multiple Methods to Assess Behavior and Results

There are multiple ways to assess employee behavior and results, and using multiple methods results in a more complete understanding of performance. In the broadest sense, evaluation methods can be categorized as either objective or subjective.

Objective assessment includes methods based on results or impartial performance outcomes. These are usually easily identifiable since they represent employee output that is visible and countable. Results performance is typically measured using objective assessment techniques. Examples of objective assessment include:

- Minutes to solve a customer problem.
- Sales calls per week.
- Completion versus noncompletion.
- Research publications published in last year.

Subjective assessment includes methods that involve human judgments of performance. Subjective assessment methods are often more contentious since they involve opinion by the manager. That does not mean they are not useful. Many aspects of employees' jobs are not easily "seen" and can't be counted. For example, objectively quantifying a consultant's relationship with clients is difficult. Yet the behavior involved in building strong client relations is central to successful consulting performance so subjective assessments often play an important role. However, since we already know managers do not always make accurate judgments of employee behavior, understanding the implications of the different types of subjective assessments is critical. Typically, managers will employ two types of subjective assessments, separately or in conjunction with one another. These are known as absolute and relative standards. An **absolute subjective assessment** involves comparing an employee's performance to that of a "model" described in the performance statement whereas a **relative subjective assessment** compares an employee's performance with another employee's performance to determine the level of performance. Let's look at some ways of accomplishing both.

Absolute Assessment Techniques

- **Graphic Rating Scale.** The most common form of absolute assessment (and evaluation in general) is known as a **graphic rating scale.** The graphic rating scale is used to assess how much of a particular behavior an employee displays on some graduated scale.
- **Behaviorally Anchored Rating Scales (BARS).** Much like behavioral interviews, a **behaviorally anchored rating scales (BARS)** compares job behaviors with specific performance statements on a scale from poor to outstanding (or similar sets of descriptors). Although BARS assessments require a little time to develop, they are the best way to keep assessments focused on behavior and provide a little more objectivity over graphic rating scales.

Relative Assessment Techniques

- **Ranking.** A ranking technique is a simple relative assessment. Managers use this technique to list all employees from best to worst. The technique is quite good for distinguishing high and low performing employees but difficult to assess employee performance in the middle of the group.

- **Forced Distribution.** This technique, also known as **topgrading,** requires the manager to assess employees based on predetermined evaluation categories and to force employees into these categories to form a desired distribution. Only a certain percentage of employees will be allowed to achieve each evaluation category. For example, three performance levels may exist in a company—poor, good, and outstanding—and only 20 percent of all employees can be rated as outstanding, 70 percent as good, and 10 percent as poor. See Management Live 5.6 for more on topgrading.

Using Multiple Sources of Data or People

Few managers have the luxury of observing their employees work throughout an entire day, much less an entire year. Thus, effective performance management involves collecting data from others about the employee's performance that can help confirm or disconfirm a manager's own observations. For example, it would be inadequate for a manager to observe her staff accountant for an hour and assume she has all the data required to evaluate performance. Other sources of data are necessary.

Peers, subordinates, project leaders, and customers can help a manager to better assess her employees. Note, however, that all sources have their limitations. For instance, an employee's peers work daily with the employee and see his behavior first-hand. Common sense would dictate giving the peers a survey and using the results as a measure of performance. Yet evidence shows that, when

Management Live 5.6

The "Topgrading" Debate

Few areas of management development have generated more passionate recent discourse among academics and business professionals than that of forced distribution, or topgrading, performance management practices. Forced ranking refers to systems in which individuals are ranked in comparison to one another. Some managers, like high-profile former GE executives Jack Welch and Larry Bossidy have extolled such practices as efficient and pragmatic means of "rewarding your doers" and "muscle-building" your organization. These and other authors often point to the success of General Electric, both in building shareholder value and developing executive talent, as evidence of the efficacy of forced ranking practices.

Many other organizations such as Heinz and SIRVA have instituted performance management initiatives based in whole or part on the process popularized by Welch and Bossidy. Even highly prestigious universities like Princeton are now topgrading. Princeton restricts the number of As to 35 percent of the student body each semester. Many students who earn high marks (say, 93 percent) will receive a letter grade of B!

Others, like well-known authors Jeffrey Pfeffer and Malcolm Gladwell, condemn forced ranking as dysfunctional and suggest that such systems will be hazardous to an organization's culture. They choose *their* examples from among such organizations as Ford Motor Co. and Enron, which have had well-publicized *unsuccessful* experiences with forced ranking systems. Among those critical of forced ranking, some take issue with the philosophy of the practice, while others contend they agree with the objectives but "not the way it is often done."

So who is right? As is typically the case, the answer probably lies somewhere in the middle. The effectiveness of topgrading probably depends on *who* is being topgraded and the culture of the organization. Cultures that are highly competitive and attract performance-oriented individuals are likely to see benefits from topgrading. In contrast, group- or team-oriented cultures would likely reject topgrading because it may be seen as pitting employees against each other. So as in many areas in management, the "right answer" depends—in this case, on the goals of the organization and what type of organizational culture they are trying to build.

peers know their ratings are used to evaluate another co-worker's performance, they provide inaccurate ratings. In some cases, they may "play" the system depending on how much they like or dislike their co-worker.[40]

Here are a few tips on how to use multiple sources of data.

- **Observe Behavior over Time.** A single observation of behavior is never enough. Make time to see performance. This may mean going along with an employee to meet a customer, working with an employee on a project, or asking for monthly progress reports.

- **Take Notes.** Research shows that managers who keep a diary or journal on each employee make more accurate performance ratings and reduce the burden associated with the evaluation process. Start a file on each employee. Schedule an hour each month to record each employee's successes and challenges over the last four weeks. Include any positive and negative data you received about the employee's performance.

- **Ask for Customer Feedback.** Customers, internal and external, should be included in assessing part of the employee's performance. This can be as simple as a few short survey questions, given periodically throughout a performance period.

- **Allow for a Self-Evaluation.** Employees themselves are a good source of data. They can highlight achievements they've made that managers may not often observe. Allow each employee to self-evaluate his or her performance.

- **Monitor Common Errors.** No matter what the source of data, if those data come from people, they are likely to have some error or inaccuracies associated with them. In Table 5.3, we discuss some of the common errors and what to do about them.

TABLE 5.3 | Common Errors in Observing Performance and How to Avoid Them

Manager's Error	What It Means	Technique to Correct
Halo Effect	• Judging all aspects of behavior or traits on the basis of a single trait or behavior. • Can be either positive or negative.	Use multiple raters of performance.
Leniency and Severity	• Consistently rating groups of employees as all high performers, or as all low performers.	Use multiple raters of performance and a forced distribution or ranking technique.
Central Tendency	• Consistently rating all employees as average. • Only using the middle of the rating scale; no high or low ratings.	Use a forced distribution or ranking technique.
Recency or Primacy	• Evaluating employee on only the most *recent* or *initial* performance, rather than performance for the <u>entire</u> evaluation period. • Could lead to false high or low ratings.	Use frequent evaluations, and require raters to maintain logs over the entire rating period.
Similarity or Contrast	• Bias due to the perceived similarity or difference between the rater's job behavior and the employee's job behavior. • *Similarity* bias will lead to inflated ratings. • *Contrast* bias will lead to deflated ratings.	Raters can be trained to correct for bias.

Providing Effective Feedback

The purpose of feedback is to influence future behavioral change, and it can do so if done properly.[41] If done improperly, feedback can actually decrease performance or reinforce poor behavior.[42] Feedback works because it generates energy that serves to motivate the individual receiving it. Feedback also guides behavior in certain directions when motivation to behave is already present. For example, feedback can serve to generate motivation by disconfirming an individual's perception and creating reward expectations. Further, it directs behavior where motivation exists by calling attention to problems that need correcting and where learning needs to occur.[43] In addition, feedback contributes to building strong interpersonal relationships. Thus, feedback can serve as a valuable tool to keep employees on track or get them back on track toward achieving their performance goals.

"The deepest principle of human nature is the craving to be appreciated."

—William James

The Principles of Good Feedback

Let's elaborate on the critical elements of *effective* feedback:

- **Be specific.** Specific feedback is more effective than vague feedback. People respond most favorably to direct examples of their past behavior.

The Height of Nonspecific Feedback

"Keep up the good work, whatever it is, whoever you are."

- **Focus on the problem rather than the person.** Feedback steeped in personal opinion and unconstructive criticism (for example, "You seem lazy")[44] is unproductive. Feedback should focus on the task not the person. Avoid people's perceived motives or attitudes.
- **Maximize absolute feedback, minimize relative feedback and comparisons to others.**[45] Feedback that says, "Sally, you just need to be more

like Timmy," won't be heard. Focus on whether Sally is meeting *her* performance goals.

- **Avoid absolutes.** Unless you work side by side with an employee daily, you can't possibly observe everything. So don't imply you can by using absolute words like "always" or "never."
- **Be timely.** Feedback is most effective when it is presented close in time to the actual behavior.[46]
- **Focus on the future.** Feedback is inherently backward looking, but what was done in the past is done. Your role is to influence future behavior by focusing on what can be done to correct undesirable behavior and continue desirable behavior.
- **Include information for improvement.** Telling an employee that her behavior is unproductive won't help unless the employee understands why it is unproductive. Effective feedback includes a statement regarding ways to improve the behavior toward performance.

Doing Feedback Well

Using the above guidelines, we have synthesized a few simple steps to keep in mind as a primer to most effectively deliver feedback:[47]

1. State the behavior you observed.
2. Describe the impact on self or others.
3. Provide information for improvement or explore improvement with the employee.

To further help you see how important phrasing feedback is, we've provided some examples of how to and not to give feedback:

Ineffective Feedback: "You don't handle your people well; you're dictating, not managing."

Effective Feedback: "I've noticed you tend not to involve your employees in making decisions. This doesn't allow them the opportunity to express their own views. In the future, I'd like to see you allow more opportunities for employee input."

> "You have to get ongoing feedback to push you out of your comfort zone."
>
> —Kevin Sharer, CEO, Amgen

The difference between the two examples is clear. In the ineffective feedback example, the employee is given a vague and general statement that is overly evaluative. In all likelihood, the employee will walk away with little information to improve performance. The effective feedback example clearly articulates the behavior observed, describes the impact of the behavior on others, and gives direction for the future. Here's another example:

Ineffective Feedback: "Your presentation of the data was unorganized."

Effective Feedback: "When you create charts with formats different than the rest of the team's, it causes confusion in data interpretation. Stick with the standard format to alleviate such confusion."

Again, the effective feedback example is highly specific and behavioral and allows for immediate correction and future focus. Managers often find themselves delivering ineffective feedback when they are angry with an employee. Instead of communicating that anger, however, managers simply provide curt and unproductive statements, masking what they really want and need to say. According to managerial psychologist Edgar Schein, this withholding of negative information that needs to be said does more harm than good. Communicate your anger about the employee's behavior, and don't lose sight of good feedback principles. Here is an example of communicating your anger in a productive way:[48]

> *Ineffective Feedback*: "You really blew that meeting John. You lack initiative and are just not aggressive enough for this kind of work."

> *Effective Feedback*: "John, I'm pretty upset about what you've done. When we got stuck on the ABC project, you seemed willing to let matters drift instead of coming up with a proposal for how to confront the problems and move forward. When the other division challenged the direction you were going, you backed off instead of showing them why your solution was the right one. I have seen both of these patterns on other projects and am concerned about the lack of initiative and aggressiveness that is implied by such behavior."

Unfortunately, although the principles are relatively simple, delivering effective feedback is hard to do and people often react negatively to receiving it.[49] Many become defensive, due to our human instinct to protect our self-image. Because defensiveness can lead to anger, managers are often reluctant to say what people need to hear. As such, quality feedback for improvement becomes obscured and hidden in platitudes and niceties. Even well-intentioned and confident managers fight their discomfort because they know how difficult it is to get candid feedback heard and acted upon.

Managing Perceptions of Fairness

Managers find managing performance and giving feedback to be so difficult in part because of the enormous burden of responsibility it represents. Coaching activities involve some of the most important and sensitive decisions within

Management Live 5.7

Revenge of the Plant Workers

A study by Professor Jerald Greenberg shows quite clearly the often hidden costs associated with perceptions of unfairness. In his research, two plants in the same company were anticipating a 15 percent pay cut for their workers. The pay cut was temporary and was to last 10 weeks. In plant A, management provided detailed explanations about why the cuts were necessary and how they would work. In addition, management expressed a great deal of regret in their announcement, acknowledging the sacrifice they were asking employees to make. In plant B, however, only a brief explanation was given, and management did not apologize or communicate regret for the decision.

Prior to these announcements, inventory (tools, supplies, and so on) in the plants were counted and were roughly equal. After the announcement, researchers measured the inventories and found that plant B had a significant increase in "missing" inventory (from 3 percent normally to 8 percent after the announcement) while plant A did not. Apparently, employees in plant B who felt a sense of unfairness in the pay cut sought retribution by stealing inventory.

The lesson is simple: Taking time to explain decisions and making decisions transparent go a long way in promoting fairness and keeping employees committed to the well-being of the organization.

Source: Greenberg, J. (1990). Employee theft as a reaction to underpayment inequity: The hidden cost of pay cuts. *Journal of Applied Psychology*, 75, 561–568.

organizations, such as promotions, performance assessments, and pay decisions. The visibility of these activities makes coaching a highly scrutinized aspect of management. Indeed, substantial research shows people respond favorably to fairness but are also highly sensitive to being treated in ways they perceive as unfair. More specifically, when employees view their job situation as "fair," they are less likely to withdraw from their work and more likely to be satisfied, perform higher, and contribute to the organization beyond their stated job requirements.[50] Thus, maintaining a persistent focus on fairness is a hallmark of a good manager. Perceptions of fairness are based on three primary factors: (1) the presence of a defined *process*, (2) a clear and communicated rule or decision model for distributing rewards, and (3) demonstrated respect for people.

- **Use a fair, defined process.** Employees view performance management as fair if they have input into the policies and procedures used to make decisions. In addition, employees want to see that the process is applied in a standard way. For example, evaluating two employees in the same job role using different performance standards is likely to lead employees to view the process as unfair.

- **Distribute rewards and resources fairly.** Employees will view performance management as fair when rewards and resources that follow from performance assessment are distributed fairly. This includes paying close attention to three potential rules for allocating rewards: (1) **equity rule,** where resources and rewards are distributed to employees based on their *contributions*, (2) **equality rule,** where resources and rewards are distributed so that each employee gets the same outcome regardless of contributions, and (3) **need rule,** where resources and rewards are distributed to those who need them most. For a practice to be just, it doesn't have to follow all three rules, but should follow at least one. For example, offering health benefits to some employees and not others violates the equality rule. Giving everyone a bonus, regardless of performance, violates the equity rule.

- **Demonstrate respect.** Respect comes in many forms. First, managers must treat people with dignity when evaluating performance. Not all employees are stellar performers, but they are all humans so treat them as such. Second, provide solid explanations and rationale for all performance management decisions. Employees understand that not all performance-related decisions are positive. What they won't understand is why you won't share the basis of your evaluation and the rationale for your decisions.

Dealing with the Problem Employee

"Managing is like holding a dove in your hand. Squeeze too hard and you kill it; not hard enough and it flies away."

—Tommy Lasorda

The logical assumption behind feedback is that providing information about performance will lead to performance improvement. But what if, after multiple attempts to correct poor or inadequate performance through feedback, nothing improves?

We use the term *problem employee* to denote an employee who after repeated feedback interventions has not improved performance. Note, we caution managers to not confuse this term with "bad person" or other disparaging or demeaning labels. Like Ken in the Manage *What?* scenario at the beginning of this chapter, there are plenty of wonderful people who simply don't perform.

The problem with the problem employee is that he can't or won't change behavior to meet acceptable levels of performance. The key to dealing with these problem situations is to determine the true source of the low performance and intervene to correct it. Great coaches apply a disciplined framework for improving performance which includes three fundamental steps: (1) diagnose the problem, (2) hold a performance improvement discussion, and (3) provide training when appropriate.

"Sometimes it's important to stop whatever break
you're taking and just do the work."

Diagnose the Problem

When multiple feedback attempts have failed, it is important to dig deeper and seek understanding of the reason for such failure. Recall that performance is a function of motivation, ability, and opportunity. No amount of feedback can replace raw talent, skills, and abilities, nor will it replace real opportunities to practice and improve. Managers must also turn the spotlight on themselves and ask what role they play in their own employee's performance failure. Sometimes, a simple reality check about this role is helpful. For example, perhaps the goals set for the employee are truly unattainable given the level of available resources. Although it is tempting to simply blame the employee for performance failure, it is not always a "person" issue. In Tool Kit 5.4 we provide a series of key questions and corresponding actions to understand the root cause of a performance failure.

Hold a Performance Improvement Discussion

When a manager can say that (1) the employee's performance is below expectations, (2) multiple opportunities for performance improvement have been provided, (3) the major cause of the performance deficiency is due to the employee, and (4) the employee wants to improve her performance, a face-to-face coaching discussion should take place. The steps and content of the discussion are outlined as follows.[52]

Step 1: Agree on the Problem

Agreement suggests that the manager and employee have a shared understanding a problem exists and of the nature of that problem. This sounds simple, but many coaches fail in this step because they tell the employee, "We've got a problem, your performance is low," and then try to fix it. Coaching experts note the employee must truly agree that his behavior is problematic and has important organizational and personal consequences. That is, the employee must "own" the problem and understand that it is his to reconcile. Until there is agreement about the problem, no further discussion can occur.

Step 2: Mutually Discuss Problem Solutions

The key question that needs to be answered is "What will you (the employee) do differently now that you understand the problem?" Nonbehavioral responses and solutions are not effective. For example, "I'll work harder, Boss," or "I'll move some things around in my schedule and take care of this," are not solutions but rather responses that generally don't lead to behavior change. An effective collaborative process requires the coach and employee to generate options and arrive at a solution.

Step 3: Create an Action Plan

Recall from Chapter 4, on motivation, that specific action plans must follow specific goals. Once an option has been selected, an action plan must be devised that the employee will commit to using to improve performance. Action plans must include: (1) steps for improving (exactly what will be done and when), (2) a timeline (with dates tied to each action step), (3) the resources required, including additional skill development if necessary, and (4) a plan for follow-up and evaluation. The fourth component is often overlooked. It is critical to document the plan and have the employee periodically demonstrate that she is moving in the right direction.

Step 4: Provide Ongoing Feedback: Reinforce Improvement

As the person attempts to improve performance, the coach must provide feedback letting the employee know if that improvement is truly occurring. In doing so, the coach is reinforcing such improvement. If improvement is occurring,

Management Live 5.8

Problem Employees: Invest or Divest?

In their popular book, *First, Break All the Rules*,[51] based on extensive research by the Gallup Corporation, authors Marcus Buckingham and Curt Coffman passionately argue that the reason organizations are so inefficient is they simply don't understand people. Most organizations, they claim, are built on two flawed assumptions about people. The first flawed assumption is that people can learn to be competent in any area they choose. The second is that people's greatest area for growth lies within their personal weaknesses. The message to managers is clear: Invest in your high performers and divest the low ones. Divesting would involve helping low performers find a job that more appropriately matches their talents rather than waste considerable company resources on attempting to develop employees outside their talent areas. The Gallup researchers note that sometimes a low performer *can* be set back on the right track. But this process is damage control and should not be confused with development. That is, the person has the talent to perform the job, but needs some slight remediation to align that talent productively with the organization goals. In contrast to the flawed assumptions, Gallup notes that the world's best managers are guided by different assumptions: that (1) each person's talents are enduring and unique, and 2) each person's greatest room for growth is in the areas of his or her greatest strength.

then the coach's role is simply to state that she sees improvement and to recognize that improvement verbally. For example, "Looks like you have made significant strides since our discussion, great work!" If improvement is not occurring, the coach needs to communicate this observation immediately. Great coaches do not reward zero improvement. That is, they do not tell an employee "good job" when it hasn't happened. Of course, providing encouragement is helpful ("I know this is going to be difficult to break your previous work habit, but you have a good plan, and sticking to it will improve your chances.") as long as it communicates that anything other than performance improvement is not acceptable.

Train Employees When Appropriate

Although managers are quick to embrace training programs, it is important to note that training is a solution to only one category of problem, namely, skill deficiency. Skills are behaviors that can be learned and practiced for consistent results. If there is an absent skill, provide training. Otherwise, do not waste time investing in training as a cure-all approach.

Making a Reassignment or Termination Decision

As one of our colleagues is fond of saying, "Sometimes Humpty Dumpty falls off the wall and *can't* be put back together." In other words, after successive attempts to coach the problem employee without positive performance results, great coaches recognize the current situation cannot continue. As a general rule, a coach can recognize this situation when she is more heavily invested in the employee's performance than the employee is. That is, when the coach is putting in more effort than the problem employee to correct the problem, reassignment or termination is likely appropriate.

Sometimes great employees are promoted or moved into roles where they become poor employees. Take, for example, a highly talented industrial engineer who is promoted based on his performance to managing a group of industrial engineers and then fails miserably as a manager. He is still a great engineer, despite the fact that he has failed as a manager. Thus, termination is not always the answer; sometimes reassignment to old positions or new posts in the organization that better utilize the employee's talent may be more appropriate. Don't lose a great employee because someone made a poor staffing decision!

At the same time, retaining those who do not improve after ample time and resources are provided hurts everyone involved. The organization suffers from lower-than-expected performance that can drain the pool of available resources. Managers' own resources are spent disproportionately on the problem person, making it difficult to advance efforts toward accomplishing goals. Co-workers of the problem employee often harbor resentment toward managers and the organization for retaining someone who does not pull his own weight. And the problem employee himself may also lose out on authentic opportunities to succeed in other environments or types of work. In general, the longer a problem employee stays without improvement, the more likely it is that the work climate will suffer.

"Creating a close connection to those you do business with has its many risks, rewards, and consequences. There are few things in business I have encountered that are more difficult than firing someone, particularly if that someone has always been, or has become, a friend. On the flipside, I have been rewarded with many friends."

—Mark Cuban

The Termination/Reassignment Discussion

Few managerial situations are feared more than that of telling an employee he or she is to be let go.[53] Managers often fear the employee will protest and the situation will become ugly. Yet if the coach has truly done her job through the performance management cycle (PMC), the decision to terminate should not shock or surprise the employee; rather, it will be seen as consistent with the manager's approach throughout. Nonetheless, few managers like to actually deliver the news. Even when termination or reassignment is the right and appropriate thing to do, it is still difficult and thus conducting the termination or reassignment meeting takes preparation and forethought (see Tool Kit 5.5 for a checklist).

Recognition and Reinforcement: Coaching the Star

Although rarely acknowledged, coaching a star employee can be just as difficult as coaching the problem employee. We use the term star employee to denote the person who consistently performs beyond expectations. Misperceptions of coaching stars include beliefs that they are completely self-motivated, will continue to perform regardless of how they are managed, and require little attention and resources. The evidence regarding coaching stars, however, suggest a more complex picture.

First, star employees may come to possess an overdeveloped sense of entitlement. They may believe their high performance merits treatment beyond what may be feasible or reasonable.[54] Second, star performance may be a function of external rewards and not intrinsic motivation. Remove the rewards (say, in difficult economic periods) and performance may decline.[55] Third, many stars have difficulty seeing the contribution others make to their own success and may be inclined to alienate co-workers and clients. Fourth, managers often allocate more resources toward problem employees, reducing attention to stars and thus offering fewer opportunities for visibility and growth. Under such circumstances, stars may be more likely to leave the organization and seek opportunities elsewhere.

Put simply, star performance does not necessarily equate to easy management. Of course, most managers prefer to have the difficulties associated with stars than those associated with problem employees but are not well informed as to how best to manage their stars.

Understanding Star Performers

Recent research has provided a very clear picture of what stars value and how to induce the highest performance and commitment from them:

- **Learning Orientation.** Star performers seek environments where they can learn and develop their skills. This includes working for managers who provide regular performance feedback that helps them exploit their strengths and improve their weaknesses.[56]
- **Selective Hiring.** Star performers want to know the manager they work for is actively seeking to hire only the best, to create a group of motivated and talented people to share the workload.
- **Reward and Recognition.** Star performers prefer to work in environments that reward individual performance and provide a high degree of

recognition for their efforts. Rewards and recognition may be in the form of frequent fast-track promotions, performance-based pay, and praise and public recognition.[57]

- **Challenging Job Assignments.** Star performers tend to want increasingly challenging work assignments that expand their areas of performance achievement and expertise.[58]

Engaging the Star Performer

Based on the preferences of star performers, we recommend important steps to ensure your star performers stay engaged and performing as stars. As we discuss in Chapter 7 on leadership, all people respond best to rewards that are contingent upon performance. That is, stars in particular want to know their exceptional outcomes will be met with rewards and recognition. Simply stated, great managers reward "doers." In fact, nothing is likely to burn out your star performers as much as equal rewards, whereby everyone receives the same reward, regardless of performance. Remember, fairness in distributing performance rewards is achieved by providing rewards commensurate with effort and results.

One common mistake managers make is to leave their star performers alone, assuming that the stars will continue to perform with a hands-off approach. While a star performer certainly will not appreciate micromanagement, it is not true that the star prefers *no* management. To the contrary, great coaches are fully involved in providing challenging job assignments to star performers to feed their need for challenge and learning. Challenging job assignments generally have one or more of the following characteristics:[59]

- **Transitional.** Assignments that involve unfamiliar, new, or broader tasks. Such assignments also involve proving one can handle the added pressure. Examples include being the inexperienced member of a team and taking a temporary assignment in a different functional area.

- **Change-Oriented.** Assignments that challenge through added responsibility to create change in the organization, to grapple with recurring organizational problems, and to handle problems with people. Examples include launching a new product, hiring new staff, resolving employee performance problems, or facilitating the development of a new vision or mission statement.

- **High Level of Responsibility.** Assignments that involve high stakes and visible results, heavy time investment, diversity of responsibility, and external pressure. Examples include taking a visible assignment with tight deadlines, representing the organization externally, or managing additional responsibilities following a personnel restructuring.

- **Non-Authority Relationships.** Assignments that require influencing others without positional power. Examples include presenting a proposal to top management, serving on a cross-functional team, or managing an internal project such as a company event.

- **Obstacles.** Assignments that provide challenge through exposure to adverse situations like financial concerns, lack of top management support, and great diversity of opinions regarding project directions. Examples include working with a talented but difficult boss, ambiguous projects, or starting a new project with few resources.

"What every individual needs—is to be recognized, by their leader and their peers, for outstanding individual performance."

—Vince Lombardi

Coaching for Employee Growth

Many people turn to their managers to provide support and guidance to navigate more effectively in an organization. And if you were to ask 10 people what they think a great coach does, you'd probably get 10 fairly similar responses: give advice. Although coaching does often involve giving advice, great coaches know that advice often falls short in efforts to help *develop* employees, to help them learn. When people give advice on solving problems (or avoiding them), they do so from their own personal experience base. That is, their advice is formed by their own assumptions about the way the world works.

In his groundbreaking book, *The Fifth Discipline*, Peter Senge argues that most people spend the majority of their work life dispensing advice or advocating their own position about the world. He notes, however, that problems are often highly idiosyncratic, and just because a method solved a similar problem in the past does not in any way guarantee it will work in the future—especially for someone else. In the end, the advice may make the advice-seeker feel better and give her something to do, but it won't necessarily help her learn to solve the problem for herself in the future. That is, the goal of coaching for growth and development is *helping people build capacity to develop and solve their own problems more effectively*.

A simple example can show why giving advice doesn't always work the way we think. Say you have a third-grade son who is just learning to multiply and divide fractions. One day, your son says, "Gosh, I'm stuck. I really don't know how to solve this math problem. What should I do?" As a parent, you have a few options:

Option 1: *Retreat.* Tell your son, sorry, but you can't help him; it's his homework and he must struggle to do it himself

Option 2: *Take Action.* Solve the problem for your son. Take his pencil and simply do it for him, saying, "See what I did there? Now you try it."

Option 3: *Consult.* Ask your son several questions about the problem that might help him solve the problem on his own, such as, "What have you tried? Have you seen this type of problem before? How did you solve the earlier problem? Are there similar rules that may apply?"

Few parents could stomach Option 1, it's just too cold. Option 2, however, is much more palatable and seems quite reasonable. Yet, in reality, the person being helped in this option is not the son, but the parent. The parent dives into action, reducing the anxious feelings over seeing his or her son struggling and needing help. Although the son may get by with what the parent has done, it is unlikely he has learned how to solve similar problems in the future. Option 3 offers a chance to help the child learn through discovery and develop the capacity to solve similar problems in the future.

Coaching for growth is no different, albeit the problems that arise may be more complex. As a developmental coach, you have a few modes of operation that can make for successful coach–employee relationships. The first mode is known as expert coaching. An **expert coach** dispenses advice, instructs, and prescribes. The second mode is known as consultative coaching. A **consultative coach** helps the employee explore alternatives and challenges the employee's thinking through asking questions. Table 5.4 shows a few differences in these two approaches.

"If it's free, it's advice; if you pay for it, it's counseling; if you can use either one, it's a miracle."

—Jack Adams

TABLE 5.4	Expert versus Consultative Coaching	
Expert Coaching		**Consultative Coaching**
Based on my experience, I would tell your co-worker to let you drive this one.	vs.	What criteria are you using to make your choice?
Budgeting always works better if you solidify your alliances early.	vs.	What are the possible political ramifications of not talking with folks about the budget ahead of time?

So which is better? That depends on the problem to be solved by the employee. We have developed a few guidelines to help guide you in your choice of which approach to take.

Use the *expert coaching* approach when:

- The problem and solution are simple and clear (for example, following federal regulations).
- There are "right" answers (for instance, technical approaches to work).
- The employee is a novice and needs to be given a lot of structure.

Use the *consultative coaching* approach when:

- The problem and solution are ambiguous (many factors are involved and one solution won't fix everything).
- The problem continues to reappear; past attempts to solve the problem have failed.
- There is relatively less urgency; work output can wait.

Concluding Note

The key princples of performance management are relatively simple to understand but a challenge to consistently execute. Execution of those principles, however, is among the most powerful lever a manager can have in driving higher performance. The most effective managers see themselves as coaches and among the most important recurring lessons of coaching are:

- **Set Performance Expectations Immediately.** Remember that settling in sends the wrong message. Use the power of goal setting to get performance up and running.
- **Give Feedback Early and Often.** The more information employees have about how they are performing at any given time, the less you will have to manage their performance. When employees don't receive feedback, they will seek it out, sometimes from unreliable sources.[60] So don't wait until the end of the year to give feedback; it will lose its motivating potential.
- **Focus on Behaviors, Not Traits.** Don't evaluate people, evaluate their performance. Observe behavior frequently and take notes.

- **Assess Both Behavior and Results.** Remember, just because someone hits their target goals does not necessarily mean they are outstanding performers. Understand the full range of performance by taking into account *how* they achieved those goals.

- **Identify and Rectify Performance Gaps.** When a performance gap exists, revisit the goal contract with the employee and agree upon interventions for closing the gap. Remember, training is not always the answer!

- **Allow for Productive Failures.** Employees need to know it is acceptable to fail or to miss the mark. What is unacceptable is to not learn from this failure and to repeat mistakes frequently. Great coaches help employees learn from their mistakes and never repeat them.

- **Reward Desired Behavior and Ensure It Repeats.** If you really want people to perform, make their rewards contingent upon reaching performance goals. Be careful that you are rewarding the behavior you desire and not inadvertently another behavior.

- **Make It Just.** Whatever you do, no matter what type of assessment is involved, ensure that the process, outcomes, and interactions with employees are perceived as fair. Fairness, not equality or happiness, is the key to great performance management.

Key Terms

absolute subjective assessment

adverse impact

assessment center

behavioral intentions

behavioral interviews

behaviorally anchored rating scales (BARS)

cognitive ability

consultative coach

disparate treatment

equality rule

equity rule

expert coach

graphic rating scale

job analysis

mentor

mentoring

need rule

objective assessment

performance management cycle (PMC)

performance tests

protégé

realistic job preview (RJP).

relative subjective assessment

situational interviews

structured interview

subjective assessment

topgrading

unstructured interview

work sample

Performance Management Tool Kits

Tool Kit 5.1   Providing a Realistic Job Preview

Every job candidate should be given a realistic job preview (RJP). Here are the minimum topics that should be presented to each job candidate. Finish the sentences below and then use them to discuss the job with each candidate.

- The essential responsibilities of the job are: _____

- The expectations for hours worked, travel, and working conditions are: _____

- The top five positive and five negative aspects associated with performing the job are: _____

- The top five positive and five negative aspects of working for the organization are: _____

- The top five positive and top five negative aspects of working for me are: _____

- The benefit package includes the following: _____

Tool Kit 5.2   Choosing the Right Assessment Method for the Job

Choosing the right person for the right job requires applying appropriate assessment methods. That is, some methods are better than others for particular jobs. Unfortunately, many factors make this decision complex, including the time frame to hire, resources available, size of the applicant pool, and type of job (for example, seasonal help versus a full-time salaried position). At the very minimum, structured interviews and a background check should be completed on all final candidates. Using other methods in addition will also improve prediction. Based on existing research regarding the validity of different assessment methods:

- Assessment for *any* job should generally include:

  - Structured Interview
  - Cognitive Ability Test
  - Measure of Conscientiousness
  - Background Check

- Jobs with a great degree of *interpersonal interaction* (customer service, sales, and so on) should add:

  - Work Sample or Simulation
  - Measures of Agreeableness and Extraversion

- Jobs with a high degree of *technical knowledge* required (such as engineer) should add:

  - Work Sample
  - Job Knowledge Test

- *Managerial* jobs should add:

  - Work Sample
  - Assessment Center or Simulation Exercises

Tool Kit 5.3   Creating and Evaluating a Behavioral Interview Question

An easy way to remember how to conduct a behavioral interview is using the STAR method. STAR is an acronym for situation, task, action, and result. Using the STAR framework can help you formulate a strong behavioral interview question based on the knowledge, skills, and abilities (KSAs) you are attempting to measure. For example, if you wanted to measure teamwork skills, you might ask:

(S) Describe a time when you were asked to be part of a team.

(T) What task were you and the group charged with doing?

(A) What did you ultimately do to accomplish the tasks?

(R) What results did you achieve?

To evaluate a response on a behavioral interview question,[61] a scoring guide must be developed. A basic scoring guide should differentiate between poor, good, and outstanding responses. On a piece of paper, draw three columns and label them Ineffective, Effective and Highly Effective. Next, brainstorm behaviors representative of each category and record them. Assign scale points to each category, recognizing that some behaviors under Effective are more or less effective than others, but are still not Highly Effective or Ineffective. Finally, leave room at the bottom to take notes. Listen to candidates' responses and record them. Go back later and evaluate the quality of the responses.

Example of STAR Rating Form for Teamwork Question

Ineffective			Effective			Highly Effective		
1	2	3	4	5	6	7	8	9

Ineffective (1–3)

- Unable to describe the purpose of the team and own the role on it.
- Did not display awareness of others' viewpoints.
- Emphasized differences and criticized others.
- Took all the credit for successes of the group.
- Changed mind in face of opposition.
- Ignored disagreements in the group.

Effective (4–6)

- Described the purpose of the team and own role.
- Related effectively to people of differing backgrounds and interests.
- Sometimes used others as problem-solving resources.
- Shared credit for group tasks.
- Mentioned an awareness of others' viewpoints.
- Highlighted and summarized areas of agreement with others.

Highly Effective (7–9)

- Described how role on team contributed to task accomplishment.
- Worked very effectively with people of differing backgrounds and interests.
- Viewed others as valuable problem-solving resources and leveraged their abilities to achieve key objectives.
- Rewarded others when their efforts made substantial contributions to the group task.
- Consistently demonstrated an awareness of others' viewpoints and feelings and modified own position when appropriate.
- Raised and discussed difficult issues/disagreements to find common ground.

Notes:

Tool Kit 5.4   Analyzing a Performance Problem[62]

This guide highlights the key questions to ask regarding a performance problem and shows the general actions to take depending on the response.

Question to Ask	Answer	Action to Take
Does the employee know what is expected of him or her?	No	Reinforce expectations and seek mutual understanding of those expectations.
Does the employee know performance can be improved?	No	Tell the employee there is room for performance improvement.
Are there obstacles the employee faces beyond the employee's control?	Yes	Remove the obstacles. If can't be done, revise the performance expectations to take this into account.
Does the employee know how to improve? Does the employee lack particular skills necessary to perform?	Yes	Provide training and practice opportunities to acquire skills.
Do negative consequences follow good performance?	Yes	Reinforce good performance with positive consequences.

Tool Kit 5.5   Terminating or Reassigning an Employee

Termination or reassignment should always be done with dignity and concern for others. Keep in mind that termination in particular has broad effects on people's families, peers, and co-workers, so taking it seriously is important. Here are the critical steps in terminating or reassigning an employee:

- **Be Prepared.** Have all your documentation regarding the employee's performance on hand and summarized in a form that can be quickly delivered. This includes the dates of each performance improvement discussion and the feedback given in each discussion.

- **Set the Right Tone: Get the Job Done.** This is not a time to schmooze or ask about the employee's family or personal life. Professionalism dictates the meeting should always be conducted face-to-face and in private and scheduled to last for 10 to 15 minutes at the most. In addition, do not attempt to relate your own termination stories or provide vague statements like "I know this is probably hard for you"; these are likely to make the situation worse.[63]

- **State the Reality.** Use effective feedback techniques. Without evaluating the person, state the reality of the situation. For example, "Jim, as you know, I have been concerned about your performance over the past 8 months, and we have met on three separate occasions to address it. Despite repeated attempts to improve performance, I have not seen such improvement to date. As I indicated in our last meeting, the next step would be separation. Thus, I have made the decision to terminate our employment relationship. And this decision is final." Do not blame others involved or side-step the issue; be direct.

- **Review Next Steps.** Organizations structure their severance and termination policies differently. The key here is to ensure you are prepared to tell the employee exactly what he or she is entitled to receive from the organization. Do this in writing and give a copy to the employee. In addition, it is important to tell the employee what to do next. For example, "OK, Jim, after we finish our meeting here, I'd like you to take 30 minutes to collect your things, return your keys, and leave the building."

CHAPTER

6

Power and Influence

"You cannot be successful in our group without building power and being able to influence customers and associates, whether or not you have any direct authority. Without power and influence, managers are about as helpful to their company as a jelly sandwich is to a drowning rabbit."

—**Scott Pickering,**
Vice President of Sales,
Urogyn Medical, Inc.

Manage *What*?

1. Influencing without Formal Authority

You are the leader on a marketing project that requires a great deal of graphic design and production work to be successful. You have design people in the firm but they do not formally report to you and seem to have little urgency to get your work done. You are a bit irritated by their lack of proactive help and know they are not nearly as busy as they let on, but you have no authority to tell them what to do or threaten them with any loss of jobs or rewards. You are reluctant to go over their heads to their boss out of fear such a move would alienate them and compromise the level of effort and quality they would ultimately bring to the project.

To meet deadlines you need some of the work done within a month. How might you get the graphics folks energized to complete your work? Are there any specific tactics you could use to get them moving? Are there any common but counter-productive tactics you should definitely avoid?

2. Selling an Idea to Your Boss

You have read a lot about the most successful companies and have picked up an idea you think would work well in your unit (operations) of the firm. Specifically, you think your department should go to an "open office" design whereby all the cubicles would be taken out and replaced with more modern collaborative workspaces. You have a host of good reasons why this would be a good idea for your unit, but your boss is a little old-fashioned and unlikely to go for this. While she has always claimed she has an open-door policy and is "constantly on the lookout for good ideas," your past attempts have been met with comments like, "We'll have to look into that," "Maybe sometime in the future we could do something like that," and "We don't have the budget for that right now."

If you really want to see this idea come to pass, how would you prepare to sell this to her? Where should you start? What would be some of the key factors to consider? Are there any tactics you should definitely avoid because they would be likely only to hurt your chances of her approval?

3. Making a Positive First Impression

Ever since you were a young child you have dreamed of working in the music business. You love music in all its forms, play an instrument yourself, and want to make your passion your vocation. However, once in college you quickly learned that, because so many people share your dream, it is exceptionally difficult to get a job in the music industry. As luck would have it, however, your current management professor has two personal friends who are senior officers (one in human resources, the other in marketing) at Sony Music, and he has invited them to make a presentation to your class. Knowing of your lifelong interest, he has asked if they would be willing to spend half an hour with you after the presentation and they have agreed. How would you prepare? How would you try to make a good first impression? How might you appropriately try to leverage your professor's relationship? Would there be any absolute taboos (things never to do) or common mistakes to avoid here?

4. Building a Personal Network that Enhances Your Power

After your first six months at a public accounting firm you are starting to see it will be very difficult to stand out until you really know the ropes and feel more connected, like all your more senior associates. All but one of your colleagues at work have been at the firm for over five years. Your fear is you will always be seen as a peon or newbie around the firm. You also know you will have a far better chance of getting things done and moving up if you have a network of people within and outside the firm who mentor, coach, and support you. You are not really willing, however, to wait five years for that to happen.

Where would you start in your attempt to get more connected? What would be specific ways to make people want to be associated with you? How would you go about building a network and finding a mentor(s)?

LEARNING OBJECTIVES

1. Describe how bases of power and norms can be used to influence behavior.
2. Use influence tactics and "weapons of social influence" to influence people over whom you have no formal authority.
3. Sell an idea to your boss.
4. Build positive relationships with employees and co-workers.
5. Create a memorable and positive first impression.
6. Build a social network.

Introduction

Although sometimes disparaged as the "dirty" side of organizational life, skilled use of power and influence is critical to managerial and personal success. For managerial purposes, **power** can be defined as the ability to exert influence to control others or events, and the capacity to defend against the influence of others.

Who has power in organizations? What are the sources of that power? What strategies will broaden our networks and increase our own power? What specific tactics have been shown to yield the most influence, especially in cases where we lack formal authority? How do we manage upward and navigate the political realities of organizational life? This chapter focuses on addressing those questions.

Although formal authority is often confused with power, it is just one *type* of power. More specifically, **authority** is the type of power a person possesses due to his position. In other words, a mother has the authority to make decisions for her 5-year-old daughter solely because she is the child's mother. Similarly, a supervisor has the authority to discipline an employee who has been late to work. A company president has the authority to sign a legal contract as a representative of the company.

Influence, on the other hand, is the *use* of power. **Influence** is power *in action*, and influence tactics serve as the means by which managers gain and exercise power. While authority can be an important tool, great managers realize they need more than just authority to be effective. Therefore, understanding what power is, where it comes from, and the most effective tactics to get beyond authority to influence others is a key to great management. Since it is unlikely most of us will ever have enough formal authority to command wide-ranging action (particularly early in careers), building personal skills associated with power and influence is important for both you personally and the organizations for which you work.

"We have learned that power is a positive force if it is used for positive purposes."

—Elizabeth Dole

As a starting place, it is important to note that power is relational. That is, power only exists where there are at least two people, and is a property of the relationship between people. A useful and popular way to think of power is that it is based on **dependence.** Dependence leads people to do things they may not otherwise do ("I am dependent upon Alice for babysitting so I will buy my new car from Alice's husband," or "Anne controls my raises so I will pay close attention to what Anne says"). Understanding such relational dependencies is key to understanding your own power and the power of others. (See Tool Kit 6.2 for ways to diagnose patterns of dependence in an organization.) It is also a useful starting point for determining the influence tactics that can help you build broad networks and influence others to get things done.

Research has shown that people who have power and use it effectively attain desired jobs more quickly, make more money, and are promoted more quickly than people without power. While this might not be particularly surprising on the surface, the way it plays out is not always obvious or self-evident. For instance, conventional wisdom suggests that it is "who you know" that leads to getting a job. Although this is sometimes the case, of course, research suggests new jobs are more often the product of the "**weak ties**[1]" of the indirect relationships one possesses rather than the "**strong ties**" of direct relationships. In other words, people ultimately tend to get jobs through a friend of a friend (weak ties) and not through people they know directly (strong ties). The implication is that having positive relationships with many people, and people who are well-connected, is an important strategy for finding a job.

The reasons why weak ties are so important may not be immediately evident. First, it is important to understand that weak ties grow exponentially when your immediate network grows. This is because each person you know has ties to numerous other people who all become weak ties in your network (for example, see Figure 6.1). For instance, just getting to know one person, could add 50 or 100 weak ties if that new friend is well-connected. In addition, weak ties serve as an important information-gathering tool. Weak ties allow a person to collect

---

MYTHS 6.1   Myths of Power and Influence

Power and influence are inherently "slimy." An old but true axiom is that power can be used for good or evil. Great managers use their power to exert influence to accomplish *positive* change in organizations.

Rationality is the best form of influence. We're taught to give people data, to influence others through the use of facts and figures. It turns out, however, that despite the popularity of the rational approach to influence, emotional approaches often win the day. People want to be inspired, challenged, and moved.

Power stems solely from one's position. Title alone is only one form of power, and it does not in any way guarantee success toward influencing others. Some of the most powerful people in organizations have unimpressive titles—for example, secretary or help-desk specialist. However, such folks often have great influence in organizations.

Involving others and sharing power weakens your own position. By and large, sharing power only *increases* your own ability to influence. Showing people you don't need to be protective because you are confident in your abilities and approaches increases your credibility and future influence potential.

First impressions and good manners are old fashioned. Hardly! Managing the impression you make always matters greatly in your ability to influence others. This includes all aspects of your work life, such as how you answer your telephone, what clothes you choose to wear, and how you introduce yourself to key clients or your boss's boss.

FIGURE 6.1 | Who Has the Power Is Not Always Obvious

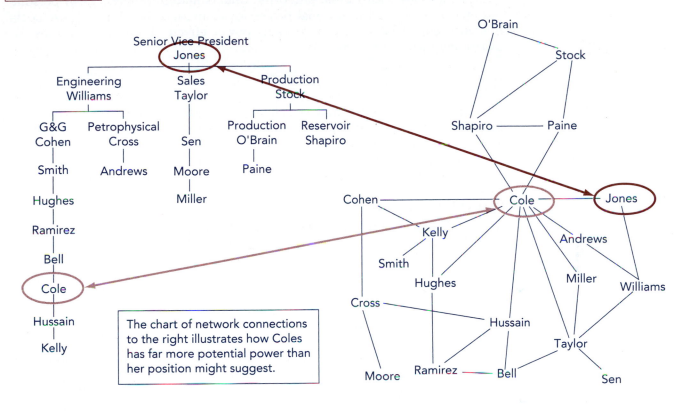

The chart of network connections to the right illustrates how Coles has far more potential power than her position might suggest.

information from a much broader network than those with fewer weak ties, which provides a significant competitive advantage; an advantage that has been shown to result in both higher wages and a higher likelihood of being employed.[2]

Thus, people with broader networks have more power and an increased number of options making them more valuable to their organization. In this light, it should not be surprising that power holders are often able to utilize their power to negotiate higher wages. Organizations are rightly willing to pay more for a person with the power and influence to get things done. For the organization, the powerful person is likely to be able to accomplish more and bring in additional resources. Thus, paying more for power would seem to be a wise investment that provides handsome returns for an organization.

Finally, research has also shown that people with well-developed power networks receive earlier promotions, have increased career mobility, and higher managerial effectiveness.[3] In short, power is advantageous to many important outcomes and thus active efforts to gain and manage your power is a step toward a successful managerial career.

The Sources of Power and Influence

Even a casual observer would notice that some people in organizations are far more able to make things happen and get what they want done than others. Think for a moment about your personal situation, your family members, and your friends. Are some of them consistently more able to get things done and to bring together the resources they need? From your own personal experience you will probably notice that the people who are able to "get things done" are not always the ones with formal authority. Understanding differences in personal power bases, networks, personal professionalism, and the ability to use social influence effectively is central to using power effectively in organizations. We expand on these four areas next.

Bases of Power

The most widely known and accepted classification of power is French and Raven's model of the five **power bases,** first introduced nearly 50 years ago.[4] Their classification has stood the test of time and become the way in which authors and practicing managers most often think about power. The five bases are reward, legitimate, referent, expert, and coercive power. (See Figure 6.2.)

Reward Power

A point emphasized throughout this text is that rewards are powerful motivators of behavior. Put simply, people are inclined to do things that will bring them rewards. There are many more forms of reward. In fact, anything we find desirable can be a reward, be it a million-dollar yacht, a promotion, a good grade on a test, or a pat on the back. What is really important is that the reward being offered is desirable to the person you want to influence. **Reward power** is thus the ability to provide others with rewards they desire in exchange for work you need accomplished.

In order to increase your reward power base you do need to control some rewards, and this may take a certain amount of creativity depending on your position. Remember, however, that social reinforcements (feedback, compliments, etc.) can be very effective rewards in some cases and that many rewards do not need to be expensive or linked to your position in the hierarchy. Simply stated, the best way to build reward power is to actually reward people and the reality is that "if you don't use it you will lose it." Few managers that have not paid anyone a compliment or provided some form of reward to people in the past five years would be seen by employees as having a strong reward power base (even if he has complete control of the budget).

Legitimate Power

"I have as much authority as the Pope, I just don't have as many people who believe it."

—George Carlin

Legitimate power is that which is invested in a role or job position (often called authority). Politicians, kings, police officers, and managers all have legitimate power. The legitimacy generally stems from some higher hierarchical level or legal mandate. A police officer has legitimate power to arrest you by virtue of laws made by elected officials. The legitimate power of a manager ultimately comes from the company's owners or shareholders.

FIGURE 6.2

French and Raven's Power Bases

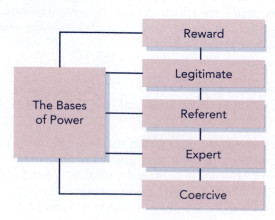

A common seduction of legitimate power is to neglect the reality that the influence associated with a role most often really stems from that position, not the *person* in the position. When people either fall from power or move onto other things, they can be surprised that those who used to fawn at their feet no longer do so. Legitimate power is often sufficient to gain compliance behavior but is less effective in inducing engaged and committed action.

Building legitimate power is often thought of as the most difficult power base to increase. This is because of its close tie to one's position in the organizational hierarchy. Remember, however, that taking a leadership role on high profile projects and being associated with important divisions within a company do not always require receiving a formal promotion, but can be effective ways of increasing your legitimate power.

Referent Power

Unlike legitimate power, **referent power** is highly associated with the person and not the position. Referent power stems from another person either admiring you or wanting to be like you. It is the power of charisma and fame and is commonly (although often curiously) wielded by celebrities as well as others in highly visible roles. No one really believes Michael Jordan is a technical expert on underwear or that golfer Arnold Palmer has a passion for motor oil. However, they are highly successful at selling products because of their referent power. The slogan "Be like Mike" is one of the most successful applications of the influence of this power base in recent memory.

In the workplace, referent power is normally associated with respect and a good working relationship. In other words, we are generally more willing to respond to a request from a person whom we admire and respect than from someone we do not know or dislike. You don't have to be friends with someone to have referent power—plenty of people are highly respected, but not necessarily liked. Referent power is one more reason why having a positive working relationship with your colleagues, bosses, and subordinates is extremely important.

Unlike legitimate power, referent power is directly under your immediate control. To increase your referent power you need to be trusted and respected. By being seen as approachable, fair, friendly, and competent, you will build your referent power and be more effective in the process. In fact, much of this textbook is geared toward helping you do exactly these things.

Expert Power

Much like referent power, **expert power** is normally associated with a person and not closely with the rank of a position. When a person possess knowledge and skill someone else requires, then she has expert power. This common form of power is the basis for a large proportion of human collaboration, including in most companies where the principle of expert specialization allows large and complex enterprises to be undertaken.

Expert power is particularly relevant in a variety of situations. Trade unions often use expert power when they encourage their members to strike for better pay or working conditions. Many information technology (IT) departments within companies are powerful due to their specialized knowledge. Expert power is also at work when you go to a doctor and she prescribes medication; you tend to accept the prescription because the doctor is supposed to "be the expert."

The most common ways for people to build their expert power is through education. Be it a college degree, advanced degree, or specific certifications (e.g., CPA, CFP, etc.) or training, education is key. Beyond the role of education, however, obtaining specific, scarce knowledge is a great way to increase your expert power. For example, a low-level computer programmer can have the most power in the company when a system for which she is responsible fails. Become a technical expert in your field and you will likely find your expert power in the organization will increase.

Coercive Power

Coercive power can be associated with either a person or the rank attached to a person's position. This is the power to force someone to do something against his or her will. Coercion often involves physical or verbal threats. It is the power of dictators, despots, and bullies. Coercion can result in physical harm, although its principal goal is to influence action. Demonstrations of personal harm are often used to illustrate what will happen if compliance is not gained.

In the workplace, coercive power can be thought of as coming in the form of disciplinary actions, demotions, or job loss. Generally, being threatened with firing is considered the most extreme form of coercive power, although threat of legal action may be used as a severe coercive inducement as well.

Actually building coercive power can be tricky business and it is not something that we would recommend in most instances. As you might imagine, building coercive power tends to undermine some of your most powerful sources of positive power. More specifically, building coercive power by "flexing your muscles" and disciplining people or assigning unpleasant work duties will likely reduce your referent power significantly. To effectively manage coercive power, the best idea is to be fair and consistent when standards are not met. We recommend building and using coercive power sparingly, perhaps only when it is absolutely necessary that you receive 100 percent compliance (e.g., legal compliance). In this way, people know that although you do not make it a practice to coerce behavior regularly, those who violate critical standards will receive a commensurate response. Remember that you don't have to use power to hold power. That people know you could coerce them is often enough to gain compliance.

Norms and Conformity

Another subtle but very powerful form of influence is found in behavioral norms. Whether overt or just understood, every group and organization possesses a set of **norms,** a code of conduct about what constitutes acceptable behavior. Some norms will be strictly adhered to while others permit a wide range of behavior, but these norms have a significant influence on behavior in organizations. Usually, sanctions from the group (such as disapproval) are applied in the case of deviations from the norm.

To illustrate, think back to the days in which you dared a friend (or maybe even "double-dog dared" if you grew up in one of our twisted neighborhoods) to do something outrageous. Such dares—like streaking naked though campus or eating bizarre amounts of restaurant condiments—are dares because they represent behavior that some reference group deems as *inappropriate* (would there be any other reason to drink an entire container of maple syrup?). Organizations of every kind are filled with such norms.

For example, if you show up late to a meeting, when the norm is to be on time, most people in the group are likely to give you the "you're late" look. These looks are designed to let you know you are violating a rule and that you should not have done so. Norms are frequently associated with clothing, language (slang, cursing), open expression of feelings, promptness, interrupting or challenging leaders, volunteering one's services, avoiding conflict, and so on. Many such norms are implicit, and new members may find it difficult to adjust—there rarely is a nice documented set of rules. Norms have great influence nonetheless.

From a managerial perspective, norms can be the source of both desirable and undesirable forms of influence. For example, you may want your employees to show up every Sunday for work. However, because this is not a general

"All in all, punishment hardens and renders people more insensible; it concentrates; it increases the feeling of estrangement; it strengthens the power of resistance."

—Friedrich Nietzsche

societal norm, you will certainly be met with resistance. Breaking norms makes people feel uncomfortable. The next time you get on a crowded elevator, start off by turning and facing the *back* of the elevator. Then, after a few seconds, start looking people in the eye. We guarantee you will not only make other people feel uncomfortable, but we suspect you will feel exceptionally awkward in bucking established norms. The important lesson is that most behavior is likely to happen "inside the norms" so it is always important to know what those norms are and how difficult it can be to influence people to break those norms.

Stemming directly from the influence of norms is the notion of conformity. **Conformity** is defined as a tendency to believe, behave, and perceive in ways that are consistent with group norms. Conformity enables us to feel as if we fit in, to feel comfortable with other people, and to have well understood codes of conduct in society at large. Conformity is an important influence on the actions of people, especially when no formal authority or power is present. Two striking examples of the extraordinary influence of conformity are provided in famous experiments conducted by Muzafer Sherif and Solomon Asch.[5]

In Sherif's study, people were invited to estimate the amount that a point of light moved and to do so in a context where each participant could hear the estimates of other participants. Results showed that group members' estimates converged on a middle-of-the-road "group estimate" indicating the presence of a persuasive urge to conform. Asch conducted a set of similar experiments focused on social pressures to conform. In his experiments, several people were seated around a table and all but one were actually in on the experiment (that is, they were working for the experimenter as confederates). The group was shown a display of vertical lines of different lengths, and each participant was asked to say which line was the same length as another displayed line. One after another, the confederate participants chose the same (but wrong) line as that which was identical in length to the other displayed line. The only real participant sat in the next to last seat so that all but one of the confederates had given an answer prior to his choice (See Figure 6.3.)

Incredibly, in repeated trials of the experiment, the real participants frequently picked the same incorrect line as the confederates, even though it was apparent to outside observers that the choice was clearly wrong. In fact, the unwitting participants (each of whom participated in a number of trials) conformed to the group response in 32 percent of the trials and 74 percent of the participants conformed at least once. It should be noted that recent research has shown some reduction in conformity since Asch's studies in the 1950s.[6] Nevertheless, his studies were instrumental in demonstrating the subtlety of conformity; a deceptively powerful source of influence.

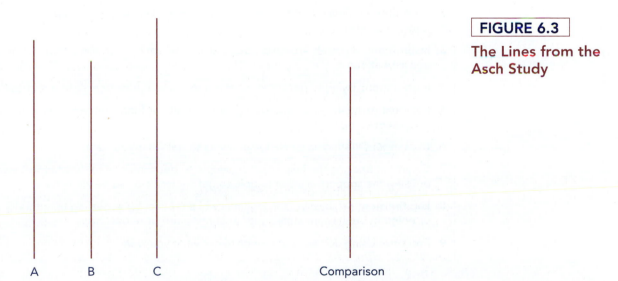

FIGURE 6.3

The Lines from the Asch Study

A   B   C   Comparison

Influencing without Authority

Thus far we have focused on understanding what power and influence are, where they come from, and how to develop them. The applied managerial skill, however, is how to use influence to get real and positive things accomplished through others, particularly in those cases where you have no legitimate power from your position. In short, you want to learn to influence without authority. Below we describe and present the supporting evidence for several approaches and tactics that have been demonstrated to be successful in such cases.

Frequency and Effectiveness of Different Influence Tactics

A variety of different tactics are used to influence others, the most common of which are described in Table 6.1.

Research regarding these nine influence tactics has uncovered interesting and important findings. First, some tactics are used far more commonly than others and certain tactics are also used much more frequently on particular targets (superiors, peers, or subordinates). Most importantly, some of the tactics are considerably more effective in achieving desired outcomes than others.[7]

More specifically, evidence shows that rational persuasion and pressure are the most frequently used influence tactics. Interestingly, the other seven tactics are used relatively rarely. With respect to the targets of influence attempts, downward influence (trying to influence a subordinate) is the most common, representing about 42 percent of the overall attempts. Upward influence (trying to influence your boss) was second, and lateral influence (trying to influence a peer) was the least common. Given the disproportionate time spent with peers, this finding is somewhat surprising.

The relative effectiveness of tactics can be defined as the reaction of the influence target in one of three ways: resistance, compliance, or commitment.

TABLE 6.1   The Range of Influence Tactics[8]

1. **Rational Persuasion:** Using logical arguments and facts to persuade someone your request will result in beneficial outcomes.

2. **Consultation:** Seeking someone's participation in planning or developing something they ultimately need to buy into.

3. **Inspirational Appeal:** Arousing a target's enthusiasm by appealing to values, ideals, and aspirations.

4. **Ingratiation:** Trying to get someone in a good mood prior to making a request.

5. **Personal Appeal:** Appealing to someone's loyalty or friendship with you to get them to do something.

6. **Exchange:** Offering an exchange of favors to get what you want.

7. **Coalition:** Seeking the help of other people to get someone to do what you want, or using the support of other people to get someone to agree with you.

8. **Legitimizing:** Establishing the legitimacy of a request by appealing to authority or pointing out its consistency with existing values or norms.

9. **Pressure:** Using demands or threats to get what you want.

- *Resistance.* The influence target is opposed to carrying out requests and will resist accomplishing what is being requested.
- *Compliance.* The target is willing to do what the influencer asks, but is not enthusiastic about it. Compliance is characterized by doing only that which is required by a request—and nothing more.
- *Commitment.* The target agrees with a request or decision from the agent and strives to carry out the request or implement the decision with energy and engagement. The target complies with the request and will often go beyond and do more than is requested.

Of course, commitment is the most effective and desirable of the influence outcomes. However, compliance may often be acceptable and may sometimes be the best that can be achieved. For example, a supervisor may be responsible for overseeing that several relatively unpleasant tasks get completed. It is unlikely anyone will be "committed" to cleaning the bathroom or to filling out an expense report so, in such cases, compliance is likely the maximum outcome. Nonetheless, gaining commitment is the gold standard of influence attempts and should be sought at every available opportunity.

Table 6.2 presents data from research that has studied the effectiveness of the nine influence tactics presented in Table 6.1. Note that personal appeal, consultation, and inspirational appeal all have "commitment" as their most likely outcome and thus are deemed the most effective of the tactics. On the other end, rational persuasion, pressure, ingratiation, and coalition are all linked most frequently with "resistance."

By bringing together the two questions of most interest—"Which tactics are most frequently used?" and "Which tactics are most effective?"—an important disconnect should be apparent. That is, the most frequently used tactics are among the least effective, and those used most infrequently are among the most effective! This would certainly seem to be a case where, in the words of humorist Will Rogers, "common sense ain't so common."

The lessons for students of influence should be clear. Do not necessarily do what you see others doing but rather do what works! Why the emotional appeals (for instance inspirational appeals and personal appeals) work so well is because they are consistent with what we know about persuasion. That is,

> "You'd be surprised how hard people work around here. They work nights and weekends, sometimes not seeing their families for a while. Sometimes people work through Christmas to make sure the tooling is just right at some factory in some corner of the world so our product comes out the best it can be. People care so much, and it shows."
>
> —Steve Jobs

TABLE 6.2 | Consequences of the Nine Influence Tactics

Tactic (listed in order of use frequency)	Outcomes (%)		
	Resistance	Compliance	Commitment
Rational Persuasion	47	30	23
Pressure	56	41	3
Personal Appeal	25	33	42
Exchange	24	41	35
Ingratiation	41	28	31
Coalition	53	44	3
Legitimizing	44	56	0
Consultation	18	27	55
Inspirational Appeal	0	10	90

there is both a rational and an emotional component that leads to change.[9] But research suggests that managers generally invest most of their influence efforts on the rational aspect even though emotional elements often lead most directly to change. Consider what persuades you most, a one hundred page report full of charts and graphs or a passionate appeal to your heart?

Most people are heavily persuaded by emotional appeals for at least two reasons. First, emotional appeals establish a sense of urgency and help to bring people together. Second, it is generally believed that thoughts and emotions are closely interrelated, and sometimes they may be in conflict. When there is a strong relationship between rational and emotional components, impacting the emotions will often bring the rational elements into line (people convince themselves that something is a good idea and then justify it with data). If however, thoughts and emotions are not in full agreement, appealing only to rational issues leaves the possibility open that people will reject the change based on an emotional objection (i.e., "I don't like the way this change feels"); one which cannot easily be overcome by data.

"You have no idea how political this place is."

© *The New Yorker* Collection 2001 Alex Gregory from cartoonbank .com. All Rights Reserved.

Political Skills

Closely related to influence tactics are a collection of behaviors broadly labeled *political skills*. Political skills combine the most effective influence tactics, resulting in a "disarmingly charming and engaging manner that inspires confidence, trust, and sincerity."[10] Like it or not, politics often play an important role in the work environment. It is often the case in organizations where the needs of two parties do not align. For example, with respect to resource allocation (pay raises, budget dollars, office space, new equipment), people and groups are often pitted against each other and respond by looking out for their own interests and ignoring the interests of others and the overall organization. In these cases using the most effective influence tactics can be especially important to your ultimate success or failure in the organization. One of the most potent forms of political skill behavior involves methods for influencing without direct authority is a concept known as **social influence**. When used appropriately, social influence can help an individual achieve positive and ethical outcomes in organizations. In the next section, we describe the most important social influence behaviors.

Social Influence Weapons[11]

Many eager, but inexperienced workers often find themselves in a bit of a quandary, anxious to get things done, but too junior in the organization to possess any real legitimate or formal authority. That is, it is often the case that we find ourselves asking the question "How am I supposed to get things done if I don't have the authority to influence people?" This is an important issue and one that thankfully has received a great deal of attention. The study of social influence provides a solid, research-backed series of tools to help people influence others in the absence of formal authority. Below we focus on six of what Robert Cialdini, the nation's leading authority on social influence, calls "weapons" of influence.

Cialdini coined the term **social influence weapons** to give people a sense of how these tactics can be used by you or against you to get you to do things you may not really wish to do. Understanding how and why social influence weapons operate to persuade us will not only enable you to influence other people, but also provide you protection from being manipulated by others in undesirable ways. Remember, these tactics may be "used for good or ill," so be aware of the power of these tactics to induce either positive or undesirable outcomes. Cialdini's six principles include (1) friendship/liking, (2) commitment and consistency, (3) scarcity, (4) reciprocity, (5) social proof, and (6) appeals to authority.

Principle 1: Friendship/Liking

A few of the tactics involved with friendship or liking are:

- **Ingratiation:** If someone likes you, they are more apt to agree with your request.
- **Self-Enhancement:** If you look good and use appealing nonverbal behavior, people will come to like your request as well!
- **Enhancing the other:** Flattery will get your request approved and gifts and favors work too.

While attractiveness plays a big role in liking (see Management Live 6.1), it does not tell the whole story. We also like people because of their similarity to us, and the flattering treatment they direct toward us. The fact that we have greater liking for those similar to us has been repeatedly demonstrated, and the wide range of comparison factors people consider in determining who is like them include age, race, gender, religion, politics, and even cigarette smoking habits.[12] People also *do* respond favorably to flattery. In a famous example, Joe Girard, a hugely successful car salesman, claimed the secret to his success was sending out a monthly card to 13,000 former customers that simply said, "I like you."

"My love for you really has less to do with how I feel about you, and more to do with how you make me feel about me."

—Unknown

The truly amazing thing is that these findings also hold in cases where flattery is obvious and where the person clearly has a motive to manipulate another person. In a controlled study where people received personal feedback from men who needed favors from them, the men who only provided positive feedback were better liked even though it was clear they had something to gain by using flattery.[13] In other words, for better or worse, we are influenced by people who like us, are similar to us, and who flatter us.

Principle 2: Commitment and Consistency

Cialdini explains that

> Once we make a choice or take a stand, we will encounter personal and interpersonal pressures to behave consistently with that commitment. Those pressures will cause us to respond in ways that justify our earlier decision. We simply convince ourselves that we have made the right choice and, no doubt, feel better about our decision.[14]

Some specific examples of how commitment and consistency can be used as influence weapons include:

- **Foot-in-the-door.** A small request is made and granted, and is then followed by a larger request.
- **Lowballing.** You agree to an offer and the other party adds unattractive details. You still follow through with the deal.
- **Bait-and-switch.** You are lured to a store by a sale, only to find that items on sale are out of stock, unavailable, or of obviously poor quality. You go find the ones in stock or of better quality and end up buying the higher quality or more expensive items.

Management Live | 6.1

Do Looks Really Matter?

However unfair, research evidence is clear that "Looks matter!" In a recent summary of studies[15] that examined the effects of attractiveness, the researchers found that:

> *"Clothes make the man. Naked people have little or no influence on society."*
>
> —Mark Twain

- Attractive individuals fared better than their less attractive counterparts in a variety of job-related outcomes.
- The attractiveness effect existed even when a lot of job-relevant information was available (so people viewed the attractiveness as being relevant even when performance levels were known).
- The biasing effect of attractiveness was present for professionals as well as for college students.
- The attractiveness effect was just as strong for attractive men as for attractive women.
- The attractiveness effect seems to be weakening over time (that is, it is not as strong as it was 20 years ago), but it is still quite significant.

Other studies have shown that attractive people are assumed to be more talented, kinder, more honest, and more intelligent than people who are less physically attractive.[16] Keep in mind these are major influences and not just relevant in some obscure cases. This effect holds for such far-reaching areas as politics (where physically attractive candidates get many more votes than unattractive ones[17]), salaries for jobs (where attractive individuals get paid 12 to 14 percent more than their unattractive co-workers[18]), and court cases (less attractive defendants are twice as likely to avoid jail as unattractive defendants). This effect also starts very young in life (elementary school teachers assume attractive children are better behaved[19] and more intelligent[20] than their less attractive classmates) and continues through adulthood.

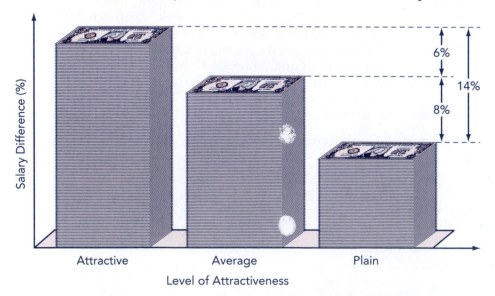

The Relationship between Attractiveness and Salary

Salary Difference (%)

6%
14%
8%

Attractive   Average   Plain

Level of Attractiveness

What is really important about all of these techniques is gaining some small degree of commitment that can then be turned into something larger. A great example of this type of influence can be seen in a classic study conducted by Steve Sherman, a psychology professor at Indiana University.[21] Dr. Sherman called a sample of local residents as part of a survey and asked them to predict what they would say if asked to spend three hours collecting money for the American Cancer Society. Notice that he did not actually ask them to collect money, but just to tell him what they would say if they were asked to volunteer. Because people did not want to appear uncharitable, a large number of people said they would volunteer. A few weeks later, the American Cancer Society called these people. As a result, there was a 700 percent increase in volunteers as compared to an earlier solicitation. You see, people really do strive for consistency!

Principle 3: Scarcity

Despite what some economics classes may have you believe, individuals are not always rational in their decision-making processes (see Chapter 3). This makes scarcity all the more powerful when it is used to wield influence. A few common tactics include:

- **Hard to Get.** Because the item is prized as being rare, you desire it even more.
- **Deadline.** A limited time offer, so you want it now!
- **One-of-a-kind.** The product is unique so you want it.

Interestingly, people are particularly sensitive to a perceived loss—more so than they are to a perceived gain of the same magnitude. Studies in medicine have shown people are more likely to fully engage in their prescribed treatment when the message received is framed in terms of what they could lose by not doing so rather than in terms of what they gain from compliance. For example, a poignant example is found in messages focusing on how many years are cut off a smoker's life versus those who do not smoke or quit. The lesson is that the positioning of a message (loss versus gain) makes a great deal of difference. Rather surprisingly, people do not need to actually *have* something to fear its loss, as they fear lost *opportunity* in much the same way they fear the loss of actual property.

This desire to preserve our options is a main component of **psychological reactance** theory, which proposes that whenever free choice is limited or threatened, the need to retain our freedom makes us want it more than before.[22] Psychological reactance makes us very susceptible to scarcity and can cloud our judgment significantly. Take the case where a company is hiring new college graduates. The company makes the assertion that you have to make up your mind in a day or two because it has so many other qualified candidates and only a few openings. The scarcity of the job opening tends to make it more attractive (even though it may not be) to job candidates.[23]

Scarcity also helps explain why attempts to ban activities or products generally do not work. Even when people do not engage in a practice, they want to feel they are free to do so if they wish. By making access to the activity "scarce," people actually want it more!

There can be great personal advantage in using the principle of scarcity. For instance, knowing a specific computer language your company uses, but that is known by relatively few people, may make you irreplaceable. The ability to speak well in front of an audience may be a very scarce commodity in some contexts. By developing skills that are scarce, you increase your value and potential influence.

Principle 4: Reciprocity

The principle of reciprocity is so widespread that sociologists and cultural anthropologists worldwide have found it to be universal across all human societies. The interdependencies created by reciprocity allow for division of labor and the creation of an organized society. If people did not generally reciprocate others' actions, we would face a chaotic environment.

It is the very widespread acceptance of reciprocity that makes it a particularly strong influence weapon. Specific tactics based upon the reciprocity principle include:

- **Door-in-the-face.** A large request is made, which is normally denied. This is followed by a smaller request, which is more often accepted.
- **That's not all.** Offer coupled with supposed added benefits before you've decided to commit to offer.
- **Foot-in-mouth.** Target gets you to feel like you're in a personal relationship and makes you feel awkward about turning down the request.

The reality in most of these reciprocity-based influence attempts is the person being influenced often did not request the service or action in the first place. A clever and familiar example of this is a tactic used by a scout troop in their attempt to sell candy bars door-to-door. Using the door-in-the face technique, the scouts first asked for a relatively large donation for an event the majority of targets would have zero interest in attending. When that offer was inevitably declined, the scouts were trained to then follow with, "If you don't want the tickets, will you at least buy some chocolate bars? They are only $1.00 a piece." Notice that this creates the appearance that both people are "giving in." In reality, the scout meets his objectives, while the buyer does not.

Managerial approaches such as "stretch goals" are examples of influence that capitalize on the reciprocity principal. Performance targets like "100 percent customer satisfaction" or "zero defects" are unlikely to ever be fully realized. However, by setting an extremely high goal at first, managers succeed in getting commitment to higher performance than would otherwise have occurred.

Resisting this form of influence can be very difficult, but a fundamental understanding at least makes you more aware of the possibility of being unwillingly trapped. Cialdini suggests we "accept the offers of others but to accept those offers for what they fundamentally are, not for what they are represented to be."[24] In other words, if the initial favor turns out to be some form of deception, we should respond as if someone is trying to take advantage of us. By looking at the influence attempt for what it is, rather than what it pretends to be, we are better able to respond in an appropriate manner that we will not regret later.

On the positive side, reciprocity can also serve as a very legitimate and important tool in your "managerial tool kit." By supporting others when they need it, by making yourself available with your expertise, and by doing the "little extra things" that need to be done, you will build a greater reservoir of influence. If you have taken care to treat other people well, it is likely others will reciprocate this treatment when you need it most.

Principle 5: Social Proof

Social proof is based on the reality that we tend to view actions as more acceptable to the degree that we see *others* performing them in the same or similar situations. Some basic social proof techniques include:

- **Repeated Affirmations.** By repeating something often enough, people believe it is true.

- **Vivid Examples.** By pointing out a single but striking or compelling example of something that worked very well (or very poorly), the impression is given that this is *always* the case.
- **Name-dropping.** Making associations with other important, well-known people.

Social proof is most influential under two conditions: (1) uncertainty, when people are unsure about what to do or the situation is unclear and can be interpreted in multiple ways, and (2) similarity, where people are more likely to follow the lead of people who are like themselves.

Local politicians certainly understand the power of this tactic. Recently, one of the authors of this book received a card supporting a local candidate for judge. However, the card was not sent by the judge himself but by a personal friend of the author. The card was inscribed with the statement, "Your friends are voting for Judge Smith. Shouldn't you?" Don't be mistaken, these influence weapons are being used all around us, everyday. They are not rare or only used by particularly savvy people.

The methods for using social proof in a positive manner are relatively straightforward. You need to have vivid examples with rich details and be able to cite several instances where your recommendation has been effective. Also, staying on point (using a few themes over and over) tends to reinforce the idea and make it more likely to be accepted by others.

Although social proof can be very powerful, we are capable of overcoming its influence. First and foremost, we need to be sensitive to clearly counterfeit evidence of what others are doing. In addition, we need to recognize that the actions of others should not form the sole basis for our decisions.

Principle 6: Appeals to Authority

Even though we frequently see bumper stickers with the message "Question authority," few people actually do. The tendency to obey legitimate authority comes from early socialization where we learned to obey our parents and teachers. Of course the tendency to obey authority is actually very important to the safety of a child (for instance, listening to others may stop a child from running into the street) and to the smooth functioning of society (people generally accept court decisions because they view the process as legitimate). Like all social influence weapons, appeals to authority can be used for good or manipulation. Some variations of this weapon include:

- **Snob Appeal.** Appealing to people's sense that they are somehow better than others. As in, "Camel filters. They're not for everybody!"
- **Appeal to Tradition.** The fallacy of asserting that something is right or good simply because it's old or because "That's the way it's always been."
- **Appeal to Novelty.** The fallacy of asserting that something is better or more correct simply because it is new, or newer than something else.

Appeals to authority are made most powerful when they concern obeying the requests of genuine authorities who possess recognized knowledge and wisdom. Problems arise, however, when we obey authority as a mindless shortcut. Accepting false authority in an unquestioning manner is a formula for manipulation.

Research has shown three kinds of symbols are most dangerous in creating artificial authority: (1) titles, (2) clothing, and (3) automobiles. In separate studies investigating the influence of these symbols (titles, clothing, automobiles), people who possessed one or another of them (and no other noteworthy credentials) were granted more obedience by others.[25] Moreover, in each case, the obeying persons underestimated the effect of authority pressures on their behaviors. That is, the people influenced generally believed that the symbols made no difference, but they actually did. It seems entirely irrational that the type of automobile a person drives would signal his or her authority, but the evidence supports it nonetheless.

We can defend ourselves against the unwanted effects of authority by asking two simple questions: Is this authority truly an expert? How truthful can we expect this expert to be in this case? The first question directs our attention away from the simple symbols and toward evidence for authority status. The second advises us to consider not just the expert's knowledge in the situation but also his or her trustworthiness in this instance. Legitimate appeals to authority can be a useful tool of influence. But be ever vigilant in ensuring your "authorities" and those of others are truly worthy of the label.

The social influence weapons offer proven strategies for influencing others when you do not have the formal authority to do so. Using the influence weapons, however, takes some thought and practice. Just as importantly, you need to be on the lookout for people trying to influence you in unwanted or undesirable ways. We have found it interesting how once you understand and recognize the basic social influence tactics how often you can see their use around you, and how effective you can be through their use.

Managing Your Boss

"Accomplishing the impossible means only that the boss will add it to your regular duties."
—Doug Larson

Many people report difficulty with the idea of "managing" their boss. This can result in a norm of politeness, where people are always courteous to their supervisors, but reluctant to pass along information that might distress them.[26] However, as one researcher put it,

> Effective organizational functioning demands that people have a healthy *disrespect* for their boss, feel free to express emotions and opinions openly, and are comfortable engaging in banter and give-and-take."[27]

"The greatest lesson in life is to know that even fools are right sometimes."
—Winston Churchill

Research indicates that the frequency and depth of effective communication between supervisor and subordinate increases each person's trust for the other, enhances managers' willingness to act on their employees' suggestions, and actually makes the manager more effective.[28] When managers don't get feedback from their subordinates regularly, it can have a negative effect on the whole organization. As mentioned in the decision-making section in Chapter 3, one study found that, of 356 decisions made in firms without significant upward communication, one-half of those decisions failed.[29]

The reality is that in almost all situations, you will have information your supervisor needs to effectively do her job. Further, your boss depends on you to make him look good, meaning your relationship with him is one of reciprocity. Your ideas have value because you are likely closer to the customer than your boss can be. You can actually help your supervisor become a better manager by giving feedback, provided you put it in a way that is constructive and that she will be willing to hear and act on.[30]

A few guiding principles have been proposed as fundamental to managing your boss.

- First, it is important to understand your boss's mindset and see the world through his lens. What is important to him? What are her goals and objectives, and how does your work contribute to those? What are his pressures? What are her strengths and weaknesses? If you understand these fundamental things, you can frame your communication in an appropriate way. You can appeal to shared values, or explain how your idea can create value relevant to your boss.[31]

- Second, aim to communicate in your boss's preferred style. Is your boss a listener or a reader? Each of us has a particular way in which we prefer to receive information, and that is usually the channel we choose to communicate with other people. If your boss consistently initiates face-to-face communication, this is likely the best way to proceed with a request. On the other hand, if your boss is a reader, it is a good idea to provide her with information in writing prior to a meeting, so she has a chance to fully absorb it.[32] But don't make this a guessing game. Ask your boss how he or she likes to communicate best and act accordingly.

- Third, you need to understand yourself. The exercises and suggestions in Chapter 1 gave you a head start on this. Understanding your own strengths, weaknesses, pressures, and goals helps you prioritize what requests you make of your boss, and gives you context when she approaches you with new challenges or opportunities.[33]

So, when approaching your supervisor, what are the best communication strategies?

- First, begin with the end in mind. Have a clear vision of your recommendation, including its strategic importance, and say it up front. Some phrases that might help you begin the conversation are "I've noticed we have a problem with X and I have a solution I'd like to propose," and "You mentioned that one of our strategic goals for this year is X and I have an idea of how we can do that." That way your boss will listen because she knows where you are headed and you won't waste her time.

- Second, outline both costs and benefits, being as specific as you can about both. Don't forget about intangible but important costs such as time and allocation of resources.

- Third, once you present your recommendation, ask for input. As a general rule, if you are going to approach your boss with a problem, *come armed with a recommendation as well*. Your solution may not be the one that actually gets implemented, but showing your superior that you are capable of understanding a problem and its ramifications could prove to be an asset to your career.[34]

> *"Listening, not imitation, may be the sincerest form of flattery. If you want to influence someone, listen to what he says. When he finishes talking, ask him about any points that you do not understand."*
> —Dr. Joyce Brothers

Professionalism: A Source of Trust and Respect

As noted earlier, power and influence derive from relationships with people. Your power and influence will therefore be tightly linked to your ability to create strong and positive relationships. You must proactively and consistently work on building such relationships—they just don't happen on their own. That may seem obvious but, unfortunately, studies show nearly half of new management hires fail in their first jobs because of their inability to build good relationships with bosses, peers, and subordinates.[35]

> *"People do not care how much you know, until they know how much you care."*
> —Unknown

When most people talk about influential managers, they tend to focus on personal characteristics and most frequently cite traits that relate to trust and respect. For example, when describing effective managers, people commonly say things like:

"He was highly organized and did what he said he would do."

"She was tough, but fair and honest, and I respected that."

"He always went out of his way to say thank you for the things I did."

"She sent the most caring and comforting note when my dad died."

Conversely, when describing ineffective managers, people commonly say things like:

"He was scattered and unfocused, and did not follow up on commitments."

"She would tell you anything to keep you happy—she sucked up to upper management and was a phony with us."

"He took the credit for our work."

"He knew nothing about me and never seemed to appreciate anything I did."

So what do the trusted and respected managers consistently do that those less successful do not? The managers who get the highest marks from their people are often not the most brilliant, nor the most versed in managerial knowledge. Rather, they are those who have devoted themselves to building relationships that bring out the best in people, and they know how to navigate social situations. We call that capability *professionalism.* When athletes are described as being "professional," it means they play the "right way," make others around them better, and represent themselves and their team well. Just as importantly, they do not do insensitive or immature things that damage their reputation or that of the team. Professional managers are the same.

Professionalism is the source of trust and respect; it brings out the best in others and strengthens your reputation and that of your organization. It is also an area where blunders can be fatal to a management career. While it can take months or years to fully gain the trust and respect of others, one breach of trust or one disrespectful outburst can damage a relationship for a lifetime. Though professionalism can include a wide variety of elements, a synthesis of the many popular management guidebooks and manuals reveals the core of professionalism concerns how you manage your relationships, your etiquette, and your social network. Attention to building and refining competence in those areas will ultimately determine the level of trust and respect you will earn as a manager.

Building Positive Relationships

"What's done to children, they will do to society."

—Karl A. Menninger, psychiatrist

Clearly, different managers have different styles and there is no "one best way" to build relationships. However, three general strategies consistently emerge as critical to creating positive relationships:

1. Get to know your people.

2. Show appreciation.

3. Under-promise and overdeliver.

Although many different labels have been used to describe those strategies, those three are the essential tools for managers most adept at relationships. Conversely, a neglect of such strategies often leads to relationship breakdowns and the derailing of otherwise promising management careers (see Management Live 6.2).

Getting to Know Your People: Showing Genuine Interest in Others

"If there is any one secret of success, it lies in the ability to get the other person's point of view and see things from that person's angle as well as from your own."

—Henry Ford

You cannot manage well without knowing those you manage. Therefore, the single most important professional behavior is to get to know those with whom you work. Unfortunately, demanding goals and busy schedules often make it difficult for managers to find the time to sit down with their people and get to know them well. A great sadness at funerals is that people often say they learned more about a deceased individual in an hour-long service than they did after working with him or her for 30 years or more. At the frantic pace of business today, learning about others is unlikely to occur naturally. Therefore, great managers proactively create opportunities to "stay in the loop" and keep abreast of the lives and concerns of their people. Specific behaviors useful to getting to know your people include:

Practice MBWA: Management by Walking Around. Make yourself visible by regularly talking and visiting with people. Every day make a point to get out of your regular office or workstation and visit with people in your workplace. If your people are not in the same physical location, then call and still occasionally visit. Don't limit your visits to just those at your level or higher. For example, secretaries and service staff often have surprising influence in organizations and, more importantly, are interesting people in their own right.

> *"You can observe a lot just by watching."*
>
> —Yogi Berra

MBWA sends positive messages to people. It reveals your interest in them and in their work, and it says you don't consider yourself "too good" to spend time with them. MBWA also enables you to stay in touch with what is going on in your department, section, or unit. So make time every week to spend time with people and aim for some contact even if you work at home or in a virtual environment. Several executives (Herb Kelleher of Southwest Airlines, for one) are beloved by people in their organizations because they take the time to visit with and take a sincere interest in people at all levels. That is a strategy worth emulating. (See Tool Kit 6.3 for a list of MBWA guidelines.)

> *"Seek first to understand, then to be understood."*
>
> —Steven Covey

Get Your Hands Dirty. One of the most common laments of first line workers is that their managers do not fully understand what they (the workers) really do. One good way to avoid that perception is to actually sample and *do* the employees' jobs on occasion. Plop down in front of the computer, pick up the telephone to deal with a customer complaint, or review a project chart. Sample their job enough to show your interest in it and to understand how it works. Think of it as a great way to connect with your frontline people and to gain a first-hand understanding of exactly what they are dealing with during

> *"The one thing I never want to be accused of is not noticing."*
>
> —Don Shula

Management Live 6.2

Managers Relating Badly

The success rate for new managers is disturbingly low, largely because of a failure to build positive relationships with people. Here are a few of the most frequent and damaging relationship mistakes that managers make:

Taking Credit for the Work of Others. A death sentence for relationships. Great managers obsess over showing appreciation and delight in the fact that their workers feel they are not taken for granted.

Failing to Follow-up on Commitments. Quickly undermines trust and creates a culture lacking in accountability. Better not to commit than to offer a promise and not live up to it. Always live by the principle: Underpromise and overdeliver.

Trying to Show Everyone Who's In Charge. One of the unfortunate misconceptions of young managers is that they need to convey complete control. They often feel any admission of weakness, or revealing of a limitation, is dangerous and probably inappropriate. Contrary to such notions, the reality is you will almost certainly be more effective when you behave authentically. So apologize when you are wrong, and do not feel you have to disguise all weaknesses.

Refusing to Ask for Help. You are not alone. Think of your group as a team and ask for their help. As a general rule, people want to help, and it is being left out of the loop that is far more damaging.

Overreliance on Title. Perhaps the hardest lesson for young managers to learn is that a management title does not elicit automatic respect and obedience. Actions speak louder than words. If you show a level of competence, and demonstrate the skills that come with your title, the respect of your workers will follow.

a typical workday. Experience what they go through in their jobs, and you will have a much richer understanding of their circumstances, be able to relate to them much better, and almost certainly gain their appreciation as well.

Arrive Early to Work and Meetings. Make it a point to arrive at least 10 to 15 minutes early for work and meetings, and visit with people at that time. Similarly, *after* meetings or other more formal events, do not always rush back to your workspace. Linger occasionally and talk shop with people there. The casual time spent in informal contexts is often the easiest and most comfortable time to get to know people. If this feels like too great a loss of "productive" work time, remind yourself that time spent building relationships is perhaps the *most* productive of management work.

Regularly Talk a Little about Yourself. People are more willing to share their own journeys with someone who has proven willing to share a bit of his or her own. So let people know about your hobbies, kids, or pets. Having some understanding and connection to your life will empower people to open up about their own lives as well. Of course, be careful not to talk so much about yourself that you are perceived as self-involved and narcissistic.

Be Authentic, Do Not Fake It. Seek to learn about others with enthusiasm and a desire to know and get the best from them as they are, not as you would want them to be. Whatever you do, *do not fake it*. If you do not have some authentic curiosity and interest in others, you will have a difficult time building relationships.

Show Appreciation. Probably the easiest to do and yet most neglected tool for good relationships is more frequent use of the words "thank you." A lack of appreciation is the cause of innumerable relationship breakdowns, and appearing to have taken credit for others' work is among the surest way to sabotage relationships. It is easy to forget to show appreciation and just move on to the next challenge. But great managers know that appreciation is the lubricant of positive relationships and are obsessive about showing it to their people whenever they can.

So take the time to pass along credit and compliments to those who have made a contribution to your cause. Always speak well of your people and point out their accomplishments to any interested party.

Under-promise and Overdeliver. Especially for new managers, the innate desire to please and be liked, and to be viewed as top performing, often creates a pressure to overpromise. However, respect derives not from idealistic intentions—however noble—but from doing what you say you will do—when you say you will do it. Indeed, there are few relationship killers like un-met expectations. People can put up with a lot, provided they feel they are being told the truth and promises made are kept, even if they originally desired something more.

Great managers, therefore, are acutely aware of the importance of managing expectations. They also know the most raving fans and highest customer appreciation often stem from delivering *ahead* of promised commitments.[36] Since the same logically holds for personal relationships, you should aim to make only those commitments and promises and deadlines you can meet or exceed—and aim to restrict a very natural inclination to promise what you cannot deliver. It bears repeating—great managers under-promise and overdeliver!

Power Etiquette and First Impressions

For many of us, the terms manners and etiquette have a way of prompting thoughts of stuffy formal events and silly, outdated conventions. Yet an understanding of modern business etiquette simply enables you to conduct yourself with ease, style,

"Nothing great was ever accomplished without enthusiasm."

—Ralph Waldo Emerson

"The deepest principle in human nature is the desire to be appreciated."

—William James

"Losers make promises they often break. Winners make commitments they always keep."

—Denis Waitley

and confidence. Manners do not make you stuffy, obnoxious, or overly formal. They make you more comfortable in situations because you know exactly what to do. Indeed, as the family and social institutions that once taught manners decline in influence, a personal command of business etiquette is now one very good way to *set you apart* from others.

Of course, there are many written and unwritten rules and guidelines for etiquette and no possible way to know them all. Possibilities to commit a *faux pas* are limitless, and chances are, sooner or later, you'll make a mistake. But it is less important that you might use the wrong fork and more critical you have a polished introduction of yourself, can use and recall names with ease, and can convey the right impression with your dress and manners. In short, we labeled this section Power Etiquette because our focus is on just a few areas of etiquette we believe have direct and powerful impact on your success as a manager.

First Impressions and Introductions

It's often very difficult to overcome a poor first impression, regardless of your knowledge or expertise. So the first rule of management etiquette is to understand the power of that good first impression and to be sure to polish your approach. People make extraordinary assumptions about your professional credibility and potential performance based upon your appearance and behavior during your first meeting or meetings.

A variety of research studies support the power of first impressions, but we are particularly taken by one very simple investigation. In that study, participants were given a description of an individual with the following order of adjectives: *intelligent, industrious, impulsive, critical, stubborn, envious.* The researchers then gave the same description of this individual to other participants, but merely reversed the *order* of the adjectives to: *envious, stubborn, critical, impulsive, industrious, intelligent.* Both sets of participants rated how likely it would be they would be friends with the person. Those with the first order of description were significantly more likely to be friends than those given the second ordering—even though both descriptions had the exact same descriptors! When positive information is given first, people are more likely to ignore later negative information. First impressions are truly important and carry considerable weight.

> *"Manners open doors that power, position, and money cannot."*
>
> —Dana Casperson

Much of your first business impression will be based on elements such as handshake, introductions, and clothing. A handshake is almost always appropriate, so develop a good, firm handshake and make a practice of rising to shake hands with anyone who enters your office or room, whether male or female. You will also want to develop a ready and refined introduction.

The goal is to make a short but memorable impression. You should generally include some hint to help people remember you and to provide a tidbit of information to draw others into a conversation. Your self-introduction may vary according to the setting and the people you are meeting. A brief, finely-tuned introduction is particularly useful when networking, beginning a conversation, or meeting someone new.

Beyond your own introduction, it is also wise to increase your skill and comfort level at introducing *others*. It is all too common for young managers to overtly avoid introductions because they are uncomfortable with how best to do it. An introduction is a courtesy to help people feel more comfortable when they meet for the first time, and it is an opportune time to demonstrate your professional acumen. Of course, some people have a knack for bringing others together, and there clearly is an art to good introductions. However, introductions really are not hard to make if you follow three simple guidelines:

- Aim to help facilitate easy and comfortable conversation between the people by weaving in information regarding their backgrounds or accomplishments.

- Try to state each name at least a couple of times to give each the best chance of picking up on the name.
- In the business world, defer to office seniority and age (not gender or social standing). This means that you introduce the younger person to the older person, and not the other way around.

Learn and Use Names

It has often been said a person's name is to that person the sweetest and most important sound in any language. However, like many others, you may likely struggle to remember names or have even noted you are "bad with names." How many times have you met someone and five minutes later not remember that person's name? While remembering names in a general way is certainly a valuable social skill, it can be *vital* to a successful management career. Remembering names and faces is a priceless and rare quality—and thus a great competitive advantage in the workplace. (Remember how important scarcity can be in making it influential.)

"Of course I remember you. You're Parasaurolophus.
I always make a point to remember names."

Fortunately, remembering names is a skill accessible to all of us. But, like all the skills we discuss here, it takes willingness to invest oneself and discipline to consistently apply a few simple memory techniques. Perhaps the best memory framework is one used to dramatic effect by Benjamin Levy, a world-renowned magician and performer. As part of his act, Levy starts out his routine by asking every member of his audience (often well over 100 people) to state their name to him. He commits all those names to memory and then reveals those later in the performance. Levy's book describing his model was named as one of *Fortune* magazine's top 75 business books of the last 75 years. His model is appropriately abbreviated as FACE—focus, ask, comment, employ—and is described in more detail in Tool Kit 6.4.

Far too many managers, young and old, resort to the excuse they are "just not good with names." Discipline yourself to use the steps of FACE, and you will stand out as one of those magical people with a knack for names.

Building Your Social Network

Few great managers have ever achieved success on their own. Rather, they build and nurture a **social network** of people whom they can learn from, turn to for advice and support, and use as resources throughout their career. An important property of power is "the ability to mobilize resources to get things done," and social networks are immensely useful to that end.[37]

Fortunately, building a social network to enhance your power and influence is not a complex undertaking, but does take superior persistence, organization, and follow-up. A few simple steps can provide an excellent basis for building a good social network.

First, it is important to have a positive outlook on needing help and about soliciting support. Many people make the mistake of assuming that needing help is a sign of weakness. As a result, they do not reach out to others and thus fail to make important connections. The truth is most people you might seek for your network have been in similar places in their careers and will often gladly offer assistance whether it is arranging for personal introductions or providing advice and counsel. In general, all people like to feel needed, and involving them in your personal network is not likely to be an unwanted imposition. Just remember to "ask for a little," and it will often lead to much greater support.

Second, be sure to get beyond your organization and become active in industry or other professional events. Clubs and professional associations offer excellent ways to both add to your expertise and to meet others in your field of interest. Make it a point to meet and talk to at least a few new people each month, and don't forget to get business cards. Always follow up with the people you meet in a quick next-day e-mail. The goal is to make an impression so they will remember you the next time you contact them.

Third, to manage the contacts you have made, use a "black book," PDA, or some other organizer that includes the names and contact information for those in your network. There will come a time in your career when knowing these people will pay off (with a job lead, a recommendation, advice) so it is important

Management Live 6.3

"Old Girls Network" Helps Bring Young Women into Technology Jobs[38]

According to a report by the American Association for University Women Educational Foundation, the adventure games and programming challenges that attract young men to computers can serve to repel girls. In fact, most women enter information technology (IT) jobs via different paths than men, the report found.

Word of these differences has encouraged female "techies" to band together to help others break into the IT field. Networking groups are revolutionizing the way women learn new technical skills and ultimately find jobs. These groups are also reaching out to children who may have a knack for technology. A good example is Web Women, an online mailing list for women interested in Internet-related careers. They recently sponsored a Take Our Kids to the Web day.

According to Eve Simon, creative director at Interactive Applications Group, a Washington, D.C., firm that creates Web sites for foundations and nonprofits, "An old girls network is a really powerful tool." That notion gains support from D.C. area hiring managers who overwhelmingly say they prefer to bring on candidates who are referred by current employees. It is also supported by research conducted by professors at Stanford Business School into the hiring patterns and organizational structures of Silicon Valley technology companies.

Leslie Forte comments that, in her eight years in the IT field, she has endured countless slights, mostly from people who didn't think she fit the stereotype of an IT person. She balances the negatives with the acknowledgement she has benefited from her network of support, which has helped her move from the help desk, traditionally a low-status position in IT, into a manager's role. Forte's boss tells her she's been rewarded because she can work comfortably in the world of computer hardware and still display soft skills, like communication. "What you're going to need is people to communicate the technology and teach people how to use it to change their lives," she says, "and for that, you're going to need people who are good with other people."

to keep your contacts "fresh." Proactively seek reasons to contact the people in your network (acknowledge an event or recognition they received, briefly report on a personal accomplishment, give them some grief on a favorite sports team defeat) and send an occasional e-mail or make an occasional phone call so that your information is up-to-date and to make sure you are not forgotten.

Finally, perhaps the most important lesson is that, just as the key to making friends is to first *be a friend*, your network will only grow to the extent you give as much as you gain. So look for opportunities to meet with and support *others* in their work.

As evidence of just how important personal networks are to career success, consider a study conducted at a major consulting firm.[39] The study was designed to determine any distinctive characteristics of high performers in terms of individual expertise, technology use, and personal networks. Results indicated that neither level of expertise nor skilled technology use differentiated average performers from high performers. It was solely the presence of larger and more diversified personal networks that differentiated the top performers from the average and low performers. Despite such findings, many of us spend an exorbitant amount of time and effort building our technical abilities and almost no time or effort building and maintaining our personal networks. Do not fall prey to that trap. Dedicate yourself to building a personal network from today forward.

"You can't know it all. No matter how smart you are, no matter how comprehensive your education, no matter how wide ranging your experience, there is simply no way to acquire all the wisdom you need to make your business thrive."

—Donald Trump

Concluding Note

Power is not a dirty word but rather essential for great management. To be effective, managers need to go beyond their formal authority and understand those influence tactics—social, political and otherwise—that have been found to be most effective in gaining commitment. Professionalism is the source of trust and respect; it brings out the best in others and strengthens your reputation. However, like power and influence, it is also an area where blunders can be highly detrimental to a career. Skilled use of power, influence, and professionalism are hallmarks of all great managers.

Key Terms

authority	norms	social influence
coercive power	power	social influence weapons
conformity	power bases	social network
dependence	professionalism	strong ties
expert power	psychological reactance	weak ties
influence	referent power	
legitimate power	reward power	

Power and Influence Tool Kits

Tool Kit 6.1   Assessing the Power of Departments[40]

In some cases, you will need to be able to determine structural components of power. For most of us, realizing if our own department has power is important in addressing issues across the organization. Jeff Pfeffer, professor at Stanford University, provides some excellent guidance on how to recognize where power may reside in your company. To assess the relative standing of the power of various departments of an organization, consider the following indicators:

- Departmental representation in general management positions—what proportion of all top-level managers are from that department.
- Departmental representation on the board of directors.
- Salary of the executive in charge of each department.
- Starting salary offered to people in each department.
- For positions in common across departments (for example, secretaries), the salaries earned by people of comparable experience.
- Whether the department is located in the headquarters building.
- Where in the building the department is located, and what the average size of offices for people in the department is.
- Growth in personnel in each department in the recent past.
- How high in the organization the person to whom the department's head reports is.
- Representation of the department on important interdepartmental task forces, teams, and committees such as those involved in new product development, capital budgeting, and strategic planning.
- Rate of promotion for people in the department, compared to that in other units.
- Reputation for influence in the firm.
- Allocation of the budget.

Tool Kit 6.2   Diagnosing Patterns of Dependence and Interdependence

Dependence is fundamental to the concept of power. If you can understand the patterns of dependence in an organization, it can also help you understand and navigate the organization's political landscape. To diagnose interdependence, ask the following questions:

1. Whose cooperation will I need to accomplish what I am attempting?
2. Whose support will be necessary to get the appropriate decisions made and implemented?
3. Whose opposition could delay or derail what I am trying to do?
4. Who will be impacted by what I am trying to accomplish? More specifically, will anything change regarding (a) their power or status, (b) how they are evaluated or rewarded, or (c) how they do their job?
5. Who are the friends and allies of the people I have identified as influential?

Tool Kit 6.3   Guidelines for Managing by Walking Around (MBWA)

The following guidelines will help you practice managing by walking around (MBWA). This important tool can give you the opportunity to practice a large number of the influence tactics discussed in this chapter. If you are not interacting with others, it is very difficult to influence others!

1. Do it to everyone.
2. Do it as often as you can.
3. Go by yourself.
4. Ask a lot of open-ended questions.
5. Watch and listen everywhere you can.
6. Get your hands dirty by trying out their work.
7. Share your dreams and expectations with everyone.
8. Bring good news as often as possible.
9. Catch them in the act of doing something right.

Tool Kit 6.4   The FACE Technique for Remembering Names

- **Focus.** The first mistake most of us make is a failure to truly focus. When trying to remember a name, the first key is to intently lock in on the name at the first opportunity. The fleeting nature of most introductions contributes to lack of focus, and right there most of us begin to believe we have a bad memory for names. However, you remember your social security number and your locker number because you have to—you know you will have to call them up later. So the first objective of remembering a name is to recognize the critical importance of locking it in at the first opportunity. The moment will pass instantaneously so you have to target your attention intensely knowing that, like your locker number, you will need that name later.

- **Ask.** Ask to clarify that you have heard the name correctly. This gets you involved with the name and activates the memory process. A side benefit is it conveys to the other person you really care.

- **Comment.** Make some comment that will help cement the name in your memory. For example, "Shannon, am I right to conclude you have some Irish heritage?" Tie it to something familiar, a question, or something that will elicit a bit of further discussion. Doing that will help lock it into your memory.

- **Employ.** A terrific aid to memory is taking new material and teaching it to someone else. That is what happens when you introduce someone you've just met to someone else. It also gives you the opportunity to use the name again.

CHAPTER

7

Leadership

"On-field leadership is critical to the success of an NFL team, but we believe that leadership is equally important to the business side of our club. We need passionate people with the ability to energize others to accomplish very aggressive objectives. The young people who get hired by the Texans will be those who have demonstrated that they have the potential to lead others."

—Jamey Rootes, President, Houston Texans

Manage *What*?

1. Making the Transition to a Leadership Position

You have been working for four years in a bank branch located in the front section of a large grocery store. For the last two years, the branch has been underperforming and a poor place to work—tellers show up late, cash drawers are often out of balance, and the customer service numbers for your branch are in the bottom quarter when compared to other branches of your bank. As a result of these problems, the branch manager was removed from your branch. Today the regional manager has offered you the job on an interim basis. The terms of your job include a three-month trial period, and, if all goes well, you will be made the branch manager. You know that the problems in your branch stem in part from the lack of trust and respect for prior leadership in the branch. While you know the employees will be happy the old boss is gone, you are not sure how they will feel about your promotion to be their new manager.

So where would you begin? How would you go about building a solid foundation of trust in your leadership? How would you address the poor financial performance? Considering you were just recently a peer of your associates, and now their manager, would there be any critical things to do or not to do?

2. Adapting Your Leadership Style to the Situation

In your position as a project manager for a large construction project, you have noticed that treating everyone the same does not seem to be working. Specifically, you have two groups of employees who seem particularly unhappy. Your senior engineers act as if the time you spend with them is unappreciated and that you are smothering them. On the other hand, your new people in purchasing complain they do not have enough direction to do their jobs well. You know your engineers have the expertise to do their jobs and that the purchasing people are still unsure of themselves. What should you do? Is it right and fair to manage some associates and groups differently than others? On what basis should you decide how to manage different groups or individuals?

3. Leading People to Performance Beyond Expectations

After your first two years as manager of a local pizza franchise store, performance is in the upper third of all stores in the firm, turnover has been low, and you enjoy good relations with your employees. However, you want to be better than just good—you want your store to be seen as great! You currently have a capable workforce, even some seemingly interested in moving up in the company, but right now they seem relatively content to just keep doing what they are doing. For your own career progress you know that to really move up you will need to get your store to have higher performance and a more notable profile in the company. Your boss has assured you that if you are able to "do great things" with your store, there will be a wide variety of options open to you within the company. You like the company and believe your boss, but are struggling to determine how to get higher performance out of your people and further your own leadership plans.

What would you do to energize your employees to take it up a notch and perform above expectations? What do leaders that transform situations like this really do? Are there any common traps to avoid making the situation worse instead of better?

4. Developing Yourself as a Leader

Even though you have been moderately successful, you are not "coming along" in your career as quickly as either your boss or you had hoped. Two years ago, becoming the regional sales manager looked like it was about three years away. Now it seems like it could be five years away. You frequently overhear your boss and his boss saying, "we have plenty of good managers but few real leaders." The inference is you and your colleagues either do not have, or have not shown, "the right stuff" of leadership.

What does it mean to be a leader? Can it be learned? How might you demonstrate it for your superiors? What specific actions could you take that have been shown to help build real leadership capability?

LEARNING OBJECTIVES

1. Discuss how personal traits are related to leadership.
2. Describe the primary behaviors associated with leadership.
3. Assess a leadership situation, and determine what style is best suited to it.
4. Build a foundation for the leadership relation using transactional leadership.
5. Lead people to performance beyond expectations using transformational leadership.
6. Create a developmental plan to improve your leadership skills.

Introduction

Leadership is perhaps the most important, yet most misunderstood, topic in all of management. The concepts of "leader" and "leadership" have been around for literally thousands of years (there are even Egyptian hieroglyphs associated with them),[1] and yet perceptions vary widely regarding what leadership is and how it can best be developed. The focus of this chapter is on the wide range of competencies related to leadership effectiveness. In our view, leadership is not genetic or a mysterious gift bestowed on just a few. It is not just one thing but a comprehensive *set* of personal characteristics, skills, and behaviors that can be learned (some are more amenable to learning than others) by anyone with the desire to do so. Consistent with our book title, the question is "What do those managers who are great leaders know and do?"

Of the many definitions of leadership, we tend to like Churchill's concise notion that "Leadership is taking people in a direction they would not otherwise go." That is, **leadership** is the ability to influence people to set aside their personal concerns and support a larger agenda—at least for a while. The most effective leaders motivate people to perform above and beyond the call of duty, and enhance group success. Leadership effectiveness is not simply who exerts the most influence or emerges to control the group, but who can achieve high group performance over time.

A great deal of attention has been devoted to the distinction between leadership and management. Leadership is generally distinguished by the necessity of followers (people) and as an influence process that takes people beyond the status quo. Leadership author Warren Bennis suggests that management is getting people to do what needs to be done, while leadership is getting people to want to go beyond what needs to be done. The most critical point, however, is that both management and leadership are important. Being a good manager won't guarantee good leadership, just as being a leader doesn't guarantee good management. Indeed, several of the most influential leadership authors summarize the relationship between leaders and managers as "leaders manage and managers lead, but the activities are not synonymous."[2] The challenge is to combine strong leadership and strong management and use each to complement the other.

"The only real test of leadership is that somebody follows."
—Robert Greenleaf

"Projects, budgets, and facilities can be managed. People need to be led."
—Ross Perot

"Leadership is like beauty; it's hard to define, but you know it when you see it."
—Warren Bennis

Leadership Matters

Leadership development has become a multibillion-dollar industry in the United States, and the amount of attention being paid to leaders and leadership has exploded in other parts of the world as well. Leadership is hugely consequential for the success of organizations and the well-being of employees and citizens. Leadership has been linked to a wide variety of important outcomes including employee satisfaction, teamwork, and financial performance.[3] Increasing evidence even suggests effective leadership is one of the best sources of sustainable competitive advantage an organization can have over its competitors.[4]

Effective leadership makes great things happen. Indeed, the most important achievements of humankind are associated with people who influenced others to achieve more than they thought was possible. On the other hand, the lack of inspired leadership has probably been responsible for more failed careers and unhappy employees than any other cause.

One interesting indication of the popularity of leadership today is that a quick search on online bookseller Amazon.com reveals well over 16,000 books currently available on the topic.[5] Just for fun, we went ahead and playfully categorized some of those many books in Management Live 7.1.

In reviewing the extraordinary range of publications on leadership, two observations stand out. First, leadership clearly matters and people are eager for ways to learn about how to more effectively lead and improve their groups and organizations. Second, the multitude of lists, models, laws, and so on make it hard to know what is really associated with leadership effectiveness and supported by more than just opinion. In this chapter, we use the best evidence available to provide guidance regarding the essential conditions and leader behaviors associated with leadership effectiveness.

As noted, leadership is an area where there is a great deal of misinformation, and myths abound. Myths 7.1 identifies a few of the most common of leadership myths. A first step toward understanding effective leadership is to first understand what is *not* true.

"The question, who ought to be boss? is like asking, 'Who ought to be the tenor in the quartet?' Obviously, the man who can sing tenor."

—Henry Ford

LEADERSHIP

Management Live 7.1

Categorizing the Vast Array of Leadership Books

To help navigate the great number of books on leadership, we thought that providing a classification of these books would be illustrative. While this is presented largely in fun, it does show the extremely broad range of books available. It also demonstrates the intense demand for leadership knowledge.

Numbers:
- Executive Charisma: Six Steps to Mastering the Art of Leadership
- Leadership Wisdom from the Monk Who Sold His Ferrari: The 8 Rituals of Visionary Leaders
- Leading Every Day: 124 Actions for Effective Leadership
- Taking Charge: 236 Proven Principles of Effective Leadership
- The Empowered Leader: 10 Keys to Servant Leadership

CEOs
We determined this category was way too large, so we just include a small sample of Jack Welch books here!
- *29 Leadership Secrets from Jack Welch
- Get Better or Get Beaten!: 31 Leadership Secrets from GE's Jack Welch
- Jack Welch and the 4 E's of Leadership
- Jack: Straight from the Gut
- The Welch Way: 24 Lessons from the World's Greatest CEO

Laws
These can also be considered a subset of the numbers category.
- The 21 Irrefutable Laws of Leadership
- The 9 Natural Laws of Leadership
- The Stuff of Heroes: The Eight Universal Laws of Leadership

Presidents of the United States
- Cigars, Whiskey and Winning: Leadership Lessons from Ulysses S. Grant
- John F. Kennedy on Leadership: The Lessons and Legacy of a President
- Lincoln on Leadership: Executive Strategies for Tough Times
- Reagan on Leadership: Executive Lessons from the Great Communicator

Religion and Spirituality
- Dynamic Spiritual Leadership: Leading Like Paul
- Leadership Prayers
- The Maxwell Leadership Bible: Lessons in Leadership from the Word of God
- They Smell Like Sheep: Spiritual Leadership for the 21st Century

Secrets
- Leadership Secrets of Jesus
- The Leadership Secrets of Billy Graham
- The Leadership Secrets of Colin Powell
- The Leadership Secrets of Santa Claus

* Denotes the winning book. This falls into the numbers, secrets, and Jack Welch categories all in one brief title.

Note: The book's authors are working on a book titled "The 12 Secret Laws of Millard Fillmore's Spiritual Army (with a forward by Jack Welch.)" We have high hopes for it!

The Full Range of Leadership

As presented in Myths 7.1, one persistent misnomer in casual discussions of leadership is that effective leadership is comprised of just *one* general skill or competency. This gives rise to questions of whether leadership can really be taught. Of course, some personal characteristics like integrity and decisiveness are not particularly amenable to change. However, leadership is multidimensional (not just personal characteristics) and many interpersonal and organizational leadership skills—such as diagnosing followers, tying rewards to performance, and creating collective goals—are certainly amenable to teaching and learning. With that in mind, we think it is most useful to address a wide variety of leadership competencies.

With respect to personal characteristics, the action focus is mostly on understanding the personal traits of importance and becoming more self-aware about your own personal profile so you can adapt when necessary and put yourself in positions where you are most likely to succeed. With respect to behavior, the key is to learn and practice those *behaviors* that promote positive transactions and transform people to go above expectations (See Management Live 7.2, for a simple but powerful example.)

Consistent with the theme of this book, and the goals of this chapter, we are presenting what research and practice have found to be the most straightforward, and up-to-date approach for understanding and practicing effective leadership. Although some of the ideas have been researched for over fifty years, the overall approach has been developed over the last fifteen years and has enjoyed both research support and success in practical application. When asked how to guide a person in a management position towards "what to do" to be successful, the combination of building a solid foundation and then focusing upon more advanced leadership behaviors offers the most solid, research-backed, behavioral prescriptions. This combination is broadly referred to as the **Full Range of Leadership Approach.**[7] In order to describe this full range approach, we begin by addressing personal characteristics and transactional leader behaviors. The remainder of the chapter is devoted to learning transformational leader behaviors.

MYTHS 7.1   Leadership Myths

Leaders are born, not made. Leadership is multidimensional and consists of a range of skills, competencies, and behaviors. Genetics play some role, of course, but mostly in terms of personal traits and what makes someone *emerge* as a leader or gain the admiration and respect of followers. Ultimate leadership effectiveness is almost exclusively related to leader behaviors (what leaders do) and those behaviors are generally learnable.

Leaders must be charismatic. While some great leaders are exceptionally charismatic, a large number of others are not. Charisma is often problematic because two people may observe the same person and disagree as to whether he or she is charismatic. Also, charisma may be helpful or harmful, depending on the situation, and charisma is certainly not a necessary condition for effective leadership.

Leadership exists only at the top. Even though we are all familiar with the names of celebrity CEOs and businesspeople (such as Bill Gates or Jack Welch), effective leadership is demonstrated by scores of people whose names you have never heard. Effective leadership can be found at all organizational levels and is *everyone's* business.

Leadership incompetence results from too little of "the right stuff." An emerging body of evidence suggests leadership failure is more related to having undesirable qualities and exhibiting toxic behaviors than it is lacking desirable ones. Sometimes having *the wrong stuff* can be just as detrimental as any right stuff we may be lacking.[6]

Personal Characteristics of Leaders

Many popular books on leadership make it sound like there is a small set of leadership traits (such as honesty, charisma, extraversion) that make a person into a successful leader. If only it were that easy. This is not to say, however, that a person's traits do not matter in the leadership process—they do. They just do not matter in the way most people think.

Early leadership research looked at successful leaders in detail to see how they differed from people who were not leaders. This early approach (circa 1850) became known as the Great Man theory of leadership[8] (there was no thought of women leading in those days) and was based on the premise that leaders were both more capable and possessed a different set of traits than followers.[9] In other words, leaders are born, not made. Interestingly, this approach was popularized by Sir Francis Galton, Charles Darwin's cousin. Today, this approach remains quite popular and implies that a particular set of traits offers some magic formula of success. This viewpoint can be seen in the titles of many popular books on leadership, which purport to have identified a set number of traits to successful leadership.

"As a young marine I learned firsthand that leaders are not born, they are made. Anyone can become a stronger leader. It's your character and abilities that make you a leader, not your job title."

—Courtney Lynch, organizational consultant

Important Personal Traits in Leadership

The evidence regarding traits is a bit more complex than those book titles suggest. While it is true that leadership is in part who you are, scientific reviews of the Great Man theory indicate traits alone won't guarantee effective leadership; rather, it's what people do with those traits that matters most. Traits are, however, good predictors of **leadership emergence,** rather than leadership *effectiveness*. In

Management Live 7.2

R. Seshasayee of Ashok Leyland

As managing director of Ashok Leyland, a leading transportation company in India whose buses carry 70 million people a day, R. Seshasayee was faced with reinvigorating the company to restore its performance after a few down years. An interview with Seshasayee suggests leadership in an Indian transportation company requires many of the same abilities as it does anywhere else in the world, or in most any workplace situation.

Seshasayee asserts, "Outstanding leaders are those who set audacious objectives and get people to own and achieve them." He continues by suggesting that leadership requires three essentials:

> [First is] setting a goal which seems impossible or needs a fundamental leap; second is to communicate to people and inspire them that the task is not so daunting; and the third is to be a living example of what can be done so that followers can refer to the leader's life and his actions and see the way to behave in given circumstances.

The leadership practices of Seshasayee go beyond the "big picture" issues described above. One of his favorite practices is to use small notes as motivational tools. He describes a habit of using pink notes as recognition tools.

> There was this employee who wrote a good report on something. I sent him a note saying that it was a 'great delight to read this report. Good show.' Later, this person left us and went to West Asia. Many years later, I ran into him in an airport and after chatting with him, he brought out his wallet and showed me the pink slip—he had preserved it all those years! The message is that little things can have a tremendous impact on people. The basic issue is to be able to relate to and touch people.

Source: Kamath, V. (2002). Leadership Has to Touch People, *Praxis 3* (4), 22–27.

other words, a set of traits has been found to be important in influencing others' *perceptions* of leadership. That is, people who possess certain traits may be more likely to be perceived as a leader by others, but these people are no more likely to be effective in a managerial role. Possession of these traits, however, seems to be linked to who will ultimately attain a managerial role and who will not.

More specifically, the personal traits of intelligence, dominance, sociability, self-monitoring, having high energy or drive, self-confidence, and a tolerance for ambiguity all do a reasonable job of predicting who will rise to the assigned position of leader. In looking at this list, these findings appear to be quite reasonable. For example, would you think a person who was bright, self-confident, had a high energy level, and so on, would be more likely to both want and be granted a management position than their counterparts (people who are not particularly intelligent, lack self-confidence, are socially passive, etc.)? This does not seem provocative in any way. What is more surprising to most people is these characteristics do not make a person noticeably more likely to be an effective leader once they reach a managerial position.

> "There are many qualities that make a great leader. But having strong beliefs, being able to stick with them through popular and unpopular times, is the most important characteristic of a great leader."
>
> —Rudy Giuliani

Characteristics that People Admire

An additional way of looking at leadership traits is to examine the personal characteristics that people admire in their leaders. Although this approach may be somewhat problematic because it is not linked to whether the person is actually effective or not, it can still be useful so we better understand what people are looking for in their leaders. We should also remember that many people who have these desireable traits might not be leaders at all. (See Management Live 7.3 for a somewhat surprising characteristic associated with success.)

Management Live 7.3

Death as a Characteristic of an Effective Leader?

On November 7, 2000, Melvin (Mel) Carnahan was elected to the U.S. Senate as a senator from Missouri. Mel Carnahan had been in a close race with John Ashcroft (who later was named the Attorney General of the United States) and trailed by several percentage points in polls taken about two months before the election. During the last few months, however, Carnahan put on a surge and ultimately beat out Ashcroft for the Senate seat. What was Carnahan's political strategy? What did Carnahan do to overcome his opponent's lead? Well, Mel Carnahan died in a tragic plane crash just three weeks prior to the election.

Scott Allison and Dafna Eylon of the University of Richmond have been researching just how such an odd turn of events can happen.[10] In laboratory experiments, Allison and Eylon presented study participants with a written description of a man named Erick Sullivan. After providing a list of impressive accomplishments relating to Erik's role in building a successful company, the researchers manipulated one important piece of information and had half of the people respond to each story. In one situation, Erik died years after he retired, and in the other case, Erik was still alive. The results of this study showed that people formed significantly more favorable impressions of Erik Sullivan when they believed he was dead than when they believed he was alive.

Allison and Eylon use the term "death positivity bias" as the inflation in ratings associated with a person's death. The authors suggest a few different explanations of the effect may be relevant. First, the social norm of respecting the dead is very strong in most cultures. Another explanation for the death positivity bias comes from commodity theory, which posits that any commodity's value increases to the extent it is no longer available. Since the death of a person is clearly an example where the person's leadership is no longer available, others may value it more highly. Perhaps most importantly, these findings illustrate the often unreliable and biased nature of trait perceptions.

Leadership authors Jim Kouzes and Barry Posner[11] started with a simple idea: They surveyed business and government executives all over the world and asked them, "What values (personal traits or characteristics) do you look for and admire in your superiors?" They have had more than 20,000 people on four continents respond. From those responses, they developed a list of 20 characteristics. The top 4 characteristics (all supported by more than 50 percent of the respondents) were:

- honest
- forward-looking
- inspiring
- competent

For students, the evidence on leadership traits and leadership emergence offers some important lessons. First, this is a prime example of the inaccuracy of common sense, in that commonly understood leadership traits are not always good predictors of leadership effectiveness. Second, it suggests a wonderful diversity in the types of people who have the propensity to be effective leaders. Third, traits that people often associate with successful leaders (self-confidence) may just end up being biases or errors people make when they are evaluating others. For instance, how many times do you think someone doesn't get a leadership position because they didn't "look or act" like a leader in a job interview? How much real leadership talent goes unrecognized because it is hidden in "packages" that do not fit most people's stereotypes of what makes an effective leader? Great managers are able to show people they have what it takes even when they do not fit the preconceived mold. And the best way to accomplish this is to *behave* as an effective leader – the topic of the remainder of this chapter.

> "Common sense is the collection of prejudices acquired by age eighteen."
>
> —Albert Einstein

Transactional Leadership

Now that you have a better understanding of the role that personal characteristics play in the leadership equation, the foundation-forming leadership behaviors need to be addressed. In the final analysis, the evidence is clear that great leadership is more about what one *does* than who one *is*. And research has shown that the basic "doing" of effective leadership involves two primary behaviors: (1) behaviors that focus on the task at hand and (2) behaviors that focus on the relationship between leader and follower. In other words, leadership involves influencing people to attain goals not just by giving them directives (task behaviors) but also by supporting the employee (relationship behaviors). Though the behaviors we discuss will be a bit more complex, the foundation of great leadership is built on these two areas of leader behavior.[12]

Understanding the Situation and Adapting

To begin our discussion of effective leadership behavior, we start with the most basic tool in a leader's toolbox—**situational leadership**.[13] What most aspiring leaders struggle with early in their leadership development is the difficult task of gauging what people need at any given time. For example,

"The beaver is very skilled at its craft. It knows exactly what to do to fix a dam. The last thing it needs is someone on the bank shouting out dam instructions."

—Grant Bright (based on "Gung Ho!" by Ken Blanchard)

some employees need a great deal of direction (say, an employee new to his career and industry), while others require little direction but more support (a seasoned accountant new to the company). In other words, situational leadership realizes that leading a group of highly motivated people with an average of 25 years of experience likely calls for a different approach than does a group of new hires unsure of what they are supposed to be doing. Understanding what employees need and adapting your style to fit those needs is the most basic of leadership skills.

To use the situational leadership approach, just a few central concepts and ideas are important. Those ideas include understanding (1) the difference between directive and supportive behavior, (2) how those two different types of leader behavior combine to form four different leadership styles, (3) the four potential developmental levels of followers, and (4) how to match style to the developmental level of your employees.

Directive and Supportive Behaviors

Directive behavior is defined as the extent to which a leader engages in one-way communication; spells out the follower(s) role and tells the follower(s) what to do where, when, and how; and then closely supervises performance. Three words can be used to define directive behavior: structure, control, and supervise. **Supportive behavior,** on the other hand, is defined as the extent to which a leader engages in two-way communication, listens, provides support and encouragement, facilitates interaction, and involves the follower(s) in decision-making. Three words can be used to define supportive behavior: praise, listen, and facilitate. Situational leadership utilizes four behavioral styles based on the different combinations of directive and supportive behavior (see Figure 7.1).

"Visibility is incredibly important. It's very hard to lead through e-mails."

—Bill Zollars, CEO, Yellow Roadway

The Four Behavioral Styles of Situational Leadership

High directive/low supportive leader behavior (S1) is referred to as **directing.** In the directing style the leader defines the roles of followers and tells them

FIGURE 7.1

Situational Leadership: The Four Leadership Styles

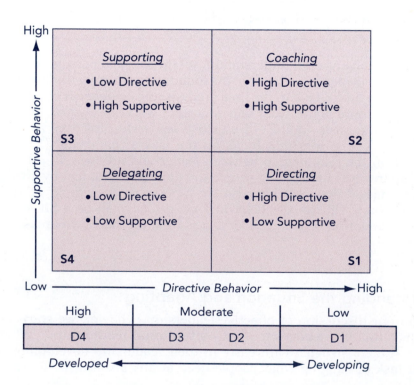

what, how, when, and where to do various tasks. Problem solving and decision-making are initiated solely by the manager. Solutions and decisions are announced, communication is largely one-way, and the leader closely supervises implementation.

High directive/high supportive behavior (S2) is referred to as **coaching.** In this style the leader still provides a great deal of direction and leads with his or her ideas, but also attempts to hear the followers' feelings about decisions as well as their ideas and suggestions. While two-way communication and support are increased, control over decision-making remains with the leader.

High supportive/low directive leader behavior (S3) is called **supporting.** In this style the control of day-to-day decision-making and problem solving shifts from leader to follower. The leader's role is to provide recognition and to actively listen and facilitate problem solving/decision-making on the part of the follower.

Low supportive/low directive leader behavior (S4) is labeled **delegating.** In this style the leader discusses the problems with subordinates until joint agreement is achieved on problem definition and then the decision-making process is delegated totally to the followers.

Using the Four Behavioral Styles

To effectively use the four styles associated with situational leadership, successful leaders recognize there is no best way and that they need to adapt their style to fit the requirements of the situation. In situational leadership, the development level of the followers is the factor that determines which of the four styles should be used. Development level is defined as the *competence* and *commitment* of your follower(s)—to perform a particular task without supervision. We use the word *competence* rather than ability because people often use ability to mean potential. They talk about natural ability to describe skills a person is born with. Competence, on the other hand, can be developed with appropriate direction and support. It is a function of knowledge or skills that can be gained from education, training, or experience. It is not something you innately have or don't have.

The Four Development Levels of Followers

Using the situational leadership model (Figure 7.1), we can identify four employee development levels: low (D1), low to moderate (D2), moderate to high (D3), and high (D4). Each of these development levels represents a different combination of competence and commitment as illustrated in Figure 7.2.

As the development level of individuals increase from D1 to D4, their competence and commitment fluctuates. When first beginning a new task where they have had little, if any, prior knowledge or experience, most individuals are enthusiastic and ready to learn (D1). Then when they begin to get into the task, individuals often find it is either more difficult to learn to perform the task than they expected or less interesting than anticipated. This disillusionment decreases their commitment (D2). If they overcome this state of development and learn to

FIGURE 7.2   The Development Levels of Situational Leadership

High Competence * High Commitment	High Competence * Variable Commitment	Some Competence * Low Commitment	Low Competence * High Commitment
D4	D3	D2	D1

Developed ◄ .... Developing

perform the task with help from their boss, most individuals then go through a self-doubt stage where they question whether they can perform the task well *on their own*. Their boss says they're competent, but they're not so sure. These alternating feelings of competence and self-doubt cause the variable commitment associated with the D3 level—commitment that fluctuates from excitement to insecurity. With proper support, individuals can eventually become peak performers who demonstrate a high level of competence and confidence (D4). In other words, given the appropriate amounts of direction and support, individuals move from one level of development to another, from being an enthusiastic beginner, to a disillusioned learner, to a reluctant contributor, to a peak performer.

When considering someone's development level, remember that people are never "fully developed" or "underdeveloped." In other words, development level is not a *global concept;* it is a *task-specific concept*. Thus the same person could be at different levels of development depending on the specific task, function, or objective he or she is assigned.

To determine the appropriate leadership style to use with each of the four development levels, match the development level to the leadership style (see again Figure 7.1). As a result, development level D1 would get a *Directing* S1 leadership style. Development level D2 would get a *high directive and supportive Coaching* S2 leadership style, and so on. Practice diagnosing the situation and applying the appropriate leader behavior. No leader will be successful without first recognizing that his or her leadership situation may require different approaches for different people.

Leading through Transactions

Few people are willing to be influenced by someone whom they do not trust or believe does not have their best interest at heart. **Transactional leadership** serves to build these important influence components. Transactional leader behavior represents an exchange, or a transaction, between the leader and follower. This exchange pursues a cost-benefit, or economic exchange strategy, whereby the leader exchanges rewards and treatment for desirable services (performance, effort, participation) from the subordinate.

These transactional leadership behaviors are important because they provide a solid foundation for the relationship between the employee and manager, and great managers realize the employee-manager relationship is the most important relationship to get right. There are numerous benefits—to employee, manager, and organization—of having a positive, constructive relationship between employee and manager, commonly referred to as the **leader-member exchange.**[14] More specifically, strong leader-employee relationships have been linked to increased employee citizenship behavior, higher employee performance ratings, increased employee satisfaction, reduced employee turnover, and a host of other positive consequences.[15]

"Your job gives you authority. Your behavior gives you respect."

—Irwin Ferderman, CEO, Monolithic Memories

Transactional Leader Behaviors

Although numerous behaviors can be considered **transactional leader behaviors,** Bernard Bass, the major contributor to the transactional leadership approach, suggests that management-by-exception (putting out fires and taking corrective action when problems occur) and **contingent reward behavior** (rewarding an employee for doing a good job) are two of the most effective transactional leader behaviors. Many people have made the parallel that management-by-exception is generally consistent with the idea of **contingent punishment**—providing an aversive consequence to reduce the frequency of a behavior.[16]

Of these two main transactional leader behaviors, research has shown contingent reward behavior consistently results in positive consequences in both employee attitudes (job satisfaction, organizational commitment) and employee behaviors (job performance, organizational citizenship).[17] Management Live 7.4 shows an interesting example of contingent reward behavior in action. Contingent reward is an essential part of effective leadership because it accomplishes the important goal of linking performance and rewards for the employee (see discussion of positive reinforcement in Chapter 4). This linkage is important because contingent rewards serve as a feedback loop that provides learning for both the employee and the organization as a whole. Thus, employees learn to see a positive relationship between what they're doing right and the rewards they receive. In most organizations, leaders control the available rewards to some extent. Since rewards are a powerful tool for showing employees what the leader desires, the use of contingent reward behavior may have important consequences for the company's overall culture, performance, and, ultimately, its long-term survival.

"A pat on the back is only a few vertebrae removed from a kick in the pants, but is miles ahead in results."

—W. Wilcox

The Role of Transactional Leader Behaviors

Transactional behaviors play an important role in effective leadership in at least three ways. First, as we have stated, they establish credibility, trust, and respect for one's manager. When a manager makes promises and more importantly keeps those promises, an employee learns to trust what his manager says. Second, transactional behaviors form the foundation upon which other effective behaviors are built. As we will see, without a trusting relationship, few employees will take a manager seriously—a critical requirement for more advanced leader behaviors. Third, transactional behaviors establish fairness in the workplace. For example, when expectations are not being met (poor performance, unsafe practices and so on), addressing the problem quickly and fairly is vital to establishing and maintaining a sense of fairness among employees. To ensure that sense of fairness, great managers need to sometimes use management-by-exception, or contingent punishment.

"Leadership without mutual trust is a contradiction in terms."

—Warren Bennis

In a plant where one of this book's authors has conducted a great deal of training, a member of a generally well-performing group engaged in some potentially dangerous behavior while driving a forklift (chasing another person and encouraging other forklift drivers to race). In this case, many managers make

Management Live 7.4

It Works for Shamu, Why Not You?

Have you ever wondered how they train killer whales to jump over a rope at Sea World and other amusement parks? Or for that matter, how they train dolphins to walk on the water and wave to the audience? Do you think they hang a rope 20 feet over the pool and then shout to the whale, "Up, up, up!" Of course not, but that is exactly how many ineffective managers treat their employees.

The way Shamu (world's most famous killer whale) and fellow killer whales are actually trained to jump over a rope is by starting the learning process with the rope *under* the water. When the whale swims over the rope, it gets rewarded. Then the rope is gradually raised. Each time the whale swims over it again, a reward is given. This continues until the whale is leaping out of the water! Now think how often managers give a reward only when the final goal is reached. Would it be more effective to provide rewards along the way as well? The killer whales seem to think so—and by the way, so do people!

a fundamental error; they ignore the behavior and say, "Overall, he is a good guy. I don't think he will do those things again."

This type of wishful thinking on the part of the manager presents a two-fold problem. It sends a message to the employee that this type of behavior is acceptable—maybe not desirable, but acceptable nonetheless. Second, and more problematic, it can also send a message to others that the workplace is not fair ("He gets away with these things because the supervisor likes him. If I did that, I'd be fired."). In this case, however, the manager called the employee in, had a brief discussion where the rules for effective negative feedback were followed well, and the behavior did not recur. More importantly, the employee understood why the behavior was reckless and others knew the issue had been handled fairly. Thus, great managers intervene early and correct problems before they become too large to handle.

When leaders perform these transactional leader behaviors well, they provide themselves with an excellent foundation. At this point, basic performance issues are addressed, relationships should be positive and productive, and employees have a sense they are being treated fairly. Great managers, however, know that what differentiates them from the rest of the pack is the ability to get people to go above and beyond expectations. In other words, it is not about getting people to do the minimum that is expected of them, it is about getting people to exceed expectations. To motivate their people to do this, great managers know people need to be able to change quickly, adapt to new demands, and seek out new challenges. Transactional leader behaviors are the way to build a solid foundation, but they will not deliver performance beyond typical expectations. Once transactional leader behaviors have established a solid foundation through transactional leadership behaviors, great managers use transformational leader behaviors to get their employees to go beyond the call.

> *"No one enjoys addressing others' deficiencies. But failure to do so sends the message that people are on track when they really aren't. And that may be the greatest disservice a leader can do to someone else."*
>
> —Eric Harvey

Transformational Leadership: Getting Performance Beyond Expectations

"We just haven't been flapping them hard enough."

Once a solid foundation has been established, **transformational leader behaviors** "seek to arouse and satisfy higher needs, to engage the full person of the follower."[18] Transformational leader behaviors engage the whole person by asking followers to transcend their self-interest for the sake of the team or organization and by raising employee awareness about the importance and values of goals. It should be noted that many different researchers have derived behaviors consistent with Bass's definition of transformational leader behavior. The content of these different models, however, are actually quite similar. Professor Phil Podsakoff and his colleagues at Indiana University noted this similarity and presented a model of six transformational leader behaviors that do a good job of synthesizing the different transformational leadership models:[19]

"You do not need leadership to eat a warm cookie."

—Scott Adams

- **Articulating a Vision.** Behavior that allows the leader to identify new opportunities for his or her group and talk positively about what that means for them.
- **Providing an Appropriate Model.** Behavior on the part of the leader that sets an example for employees to follow that is consistent with the values the leader espouses.
- **Fostering the Acceptance of Group Goals.** Behavior on the part of the leader aimed at promoting cooperation among employees and getting them to work together toward a common goal.
- **Communicating High Performance Expectations.** Behavior that demonstrates the leader's expectations for excellence, quality, and high performance on the part of followers.
- **Providing Individualized Support.** Behavior that indicates the leader respects followers and is concerned about their personal feelings and needs.
- **Providing Intellectual Stimulation.** Behavior on the part of the leader that challenges followers to re-examine assumptions about their work and rethink how it can be performed.

Transformational leadership was once thought to be a heroic type of leadership performed only by gifted people at the top of organizations. Twenty years of research, however, now suggests it is not restricted to any particular function, managerial level, or type of organization. Most importantly, the six major behaviors above appear to be quite amenable to learning. All of this is good news when you consider the great benefits that follow from engaging in these six transformational leadership behaviors.

For example, in a study of 1,539 people, Podsakoff and his colleagues found the six transformational leader behaviors were associated with increased employee satisfaction, employee trust in their leader, and job performance (Figure 7.3).[20] Figure 7.3 shows that transformational leader behaviors are not just "nice to do" but have been shown to significantly work outcomes that matters! Other research has shown the effectiveness of transformational leadership in all sorts of industries and organizations. Here is just a sampling of that research:

- Methodist ministers rated high in transformational leadership had greater Sunday church attendance and membership growth.[21]
- In multiple banks, financial performance and commitment increased for 20 managers trained in transformational leadership versus the performance of a group of managers who did not receive the training.[22]
- German bank unit performance was higher in banks led by transformational leaders.[23]
- Sales managers who used transformational leadership behavior had sales representatives that had increased sales performance.[24]

Average Correlations between Transformational Leader Behaviors and Satisfaction, Trust, and Job Performance[25]

In other words, when leaders engage in transformational leadership behaviors, employees are more satisfied, more optimistic about the future, less likely to leave their jobs, more likely to trust their leader, and perform higher than employees who work for leaders who do not display these key behaviors.

As we noted, an important consequence of performing transformational leadership is that followers tend to give their transformational leader extra effort or performance beyond stated expectations. This extra effort comes in many forms, one of which has been termed **organizational citizenship behavior (OCB).** These are discretionary behaviors (not required to perform one's job) that are beneficial to the organization but not explicitly recognized by the formal reward system. Leading OCB author, Dennis Organ, conceptualized the ideas behind OCB and asserted that, overall, OCBs "promote the effective functioning of the organization" – and it is easy to see why.

Imagine your co-worker is having a problem with his computer and is becoming increasingly frustrated. Do you offer to try to help him or, knowing that it's not really your job to deal with computer problems, let him figure it out on his own? Helping your co-worker is an example of an OCB; you are certainly not required to help, but doing so increases the likelihood he will be productive and your manager will be happy you pitched in. In Table 7.1, we describe the various types of OCBs that employees exhibit, particularly when a leader engages in transformational leadership behavior.

Articulating a Vision

Articulating a vision has long been recognized as an important leadership behavior. Podsakoff and his colleagues defined the behavior as being aimed at "identifying new opportunities for his or her unit and developing, articulating, and inspiring others with his or her vision of the future." While the ability to develop a vision that will capture people's hearts and minds may be beyond our scope here, the ability to communicate such a vision is exactly what research evidence suggests you can be taught.[26] More specifically, to increase your ability to articulate a vision you should:

1. Repeat the vision often.
2. Explain the significance of the vision.

"Our vision is to create the world's most competitive enterprise."

—Jack Welch, former CEO of General Electric

TABLE 7.1 | Organizational Citizenship Behaviors (OCBs)

Altruism. Behaviors that have the effect of helping a specific other person with an organizationally relevant task or problem.

Civic Virtue. Behaviors regarding responsible participation in the political life of the organization. Dennis Organ explains that civic virtue "implies a sense of involvement in what policies are adopted and which candidates are supported. Behaviorally, civic virtue takes such mundane forms as attending meetings, reading mail, discussing issues on personal time, voting, and 'speaking up'."[27]

Conscientiousness. Employee behavior that goes well beyond the organization's role requirements, in the areas of attendance, taking breaks, and obeying organizational policies.

Courtesy. Actions such as touching base with those parties whose work would be affected by one's decisions or commitments. Providing advance notice, reminders, and passing along information are all examples of courtesy.

Sportsmanship. Behavior indicating an individual's willingness to tolerate less-than-ideal situations by not filing petty grievances or complaining about minor issues. An employee who exhibits sportsmanship behavior can be described as being a good sport.

3. Appeal to your audience's values.
4. Use metaphors.
5. Use emotional appeals.
6. Speak in positive terms.
7. Use the term "we" instead of "I."

Additional research suggests effective visions should be appropriate for the level of the employee to which they are being communicated and that they should not contradict higher level visions. In other words, when a first-line supervisor communicates a vision to her work team, it should be put into different terms than how the CEO originally presented the company's vision, but also should not work against it. For example, the vision that Jack Welch presented for General Electric—"to create the world's most competitive enterprise"—would need to be converted into action by the lower levels of the organization. In this case, a lower level maintenance supervisor may have presented the vision to his employees as "We need to constantly maximize our machine uptime if we are going to make this place as competitive as it can be."

Great managers also realize visions need to be described in future terms and be short. The best visions tend to lend themselves to creating a mental image in the mind of those who hear it. The mental image helps create enthusiasm and assists in directing the day-to-day actions of the group. Please see Tool Kit 7.3 for more ways to effectively calculate a vision.

Some additional specific techniques for effectively articulating a vision on the job include:

- Create a positive picture of the future for the work group.
- Stand up for what is important.
- Adjust plans and action as necessary in dynamic situations.
- Communicate the strategy of the organization as a whole and make sure your actions are in concert with that overall strategy.
- Involve the right people in developing the strategy for your area.

"I remember sitting in the audience at a meeting where Jack (Welch) said GE would be the No. 1 market-cap company in the world. This was at a time when IBM seemed untouchable. I thought to myself, 'I don't know if that was brave or delusional, but I will sign up for that.'"

—Kevin Sharer, CEO
Amgen

"You can only lead where you yourself are willing to go."

—Lachlan McLean

"Leaders need to be optimists. Their vision is beyond the present."

—Rudy Giuliani

Providing an Appropriate Model

Providing an appropriate model is leader behavior that sets an example for employees to follow that is consistent with values the leader and the organization espouses. Why role modeling is such a powerful tool can be further explained by Bandura's social learning model (originally discussed in Chapter 1). Basically, role modeling sets an environmental cue in the mind of a person that this behavior is important and should be emulated. Thus, if a leader has done a good job expressing a vision, and then behaves in a way consistent with that vision, these messages come together in employees' minds and provide a clear message this vision is important and that others are treating it that way. See Tool Kit 7.4 ways to provide an appropriate model.

Consider for a moment what happens when people in leadership positions do not provide appropriate models to their employees. Assume that the vision of your company is to achieve "success through wasting nothing." The company posts "success through wasting nothing" banners around the offices, you get new business cards with the vision printed on them, and you see the company is recycling their paper now to underscore the importance of the vision. Now suppose you learn the CEO and her family are using the corporate jet to take a family vacation to Fiji and that this costs the company $100,000. What would the CEO's behavior do to your motivation? If you are like most people, this type of behavior would send a message that "success through wasting nothing" must only apply to the average worker. It is also likely you would now view the entire vision as a joke and behave in ways that might be contrary to what the CEO espoused.

Providing an appropriate model is not only important for senior executives, however, but for anyone in a leadership position. The old adage—behavior speaks louder than words—is true, and even seemingly innocent behavior can speak volumes. For instance, if you stress being on time to other people, you had better be on time yourself. Kouzes and Posner provide a straightforward prescription for effective leader modeling: DWYSYWD—Do what you say you will do. They point out that DWYSYWD has two essential elements—*say* and *do:*

> To set an example, leaders must be clear about their values; they must know what they stand for. That's the "say" part. Then they must put what they say into practice: They must act on their beliefs and "do."

Fostering the Acceptance of Group Goals

Fostering the acceptance of group goals is behavior on the part of a leader aimed at promoting cooperation among employees and getting them to work together toward a common goal. The most common example of this behavior is the setting of a **superordinate goal.** Superordinate goals are achievable only when *all* group members exert effort; individual effort alone will not result in goal achievement.

Importantly, these superordinate goals can be either top-down or bottom-up in nature. For example, a newspaper in Washington was in danger of closing because it was consistently losing money, as most readers in the area subscribed to the much larger *Seattle Times*.[28] The smaller newspaper's staff held brainstorming sessions to come up with ways of saving the paper, and a superordinate goal was set around establishing a new identity for the paper. The superordinate goal was that the paper should become "the source of news for the county." In other words, a decision was made to change the emphasis of the paper to county-specific news (the county had more than 900,000 residents). As a result, the paper became profitable and remains so at this time.

"Nothing is so potent as the silent influence of a good example"

—James Kent

"If you're not excited, how can you get others excited? People will know. It's like how kids and dogs can sense when people don't like them."

—Carol Bartz, CEO
Autodesk

Fostering the acceptance of group goals works because the process brings people together to accomplish feats they previously thought were not possible. Group goals provide a sense of purpose, a rallying point, and common objectives to groups of people who are all too often caught up in internal competition and political infighting. Another specific reason getting people to accept group goals works is the goals have a self-managing feature about them. They serve as useful benchmarks to let people know "how they are doing" by thinking about whether or not the goal has been accomplished (see both Chapter 1 and Chapter 4 for further discussion of the importance of goals). For specific guidelines on fostering the acceptance of group goals see Tool Kit 7.5.

Communicating High Performance Expectations

High performance expectations are behaviors that demonstrate the leader's expectations for excellence, quality, and high performance on the part of followers. In other words, great managers know if they expect a lot out of people, they are likely to get it. Yet setting high performance expectations for many managers is counterintuitive. They often fall into the trap of thinking, "I'll set the bar low so my employees can feel success," or "I'll meet my quarterly goals by not challenging people and getting some quick wins." The evidence is clear, however; if you want high performance, setting the performance bar low will do one thing—produce low performance.

The reason why communicating high performance expectations works is due in part to what has been termed the Pygmalion effect (See Management Live 7.5 for a summary of the research findings). Basically, the **Pygmalion effect** (also

> *"You have to expect things of yourself before you can do them."*
>
> —Michael Jordan

> *"High expectations are the key to everything."*
>
> —Sam Walton

Management Live 7.5

The Power of Pygmalion on the Job

A large and growing body of evidence supports the power of high expectations and self-fulfilling prophesies in the workplace. Recent research conducted by Brian McNatt examined 12 separate research studies from different work settings, involving a total of 2,874 participants. Each study randomly assigned employees to two groups and told supervisors that one group of employees had considerably greater potential than the other group. Thus, a positive view was fostered on the part of supervisors about one group of employees who were actually *no different* than other employees.

With only two exceptions, employees in the groups about whom the supervisors were given positive information responded with greater productivity. The magnitude of these gains seemed to be dependent on the circumstances of the work relationship. The greatest gains were seen in military training settings. The researchers suspect this is because in the military it is easier to control the information supervisors receive. In a business situation, word of mouth and reputation may bleed into the situation, making the positive information received by the supervisor less believable.

The second greatest gains were had in the situations where disadvantaged workers (those that for whatever reason were less likely to be successful) were randomly assigned to two groups. The group about whom the supervisor was given positive information made significant gains over the group about whom the supervisor was not given positive information. It is suspected that people with low self-esteem and self-efficacy (confidence) are more likely to respond to positive feedback. This indicates that supervisors have the potential to help employees become higher performing. However, they do need to believe the employee has potential—the Pygmalion effect. This is probably because the employee is more fully engaged and motivated when working for a positive-thinking supervisor, allowing the organization to fully tap into that employee's capabilities.

Source: McNatt, D.B. (2000). Ancient Pygmalion Joins Contemporary Management: A Meta-Analysis of the Result. *Journal of Applied Psychology, 85*, 314–322.

called self-fulfilling prophecy, and named after the Greek mythology character who "willed" his stone beloved to come alive) is based on the premise that:

- We form certain expectations of people.
- We communicate those expectations to others through behavioral cues.
- People tend to respond to these behavioral cues by adjusting their behavior to match them.
- The result is that the original expectation comes true.

It should be pointed out that self-fulfilling prophecies have been shown to work across a wide variety of situations. And we say a wide variety of situations, we just don't mean with different types of people, doing different jobs, in different types of organizations. While all of these are true the effect goes much further. Even rats respond to self-fulfilling prophecies![29] Further, these self-fulfilling prophecies are incredibly powerful as evidenced by the following research findings:

1. High performance expectations lead to higher performance.
2. Low performance expectations lead to lower performance.
3. Better performance resulting from high expectations leads people to like someone more.
4. Lower performance resulting from low expectations leads people to like someone less.

"Treat a man as he is and he will remain as he is. Treat a man as he can be and should be, and he will become as he can and should be."

—Johann Goethe (1749–1832)
German poet, novelist, playwright, courtier, and natural philosopher

Put simply, if you truly think a person will succeed or fail, they generally will! There are several ways to actually communicate to others your expectations of them. When you set challenging goals or express confidence in another person's ability, you are communicating an expectation. When you assign tasks, you are providing a measure of your expectations. Regardless of which of the preceding behaviors you use to communicate high performance expectations (the more behaviors, the better), you want to be aware of your expectations and engage in frequent checks regarding others' expectations of themselves. Great managers understand that a key to getting high performance is to set the bar high. When the people around you start to set their own bars high as a result of your actions, consider this the ultimate success of communicating high performance expectations (see Tool Kit 7.6 to more effectively communicate high performance expectations).

THE RETURN OF GUARDED OPTIMISM

Providing Individualized Support

Providing individualized support is leader behavior that indicates he or she respects followers and is concerned about their personal feelings and needs. It shouldn't be surprising why this type of behavior is effective; individualized support makes people feel valued, capable, and liked. There is perhaps no more central explanation to an effective relationship than mutual liking.

Examples of individualized support can readily be seen. Some are heroic in scope, but most are relatively simple. By placing yourself in the position of the other person (using empathy), you are better able to consider what the person may need. If you realize that person has been under a great deal of stress at work (due to major projects being due or working on a particularly frustrating problem), finding out what you can do to help is an important means of showing individualized support. It requires being attuned to employees' needs and paying attention to what people are saying and doing (recall the Chapter 1 discussion of the importance of awareness). Other everyday examples include:

"You can't be a good leader unless you generally like people. That is how you bring out the best in them."

—Richard Branson

- Making interpersonal connections with employees (such as asking about that movie he just saw).
- Genuinely caring and showing compassion in actions.
- Encouraging continuous development and growth of employees.
- Sending the message, "I care about you and am looking out for your best interest."

These behaviors are not complex, yet the payoff for understanding the unique needs of each employee is great. Research shows that providing individualized support can actually serve as a major buffer to employee stress and burnout. Further, individualized support has been shown to be associated with increased employee citizenship behavior, increased employee job satisfaction, enhanced organizational commitment, increased employee organizational citizenship behavior, and improved performance. For further ways to provide individualized support, see Tool Kit 7.7.

Providing Intellectual Stimulation

The final transformational leader behavior identified by Podsakoff and his colleagues is intellectual stimulation. **Intellectual stimulation** is defined as leader behavior that challenges followers to re-examine assumptions about their work and rethink how it can be performed. Leaders who engage in intellectually stimulating their employees refute remarks like "That's the way we've always done it," or "I'm not sure, that's not my job." These are clear signs employees are not being asked to question old assumptions. Great managers know that without intellectual stimulation employees become cogs in the wheel, resigned to performing their jobs with little passion or inspiration. In most cases, a little stimulation can go a long way.

Common ways of showing intellectual stimulation include:

- Encouraging the imagination of employees.
- Challenging the old ways of doing things.
- Looking for better ways to do things.
- Encouraging your followers not to think like you.
- Being willing to take risks for potential gains.
- Sending the message, "If we change our assumptions, then. . ."
- Making it acceptable to fail if learning from the failure takes place.

Some of the most intellectually challenging people we have heard of happen to work in the restaurant industry. This may not be a coincidence. Think of how much competition most restaurants face—and when good restaurants stop reinventing themselves, they tend to stagnate and not be as successful as they once were. A great example of intellectual stimulation can be seen by the practices of Allen Susser of Chef Allen's in North Miami Beach. Susser gives servers and cooks $50 each to dine at any restaurant with cuisine similar to that of Chef Allen's. Employees return with a short written and oral report on what they have learned.

Another example can be seen by actions of Matthew Mars and John D'Amico, proprietors of Chez Francois restaurant in northern Ohio. Every January and February they close their restaurant and travel around the world looking for new ideas to bring back and inspire their staff with. In 2005 they traveled to Argentina, Italy, Mexico, Miami, New York, and Las Vegas to see what new ideas and trends they could identify. Keep in mind, this is to run a restaurant located in a town of about 11,000 people! Not surprisingly, Chez Francois has become a destination for people in the region and is one of the top restaurants in Ohio.

Regardless of the industry, it is always important to keep an eye out for innovative or potentially useful ideas. The real power, however, comes from organizations of people who are all observing what is going on around them and who feel free to share these observations. See Tool Kit 7.8 for more ways to intellectually stimulate others.

To intellectual stimulate others on the job, Kouzes and Posner in their book *The Leadership Challenge* offer some additional specific suggestions:

- Send people shopping for ideas.
- Put idea gathering on your agenda.
- Make it safe for others to experiment.
- Eliminate firehosing (the process of dousing good ideas with reasons why they will not work).
- Honor your risk takers.
- Debrief every failure as well as every success.
- Encourage possibility thinking ("What if. . .?").

> *"Innovation comes from people meeting up in the hallways or calling each other at 10:30 at night with a new idea, or because they realized something that shoots holes in how we've been thinking about a problem. It's ad hoc meetings of six people called by someone who thinks he has figured out the coolest new thing ever and who wants to know what other people think of his idea."*
>
> —Steve Jobs

Putting the Full Range of Leadership into Action

The combination of transactional and transformational leader behaviors offer a powerful set of tools to leaders. The full range of the leadership model is based on the idea that leaders need to use transactional leader behaviors to build trust and to assure fairness in the work setting. Then the transformational leader behaviors can be used to build upon this basic fair exchange to get workers to excel by inspiring them with treatment that goes beyond the basic exchange of treatment for performance. Thus, it is the pairing of the transactional leader behaviors (needed to put a good foundation in place) and the transformational leader behaviors (needed to satisfy the higher level needs of employees) that will allow leaders to be maximally effective. This is something that great managers know and put into action!

Obviously, leadership is a complex subject and there is a great deal of information to digest. However, it can be manageably boiled down to trying to increase your competence across the three dimensions of leadership: personal characteristics, transactional behaviors and transformational behaviors. Within the domain of personal characteristics, your charge is to know yourself and act in ways proven to earn admiration. Recall that the recurring traits people admire in leaders are integrity, decisiveness, competence, and the ability to be forward-looking. For an example of someone who effectively uses the full range of leaderships see Management Live 7.6 about Jeff Beros, the CEO of Amazon.com.

With respect to transactional behaviors, diagnose your followers and customize your actions to their needs. Learn the situational leadership model and when and how you will want to emphasize directive or supportive behaviors, or both. Be clear about what you want from your people and be sure the rewards and punishments you use are tied to those behaviors and *only* those behaviors.

Finally, strategize how you can bring the transformational behaviors to life in your situation. Can you identify and transfer a compelling vision people will

Management Live 7.6

Jeff Bezos and the Full Range of Leadership Model

Without doubt, most successful leaders rely upon a combination of transactional and transformational leader behaviors in their day-to-day actions. Microsoft's Bill Gates has set up systems that reward employees for their hard work and that weed out underperformers. But Gates is also credited with communicating compelling visions of where Microsoft is headed, he has set goals requiring people to work together, and he has served as model of hard work. The same can be said for several other leaders including Jack Welch of General Electric, Terry Semel of Yahoo!, and Scott McNealy of Sun Microsystems. One case, however, that deserves special mention is Jeff Bezos, the CEO of Amazon.com.

There is no question that Bezos uses transactional leadership and analytical tools effectively. He likes to enumerate the criteria, in order of importance, for every decision he has made—even why he married his wife. The No. 1 reason for that particular choice? He wanted someone who would be resourceful enough to get him out of a Third World prison!

When it comes to being the CEO of Amazon.com, Bezos manages by the numbers. According to Steve Risher, Amazon.com's former vice president of marketing who now teaches business at the University of Washington, "there are fun moments in the four-hour meetings [at Amazon.com], but they aren't fun meetings. If someone comes in without the numbers, it can get ugly pretty quickly." Another indication of Bezos's numerical focus is one of his favorite phrases when someone has a good idea is, "We can measure that," according to Patty Stonesifer (a former Microsoft executive who's now an Amazon.com director). But, she adds, "It's one thing to be a data junkie who just looks at history, but Jeff takes a prospective view. He takes risks and he changes and changes." It is the combination of these skills that has made Jeff Bezos a successful leader for Amazon.com.

Bezos sees himself as a "change junkie," and the culture he has created is adept at coming up with innovations, but he's also unapologetic about copying ideas from competitors. In short, Bezos is a leader who understands how to take advantage of all the tools available to him. Whether it's rewarding a good idea, setting challenging goals, or getting people to work together, Bezos uses all of the tools at his disposal to be the best leader he can for Amazon.com.

As a prime example of Bezos's ability to convey vision and get people to think about things in new ways, in 2005 Amazon was faced with whether it should make its huge warehouse of data available to outside parties, that is, data that had taken more than 10 years and $1 billion dollars to build, organize, and safeguard. At the end of a spirited debate, Bezos jumped up from his seat and, mimicking a flasher opening up a trench coat, declared that Amazon would "aggressively expose ourselves!" This move will undoubtedly open different possibilities for Amazon and change the way it does business. While this move will certainly be a risk, it also provides an opportunity for new growth and undoubtedly will get Amazon's employees to think about their business in new ways. This is what makes Bezos a good example of a leader who establishes a transactional base and then excels with transformational behaviors.

Source: Deutschman, A. (2004). Inside the Mind of Jeff Bezos, *Fast Company*, 85, 52.

want to sign on for? What are your collective goals? How are you supporting others? In what ways are you seeking to provide intellectual stimulation to your associates, and so on. The full range of leadership approach is not a simple cookbook recipe, but an evidence-based model of leadership effectiveness that can and should guide your thinking about how to go forward in a leadership position.

Becoming a Leader

"Leaders develop themselves."
—Warren Bennis

Leadership development is a lifelong journey and it is never too early too start. The primary responsibility for your leadership development rests with you. At the same time, successful organizations are so aware of the importance of leadership development they have put in place a variety of tools and programs that can facilitate personal growth. For example, one recent study of corporate leadership development asked 350 organizations, "What programs or activities have most positively impacted the development of leaders in your company?" A summary of the results is presented in Figure 7.4.

FIGURE 7.4

Key Actions that Impact Leadership Development Success

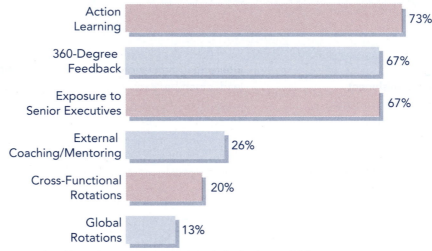

Notes: Adapted from Linkage Inc., Best Practices in Leadership Development (2000).

Although that study was targeted to organizational leadership development efforts, the findings have direct implications for your own personal development. For example, consistent with the theme of this book, all successful development efforts start with assessment. So getting external feedback from multiple sources (360-degree feedback) can be a strong catalyst for personal growth. Further, an assertive effort to get cross-functional roles and stretch assignments seems to be a leadership development facilitator. Third, a very clear message from those findings is you do not develop as a leader by *yourself*. Rather, those with a mentor or mentors and a network of support are more likely to build leadership capacity early in their careers.

"One of the things we have done for years is 360-degree reviews. It's amazing when you go to a leader and say, 'There are 30 people who reviewed you, and 30 of them trust you. But all 30 say you don't listen well.' It has an impact."

—Hank Paulson, CEO, Goldman Sachs

The most important thing for your leadership development, however, is to actively engage in leadership opportunities wherever they might present themselves. These opportunities may be within the context of an existing job (project assignments, job rotation, task force or other special teams) or a social organization. For students, the leadership chances may be in a club or other extracurricular role. Becoming an effective leader is about stepping up and being willing to lead people in a new direction. Put simply, leadership competence comes to those who choose to lead.

Concluding Note

Dare to Lead

Some would say leadership is the most important yet elusive skill set in all of management. There is no question that organizations of all kinds are desperate for good leadership—so the need is large, and the opportunity is great. Effective leadership consists of multiple dimensions and is a function of personal characteristics as well as transactional and transformational behaviors that influence positive action in others.

In this chapter we have reviewed the evidence base for different leadership dimensions and have hopefully stimulated thought about what it takes to earn respect and take a group in a direction they would not otherwise go. Now summon your resolve and dare to lead at your next opportunity.

Key Terms

articulating a vision

coaching

contingent punishment

contingent reward behavior

delegating

directing

directive behavior

fostering the acceptance of group goals

full range of leadership

high performance expectations

intellectual stimulation

leader-member exchange

leadership

leadership emergence

organizational citizenship behavior (OCB)

providing an appropriate model

providing individualized support

pygmalion effect

situational leadership

supportive behavior

superordinate goal

supporting

transactional leader behavior

transformational leader behavior

Leadership Tool Kits

Tool Kit 7.1 Steps to Providing Contingent Rewards

1. Describe the desired behavior (push high margin products, helping others, share expertise with marketing task force).
2. Explain the benefits that the desired behavior will cause (increased profits, happier people, improved customer service).
3. Explain rewards associated with the desired behavior (increased performance ratings, raise, bonus, promotion, more responsibility, interesting work assignments).
4. Provide examples and answer questions regarding desired behaviors.
5. Monitor behavior and reward desired behavior.
6. Follow through with the reward promised should the desired behavior occur.

Tool Kit 7.2   Steps to Effective Contingent Punishment

1. Meet privately. Never punish in public.
2. Describe the undesirable behavior (poor customer contact, not meeting sales goals, bypassing of safety policies).
3. Explain the problems the undesirable behavior is causing (low employee satisfaction, customer complaints, lost sales).
4. Allow questions and opportunities for clarification.
5. Explain consequences if the undesirable behavior does not change (probation, formal discipline procedures, termination).
6. Provide examples and time for questions regarding desired behaviors.
7. Monitor behavior and reward desirable behavior.
8. Follow through with appropriate response to behavior (aversive consequence if the behavior has not changed or positive outcomes if the behavior has changed).

Tool Kit 7.3   Guidelines for Effectively Articulating a Vision

- Make the vision as short as possible.
- Present the vision in future terms ("We will be. . .").
- Design the vision to match the level of the audience. For example, while growth may be relevant to top managers, sales numbers over the next year may be more relevant for salespeople, and reject rates may be more important for manufacturing employees.
- Make eye contact with your audience.
- Vary the speed and volume of your voice.
- Repeat the vision often.
- Explain the significance of the vision by linking it to what your audience finds important—appeal to their values.
- Speak in positive terms.
- Use the term "we" instead of "I."

Tool Kit 7.4   Providing an Appropriate Model

- Be clear about your expectations of other people.
- Hold yourself to the same standards and expectations to which you hold others.
- Be consistent in your display of the desired behavior.
- Remember that even small indiscretions can have major consequences. For instance, if you were trying to encourage cost savings, staying in an expensive hotel would undermine your credibility.
- Perform desirable behaviors where they can be observed. If no one sees you doing something positive or knows about the behavior, the positive behavior cannot serve as a model.

Tool Kit 7.5   Fostering the Acceptance of Group Goals

- Set a superordinate goal.
- Make sure that the goal is SMART (specific, measurable, attainable, relevant, and time-bound).

- Encourage people to work together by moving them closer together, and by encouraging informal contact (lunches, after work gatherings).
- Continually remind people that everyone is "in it together" and that success for each person depends upon the group's success.

Tool Kit 7.6   How to Communicate High Performance Expectations

- Set high standards for your people.
- Communicate the high standards and your confidence in their ability to achieve those standards.
- Let people know you are there to help them accomplish the high performance.
- Encourage workers to seek you out for help whenever they feel it would be helpful.

Tool Kit 7.7   Providing Individualized Support

- Work to build positive relationships with others so they feel comfortable approaching you.
- Determine how much support and what type of support each person needs. This can be done by observing their behavior as well as asking each person what he or she needs from you.
- Encourage the continuous development and professional growth of others.
- Show you care about others by genuinely caring and showing compassion in your actions.
- In all interactions with employees, you should be sending the message, "I care about you and am looking out for your best interest."

Tool Kit 7.8   Intellectual Stimulation of Others

- Create an environment where new ideas are encouraged and implemented (solicit ideas from people, reward new ideas, implement new ideas even if they only make small changes to show ideas are taken seriously).
- Challenge old ways of doing things and encourage others to look for better ways of doing them.
- Encourage followers not to think like you do.
- Send the message to others, "If we change our assumptions, then. . ."

Tool Kit 7.9   Becoming an Effective Leader

Unlike many other areas of personal skill development, developing yourself into an effective leader is likely to take years to accomplish, rather than weeks or months. As a result, a long-term plan is needed to do this effectively. This plan should consist of the following:

1. Initial Diagnosis: What do you value? What do you want out of your career? Where do you see yourself being in 5, 10, and 20 years?
2. Assessment: Seek feedback from others and utilize as many tools as possible (personality measures, career preferences) to enhance your understanding of yourself.
3. Design: While it is impossible to create a detailed plan for the next 20 years, you can seek out opportunities that help you fill in the gaps in your background compared to the requirements of the positions you seek.
4. Implementation: Take advantage of opportunities when they present themselves. Even if the timing may not be great, sometimes people only get a few major chances in their lifetimes. When key mentoring

opportunities, job rotation chances, or global assignments present themselves, these opportunities need to be seized when they help contribute to your personal development.

5. Support: Continually seek out feedback and development opportunities. Many successful leaders have had to take a wide variety of job assignments so they have a better understanding of the business and increased visibility in their corporate environments.

6. Evaluation: Every few years measure your progress. Are you ahead of schedule or behind? Why? What opportunities should you be seizing that you are not? Only through ongoing evaluation will you be able to continually develop your leadership ablities

Team Effectiveness and Diversity

"If you are not an effective team player in our organization, you are destined to fail. We build it into our reward systems and we promote those who have it. Most people who have worked in a number of teams think they are pretty good team players. They are not. At least not with respect to what we demand of our teams. I did not get nearly enough team training in college and I would recommend that any person who wants to work here, or places like this, take every opportunity to experience teams and get some practice in helping make them effective."

—David Pierce, CEO, Atari, Inc.

Manage *What*?

1. Helping the Highly Cohesive but Low-Performing Team

"I don't know what the problem is," says a member of a team formed two months ago. "We don't bicker or fight, and we all get along so well. We seem like a very cohesive team, we are really well organized, and we have great members. But the products of our work are disappointing." Another member puts it a bit more succinctly, "I love our team, but our performance stinks."

Assuming that the team does have capable members, what would be potential causes of the team's low performance? How would you go about trying to diagnose what is wrong? What suggestions would you give the team for ways they might go about producing higher quality outcomes?

2. Getting a Team Started: Leading the First Meeting

One of the more awkward moments is when a team first meets and tries to figure out what they are supposed to do and how they will work together. You have just been assigned to a new team, and, after all members have arrived at the first meeting, you find no one really wants to say much and you fear this group has a good chance of floundering. If your goal is to help make this group a high-performance team, what strategies would you recommend to get them kick-started and on their way to being effective?

3. Making a Diverse Team Productive

You have just been honored by being appointed to one of three project action teams, chartered by your company's senior leadership officers, to work on a current strategic issue in the firm. You have been asked to complete your work in three months and make a presentation at the top management retreat in front of the CEO, the vice president of marketing, and other decision-makers. Your team's charge is to explore how your firm might better recruit the best young talent worldwide. The team is composed of eight people from across the company and is the most diverse team you have ever been on.

More specifically, the team consists of six men and two women; an age range of 24 to 62; three American Caucasians, one African American; one Hispanic American, and one national representative each from company units in India, China, and Brazil, who are all currently on assignment in the United States. Everyone speaks English, although the Chinese woman seems exceedingly shy and not particularly comfortable with her language skills.

Recognizing it is demanding enough to achieve quality team outcomes with people you know well and understand, you are concerned it's going to be very difficult to pull this group together quickly, communicate effectively, and achieve the kind of work product you will want to present in three months. So what would you recommend that could help bring this team together? How would you attempt to minimize some of the communication and coordination challenges known to face diverse teams? Conversely, how might you best bring out the potential creativity and idea generation that is the promise of diversity? In short, what could you do to help create a productive and diversity-friendly team?

4. Dealing with a Problem Team Member

You have been working as part of a five-person team for several months, and it is now painfully clear to you and three other members of your team that the fifth member is not motivated and is just not "pulling his weight." One of your teammates wants to "kick the slacker off the team" and you are prepared to do that if the person continues to contribute so little to the team's performance. The poor performer, however, was included on the team because of his excellent skills and expertise that, if applied, could help you greatly. So your first preference would be to keep the team together, motivate this member to contribute more fully, and generate higher performance as a unit.

So where would you start? How might you approach the problem member with the issue? Are there others you would involve? Are there particular traps to avoid here? Does your approach change any if this free rider is a minority in the group (for example, the only female), much older, or from a different culture?

LEARNING OBJECTIVES

1. Determine when using a team makes sense.
2. Develop a team which exhibits the five dimensions of high performing teams.
3. Diagnose team problems, particularly with regard to team dynamics, and take steps to overcome them.
4. Explain how diversity affects team processes.
5. Use team-building interventions to stimulate team performance.
6. Contribute to team success, using those task and interpersonal behaviors known to be characteristic of the most productive team members.

Teams in the Workplace

Teams are a hot topic these days, but they represent a paradox. When they are effective, teams make better decisions than individuals and greatly outperform their best member. Teams can generate higher productivity and more rapid innovation and creativity, especially for complex work. They can also create more satisfying work environments and places where people are attracted to work and stay. Authors Jon Katzenbach and Douglas Smith, authors of *The Wisdom of Teams*, have even suggested teams are the single best tool organizations have for meeting today's performance and change challenges.[1]

One terrific example of adaptive teamwork can be found at Southwest Airlines. Under the leadership of an airlines industry maverick, Herb Kelleher, Southwest became the most consistently profitable, productive, and cost-efficient carrier in the airline industry. It has also earned the Triple Crown award for best on-time performance, baggage handling, and customer satisfaction for several years running.[2] A financial analyst once asked CEO Kelleher if he was afraid of losing control of the organization. Kelleher told him he has never had control and never wanted it. "If you create a team environment where the people truly participate, you don't need control. They know what needs to be done, and they do it. And the more that people will devote themselves to your cause on a voluntary basis, a willing basis, the fewer hierarchies and control mechanisms you need." Southwest Airlines is a great example of creative team building on a very large scale.

But while teams hold great potential for positive outcomes, they also frequently fail.[3] For most people, the very word *team* produces both positive and negative reactions. Although it is said that two heads are better than one, we are also warned that too many cooks spoil the broth. For every case of team success, there is an equally compelling case of team failure. Although some people are

"Great teams can outperform collections of individuals, even when the individuals are more talented."

—John Chambers, CEO, Cisco Systems

"A camel is a horse put together by a committee."

—Unknown

energized by teamwork and excel in teams, others are not well suited to team-work and dislike being part of a team.

Experience suggests there are several common misconceptions and unfound-ed assumptions regarding what makes effective teams. And since a key step to behaving effectively is to first recognize and avoid what *not* to do, here is a brief description of four of the most pervasive team myths that often get in the way of team performance are presented in Myths 8.1.

MYTHS 8.1   **Myths of Teamwork[4]**

Teams are always the answer. While stirring sports and military analogies can lead us to believe that teams are universally wonderful, they are often *not* the best way to accomplish a task. If the proper conditions for teamwork are not present, you are better off making individual assignments.

The key to team performance is cohesion. It is common for people to talk about their best team experiences in terms like "We all got along so well" or "everybody liked one another." But high cohesion is not a sufficient, or even the most critical, element for team performance. It sometimes even causes teams to make bad decisions and flounder.

The team leader is the primary determinant of team performance. Team leaders have an important role, especially at the beginning. But teams with leaders who control all the details, manage all the key relationships, and have all the good ideas are usually underproductive.

The best individual performers will create the highest performing team. The highest performing teams have *complementary* members, willing and capable of playing differ-ent roles, and are often *not* characterized by the highest level of individual talent.

So when should we use teams? How do we know productive, high-performing teams when we see them? What are the most common threats to team performance? How can we intervene to help struggling teams and deal with free riders? What really makes a good team member? Those questions are the focus of this chapter.

When Do Teams Make Sense?

With some proclaiming the wonders of teams, and others pointing to their lim-itations and failures, how do we decide when and where teams are most ap-propriate? Teams make the most sense for particular objectives and under certain circumstances.[5] In other words, teams do not represent a solution for all situations.

First, teams are better when no individual "expert" exists. When there is no clear individual expert to handle a problem situation, teams tend to make bet-ter judgments than the average individual acting alone. With a team, labor and information can be shared, more knowledge and information can be applied to a problem, a greater number of alternatives can be examined, and tunnel vision can be avoided.

Second, teams are often superior in stimulating innovation and creativity. Teams are better when risk is desirable. Because of their tendencies to make more

"If you see a snake, just kill it. Do not appoint a committee on snakes."

—Ross Perot, Founder, EDS

extreme decisions, teams are often more creative and innovative in performing tasks than individuals.

Third, teams can help create a context where people feel connected and valued. Human beings crave contact with other human beings and teams can serve to create a sense of community and support, reduce work stress, and perhaps induce people to join or stay in a particular role.

The first team skill, then, is the ability to assess when and where a team is even appropriate. If you cannot clearly point to the existence of one or more of the three conditions above, do *not* create a team. At their worst, teams slow decision-making, create confusion, and serve to detract from individual effort. The key is to use them when they make sense and to understand what makes them high performing. Even if a team is not appropriate, a meeting still may be needed. We have provided a set of guidelines in Tool Kit 8.1 to increase the effectiveness of any meeting.

High-Performing Teams

While the word **team** is used in several different ways, we use it specifically to refer to a group of people who are collectively accountable for definable outcomes and have a high degree of interdependence and interaction. By our definition, a team is not just people who work for the same manager or whose workspaces are located near one another. Rather, a team is a group that shares responsibility for producing something together. People often confuse interdependence with personal contact. Simply working closely with others, however, does not make a team. Teams are unique because each member cannot complete the work without the work of other members.

"Wearing the same shirts does not make you a team."

—Steve Bucholz & Thomas Roth, Authors, *Creating the High Performance Team*

As we noted earlier, just because a team is brought together hardly ensures it will be high performing. Below we highlight what defines a high-performance team and the key characteristics, or disciplines, that contribute to such performance.

The High-Performance Team Scorecard

The scorecard for determining whether a team is high performing consists of three dimensions:[6]

Production Output. The products or outcomes of the team meet or exceed the standards set in that context. For example, a manufacturing team that exceeds its quota would get high ratings.

Member Satisfaction. Being part of the team provides people with satisfaction. Members find belonging to the team to be a good experience both professionally and personally.

Capacity for Continued Cooperation. The team accomplishes its tasks in a way that will maintain or enhance its ability to work together in the future. That is, effective teams do not exhaust all their resources and goodwill, but get better at working together for the next project and continually strive to learn from mistakes.

A high-performance team, then, is one that produces high-quality work but also has members who derive value from being part of the group and who are able to learn from each project in ways that make them able to cooperate even better in the future. Any team can stumble on to some success. Great teams, however, strive to understand the reasons behind their performance so they are able to repeat that success consistently.

The Five Disciplines of High-Performing Teams

One look at the hundreds of books devoted to teams would reveal a bewildering list of characteristics that are allegedly critical to creating high performance. Obviously, every team and context is different and so it is impossible to specifically pinpoint any one ideal team success profile. However, recent research on teams has concluded that, across many different types of teams and contexts, five disciplines consistently emerge as essential to high performance: (1) small size, (2) capable and complementary members, (3) shared purpose and performance objectives, (4) productive norms and working approach, and (5) mutual accountability (Figure 8.1). Other commonly identified disciplines (for example openness and communication) remain important, but none are as critical or as manageable as these five.[7]

What stands out about this short list is that none of the five disciplines are provocative, novel, or difficult to understand. But isolating and understanding the essential disciplines have proved to be much easier than actually *applying* those disciplines to achieve team performance. *Disciplines* is absolutely the right word because it conveys the importance of consistent application as opposed to just knowing or identifying the characteristics.

Team expert Jon Katzenbach likes to make this point using an analogy from weight-loss efforts. That is, there are only a very few simple, widely known, and accepted behaviors for losing weight based on some essential principles (eat less, eat more wisely, exercise). However, if you do each of those three things only once, and then check them off your list, you will not lose weight. Only through repeated and disciplined application of all three can you expect to meet significant weight-loss goals. Similarly, it is only through the repeated and disciplined application of the team dimensions that your team will achieve high performance. Simply stated, the research suggests you really have to get high scores on all of the disciplines, and do so consistently, if you want to deliver team performance.[8]

> *"We have always found that people are most productive in small teams with tight budgets and time lines and the freedom to solve their own problems."*
>
> —John Rollwagen, CEO, Cray Research

FIGURE 8.1

Five Disciplines of High-Performing Teams

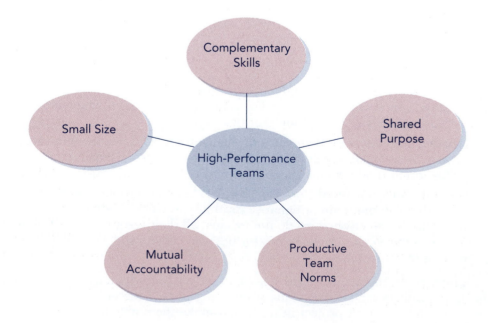

Small Size

It is seductive to believe that if two heads are better than one, maybe 15 heads would be better than five. That is, however, not the case. Just as one glass of wine a day is good for your heart but five may kill you, there is a point of diminishing returns with respect to team size and performance. Research has shown that, on average, people working in smaller groups work harder, engage in a wider variety of tasks, assume more responsibility for the team's performance, and feel more involved with the team.[9] The larger a team gets, the harder it is for people to meet either in person or virtually, gain shared understanding and commitment, share leadership roles, and so on.

We think Amazon CEO Jeff Bezos's "two pizza group" is an appropriate guideline.[10] High-performing groups are rarely more than 10 people and ideally are between five and eight members. If you have some influence over team size, aim for the smallest number of people who would bring enough complementary skills to accomplish the objectives. Do not be seduced into thinking more is better, and if a natural grouping exceeds 10, break it into smaller subgroups.

> *"I believe in the 'two pizza' group. If you can't feed the group with two pizzas, it is too large."*
>
> —Jeff Bezos, CEO, Amazon

Capable and Complementary Members

People commonly believe they are good team players and have good team skills because they get along well with others or have always been well liked. However, as noted by Atari CEO, David Pierce in the opening quote of this chapter, that perception is often inaccurate. The reality is that teamwork is *not* for everyone, and some people are far better suited to making team contributions than others but it is often not obvious who those people are. A typical team selection trap is to neglect consideration of specific skills and instead opt for people who are either readily available or seem to have the right functional background.

> *"There is no 'I' in team. But there is an 'I' in win."*
>
> —Michael Jordan

Of course, every team needs enough functional or technical skills to do the tasks they have to do. If the team's job is house construction, then a group of chemists is unlikely to be optimal. However, it is not enough for team members to simply perform their functional area of expertise. The team also needs task management and interpersonal skills, and it is often much more elusive to determine whether potential members have those skills.

Fortunately, while "good team player" may seem like a rather fuzzy and ill-defined notion, recent research work has begun to very clearly identify the skills and competencies that characterize effective team members.[11] For example, team researchers have developed a 35-question paper-and-pencil test that assesses how an individual responds to a variety of common teamwork situations.[12] The test measures five dimensions of teamwork knowledge, skills, and abilities (KSAs) and 14 specific teamwork competencies (see Table 8.1). Research studies have shown that scores on the teamwork test are related to team effectiveness as measured by peers and supervisors.[13]

Other recent research has shown general cognitive ability and the personality characteristics of conscientiousness and agreeableness (recall the research from Chapter 5 on selecting people for jobs) to be associated with higher team member ratings and performance outcomes.[14] The implication of these findings for team performance is to not take for granted that people have the requisite skills to excel on a team. Look for ways to gather information about potential team members in order to make informed and systematic judgments about selection rather than rely solely on gut feel or demonstrated functional expertise (Chapter 5 offers a number of ways to do exactly this).

> *"Teams do not really become successful until they have rejected a candidate for their team."*
>
> —John Mackey, CEO, Whole Foods Market

> **TABLE 8.1**   **The Knowledge, Skills, and Abilities (KSAs) Requirements for Teamwork**
>
> 1. **Conflict Resolution.** The KSA to recognize and encourage desirable, but discourage undesirable, team conflict.
>
> 2. **Collaborative Problem Solving.** The KSA to recognize the obstacles to collaborative group problem solving and to implement appropriate corrective actions.
>
> 3. **Communication.** The KSA to listen non-evaluatingly and to appropriately use active listening techniques.
>
> 4. **Goal Setting and Performance Management.** The KSA to help establish specific, challenging, and accepted team goals.
>
> 5. **Planning and Task Coordination.** The KSA to coordinate and synchronize activities, information, and task interdependencies between team members.

Source: Stevens, M.J., & Campion, M.A. (1999). Staffing work teams: Development and validation of a selection test for teamwork settings. *Journal of Management, 25* (2) 207–228.

"As a coach, I play not my eleven best, but my best eleven."

—Knute Rockne

"We didn't have the twenty best guys. We had the twenty right guys."

—Herb Brooks, Coach of 1980 "Miracle on Ice" U.S. Hockey Team

In thinking about team composition, it is also important to recognize every successful team needs a mix of skills and talent to deliver its performance objectives. That is, the key is not necessarily to search for people who bring high levels of *all* skills. Since people more often excel in limited areas, the focus should be on diversifying the team and considering multiple dimensions and potential interactions rather than solely evaluating members on their individual merits. As coaches Brooks and Rockne astutely noted in the nearby margin quotations, just having a group of individual stars is not the key to success. It is *complementary* members, capable of playing roles and who together bring technical, problem-solving, and interpersonal skills that are the key to team success. A truly great example of this was seen when the Greek national basketball team beat a team of NBA all stars 101-95 in 2006. It is important to note that the Greek team did not have a single NBA player on its roster. "We have to learn the international game better," U.S. coach Mike Krzyzewski said. "We learned a lot today because we played a team that plays amazing basketball and plays together."

Management Live 8.1

Warren Buffett on Working with Winners

My managerial model is Eddie Bennett, who was a batboy. In 1919, at age 19, Eddie began his work with the Chicago White Sox, who that year went to the World Series. The next year, Eddie switched to the Brooklyn Dodgers, and they too won their league title. Our hero, however, smelled trouble. Changing boroughs, he joined the Yankees in 1921, and they promptly won their first pennant in history. Now Eddie settled in, shrewdly seeing what was coming. In the next seven years, the Yankees won five American League titles. What does this have to do with management? It's simple—to be a winner, work with winners.

Source: Berkshire Hathaway. (2003). Letter to the Shareholders. *2002 Annual Report.* Omaha, NE.

Of course, many groups and managers do not have the opportunity to provide input on selecting their team members. But having the right skill sets in the team remains one of the disciplines of high performance—without that, no amount of process excellence will suffice. So it often makes sense to better understand the skill sets that exist in an assigned team and to consider strategies for filling gaps or reducing redundancies. There is also the possibility existing members might learn and grow into the skills the team ultimately needs.

Shared Purpose and Performance Objectives

High-performing teams have both a clear understanding of the purpose of the team and a belief that the goal is worth pursuing. The best teams are also able to translate their purpose into a clear understanding of the outcome-based goals to be achieved. Indeed, there is growing consensus among team experts that the single most powerful engine for teams is a clear and compelling performance challenge. Without a clear performance imperative, little else matters. High-performing teams know explicitly what they are expected to accomplish and how they will be measured and evaluated as a team.[15]

> *"The single most important factor for effective teams is that they have a clear goal. When they don't have a goal, they tend to flounder, because they have nothing to work toward."*
>
> —Jeff McHenry,
> Director of Executive Development,
> Microsoft

One of the more straightforward, but curiously neglected, prescriptions is to articulate *outcome*-based, rather than just *activity*-based, goals (see Table 8.2). This is a point similar to one discussed in Chapter 4 on motivation. **Outcome-based goals** describe the specific outcomes by which success will be determined, while **activity-based goals** describe just the activities. Marriott Hotels, for example, use their Guest Service Index to assess performance of their hotel service employees. FedEx has a similar measure whereby employees evaluate their managers. Outcome-based goals answer the questions: How would we know success? or When would we declare victory? Unless a group comes to terms with their specific goals, the group's members are destined to struggle and unlikely to ultimately achieve high performance. To be blunt, if you cannot create shared performance objectives, *disband the team*.[16]

Just as goals strengthen the motivation of individuals, they can also enhance the motivation in groups. For example, in a study of U.S. Air Force personnel, a group goal-setting and feedback program increased productivity by 75 percent.[17] In a study of the Notre Dame University hockey team, specific goals for aggressive behavior led to a 141 percent increase in legal body checking over two years.[18] Studies of United Way campaigns have found those communities that set challenging financial goals for their campaigns had better results than those with lower goals.[19] Obviously, group goals can have significant efforts.

Team Development

The development of teams typically occurs in four phases, and key to the journey to high performance is the establishment of shared and productive norms and a working approach whereby the team can effectively manage—not eliminate—conflict.

One way to improve the internal operations of teams and facilitate team effectiveness is to recognize different stages of team development. Team effectiveness may be influenced by how well group members and leaders deal with the problems of each stage of development. The four stages of group development are forming, storming, norming, and performing.[21] All high performing teams ultimately go through all four stages, while some unsuccessful groups never make it past the forming stage. A key teamwork skill is to help accelerate the process of development.

TABLE 8.2 | **Examples of Outcome vs. Activity Goals**[20]

Outcome Goal: Win three new accounts in the next quarter.   **Activity Goal:** Develop a plan for winning new accounts.
Outcome Goal: Reduce the average duration of patient days by one day over the next five months.   **Activity Goal:** Save money through reducing patient days.
Outcome Goal: Cut in half the time it takes to process and approve new software licenses.   **Activity Goal:** Re-engineer the new software license process.
Outcome Goal: Improve the retention rate among top-rated performers by 20 percent this year without incurring any additional salary or benefit costs.   **Activity Goal:** Make this company the best place to work.
Outcome Goal: Generate at least one-fifth of our revenue from products less than two years old.   **Activity Goal:** Build a culture of innovation and new product development.

"The life expectancy of a team is about eight months. The next year, it's a whole new team."

—Mike Krzyzewski

Forming Stage. In the forming stage of group development, a primary concern is the initial entry of members into a group (see Tool Kit 8.2 for some good icebreakers). At this point, individuals ask several questions as they begin to identify with other group members and with the group itself. Among their concerns are: "What can the group offer me?" and "What will I be asked to contribute?" People are interested in discovering what acceptable behavior is, determining the real task of the group, and defining group roles.

Storming Stage. The storming stage of group development is a period of high emotion and tension among the members. Hostility and infighting between members may occur, and the group typically experiences some changes. Membership expectations tend to be clarified and further elaborated. Attention tends to shift toward obstacles standing in the way of group goals. Outside demands, including performance pressure, may create conflict in the group during this stage. Conflict may also develop over leadership and authority, as individuals compete to impose their preferences on the group and to achieve their desired status position.

Norming Stage. The norming stage is the point at which the group begins to come together as a coordinated unit. The interpersonal probes and jockeying behavior of the storming stage give way here to a precarious balancing of forces. The group as a whole will try to regulate behavior toward a harmonious balance. Minority viewpoints and tendencies to deviate from or question the group direction will be discouraged. Indeed, holding the group together may become more important to some than successfully working on the group's tasks. The sense of premature maturity needs to be carefully managed as a stepping-stone to a higher level of group development and not treated as an end in itself.

Performing Stage. The performing stage of group development sees the emergence of a mature, organized, and well-functioning team. The group is now able to deal with complex tasks and to handle membership disagreements in creative ways. Group structure is stable, and members are motivated by group goals and are generally satisfied. The primary challenges of this stage relate largely to continued work on task performance but with a strong commitment to continuing improvement and self-renewal.

Productive Norms.   **Norms** are generally unwritten rules or standards of behavior that apply to team members and can be either prescriptive—dictating what should be done—or proscriptive—dictating behaviors that should be avoided. Norms allow members to predict what others will do, help members gain a common sense of direction, and reinforce a team culture.[22] Teams operate with many types of norms (communication, punctuality, level of formality), but among the most critical are those related to effort, meetings, and trust. Examples of productive and unproductive team norms are presented in Table 8.3.

Teams with norms that encourage preparedness and hard work on behalf of the team tend to be more successful in accomplishing their tasks. In a high-performing team, when someone violates a team norm, other members typically respond in ways that attempt to enforce the norm. These responses may include subtle suggestions, direct criticisms, reprimands, or even expulsion from the team. Strong norms create a team culture where members can rigorously, maybe even brutally, challenge each other without taking it personally or getting upset and defensive. Make no mistake, the difference between teams that achieve

---

TABLE 8.3   **Examples of Productive and Unproductive Team Norms**

Common norms in work teams deal with relationships with supervisors, colleagues, and customers, as well as honesty, security, personal development, and change. The following list gives examples of how such team norms may be both positive and negative.

Organizational and Personal Pride Norms
- Productive Norm: Around here, it's a tradition for people to stand up for others who are unfairly criticized.
- Unproductive Norm: In our team, it is everyone for herself.

Performance Excellence Norms
- Productive Norm: In our team, people always try to improve, even when they are doing well.
- Unproductive Norm: Around here, there's no point in trying harder—nobody else does.

Teamwork Norms
- Productive Norm: Around here, people are good listeners and actively seek out the ideas and opinions of others.
- Unproductive Norm: In our team, it's dog-eat-dog and promote yourself.

Leadership Norms
- Productive Norm: Around here, people respect leaders and seek to take leadership roles.
- Unproductive Norm: In our team, everybody avoids the burden of leadership.

Punctuality Norms
- Productive Norm: To be on time is to be late; to be early is to be on time.
- Negative Norm: Don't worry about showing up on time, nothing ever gets accomplished in the first 10 minutes anyway.

Straight Talk Norms
- Productive Norm: In this team, people say what they mean and mean what they say. We do not walk on eggshells.
- Unproductive Norm: Around here, if you use enough business jargon, you can "BS" your way through anything.

Productivity Norms
- Productive Norm: In our team, people are continually on the lookout for better ways of doing things.
- Unproductive Norm: Around here, people tend to hang on to old ways of doing things even after they have outlived their usefulness.

high performance and teams that don't is very often the productive norms that are established and enforced.

Mutual Accountability

In a high-performing team, members pull their own weight, are rewarded for contributing, and challenged for slacking. Effective teams are characterized by high mutual trust among members and are concerned about the culture of the team. High performance is rarely achieved if there is not a belief members can be trusted and will act in the best interests of others on the team. Effective teams find a way to reward those who contribute, and accountability is determined in part by the team reward structure.

There are two fundamentally different types of team rewards: cooperative and competitive.[23] **Cooperative team rewards** are distributed equally among team members. That is, the group is rewarded as a group for its successful performance, and each member receives exactly the same reward. This type of reward structure does not recognize individual differences in effort or performance. Cooperative reward systems ignore the possibility that some members make greater contributions to group task performance than others. This type of inequity can demotivate team members who are high performers (see Management Live 8.2).

Under a **competitive team rewards** system, members are rewarded for successful performance as individuals on the team. They receive equitable rewards that vary according to their individual performance. It provides strong incentive for individual effort. It can also pit members against each other.

> *"I have never put players' names on the backs of their jerseys because I was under the impression they were playing for the name on the front."*
>
> —Bob Knight

Management Live 8.2

Cooperative Team Rewards in Action[24]

RR Donnelley & Sons is one of the largest commercial printers in the United States with products including books, catalogs, direct mail, and phone books. RR Donnelley has a very interesting strategy for implementing cooperative team rewards.

At Donnelley, the team reward system is based on a "game" concept. A Donnelley press operator created one game called NASCAR '98 with help from his frontline peers, all stock car racing fans. For the game, a "racing crew" consisted of a team working on an offset press. The game's purpose was to reduce materials waste and the goal of the game was to reduce waste compared to the previous year.

Each press crew chooses a real NASCAR driver and a Matchbox car which are then displayed on the wall. Velcro on the bottom of the cars allows the cars to stick onto the Velcro track. Cars are positioned on the track based on how the press they represent is doing that month against its own waste-reduction goals. Competition against the team's prior performance is the main idea because Donnelley wanted to make the goals purely collaborative; they did not want inter-team competition.

There is a winner each month—the press that performs best against its own goals. Each winner receives an actual NASCAR checkered flag, which many of the winning press operators hang in the work areas. In addition, the winning team is featured in the Gallery of Winners photo display next to the scoreboard for the entire year. These monthly winners also receive $40 individual gift certificates that each team member can use at a local shopping mall. If other press crews beat all of their goals in a given month, but aren't the overall department winner, each crew member receives a $20 gift certificate to the mall.

Playing the games has taught the workforce about Donnelley's business in ways classroom training never could. Not only do the games increase awareness of strategic business goals, but they're also much more fun and engaging than classroom training. Perhaps most importantly, the games provide a context where cooperative rewards have proven to be appropriate and motivational.

Competitive team rewards differentially reward team members based on their effort or performance. While competitive team rewards may please high performers, they may also undermine the team's cohesiveness.

Which of these two reward systems is most appropriate depends on the degree of task interdependence. Pairing cooperative rewards with low interdependence will encourage unnecessary cooperation, may stifle individual performance, and may also promote social loafing. A similar mismatch can occur when competitive rewards are coupled with high interdependence. In this case, members desiring to secure a payoff from their own efforts will detract from the collective spirit of the team.

In many team-based organizations, reward structures are constructed so that at least some portion of team members' pay is contingent on the performance of the team as a whole.[25] This promotes cooperation and reduces the incentive for competition among members. How rewards are allocated should also be based on how demonstrable (easily observed) the individual contributions are. In the case of a baseball player, for example, it is relatively easy to demonstrate individual performance. However, for a football player, performance is often heavily dependent on how other players performed; thus, cooperative rewards are more appropriate.

Because team performance is more difficult to track and the actions that people take and the results of the team are often blurry, the use of several sources of appraisal (such as peers and customers) makes particular sense with teams. Peer evaluations can allow members to get direct feedback about their performance and help a team enforce performance norms (see Tool Kit 8.3).

In short, the high-performing team challenge can be boiled down to: (1) keep the group small, (2) focus on complementary skill sets, (3) set clear outcome-based goals, (4) enforce productive norms and conflict management, and (5) match rewards to contributions, making at least some portion cooperatively based (see Tool Kit 8.4).[26]

It all sounds simple enough. However, we hasten to remind you the battle is maintaining the discipline to *execute* those simple rules.

> *"I don't give Cs in this course, but you do."*
>
> —Professor explaining the importance of team peer evaluations to her students

Managing Threats to Team Performance and Decision Making

Just as a company can become more profitable in two ways—selling more or spending less—a team can improve its performance through either building synergies (those activities that go better in a team compared with individuals working independently) or reducing threats. Threats refer to anything that can go wrong with a team. It may often be easier to control threats than stimulate synergies.[27] Below we identify the most common threats to team performance— information processing biases, social loafing, and social conformity—as well as strategies for controlling them.

Over the last 50 years, research on group dynamics has revealed that the effects on people of being in a team are exceptionally powerful and sometimes even scary. Four illustrations are:

- **Risky Shift.** When people are in groups, they make decisions about risk differently than when they are alone.[28] In the group, they are likely to make riskier decisions, as the shared risk reduces personal risk. On the other hand, group members may not want to let their colleagues down and hence can become risk-averse (sometimes called cautious shift). The bottom line is that when individuals come together in a team, they often make more extreme decisions than they might as individuals.

- **Innocent Bystander.** Membership in a team can sometimes create a **diffusion of responsibility** whereby members feel their personal responsibility is limited because others will step up and act. An extreme state of diffusion of responsibility among people is known as the **innocent bystander effect.** Perhaps the most horrific example of that is the case of Kitty Genovese, a woman who was on her way home late one evening in New York and was attacked and stabbed to death. Thirty-eight of her neighbors in the apartment building where she lived witnessed the attacker approach and kill her; however, not a single person so much as called the police. While some people are quick to explain this scenario as a symptom of social and moral decay, it is actually a predictable social phenomenon. Observers in Kitty Genovese's apartment building knew others were watching and felt less responsible and so less inclined to intervene. They assumed someone else had probably already called for help and they felt as if they were just innocent bystanders.[29]

- **Choking.** As human beings, we are born with an innate tendency to be stimulated when others are watching. Indeed, one of the great promises of teams is they promote social facilitation whereby individual motivation and performance are enhanced by the presence of others. The presence of others can create so much pressure and anxiety, however, that individual team members' performance can actually be hindered or below what they could do in isolation. This effect is commonly known as **choking** and research has found it is particularly likely when people are not experts at the tasks at hand.[30]

- **Escalation of Commitment.** A situation where team members will persist with a losing course of action, even in the face of clear evidence of their error, is known as **escalation of commitment,** which we discussed in Chapter 3 as an individual decision bias as well. Perhaps worst of all, the bigger the investment or the more severe the potential loss, the more prone team members are to escalation.[31]

Information Processing Biases

Most people take communication for granted in their interaction with team members but, of course, nothing magical happens just because you get together. Indeed, one of the most difficult challenges is to overcome naturally occurring information processing biases, including narrow perspectives and uneven communication.

First, people are remarkably poor at taking others' perspectives. For example, people privy to information and knowledge they know others are not aware of still tend to act as if others are aware of it, even in cases where it would be impossible for the others to have such knowledge.[32] Studies show we often grossly overestimate the overlap between our knowledge base and that of others.[33] Further, people wrongly assume others share the same underlying assumptions about the world.

Second, left unmanaged, in any team a handful of people will do the majority of talking, and this inevitably leads to uneven communication. For example, in a typical four-person group, two people do over 70 percent of the talking. Of course, this is not always dysfunctional, but some evidence suggests the people doing the talking may *not* be the most informed about the problem.[34] Moreover, the power of group decision making is lost if one or two people dominate the discussion or overly influence decisions.

An Information Processing Bias at Work

A persistent threat to be addressed is that unique information does not always emerge in team interactions as team members are more likely to discuss information that everyone already knows rather than the unique information each may have. Thus, decisions will be biased in the direction of whatever information happens to be commonly shared. This often means that technical information is not given the weight it should have because it may be held by only one member, and teams often fail to make the choices that would have been supported if all members had full information about those choices.[35]

Effective teams are able to muster the discipline to efficiently process the information that resides within the team and involve all members in generating ideas and making decisions. High-performing teams direct discussion toward unique information, minimize status differences, and frame tasks as problems to be solved (via accumulated evidence) rather than opinion-based judgments to be made. To ensure you get the relevant information into team discussions, make frequent use of "go-arounds" (formally allowing each member air time) and direct solicitations of those with known interests and expertise.

Another category of threats are social in nature and include social loafing (people will opt to be free riders) and conformity (people make poor decisions in an effort to be liked or accepted by the team).

"We've got to go into an absolute new revolutionary era in the sharing of information."
—Rudy Giuliani

Social Loafing

Perhaps the most well-known and despised threat to effective team process is known as **social loafing** or, more simply, free-riding. Most of us are well acquainted with this phenomenon based on prior experiences in teams. Max Ringelmann first formally identified this tendency in a simple experiment. He asked people to pull as hard as they could on a rope, first alone and then in a group. He found the average individual effort dropped as more people joined the rope pulling task (see Figure 8.2).[36]

Today the term **Ringelmann effect** is used to describe the situation in which some people do not work as hard in groups as they do individually. The cause of the effect is a lack of actual or perceived individual accountability. On the one hand, a social loafer may recognize that his or her contributions are less noticeable in a group setting; on the other, a social loafer may simply prefer to let others carry all or most of the workload given the task at hand.

FIGURE 8.2

Social Loafing Increases as a Function of Group Size[37]

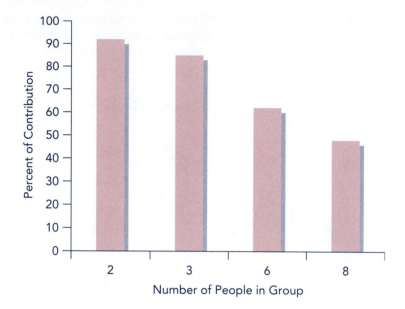

As a general rule, most of us want equitable work sharing and abhor free riders. Team members are commonly concerned they will be left doing all the work and getting little or no credit. This can lead to what is known as "sucker aversion." Because everyone wants to avoid being taken advantage of, team members hedge their efforts and wait to see what other members will do. Obviously, when everyone does this, no one contributes. When people see others not contributing, it confirms their suspicions and they avoid being a sucker ("I'm no sucker. If these guys aren't going to contribute, why should I?").

Perhaps the best strategy for addressing social loafing is **identifiability.** That simply means to find ways to get each member's contribution to a task somehow communicated or displayed where others can see it. In such cases, people are less likely to loaf or slack off than when only overall group performance is made available. A team contract that stipulates consequences for free-riders and peer evaluations are good identifiability strategies and can help avert free-riding. Social loafing may also be reduced if the task is sufficiently involving, attractive, or intrinsically interesting.[38]

"Teamwork is the quintessential contradiction of a society granded in individual achievement."

—Marvin Weisbord

Social Conformity

Another recurring pitfall of teams, though sometimes subtle, frequently constrains the effectiveness of good decision-making. **Social conformity** involves social pressures to conform to the perceived wishes of the group. That is, members of a team strive so hard to maintain harmony and cohesion they end up avoiding the discomforts of disagreement.[39] But in so doing, they make poor decisions. Social psychologist Irving Janis called this **groupthink**—the tendency of members in highly cohesive teams to lose their critical evaluative capabilities.[40] Janis noted that pressure to conform in highly cohesive teams causes members to self-censor personal views and become unwilling to criticize views offered by others. Desires to hold the team together become more important than the quality of the decision under consideration. To avoid unpleasant disagreements, there is an overemphasis on concurrence and an underemphasis on realistic appraisals of alternatives. Such situations can result in poor decisions.

One of the most famous examples of groupthink is the presidential advisory group that almost led President John F. Kennedy into invading Cuba and potential nuclear war in the 1961 Bay of Pigs affair. The first Challenger space shuttle disaster was another groupthink situation in which NASA officials disregarded engineers' concerns and placed great pressure on them ultimately leading them to change their initial no-launch decision despite evidenced-based concerns.

A form of social conformity related to groupthink is known as the **Abilene paradox.**[41] The paradox drew its name from an exceptionally clever parable describing four adults sitting on a porch in 104-degree heat in the small town of Coleman, Texas, some 53 miles from Abilene. They are engaging in as little motion as possible, drinking lemonade, watching the fan spin lazily, and occasionally playing a game of dominoes. The characters are a married couple and the wife's mother and father. At some point, the wife's father suggests they drive to Abilene to eat at a cafeteria there. The son-in-law thinks this is a crazy idea but doesn't see any need to be obstinate, so he goes along with it, as do the two women. They get in their car with no air conditioning and drive through a dust storm to Abilene. They eat a rotten lunch at the cafeteria and return to Coleman exhausted, hot, and generally unhappy with the experience.

It is not until they return home that it is revealed that *none* of them really wanted to go to Abilene—they were just going along because they thought the others were eager to go. That hidden pressure toward agreement is an insidious pitfall for many groups. Contrary to our basic human fears that conflict will lead to our team's ultimate demise, it is sometimes precisely the opposite! Often the real performance threat to a team is the inability to manage *agreement*. If you would like to experience the paradox first-hand, just suggest that your team order a couple of pizzas for their next meeting and then ask them, "What would you like on them?" We suspect that the ultimate pizzas delivered are unlikely to be what any member would have ordered individually. Of course, this may represent effective compromise. It also may reflect members' desire to go along and do what others want—a formula for poor group decisions.

So how do you avoid the various forms of social pressure to conform? Of course, you can never fully inoculate a team from a bias toward agreement, but Tool Kit 8.5 outlines several actionable steps that can help a team steer clear of Abilene and the consequences of groupthink.

Managing Diversity

Working with teams of people very similar to us is tough enough; working with those who are *dissimilar* is often even more challenging. Of course, varying factors, both new and enduring, such as the globalization of our economy, an aging workforce, an influx of immigrants, and a rise in the number of working women all mean that, in most organizations, team diversity of varying degrees will become, or already has become, the norm. Even those firms with a solely U.S. presence already face an exceptionally diverse population. Clearly, the ability to effectively work with diversity in ways that make it productive, not destructive, is essential to achieving successful team outcomes.

"We all live with the objective of being happy; our lives are all different and yet the same."

—Anne Frank

Current research suggests teams composed of individuals with diverse backgrounds face special challenges in functioning effectively, but also have potential advantages that can enhance their performance. Group functioning is made more difficult because diverse people are less likely to see or understand situations in similar ways. People from like backgrounds trust each other more readily, while diversity increases the chance for misperception and confusion in the group process. Time spent by the group clarifying confusion thus increases the time needed to achieve outcomes and diminish productivity. Put simply, diversity

FIGURE 8.3

Phases of Success for a Diverse Team

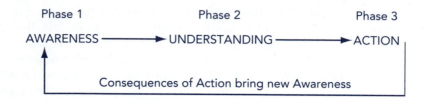

makes communicating and reaching agreement within a group more difficult and time consuming.

At the same time, diverse teams do also have the *potential* to achieve better outcomes than homogeneous teams because their wider range of human resources enables them to invent more options and create more solutions. Diversity makes it easier for teams to consider more ideas, avoid groupthink, and actively attend to fellow team members' ideas and contributions. Diversity is most advantageous for teams facing ambiguous and creative tasks. Diversity is most challenging for teams facing implementation-type tasks that require reliable, fluid, and frequent interaction.

The managerial skill challenge, then, is to find ways to minimize potential process deficits and harness the potential of diversity to positively influence team outcomes. The successful diverse team is generally one in which members are *aware* of and open about important differences not just surface ones, *understand* how those differences might influence team process and member engagement, and *take explicit action* to bring the team together and communicate most effectively (Figure 8.3).

Awareness

Any managerial focus on diversity should stem from the reality that not everyone is motivated by the same things nor do they prefer to interact in the same way. At one level, this reality makes teamwork more difficult. But given both the productive potential of diverse teams, and their inevitability in today's workforce, it does little good to worry about that. Rather, a first step in being diversity savvy is to be aware of the situation, embrace it, and make the most of it.

"It is not best that we should all think alike; it is difference of opinion that makes horse races."

—Mark Twain

With respect to diversity awareness, three common traps often befall teams. One is a tendency to romanticize diversity, whereby *any* differences are deemed important and the presumption is that diversity somehow magically leads to positive team outcomes. That is nonsense. As noted above, the research is clear that diversity generally makes team challenges *more* demanding and, for some types of teams and team purposes, will be a detriment rather than an enabler.[42]

A second trap is to deny or ignore important differences and the potential for those differences to affect team process and outcomes. Being strictly "diversity blind" may sound like a fair and high-minded approach but, in reality, is often a recipe for team failure. People differ in important ways that affect their perceptions, motivations, and actions on behalf of a team. To neglect that reality is to destine teams to fail.

A third trap is that, when most people use the term diversity, they are talking only about observable or **surface-level diversity.** Surface-level diversity refers to differences that are easily seen and generally verifiable via a quick assessment of physical characteristics, including gender, age, race, and national origin/ethnicity. However, diversity exists on many levels. Indeed, while surface-level diversity factors heavily into people's unique cultural background and experience, important diversity also exists below the surface and is not so easily observed. This type of

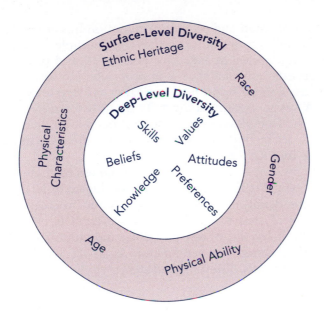

FIGURE 8.4

Surface-Level and Deep-Level Diversity

diversity has been called **deep-level diversity** and reflects differences among people such as attitudes, beliefs, knowledge, skills, and values.[43] This level of diversity can only be understood by seeking to learn about different perspectives and observing behavior over time. The most prevalent and insidious danger is to assume the surface-level diversity you *can* observe is indicative of a deeper-level diversity you *cannot* observe (Figure 8.4).

As you might suspect, people who make such assumptions and are only concerned with surface-level diversity miss the real underlying power associated with deep-level diversity. For example, research has shown that managers who want to form an effective diverse work team should do so on the basis of factors relating to differences in skills, personality traits, values, and attitudes, rather than surface-level characteristics.[44]

This is not to say that attention to surface diversity is never warranted. It clearly is a good place to start to ensure equity in the workplace. In too many

Management Live 8.3

Diversity Philosophy at Booz Allen Hamilton

A great example of the importance of broadly conceived diversity (that is, at both surface- and deep-level) can be found in the following comments from Tony Mitchell, a managing principal for Booz Allen Hamilton Inc. "As a consulting firm, one of the most important aspects of our ability to support our clients is intellectual capital—or what we call *thought leadership*. Diversity comes into play here as diversity of thought. If we have people who all have the same backgrounds, who all went through the same type of formal training and education, and who all had the same experiences in terms of corporate America, we limit our ability to refine our thinking on how we can improve our clients' probability of success—no matter what the specific problem is. That includes diversity in the traditional sense of race and ethnic background, but we try to ensure that we capture diversity in the broadest sense."

Source: http://www.nytimes.com/marketing/jobmarket/diversity/booz.html

cases, a history of exclusion and even discrimination has created a lack of representativeness of certain groups of minorities (for example, a glass ceiling clearly exists where few women are in executive positions), and proactive attempts to create a more representative balance is appropriate. However, surface diversity is often treated as a more important indicator of deep-level diversity than it really deserves. A key to creating a diversity-friendly team is to recognize diversity is more than surface or skin deep and that deep-level diversity is the key to more productive work environments. For some specific ways to get past surface-level diversity, see Tool Kit 8.6.

True diversity awareness comes from a willingness to challenge assumptions and avoid stereotyping. For example, research conducted by IBM's Geert Hofstede (discussed in more detail shortly) has found some interesting differences in certain populations of ages and cultures. However, it is critical to remember the perceptions and behaviors of any particular individual of a given group may not conform to the averages or tendencies. As Table 8.4 illustrates, diversity awareness is fundamentally different than stereotyping.

Understanding

The most prevalent myth about diversity is that people are more different than alike. It is tempting to assume that people's visible differences will somehow lead them to behave in a stereotypical way. The opposite, however, is frequently true. With respect to most of the surface-level dimensions of diversity, surprisingly few evidence-based differences are relevant to team performance.

Three surface dimensions where research *has found* interesting differences among people are ethnic heritage (culture), age, and gender. These research findings are intuitive to most managers who often note their most difficult challenges are: (1) managing people from different cultures, (2) managing those considerable age differences, and (3) communicating with the opposite sex.

Cultural Differences

The most well-known research on cultural differences was conducted by Geert Hofstede in his role as a psychologist for IBM. Hofstede collected data on employee values and perception of the work situation from more than 116,000 IBM employees in 64 countries. Based on his surveys, he identified five dimensions along which people from national cultures tend to differ (see also Table 8.5).

TABLE 8.4   Diversity Awareness vs. Stereotyping

Diversity Aware	Stereotyping
Based on differences verified by empirical research on actual intergroup differences.	Frequently based on false assumptions and anecdotal evidence or even impressions, without any direct experience with a group.
Views cultural differences as neutral.	Judges traits of a group as positive or negative, or ascribes motives for group members' behavior.
Assumes a higher probability that members of a group share the traits of the group, but allows for individual differences.	Assumes characteristics thought to be common to a group apply uniformly to every member of that group.

| TABLE 8.5 | Hofstede's Cultural Attitudes Profile for 10 Countries |

Country	Power Distance	Individualism	Achievement Orientation	Uncertainty Avoidance	Long-Term Orientation
United States	L	H	H	L	L
Germany	L	H	H	M	M
Japan	M	M	H	H	H
France	H	H	M	H	L
Netherlands	L	H	L	M	M
Hong Kong	H	L	H	L	H
Indonesia	H	L	M	L	L
West Africa	H	L	M	M	L
Russia	H	M	L	H	L
China	H	L	M	M	H

H = top third, M = middle third, L = bottom third among 53 countries and regions for the first four dimensions and among 23 countries for the fifth.

Source: Hofstede, Geert. February 2003. *Culture's Consequences, Comparing Values, Behaviors, Institutions, and Organizations Across Nations*, Second Edition. Newbury Park, CA: Sage Publications.

1. **Power Distance.** Hofstede used **power distance** to refer to the degree to which people accept economic and social differences in wealth, status, and well-being as natural and normal. Countries that allow inequalities to exist or believe they are natural are high in power distance; those that dislike and prevent the development of strong inequities between citizens are low in power distance. Highly industrialized Western countries tend to score lower in power distance, while developing countries, particularly those in Latin America, tend to score higher on this measure.

2. **Individualism versus Collectivism.** This dimension focuses on the values that govern relationships between individuals and groups. Countries high in individualism value individual achievement, freedom, and competition. In countries high in collectivism, values of group harmony, cohesiveness, and consensus are very strong, and the importance of cooperation and agreement is paramount. In collectivist cultures, the group is viewed as more important than the individual. Japan epitomizes a country dominated by collectivist values, while the United States is the most-often-mentioned example of an individualistic country.

3. **Achievement vs. Nurturing Orientation.** Countries that are achievement oriented value assertiveness, performance, success, and competition and are results oriented. Countries that are nurturing oriented value quality of life, warm personal relationships, and service and care for the weak. People from Japan and the United States tend to be achievement oriented, while those from the Netherlands, Sweden, and Denmark tend to be nurturing oriented.

4. **Uncertainty Avoidance.** People from different countries have been found to differ in their tolerance for uncertainty and their willingness to take risks. Countries low on uncertainty avoidance are relatively easygoing and comfortable with ambiguity (such as the United States and

Indonesia); they also tend to be tolerant of differences in what people believe and do. On the other hand, those high in uncertainty avoidance (such as Japan and France) tend to be more rigid and intolerant of difference. In high uncertainty avoidance cultures, conformity to the values of social and work groups to which a person belongs is the norm, and structured situations are preferred because they provide a sense of security.

5. **Long-Term versus Short-Term Orientation.** The last dimension that Hofstede identified concerns whether citizens of a country have a long- or short-term orientation toward life and work. A long-term orientation derives from values that include saving and persistence in achieving goals. A short-term orientation reflects values such as a concern for happiness or stability and living for the present. Japan and Hong Kong are known for their high rates of per capita savings; they have long-term orientations. Citizens in the United States and France, on the other hand, tend to spend more and save less, reflective of their short-term orientation.

One of the most important contributions of Hofstede's work for working with diversity in teams is the notion of **diversity distance.** For example, a group that consists of Norwegians and Swedes is not as diverse as a group that consists of Norwegians and Saudis, which in turn is not as diverse as a group of Norwegians, Saudis, and Americans. Understanding such distance and some typical patterns of perceptions and motives can be useful as a starting point in working with team members from diverse cultures.[45]

Generational Differences

"Every generation needs a new revolution."

—Thomas Jefferson

Another area where recent research has highlighted patterns of differences is on the core dimension of age (generation). Rather than relying solely on demographic birth patterns, author Claire Raines has identified four generations of workers.[46] Each has a unique history and set of common life experiences not shared by other generations. The evidence suggests these generational experiences shape work attitudes and perceptions in important ways. The four categories of generations are (1) traditionalists, (2) baby boomers, or boomers, (3) Generation X, or Xers, and (4) millennials.

- **Traditionalists.** The traditionalists were born between 1922 and 1943 and entered the workforce in the mid-1940s and 1950s. Often referred to as "the greatest generation" because of their survival and ingenuity during the years of the depression and World War II, these workers tend to embrace strong work ethic values. These values include hard work, a conservative approach to business, and intense organizational loyalty. Not surprisingly, this generation tends to not be comfortable publicly questioning the hierarchical chain of command.

- **Boomers.** Born between the mid-1940s and early 1960s, boomers were named as a result of a large increase in the birth rate during this time period—some 4.3 million births per year at the trend's peak. Boomers' work values tend to focus on quality of life and nonconformance (think hippies and Vietnam war protests). At the same time, they seek recognition and also place value on respect.

- **Generation X.** The Xers were born during the mid-1960s through about 1980 and grew up in an era that saw a large increase in nontraditional families (single parenting). They watched as their parents underwent the downsizing of the 1980s and developed a new sense of values about the world of work, which included some cynicism toward organizations, a focus on work–life balance, flexibility, and loyalty not to the company but to relationships with others.

- **Millenials.** Born in the early 1980s through the turn of the century, millenials are the first generation to be truly surrounded by technology and a media-driven world. They, like Xers, also tend to believe the workplace is more than just a place to make money, but a place to express oneself and often socialize. In addition, millenials place more value on global awareness, heroism, and goal achievement (see Tool Kit 8.7).

"I'll have someone from my generation get in touch with someone from your generation."

Gender Communication Differences

A third area of diversity understanding related to team functioning concerns gender—particularly communication style differences between men and women. For example, research observing men and women interacting in group settings has found that, for males, conversation is for solving problems, maintaining status, and preserving independence, not necessarily building closeness or community. For men, activities and doing things together is central, and just sitting and talking is not an essential part of closeness. Men are typically friends with other men they *do things* with. Females, on the other hand, use conversation to negotiate closeness and intimacy. For them, talk is the essence of intimacy, so building closeness and community means sitting and talking. Author Deborah Tannen succinctly describes these differences as "women talk to establish rapport . . . while men talk to report."[47]

From a team-building perspective, it is not hard to see how these differences can potentially influence the effectiveness of a gender-diverse team. In general, men will tend to be most focused on team *outcomes* and *solutions*, while women will be as concerned with the problem-solving *process*. Consistent with this, one study of team member perceptions (among men and women on the same set of teams) found male participants were most comfortable and satisfied with their team when the team's objectives were clarified to the greatest extent possible and the individual roles of team members were well-defined.[48]

Women, on the other hand, were most comfortable when communication and other group maintenance activities were clearly valued in addition to task

"The quickest way to a man's heart is through his chest."

—Roseanne Barr

activities. Women were also more comfortable than men with collective, team-based evaluations and rewards. More specifically, "poor sharing of information" was the top reported problem for females, while for males the top problem was "unclear or inappropriate expectations." These findings seem consistent with gender theorists' claim that women value relationships based on communication and understanding and that men's roles tend to be defined by role and status.

As with cultural and age generalities, it is worth noting once again that perceptions and behaviors of any particular individual of a given group may not conform to averages or tendencies. However, understanding the patterns that have been documented is useful to help move beyond surface levels of core differences (old/young; American/Chinese; male/female) to a richer understanding of how such differences may manifest themselves in team member perceptions and behavior.

Action

Armed with an awareness of the diversity in your team and an understanding of both misconceptions and real differences in general populations, you can ultimately be more effective in trying to make a diverse team productive. Several prescriptions useful in that regard are highlighted here:

Heighten Attention to Good Management Fundamentals

At the most basic level, good diversity management is simply good people management—only harder and more important without the lubricant of natural trust that comes from similarity. That means you need to focus on job-related behaviors and earn the trust and respect of others by treating them with respect and dignity. People of diverse backgrounds rarely need preferential treatment, just fairness. For example, if you need a good scribe or secretary, focus on the characteristics of the role, not on finding a young woman. If you need a team member to act in a leadership role, look closely at members' organizational and interpersonal skills, not on finding someone of a particular gender, race, or age. Do not succumb to allowing your stereotypical understanding of others, or your impressions based on superficial diversity, to bias your decisions. Put simply, the rules of good management do not change with diverse people—they just take on added importance.

Heighten Attention to Good Team Fundamentals

Here again, the presence of diversity only accentuates the need for even greater focus on the fundamental team disciplines discussed earlier in this chapter. More specifically, it is especially important to keep diverse teams small and pick members on the basis of some expertise other than just their diversity. In some circumstances, you may want to proactively seek those in protected classes for some roles—but always keep an eye on the outcome goals of the team. Tokenism for the sake of appearances, or for appeasing external pressure, is unlikely to be a productive approach and often backfires.

Similarly, be obsessive about clarifying shared outcome goals and group norms of behavior. With diverse group membership there is additional importance in being absolutely clear that everyone knows and agrees what the group is ultimately charged to accomplish, and how decisions will be made and work accomplished. Finally, seek mechanisms of mutual accountability. It is very easy in diverse teams for members to feel that their representation and input is enough. But without a shared stake in the outcome there is little chance the promise of diversity will truly be achieved.

Actively Challenge Your Assumptions

Although relevant differences in diverse team members do exist (language, culture, generation), we often perceive differences that are really *not* there. For example, with respect to gender, researcher Janet Hyde has recently shown that, while men and women certainly do differ in some straightforward ways, they are more *alike* than they are different. In her research, Hyde reviewed some 45 meta-analyses (large studies of other studies—in this case, 124 results overall) examining research that investigated almost every potential gender difference, including cognitive abilities, communication, personality, psychological well-being, work behavior, motor skills, and moral reasoning. What she found is that 78 percent of all these studies found *no meaningful differences* between men and woman. In other words, the data point more to similarities than differences.

Further, some disturbing research suggests perceptions of difference can influence important decisions. For example, an analysis of studies over a 20-year period showed that employees who were similar to their managers' ethnicity received higher performance ratings than employees who were dissimilar in terms of ethnicity.[49]

The key point here is the reasons for differences in performance were not *because* of age, race, or gender, but because of *perceptions* that age or race matter in performance. Do not confuse the two. A belief that race matters is very different than whether it *actually* matters. Unfortunately, people often pay a high price for these mythical managerial perceptions about surface-level diversity.

Recall that the best managerial outcomes come from treating people as individuals and seeking to understand their unique styles, values, and motives. So discuss with each team member their expectations—what they need and don't need and how you can be most helpful to them. In turn, you should articulate your expectations as well.

> *"Don't make assumptions. Find the courage to ask questions."*
> —Don Miguel Ruiz

Increase Interaction and Inclusion

Increasing interaction between individuals reduces the influence of stereotypes and improves team functioning. As people get to know others, stereotypes are replaced by more accurate knowledge of each other, which can result in reduced prejudice and greater cohesion. Be diligent about including diverse others in all key meetings and interactions. Unfortunately, diversity often makes us far less comfortable in interacting with others and thus the level of communication is likely to be typically *less* in such teams, particularly initially. Moreover, based on past experience, diverse members may have a fear of exclusion so it is doubly important to be sure all team members are included and important interactions are conducted in contexts accessible and comfortable to all.

"Aha! Just as I suspected!"

With that in mind, be bold in trying to better know your team members and seek to recognize and uncover important differences. If you are in doubt, go ahead and ask! Most people will give you the benefit of the doubt if they sense you are respectful and making a good faith effort to understand and be sensitive to their interests. Moreover, increase the use of process checks (Tool Kit 8.8) to be sure the group is on target. Seek two-way understanding by sharing your perceptions and style preferences and actively inquiring and listening to other team members share their own. By initiating dialogue, you will aid your own understanding and establish stronger relationships with team members.

Effective Team Interventions

Given an understanding of the basic disciplines of high-performing teams and the most common and insidious threats that derail them, we felt it was important to explore what can be done to effectively intervene to stimulate performance and avoid dysfunctions. We highlight four types of interventions that have proven useful in building various aspects of high-performance teams: (1) understanding member profiles, (2) building team cohesion, (3) conducting after-action reviews and process checks, and (4) dealing with a free rider.

Understanding Member Profiles

Most of us intuitively sense a team will perform better if the members get to know one another. While certainly true at some level, the unfortunate reality is what we ultimately come to know about others is often superficial (family, hobbies) and has little to do with how we might function effectively together in a team.

"Our team is well balanced. We have problems everywhere."

—Tommy Prothro, Former Professional Football Coach

One tool widely used in helping teams build better understanding of each other on such dimensions is the Myers-Briggs Type Indicator (MBTI) assessment of style preferences. As discussed in chapter 1, the MBTI is widely used as a stand-alone individual assessment of one's personality preferences. Yet, it can also be useful for team building. That's because the MBTI reveals individual preferences with respect to important team-related interactions such as how people prefer to gather information, order discussion, and make decisions.

Collectively reviewing the different MBTI profiles in a team can have a variety of potential benefits including identifying sources of conflict, providing a basis for improving communication patterns, distributing work according to preferences (assuming people agree with their preference profile), supplying a framework to better understand and resolve conflict, and increasing understanding of how to best utilize all members for useful and effective problem solving.

Building Team Cohesion

The extent to which members of a group actually conform to its norms is strongly influenced by the group's level of cohesiveness—the degree to which members are attracted to and motivated to remain part of a group. Persons in a highly cohesive group value their membership and strive to maintain positive relationships with other group members (see Management Live 8.4).

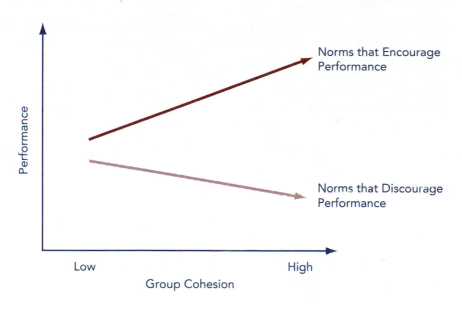

FIGURE 8.5

Cohesiveness and Performance Norms

The more difficult it is to get into a group, the more cohesive the group typically becomes. The hazing through which fraternities put their pledges is meant to screen out those who don't want to "pay the price" and to intensify the desire of those who do to become fraternity actives. But group initiation needn't be as blatant as hazing. The competition to be accepted to a good medical school results in highly cohesive first-year medical classes. The common initiation rites—applications, test taking, interviews, and the long wait for a final decision—all contribute to creating this cohesiveness.[50] For specific ways to build team cohesiveness, see Tool Kit 8.9.

Members of highly cohesive groups tend to be concerned about their group's activities and achievements. In contrast to people working in less cohesive groups, they tend to be more energetic, less likely to be absent, happier about group successes, and more upset about failures.[51] However, as noted in the section on myths, cohesive groups do not always result in high performance. The critical question is whether the cohesiveness supports high-performance task outcomes. Figure 8.5 helps to answer the question: "How do different norms and levels of cohesiveness combine to influence performance?"

Management Live 8.4

Safe Return Doubtful

One of the most powerful historical examples of extraordinary cohesion emerging in a team is the story of Sir Ernest Shackleton and his voyage to Antarctica. The story has been chronicled in an IMAX film and is the focal point of an innovative management training program created by Philip Morris Co. In the course of the training, managers are asked to place themselves in the roles of members of Shackleton's expedition, and it becomes a rich and authentic illustration of the power of a common purpose.

One of the more interesting aspects of the adventure was that Shackleton advertised for his crew with an ad that read: "Join an Antarctic Expedition! We promise you: low pay, poor climate, and *safe return doubtful*." Yet he still got well over 5,000 applicants! If people perceive an opportunity for an adventure and share in the values and common purpose, it is remarkable what they will tolerate and sacrifice on behalf of the team.

Source: Block, P. (2000 June). Safe Return Doubtful. AQP News for a Change, 1–3.

When the performance norms encourage performance and the group is cohesive, the figure shows this to be the best-case or high-performance situation. But in a highly cohesive group, where norms exist that discourage performance, the group is less likely to perform well. This creates the worst-case or low-performance situation in the figure. Members will behave in ways that conform to shared low-performance expectations.[52] The bottom line is that cohesion is important for team performance, but the norms present in the group will dictate whether or not that cohesion is channeled towards high or low performance. Remember, although norms are unwritten they have a powerful influence on people who simply want to do most anything to avoid the discomfort of breaking those norms. So, while it's important to increase cohesion in the group, it is equally important to pay attention to the types of norms (i.e., productive vs. unproductive) being set.

Conducting After-Action Reviews and Process Checks

The ability to learn from experience and work smarter as a group is an essential element of high performance. Great teams have "productive failures" whereby mistakes are not seen as cause for punishment but opportunities for growth and development. High-performing teams do not repeat their prior mistakes, they learn from them!

Military commanders have long recognized that, in life-or-death situations, making the same mistake twice, or not learning from prior failures, can be catastrophic. Tool Kit 8.8 is adapted from a U.S. Army best practice and represents a targeted process for ensuring that teams are conscious about what they are doing well—and not so well (these are also discussed in Chapter 3).

Dealing with a Free Rider

With respect to dealing with social loafing, you should consider three preliminary steps before approaching a slacking teammate. The first step is to correctly state the issue in terms of the demonstrated behaviors, not labels like "unmotivated" or lazy. Second, ask yourself whether it is legitimate for you to give feedback about the perceived problem. That is, does their behavior affect the team's or other members' ability to get results or is his behavior damaging a working relationship within the team? Third, consider whether you have collected a *balanced* set of facts about the situation? Often when we draw conclusions (as reflected when general labels are used to describe a situation), we really don't have sufficient facts on which to make a judgment.

One strategy for trying to actively reduce loafing is to address the issue before it happens, by creating spoken norms within the team. That is, before a goal gets set, a task assigned, or work divided, the team might discuss and agree upon the consequences for members who do not pull their own weight. This type of **social contracting** can help create a higher level of accountability and will allow for a common reference point all members can refer to should freeloading occur.

Thomas Watson, founder of IBM, was once asked, "Mr. Watson, how many people do you have working for you?" His response: "About half."

Creativity in Teams

As global competition rises and organizational challenges become ever more complex, there is an increasing premium on *creativity* in teams. Creativity is bringing into existence a new or novel idea, and this ability can often be hard to cultivate in teams. It might be tempting to think creativity stems from a lack of structure and procedure, but managing for more creativity in teams is not all about "letting go." Teams that produce creative results generally have an environment that encourages and rewards creativity—they don't just *hope* it happens. As management expert Peter Drucker has said, "Most of what happens in successful innovations is not the happy occurrence of a blind flash of insight but, rather, the careful implementation of an unspectacular but systematic management discipline."

The two critical success factors that promote more creativity in teams are: (1) a climate of trust and risk taking, and (2) the disciplined use of creative problem-solving tools and processes.

A Climate of Trust and Risk Taking

A team where creativity blossoms has a safe environment marked by openness, mutual trust, and a willingness to challenge each other's ideas. On such teams, members are willing to share information and to fully express differences in assumptions and interpretations. Team members see mistakes as learning experiences and part of the creative process. The team avoids "idea killer" phrases and places a premium on "idea growers" (Table 8.6).

Creative Problem-Solving Techniques

Having a set of techniques to help take advantage of the different talents of your team is a second key to creative team problem solving. Among the most successful methods for generating creative thought are an encouragement of divergent thinking, subdivision, analogies, and problem reversal.

One of the keys to creativity is to use language that embraces and encourages creative ideas rather than prematurely suppresses them. Below are two sets of common phrases in organizations:

TABLE 8.6   **Idea Growers vs. Idea Killers**

Idea Killers
• We tried it before.
• That will never work.
• It would cost too much.
• That's not our job.
• You can't do that here.
• Our customers would never go for that.
• That's not how we have always done it.
• What we have is good enough.
• You may be right, but. . .
• If it ain't broke, don't fix it.

Idea Growers
• How could we improve. . .?
• Who else can build on that?
• How many ways could we. . .?
• May I ask a question?
• What have we missed?
• Who else would be affected?
• What would happen if. . .?

Source: Gorman, C.K. (2000). *Creativity in business: A practical guide for creative thinking.* Menlo Park, CA: Crisp Publications.

Divergent Thinking

Most intuitive attempts to solve problems rely on **convergent thinking**—starting with a defined problem and then generating alternatives to solve it. Convergent thinking is oriented toward deriving the single best (or correct) answer to a clearly defined question. It emphasizes speed, accuracy, and logic and focuses on accumulating information, recognizing the familiar, reapplying set techniques, and preserving the already known. It is based on familiarity with existing knowledge and is most effective in situations where a ready-made answer exists and needs simply to be recalled from stored information.

Divergent thinking, by contrast, involves producing multiple or alternative answers from available information. It requires making unexpected combinations, recognizing links among remotely associated issues, and transforming information into unexpected forms. Answers to the same question arrived at via divergent thinking may vary substantially from person to person but be of equal value. They may never have existed before and thus are often novel, unusual, or surprising.

Subdivision

One stimuli for divergent thinking is **subdivision,** or the process of breaking things, such as problems, products, or services, into their smallest component parts or attributes. Once a problem or item is subdivided, think about changes to each individual part, including those that seem on the surface like they could never work. The number of alternatives generated is likely to be far greater, and often the best creativity stems from the wild and "out there" ideas included in a longer list.

In a similar fashion, it can be useful to have a question checklist to push creative buttons in a team. Useful questions for prompting creativity include:

- What else could this be used for?
- What else could be used instead?
- How could it be adopted or modified for a new use?
- What if it were larger, thicker, heavier, or stronger?
- What if it were smaller, thinner, or lighter?
- How might it be rearranged or reversed?
- In my wildest dreams, how would this problem be resolved?

Analogies

One well-tested technique for improving creative problem solving involves using **analogies.** The goal of analogies is to help make the strange familiar or the familiar strange. That is, team members put something they don't know in terms of something they do, or they expand thinking by taking a familiar issue and relating it in a new or distinctive context. Some good questions to ask when forming analogies are:

- What does this remind me of?
- What does this make me feel like?
- What is this similar to?
- What *isn't* this similar to?

Many creative solutions have been generated via the use of analogies. FedEx was modeled after the hub and spokes of a wheel. Taco Bell, in turn, used the FedEx model as an analogy to help conceive how to get small stores in diverse locations the inventory they needed. When using analogies it is important to find analogs that can be readily visualized or pictured by your audience (for example, football games, crowded malls, making breakfast).

"Creativity is more than just being different. Anybody can be plain weird, that's easy. Making the simple awesomely simple, that's 'creativity'."

—Charles Mingus, Jazz legend

"Analogies, it is true, decide nothing, but they can make one feel more at home."

—Sigmund Freud

Problem Reversal

A final technique for generating creative ideas is **reversing the problem.** As we discuss in Chapter 3, reframing a problem is sometimes all it takes to redirect energy towards creative solutions. So, take a problem and think of the opposite approach, and force seemingly unrelated attributes together. For example, suppose you work at a restaurant and are faced with the problem that guests are unhappy with the service. Maybe one angle would be to treat the guests *as servers* and allow them to help prepare and serve their own meal (open grills are now very popular). ATMs were conceived in that same way (that is, have less employee service and more convenient opportunity for customers to serve themselves). The idea is to reverse or contradict the existing understanding of a problem to expand the alternatives considered. So maybe the way to higher student satisfaction is to make a course *harder*, not easier, or that the service in a retail store is *too* fast, or a map too detailed. Such opposite and upside-down perspectives often challenge and provoke and can serve to enhance team creativity.

Virtual Teams and Meetings

Not long ago, the mention of a team evoked images of a group of people in a nice meeting room, huddled around a conference table, with someone writing notes on a flip chart. Today, teams are often virtual, with people working in remote locations. Virtual arrangements can save time and travel expense and can allow for people to belong to a team whether or not they live or work in close proximity to each other. Virtual membership also allows people to more easily accommodate their personal and professional lives.[53]

"Technology . . . the knack of so arranging the world that we don't have to deal with it."
—Max Frisch, Swiss author, 1957

While much has been made of the virtual revolution and the need to develop a new set of virtual skills (virtual communication skills, virtual collaborative skills, and so on) the truth is that the five fundamental disciplines of high team performance remain the same. Indeed, the most significant difference is that, because people are dispersed and there is no naturally occurring monitoring and social pressure, virtual teams demand even higher attention to those disciplines. That is, for virtual teams to achieve high performance it is even more critical to ensure that the group is kept to a manageable number, the right members are selected, goals and norms are established and shared, a productive working approach is facilitated, and members feel a mutual accountability for team outcomes.[54]

For example, one study of 29 virtual teams that communicated strictly by e-mail over a six-week period found the most successful teams shared three specific characteristics. First, they began their interactions with a series of social messages—introducing themselves and providing some personal background—before focusing on the work at hand. Second, they set clear goals and roles for each team member, thus enabling all team members to identify with one another. Third, all team members consistently displayed eagerness, enthusiasm, and an intense action orientation in their messages (mutual accountability).[55]

Electronic Meetings

Whether a team is geographically dispersed and primarily virtual or not, some evidence suggests that electronic meetings (systems that allow for simultaneous discussions) can be superior to face-to-face gatherings, at least for certain types of group tasks. The major advantages of electronic meetings are anonymity, honesty, and speed. Participants can anonymously type any message they want and it flashes on the screen for all to see. It also allows people to be brutally honest without penalty or the pressures of social conformity. And it's fast because chitchat is eliminated, discussions don't digress, and many participants can "talk" at once without stepping on one another's toes.

More specifically, some studies have found that electronic meetings can be as much as 55 percent faster than traditional face-to-face meetings.[56] On the other hand, electronic meetings are not always advisable. For example, they are not good for establishing relationships, dealing with sensitive issues, or persuading a team to fully commit to a course of action. The bottom-line implication is that it makes sense to use electronic meeting technologies for one part of the team process. If you really want to get creative, innovative, high-quality ideas, then electronic discussion is clearly better than verbal discussion. On the other hand, if you want to build a good team, strengthen the relationships, and allow for opportunities for mentoring and individual growth, verbal discussion is better. Tool Kit 8.10 provides a nice template for determining whether an electronic or face-to-face meeting would be most productive.

Great Team Members

"You are either part of the solution, or you are part of the problem."
        —Anonymous

If you want to be a part of great teams, you need to be a great team player yourself. Teams need members who perform both task and maintenance (interpersonal) roles, and the best contributors are individuals who know what they do well and can match that to the needs of their team. Table 8.7 is a useful typology of the different roles a team member could potentially perform to contribute to a team. It also makes a nice team audit for assessing contributions of members and the gaps that, if filled, might help a team function more effectively.

TABLE 8.7 | **Possible Team Member Roles[57]**

Task Roles	Interpersonal Roles
• **Initiating:** Suggesting new goals or ideas.	• **Encouraging:** Fostering team solidarity by reinforcing others.
• **Information seeking:** Clarifying key issues.	• **Harmonizing:** Mediating conflicts.
• **Opinion seeking:** Clarifying attitudes, values, and feelings.	• **Compromising:** Shifting one's own position on an issue to reduce conflict in the team.
• **Elaborating:** Giving additional information about points made by others.	• **Gatekeeping:** Encouraging all team members to participate.
• **Coordinating:** Pulling together ideas and suggestions.	• **Reflecting:** Pointing out the positive and negative aspects of the team's dynamics and calling for change if necessary.
• **Orienting:** Keeping the team headed toward its stated goals.	• **Standard setting:** Expressing, or calling for discussion of, standards for evaluating the quality of the team.
• **Recording:** Performing a "team memory" function by documenting discussion and outcomes.	
• **Challenging:** Questioning the quality of the team's method, logic, and results.	

Concluding Note

As we have repeatedly emphasized throughout this book, many principles and tools of great managers are very straightforward and make so much intuitive sense that they start to sound easy—and that is a grave trap. Team building is exceedingly hard work and it takes time and discipline. Remember that not all great team members or team processes started that way. The predictable reality is you will be a part of teams that flounders and your results will sometimes be disappointing. One goal you should have with any team you join is to learn something you can take with you as you navigate a world filled with organizational teams that could use your help. When things do not go well, ask yourself (and your team), "What can we learn from this?" and go on bravely with a tolerance and enthusiasm for the struggle. In the end, few things are more satisfying and outright fun than being on a team that really works.

"Nothing great was ever achieved without enthusiasm."
—George Bernard Shaw

Key Terms

Abilene paradox

activity-based goals

analogies

choking

competitive team rewards

convergent thinking

cooperative team rewards

deep-level diversity

diffusion of responsibility

divergent thinking

diversity distance

escalation of commitment

forming stage

groupthink

identifiability

innocent bystander effect

norming stage

norms

outcome-based goals

performing stage

power distance

reversing the problem

Ringelmann effect

risky shift

social conformity

social contracting

social loafing

storming stage

subdivision

surface-level diversity

team

Team Effectiveness and Diversity Tool Kits

Tool Kit 8.1   Essentials for Effective Meetings[58]

First and foremost, get in the habit of starting every meeting by asking: (1) What are the two or three most important things we need to get done at this meeting? and (2) How much time does everyone have? Just that opening can help create the sense of direction and urgency that helps avoid the wasted time and lack of direction characterizing all too many meetings. If you feel a need to socialize (often entirely appropriate to help build team spirit and morale), focus on the goals of the meeting first, then socialize. But try to keep it short—shorter is always better. Try to do a few things at a brisker pace.

You should also:

- *Always* work from an agenda, ideally distributed in advance but at least established at the very start of the meeting.
- Appoint a scribe to record the discussion and outcomes of the meeting.
- Use "go-arounds" and direct solicitations of those with known interests and expertise to ensure you get all relevant information into the discussion.
- Explicitly attach action assignments to specific members and get public ownership (in front of the group) of their willingness to complete the task by a deadline date.

- Even in a short meeting, avoid leading all the discussion yourself. Maximize participation by inviting members to lead different aspects of the discussion.
- Push the team to stay focused on the key meeting objectives identified at the start. Use "parking lots" for good off-task ideas and defer discussion until future meetings.
- Close every meeting with a brief review of what was accomplished, clearly reiterate any action items and which members "own" those items, and push to schedule a time for the next meeting.

Tool Kit 8.2   Three Terrific Icebreakers for a Team Start-Up

- **Commonality Amidst Diversity** Working together, the group identifies three things (such as background, experiences, possessions) that all members of their team have in common, but that no other team would likely share.
- **Two Truths and a Lie** Present two truths and a lie about yourself and let the team figure out which is the lie.
- **Learning Names** Have everyone share just a few minutes of background and then give everyone in the team a nickname based on that brief bio. Or ask each person to match the first letter of their name with the first letter of a car, vegetable, or fruit. Then go around and have everyone attempt to recall the phrase for everyone else in the group. It is remarkable how this simple labeling process can enhance the stickiness (memory recall) of names and bios.

Tool Kit 8.3   Peer Evaluation Items

This team member:

1. Consistently shows up to meetings on time.
2. Demonstrates flexibility in setting meeting times.
3. Prepares work assignments prior to meetings.
4. Contributes a shared amount of the workload.
5. Encourages innovation among team members.
6. Maintains focus on team goals.
7. Maintains an appropriate balance between talking and listening.
8. Changes his or her opinion when appropriate.
9. Communicates ideas effectively.
10. Shows respect for all group members.
11. Provides feedback effectively.
12. Is receptive to, or non-defensive about, feedback.

Tool Kit 8.4   Disciplines of a High-Performing Team

Focus on the elements below to prevent most problems that keep teams from being effective and enjoyable. If your team is working well, you're probably practicing all of these in some fashion. If your team is experiencing difficulty, check each step as a team, and you'll most likely figure out what needs to be worked on to bring about success.

1. Keep to an optimal group size (3–10). "If we have too many members, we'll assign subgroups and choose representatives to be a small coordinating team."
2. Ensure complementary skill sets. "We have the technical (functional), problem-solving and interpersonal skills we need. Based on this work, no one is redundant; everyone has unique skills to contribute."
3. Establish a shared purpose and clear outcome. "Here are *our* goals and here are *my* individual roles and outcome goals." "We will measure our success by. . ."

4. Establish productive norms and working approach. "We enforce norms regarding effort, meetings, and conflict management. We encourage spirited discussion and confrontation but with personal support. Our meetings are tight and disciplined."

5. Create mutual accountability. "Here's what we're accountable for, why we have to do it together, and how we are each rewarded if we succeed."

Tool Kit 8.5   Strategies to Help Teams Avoid Social Conformity [59]

- Ask each member to be a critical evaluator.
- Encourage a sharing of objections.
- Don't let the leader become partial to one course of action.
- Create subgroups with different leaders to work on the same problem.
- Have members discuss issues with outsiders and report back.
- Invite outside experts to observe and react to group discussions.
- Have a different member act as "devil's advocate" at each meeting.
- Write alternative scenarios for the intentions of competing groups.
- Hold "second-chance" meetings once an initial decision is made.
- Make use of pre-votes and anonymous decision votes.
- Use electronic meeting formats.

Tool Kit 8.6   Getting Underneath Surface Diversity

To know that a person is of a certain race, gender, or ethnic background does not by itself tell us much about that person's perceptions, values, or behaviors. However, it clearly does alert us to possible *sources* of miscommunication. We can then take the opportunity to learn more.

The following list includes several practical strategies for learning more about those who differ from us. Not surprisingly, the key ingredient to establishing a relationship with people of difference is mutual respect and a desire for understanding.

1. Create informal time together. Invite fellow members to meals—ideally in your home. Show respect for their culture and language and signal to them that you honestly want to learn about them and their culture. Ask, "How would I feel if I were in their shoes?"

2. Learn how to pronounce names correctly. Their name is as important to them as yours is to you. Practice saying it until you get close to how it should be pronounced.

3. When speaking English, do so slowly and clearly. Remember, raising your voice and speaking louder does not make English more understandable.

4. Listen, observe, and ask a lot of questions. A key question might be, "Would you help me understand?"

5. Be careful about promises. In English we express the subjunctive (possibility, probability, or contingency) in a way that is sometimes misunderstood by internationals.

6. Don't allow cultural differences or preferences to become the basis for criticism and judgments. Differences are neither good nor bad. What we do with them is the key. Seek and promote any organizational diversity initiatives (training seminars, mentoring, language seminars) that might help your cause.

Tool Kit 8.7   Six Principles for Managing Millennials

So how do you translate what you've read so far into your day-to-day life on the job? What do today's young employees want? If we're designing recruiting programs and management systems based on their values and needs, how do we proceed? What kind of work environments attract, retain, and motivate millennial co-workers? Here are their six most frequent requests:

1. **You be the leader.** This generation has grown up with structure and supervision, with parents who were role models. Millennials are looking for leaders with honesty and integrity. It's not that they don't want to be leaders themselves, they'd just like some great role models first.

2. **Challenge me.** Millennials want learning opportunities. They want to be assigned to projects they can learn from. A recent Randstad employee survey found that "trying new things" was the most popular item. They're looking for growth, development, a career path.

3. **Let me work with friends.** Millennials say they want to work with people they *click* with. They like being friends with co-workers. Employers who provide for the social aspects of work will find those efforts well rewarded by this newest cohort. Some companies are even interviewing and hiring groups of friends.

4. **Let's have fun.** A little humor, a bit of silliness, even a little irreverence will make your work environment more attractive.

5. **Respect me.** "Treat our ideas respectfully," they ask, "even though we haven't been around a long time."

6. **Be flexible.** The busiest generation ever isn't going to give up its activities just because of jobs. A rigid schedule is a surefire way to lose your millennial employees.

Tool Kit 8.8   Team Process Checks

To help assess whether your team is operating effectively, have each team member complete a process check form, rating the team's functioning on a 10-point scale on a set of dimensions that ensure good team functioning. Questions might include:

- How satisfied are you that your ideas are heard by the team?
- Our team outcome goals are clear and understood by all team members.
- Rate the quality of decision-making in the team.
- How well does the team follow its agenda and meet agreed-upon deadlines?
- How well does the team follow its own ground rules?
- How well does the team fully utilize people's skill sets?
- Rate your level of comfort in asking other team members for help.
- How well does the team resolve differences of opinion?
- Overall, how would you rate the quality of the team's functioning ability?

Tool Kit 8.9   Building Team Cohesiveness

- Schedule nontask time together.
- Get agreement on group goals.
- Focus attention on competition with outside groups.
- Reward members for group results (cooperative rather than competitive rewards). Isolate the group.
- Reduce contact with other groups.
- Create a sense of performance "crisis."

The opposite steps may be taken to reduce the cohesiveness of a group. Such actions may become necessary when members of a highly cohesive group are operating with negative performance norms and efforts to change these norms have failed.

Tool Kit 8.10   When to Meet Face-to-Face vs. Electronically

Face to Face

- First meetings when team members are trying to create a common identity, establish goals, and hammer out a productive working approach.
- When the goal of the meeting is to persuade members to commit to a particular course of action.

- When the team must deal with highly sensitive issues.
- When conflicts must be resolved.
- When the team is acknowledging important milestones or celebrating successes.
- When privacy and confidentiality of team discussions must be maintained.

Electronically

- When generating new ideas.
- When the goal is fact-finding or solving problems that have one right answer.
- When gathering preliminary information and opinions prior to a face-to-face meeting.
- When keeping team members informed between meetings.
- When the goal is to reduce status effects or groupthink.

CHAPTER

9

Conflict and Negotiation

"Win-win negotiating is not just academic talk to us. We need more people who are good at protecting the firm's interest without alienating our clients and associates. When we can bring in people who really 'get it,' everybody is much better off. Those who 'don't get it' don't last very long in this business."

—Sherri Bachmann,
Managing Partner,
Bachmann Global Associates

1. Resolving a Team Dispute

You are a team leader and just returned to your office after a miserable meeting. At the end of the meeting, one of the members, Pat, stood up and said some very offensive and controversial things. Jordan briefly responded and stormed out. You asked for other feedback and rebuttal, but no one else said anything and the meeting was adjourned. But you have already gotten an e-mail from two other members claiming they were offended and felt "silenced" and that you better do something about this or they will take their concerns to a higher level.

Given that this has been a very productive team, how do you go about holding it together? What steps should you take? Would you bring Pat and Jordan together, and, if so, how would you mediate the meeting? Would you involve others? What traps would you want to avoid that would likely only escalate the dispute?

2. Negotiating an Agreement Between Conflicting Parties

You are the chair of the student facilities committee at the Ballton learning-living center (dormitory) on your campus and find yourself in the middle of a sticky debate. When it was built in the 1940s, the hallmark of the center was a clock tower that has now fallen into disrepair, to the point of leaking and causing water damage. The clock tower was originally paid for by a special gift from the Ballton family, a large and continuous donor to the university to this day. Rumor has it that the key donors in the family are quite disappointed the tower has been neglected.

Part of your committee is adamant about the importance of repair, not only to appease the Balltons, but also for the historical significance of the structure and the aesthetic attractiveness of the center. The other part of your committee is equally adamant and wants to spend only the absolute minimum necessary to repair the leak and use the remainder of your budget dollars on other facilities improvement including revamping the workout and recreational rooms in the lower level of the center. One member of that group is particularly vocal and you overheard him comment that "It would be stupid to spend the money on something nobody in the dorm uses or cares about."

You know both sides have compelling arguments and it would not be wrong to take either side. So how would you go about negotiating a plan that would potentially satisfy both factions of your committee? Where would you start? How would you go about structuring a negotiating process here? What traps would you want to avoid to not further polarize the groups? What if you were to make a decision yourself and tell both sides to deal with it?

3. Getting Beyond Failed Negotiations

You are assistant manager at a large retail store where two of your sales associates, Chris and Terry, have been at each other's throats to the point where the conflict is now affecting work at the store and bothering others. When it first started, you brought the two together for a meeting, but you did not really know what to do and did not take an active role, and the meeting was essentially a disaster. Because they are part of your unit, the store manager has told you to "Please deal with this ASAP and let me know what I can do to help."

So what would you do? What would be your first actions? How would you structure a mediation meeting that would be more likely to yield better results than last time? Any traps to avoid? Would you ask your boss to help in some way?

Introduction

An inescapable reality for anyone who works with people in organizations is **conflict.** Conflict can take many forms: It may be a disagreement about how to complete a task or allocate money or a personality clash between two associates, but it is an inevitable part of organizational life.[1] As we will see, conflict is not always bad for a group or organization, but, improperly diagnosed or left unchecked, it can be a highly destructive force. Too much conflict can create a toxic workplace environment where satisfaction and performance are low and absenteeism and turnover are high. Great managers know this and take great care to prevent conflict from becoming destructive.

"Where all think alike, no one thinks very much."

—Walter Lippmann

Conflict Can Get Ugly

"The suggestions are supposed to go in the box."

Conflict, of course, is a big topic, and entire college courses are devoted to coverage of conflict negotiation, mediation, and resolution. However, from a skills perspective, we believe a few focal points are key for managers. First, all conflict is not the same. Thus, knowing the different types and sources of conflict is useful as a diagnostic aid when faced with disputes and disagreements.

MYTHS 9.1   **Myths of Conflict and Negotiation**

- *Conflict is always dysfunctional.* Conflict can be destructive; however, in the right form and managed well, it can also stimulate innovation and improve group decision-making.

- *Conflict is generally a "personality" problem.* Most conflict has less to do with personality and more to do with different perceptions and scarce resources. A recurring lesson of conflict management is to separate the people from the problem.

- *Negotiation creates a winner and loser.* Sometimes there will be a winner and loser, and sometimes people have to agree to disagree or find an equal place to call it a draw. But the ultimate and often possible resolution is to break out of a win-lose mind-set and seek outcomes where both parties feel like winners.

- *Good conflict mediators are born, not made.* Some people do have personal traits that make them well-suited to bringing people together (grandmas often have this knack). But like almost everything else we have addressed in this text, effective mediation is a learned skill. The evidence is clear that those who wing it are generally far less successful than those who learn and execute a known set of effective principles.

Second, there is an impressive body of evidence regarding different *styles* of conflict resolution and their relative pros and cons. An understanding of your own style preferences and an awareness of the different styles available (and the importance of adapting one's style to the situation) are important conflict management tools.

Third, there are few more unnerving events for new managers than to be thrust into conflict situations and being asked to mediate between conflicting parties or help negotiate an agreement. Conflict situations are often highly charged and emotional and can cause great stress. Hence, an understanding of the fundamental principles of effective negotiation and mediation is critical for success in such contexts. In short, managers do not have to have the solution to every conflict. They should, however, be capable of diagnosing conflict and facilitating resolutions and agreements. This chapter is focused on those competencies, but first note the common myths associated with these areas that are shown in Myths 9.1. Remember that an important step toward doing the "right thing" is knowing what not to do.

Types of Conflict and Their Effects

At the most general level, two kinds of conflict occur in organizations.[2] **Task conflict** is conflict over tasks, ideas, and issues and is divorced from evaluations of people's character. **Relationship conflict** is personalized and, therefore, highly threatening and damaging for personal relationships, team functioning, and problem solving.

Conflict can be compared to cholesterol: Both have good and bad forms (and in case you were wondering, HDL is the good cholesterol and LDL is the bad cholesterol). Relationship conflict is the "bad conflict." It threatens productivity and interferes with the effort people put into a task because they are preoccupied with retaliation, increasing their personal power, or attempting to restore cohesion, rather than working on the task. For the most part, relationship conflict is probably what comes to mind when you think about conflict. It causes managers a great deal of stress and is associated with mainly negative consequences.

TABLE 9.1 Positive and Negative Effects of Conflict

Positive Effects of Conflict	Negative Effects of Conflict
Brings problems into the open that might otherwise be ignored.	Can lead to negative emotions and stress.
Can motivate people to try to understand others' positions and ideas.	Often reduces communication between participants, which can hurt work coordination.
Encourages people to voice new ideas, facilitating innovation and change.	May cause leaders to avoid participative leadership and instead rely on "top-down" authoritarian decisions.
Forces people to challenge their thinking and assumptions, often improving the quality of decisions.	Can result in negative stereotyping and work-group divisions, since members of opposing groups tend to emphasize the differences between themselves and the opposition.

In contrast, task conflict can be seen as the "good conflict." It can be beneficial to more effective decision making and problem solving and can lead to greater accuracy, insight, and innovation.[3] Task conflict may induce a healthy level of constructive criticism and the stimulation of more spirited and evidence-based discussion. In other words, task conflict is what managers may want to stimulate to "shake things up". Stimulating relationship conflict is a recipe for disaster.

In one study of 48 top management teams' decision making quality and team member commitment, team members were asked to assess how much relationship conflict (anger, personal friction, personality clashes) and task conflict (disagreements over ideas, differences about the content of the decision) was present in their respective groups. Results showed the presence of task conflict was associated with higher decision making quality, higher commitment, and more decision acceptance. In contrast, the presence of relationship conflict significantly reduced those same outcomes.[4]

Table 9.1 outlines several of the more evidence-based positive and negative consequences of conflict in the workplace. Consistent with the above findings, other studies have found a low to medium level of task-related conflict can stimulate more careful thinking and conscientious work.[5] Other evidence has found a leading cause of business failure is too much *agreement* among top management; thus, task conflict that fosters alternate viewpoints and less complacency can be very useful.[6]

"Don't be afraid of opposition. Remember, a kite rises against, not with, the wind."

—Hamilton Mabie

While task conflict can and does have beneficial effects, and the good conflict/bad conflict distinction has been conventional wisdom for many years, task conflict certainly does not *always* have such effects. Indeed, the potential damaging effects of conflict was highlighted in a recent meta-analysis that examined 28 separate studies of conflict in teams and found the presence of conflict in work teams has a generally detrimental effect on team member satisfaction and often even on team performance.[7]

These most recent findings confirm that relationship conflict is certainly dysfunctional in organizations and that too much task conflict is generally bad as well. Findings on the beneficial effects of a small to moderate amount of conflict are mixed. Factors that help explain when and where task conflict may be beneficial are the timing and handling of the conflict in the course of a decision process. That is, *when* the conflict occurs (early or late in the process) and *how it is addressed* by the manager or team, seem to be important to whether the task conflict ultimately has good or bad effects.

TABLE 9.2   **Effects of Conflict in Project Teams**

Conflict Type	Project Stage (High-Performing Teams)		
	Early	Middle	Late
Relationship	Low	Moderate	Moderate
Task	Low	Moderate	Low

Conflict Type	Project Stage (Low-Performing Teams)		
	Early	Middle	Late
Relationship	Low	Low	High
Task	Moderate	Moderate	Very High

For example, one recent study explored the conflict profiles of a set of both high- and low-performing teams over a 13-week period.[8] As shown in Table 9.2, the intriguing results suggest high-performing teams had very little conflict *early* in the project whereas conflict in the low-performing teams was present from the beginning. During the middle period of the project, the high-performing teams experienced moderate levels of conflict, whereas the low-performing teams maintained a relatively consistent level of conflict. Finally, late in the project the low-performing teams had a high degree of conflict, whereas the high-performing teams experienced much less. These findings and others are important in managing conflict because they prescribe when and how it can be either beneficial or detrimental. For a structured list of questions to diagnose the sources of conflict, see Tool Kit 9.1.

Managing Conflict

"There is an immutable conflict at work in life and in business, a constant battle between peace and chaos. Neither can be mastered, but both can be influenced. How you go about that is the key to success."

—Philip Knight, former CEO, Nike

So what do great managers do when conflict arises? Clearly, the goal isn't to eliminate conflict (that's impossible anyway) but to manage it in a way that reduces its potential harm to engagement and performance. An important first step in this direction is to be able to diagnose a conflict situation to determine its source. That is, as we have noted in several places in this text, there should be no treatment without diagnosis. To do so is managerial malpractice!

Diagnosing Conflict Sources

As noted, the first diagnosis to make about conflicts is whether they are focused on relationships or on tasks. Relationship-centered disputes can be nasty—they stem from what has transpired between two or more people and often deteriorate into name-calling sessions or even worse. These are disputes about things like accusations of harm, demands for justice, or feelings of resentment, and are often played out in confrontations where emotions run high. Relationship conflict is sometimes outside the manager's scope to mediate and the best solution may well be to separate (reassign, relocate) the conflicting parties if no reasonable working solution can be found.

Task-centered disputes, on the other hand, are debates over competing ideas, proposals, interests, or resources. They can be, though not always are, conducted in a healthy manner. In most of such conflicts, emotions run "cooler" than they do in relationship-centered disputes, and participants are generally more receptive to solutions.

Several questions are useful starting points for diagnosing conflict and represent the major sources of conflict:

- Do the disputants have access to the same information (informational)?
- Do the disputants perceive common information differently (perceptual)?
- Are the disputants significantly influenced by their role in the organization (role)?
- What stressful factors in the environment might disputants be reacting to (environment)?
- In what way do disputants' personal differences play a role in the dispute (personal)?

Informational Factors

Informational factors come into play when people have developed their point of view on the basis of a different set of facts. The parable of the blind men and the elephant vividly illustrates this point.[9] The parable describes a group of blind men who traveled to visit an elephant. When they encountered the animal, each approached a different part of it: One felt the elephant's trunk, another its leg, another its side, another its tail, and so on. Consequently, each man believed the elephant was something different: The one that felt the trunk argued that the elephant was like a snake, while the one who felt the leg maintained it was more similar to a tree trunk. Because each of the men had a different piece of information about the elephant's body, they had vastly different interpretations of its nature.

Such differences in information are often the source of conflict. In an organization, if two people have different information about, say, the budget allocations for a project or the deadline for filling a customer request, they are likely to find themselves in conflict as a result of their different understandings.

> "Get your facts first, and then you can distort them as much as you please."
> —Mark Twain

Perceptual Factors

Perceptual factors exert their influence when people have different images or interpretations of the same thing. In this instance, each person selects the data that support his or her point of view and tend to devalue information that does not support it. Say, for example, you have an instructor who assigns a team paper with no set page limits. When you ask for clarification on the length, the instructor tells you that she doesn't think you can cover all the information in less than seven pages. It is very likely that members of your work team could disagree on what this means: Some will contend the paper is to be seven pages long; others will argue it probably needs to be longer to fulfill the instructor's expectations. You all have the same objective (if somewhat vague) information, but you interpret it differently. This difference in perception is a common source of frustration and of conflict.

Role Factors

Role factors have the potential to contribute to conflict when people believe their roles within an organization are somehow in conflict or that the "turf" associated with their position is being challenged. This may occur when division managers believe they have to fight for their work unit in budget allocation meetings, but it can also occur at the interpersonal level. Assume your best friend becomes your boss. It is not hard to see how the roles of friend and boss might be difficult to navigate in this circumstance. A similar problem can occur between the role of parent and friend, of boss and employee, and a host of other combinations. While many people can work through such conflicts, the possibility of conflict certainly exists when incompatible roles are imposed on an interpersonal relationship.

Environmental Factors

Several environmental factors can cause, or at least intensify, conflict situations. When an organization is forced to operate on a shoestring budget, its members are more likely to become involved in conflict over scarce resources. Scarcity of any kind tends to lower the levels of trust people have in one another, which in turn increases the potential for conflict. For example, when a large East Coast bank announced a major downsizing, the threat to employees' security was so severe it disrupted long-time, close working relationships. Even personal friendships were not immune: Long-standing golf foursomes and car pools were disbanded because tension between members was so high.

Another environmental factor is uncertainty. When people feel uneasy about their status in an organization, they tend to become anxious and more prone to conflict. This kind of "frustration conflict" often occurs when employees experience rapid, repeated change in their environment. If task assignments, management philosophies, work procedures, or lines of authority are changed frequently or with little notice, the resultant stress can cause sharp, bitter conflicts over seemingly trivial problems.

Finally, an important aspect of conflict stemming from the environment is the degree to which competition is present. In many instances, a little healthy competition can be an inducement for higher effort and engagement. For example, creative sales managers routinely develop contests to stoke the competitive juices of their people who respond because they want to win any game. Unfortunately, it is also possible that competition can interfere with overall group success. Often called a **mixed-motive situation,** employees are placed in a position where they are rewarded if they compete aggressively but told they should work toward the department's overall outcome as a whole.[10] As you can imagine, competing can often be a **zero-sum game** whereby the success of one employee means the failure of another. Such situations can lead to intense conflict when one employee leads another to believe they are both working toward the common good, the latter employee finding out later that the other employee was in it for himself.

"Science cannot resolve moral conflicts, but it can help to more accurately frame the debates about those conflicts."

—Heinz Pagels

Personal Factors

Personal factors are perhaps the most intractable of conflict sources. Conflicts stemming from incompatible personal values are very difficult to resolve. They can become highly emotional and take on moral overtones. In this kind of conflict, disagreements about *what is factually correct* can easily turn into bitter arguments over *who is morally right*.

Other types of personal factors that can contribute to conflict include different personalities as well as differing long- and short-term goals for the parties involved. Interestingly, even cases where people are very much alike and want to play the same role (for example, two people want to set the agenda or to "take charge") can lead to conflict. You have probably experienced situations where two people did not get along because they were so much alike!

When facing a particular conflict, understanding the five potential sources is a good first step in diagnosing the situation and deciding on a course of action. Armed with an idea of what the nature of the conflict is, you can then move into conflict management mode.

Matching Conflict Styles with Situations

As with all people situations, there is no one best way to manage conflict, either as an involved adversary or as a neutral third party. Rather, there are several

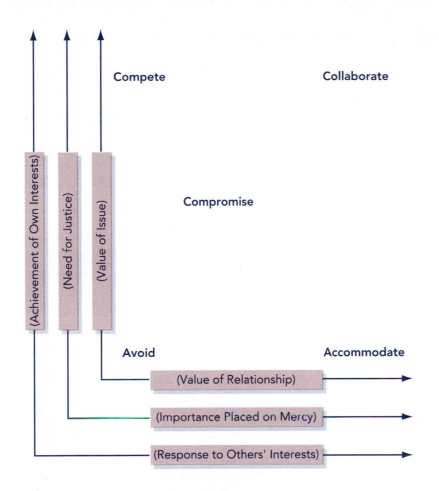

FIGURE 9.1

Thomas Kilman Conflict Resolution Grid

styles and strategies you can use, and their effectiveness for you will depend on a variety of factors. One of the most well known assessments for measuring your conflict style is the Thomas-Kilman Conflict Mode Instrument. That assessment is based on a model of five conflict resolution strategies: competition, accommodation, avoidance, compromise, and collaboration. Although most people find they have one dominant conflict management style, you might find your preferred style is balanced between two or more. This may indicate flexibility in your conflict management style and may help you to adapt your style as the situation dictates—an important capacity for most effective conflict management. Figure 9.1 provides an overview of the five conflict management types and how the styles relate to one another.

Two often-misunderstood points regarding conflict management styles are important to keep in mind. First, there are no necessarily good or bad styles. That is, *all* five styles can lead to successful strategies, it just depends on the situation. So the key is to develop the ability to recognize when a style would be appropriate and be able to adapt your style to that circumstance. There are, however, ineffective techniques of applying any of these conflict management styles, which you would be better off avoiding. These are illustrated in Table 9.3.

Second, do not confuse conflict management styles with stable personal characteristics (such as height), abilities (such as cognitive ability), or personality traits (such as extraversion). Conflict styles are preferences, your natural reactions or behavioral responses. For example, if your natural style is to prefer avoiding conflict, it does not mean you cannot, or will not, confront. It does mean, however, you will have to be more conscious of the appropriate situations for confrontation and expend more energy to execute that particular approach.

We will now describe each of the five styles in more detail.

"You can't shake hands with a clenched fist."

—Indira Gandhi

"The direct use of force is such a poor solution to any problem, it is generally employed only by small children and large nations."

—David Friedman

TABLE 9.3 *Ineffective* Conflict Management Techniques
• After listening to the other person for a short time, begin to nonverbally communicate your discomfort with their position, for example, sit back, fidget, shake your head, and so on.
• Have serious conflict management conversations in public places, or with frequent interruptions.
• Discourage the expression of emotion. While you don't want people to get overheated, it is often inappropriate to require them to be dispassionate.
• Minimize the seriousness of the problem, particularly if someone else brought it to your attention.
• Publicly or privately make derogatory jokes about the conflict situation or other parties to the conflict.
• Express displeasure that conflict is being experienced. Remember, conflict can be a *good* thing too.
• Tell the other party they are irrational or incompetent.

Competition

Competition is characterized as being dominant and nonsupportive. In this mode, individuals pursue their own concerns relatively aggressively, often at the expense of other people's concerns. This is a power-oriented mode, where people use whatever power seems appropriate to win their position—their organizational status, their ability to be persuasive, or even threats of punishment for noncompliance. Competing could mean standing up for your rights, defending a position you believe is correct, or simply trying to win.

Although you might think a competitive strategy would be outdated in today's collaborative, team-based business environment, that is not the case. Many situations make it is absolutely necessary to use this kind of style.

Consider situations where someone has to be in charge to effectively coordinate complex systems, for example, situations where safety is on the line. Would we really want an air traffic controller trying to negotiate with every pilot who is landing a plane? Similarly, the competition approach may be helpful when you notice a dispute has perception issues that need to be resolved. If two of your associates disagree about your desired work standards, it would be appropriate for you to assertively make your wishes known so that they can be on the same page. Similarly, it is appropriate to use the competitive style on important issues when unpopular actions need implementing, such as cost cutting, enforcement of unpopular rules, or discipline. Competition also can be valuable against people who take advantage of noncompetitive behavior.

However appropriate competition can be in some circumstances, it can also be highly unpopular. With that in mind, here are a few tips for using this approach most effectively:

- **Be direct.** Use declarative and precise statements, and keep them simple. Make sure people know *exactly* what you want them to do. This is not the time for ambiguity or showing others you are unsure. For example, say you see a child about to run into the street in the path of an upcoming car. Your best response would be a loud, clear, "Timmy! Stop right there!"

- **Explain later.** To avoid having to use this technique often, take a minute to explain your rationale to the other person once the emotions or stress of the conflict situation have diminished. For example, once you have caught your breath and slowed your heart after Timmy's near miss, it would be a good idea to explain basic traffic safety principles.

- **Use this strategy selectively.** We all know people who yell direct commands about every little thing. Over time, we tune them out; their competing conflict management style loses its effectiveness when they use it too often. This is a good weapon to have in your arsenal when you really need to use it, but using it too often can damage your work team's morale and lessen your personal credibility in future conflicts. Think about it. If you bark commands at Timmy all the time, he is less likely to respond when he absolutely must.

Accommodation

Accommodation is behaving in a supportive, submissive, unassertive and cooperative manner. It is generally the opposite of competition. When accommodating, individuals neglect their own concerns to satisfy the concerns of others. There is an element of self-sacrifice in this mode. Accommodating might take the form of selfless generosity or charity, obeying another person's order when you would prefer not to, or yielding to another person's point of view. Basically, when someone goes along with you when you are in competition mode, they are in accommodating mode.

Put simply, if this is your most frequent conflict management style, others will ultimately not respect you at work. They may like you a lot, but chances are good you (and ultimately the people you represent) will eventually be exploited. Fortunately, most people who practice accommodating in their interpersonal conflicts can easily make the transition to a more assertive style by recognizing that, when they accommodate everyone else's interests at work, they are essentially cheating the company they represent. One of your primary duties as a manager is to protect the interests of your organization and your workers, and it is difficult to do this through accommodation.

So when *is* accommodation a viable option, and how do you do it effectively should you choose to use it? Accommodation is a good idea if an issue is just not that important to you. Say, for example, one of your people wants to come in at 8 a.m. rather than 8:30 a.m., leaving a half hour earlier in the afternoon. Ask yourself, is this a big deal? If it isn't critical the person be in the office at the close of business, why not take the opportunity to accommodate him?

Similarly, occasional accommodation is good when you engage in a series of negotiations with another person. Giving in on issues that aren't that critical can earn you "goodwill points" that could prove useful in future encounters. Finally, accommodation is also a good strategy if you think your safety could be jeopardized and someone else knows more about the situation than you do. For example, accommodation is the perfect strategy for those rare occasions when a firefighter gives you instructions to leave a burning building. More pragmatically, accommodation may be an appropriate strategy if there are status or power differences in a dispute, and you are simply outranked by the other person. Accommodation is also a good idea when you find out you are wrong, since it allows a better position to be heard and allows you to simultaneously learn and show your reasonableness.

In these or similar circumstances, here are some strategies for using accommodation effectively in your managerial role:

- **Acknowledge the accommodation.** We don't mean you should try to make yourself out to be a martyr, but it is important to let the other person know you are consciously giving them what they want.

- **Have a rationale.** Remember that one of the most important things you need to do as a manager is to treat all people fairly. If you accommodate the wishes of one employee, you need to have a reason that is palatable to other employees if you hope to avoid their resentment or looking like you are playing favorites. Similarly, having a rationale will help you decide what to do if other people ask for the same accommodation.

Avoidance

Avoidance is behaving in a submissive, nonsupportive, unassertive and uncooperative manner. People in this mode do not immediately pursue their own concerns or those of the other person. They simply do not address conflicts. Avoiding might take the form of diplomatically sidestepping an issue, postponing an issue until a better time, or simply withdrawing from a threatening situation.

As we have previously noted, managers who ignore or fail to manage conflict are likely to incur the disadvantages of conflict without enjoying any of the advantages. If this is your dominant reaction to conflict, you might want to consider role-playing or practicing other conflict styles so you become more comfortable actually engaging in conflict.

"All problems become smaller if you don't dodge them, but confront them."

—William F. Halsey

Still, in some situations, avoiding is a good strategy. Basically, you can use avoiding as a way of delaying issues until they are more appropriate to address. If an overworked, overstressed co-worker on a tight deadline starts to argue with you, it might not be a bad idea to simply walk away, pledging to address the issue at a specific, but later time. Similarly, if a conflict has information issues, your best strategy might be to provide everyone with the same information and then insist on some reflection time before the discussion continues. Sometimes, having time to reflect on a dispute can help the parties to absorb new information without feeling defensive about it. Avoiding is also appropriate when an issue is trivial, or more important concerns are pressing. Similarly, this strategy is useful when others can resolve the conflict more effectively. For example, it might not be appropriate for you to try to manage a conflict occurring between people with whom you are not directly involved.

If you are going to employ the avoidance strategy, here are some guidelines to do it effectively:

- **Set time limits.** Rather than merely saying you will deal with a conflict *later*, specify (in your own mind, if not with the other parties) when you will get back to it—and then do it. Allowing conflicts to fester for too long only makes them more difficult to handle in the long run.

- **Set goals for the time out period.** It is important that people know what they are supposed to be working toward while they are avoiding a conflict. If they should be absorbing new information, getting additional information, or even just calming down, be sure everyone knows what they should try to accomplish.

Compromise

Compromise is the intermediate style. The objective of people who use this style is to find some expedient, mutually acceptable solution that partially satisfies everyone involved. It falls into the middle ground between behaving in a supportive and nonsupportive manner and between behaving in a dominant and submissive way. Compromising might mean splitting the difference, exchanging concessions, or seeking a quick middle-ground position.

When is it appropriate to use the compromising style? If the conflict involves scarce resources that cannot be expanded, then some form of compromise is usually required to reach a fair outcome. For example, if the organization's budget only allows two new employees to be hired, and three managers each need a new employee, they are going to have to negotiate to determine the best distribution of the limited number of people that can be hired. Compromise is also most appropriate when the conflict has significant role factors. If you are a party to the conflict simply because of your position in the organization, then you will likely find yourself in a position where you will need to also defend your own department's interests against the competing demands of other departments. Compromise also works to obtain temporary solutions when some interim action must be taken, but future study is required. It is also a good way to arrive at solutions when you are under time pressure. As a last resort, compromise also can be utilized when previous attempts at collaboration or competition are unsuccessful.

Collaboration

Finally, **collaboration** represents behaving in a both dominant and supportive, assertive and cooperative manner. It is the opposite of avoiding. Collaborating means digging into an issue to identify the underlying concerns of the two conflicting individuals and then finding an alternative that meets both sets of concerns. Collaborating might take the form of trying to learn from each other in the course of a disagreement or jointly seeking solutions to problems involving scarce resources. Collaborators value the insight they gain from learning about others' interests and perspectives. They enjoy taking a creative approach to problem solving and won't leave the table until everyone is fully satisfied with the outcome.

A collaborative negotiation is one in which both parties consider their relationship and the outcome so important that they must work together to maximize both. The collaborative negotiation is also referred to as *win-win* because it strives to ensure both sides achieve winning positions. Collaborators put their attention to creative problem solving, rather than the competitive tactics of compromising.

Collaboration is often touted as the most important conflict management strategy in organizations, with good reason. Collaborative approaches to conflict management take relationships into account, and allow for healthy debate and expression of diverse ideas within the confines of mutual respect and a commitment to ultimately reach a solution under which everyone benefits. Collaboration is appropriate when part of your objective is to learn more about the other party, when you wish to merge insights or perspectives from other people or groups, or when you need to work through feelings that have interfered with a relationship. Collaboration also has the benefit of making people feel committed to the solutions decided on, since they feel that they have been part of the decision-making process. Consequently, collaboration is particularly useful when you need to gain commitment by incorporating everyone's concerns into a consensus decision. We should note, however, that collaboration—though one of the most positive options in this arsenal of approaches—is also the most time-consuming.

"Truth springs from argument amongst friends."

—David Hume

Table 9.4 provides a concise summary of the five conflict approaches and the appropriateness of their use in different situations.

TABLE 9.4 | When to Use Each of the Conflict Management Styles

Situational Consideration	Competition	Accommodation	Avoidance	Compromise	Collaboration
Issue Importance	High	Low	Low	Medium	High
Relationship Importance	Low	High	Low	Medium	High
Relative Power	High	Low	Equal	Equal	Low–High
Time Constraints	Medium–High	Medium–High	Medium–High	Medium–High	Low

Situational considerations are defined as:
• Issue Importance: How important is the disputed issue? (High = Extremely important; Low = Not very important)
• Relationship Importance: How important is the relationship? (High = Critical, ongoing, one-of-a-kind partnership; Low = One-time transaction, for which there are many other alternatives available)
• Relative Power: What is the relative level of power, or authority, between the disputants? (High = Boss to subordinate; Equal = Peers; Low = Subordinate to boss)
• Time Constraints: To what extent is time a significant constraint in resolving the dispute? (High = Must resolve the dispute quickly; Low = Time is not a salient factor)

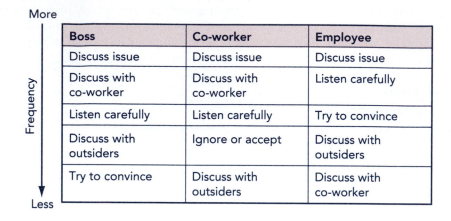

FIGURE 9.2

FIGURE 9.2

How People Actually Respond to Conflict

More

	Boss	Co-worker	Employee
Frequency	Discuss issue	Discuss issue	Discuss issue
	Discuss with co-worker	Discuss with co-worker	Listen carefully
	Listen carefully	Listen carefully	Try to convince
	Discuss with outsiders	Ignore or accept	Discuss with outsiders
	Try to convince	Discuss with outsiders	Discuss with co-worker

Less

While adapting conflict style to the situation is the ideal, the reality is that it is often difficult to do. Unfortunately, evidence suggests that the conflict style we actually use is often based less on the situational considerations outlined in Table 9.4 and more on either our dominant style or the positions of the parties involved. For example, one study found that, despite widely varying types of conflict, people tended to use their one dominant style.[11] Other evidence, summarized in Figure 9.2, reveals that the choice of conflict management strategy is heavily influenced by whether the conflict is with a boss, co-worker, or employee. Note that when a conflict is with a boss, people try to "convince" less frequently than if the conflict were with employees.

Management Live 9.1

The Robbers Cave and the Superordinate Goal[12]

In 1954, researchers Muzafer and Carolyn Sherif set out to study prejudice in children's social groups. With a group of 22 boys at a Boy Scout camp at Robbers Cave State Park in Oklahoma, the Sherifs split the boys up into two groups (the Eagles and the Rattlers) and set up four days of competitions between the groups, promising rewards such as medals and camping knives to the winners. As the competition proceeded, conflict between the two groups developed. The conflict was first evidenced by the boys' incessant taunting of those outside their own group. As the competition continued, the conflict intensified and the Eagles burned the Rattlers' flag. Seeking retribution, the Rattlers trashed the Eagles' cabin. The groups became so aggressive with each other that the researchers had to physically separate them.

In order to reduce the conflict, the Sherifs first attempted to allow the boys from each group to talk with each other or have contact. This only served to intensify the situation. Next, the Sherifs forced the boys to work together to accomplish superordinate goals such as repairing a broken-down vehicle. These superordinate goals drastically reduced the conflict between the two groups. The lessons from the Robbers Cave study play out in organizations today. It's not enough to put people in a room and tell them to get along. A manager must discover a common purpose that employees can rally behind and thus transcend their disputes.

Seeking Superordinate Goals

One universal strategy that is valuable across all styles and situations is seeking a **superordinate goal**.[13] A superordinate goal is an objective so valuable to both parties that it transcends the dispute. As one example, social scientists have learned that one way to reduce conflict between some groups (and individuals) is to have them work together on a project of mutual interest. The project must be of high importance and value to each party and cannot be completed without the successful input from both parties. Management Live 9.1 is a classic illustration of a superordinate goal being used in a youth group context.

Effective Negotiations

People commonly think of negotiation as something that takes place in a limited set of arenas such as international diplomacy, organized labor, or car dealerships. However, in reality, most of us negotiate many times each day. For example:

- We negotiate with associates to get them to take on a new assignment or to take a trip to another city.
- We negotiate with our manager to get assigned to high-profile projects.
- We negotiate purchases from vendors as well as discounts and deals.
- We negotiate deadlines with customers, colleagues, or vendors.
- We negotiate in group meetings to get other people to support our proposed initiatives.

"In business, you don't get what you deserve, you get what you negotiate."

—Chester Karrass

Although every negotiation has unique features, effective interactions share the common elements of preparation, execution, and evaluation. In this section we touch on key points and skills associated with each of these elements. The goal is for you to become a more effective negotiator in a variety of settings.

To Negotiate or Not? Recognizing Negotiation Situations

Two points regarding the recognition of negotiation situations are important. First, it is important to question whether an issue that appears to be nonnegotiable or that someone states as being so truly is. For instance, if you have a job offer and the company has indicated the salary is nonnegotiable, you should fully consider and investigate whether that is really the case. If salary truly is nonnegotiable, maybe the amount of vacation, expense accounts, or a company vehicle *are* negotiable items, which may lead to significant increased value for you (see Tool Kit 9.2).

"Only free men can negotiate."

—Nelson Mandela

Second, if there is no way to create added value for yourself in a negotiation, you should not be negotiating in the first place. For instance, a supervisor should never negotiate over a safety rule or unexcused absences from work. Similarly, parents are often duped into negotiating things with children that should have been clearly stated as nonnegotiable (wearing seat belts, eating junk food before dinner). In such cases, negotiating only undermines legitimate authority and can add no value. Even worse, negotiating in these cases can actively lead to having to negotiate for everything. This is not a path you want to travel down.

The Negotiation Scorecard: Outcomes of an Ideal Negotiation

Before we can start the negotiating process, we need to know what an effective negotiation should produce. In this case, the scorecard for an effective negotiation consists of three outcomes:[14]

1. **All parties believe they made a good deal.** Ideally, you want the other parties to believe they have helped themselves—rather than hurt themselves—by working with you.

2. **The relationship is maintained or even improved.** Usually you negotiate with people you have ongoing relationships with so you hope to sustain a positive relationship after the negotiation is complete.

3. **Each negotiator's constituents are satisfied with the agreement.** When you negotiate, other people have to accept the agreement you reach. Examples include your boss, partners, employees, or customers.

The most successful negotiations are characterized by all three of these outcomes.

A Win-Lose Negotiating Mindset

"It's not enough that we succeed. Cats must also fail."

Win-Win Negotiation

"If you are planning on doing business with someone again, don't be too tough in the negotiations. If you're going to skin a cat, don't keep it as a house cat."

—Marvin S. Levin

Largely because we are all intimately familiar with courtroom debate and high-profile negotiations in the news, we commonly assume a competitive or "win-lose" approach to the negotiations we regularly face. Buying a car is a common example of this. If you choose a competitive strategy to negotiate, you have to accept the possibility of losing. **Win-lose negotiation** means someone has to lose in the negotiation process, and odds are it will sometimes be you.

However, in many situations, the possibility of losing is not acceptable. Examples of such situations include negotiating with:

- Your boss.
- Your peers, both individually and as a group.
- Major clients your company has had for multiple years.
- Potential partners for long-term ventures.

With some of these—for example, a major client—you don't even want to accept the possibility that the *other party* will lose. Parties who lose in negotiation often seek other relationships, and you clearly don't want that with a major client. So while you might use a win-lose approach to negotiate for a car deal or to decide a lawsuit, in ongoing relationships you ultimately want "win-win" outcomes—whereby both parties walk away from the agreement feeling good about it and believe the relationship has been maintained or even improved. Remember, when people feel that they have lost, they are not likely to want to do business with you again or may even be looking to get even. Neither of these outcomes is good for building long-term relationships.

TABLE 9.5	Characteristics of Win-Win Negotiation
• A focus on common interests rather than differences.
• An attempt to address needs and interests rather than bargaining positions.
• A commitment to helping the other party meet their needs also.
• An exchange of information and ideas.
• The creation of options for mutual gain—creating value for both parties.

Win-win negotiation is focused on cooperative problem solving. This does not mean you give in or compromise easily just to maintain a good relationship with the other party. It means you treat the conflict as being separate from the relationship and work to seek a mutually acceptable solution to the conflict. The way to maintain the relationship is not to win the fight, but to solve a problem, in a way that meets the needs of both parties and creates value for both. You don't need to defeat the other party; in fact, the best way to get them to agree to a settlement that benefits you is for the settlement to also benefit them. In win-win negotiation, a critical challenge is to propose a solution that helps the other party meet their needs, along with your own. Table 9.5 presents the characteristics of win-win negotiations. A collaborating conflict management style best represents the win-win approach to negotiations.

"You say it's a win-win, but what if you're wrong-wrong and it all goes bad-bad?"

"My father said: 'You must never try to make all the money that's in a deal. Let the other fellow make some money too, because if you have a reputation for always making all the money, you won't have many deals.'"

—J. Paul Getty

Stages of Effective Negotiations

As a way of attempting to resolve conflicts, negotiations are generally thought of as the most common and easily implemented remedy. Like any good tool, negotiations involve a series of steps that, when done properly, will help to increase the likelihood of success. The major steps involved with the negotiation process can be broken down into preparation, understand needs, list and discuss options, process tactics, ending, and evaluation (Figure 9.3).

FIGURE 9.3 The Stages of the Negotiation Process

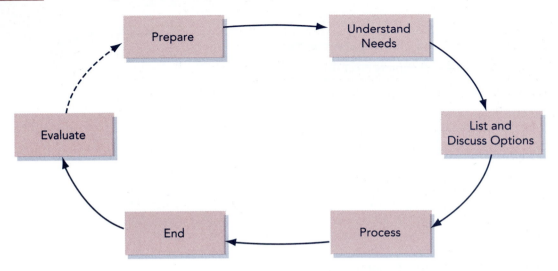

Negotiation Preparation

People who frequently negotiate (such as purchasing agents or insurance adjusters) say in surveys that the most important part of negotiation is the planning and preparation.[15] Even though it is extremely important, negotiators from many other countries have the impression that Americans don't take the task of negotiation planning seriously enough. It is very easy to be careless or superficial in this step, so don't fall into that trap. The following tips apply to good negotiation preparation.

Organize the Issues

"Start out with an ideal and end up with a deal."

—Karl Albrecht

Begin by identifying and defining the issues. For example, if you are being asked to take a promotion and transfer to Sao Pãulo, Brazil, you need to list the issues you want to bring into the negotiation. You will likely want to discuss pay, moving expenses, how much time you will have to move, expenses of travel if your family moves at a different time than you do, among other issues. Try to consider the issue from multiple levels. Are you negotiating just your move to Brazil or also your future with your current firm? This may not always be obvious at first, but some serious thoughts about these types of issues can prove useful.

You will want to list the issues in writing. Organize the issues into priorities. For a few issues, simply order 1, 2, 3, and so on. For more issues, divide them into high and low priority groups. This is also a good place to utilize the decision making skills that were presented in Chapter 3.

Talk to Other People Who Have Information You Need

1. **Seek out other people you know who have conducted similar negotiations.** For example, if you are being asked to take that transfer to Brazil, look for people you know who have been asked to take international transfers. You want to ask these people what issues were negotiable for them and what issues were not. Ask them about the agreement they reached. This is analogous to buying a house. If you've done this a few times, you know some issues are negotiable and some aren't. Don't reinvent the wheel. Learn from other people's experiences. This is especially important because it is unlikely you will have a good knowledge base

of first-hand information if you've never been in this type of situation before. By finding out as much as possible from people who have experience, you will put yourself in a much stronger position.

2. **Talk to your constituents.** When you negotiate, you usually represent constituents who must accept the agreement you reach. For the move to Brazil, it may be your spouse and children. If you are negotiating a new hire, it may be the HR department or your boss. If you don't address your constituents' concerns in the negotiation, you'll have difficulty reconciling them later.

3. **Talk in advance to the other parties.** In some formal situations such as international diplomacy, it makes sense to agree on the topics to be negotiated (and not negotiated), timetables, schedules and locations of meetings, deadlines, and who may attend the meetings. Many of the negotiations you will be involved in are not this complex, but some are. If they do become complex, consider whether these sorts of agreements before the negotiation would be useful.

Research the Parties You'll Be Negotiating With

Like you, the other parties involved are only going to negotiate if they believe they can serve their interests better by negotiating than by not negotiating. Therefore, gaining an understanding of their interests will be helpful to you. If they have chosen to negotiate with you, they have a reason they are willing to negotiate. You have more to work with if you understand that reason.

"To measure the person, measure their heart."
—Malcolm Forbes

It also is helpful to know whether each of the other parties plans to use a competitive or cooperative approach to the negotiation. To help determine that, consider five indicators (see also Table 9.6):

1. Learn their reputation. Do they have a pattern of being competitive or cooperative in past negotiations?

2. Do the issues seem to be scarce resources like money or time? If so, they may move toward a competitive style.

TABLE 9.6 | **Types of Difficult Negotiators**[16]

- **Aggressive Opener** Negotiator unnerves others by making nasty comments about their previous performance or other remarks to belittle the opponent.

- **Long Pauser** Will not answer immediately; appears to give comments substantial thought with long silences; hopes silence will get the other side to reveal additional information.

- **Mocker** Mocks and sneers at the other party's proposals to anger the other side so that they will say something they may later regret.

- **Interrogator** Challenges all comments with searching questions meant to suggest the other party has not done their homework; contests any answers and asks the opposition to explain further what they mean.

- **Sheep's Clothing** Appears to be reasonable while making impossible demands.

- **Divide-and-Conqueror** Produces dissension within other party to create internal conflict; allies with one member of the team and tries to play him or her off against the other members of the team.

- **Dummy** Pretends to be dense and by doing so exasperates the opposition in hopes of drawing out more information or lulling the opponent into a false sense of superiority.

3. Do you believe they have an interest in maintaining a good relationship? Such an interest suggests a cooperative approach.

4. Is this an ongoing relationship or a one-time negotiation? Parties are often more competitive in one-time negotiations.

5. Do you think they will trust you with all the information they have on the topics to be negotiated? Lack of trust and information hoarding are characteristic of competitive negotiations.

Consider Your BATNA (best alternative to a negotiated agreement)

We negotiate in order to get a better outcome than we could get if we did not negotiate. Therefore, it is critical to know what alternative we will be left with if we *cannot* reach a negotiated agreement or what is known as the best alternative to a negotiated agreement (**BATNA**).[17]

The BATNA is the yardstick against which you measure any possible agreement.

- An agreement better than your BATNA should be accepted.
- An agreement worse than your BATNA should not be accepted.

By putting a little different twist on our example of a transfer to Brazil, we can see how the BATNA works in practice. Let's say that you are trying to get an employee, Bob, to accept a promotion and transfer to go to São Paulo, Brazil. You want Bob for the promotion because he seems to have the right skill set to be successful. Unfortunately, Bob may not want to go to Brazil, and his skill set is already highly marketable in his current city. Let's say that if you can't get Bob to go to Brazil, your best alternative is Pat from a local office. Pat has relatives in Brazil and is interested in going there. Pat would do an acceptable job, but in your estimation, Pat is not as good a match for this assignment as Bob.

In this case, Pat is your BATNA. This is the yardstick against which you measure the possible negotiated agreement with Bob. If you have to agree to buy Bob's house, give him a $40,000 pay raise, and wait two months to get Bob to go to Brazil, you compare that against having Pat in the job in São Paulo.

If your BATNA is very good, you are in a strong negotiating position when you meet with Bob. However, if your BATNA is not acceptable to you, you must be more willing to make concessions to Bob. A good BATNA reduces your dependence on the other party. A very weak BATNA can lead you to accept very undesirable situations. Think of people who are desperate. A person driving across the desert does not have a very good BATNA when they pull up to the only gas station for 100 miles.

"The best way to make a good deal is to have the ability to walk away from it."

—Brian Koslow

Understanding the Needs of Other Parties

Many people begin negotiating by stating their positions. Positions are what people claim they want. For example, "I want you to accept a promotion to lead our office in São Paulo, Brazil. I want you there two weeks from today." Unfortunately, positions don't really give much information. They tell what we want, but not the true underlying *reasons* why we want it.

If we are going to view negotiation as a mutual problem solving situation, we have to share information so the other party understands the problem to be solved. In the Brazil example, it may be that our current manager, who was doing a very poor job, just resigned unexpectedly. It's a good opportunity to replace a poor performer, but we need a seasoned person who can move quickly. If we share these underlying needs with the other party, they are more capable of helping solve the problem.

If they know our true needs, they have the ability to offer possible options we may have never considered. For example, "I don't want to go to São Paulo to manage the operations there. However, I would consider going for a temporary assignment for six months to train a new manager." That option might be better than your BATNA. If you consider Bob's offer of going for six months better than sending Pat, then Bob should be sent because this is better than your BATNA.

So try to never begin a negotiation by stating positions. Begin by discussing the needs and interests of the parties. Listening to their needs and interests is critical. Many skilled negotiators rank listening as being one of the most important negotiation skills.[18] Being able to "put yourself in their shoes" is critical to creating a solution.

> *"Problems cannot be solved from the same level of awareness that created them."*
> —Albert Einstein

List and Discuss Possible Options

Once the parties have an understanding of the needs and interests of each other, you are ready to move to discussing options. Options are possible solutions or parts of possible solutions. Given that we negotiate multiple issues, a partial solution that addresses one issue is often a helpful building block for a complete solution. Generating multiple creative options to discuss is a source of power for a negotiator. If you can offer four or five possibilities that meet the needs of both parties, then you have great potential to control what the solution looks like. However, this only works if you are committed to finding a solution that lets all parties meet their needs. We can't forget the other party only wants to reach an agreement with us if the agreement creates value for *them*. This is because others are rarely motivated to do things that only benefit you!

Complex negotiations often happen in stages across time. Once you understand the other parties' interests, this might be a good time to pause the negotiation and let each party discuss possible options with their constituents. You also might find this to be a good time to do additional research on the issues and alternatives to negotiating a settlement with this party (for example, discussing the proposed project with another potential partner).

Choosing Among the Options

As you continue discussing options with the other party, it is often helpful to talk in **hypotheticals.** An example might be to ask, "If we were able to move the roll-out date forward by six months, would you be able to commit more engineers to the project?" Using hypotheticals lets you explore creative possibilities with less pressure and helps both parties think through issues they may not have previously considered. This process can be helpful in the generation of new solutions and new opportunities. Mutual gain can often be created when the priorities of the two parties are different. For example, the other party may want an immediate start-up date for the project, to balance off personnel demands on other projects. Maybe the start-up date is not important to you because your segment of the project begins during the second month of the project. Trade-offs may work here because the priorities are different.

To be successful at this stage, look for ways to improve options that are already on the table. You can create considerable goodwill if you point out to the other party how their idea could be altered to serve their needs better without causing you any harm. Conversely, you may see ways to serve your needs better without negatively affecting their outcome.

Use of Objective Standards and Norms

The vast majority of people we negotiate with want to appear reasonable. Therefore, when confronted by what appears to be reasonable standards, most negotiators will have difficulty ignoring those standards. The key then is knowing where to look for these standards and norms.

Try to look for objective standards or precedents that are supportive of what you want in a negotiation. For example, "I thought you gave a 10 percent discount to all customers who place orders this large." If that standard is true, the other party feels unreasonable if they don't provide you the same discount. Having a good grasp of your industry and what your competitors are offering is extremely helpful in this situation.

However, be aware that multiple objective criteria might apply to a negotiation. For example, "Yes, but we don't give the 10 percent for the initial order because of the overhead costs in setting up the account. We do give the 10 percent in subsequent orders." Obviously, you want to look for the objective criteria most consistent with your needs. Be aware that the other party you are negotiating with has constituents that they must satisfy. Sometimes they are looking for you to give them the objective standards they can use to go back and convince those constituents.

Employing Process Tactics During Negotiations

Once you have your list of options on the negotiating table and are discussing them, consider employing these process tactics to achieve your objectives:

Look for Key Information from the Other Party

Information is the lifeblood of negotiation. As the negotiation opens, you want to start looking for information. Ask probing questions: why, how, what if, what would be wrong with. . . ?

Since a strong BATNA provides an advantage, you would like to determine your negotiating party's BATNA. For example, let's say you are trying to decide between three job offers. Do these companies have other job candidates in mind? If so, what are the qualifications of the others? If one of the companies has no other good candidates, that helps your negotiating position. If the company has other qualified and attractive candidates, you should know that early in your negotiation. More specifically:

"Information is a negotiator's greatest weapon."
—Victor Kiam

1. You want to understand the other party's underlying needs and interests. Like you, they have decided to negotiate for some reason. You have more information to work with if you understand that reason.
2. If they have a deadline, you want to know it. For example, do they need to reach an agreement before their flight to London tomorrow? Evidence shows people will make more concessions as their deadline approaches. Not all negotiators have a deadline, but if they do, you want to know it.

Making Concessions

People enter negotiations expecting concessions to be made on both sides. With that in mind, experienced negotiators will always leave themselves room to make at least some concessions.

There is clear evidence that parties feel better about a settlement when the negotiation had a progressive set of concessions than when it did not. This is because negotiators want to believe that they are capable of shaping the other's behavior. When one peson makes a concession and the other does not, reciprocity is not fulfilled (see Chapter 6) and the party who made the initial concession can experience a deep-rooted sense of betrayal. It is very frustrating to negotiators to see they have not shaped the outcome and influenced the other negotiator's behavior.

In the 1950s, GE used an extremely aggressive tactic in negotiating with its labor unions. The company claimed it had done all the appropriate research, its offer was fair, and the offer represented a nonnegotiable final offer. This was referred to as GE's "take it or leave it" strategy and was later called "Boulwareism" after GE's labor negotiator Lemuel R. Boulware.[19] Regardless of the offer's actual fairness, the unions hated this tactic because they felt they had no influence on the other party or outcome. It should be pointed out that a "take it or leave it" or Boulwareism approach is generally seen as a case of negotiating in bad faith and is not recommended. Remember that in an ideal negotiation all parties believe they have made a good deal. *How* you go about negotiating can influence that perception. Management Live 9.2. gives an interesting example of how everyone can be better off through obtaining a **Pareto efficient** outcome.

One common question concerns what to do if the opposing side is more powerful. There is no easy answer, but your best strategy is to be very clear on your BATNA. The better your BATNA, the better your position. So search for ways to improve your BATNA and be prepared to predict *their* BATNA. A related question is what if the other party won't participate in a win-win process? In such cases your best option is to try to place the focus on the integrity of the process instead of the opposing positions. If you really feel unable to keep the negotiations going in the right direction, you may want to consider using a third party to facilitate the negotiation.

Some Common Forms of Leverage

Discussions of who has more power among negotiating parties and who will not negotiate are related to leverage. Leverage refers to the principle of using a small advantage, or merely a perceived advantage, to gain a much larger benefit. Leverage in negotiations can take several forms, a few of which we highlight here (see also Management Live 9.3).

Leverage of Legitimacy.   The goal of this form of leverage is to give the impression an issue is not negotiable. To the extent that the other party believes it is nonnegotiable and does not attempt to negotiate, you have been successful. If a customer goes into an appliance store planning to buy a refrigerator, the store

Management Live 9.2

Pareto Efficiency

The ultimate goal of negotiations is to be Pareto efficient. A Pareto efficient outcome (the term is named after Italian economist Vilfredo Pareto who brought us the Pareto (80–20) rule as well!) is one in which two parties reach an agreement resulting in both parties being better off and no other change to the agreement could bolster both equally (i.e., one party would ultimately benefit more). If there is an outcome that would have made both better off, the decision reached is not Pareto efficient.

Consider Barry and Nancy, who are going out to dinner. Barry likes Indian food best but cannot eat Chinese food. Nancy greatly prefers Chinese food but finds Indian dishes too hot. There is a range of possible solutions. They could go to a Chinese or Indian restaurant or choose among numerous other types of cuisine. They find Italian food acceptable but both prefer Thai to Italian.

It is possible to plot out all of these choices on a graph. On one axis are Barry's preference values. On the other axis are the values Nancy attaches to each preference. For Barry, Indian food has the highest value, Thai is next, then Italian, and Chinese last. For Nancy, Chinese is highest followed by Thai, Italian, and Indian last.

In this case we conclude that Thai Pareto exceeds Italian. That is, a decision to go to a Thai restaurant results in both Barry and Nancy being better off than if they had gone to an Italian restaurant. The Thai choice is also Pareto efficient because the only choice that is better for Barry (Indian) leaves Nancy worse off. Similarly, the only decision better for Nancy (Chinese) leaves Barry worse off.

Collectively, negotiators "leave money on the table" when they settle for a Pareto inefficient agreement. Pareto notions are a good mind-set for seeking win-win agreements.

may have a very official-looking price tag on each refrigerator that says "Holiday Sale $759.99." Most people will not attempt to negotiate the price of the refrigerator in such cases because it appears nonnegotiable. Some recent evidence does suggest, however, that more things truly are negotiable than generally believed.

In any case, there are two lessons to learn about the leverage of legitimacy.

1. *Make it look nonnegotiable.* If you don't want something to be negotiated, think of ways to make it appear nonnegotiable. Vendors do this by having an "official price sheet." They are attempting to give the impression that the terms of the sale are not negotiable. If the customer agrees to the sale without challenging any of the items in it, they have been successful in establishing legitimacy.

2. *Ask.* There is generally no or minimal risk in asking whether an issue that appears to be nonnegotiable truly is. If the vendor absolutely will not sell for any other price, you'll pay the same price whether you ask or not. If a vendor absolutely will not waive the restocking fee for returns, you haven't lost anything by asking.

Leverage of Timing.   A common tactic in negotiation is to get up to leave, saying, "Let me think about it. I'll be back." This has traditionally been a very effective tactic when buying a new car because salespeople do not want to see a customer who is willing to buy walk out the door. A variation of this tactic can be used by telephone as well.

You may gain several benefits by using this tactic:

1. You control the timing of when the negotiation will continue.

2. You get the opportunity to collect your thoughts and plan the next step in negotiating. This is particularly useful in complex negotiations.

3. You gain an opportunity to consult with other people, possibly including your own constituents, and collect further information.

4. You can use the time to talk to other parties to see if a better deal is possible elsewhere.

5. You can put pressure on the other party, if the other party is facing a deadline. For example, if a delegation has traveled from Argentina to discuss a

Management Live 9.3

The Leverage of Limited Authority

All things equal, most people would say they prefer more authority to less. However, in negotiation, we gain an ironic benefit by having our authority limited by our boss or by some other entity.

For example, if you have been interviewing candidates for a job and have decided which one to make an offer to, your boss telling you a maximum salary to offer gives you an advantage. You are less pressured to accept an agreement you, your boss, and possibly others don't want. Your bottom line is carved in stone by someone else. You can even say, if pushed, "I wish I could help you, but my hands are tied. If it were up to me, I'd accept your offer." You are unable to make any further concessions, so the logical route of progress is for the other party to make concessions.

As you might suspect, overuse of this tactic can frustrate the other party so much they break off negotiations if they have a reasonable BATNA. If this tactic is used on you, one response is to attempt to circumvent the person with no authority and negotiate with the person who *has* authority.

joint venture with you, they incur a cost by extending the negotiation and letting you control the timing. This same principle may hold for sales quotas and the ending of a month or a quarter.

Bluffing Carries a Risk

With all of the recent attention to Texas Hold'em poker, you may be wondering about the stone-cold bluff. Bluffing is a common tactic in negotiation, but be aware that bluffing incurs two risks. First, heavy-handed bluffing can strain relationships. Remember that one outcome of the ideal negotiation is that the relationship is maintained or even improved. Bluffing is an especially high-stakes risk in ongoing relationships. Second, if the bluff fails, the negotiation can be over. In this case, you may have sacrificed an outcome superior to your BATNA because of the failed bluff.

As an example of overplaying a bluff, assume you tell a vendor you absolutely must have shipment within 48 hours or there is no deal. However, you are bluffing. You know this is the only vendor that can fill your order with the specifications you want and that you would wait as long as necessary to get the order from this vendor. You just bluffed to get a faster shipment. Suppose the vendor replies, "We absolutely can't ship it that fast; I guess we'll have to lose out on your order. Maybe we could do business in the future." At that point, you begin to backpedal and the vendor realizes you were bluffing—and that they can make the delivery any time they want. If you were heavy-handed in the way you posed your bluff, you may have even strained the relationship. In that case, the vendor may choose not to expedite the order at all. The failed bluff showed the vendor that it didn't need to negotiate to get your business.

"During a negotiation, it would be wise not to take anything personally. If you leave personalities out of it, you will be able to see opportunities more objectively."

—Brian Koslow

The End of the Negotiation

When a negotiation draws to its close, always keep multiple issues on the table until the very end. That gives you the opportunity to make trade-offs so each party believes they made a good deal. If you let the end of the negotiation come down to one issue, with all other issues taken off the table, you'll have much more difficulty reaching an agreement whereby both parties believe they made a good deal.

Once you have made an agreement, you'll want some level of documentation of the terms of the agreement. This might range from a verbal agreement and handshake to a formal contract prepared by attorneys. You'll need to decide what level of documentation you want. Either end of the continuum carries a risk.

If you ask for the agreement in writing:

- You can offend the other party. This is a particularly common problem in cross-cultural negotiation. In many cultures, a personal relationship of trust is paramount, and asking for a contract prepared by attorneys is offensive because it implies a lack of trust in the relationship. This is especially true in Japan and many South American countries.
- You strain the relationship. Think of what it would do to the relationship if you negotiated with your spouse over the specifics of an upcoming vacation and then insisted on putting the terms of the negotiation in writing.

If you don't ask for the agreement in writing:

- The other parties can later disagree about the terms of the agreement.
- One or more parties may back out of the agreement.
- The resources you are investing are at more risk.
- Your constituents, particularly your boss, may not be satisfied with a verbal agreement.

TABLE 9.7 | Actions of Superior Negotiators

Evidence shows that superior negotiators demonstrate behaviors average negotiators are less likely to exhibit. Compared to average negotiators, they:

In negotiation planning:

1. Consider more possible solutions and options.

2. Spend more time looking for common interests.

3. Think more about long-term consequences.

In the actual negotiation:

4. Are more likely to begin by taking a cooperative rather than competitive stance.

5. Make fewer immediate counterproposals.

6. Make a greater effort to understand the other party's interests.

7. Ask more questions, especially to test understanding.

8. Are less likely to describe their offers in glowing, positive terms.

9. Have a greater frequency of topic changes.

10. Summarize the progress made during the negotiation.

Evaluate How Well It Went

"I am a woman in process. I'm just trying like everybody else. I try to take every conflict, every experience, and learn from it. Life is never dull."

—Oprah Winfrey

Most negotiators naturally neglect thinking about the process of negotiation itself. Instead, they focus exclusively on the content of the specific negotiation—the problem, their needs, the issues, the proposals, and the counterproposals. As the stakes get higher, the process gets pushed even farther into the background.

When the negotiation is over, however, it is always a good idea to take time to analyze how the process went. Think about your strategy and tactics. In retrospect, were they appropriate? What information was critical to the process, and how did you seek it? Did you recognize the strategy and tactics used by the other party? Did you respond effectively to that strategy and those tactics? If this was a negotiation in an ongoing relationship, what did you learn that might help in the next negotiation? Did the other party use any tactics you would like to adopt into your negotiating style? Please look to Tool Kit 9.3 as a helpful tool to evaluate the negotiation.

This is yet another situation where it's important to learn from our experiences. We all know people who repeat the same mistakes. In negotiation, learning from your mistakes means analyzing the process afterward when you have time to focus on process. Evidence shows that superior negotiators are more likely than average negotiators to analyze the negotiation process after the negotiations are over (see Table 9.7).

Mediation

"Ever negotiate with lawyers at a huge company? If they saw you drowning 100 feet from the shore, they'd throw you a 51-foot rope and say they went more than halfway."

—Paul Somerson

To imply that all negotiation creates a happy ending is nonsense. Negotiation between parties often breaks down or creates unsatisfactory outcomes. Fortunately, if negotiation does break down, you are not entirely out of options. Perhaps the most straightforward of those options is some form of mediation using a third party (maybe you, if you have two conflicting associates). Mediation has a long history of facilitating conflicts and can sometimes create the discipline and focus to resolve a dispute when negotiation has failed (see Tool Kit 9.4 for a very detailed, step-by-step mediation guide).

In some cases, a mediator is an outside party who specializes in helping people in conflict reach an amicable agreement. In other cases it can simply be a manager with two conflicting associates or a friend trying to help resolve a dispute between two other friends. A mediator is typically necessary where a lack of trust between two parties makes negotiation ineffective. In such cases, only when the disputing parties feel there will be some sense of fairness and justice will disputes be resolved.

"Progress in mediation comes swiftly for those who try their hardest."

—Patanjali

Trust Building in the Mediation Process

An effective mediator must convince the parties to trust him or her, then to trust the negotiation process itself, and finally to begin to trust each other.[20] To help the parties involved trust the mediator, a few important guidelines for the mediator include:

- Choose a comfortable, neutral space away from any party's "turf."
- Schedule short meetings and be involved for as short of a time as possible.
- Listen with an open mind and do not say much.
- Be respectful and express only positive opinions of the parties involved.
- Emphasize a desire to help. Do not pick sides.
- Assure parties that all conversations are held in strict confidence.
- Be a role model and build a strong reputation for staying on task and doing what you say.

Trust in the process is facilitated by focusing only on procedural matters in the beginning. For example, getting parties to agree on where to hold the meetings and some ground rules for discussion may help convince them the process may work. It is best to avoid all substantive issues until both parties have made some small agreements. These small successes build momentum that a solution is possible.[21]

An effective mediator also (1) is dogged in learning and applying facts, (2) frames the disputed claims into the real issues, (3) maintains neutrality, and (4) seeks to understand the underlying interests of each party, validating both sides. These skills are nicely illustrated in the following example of mediation of a trucking accident dispute.

"To be a good mediator you must be a good listener. . . . You have to listen to not only what is being said, but what is not said—which is often more important than what they say."

—Kofi Annan

Mediation in Action

Several years ago, a large trucking company received a call from a customer that a truck had recently caused damage to the customer's loading dock, but that the trucker would not compensate the manufacturer for the repairs. After some discussion, mediation was recommended.

The opening statements were predictably accusatory, with the manufacturer expecting compensation and the trucking outfit denying any involvement. The mediator sought and introduced the undisputed facts that emerged in the discussion to help both sides understand what really happened and when.

The mediator listened as each side presented its positions and then followed up with a line of questions designed to reframe the discussion in terms of issues. The manufacturer stated that the container door swung open as the truck pulled out, damaging the frame and bending the rails that allow the steel shutters to seal the opening, resulting in several thousand dollars of damage. On the other hand, the trucking outfit noted that several days had gone by before it was notified of a claim, and it was not sent any evidence of the damage.

Through each party's responses, the mediator began to clarify each party's underlying interests. While it was obvious the manufacturer wanted monetary compensation, the trucking outfit wanted to ensure the manufacturer was not taking advantage. In essence, the trucking outfit was not inclined to accept any liability for the events in question before being shown it was responsible.

The mediator then validated the motivations and acknowledged the feelings of each party explicitly, giving all sides a reason to buy into the mediation and continue. When both sides agreed that it is industry standard for the truck driver to be responsible for properly securing the container door before departure, and the mediator pointed out that the driver would be unlikely to volunteer information to his own employer about any sort of incident, the trucking outfit agreed to settle the matter upon two conditions. One was a follow-up discussion with the driver who had handled that day's shipment and the second was receipt of the manufacturer's internal documentation (including pictures) noting what had happened.

This mediation was successfully concluded in under an hour and did not require further mediator intervention to uphold the bargain. Without the mediation, the conflict would likely have deteriorated to the detriment of both parties—not only would the trucking outfit have lost a valued customer, but the manufacturer would also have limited its own scheduling options and pricing power by severing all ties to an established local trucking outfit. In this case, the relationship between the trucking outfit and the manufacturer was preserved and the parties were able to continue working together going forward to their mutual benefit.

Of course, things don't always work out so smoothly. However, they are far more likely to work out if you avoid the tendency to wing it in the pressure of conflict situations and instead practice the known principles of mediation success.

Concluding Note

Conflict situations are inevitable and frequent in organizational life and generally are among managers' most unnerving experiences. Two fundamental guidelines are to always diagnose before acting and to know the different alternatives for conflict resolution so you can adapt your own natural inclinations as appropriate. Becoming familiar with a few simple, but powerful, principles for negotiating agreements and mediating disputes is also critical to competence in managing conflict. Perhaps the most important lesson is that conflict can be a powerful source of growth. That is, properly managed, it can be an opportunity to implement change in the way people interact and improve their problem-solving skills. It can also result in increased innovation and strengthened relationships. To quote William Ellery Channing, "Difficulties are meant to rouse, not discourage. The human spirit is to grow strong by conflict."

Key Terms

accommodation	conflict	task conflict
avoidance	hypotheticals	win-lose negotiation
BATNA	mixed-motive situation	win-win negotiation
collaboration	Pareto efficient	zero-sum game
competition	relationship conflict	
compromise	superordinate goal	

Conflict and Negotiation Tool Kits

Tool Kit 9.1   Diagnosing Conflict Sources

The following questions are useful tools for you to diagnose where conflict is originating. By being able to determine its cause, conflict becomes easier to understand and to ultimately manage.

- Do both parties have access to the same information? (if not, then informational factors are a likely source of conflict)
- Do the parties perceive known information in the same manner? (if not, then perceptual factors are a likley source of conflict)
- Are the parties able to discuss the issues without being heavily influenced by their roles in the organization? (if not, then role factors are a likely source of conflict)
- Is the environment in which the parties are operating relatively calm and supportive of agreement? (if not, then environmental factors are a likely source of conflict)
- Do the parties have mutual respect for each other and share a certain level of personal liking? (if not, then personal factors are a likely source of conflict)

Remember that multiple sources of conflict may exist simultaneously. Just because one source of conflict is uncovered, do not stop looking. There may well be other sources at work.

Tool Kit 9.2   To Negotiate or Not? That Is the Question

Like many cases, to negotiate or not can be thought of as a cost/benefit analysis. If the benefits of a negotiated solution compared to your BATNA is larger than your costs of negotiating, then negotiating should be done. To calculate the benefits of negotiating, consider:

- Current BATNA
- Liklihood of favorable negotiated outcomes.
- Direct costs of negotiating (travel, personnel, meeting facilitites, etc.).
- Indirect and opportunity costs (lost work time of personnel, secretarial support, etc.)

Then, if the incremental benefits (negotiated outcome minus BATNA) are greater than the incremental costs (direct plus indirect costs), then negotiating makes sense. If not, the effort of negotiating may not be worthwhile.

Tool Kit 9.3   The Negotiation Scorecard

In evalauting a negotiation, it is useful to debrief any negotiation experience using a scorecard like the one below. You may need to modify the scorecard for specific instances, but the framework provided here is pretty flexible and generally will do a good job of letting you know whether or not the negotiation was truly a win-win outcome.

	Yes	Maybe	No	Not Relevant
All parties believe they made a good deal				
You believe you made a good deal				
Your boss believes you made a good deal				
The other party believes they made a good deal				
The relationship is maintained or improved				
You wish to do more business with the other party				
The other party wants to do more business with you				
Constitutents are satisfied with the deal				
Your constitutents (boss, peers, partners, and other stakeholders) are satisfied with the deal				
The other party's constitutents are satisfied with the deal.				

A truly win-win deal should not have any entries in the "no" category above. One or two "maybes" may exist, but ideally, a "yes" should appear in every row.

Tool Kit 9.4   A Mediation Guide
Step 1: Stabilize the Setting

- Greet the parties.
- Indicate where each of them is to sit.
- Identify yourself and each party by name.
- Offer water, paper and pencil, and patience.
- State the purpose of the mediation.
- Confirm your neutrality.
- Get their commitment to proceed.
- Get their commitment that only one party at a time will speak.
- Get their commitment to speak directly to you.

Step 2: Help the Parties Communicate

- Explain the rationale for who speaks first.
- Reassure them that both will speak without interruption, for as long as necessary.
- Ask the first speaker to tell what has happened.
  - Take notes.
  - Respond actively.
  - Calm the parties as needed.
  - Clarify with restatements.
  - Focus the narration on the issues in the dispute.
  - Summarize, eliminating all disparaging references.
  - Check to see that you understand the story.
  - Thank this party for speaking, the other for listening quietly.
- Ask the second speaker to tell what has happened, and follow the same list of instructions as you did for the first speaker, from taking notes to thanking both parties.
- After both speakers have had their say, ask each party in turn to clarify the major issues to be resolved.
- Inquire into basic issues, probing to see if something else, instead, may be at the root of the complaints.
- Define the problem by restating and summarizing.
- Conduct private meetings if needed.
- Summarize areas of agreement and disagreement.
- Help the parties set priorities on the issues and demands.

Step 3: Help the Parties Negotiate

- Ask each party to list alternative possibilities for a settlement.
- Restate and summarize each alternative.
- Check with each party on the workability of each alternative.

- Restate whether the alternative is workable.
- In an impasse, suggest other alternatives.
- Note the amount of progress already made, to show that success is likely.
- If the impasse continues, suggest a break or a second mediation session.
- Encourage them to select the alternative that appears to be workable.
- Increase their understanding by rephrasing the alternative.
- Help them plan a course of action to implement the alternative.

Step 4: Clarify the Agreement

- Summarize the agreement terms.
- Recheck that each party understands the agreement.
- Ask whether other issues need to be discussed.
- Help them specify the terms of their agreement.
- State each person's role in the agreement.
- Recheck with each party that each knows when to do certain things.
- Explain the process of follow-up.
- Establish a time for follow-up with each party.
- Emphasize that the agreement is theirs, not yours.
- Congratulate the parties on their reasonableness and on the workability of their resolution.

CHAPTER
10

Making Change

"It used to be that change leadership was restricted to people at the very top of the organization. Today, however, especially in a rapidly changing industry like telecommunications, we need people who can make change at every level. If you want to move up the ranks here, show that you can lead people to make a change."

—Matt Collins,

Director of Marketing,

Forum Nokia

Manage **What**?

1. Converting an Organizational Problem into an Achievable Change Initiative

It's your senior year of college and, in an attempt to build your resume, you agreed to run for president of the campus professional business fraternity. No one else ran so you won in a landslide. But now you are faced with a big challenge as your returning vice president tells you the organization is a mess. She further notes that nobody is motivated and the members just want something to put on their resume. She observes it is really hard to get people to take initiative on fraternity events and that new membership and attendance at events dropped to an all-time low last term.

Clearly, this seems like a situation ripe for change management, but how would you proceed in ways that might really yield improvement? Where do you begin? What common traps should you avoid? Who, if anyone, would you want to involve in the process? What resistance might you predict? At the end of the year, how would you judge whether you were successful as a change agent?

2. Creating Urgency for a Change

You are in sales with a pharmaceutical firm and the major drug in your portfolio is one of three patented products that are widely prescribed by physicians (the other two are manufactured by two competitor firms). You are starting to see that the other firms are gaining an advantage with their aggressive and innovative promotion campaigns and marketing efforts. Sales of your product have not fallen off much yet, but you can see that the doctors you call on are starting to be more and more impressed with the competitor products while interest in your drug is waning. Unfortunately, your superiors are complacent and do not recognize what is happening. Other salespeople have tried to make similar cases in the past but have often been dismissed as whiners (because their own sales were dropping) or as "Chicken Littles" who acted as if the sky was falling when it was only a passing phase that happens with all product cycles.

From your relatively low level in the firm, how might you build urgency for a change here? What might you do knowing you have little authority to get anyone to comply? What common traps should you avoid? Are there tactics that might seem intuitive or obvious but that might only raise resistance and create obstacles rather than urgency?

3. Dealing with Change Resistors

You are working as assistant manager in a restaurant where a new manager has just been hired away from a very popular and successful competing restaurant chain. The new guy is bright and energetic and eager to bring some of what he learned in his prior job to his new role. More specifically, he wants to overhaul the way your hosts and servers interact with diners. He is particularly interested in a team approach (whoever is available brings ready food to a table regardless of who took the order) and is encouraging more proactive exchanges with diners. For example, he wants servers to make recommendations and encourage diners to try various specialty items on the menu. The recommended approach is not forceful or aggressive, but is a reasonable way of ensuring that guests are given every opportunity to sample some of the best food and drink and to help create a more memorable dining experience. You really like the new approach and think it can lead to higher store performance and ultimately translate into better bonuses and merit increases for the staff. But you know there will be resistance.

What different forms might the resistance take? What recommendations would you make for how to present the change in a way that might unfreeze that resistance? What common traps should you avoid?

LEARNING OBJECTIVES

1. Use models of the change process to describe a planned organizational change.
2. Structure an organizational problem so that it becomes an achievable change initiative.
3. Collect and feedback data needed to increase change readiness.
4. Provide feedback about change results.
5. Implement interventions that have the most likelihood of creating desired change.
6. Evaluate change results.
7. Create an environment which sustains planned change.
8. Suggest strategies for overcoming resistance to change.

Introduction

Making change is the appropriate title for this chapter, and it is rightly placed at the end of the book. It is the right title because, unlike many discussions of change in organizations, our focus is *not* primarily on large-scale organizational transformations or cultural shifts. Rather, our goal is to help you develop the skills of an effective **change agent** whatever the scope of your desired change and regardless of your level in an organization.

Consistent with the opening quote above, our belief is that change leadership can and does happen at every level in an organization. It *needs* to happen at all levels if an organization is to thrive in today's dynamic business environment. Though few of us will soon be responsible for a new product launch, an international relocation, or a large-scale quality improvement effort, we will all have the opportunity to observe gaps in our organizations between what is and what should be. Even the lowest level employees have the opportunity to facilitate, support, and execute change.

Making change is appropriately at the end of the book because it goes well beyond a one-dimensional skill or capability. It involves a reliance on almost every skill covered in this text. For example, the successful change agent will often need to define and frame problems, communicate persuasively, motivate and lead others, manage conflict, build teams, and so on. Thus, you might think of making change as a capstone management skill and one that brings together many pieces of your journey in managerial skill development.

Managers in every type of organization (government, business, religious, family) have always struggled with change. The key element in change is people, and getting people to buy into a new way of doing anything is often difficult and inevitably involves resistance. As you saw in Chapter 1, significantly changing the behavior of a single person (yourself) can be exceptionally difficult work. So helping others change their behavior, in an effort to get something new accomplished in an organization, offers particularly complex challenges.

Although getting people to change is undeniably challenging, much is known about change, why it fails, and when it succeeds. In this chapter we review what is known about making successful change and present practical frameworks and tools that can help you develop a greater capacity to identify and create positive change.

The Challenge of Change

Any unit you join will surely have to change and adapt if it hopes to survive and thrive. Many types of changes can occur in organizations (new products, new work processes, new employees) and many of those changes are unplanned. That is, unplanned change is the result of external forces that require some reaction and organizational adaptation. Our focus in this chapter is on *planned* change resulting from managers' and others' deliberate attempts to improve organizational operations. As seen in Management Live 10.1, planned change can succeed.

In some cases, managers at higher levels have the power and influence to force change in an organization. That is, by virtue of their authority and control over key organizational reward systems, they can dictate a change from the top and people in the organization will be forced to comply (at least temporarily). However, in most cases, particularly for lower level managers and associates, no such power or influence ensures such compliance.

Therefore, the challenge of change is most often how to influence people when you do *not* have the formal authority to dictate a desired new direction. To do so requires an understanding of how change happens and what can be done to positively influence the process. Moreover, the ultimate goal of any change initiative should be to get beyond simple compliance to commitment. Compliance behaviors are unlikely to last or to create any positive momentum (they often just make people mad or dissatisfied), and they will not ultimately yield the long-term behavioral change most desired in change efforts.

Before we focus on how to make change, it is a good idea to dispel a few of the more persistent myths that exist in this area (see Myths 10.1).

MYTHS 10.1   Myths of Making Change[1]

- *Crisis is a guarantee of change.* Urgency is important, but crisis hardly ensures change will occur. Consider that 90 percent of patients who have had coronary bypass surgery *do not* sustain changes in the unhealthy lifestyles that worsen their severe heart disease and greatly threaten their lives.

- *Change is best motivated by fear.* It's too easy for people to go into denial over the bad things that might happen to them. Compelling, positive visions of the future are a much stronger inspiration for change.

- *Compelling facts are the key to change.* For better or worse, our thinking is guided by emotions and stories, as much as, if not more than, by facts. When a fact does not fit how we make sense of the world, we ignore or reject it. Facts alone, without some personal emotional connection, rarely inspire significant change.

- *Old dogs can't learn new tricks.* Our brains have extraordinary plasticity, meaning we can continue changing and learning new things throughout our lives. The key is to have significant motivation and understanding of the need for change; age has little to do with it.

General Models of the Change Process

The reality is that many change efforts fail—even when it seems profoundly logical or imperative that change should occur. One reason is that change initiatives are often haphazard and not managed in line with what is known about what causes them to succeed and fail. Investment managers would not think of investing funds without considering models of risk, portfolio performance, and so on. Doctors would not prescribe medicine without evidence of the effects of the prescribed drugs. Yet change efforts are often curiously free of any adherence to the change process models shown to predict and explain when and how change will occur. We briefly describe here several models of change that can help you think about how change unfolds. We then present a more specific framework for planned action and a set of practical strategies for converting an organizational problem into an achievable change initiative.

Lewin's Unfreeze-Change-Refreeze Model

The renowned sociologist Kurt Lewin developed one of most enduring, conceptions of organizational change[2] which was a direct extension of his *field theory*. In general, he conceived of fields of force that struggle to maintain the status quo as depicted in Figure 10.1.

"There is nothing so practical as a good theory.

—Kurt Lewin

Lewin's model described change as a three-stage process of unfreezing, changing, and refreezing. In Lewin's **unfreeze-change-refreeze model,** the first stage, *unfreezing*, involves overcoming inertia and breaking down existing ways of thinking. Resistance has to be overcome and a readiness or willingness to get involved with a change has to be sparked. Lewin felt this stage is often neglected because eager and excited change agents—people responsible for making or communicating a change—often dive right in and try to sell their change without first diagnosing and dealing with the resisting factors.

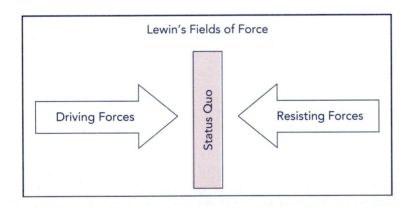

Lewin's Fields of Force

Driving Forces → Status Quo ← Resisting Forces

FIGURE 10.1

Lewin's Force Field Analysis

Management Live 10.1

Your Planned Change Can Succeed

It is popular today to talk about the high failure rate of change and the imposing odds against most attempts to make change in organizations. However, the evidence is that planned change efforts, relying on sound frameworks of the change process, have been quite successful. For example, several comprehensive reviews summarizing research evidence regarding the effectiveness of change interventions, have found positive results. For example, one study identified 35 reported change interventions that were evaluated by rigorous methods. Using outcome measures such as performance, turnover, and productivity, researchers found there was significant positive change in 51 percent of the cases.[3] Other reviews have found gains in productivity associated with change interventions in over 80 percent of studies investigated.[4, 5]

The second stage is what Lewin called *changing* and refers to when the change intervention is started and ongoing. Changing is often a period of anxiety and tension as old ways are challenged and the reality of a new way is first truly experienced. New information and rewards are introduced and comfort zones are pushed. The third and final stage is what Lewin called *refreezing*. Ideally, a new mind-set and behavioral pattern is created for those involved, and the change yields positive benefits for the unit or organization.

Lewin's model is always a good starting point in a situation where change is desired because it draws attention to the most important questions:

1. What is preventing change and why hasn't it happend yet?
2. What actions might influence change?
3. How can change be sustained?

Based on his theory, Lewin developed the concept of a **force field analysis** (see Tool Kit 10.1 for steps to conduct a force field analysis). The current state or status quo is a function of the driving forces and the resisting forces. Driving forces are pushing for change while resisting forces exist because push back against the driving forces in order to maintain the status (see Figure 10.1).

Lewin argued that the effective path to change is to focus first and primarily on removing the restraining forces rather than trying to dramatically increase the driving forces. While that may seem counterintuitive, the logic is that increasing the driving forces can often result in an increase in the resisting forces against the change—people dig in and push back. Removing the obstacles and restraining forces can, therefore, be the least disruptive and quickest path to change.

Although simple in concept, Lewin's model provides a general overview of change that has had profound influence on change research and practice. Indeed, most models of change developed since then acknowledge his influence and simply elaborate on his elegant three-stage model of the organizational change process.[6, 7]

Bridges' Model of Transitions

One model very similar in form to Lewin's is the **model of transitions** created by William Bridges.[8] In studying a variety of failed change efforts, Bridges became convinced it is impossible to achieve any desired objectives without getting to the "personal stuff." Bridges asserts that *transition* is not the same as change. A change occurs when something in our external environment is altered, such as changes in leadership, organizational structure, job design, systems, or processes. Transition, however, is the *internal* process that people must go through to come to terms with a new situation.

According to Bridges, individuals experience three stages of transition while undergoing change (Table 10.1). Further, Bridges believes the failure to identify and prepare for the inevitable human psychological transitions that change produces is the single largest problem with most change initiatives—and why they too often fail. Although many changes can be physically put in place quickly, the psychological process of transitions takes time. Indeed, transitions can take a very long time if they are not well managed, so the *acceleration* of transitions becomes critical.

If any change is going to be sustained, people must own it. And unless they go through the inner process of transition, they will not develop the new behavior and attitudes the change requires. As a result, change efforts that disregard the process of transition are doomed. The critical lesson is to both recognize

| TABLE 10.1 | Bridges' Model of Transitions |

Stages	Transition	Internal Change	Associated Feelings
1	Endings	Dealing with Loss	Anxiety, Blame, Fear, Shock
2	Neutral Zone	Transitional Period	Anxiety, Confusion, Uncertainty
3	Beginnings	Setting New Goals	Integration, Reinventing Yourself

the nature of personal transition and to learn basic transition management strategies that can help accelerate the process.

Kotter's Eight Stages of Change

For many years, a leading authority on change has been John Kotter, a Harvard Business School professor. **Kotter's change model** is another useful way to think about the critical elements necessary to create successful change interventions.[9, 10]

Increase Urgency

Kotter contends that raising a feeling of urgency is the first and most critical step in successful changes. Reports and spreadsheets are not enough; you need to demonstrate actions that make people aware, even shock or jolt them, into understanding the need for the change you've determined.

> *"Change is not made without inconvenience, even from worse to better."*
> —Richard Hooker, 1554–1600

The goal is to get people out of their established routines and comfort zones and ready to move. Kotter notes one way to do that is to create dramatic presentations with compelling objects people can actually see, touch, and feel. He suggests showing customer-service people a videotape of an angry customer rather than handing out a two-page memo filled with negative customer data. You want people telling each other, "Let's go, we need to change things!"

A favorite example of Kotter's is taken from an organization that had a very fragmented and disorganized purchasing system. One result of that poor system was the company was paying significantly different amounts for the same products but, because people across units were not aware of what others were doing, few felt any pressing need for change. To heighten the sense of urgency, one middle manager in the company collected and made a display of all *424 different types* of rubber gloves the company regularly purchased and the wide range of prices paid for those gloves. The display was then prominently exhibited throughout the company to alert people to the reality that the firm was purchasing the same product from multiple vendors and at very different prices. Although many people in the company already knew there were significant problems with the purchasing system, the exhibit created a buzz and had people saying, "*Now we have to do something!*"

Create a Guiding Coalition (Identify Your Champions)

Every good change initiative needs a group of influential, effective champions. It is important to find the right people who are fully committed to the change initiative and who can help you influence others and manage resistance. Senior managers with some clout in the organization are often good champions. However, in some cases the best champions are those thought to be skeptical of change or who would be seen as cynics or tough sells. For example, those responsible for

"Thank you, Bentley. We get the picture."

addictive behavior counseling for teenagers often rely on recovering addicts—those who have experienced the lows of addiction first-hand—as champions of their message and sources of moving testimonials.

Get the Vision Right

While creating a shared need and urgency for change may push people into action, it is the vision that will steer them in the new direction. Kotter emphasizes you want to construct a relevant vision that will help people visualize possible futures. The ideal is a clear picture of a post-change future, no matter how small, that can be articulated in one minute or written up on one page or less. To commit to change, people need a clear sense of where they are going and why that future state will be better or the existing state more undesirable.

Communicate for Buy-In

"The view only ever changes for the lead dog."

—Yukon Dog Sledder

Once a vision and set of goals have been developed, they must be communicated in order to promote understanding. Sending clear and credible messages about the direction and progress of change establishes buy-in, which in turn gets people ready to act.

You are generally best off keeping communication simple and heartfelt. Find out what people are really feeling and then speak directly to their anxieties, confusion, anger, and distrust. Aim to help people get information relevant to their specific needs. Do not rely on memos and reports that will simply get lost in the clutter.

Empower Action

To empower means to bolster confidence that the job can be done and to recognize and reward in ways that inspire, promote optimism, and build self-confidence. Actively encourage input and participation of those who will be involved with the change, be as open with information and feedback as you can, and keep making the case to resistors so they feel the need for change.

Rather than viewing empowerment as simply handing out power, Kotter describes it as removing barriers, or unfreezing those whom you want to take part in the change effort. This is akin to Lewin's suggestion to aim to remove or diminish the resisting forces. This removing of obstacles helps inspire people to take action and avoid a "wait and see" approach.

Create Short-Term Wins

Creating short-term wins is a recurring method for success and one emphasized by every popular model of change.[11] Short-term wins nourish faith in the change effort, emotionally reward the hard workers, keep the critics at bay, and build momentum. By creating short-term wins, and being honest with feedback, the change is seen as working and thus energizes people further.

If you can produce enough short-term wins fast enough, you can energize your change champions. So be on the lookout for small wins that are visible, timely, clear, and meaningful to others. Focus publicly on just two to four goals instead of 15, and make sure no new initiatives are added until one of those first goals is achieved and celebrated.

Consolidate Gains and Don't Let Up

You're not done until the change has been entrenched in the organization. This is a good time to revisit Kurt Lewin's force field analysis. Frequently, successful change can slide back into past habits when the new behavior does not become commonplace. Successful change agents follow up regularly to ensure the new change remains supported, and continue to highlight small wins and progress in relation to goals.

Anchor Change in Your Culture

The final and ultimate goal is to build a hardiness and capacity for future changes in your workplace. Successful efforts build on the momentum from one change to stimulate *other* needed changes and initiatives. Highlight the connections between making change and career success by finding ways to reward risk-taking and change makers. Aim to help make your workplace a "change-ready" culture. Management Live 10.2 gives an interesting take on how Jack Welch viewed the issue making changes work—and last.

Management Live 10.2

Schools, Media, and Police: Powerful Levels of Change

Former GE CEO Jack Welch once noted that the most rapid political and societal change has come about when a change maker sought and gained control over the schools, the media and the police. Although not identical in form, corporations have their equivalents of all three, and therein lies a basic lesson for making change in organizations. Put simply, if you can exert influence over the schools, media, and police in your context, you have a very good chance of making change.

In organizations, schools include training and development seminars but also less formal discussion forums, e-learning, and on-the-job mentoring and coaching. The media include internal publications, employee magazines, newsletters, e-mail, and the grapevine. The police can be the accountants or managers who review decisions and control how money is spent and people are rewarded or sanctioned.

As a change agent you are looking for the most influential levers to get your change accomplished. And there are few more powerful levers in organizational life than the schools, media, and police. If you want to make change, find ways to influence what people are learning, and hearing, and how they are rewarded and punished.

Source: Tichy, N., & Sherman, S. (1994). *Control your own destiny or someone else will: Lessons in mastering change—The principles Jack Welch is using to revolutionize General Electric.* New York: Harper Business.

A Practical Model of Planned Change

The models of change presented above hopefully stimulate ideas about why change often fails and how one might *generally* strategize to make a successful change in an organization. However, many inexperienced change agents need an even more concrete and practical blueprint. With that in mind, we present and illustrate a model of change here that draws heavily on the work of Lewin and Kotter as well as Robert Schaffer, Peter Block, and others who have been influential in researching successful change.[12]

"Change is like manure. It smells terrible, but it makes things grow."

—Dan Gottlieb

Reduced to the essential elements, all planned change efforts can be thought of in terms of:

1. Structuring the problem and contracting with key parties.
2. Collecting data and feedback.
3. Implementing interventions.
4. Evaluating and sustaining the change.

However, it is important to note that such discrete phases are isolated and separated only for purposes of explanation and illustration. Real change in organizations is rarely a straightforward, linear process and usually involves considerable overlap and skipping among the phases.[13] For example, data collection can easily lead to a restatement of the problem, more data can come to life in the process of an intervention, and so on.

To help illustrate how a planned change process might actually evolve through the four phases, we first describe an actual organizational change scenario and use that example throughout the proceeding discussion.

The Stand

A few years ago, Indiana University agreed to allow the student entrepreneurship club in the Kelley School of Business to establish a new food and drink stand (rather unimaginatively called The Stand) to be created in the lobby of the Business School building, one of the biggest and busiest buildings on campus. The agreement was that the MBA entrepreneurship club would run it. In turn, the club would share the profits with other business clubs whose members provided staff workers for the operation.

The prospect of The Stand created excitement among student groups, faculty, and administrators. There was no other food service in the building or nearby so fresh coffee, bagels, sandwiches, and other treats were eagerly anticipated. Profits from The Stand were intended to be a source of significant revenue for several clubs, and formation and management of The Stand was hoped to create hands-on learning opportunities for students.

All things considered, it appeared to be a great new initiative—except that it did not work! More specifically, after its first year of operations, the president of the entrepreneurship club declared The Stand to be "very unsuccessful." She further noted that net revenues were a fraction of what they were projected to be and "hardly worth the effort." Business clubs' interest in staffing The Stand had been spotty all year and dropped off significantly toward the end of the academic year.

Structuring the Problem and Contracting with Key Parties

"In any organization there is always something that can be done right away to improve performance."

—Robert Schaffer

Although sometimes unfortunately bypassed in an urgency to *do something* quickly, the first step in any effective planned change process is to structure the problem to be addressed and to "contract" with the key parties involved.

Structuring a Problem

Structuring a change problem involves addressing two fundamental questions:

- Who is/are the customer(s) of the change?
- What is the scope of change (how broad, how much)?

Unless you explicitly address those questions, and structure the change initiative accordingly at the outset, you run the great risk of proceeding without a clear understanding of what you are trying to do or for whom you are doing it. Most change projects in organizations are likely to have a broader effect than originally thought and may produce unforeseen results. Further, change has a ripple effect, and even a small change in one part of an organization can have effects on individuals and groups in other areas. For these reasons, it is critical to clarify the nature of the problem and the relevant parties (often called stakeholders).

"Regardless of your role in today's organization, if you do not have a customer, you have a problem."

—Frank Morgan, Former Chief Learning Officer, Dow Chemical Co.

Contracting with Those Involved in the Change

Never try to make change alone. Any change done *to* people is less likely to be as effective as change in which people felt involved from the beginning. Far too often, a *joint* diagnosis of problems is neglected in favor of expediency or rapid movement. However, by encouraging people to develop a shared view of what is wrong or what is needed, an initial commitment to change is more likely to be established and mobilized.

"A big problem with both parents and managers is that they want to judge before they understand."

—Unknown

While the term **contracting** is often used to refer to an external vendor or consultant, it actually carries a much broader meaning. The idea is to get those connected to the change involved in doing a **gap analysis** together. That is, where are we now and where do we want to be? The more transparent (not hidden or kept secret) you make all information pertaining to the change and involve those who will be connected with the change, the better the chance for success.

Smart change agents also work to clarify their *own* role in the change process. That is, situations differ in their need for direct or supportive change

Management Live 10.3

Robert Schaffer's Five Fatal Flaws of Consulting

In many ways, the role of change agent can be likened to being an "internal consultant." A good consultant works with a client to frame a problem and gathers data to diagnose situations and propose potential solutions. Author Robert Schaffer, whose writings on change are among the most widely reprinted articles in Harvard Business Review, suggests the reason many change/consulting relationships fail can be traced to five fatal flaws. Of course, not every project is marked by all five flaws, but even a few can block the path to success.

- Projects are defined by the work to be done not the *change results* to be achieved.
- The scope of the project ignores readiness to implement.
- Projects aim for one big solution rather than incremental small wins.
- Projects entail a sharp division of responsibility between client and consultant and little room for partnership.
- Projects make labor-intensive use of consultants rather than leveraged use whereby the targets of change can become self-dependent.

By actively reversing each of the five flaws of conventional practice, Schaffer suggests that change initiatives can be set up to succeed, rather than fail, and are far more likely to truly reach the objectives for which they were designed.

Source: Schaffer, R.H. (2002). *High-impact consulting: How clients and consultants can work together to achieve extraordinary results.* San Francisco: Jossey Bass.

consultation. Author Ed Schein has suggested the change agent role can vary from being a "pair of hands" (using your expertise to fix the problem yourself) to a doctor–patient (providing the diagnosis and recommended treatment) to a process consultation (acting more as an advisor/facilitator of the process). The appropriate role will differ depending on the circumstances, of course, but assume people will be curious about your agenda and your role as change agent. So the more you are able to communicate this information to them, the more people will feel comfortable with the process and, again, will be more likely to embrace and commit to making the change.

Returning to The Stand scenario, if you were involved in being a change agent, it would seem essential to meet with the head of the MBA entrepreneurship club, probably some students who serve as staff, and perhaps some of the other club heads with a stake in the operation's success. As you may recall from the chapter on problem solving (Chapter 3), a recurring trap is to solve the *wrong* problem precisely. So, before you embark on setting goals and intervening, first connect with the key players to: (1) understand their perspective on the problem(s), and (2) lay the groundwork for getting their commitment in finding a solution. Further, clarify your role and interest in the change and how you are personally involved and committed to seeing it through. See Management Live 10.3 for important issues related to the early stages of any consulting project.

Externalizing the Threat/Enemy

Any significant change effort will inevitably involve resistance. But one way to almost surely create *more* resistance is to frame the problem as caused from *within*. That is, if the motivation for the change is perceived as being the result of internal incompetence or negligence (for instance, by current staff or managers), then the change will almost certainly encounter defensive backlash from those very groups who will feel attacked and therefore look to undermine any change. So smart change agents attempt to *externalize* the enemy or threat, that is, provide an externally caused need for change. Good candidates for external enemies are competitors, market forces, rapid environmental shifts, government and regulation, higher customer demands, and simply "changing times." For example, at The Stand it is likely that blaming either current leaders or student staff members (however much such blame may be deserved) would almost certainly derail any change. If you really want to mobilize commitment, you need to be focused on an external enemy such as unforeseen competition. If together you are fighting an external threat, you have a much better chance of uniting and getting behind a change. Note that the root cause of the problem may very well be an internal issue or multiple issues. But getting people to rally early on in the process can help galvanize their attention towards ultimately solving the real issue at hand.

Defining Goals in Terms of Results Instead of Activities

Presuming you structure the problem and get the right people involved with energy to make change, the next key is to establish a set of measurable objectives. While that may seem obvious, it is often (if not usually) violated in the initiation of change projects. Change projects are too often defined in terms of activity or actions to be taken and not in terms of specific outcomes or results to be achieved. Of course, the assumption always is that the activities will translate into the desired results. But that is only an assumption; it is rarely part of the formal framing of a change or contract. Indeed, making measurable results the primary, immediate goal of a change project is one of the most important elements of successful change.[14]

The value of results-oriented goals is threefold:

1. They lead to more direct and urgent strategy development (How do we most directly and quickly achieve those goals?).
2. They lend themselves to more objective and meaningful evaluation and measurement (What has worked and not worked?).
3. They promote accountability and produce a healthy culture of ownership among those involved.

Not incidentally, achieving and celebrating real value-added outcomes is rewarding and often fun. When the goals are in terms of outcomes, you can take aim from the very first moment at achieving tangible results—not just programs, reports, or a set of recommendations.

Even with a focus toward the measurable, a second trap is to think solely of a *singular* goal. However, recent research has begun to demonstrate the value of a more **balanced scorecard,** which argues for developing goals around *multiple* factors.[15] A balanced scorecard approach is based on the notion that a single goal may often be insufficient to truly assess the impact of an initiative. So if you have a change project designed to get at a sales problem, then the goals might be in terms of sales performance, customer satisfaction, new accounts generated, and salesperson product knowledge. If your change involves cost-cutting and budget savings, then goals might be in terms of dollars saved, budget efficiency, process steps reduced, and so on. If your problem is declining membership in some unit, then the goals should be built around membership totals, new contacts made, and so on.

Based on the discussion above, at The Stand a set of results goals might include a defined increase in revenue and profit, percentage increases for particular clubs attached to measured customer satisfaction on their shifts, and reduction in inventory waste. The common trap here would be to establish objectives that point to a new ordering or inventory system, a new commission structure for staff, or a new supplier selection process. Those may well be *paths* to results goals but, by themselves, are activities and not results.

Collecting Data and Providing Feedback

Once we have structured the problem and contracted to determine our own role and that of others, it is important to collect information that will help determine what intervention or activities will be most likely to achieve the goals set and make effective change occur. One way to focus the diagnosis is to ask, "Where is the real pain we want to address?" The challenge is to look beyond the symptoms and identify the root issues that need to be targeted. In The Stand case, the real pain likely stems from the low revenue that goes to the various clubs involved. So, if we want to make change that will have real impact and be of true value, then we need to focus explicitly on how to increase revenue to those clubs and alleviate that pain.

"First seek to understand, then to be understood."

—Stephen Covey

Different Methods of Collection

Various methods can be employed to collect information (interviews, small groups, financial or operational data, customer surveys). Usually it's preferable to use more than one method to obtain multiple data points or perspectives.

A multimethod approach usually includes interviews. Interviews offer many advantages such as gaining a wide range of information while simultaneously building a relationship with the interviewees. The people interviewed generally are those likely to be involved in the change process, and thus the change agent can spend time during the interview explaining his or her approach, which begins the necessary unfreezing process.

However, interviews also have their challenges and drawbacks. For example, arranging and conducting interviews can take a great deal of time, and the process itself can lead to bias and selective information. Therefore, although the interview is generally the starting point of data collection for most change, change agents should keep an eye toward using other methods such as questionnaires, archival information review, and even simple personal observation.

Understanding Before You Judge

A common postmortem observation of failed change initiatives is that the change agents were *quick to judge* but slow to really *understand* the context of their change. To keep you aware of that common oversight, we present here some of the best approaches for getting a more thorough and actionable diagnosis.

Find out who benefits from the current situation.[16] Rare is the change that does not create some "loser" (or at least a *perceived* loser) in the process. Such people can be the turning point for your change so try to first understand who is going to *lose* the most from your proposal.

Write down everything you do *not* know.[17] Ed Schein has proposed one good way to stimulate good diagnosis and learning is to formally write down everything you really do *not* know about how a system or process works. Authentic inquiry and experience can significantly enhance the chance of a collaborative relationship with others and slow down a premature diagnosis and a neglect of the unfreezing phase in making transitions.

Use appreciative inquiry. Appreciative inquiry involves looking for what is *right* and effective in any system.[18, 19] As its name suggests, it is based on discovering the *best* of what works in an organizational context. Too often, attempts to introduce change send a signal that those involved have failed or that prior incompetence led to the need for change (that is, internalizing rather than externalizing the enemy). Appreciative inquiry seeks to highlight what is right and working and thereby avoid a strictly negative tone and emphasis on weaknesses. Appreciative inquiry recognizes that people are most motivated by their own stories of success and tries to use that to spur commitment to make something new, better, or more productive in the organization.

Discuss the undiscussables. Author Roger Schwartz[20] has observed that change agents often choose not to discuss the most critical problems and issues because they seem delicate, political, or otherwise problematic. They reason that to raise such issues would only make some people feel embarrassed or defensive and to discuss them would not be sensitive or compassionate. The unfortunate result, however, is to overlook the *uncompassionate* consequences created by *not* raising undiscussables and a resulting failure to address the biggest obstacles to change. To raise an undiscussable issue with compassion for others and yourself, try using the following approach suggested by Schwartz: "I want to share some observations and raise what may be an undiscussable issue. I am not raising it to put people on the spot, but to see if there is an unaddressed issue that is preventing us from being as effective as we want to be. Here's what I've observed . . . ."

Providing Feedback

A key change tool in the data collection process is to provide feedback of any information gathered. Feedback is an attempt to heighten awareness and build urgency for change. Energy created by feedback comes from two sources: the process and content. As noted earlier, people can be energized when they are involved, and when they see a gap between a current and a desired state. Probably the most important aspect of data feedback is to "get the system into the room."[21] That is, if there are people directly associated with the data, then these individuals should be present. In addition, if the group is to build their own capacity for solving problems, individuals who have the power to make decisions and affect change need to be present.

You always need to be aware, however, that people will bring various feelings into a feedback meeting. For example, there may be anxiety and defensiveness as well as hope that true change will occur. The key point is that if you are going to collect information in your organization, then you need to plan how you will feed that information back and to whom.

One way to help people structure data was developed by the consulting firm McKinsey & Company and is known as MECE (pronounced "me-see").[22] **MECE** stands for *mutually exclusive and collectively exhaustive*. The concept is that problems can be best addressed when structured in a systematic way. Using MECE, you attempt to first identify all relevant issues and approaches to a particular problem and then reduce them to the smallest list possible. When each item is a separate and distinct issue, then your list is ME, or mutually exclusive.

The second issue is whether each aspect of the problem can be categorized under one and only one of these issues—that is, have you thought of everything? If so, then your list is CE, or collectively exhaustive, and is thus a concise frame for analyzing your options and selecting an intervention. In the end, you can sort every piece of data you collect into broad categories for potential discussion and action.

To illustrate, let's practice MECE on the situation facing The Stand. About all we know is that revenue is down and staffing has been problematic. That is often about as much information as exists in the first stages of change. So what might be our potential courses of change action? A reasonable preliminary list might include:

1. *Changing what we offer and how we market and promote those offerings.* The Stand may not be offering an attractive variety of what the customer base wants at acceptable prices. It may be that customers do not know what we have nor find it convenient or easy to get what they want from The Stand.

2. *Changing how we manage the workforce and deliver better customer service.* It seems likely the part-time, transient workforce does not deliver consistent product quality (for example, coffee is made wrong or differently) or high levels of customer attention and service. Poor attention to inventory control may lead to shortages of high-demand product, excess waste, and poor cost control.

3. *Changing our supplier selection and evaluation.* It may be that our suppliers are not consistently delivering quality products at price points whereby The Stand can make a material profit.

As you work through the analysis, other ideas will likely surface. The idea is to condense them into the shortest list that is still MECE. If you collected data that suggests maybe changing the staffing model, that would logically fit as a sub-bullet under point no. 2. Data suggesting a new concept for placing flyers and taking The Stand products into classrooms would fit under point no. 1. If you find several additional options you cannot readily categorize into one of the major items, then simply create a new item called "other issues" and move on. But keep the list short—three or four categories are usually best to stay at the heart of the matter. The idea is to tighten the focus and bring some clarity to

"Anything not worth doing is not worth doing well."

—Unknown

ambiguous situations, so long lists become counterproductive. MECE is a good place to start the translation of a general problem into an actionable change initiative because it prompts you to be complete and thorough without creating excessive overlap and confusion.

Diagnosing Change Readiness

"We do not have to change, because staying in business is not compulsory."

—W. Edwards Deming

The best change in the world is only valuable if the targets of change are ready to accept, implement, and sustain it. Robert Schaffer uses the example of a home furnishing consultant who redesigned a family closet with new fixtures and organization schemes.[23] The family loved it and the project was deemed a smashing success, but a few weeks later the closet was just as messy as before the change. The problem was the family had not contributed to the solution and was not ready to sustain it. This example illustrates the importance of Lewin's notion of first *unfreezing* prior to any intervention.

Independent of the appropriateness of any change, the chance of success will be heavily influenced by what the targets of change are actually ready and able to do. Several researchers have pointed to the importance of a "felt need" or overt desire to make a change.[24] In the treatment of obesity and addictive behaviors, for example, it is well-known that those patients who accept personal ownership of the problem ("I am Tim and I have an eating problem") and an overt desire to improve their condition are far more likely to actually succeed in a change than those without such a felt need. In organizational contexts, one element of readiness testing is an identification of the level of felt need among the people whose approval or cooperation will be essential for success. Other elements include the level of perceived support from management for the change and the existing cynicism regarding prior change initiatives (discussed in some detail in the section on managing resistance that follows). Often the readiness is higher if a change can be framed in terms of a small scope and a quick start.

Put simply, you want to be sure you do not embark on a well-intentioned change effort that is destined to fail. Tool Kit 10.1 at the end of this chapter includes a description of how to conduct a force field analysis. As discussed earlier, a force field analysis is a form of readiness assessment that focuses on finding and reducing forces leading to complacency and discovering whether people involved in a change will be sufficiently ready to carry it out. Common sources of complacency include an absence of urgency, measurement of the wrong performance indices, lack of feedback from external sources, a denial of problems, and too much conformity and acceptance of low performance norms (also known as "happy talk").

Returning to our Stand scenario, our student leaders and staff need to understand the nature of the revenue problem. In this case, it is likely the student staffers do not fully appreciate how revenue is made, the importance of inventory management, attentiveness to customers and so on. The crux of the data collection and feedback is to determine where the pain is greatest and what can be done (which interventions will address the existing problems). Whatever change is decided, however, it will have to be owned by the key parties or it is destined to fail before it ever begins.

Looking for Small Wins to Generate Momentum

A natural tendency in any change context is to think big and aim for a comprehensive solution to an identified problem. Once a need or problem is defined, most of us like to think in terms of a complete remedy. Why not fully solve the problem once we have identified it? However, it is short-term gains and highly visible rapid changes that will help embed the change and gather momentum. In other words, the big solution will often take so long people will lose track of the solution. By proceeding with changes in smaller, more definable units, people have the chance to see progress, know why something happened, and then turn their attention to making more changes. So do not think solely of big gains and wide scope. Aim for small gains and short-term wins.

At The Stand, small wins might be a 10 percent cut in inventory waste during one week, a week of perfect staff attendance, or a certain growth in store traffic for a targeted day. Even *before* you begin the implementation, it is wise to target potential small wins. They will build momentum and raise expectations that, although the process will be difficult at times, in the end the change will be beneficial.

Implementing Interventions

Once we have a feel for our scope, goals, and rationale, the next step is to actually execute the alternatives that have the most potential to create the change we desire. When attempting to address some organizational problem, a change agent might reasonably ask, "What are my options?" or "What are the different things I might do to address any particular problem?"

Types of Interventions

Of course, an infinite number of specific change activities might be selected. However, work in the **organizational development** field has synthesized the types of change interventions into four distinct categories that can provide a good menu or starting point for the type of intervention you might undertake:[25]

- **Strategic.** Strategic interventions might involve organization structure, reporting relationships, target markets and customers, and new product/ service introductions. At The Stand, changing the mix of offerings or targeting a low cost market segment would be a strategic intervention.

- **Social and Human Resource.** Social and human resource interventions deal with culture, teamwork, selection, performance evaluation, training, and rewards. The focus is on how people communicate, solve problems, and are selected, trained, and rewarded. At The Stand, instituting a new team-based approach to cost containment or a commission-based reward system for student staffers would be examples of social and human resource interventions.

- **Structural.** Structural interventions deal with changes in work area configurations, workflow design, dividing labor, and so on. Reducing the number of steps in making a bagel sandwich, or determining how best to move a customer through from order to payment would be examples of structural interventions that might be undertaken at The Stand.

- **Technological.** Technological interventions deal with tools, equipment and machinery, and computing systems. At The Stand, new inventory software or tracking systems would be possible technological interventions.

Obviously, there are an almost infinite number of things you might do in pursuit of change. The importance of the above categorization is it helps structure decisions about what type of intervention to undertake in a concise and meaningful way. Consistent with the MECE (mutually exclusive and collectively exhaustive) analysis discussed earlier, the four categories of interventions are a good starting point for thinking about the distinct options you have in attempting to make change. Depending on the nature of the organizational challenge, the resources you have at your disposal, and the scope of the effort, different interventions will be appropriate. Perhaps most importantly, many organizational challenges are likely to be solved using a combination of intervention types. The key then is to select a set of interventions and aim to ensure they are consistent and fit together. Interventions must be selected and coordinated carefully, since either an inappropriate intervention or the lack of consistent interventions (where they end up working against each other) will doom the effort.

Framing, Reframing, and Selecting Interventions

Another useful model for thinking about change interventions is the **four frames model** developed by authors Lee Bolman and Terrence Deal.[26] They suggest that four frames exist in organizations of every kind: structural, human resource, political, and symbolic. The four frames can be respectively likened to factories, families, jungles, and theaters or temples.

- The *Structural Frame* (factory) relates to how to organize and structure groups and teams to get results.
- The *Human Resource* Frame (family) concerns how to tailor organizations to satisfy human needs, improve human resource management, and build positive interpersonal and group dynamics.
- The *Political Frame* (jungle) deals with how to cope with power and conflict, build coalitions, hone political skills, and deal with internal and external politics.
- The *Symbolic Frame* (theater or temple) is focused on how to shape a culture that gives purpose and meaning to work, to stage organizational drama for internal and external audiences, and to build team spirit through ritual, ceremony, and story.

Bolman and Deal suggest frames are tools that can help change agents identify the various options inherent in any situation. Their most powerful prescription is that of **reframing,** which means simply to explore organizational issues through multiple lenses or frames and to use those frames to uncover new opportunities and options in confusing or ambiguous situations.

Looking at situations through more than one frame can help you choose among different alternative approaches and not get mired or narrowly focused on a single frame that may seem intuitive or reflect solely your own personal style or orientation. Using multiple frames has been shown to lead to better decision-making and fewer dysfunctional change efforts.[27] Conversely, the failure to see the world through more than one frame has been associated with many well-documented and notorious organizational blunders.[28]

To illustrate, suppose our focal organizational problem was the high student dropout rate at our university. The structural frame would lead us to investigate our current systems for helping struggling students and the efficiency of the existing bureaucracy. Questions asked might include: What is currently in place for students to get help? How easily can we identify and reach struggling students before it is too late?

A human resource frame would focus on the *students* themselves and the ways in which they are admitted into the university and graded and developed while they are on campus. Within that frame we might be interested in how students create support groups, find their identity on campus, and connect with others in the campus community.

A political frame would direct the focus toward the university culture and who really "owns" the problem of student dropouts. We might explore the reward system for faculty and others and even the *disincentives* to keep students in school (for example, a more elite student population, less remedial instruction, more time for research and consulting). How might different groups work together to help address the problem and what would be the rewards and incentives for doing so?

A symbolic frame would explore perceptions of how we label and discuss "at risk" students and the sense of embarrassment associated with needing help. How might we reduce some of the stigma attached to those needing remedial instruction and create a more inviting environment for those who need help so they will proactively seek it?

Focusing on the different frames makes it possible to reframe, that is, view the same problem or challenge from multiple perspectives and avoid the quick intuitive calls that are often superficial and uninformed. When the world seems confusing and it is difficult to decide what to do, reframing is a powerful tool for gaining clarity, generating new options, and finding strategies that work.

The central enduring point is no one best type of intervention or change approach is clearly best. The best intervention depends on the situation because interventions are not one-size-fits-all. The challenge, therefore, is to have one or more frameworks that help you generate and explore the range of options open to you. Both the typology of organizational development interventions and Bolman and Deal's four frames model are time-tested tools that are useful in that regard.

"There is no one best way. But all ways are not equally effective."

—Jay Galbraith

Communicating What You Are Doing

The mantra of successful real estate people is location, location, location. The analogous axiom for change agents should be communicate, communicate, communicate! Whatever you decide to do, a critical factor in your success will be how well you are able to communicate the whys and whats of your change intervention as clearly and as often, and in as many different ways as you can. The best change agents think in terms of multimedia and use targeted communication. That is, an overall e-mail or memo is unlikely to successfully communicate your message. Rather, think of how you can really reach the targets of your change, authentically address their most frequently asked questions, and identify and leverage key people who might most effectively communicate your message (see Management Live 10.4).

Management Live 10.4

The Law of the Few: Finding Your Best Communication Champions

It is well-known that one critical element in the communication of any message is the nature of the *messenger*. In his best-selling book, *The Tipping Point*, author Malcolm Gladwell makes a compelling case for the "law of the few," which refers to the reality that it is just a select few individuals who create epidemics and rapid societal changes. The key is to find those exceptional people or *senders* who are capable of starting epidemics. Gladwell specifically identifies three distinct types of senders, which he labels *connectors*, *mavens*, and *salespeople*. Connectors are people who know lots of people and have a particular knack of making friends and social connections. They have a link to many different worlds and an ability to bring them together. Mavens are information specialists who like to figure things out and, once they do, want to tell others about it too. Salespeople are those with the skills to persuade us when we are unconvinced of what we are hearing. From the perspective of a change agent, the lesson is that your biggest impact will come from concentrating your time and resources on connectors, mavens, and salespeople. Who are those people in your context and how do you find and energize them on behalf of the change you seek?

Source: Gladwell, M. (2000) *The tipping point: How little things can make a big difference.* New York: Little Brown.

Evaluating and Sustaining Change Efforts

Successful change must have made meaningful progress on the results established at the outset. It is important to do some evaluation to verify success, identify needs for new or continuing activities, and improve your change process itself to help make future interventions more successful.

Also, recall that any change in organizations is likely to have a broader effect than originally thought. Any initiated change may produce unforeseen and potentially undesirable side effects in addition to the expected result. Further, change has a ripple effect, in that even a small change in one part of an organization can have effects on individuals and groups in other areas. For this reason, it is critical to get evaluation data from all stakeholders.

Frequently, a successful change can slide back into the past when the new behavior does not become tradition or "the typical way things get done around here." So it is important to remain diligent and attempt to create a new, sufficiently strong support for the change to remain. Do not declare victory too soon as the resisting forces are always waiting to make a comeback.

Sustaining change is never easy. Peter Block notes that what makes sustaining change so difficult is our natural tendency to believe change can be installed, managed, engineered, and forgotten. That engineering model works well for solving mechanical problems but is incomplete in trying to change human systems. Change cannot be installed and engineered, and so it always takes longer and is more difficult than people usually imagine.[29]

Overcoming Resistance to Change

No matter how well planned your change efforts, you can't avoid resistors. Resistance is an inevitable reality of change management, and for any significant change there will be naysayers, cynics, victims, and people who will dig in their heels and push back. It is tempting to view opposition as being strictly negative and those resisting change as troublemakers or bad apples who need to be removed. However, we have been careful here not to talk about *eliminating* resistance but overcoming or managing it. There can, of course, be legitimate reasons to resist change efforts. For example, proposed changes may not be well directed and thus not worthy of support. Moreover, even when change is warranted, resistors can provide some of the best information for how to frame, communicate, and modify change initiatives for the better.

Resistance to change can come about for many reasons (see Table 10.2). However, resistance is usually related to uncertainty about the effects of the proposed changes or experience with previous changes that have failed. We all enjoy the comfort of established routines; therefore, any change in approach or scope can be disruptive and make us less productive and insecure in our activities. In general, resistance can be traced to people (1) not fully understanding the change or need for it ("I don't know what I will have to do"), (2) fearing they will not be able to thrive in the new changed reality ("I don't think I can do it"), or (3) not seeing any sufficiently rewarding or punishing consequences linked to the change ("What's in it for me?"). As one of our colleagues reminds us, people don't resist the change itself as much as they resist the threat of *being* changed.

TABLE 10.2	Why People Resist Change

- **Loss of Control** Individuals feel change is being done to them rather than done with or by them.
- **Loss of Face** When changes being suggested result in people loosing face or status.
- **Loss of Identity** People who build an identity around their role do not like any loss of symbols, tradition, or status.
- **Loss of Competence** People do not like having their competence challenged by being put into situations where they lack the necessary competencies.
- **Excessive Personal Uncertainty** The individual is not aware or is uncertain of how the changes will affect them.
- **More Work** Change often brings fear of additional work for those involved.
- **Unintended Consequences** Change in one area often has unintended effects in another.

Accelerating Change, Reducing Opposition

Urgency—But Not Fear

It has become popular in discussions of change resistance to talk about "burning platforms" that force people to jump away from their comfortable positions. Burning platforms can work, but they can also create a panic that prevents action. Unless fear is converted to a positive urgency and with some speed, it can create a source of resistance rather than an impetus for action. With too much fear, some people will focus on the immediate source of anxiety and nothing else. Some will freeze, hide, or become self-protective. Fear can produce movement, but it is not the best sustaining force. It is urgency that sustains change; you do not want self-preservation as the No. 1 goal.[30]

In today's competitive organizational cultures, the reality is that organizations not only want and need to make change, they want to accelerate the change process. One manager described his situation as needing "big change fast." As Lewin noted, it may often be more productive to explore and seek to counter the resisting forces than it is to create a wave of momentum in favor of the change. Indeed, your best hope of accelerating the change process probably lies in the success of strategies to overcome resistance and several factors will affect the choice of how best to overcome resistance. Part of the skill of a change agent is recognizing the appropriate strategies to employ. Some common factors should influence the choice of these including:

The urgency of the need for change. The stronger the threat or importance of change, the stronger the case for quick-change strategies.

The degree of opposition or resentment. The more opposition you expect to the changes, the more appropriate strategies that involve the largest amount of key people are. The rate of change also needs to be considered, as this strategy often takes longer.

The power of the individual/group initiating the change. It may be possible to implement fast change strategies, even if there is opposition, if the individual or group initiating the change is powerful enough.

The necessity for information and commitment. If the change can only be achieved and sustained by commitment and education of those affected (very often the case), full involvement in the change is essential.

In the end, the diagnosis of resistance and the effectiveness of strategies to manage it will be among the best predictors of your change success. Do not fear resistance. Resistors often hold a value many change agents never bother to exploit. The key is to learn to isolate areas of resistance and then seek to understand them, make use of them, and strategize to most effectively manage and ultimately overcome them.

Strategies for Overcoming Resistance

There are six general strategies for overcoming resistance.[31]

Education and Communication

Coupled with education efforts, in the context of change, some experts have noted it is virtually impossible to *overcommunicate*. Let people know what and why at every opportunity. Some successful change agents post a regular frequently asked question (FAQ) in an attempt to keep people posted. The trap, however is to focus solely on the frequency of the communication. As such, do not send out the same memo or communication everyday assuming you'll just pound the message into peoples' heads. It's the quality of communication that matters more than the frequency. So, plan ways to communicate that are varied and tailored to different stakeholder groups.

Participation and Involvement

As emphasized previously, it is far more unlikely, even difficult, for people to resist changes they help bring about themselves. Participation enhances understanding and feelings of control. It also reduces uncertainty and promotes a feeling of ownership.

Facilitation and Support

By accepting people's anxiety as legitimate and appropriate, you have a better chance of gaining the respect and commitment needed to make the change work. When you acknowledge and respond to FAQs, a concern of the month, and other such needs for information, your approach provides people with the sense that their concerns are being heard and attended to. Testimonials from those at the front of the change can be a powerful influence if used appropriately.

Negotiation and Agreement

Often necessary when dealing with powerful resistors, negotiation and agreement normally involve specific exchanges and incentives in return for a person or group's agreement to support a change. Examples of this may include providing assurances certain employees will not be laid off as part of a restructuring effort or that a particularly powerful department head will be able to maintain her budget.

Manipulation and Co-optation

Manipulation and co-optation involve selectively using information and implied incentives. The aim—a risky one—is to get the compliance of resistant parties by promising them certain rewards and benefits linked to their "going along with" the change.

Explicit and Implicit Coercion

In some cases, the use of authority and threat of punishment may be necessary. As with manipulation, using coercion is a risky process because people will likely resent forced change. But in some situations speed may be essential and the changes will not be popular regardless of how they are introduced, so coercion is among the only options.

Although these six strategies have been described independently, they are not mutually exclusive, and a range of strategies can be employed to manage resistance. The key is to fully understand the pros and cons of each method and to be aware of your own change situation. Table 10.3 summarizes the six different methods and their advantages and disadvantages.

TABLE 10.3   **Different Approaches to Overcoming Resistance**

	Approach	Commonly used when . . .	Advantages	Disadvantages
1	Education and Communication	There is a lack of information and analysis.	Once persuaded, people will often help implement the change.	Can be very time-consuming if many people are involved.
2	Participation and Involvement	The initiators do not have all the information they need to design the change, and others have considerable power to resist.	People who participate will be committed to implementing change, and any relevant information they have will be integrated into the change plan.	Can be very time-consuming if participants design inappropriate change.
3	Facilitation and Support	People are resisting because of adjustment problems.	No other approach works as well with adjustment problems.	Can be time-consuming and expensive and still fail.
4	Negotiation and Agreement	Some person or group with considerable power to resist will clearly lose out in a change.	It can sometimes be a relatively easy way to avoid major resistance.	Can be too expensive if it alerts others to negotiate for compliance.
5	Manipulation and Co-optation	Other tactics will not work or are too expensive.	It can be a relatively quick and inexpensive solution to resistance problems.	Can lead to future problems if people feel manipulated.
6	Explicit and Implicit Coercion	Speed is essential, and the change initiators possess considerable power.	It is speedy and can overcome any kind of resistance.	Can be risky if it leaves people angry with the initiators.

Managing Organizational Cynicism

In recent years how people view their relationships with organizations has changed dramatically. Rampant mergers and acquisitions have often resulted in mass lay-offs. And though labeled as "right-sizings" or restructurings, such changes have not been well received in the ranks of the workforce. Unethical corporate leadership and greed have further contributed to employee negativity. Indeed, many employees have become increasingly cynical and the popularity of cartoon strips such as Dilbert and television shows such as "The Office" are further evidence that people may hold rather negative impressions of managers and management.

From the perspective of a change agent, research on **organizational cynicism** has revealed at least three important considerations. First, such cynicism may be entirely rational. That is, a firm may well have a history of dishonesty and unmet promises and thus resistance to a change effort may be based on past organizational behavior. Second, rational or not, cynicism's existence will heighten resistance. Salaried employees have often been found to be cynical about organizational change, perhaps because they are frequently the population that stands to be most directly affected. Third, cynicism is particularly difficult to overcome if prevalent in the organization's leadership. Cynicism among middle managers, for example, greatly magnifies the challenge of change in an organization.

A cynical environment will make resistance even more pronounced and makes the importance of diagnosing and managing that resistance even greater. That said, some research has shown that cynics are often more deeply concerned about the organization and could, if turned around, make the best change agents.[32]

Concluding Note

Stay Focused on the Basics

Throughout this chapter we have presented several different frameworks, models, and charts, which can all become rather bewildering. Change in organizations is a complex process, making it easy to get overwhelmed and frustrated about how to actually proceed. Fortunately, although different writers and professionals certainly have multiple perspectives, the good news is that relatively few core ideas are repeatedly referenced. Below is a Top 10 list of the most fundamental lessons of change:

1. Change only when it is important. Do not change for change's sake.
2. Know your customer. If you don't have one, find one.
3. Seek participation and involvement in both planning and execution.
4. Define your change goals in terms of *results*.
5. Listen to learn about rationales for resistance, rather than get defensive over them.
6. Make sure people know the *whys* of change.
7. Plan for, seek, and celebrate small wins in the process of change.
8. Communicate often with whatever you know, and in different forms.
9. Find the key champions for your cause.
10. Frequently highlight and discuss the post-change future.

In earlier times a CEO or a few leaders at the top with a change agenda were enough. But now it takes a company *full* of change agents to really adapt and thrive in a competitive world.[33] There is no reason a young supervisor cannot be an agent of change in the way that hourly employees are treated, a young engineer cannot orchestrate the redesign of a quality control system, or a young restaurant manager can't champion a new way to serve diners. You do not need to be at the top to bring new ideas and enhance your organization. What you do need is an understanding of the process and a little passion to add value to your workplace. *No matter where you are in an the organization, just do it.* In the end, the most important elements in your success as a change agent will be your heartfelt belief that change is possible and your motivation to make something happen. The world around you may seem like an entirely immovable place, but it almost never is. Intelligent action can make a difference with the right pushes in the right places. There is an extraordinary need for people who are willing and able to seek positive change in our world. So now go make change!

Key Terms

appreciative inquiry	four frames model	model of transitions
balanced scorecard	gap analysis	organizational cynicism
change agent	Kotter's change model	organizational development
contracting	unfreeze-change-refreeze model	reframing
force field analysis	MECE	

Making Change Tool Kits

Tool Kit 10.1   Conducting a Force Field Analysis

Force field analysis is a powerful tool that can be used in several different contexts. The basic premise is that, for every problem or current state of affairs (the status quo), a desired condition or future state also exists that has not been achieved. The status quo is held constant in an organizational system by two opposing forces: (1) driving forces (positive aspects of the problem), and (2) resisting forces (negative aspects of the problem). A force field analysis will help you understand all sides of the problem and where to begin looking. According to the creator of this tool, Kurt Lewin, if you really want to solve the problem, you should begin by removing the restraining forces. Brainstorm with your team to identify the driving and restraining forces that currently exist or that may be present in the near future.

1. On a piece of paper or flip chart, write "Current State" at the top center and write your problem statement underneath. To the right of your current state, write your Desired Condition and write the ideal state if the problem were solved.

2. Draw a line down from the center of Current State. Label the left side Driving Forces and the right Resisting Forces.

3. Now answer the following questions and record the answers on the appropriate side:

   • What are the *drivers*, those things that are driving you toward success and goal achievement?

   • What are the *resisters* for the project or change effort, those things that are restraining you from reaching success and goal achievement?

4. Draw a horizontal arrow underneath each driver and restrainer that demonstrates the relative strength of each. Point the arrow toward the center. Your longest arrow indicates the strongest field of force that is currently operating. Similarly, the shortest arrow indicates the least powerful force. Thus, there should be a range of arrow lengths.

Now that you have a map of the various driving and restraining forces affecting your problem, as well as their varying levels of strength, you are ready to act. Now, your team can make a game plan for how to diminish or remove the forces that are a barrier to you implementing your change.

Tool Kit 10.2   Finding Cost-Cutting Opportunities

One place to make quick inroads with change in most organizations is to look for cost-cutting opportunities. Several authors have made the case that the long-standing entrenched traditions in organizations (the sacred cows) often can be the most effective targets for cost reduction.[34] With that in mind, one strategy is to observe your organization (or unit within) and fill in the following sentences:

- What a pain it is to _____
- This job would be great if I didn't have to _____
- No one reads this so why am I doing it? _____
- It's a waste of time to _____
- I could be much more productive if I didn't have to _____
- We could save a lot of money if we stopped _____

How you respond to these questions will often lead you to important change areas. In a similar vein, other organizations have instituted "Save a buck a day" programs and other ways to alert and empower people to keep an eye out for waste and inefficiency.

Tool Kit 10.3   Communicating to Avoid Clutter

According to John Kotter, the total amount of communication going to the average employee in three months is 2.3 million words or numbers. The typical communication of a change project uses 13,400 words. That means that the change-associated communication the average employee sees is .058 percent of what that same employee sees overall. With that in mind, several elements of effective communication are key and include:

- **Simplicity.** Try to keep all jargon and technical terminology out of messages.
- **Analogy and Example.** A picture, chart, or illustration is worth a thousand words.
- **Multiple Forums.** Big meetings, small forums, memos, and newsletters are all effective for spreading the word (recall the concept of controlling the schools, media, and police).
- **Repetition.** Ideas sink in only after they've been heard many times.
- **Modeling the Way.** Visible people behaving inconsistently with the vision overwhelms other forms of communication.
- **Explanation of Seeming Inconsistencies.** Unaddressed inconsistencies undermine the credibility of all communication.
- **Give and Take.** Two-way communication is always more powerful than one-way communication.

Tool Kit 10.4   How to Tell an Effective Change Story

Most people trying to make change in an organization likely do not think of themselves as storytellers. That is unfortunate because recent evidence suggests a good story or stories can be a critical element in executing successful change. A carefully crafted and chosen story can help a change agent translate an abstract concept into a meaningful mission for others. The key is to know which story strategies are right for what circumstances. The chart below offers several dos and don'ts for organizational storytellers, along with examples of stories that get results.

If your objective is:	You will need a story that:	In telling it, you will need to:	Your story will inspire such phrases as:
Sparking action	Describes how a successful change was implemented in the past, but allows listeners to imagine how it might work in their situation.	Avoid excessive detail that will take the audience's mind off its own challenge.	"Just imagine. . ." "What if. . ."
Communicating who you are	Provides audience-engaging drama and reveals some strength or vulnerability from your past.	Provide meaningful details but also make sure the audience has the time and inclination to hear your story.	"I didn't know *that* about him!" "Now I see what she's driving at!"
Transmitting values	Feels familiar to the audience and will prompt discussion about the issues raised by the value being promoted.	Use believable (though perhaps hypothetical) characters and situations, and never forget that the story must be consistent with your own actions.	"That's so right!" "Why don't we do that *all* the time!"
Fostering collaboration	Movingly recounts a situation that listeners have also experienced and that prompts them to share their own stories about the topic.	Ensure that a set agenda doesn't squelch this swapping of stories—and that you have an action plan ready to tap the energy unleashed by this narrative chain reaction.	"That reminds me of the time that I . . ." "Hey, I've got a story like that."
Taming the grapevine	Highlights, often through the use of gentle humor, some aspect of a rumor that reveals it to be untrue or unreasonable.	Avoid the temptation to be mean-spirited—and be sure that the rumor is indeed false!	"No kidding!" "I'd never thought about it like *that* before!"
Sharing knowledge	Focuses on mistakes made and shows, in some detail, how they were corrected, with an explanation of why the solution worked.	Solicit alternative—and possibly better—solutions.	"There but for the grace of God. . ." "Wow! We'd better watch that from now on!"
Leading people into the future	Evokes the future you want to create without providing excessive detail that will only turn out to be wrong.	Be sure of your storytelling skills. (Otherwise, use a story in which the past can serve as a springboard to the future.)	"When do we start?" "Let's do it!"

Source: Reprinted with permission from Denning, S. (2004 May). Telling tales. *Harvard Business Review, 82* (5), 122–129.

Tool Kit 10.5   Change What? Isolating a Problem That Matters[35]

Change merely for the sake of change is counterproductive, so the first challenge of any change agent is to be sure he or she is pursuing change that is important and matters. Determining what is important is always subjective, of course, but four general areas within any organizational unit are good places to start.

- **Markets and Customers.** How might we add value to the product or customer? How might we improve our service levels? Your challenge might deal with the way your unit will, or should, view and segment its markets and customer base. Similarly, it may deal with the scope and variety of services you provide (perhaps heading up a new market initiative) or might involve partnerships *within* the firm (other departments or divisions within the firm) or *external* to the firm (customers, suppliers).

- **Business Processes/Organizational Structures.** Your change may be focused on a gap in the way your unit's processes operate now and the way they will need to operate in the future. This may involve different types of structural configurations or performance or financial measures.

- **Technologies.** Your change vision may reveal a gap between the technologies in place today and those needed to be competitive in the future.

- **People and Reward Systems.** Your change vision may include differences in the kinds of people you will need, systems and measures for selecting, training, and rewarding them, and the way you work together (teams).

If you find yourself in a position where you are eager to add value, but are not sure where to focus your attention, it can be also productive to explore questions such as: What problems are most likely to keep your boss up at night? How might we improve communication? How might we encourage innovation? How could we improve morale? How do we speed up decision-making? Or, most directly, how do we cut costs?

Building High Performance Organizations and Great Places to Work

"Nothing is more important to the success of an organization than the way people are managed."

—Conclusion from Gallup Company research[1]

EXPANDED CHAPTER OUTLINE

INTRODUCTION

HIGH PERFORMANCE VS. TOXIC CULTURES: THE OUTCOMES OF GREAT PEOPLE MANAGEMENT

THE PRACTICES OF HIGH PERFORMANCE MANAGEMENT
- Selective Hiring of New Personnel
- Decentralized Decision Making and Employee Involvement
- Comparatively High Compensation Contingent Upon Performance
- Extensive Training
- Employment Security
- Reduced Status Distinctions and Barriers
- Extensive Sharing of Information Throughout the Organization

HOW DO I HELP CREATE A GREAT PLACE TO WORK?

SOME SUCCESS STORIES
- Whole Foods
- The Men's Wearhouse
- AES Corp.

CONCLUDING NOTE

Introduction

"Our true 'core competency' today is not manufacturing or services, but the global recruiting and nurturing of the world's best people and the cultivation in them of an insatiable desire to learn, to stretch, and to do things better every day."

—GE 2000 Annual Report[2]

The ultimate goal of learning management skills is to help create organizations that are simultaneously productive and great places to work. Organizational success comes through people, and the most powerful influence on people is their direct manager. If managers are performing the critical skills and the environment has been properly shaped, the organization has powerful tools for achieving extraordinary results.

In the chapters of this book, we have intentionally separated the management skills into digestible learning sections. Mastering something new requires focus and attention, and thus separating the specific skills makes a great deal of sense for learning how to perform them.

In practice, however, great management rarely involves the singular use of a particular skill. That is, managers do not typically report that they face motivation or decision making or communication problems; managers just face *problems*. In this vein, one CEO of a large pharmaceutical company jokingly noted that, when he faces a problem, "he can not remember what class he is in."[3] The reality is that effective people management ultimately involves a combination of skills and, just as important, the motivation to consistently apply such skills.

"I've got some skills—I'm just not sure they add up to a 'set.'"

When great people management skills are consistently applied in organizations, remarkable things can happen. People get fired up about their firms and their jobs, firms are drawn to support and reward those people in exceptional ways, and the job of manager is infinitely more fulfilling and rewarding. Managers who most contribute to high performance cultures and great places to work share three things: (1) a belief in the power of people management to influence organizational success, (2) an understanding of the people management practices that most influence commitment and performance, and (3) motivation, even courage, to manage in a way that puts people first, even in organizations with little traditional support for such behavior. We build on and illustrate each of these shared beliefs here.

High Performance vs. Toxic Cultures: The Outcomes of Great People Management

Great strategy, breakthrough products, innovative technology, clever marketing, and even luck significantly influence organizational success. However, it is also true (but for some reason a much bigger secret) that people management practices are among the most important and sustainable source of competitive advantage in organizations today.[4] Indeed, several recent investigations have found that, more than product, industry, technology, or strategy, how people

"Because our people measures determine our success, we need to make this a people leadership company."
—Peter Dunn, CEO, Steak n Shake

Management Live C.1

Five Cases for High Performance Management

Studies in a wide range of manufacturing and service industries show that people-oriented management practices achieve greater productivity, quality, and cost efficiency than systems that impose direct control. Highlights of five studies suggest just how much people can deliver when supported by effective management.

- Among 702 large firms representing several industries, being one standard deviation better on an index of high-commitment human resource practices resulted in an increase in shareholder wealth of $41,000 per employee.[6]
- Motor vehicle manufacturing firms implementing flexible production processes and associated practices for managing people enjoyed 47 percent better quality and 43 percent better productivity than firms relying on traditional mass-production approaches.[7]
- The five-year survival rates of firms issuing initial public offering showed that those whose human resource practices scored in the top one-sixth of IPO firms had a 33 percent higher probability of surviving than those in the lowest one-sixth. Firms in the top one-sixth in providing financial rewards to all employees, not just managers, had almost twice as much chance of surviving for five years than those in the bottom one-sixth.[8]
- Steel mini-mills using a high-commitment approach to management required 34 percent fewer labor hours to make a ton of steel and had a 64 percent better scrap rate than mini-mills using a command-and-control approach.[9]
- Apparel manufacturing firms that had changed to modular production and relied on teams of multiskilled people paid on a group basis had 65 percent better operating profit as a percent of sales, 22 percent higher gross margins, and 49 percent more growth in sales over a four-year period, compared to firms that relied on traditional bundle manufacturing and paid single-skilled operators on the basis of individual piecework over the same period.[10]

are managed in a firm has the most profound effects on numerous organizational outcomes, ranging from quality and productivity to the survival rate of new firms (see Management Live C.1).[5]

For example, a recent large-scale study of 750 publicly traded companies found that those with superior people management practices had as high as a 47 percent jump in financial return to shareholders. Moreover, by using data collected over time, the results refute the notion that only companies doing better financially can "afford" to use high performance management practices. The data suggest no company can afford *not* to use such practices. It pays—literally—to manage people well.[11]

Similarly compelling evidence of the importance of people management practices comes from service firms (restaurants, hotels, banks, retail stores), where year in and year out, a few select firms selling the same type of products to the same type of customers consistently outperform their competitors. Managers at Southwest Airlines, MBNA, Best Buy, Ritz-Carlton Hotels, and the Merry Maids subsidiary of ServiceMaster understand financial performance is linked to customer loyalty and satisfaction and that such loyalty stems directly from *employee* loyalty, satisfaction, and productivity. Put simply, it takes satisfied and committed employees to get satisfied and loyal customers.

Perhaps the most comprehensive recent investigation of the relationship between people management and various metrics of organizational performance was conducted by The Gallup Organization. Gallup tapped into its database of more than 1 million surveys of workers around the world. The central focus of the investigation was to uncover an answer to the question: "What does a strong and healthy workplace look like?" The researchers eventually distilled 12 core issues (called the Q12) that they contend can represent a simple barometer of the strength of any work unit (see Management Live C.2). Employees who more

Management Live   C.2

12 Questions That Matter

If you want to build the most engaged workforce, then your first job is to help every employee generate compelling answers to 12 simple questions about the day-to-day realities of his or her job. These factors, maintain Marcus Buckingham and his colleagues at The Gallup Organization, determine whether people are engaged, not engaged, or actively disengaged at work. Employees are fully engaged when they can answer each question with and emphatic yes!

1. Do I know what is expected of me at work?
2. Do I have the materials and equipment I need to do my work right?
3. At work, do I have the opportunity to do what I do best every day?
4. In the past seven days, have I received recognition or praise for doing good work?
5. Does my supervisor, or someone at work, seem to care about me as a person?
6. Is there someone at work who encourages my development?
7. At work, do my opinions seem to count?
8. Does the mission or purpose of my company make me feel my job is important?
9. Are my co-workers committed to doing quality work?
10. Do I have a best friend at work?
11. In the past six months, has someone at work talked to me about my progress?
12. This past year, have I had opportunities at work to learn and grow?

Source: Buckingham, M., & Coffman, C. (1999). *First, break all the rules: What the world's greatest managers do differently.* New York: Simon & Schuster.

favorably endorsed these 12 questions were seen as being more "engaged" in the organization and their work.

What is most impressive is how individuals' *subjective* answers to the Q12 index relate to *objective* business results. Indeed, the relationships between those questions and a variety of performance measures were substantial. For example, the most "engaged" workplaces (those in the top 25 percent of Q12 scores) were more likely to have lower turnover, higher-than-average customer loyalty, above-average productivity, and more likely to report higher profitability.

At a more specific level, the electronics retailer, Best Buy, has embraced the Q12 approach with some interesting findings. When it first started surveying its employees in 1997, the company was in the 45th percentile of the Q12 database. Within four years it was in the 70th percentile. More important, in those four years, 99 stores improved their Q12 scores significantly, while just 18 stores had scores that fell. The 99 stores that improved their engagement level dramatically improved store profits. The stores whose engagement level fell missed their targets. Not surprisingly, the company found that its store with the highest Q12 score ranks in the top 10 percent of Best Buy stores as measured by P&L budget variance—and the store with the worst Q12 score falls in the bottom 10 percent.

At Steak n Shake restaurants, a focus on leadership development and improved associate work satisfaction has dramatically cut both manager and associate turnover, and significantly increased guest satisfaction and store earnings. CEO Peter Dunn calls it the "virtuous cycle". That is, when a firm takes care of its managers, they will in turn take care of associates, and those associates will then take care of customers. Well-treated customers drive the growth and financial success of an organization—particularly in a high customer-interaction business like food service.

Despite such evidence of these successful practices, the number of "toxic" workplaces remains depressingly high. Reports of organizations where bosses scream at and threaten workers, allow little involvement in decision making, neglect the hiring process, horde information from associates, and otherwise fail to employ the skills covered in this text are all too frequent. In such cases, the results are predictable. Good people leave, and those that stay do not fully commit to the business and are far less inclined to recommend ways to improve the organization's products and services or work harder to satisfy customers.

"Do you mind if I give you a little destructive criticism?"

In short, the kind of workplace that great management creates matters as much or more than virtually any other organizational element. An environment where people work with high levels of trust and support is likely to generate greater commitment and foster greater innovation and creativity. Investing time and resources into making a company a *great place to work* is likely to pay off with direct impact on the bottom line.

The Practices of High Performance Management

"95 percent of my assets walk out the door every night. My job is to bring them back."

—Jim Goodnight, Founder, SAS

Demonstrated relationships between organizational success and people management practices rightly prompt questions regarding just what the most influential and important practices are. Of course, many management practices can be supported on a humanistic level, but ultimately carry no supporting evidence that they actually contribute to high performance cultures. Those people management practices that *have* been shown to relate strongly to organizational performance should now be familiar as they really are just the organizational extensions of many of the individual managerial skills and practices discussed in this text. Professor Jeffrey Pfeffer of Stanford has pioneered the synthesis of high performance people management practices, and we draw heavily on his influential work in the following discussion.[12] Given an emerging body of evidence that has explored these practices with supporting evidence, we think any great manager should be aware of, and engaged, in trying to create such practices in his or her own organizational role.

Selective Hiring of New Personnel

Too many firms spend more time and energy picking a copy machine than they do hiring new associates. That is unfortunate because the linchpin for all people-first management strategies is a base of capable and willing (not necessarily extraordinary) people. The performance management skills outlined in Chapter 5 are essential to creating a truly great place to work. It may often make sense to let high performing peers participate in the hiring process because good people *hire other good people,* creating something of a rolling snowball effect whereby the organization keeps collecting more and more stars. Southwest Airlines even allows some customers to get involved in some phases of their flight attendant selection.

Firms commonly can get so desperate to fill a position that they go against their own guidelines. But a bad hire is far worse than no hire. Involve senior management and others to emphasize the importance of hiring.

Think of an extreme case of selective hiring. If you have ever seen the television show "The Apprentice," Donald Trump picks one employee from an applicant pool of hundreds of thousands of people after seeing the finalists perform a series of difficult tasks. In this case, do you think that Trump should be able to find a well-qualified person? We would certainly hope so!

While it is very unlikely your company will be as popular as "The Apprentice," selective hiring can be practiced in most organizations. Companies that really get this right, however, do not stop with the hiring; they continually adjust their hiring practices to make sure the people they get are successful in the jobs for which they apply.

Decentralized Decision Making and Employee Involvement

Assuming good people have been hired, great organizations then let those people go to work. These organizations may provide good training and give a lot of direction, but letting people do the job for which they were hired is just as important. This provides a sense of ownership and challenge and often supports a customer service orientation. By encouraging employees to go beyond the literal boundaries of their jobs, you gain not just a part, but the full potential, of their contributions to the organization.

An emphasis on decentralized decision making can take several forms. In some cases, it may involve the creation of self-managed teams, which may reduce the necessity of administrative oversight and closer customer contact. In other cases, it may simply mean giving associates greater discretion to use their heads in making good decisions—often to satisfy customers. Nordstom, a high-end department store, is famous for an employee manual that consists solely of:

Rule 1: Use your good judgment in all situations.

Rule 2: Refer to Rule 1—there will be no additional rules.

Trusting people to use their brains and abilities has even broader effects than you may think. Because people tend to manage others the way they were managed, managing with a focus on trust helps build a positive organizational culture. A culture that allows for input and involvement in decision making has a cascading effect in an organization over time.

> "As is done to children, they will do to society."
>
> —Karl Menninger

You can divide any working population into three categories: people who are engaged (loyal *and* productive), those who are not engaged (just putting in time), and those who are actively disengaged (unhappy and spreading their discontent). Some recent estimates suggest the U.S. working population is no more than 26 percent engaged and up to 20 percent actively disengaged. One of your most important tasks as a manager is to increase the percentage of *your employees* who are engaged.

Comparatively High Compensation Contingent Upon Performance

Although labor markets are far from perfectly efficient, a relationship does exist between what a firm pays and the quality of the workforce it attracts. Put simply, higher wages attract more qualified people. A firm does not need to be at the *very* top; many other factors matter. But to the extent you can pay well, the better your chance of attracting the highly qualified, capable people your organization needs to be successful.

> "No matter how much we invest in our employees, they give us more in return."
>
> —Robert Wegman, CEO, Wegmans Food Markets

An important distinction needs to be made regarding high wages. Decision makers in organizations frequently claim "we cannot be competitive if we pay higher wages than our competitors." However, such a statement may reflect a failure to understand that high labor *costs* are not the same as high labor *rates*. For example, at some of its properties, hotel chain Marriott hired fewer maids to clean rooms, but then paid a higher wage to those they did hire to do more rooms at higher quality—creating a higher labor rate but sustaining a similar overall labor cost. The result was a group of maids who were more committed, produced higher quality work, and ultimately satisfied more customers. In many cases it is possible high wages can be a win-win situation for the employee and the employer alike.

> "Money is not everything, but it is hard to imagine a situation where having lots of money made it worse."
>
> —Robert Byrne

Of course, whatever the pay level, your main aim is to reward people for those activities and behaviors that are central to organizational performance. So, measuring what really matters, not just what your current software system can easily produce a report of, is absolutely critical. Many of the most progressive firms at managing people have developed unique standards of performance that often involve people, not just sales or technical accomplishments. For example, Pfeffer refers to the following measurements when discussing what separates "the best from the rest":[13]

- Hewlett-Packard evaluates managers on their *subordinates' assessment* of managerial behavior and adherence to HP values. FedEx has a similar leadership assessment process.
- Motorola has traditionally had a goal of giving each employee at least 40 hours of training per year, and measures managers by the proportion of their people who get that amount of training.
- Singapore Airlines spends 15 percent of its payroll costs on training. Most important, however, is that the firm takes its commitment to training seriously enough to track it.
- SAS Institute measures key employee turnover and holds all managers accountable for that metric. As a result, managers are acutely aware of the turnover rate and talk and strategize with others to keep the number down.
- Southwest Airlines tracks the number of its job applicants (currently more than 120,000 a year). Some would see processing so many applicants as a waste of resources, but Southwest views this activity as critical to ensuring access to the best possible workforce.

Extensive Training

Today's workforce is aware of the uncertainty of jobs and organizational success and, thus, more than ever, is acutely interested in growth and employment viability. The cost of training and educational opportunities for people can be high, but evidence suggests the investment is returned. A recent study by the American Society for Training and Development found that top performing organizations consistently showed a higher percentage of their budget devoted to training and had a higher percentage of their total workforce involved in training compared to lower performing companies.

"What if we train all these people and they leave? What if we don't and they stay?"

—Anonymous

Extensive training is an important piece to the overall puzzle. Training will allow employees to possess the skills they need to be fully engaged decision makers. Training's effect should be enhanced performance that allows for higher wage rates to be paid.

An excellent example of an organization known for its training is Motorola. Motorola begins by taking a broad look at the goals of the organization and the current business environment. Then, to get a measure of where its current skill levels rank, the company reviews performance excellence scorecards and conducts interviews with senior management. The gaps identified from the scorecards and the interviews are then compared with current critical business goals to determine and prioritize individual, team, and the organization's learning needs. Training priorities and opportunities that align to critical business needs are communicated directly from senior leadership through manager briefings, e-mail messages, and quarterly Town Hall meetings. As a result of these communications learning skill guides are created that list the company's priorities according to functions, groups, and regions. Employees can refer to these guides and identify training opportunities available for their own individual development needs.

At the individual level, Motorola identifies training needs through its Personal Commitment process. During this process, individuals discuss training and career development with their managers. Within these dialogues, career aspirations, feedback from managers, linkage with overall business and group objectives, and recommended training from the learning skill guides are covered.

These plans are jointly reviewed and agreed upon by both the employee and the supervisor. Training opportunities for employees include instructor-led, classroom-based training, e-learning via the Web or CD-ROM, and self-study opportunities such as reading industry publications and participating in communities of practice.

Smart companies recognize that a significant commitment to employee training is critical to continued success.

Employment Security

From a simple psychological perspective, people will work more effectively when they can focus on doing their job rather than worrying about *keeping* it. Similarly, if employees are your company's greatest assets, then it makes sense to ensure they're not working for your competition. Keep in mind if you have been selective about who you have hired—well-paid, involved decision makers whom you have invested a lot in training—why would we want them to worry about losing their job?

Although this may seem like common sense, many organizations practice uncommon sense and get sucked into the performance death-spiral. For example, a first action of many new CEOs is to initiate layoffs. If competitive success is truly achieved through people, then it is important to build a workforce that can achieve competitive success and that others cannot readily duplicate. Ironically, the recent trend toward using temporary help, part-time employees, and contract workers, particularly when such people are used in core activities, flies in the face of the changing basis of competitive success. This trend raises questions about why these practices seem to be growing, what effects they have on the ability to achieve advantage through people, and what the implications are for organizations that might follow a different strategy.

Providing your people a sense of employment security is not always fully possible, but is a valuable practice worth striving towards. The practice of maintaining employment security does not mean poor performers have a job for life, quite the contrary. As we discussed in Chapter 5, effective performance management dictates communicating extensively to a company's star performers so they feel valued and that their jobs are secure. Valuing performance and rewarding the doers has positive effects on organizational culture. In contrast, tolerating slackers and deadwood can ultimately poison the culture; great managers actively manage poor performers to maintain a high performing environment.

Reduced Status Distinctions and Barriers

The trappings of executive life are seductive at some level, but in reality most people *hate* status distinctions, and such distinctions generally depress morale, innovation, and people's satisfaction with their jobs. In short, people do not like to be reminded they are somehow lower in the pecking order than others.

Typical ways status is communicated include:

- *Dress.* Managers wear white hard hats in plants, while workers wear yellow, or managers wear ties, and employees are in company uniforms.
- *Parking Spaces.* Executives have reserved spaces while others use an open lot.
- *Expense Budgets.* While on company business, companies often have two different sets of standards for travel. Executives stay in expensive hotels and the company pays for expensive meals, whereas lower ranking employees have strict limits and often have to go through a laborious process to get their reimbursements.

- *Benefit or Compensation Packages.* Managers are eligible for bonuses or stock options whereas others are not. Also, large differences exist in executive pay when compared to average workers (see Management Live C.3).
- *Office Size and Furniture.* Executives have corner offices, managers have offices, the rest have cubicles.
- *Equipment.* Executives and managers often have huge computer monitors and up-to-date new computers while employees, who use their computers for a much higher percentage of the day, have smaller screens and slower computers.
- *Access.* In many banks and other large headquarters buildings, executives have their own elevators with special key cards. These key cards guarantee

Management Live C.3

Executive Pay

How much more should the people in the top of an organization earn over the people at the bottom? The question can be approached in many ways. For example, we might take a moralistic approach and argue for certain rights or living wages. We might suggest an answer more consistent with capitalism and survival of the fittest. Or we might examine the business case, which a recent study set out to do. In particular, he examined the ratios of the top-to-bottom pay scales in organizations and looked at performance metrics for both individuals and organizations. Results showed that, as organizations increase the disparity between the top and bottom, *both* individual and organizational performance decreases. In other words, people at the top may perform better, but people at the bottom (of which there are many more, explaining the overall decline in the organization's performance) perform worse. Given these findings, it is difficult to justify the large dispersion between the top and bottom—it just doesn't make good business sense. Yet, as the chart below shows, U.S. corporations are leading the way (almost double) among the most industrialized countries in pay dispersion. A wide disparity in wages from top to bottom can be particularly damaging to the morale of the workforce when senior executive wages are *not* tied to the overall peformance of the firm.

The U.S. CEO-to-Worker Pay Ratio is Much Higher than Those of Other Industrialized Countries

Ratio of CEO-to-Worker Compensation (2001)

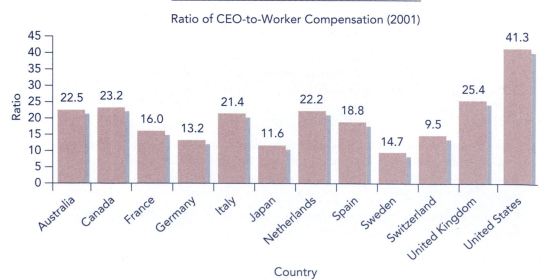

Source: Towers Perrin 2001-2002 Worldwide Total Remuneration Study

Note: Worker figures based on average salary of a manufacturing worker.

that no other employees can access the floors on which the executives work or gain entrance to the executive cafeteria.

Clearly, the symbols of workplace status differences surround most people on a daily basis.

A good example of a company that has removed most status differences is Wainwright Industries, headquartered in St. Louis, Missouri. Wainwright manufactures stamped and machined parts for customers in the automotive, aerospace, home security, and information processing industries. In 1994, the company won the U.S. National Institute of Standards and Technology's prestigious Baldrige Award. In 1996, Industry Week tapped Wainwright's company as one of the best-run plants in America. As part of creating Team Wainwright, all employees (including the CEO) wear the same uniform on the job. In addition, Wainwright has no assigned parking spaces, and all of the office walls were removed and replaced with glass so that anyone walking by a manager's office (including the CEO's) could see what that person was doing. Don Wainwright, the CEO, asserts that "If I can walk out on the shop floor and see what a person is doing, then anyone should be able to see what I am doing." This level of equality is rarely seen in U.S. companies, but does wonders for showing people that "everyone here counts regardless of status."

Extensive Sharing of Information Throughout the Organization

At the most basic level, you build trust by treating all members of an organization as though they can be trusted. This means, among other things, sharing information with everyone. When John Mackey, CEO of Whole Foods Market, was asked why his firm shared all of its performance information with everyone, and even made it possible for each team member to know the salary of everyone else in the company by name, he replied that to keep secrets implied the organization didn't trust those from whom information was withheld. Knowledge is power, and sharing information entails sharing power. Not sharing information suggests some in the organization can be trusted with its secrets, and others can't. This is the wrong message to send if you want to harness the efforts and energy of everyone in the organization.

You cannot build trust without treating people with respect and dignity. Layoffs in which those let go are immediately escorted off the premises by uniformed security guards send a clear signal of distrust. This process deprives those people who have been laid off of the opportunity to say goodbye and, more fundamentally, signals distrust and disrespect. Consider instead New Zealand Post, which in 1987 became a state-owned enterprise expected to operate on a profitable basis. It has since accomplished amazing things, for instance, actually *reducing* the cost of a stamp! People laid off were offered generous severance, given parties on their leaving, and recognized for their contributions to the company. Indeed, the organization even let the staff help decide who would go and who would stay—for it turned out some people the organization intended to keep wanted to leave or retire and others wanted to stay.

Building trust also means taking the organization's values seriously. The 2005 annual report for AES Corp., one of the world's largest independent producers of electricity, discusses how well the organization is doing in living up to its four core values of safety, integrity, honoring commitments, striving for excellence and having fun through work. Whole Foods Market's annual report prominently displays the results of its employee satisfaction survey. These organizations signal they take seriously their commitments to both their values and their people by publicly discussing where they are succeeding and where they are falling short—and what they are going to do about it.

Today many firms spend a great deal of time benchmarking best practices in other companies. They want to know how they're doing relative to their peers.

In reality, however, most managers can often learn much from examining what is done well in their own company. In other words, learn from your own people first.

As an excellent example of sharing information inside of the business, let's return to the example of Best Buy used earlier in this chapter. Interestingly, across 400 stores (which for all practical purposes are identical to each other), employees are engaged to vastly different degrees. In the Best Buy store that had the highest

Management Live C.4

The Great Place to Work Institute Model

Every year, the Great Place to Work Institute conducts a survey to determine the 100 Best Companies to Work for in America. The Institute defines a great place to work as one in which you "trust the people you work for, have pride in what you do, and enjoy the people you work with." To score well in this survey, employees of companies respond to both a Trust Index and a Culture Audit. The model of a Great Place to Work that the organization has developed is as follows.

Dimension	How it plays out in the workplace	
	Credibility • Communications are open and accessible. • Competence in coordinating human and material resources. • Integrity in carrying out vision with consistency.	**T**
	Respect • Supporting professional development and showing appreciation. • Collaboration with employees on relevant decisions. • Caring for employees as individuals with personal lives.	**R** **U** **S**
	Fairness • Equity - balanced treatment for all in terms of rewards. • Impartiality - absence of favoritism in hiring and promotions. • Justice - lack of discrimination and process for appeals.	**T**
	Pride • In personal job, individual contributions. • In work produced by one's team or work group. • In the organization's products and standing in the community.	
	Camaraderie • Ability to be oneself. • Socially friendly and welcoming atmosphere. • Sense of "Family" or "team".	

scores on the Gallup surveys, 91 percent of employees strongly agreed with the statement, "I know what's expected of me at work." In the store with the lowest score, just 27 percent agreed. What would account for those kinds of differences? How should a company like Best Buy or any other store for that matter capitalize on those types of discrepancies across locations? By the *sharing of information*. What do the store managers in the store with a high level of engagement do differently from the store with low employee engagement? Are they selecting their workers the same? Treating them the same? Probably not. But only through sharing this type of information will managers at the poor store be able to learn from managers at the successful store.

Again, some may say the practices described above are just common sense and should come naturally to managers. That is absolute nonsense. Great management is neither common nor easy, and the existence of so many ineffective managers and toxic organizations attests to that. If great management was natural, wouldn't great managers and great organizations be far more common? If it is common sense, then more such sense is sorely needed in our organizations today.

An organization need not be born doing the right thing with respect to people. New Zealand Post wasn't born to the right thing, and Motorola, Best Buy, and Wainwright Industries certainly weren't always standards by which others were judged. As long as leaders recognize the importance of building business success around their people and learn to manage with trust, encourage change, and ensure their measurement systems contribute to solving rather than causing problems, organizations of all sizes and in all sectors can accomplish great things. Organizations just require leaders to focus on what is, after all, their most important asset—their people.

How Do I Help Create a Great Place to Work?

Clearly, great management requires skill development and acquired expertise. However, as you may recall from Chapter 4 on motivation, any performance is a function of ability, motivation, and opportunity. Put another way, holding ability constant, those that *really want to be* good managers, with a little courage and willingness to dare to be great, have a decided edge on their competition.

Creating a committed workforce and a high performance culture is sometimes thought to be outside the control of individual managers, especially young managers with little experience in an organization. However, one of the most compelling findings of the Gallup research discussed earlier is that there was more variation in Q12 scores *within* companies than *between* companies. That is, within each of the more than 200 organizations analyzed, Gallup found some of the most-engaged groups and some of the least-engaged groups. Thus, high performance cultures are not so much characteristic of an entire organization as they are within *particular units* of an organization.[14] So it is imminently possible to make the journey to great management, provided you have the awareness, the willingness, and a little courage to make it happen.

Examples of individual managers making a difference are all over. For example, author Marcus Buckingham tells the story of Ralph Gonzalez, a manager at Best Buy who was charged with resurrecting a troubled store in Hialeah, Florida.[15] He immediately named the store the Revolution, even drafted a Declaration of Revolution, and launched project teams, complete with army clothes. He posted detailed performance numbers in the break room and deliberately overcelebrated every small achievement. He gave every employee a whistle

"The only things in life you regret are the risks that you didn't take."

—Unknown

and told them to blow it loudly whenever they caught anybody (co worker or supervisor) doing something "revolutionary." As a result of Ralph's efforts, the Hialeah store became one of Best Buy's best in terms of store performance and employee satisfaction.

Put simply there is no knowledge advantage without an *action* advantage. Knowing what to do but not doing it does not get you far. Our hope is that our demonstration of the connection between people management and organizational performance, and an awareness of management practices that really do make a difference, will help close the gap between knowing and doing in how we manage people.

Some Success Stories

Managers in workplaces all across the world implement some of the practices described in this book. The rare company, however, has built a culture where these skills are implemented on an ongoing, consistent basis. That is, pockets of excellence exist all over, but truly excellent performance at the corporate level is still pretty rare. The companies discussed below provide illustrations of great people management practice and demonstrate how ordinary people can achieve extraordinary results.

Whole Foods

Whole Foods, which grew in the 1990s from $100 million to $1 billion in sales—in the grocery business, no less—is rightfully well-known for its use of self-managed teams. The company shares detailed performance and financial information with all its people—so much information that, because many people own stock in the company, all employees are considered insiders for purposes of Securities and Exchange Commission regulations. The company even makes data about individual salaries available to *all* its employees. It also shares productivity gains with its people through team-based incentive compensation, as part of fostering decentralized decision making.

The Men's Wearhouse

The Men's Wearhouse has succeeded in the retailing industry, which is notorious for its use of part-time, low-paid, undertrained, and poorly treated help. The company has achieved this success by doing exactly the opposite of what the industry is known for: It has invested heavily in training, uses relatively few part-time staff, pays above-industry-average wages, and encourages employee stock ownership. The company recognizes that what's important is not what people *cost*, but what they *do*.

AES Corp.

AES Corp., a global developer and operator of electric power plants, has succeeded by fostering radical decentralization, sharing financial and performance information (all of its people, like Whole Foods, are also insiders), recruiting on the basis of cultural fit, and eschewing bureaucracy. How many companies with several thousand employees do you know that have no human resources staff and that make business development and strategic planning part of everyone's job, not just the responsibility of centralized staff?

Concluding Note

Become a Positive Force

It is not overstating the case to say that today's organizations are *desperate* for great managers. Global competition puts more pressure than ever on managers to get the most out of their workforce, and that workforce is more diverse and thus more complex to manage than it has ever been. At the same time, the pressures on managers to be models of ethical behavior and social responsibility are higher than ever before.

"The only regrets you are likely to have in life are the risks you did not take."

—Anonymous

The great American philosopher William James was fond of saying that, when some outcome was in question, we would do well to believe the most positive outcome will happen. For example, in a situation where we are wondering if someone will be a friend or foe, we are better off assuming they will be a friend because then we will act in a friendly way toward them and the act can become a self-fulfilling prophecy. Similarly, if we are attempting some difficult task, it is better to believe we can do it because then it becomes a challenge to be tackled.

The challenges of being a great manager are large, but so too are the rewards. Managers make a profound difference in the lives of people and the success of organizations. The number of great managers is far too low; this book was written in the spirit of increasing their number. Your place in life is not too small to do something great. You have the tools to make a real difference in the lives of people and the success of organizations. Now onward to management greatness!

Endnotes

Intro

1. Goleman, D. (1995). *Emotional intelligence.* New York: Bantam. See also Sternberg, R. (1997). *Successful intelligence.* New York: Simon Schuster. Silberman, M. (2000). *People smart: Developing your interpersonal intelligence.* San Francisco: Berrett-Koehler.
2. Goleman, D. (1995). *Emotional intelligence.* New York: Bantam; Goleman, D. (1998). *Working with emotional intelligence.* New York: Bantam.
3. Williamson, E. (1999, October 5). Thanks to emotional intelligence. *The Wall Street Journal.*
4. Feist, G.J., & Barron, F. (1996, June). *Emotional intelligence and academic intelligence in career and life success.* Paper presented at the American Psychological Association Convention, San Francisco, CA. Kelley, R. E.(1998). *How to be a star at work.* New York: Times Books.
5. www.greatplacetowork.com; Levering, R., & Moskowitz, M. (2005). *The 100 best companies to work for in America.* New York: Penquin.
6. Huselid, M.A. (1995). The impact of human resource management practices on turnover, productivity, and corporate financial performance. *Academy of Management Journal, 38,* 647. Huselid, M.A., & Becker, B.E. (1997). The impact of high performance work systems, implementation effectiveness, and alignment with strategy on shareholder wealth. *Academy of Management Best Paper Proceedings,* 144–148. Pfeffer, J., & Veiga, J.F. (1999). Putting people first for organizational success. *Academy of Management Executive, 13,* 37–48. Pfeffer, J. (1998). *The human equation: Building profits by putting people first.* Boston: Harvard Business School Press. Pfeffer, J. (1995). Producing sustainable competitive advantage through the effective management of people. *Academy of Management Executive, 9,* 55–72.
7. Harter, J.K., Schmidt, F.L., & Hayes, T.L. (2002). Business-unit-level relationship between employee satisfaction, employee engagement, and business outcomes: A meta-analysis. *Journal of Applied Psychology, 87,* 268–279.
8. Buckingham, M., & Coffman, C. (1999). *First, break all the rules: What the world's greatest managers do differently.* New York: Simon & Schuster.
9. McCall, M.M., Jr., & Lombardo, M. (1983). What makes a top executive? *Psychology Today, 26,* 28–32. See also Shipper, F., & Dillard, J.E. (2000). A study of impending derailment and recovery of middle managers across career stages. *Human Resource Management, 39,* 331–345.
10. Carens, K., Cottrell, D., & Layton, M.C. (2004). *Management insights: Discovering the truths to management success.* Cornerstone Publishing: Dallas, TX.
11. Buckingham, M., & Coffman, C. (1999). *First, break all the rules: What the world's greatest managers do differently.* New York: Simon & Schuster; Devries, D.L., &

Kaiser, R.B. (2003). Going sour in the suite. In Steckler, S., Sethi, D., & Prescot, R.K. (coordinators). *Maximizing executive effectiveness.* Workshop presented by the Human Resources Planning Society, Miami, FL.
12. Tulgan, B. (2004). www.rainmakerthinking.com.
13. Whetton, D.A., & Cameron, K.S. (2005). *Developing Management Skills* (6th ed.). Upper Saddle Ridge, NJ: Pearson Prentice Hall.
14. Ibid.
15. Baldwin, T.T. (1992). Effects of alternative modeling strategies on outcomes of interpersonal skill training. *Journal of Applied Psychology, 77,* 147–154.
16. McCall, M., Lombardo, M.M., & Morrison, A. (1998). *Lessons of experience.* Lexington, MA: Lexington Books.
17. Rubin, R., Bommer, W., & Baldwin, T.T. (2002). Using extracurricular activity as an indicator of interpersonal skill: Prudent evaluation or recruiting malpractice? *Human Resource Management, 41* (4), 441–454.

Chapter 1

1. Drucker, P. (2002). *The effective executive.* New York: Harper Collins.
2. Baldwin, T.T. (1992). Effects of alternative modeling strategies on outcomes of interpersonal skill training. *Journal of Applied Psychology, 77,* 147–154.
3. Mabe, P.A., & West, S.G. (1982). Validity of self-evaluation of ability. A review and meta-analysis. *Journal of Applied Psychology, 67* (3), 280–296. See also, Bass, B.M., & Yammarino, F.J. (1991). Congruence of self and others' leadership ratings of naval officers for understanding successful performance. *Applied Psychology International Review, 40,* 437–454. Church, A. (1997). Managerial self-awareness in high performance individuals in organizations, *Journal of Applied Psychology, 82* (2) 281–292.
4. Bandura, A. (1977). *Social Learning Theory.* New York: General Learning. Bandura, A. (1986). *Social Foundations of Thought and Action.* Englewood Cliffs, NJ: Prentice Hall.
5. Ibid.
6. Ibid.
7. Collins, D.B., & Holton, E.F. (2004). The effectiveness of managerial leadership development programs: A meta-analysis of studies from 1982 to 2001. *Human Resource Development Quarterly, 15*(2), 217–248. Baldwin, T.T., & Rubin, R. (2004). Making better managers: A meta-analytic review of management development interventions (1951–2003) and an agenda for future research. *Academy of Management Best Paper Proceedings.*
8. Manz, C.C., & Neck, C.P. (2003). *Mastering self-leadership: Empowering yourself for personal excellence.* (3rd ed.). New York: Pearson Prentice Hall. Manz, C.C., & Sims, H.P. (1989). *SuperLeadership: Leading others to lead themselves.* New York: Prentice Hall.
9. Ibid.

10. Edmondson, A.C. (1996). Learning from mistakes is easier said than done: Group and organizational influences on the detection and correction of human error. *Journal of Applied Behavioral Science, 32* (1), 5–28. Edmondson A.C. (1999, December). Psychological safety and learning behavior in work teams, *Administrative Science Quarterly, 44* (4), 350–383.

11. Latham, G.P. (2004). The motivational benefits of goal setting. *Academy of Management Executive, 18,* 126–130.

12. Locke, E.A., & Latham, G.P. (1990). *A theory of goal setting and task performance.* Englewood Cliffs, NJ: Prentice Hall.

13. Skinner, B.F. (1971). *Beyond freedom and dignity.* New York: Knopf.

14. Marx, R.D. (1982). Relapse prevention for managerial training: A model for maintenance of behavior change. *Academy of Management Review, 7* (3), 433–441. Marx, R.D. (1986). Self-managed skill retention. *Training and Development Journal, 40* (1), 54–57.

15. George, J.M., & Jones, G.R. (2002). *Individual difference: Personality and ability. Understanding and managing organizational behavior.* Upper Saddle River, NJ: Pearson Education, Inc. Digman, J.M. (1990). Validation of the five-factor model of personality across instruments and observers. *Journal of Personality and Social Psychology 52,* 81–90. Barrick, M.R., & Mount, M.K. (1991). The big 5 personality dimensions and job performance: A meta analysis. *Personnel Psychology, 44,* 1-26. Barrick, M.R., Mount, M.K., & Strauss, J.P. (1993). Conscientiousness and performance of sales representatives: Test of the mediating effects of goal setting. *Journal of Applied Psychology, 78,* 715–722. Witt, L.A., Burke, L., Barrick, M.R., & Mount, M.K. (2002). The interactive effects of conscientiousness and agreeableness on job performance. *Journal of Applied Psychology, 87,* 164–169.

16. Lubinsky, D., & Dawis, R.V. (1991). Aptitudes, skills and proficiencies. In M.D. Dunnette, & L.M. Hough (Eds.), *Handbook of Industrial Psychology.* (2nd ed., vol. 3, pp. 1–59)., Palo Alto, CA: Consulting Psychologists Press.

17. George, J.M., & Jones, G.R. (2002). *Individual difference: Personality and ability. Understanding and managing organizational behavior.* Upper Saddle River, NJ: Pearson Education, Inc.

18. Schmidt, F., & Hunter, J. (1998). The validity and utility of selection methods in personnel psychology: Practical and theoretical implications of 85 years of research findings. *Psychological Bulletin, 124,* 262–274.

19. Ashkanasy, N.M., & Daus, C.S. (2005). Rumors of the death of emotional intelligence in organizational behavior are vastly exaggerated. *Journal of Organizational Behavior, 26,* 441–452. Daus, C.S., & Ashkanasy, N.M. (2005). The case for the ability-based model of emotional intelligence in organizational behavior. *Journal of Organizational Behavior, 26,* 453–466.

20. Rubin, R.S., Munz, D.C., Bommer, W.H. (2005). Leading from within: The effects of emotion recognition and personality on transformational leader behavior. *Academy of Management Journal, 48,* 845–858. Daus, C.S., & Ashkanasy, N.M. (2005). The case for the ability-based model of emotional intelligence in organizational behavior. *Journal of Organizational Behavior, 26,* 453–466.

21. Caruso, D.R., & Salovey, P. (2004). *The emotionally intelligent manager: How to develop and use the four key emotional skills of leadership.* San Francisco, CA: Jossey-Bass.

22. Rubin, R.S., & Riggio, R.E. (2005). The role of emotional intelligence in ethical decision making at work. In R. Giacalone, C.L. Jurkiewicz, & C. Dunn (Eds.), *Positive psychology in business ethics and corporate social responsibility* (pp. 209–229). Greenwich, CT: Information Age Publishing.

23. Ang, S., Van Dyne, L., & Koh, C. (2006). Personality correlates of the four factor model of cultural intelligence. *Groups and Organization Management. 31(1);* 100–123. Earley, P.C., & Mosakowski, E. (2004). Cultural intelligence. *Harvard Business Review, 82,* 139–153

24. Earley, P.C., & Ang, S. (2003). *Cultural intelligence: Individual interactions across cultures.* Palo Alto: Stanford University Press.

25. Van Dyne, L., & Ang, S. (2005). *Cultural intelligence: An essential capability for individuals in contemporary organizations.* East Lansing, MI: GlobalEDGE.

26. Hurtz, G.M., & Donovan, J.J. (2002). Personality and job performance: The Big 5 revisited. *Journal of Applied Psychology, 85,* 869–879.

27. Thanks to Vicki Staebler-Tardino for making this point so elegantly.

28. Jung, C.G. *Psychological Types.* (1921/71). *CW 6.* Princeton: Princeton University Press.

29. Rokeach, M. (1973). *The nature of human values.* New York: The Free Press.

30. Fisher S.G., Macrosson W.D., & Yusuff M.R. (1996). Team performance and human values. *Psychological Reports, 79,* 1019–1024.

31. Cable, D.M., & DeRue, D.S. (2002). The convergent and discriminant validity of subjective fit perceptions. *Journal of Applied Psychology, 87* (5), 875–884. Meglino, B.M., & Ravlin, E.C. (1998). Individual values in organizations: Concepts, controversies, and research. *Journal of Management, 24* (3), 351–389. Cable, D.M., & Judge, T.A. (1996). Person-organization fit, job choice decisions, and organizational entry. *Organizational Behavior and Human Decision Processes, 67,* 294–311.

32. Fritzsche, B.A., McIntire, S.A., & Yost, A.P. (2002). Holland Type as a moderator of personality-performance predictions. *Journal of Vocational Behavior, 60,* 422–436.

33. Mauer, T.J., & Tarulli, B.A. (1997). Managerial work, job analysis and Holland's RIASEC vocational environment dimensions. *Journal of Vocational Behavior, 50,* 365–381.

34. Fletcher, C., & Baldry, C. (2000). A study of individual differences and self-awareness in the context of

multi-source feedback. *Journal of Occupational and Organizational Behavior, 73*, (3), 303–319.

35. Ibid.

36. Hazucha, J.F., Hezlett, S.A., & Schneider, R.J. (1993). The impact of 360-degree feedback on management skills development. *Human Resource Management, 32* (2–3), 325–351. London, M., & Beatty, R.W. (1993). 360-degree feedback as a competitive advantage. *Human Resource Management, 32* (2–3), 353–372.

37. Van Velsor, E., Taylor, S., & Leslie, J. B. (1993). An examination of the relationships among self-perception accuracy, self-awareness, gender, and leader effectiveness. *Human Resource Management, 32* (2–3), 249–263.

38. Buckingham, M., & Coffman, C. (1999). *First, break all the rules: What the world's greatest managers do differently.* New York: Simon & Schuster. Buckingham, M., & Clifton, D.O. (2001). *Now discover your strengths.* New York: Free Press. Clifton, D.O., & Nelson, P. (1996). *Soar With Your Strengths.* (2nd ed.). New York: Dell Books.

39. DeFrank, R.S., & Ivancevich, J.M. (1998). Stress on the job: An executive update. *Academy of Management Executive, 12* (3), 55–66.

40. Auerbach, S.M. (1998). *Stress management: Psychological foundations.* Upper Saddle River, NJ: Prentice Hall.

41. Selye, H. (1974). *Stress Without Distress.* New York, NY: Lippencott and Crowell Publishers.

42. Kanner, A.D., Coyne, J.C., Schaefer, C., & Lazarus, R.S. (1981). Comparisons of two modes of stress measurement: Daily hassles and uplifts versus major life events. *Journal of Behavioral Medicine, 4*, 1–39.

43. Zohar, D. (1999). When things go wrong: The effect of daily work hassles on effort, exertion, and negative mood. *Journal of Occupational and Organizational Psychology, 72*, 265–283.

44. Brandon, J.E., & Loftin, J.M. (1991). Relationship of fitness to depression, state and trait anxiety, internal health locus of control, and self-control. *Perceptual and Motor Skills, 73* (2), 563–566.

45. Lupinacci, N.S., Rikli, R.E., Jones, C.J., & Ross, D. (1993). Age and physical activity on reaction time and digit symbol substitution performance in cognitively active adults. *Research Quarterly for Exercise and Sport, 64*, 144–150.

46. Shepard, R.J. (1999). Do work site exercise and health programs work? *The Physician and Sportsmedicine, 27*, 48–72. Frew, D.R., & Bruning, N.S. (1988). Improved productivity and job satisfaction through employee exercise programs. *Hospital Material Management Quarterly, 9*, 62–69. Edwards, S.E., & Gettman, L.R. (1980, November). The effect of employee physical fitness on job performance. *Personnel Administrator, 25*, 41–61.

47. Neck, C.P., Mitchell, T.L., Manz, C.C., & Thompson, E.C. (2004). *Fit to lead: The proven 8-week solution for shaping up your body, your mind, and your career.* New York: St. Martin's Press. Neck, C.P., & Cooper, K.H. (2000). The fit executive: Exercise and diet guidelines for enhancing performance. *Academy of Management Executive, 14* (2), 72–83.

48. Maddi, S., & Kobasa, S.C. (1984). *The hardy executive: Health under stress.* Homewood, IL: Dow Jones–Irwin.

49. Ibid.

50. Maddi, S., Kahn, S., & Maddi, K. (1992). The effectiveness of hardiness training. *Consulting Psychology Journal: Practice and Research, 50* (2), 78–86.

51. Ibid.

52. Fredrickson, B.L. (2001). The role of positive emotions in positive psychology: The broaden-and-build theory of positive emotions. *American Psychologst, 56*, 218–226.

53. Tugade, M.M., & Fredrickson, B.L. (2004). Resilient individuals use positive emotions to bounce back from negative emotional experiences. *Journal of Personality and Social Psychology, 86* (2), 320–333.

54. Covey, S. (1989). *The 7 habits of highly effective people: Powerful lessons in personal change.* New York: Simon & Schuster. Lakein, A. (1973). *How to get control of your time and your life.* New York: Signet.

55. Allen, D. (2003). *Getting things done: The art of stress-free productivity.* New York: Penguin Books.

56. Lakein, A. (1973). *How to get control of your time and your life.* New York: Signet.

57. Cited in Kay, M. (1995). *You Can Have It All : Lifetime Wisdom from America's Foremost Woman Entrepreneur.* New York: Prima Lifestyles Books. pp. 68–69.

58. Lakein, A. (1973). *How to get control of your time and your life.* New York: Signet.

59. *If you drop it, should you eat it? Scientists weigh in on the 5-second rule.* (2003, September 2). ACES News Services.

60. Winston, S. (1991). *Getting Organized: The Easy Way to Put Your Life in Order.* New York: Warner Books.

61. Roberts, H.V., & Sergesteketter, B.F. (1993). *Quality is personal: A foundation for total quality management.* New York: Free Press.

Chapter 2

1. Quoted in Matson, E. (1997, February/March). Now that we have your complete attention . . . . *Fast Company, 7*, 124–125.

2. Conger, J.A. (1998, May–June). The necessary art of persuasion. *Harvard Business Review*, Reprint 98304. Mayfield, M., & Mayfield, J. (2004). The effects of leader communication on worker innovation. *American Business Review, 22*, 46–51.

3. See, for example, Clutterbuck, D., & Hurst, S. (2002). Leadership communication: A status report. *Journal of Communication Management, 4*, 351–356. Curry, M.J. (1996). Teaching managerial communication to ESL and native-speaker undergraduates. *Business Communication Quarterly, 59*, 7–30.

4. Mayfield, M., & Mayfield, J. (2004). The effects of leader communication on worker innovation. *American Business Review, 22*, 46–51.

5. Hanft, A. (2005, June). It's the sound bite, stupid. *Inc.*, 128.

6. Harmon, R R., & Coney, K.A. (1982). The persuasive effects of source credibility in buy and lease situations. *Journal of Marketing Research, 19*, 255–260.

7. Conger, J.A. (1998, May/June). The necessary art of persuasion. *Harvard Business Review,* Reprint 98304.

8. Hovland, C.I., & Weiss, W. (1951). The influence of source credibility on communication effectiveness. *Public Opinion Quarterly, 15,* 635–650. Hovland, C.I., Janis, I.L., & Kelley, H.H. (1953). *Communication and persuasion.* New Haven, CT: Yale University Press.

9. Conger, J.A. (1999). Learning the language of leadership. *Human Resource Management International Digest, 7,* 25–27.

10. Chaiken, S. (1979). Communicator, physical attractiveness, and persuasion. *Journal of Personality and Social Psychology, 37,* 1387–1397. Eagly, A.H., Wood, W., & Chaiken, S. (1978). Causal inferences about communicators and their effect on opinion change. *Journal of Personality and Social Psychology, 36,* 424–435.

11. Cialdini, R.B. (1984). *Influence: The psychology of persuasion.* New York: Quill.

12. Kaufman, B. (2003, March/April). Stories that sell, stories that tell. *The Journal of Business Strategy, 24* (2), 11–15.

13. Dennehy, R.F. (1999, March). The executive as storyteller. *Management Review, 88* (3), 40–44.

14. Etgar, M., & Goodwin, S.A. (1982). One-sided versus two-sided comparative message appeals for new brand introductions. *Journal of Consumer Research, 9,* 460–465. Golden, L. L., & Alpert, M. I. (1987). Comparative analyses of the relative effectiveness of one-sided and two-sided communications for contrasting products. *Journal of Advertising, 16,* 18–28. Kamins, M. A., & Assael, H. (1987). Two-sided versus one-sided appeals: A cognitive perspective on argumentation, source derogation, and the effect of disconfirming trial on belief change. *Journal of Marketing Research, 24,* 29–39. Pechmann, C, (1992). Predicting when two-sided ads will be more effective than one-sided ads: The role of correlational and correspondent inferences. *Journal of Marketing Research, 29,* 441–453.

15. Crowley, A.E., & Hoyer, W.D. (1994). An integrative framework for understanding two-sided persuasion. *Journal of Consumer Research, 20,* 561–574.

16. Hattersley, M. (1997, April). Using logic to make your argument. *Harvard Management Update.*

17. Wiethoff, W.E. (1994). *Writing the speech.* Greenwood, IN: Alistair Press.

18. Buda, R. (2003). The interactive effect of message framing, presentation order, and source credibility on recruitment practices. *International Journal of Management, 20,* 156–163. Pham, M.T., & Avnet, T. (2004). Ideals and oughts and the reliance on affect versus substance in persuasion. *Journal of Consumer Research, 30,* 503–518.

19. Minto, B. (1996). *The Minto pyramid principle: Logic in writing, thinking, and problem solving.* London: Minto International.

20. Quoted in Matson, E. (1997, February/March). Now that we have your complete attention . . . . *Fast Company, 7,* 124–125.

21. Bozek, P.E. (1998). *50 one-minute tips to better communication.* Menlo Park, CA: Crisp Learning.

22. Lopez, E.J. (2005). *The art of using visual aids.* The 2005 Sourcebook for Advanced Practical Nurses, 15–16.

23. DuFrene, D.D., & Lehman, C.M. (2004). Concept, content, construction, and contingencies: Getting the horse before the PowerPoint cart. *Business Communication Quarterly, 67,* 84–88.

24. Adapted from Simons, T. (1998, March). Study shows just how much visuals increase persuasiveness. *Presentations, 12* (3), 20.

25. Adapted from Becker, R.A., & Keller-McNulty, S. (1996). *The American Statistician, 50,* 112–116.

26. Daft, R.L., Lengel, R.H., & Trevino, L.K. (1987). Message equivocality, media selection, and manager performance: Implications for information systems. *MIS Quarterly, 11,* 355–366.

27. Ibid.

28. Carlson, J.R., & Zmud, R.W. (1999). Channel expansion theory and the experiential nature of media richness perceptions. *Academy of Management Journal, 42,* 153–171.

29. Alge, B.J., Wiethoff, C., & Klein, H.J. (2003). When does the medium matter? Knowledge-building experiences and opportunities in decision-making teams. *Organizational Behavior and Human Decision Processes, 91,* 26–40.

30. Quoted in Ransom, D. (2005, February). Bad news bearers. *Fast Company, 91,* 28.

31. Augustine, N.R. (1995, November/December). Managing the crisis you tried to prevent. *Harvard Business Review, 73* (6), 147–159.

32. Rice, E.J. (1998, May). Are you listening? *Quality Progress, 31* (5), 25–29.

33. Robinett, B. (1982). The value of a good ear. *Personnel Administrator, 27,* 10.

34. Kanter, R.M. (1983). *The change masters.* New York: Simon & Schuster, 70.

35. Bormann, E.G., Howell, W.S., Nichols, R.G., & Shapiro, G.L. (1969). *Interpersonal communication in the modern organization.* Englewood Cliffs, NJ: Prentice Hall.

36. Eckman, P., & Friesen, W. (1971). Constants across cultures in the face and emotion. *Journal of Personality and Social Psychology, 17,* 124–129.

37. Morsbach, H. (1973). Aspects of nonverbal communication in Japan. *Journal of Nervous and Mental Disease, 157,* 265–272. Barna, L. M. (1988). Intercultural communication stumbling blocks. In L. A. Samovar & R. E. Porter (Eds.), *Intercultural communication: A reader* (pp. 102–125). Belmont, CA: Wadsworth.

38. McCaskey, M.B. (1979, November–December). The hidden messages managers send. *Harvard Business Review, 57,* 146–147.

39. Kratz, D.M., & Kratz, A.R. (1995). *Effective listening skills.* Boston: McGraw-Hill.

40. Pearce, C.G., Johnson, I.W., & Barker, R.T. (2003). Assessment of the listening styles inventory. *Journal of Business and Technical Communication, 17,* 84–103.

41. Kratz, D.M., & Kratz, A.R. (1995). *Effective listening skills.* Boston: McGraw-Hill.

42. Hamilton, M.A. & Stewart, B.L. (1993). Extending an information process model of language intensity effects. *Communication Quarterly, 41,* 231–246.

43. Unknown. (2000). The basic presentation checklist. *Harvard Management Communication Letter,* Reprint C0010B.

44. Adapted from Half, R. (1991, December). Managing your career: How can I write an effective memo? *Management Accounting, 73* (6), 11.
45. Bozek, P.E. (1998). *50 one-minute tips to better communication.* Menlo Park, CA: Crisp Learning.

Chapter 3

1. Nutt, P.C. (1999). Surprising but true: Half the decisions in organizations fail. *Academy of Management Executive, 13* (4), 75–90.
2. Winerman, L. (2005). What we know without knowing how. *Monitor on Psychology, 36* (3), 50–52.
3. Gladwell, M. (2005). Blink: The power of thinking without thinking. New York, NY: Little, Brown & Company.
4. Argyris, C. (1985). *Strategy, change, and defensive routines.* Boston, MA: Pitman.
5. In this section, we relied heavily on Max Bazerman's outstanding synthesis of the most important research on judgment biases and errors. Bazerman, M. (1998). *Judgment in managerial decision making.* (4th ed.). New York, NY: Wiley & Sons. We also draw heavily on the work of Michael Metzger, Business Law professor at the IU Kelley School of Business where he teaches a highly acclaimed course on critical thinking.
6. Dawes, R.M. (2001). *Everyday irrationality: How pseudoscientists, lunatics, and the rest of us fail to think rationally.* Boulder, CO: Westview Press.
7. Kahneman, D., & Tversky, A. (1972). Subjective probability: A judgment of representativeness. *Cognitive Psychology, 3,* 430–454.
8. Gilovich, T., Vallone, R., & Tversky, A. (1985). The hot hand in basketball: On the misperception of random sequences. *Cognitive Psychology, 17,* 295–314.
9. Ibid.
10. Tversky, A., & Kahneman, D. (1974). Judgment under uncertainty: Heuristics and biases. *Science, 185,* 1124–1131.
11. Myers, D.G. (1980). *The inflated self.* New York: Seabury Press. Svenson, O. (1981). Are we all less risky and more skillful than our fellow drivers? *Acta Psychologica, 47,* 143–148.
12. Plous, S. (1993). *The psychology of judgment and decision making.* New York: McGraw Hill.
13. Christensen-Szalanski, J., & Bushyhead, J. (1981). Physicians' use of probabilistic information in a real clinical setting. *Journal of Experimental Psychology: Human Perception and Performance, 7,* 928–935.
14. For example, see Koriat, A., Lichtenstein, S., & Fischhoff, B. (1980). Reasons for confidence. *Journal of Experimental Psychology: Learning, Memory, and Cognition, 6* (2), 107–118. Lichtenstein, S., & Fischhoff, B. (1980). Training for calibration. *Organizational Behavior and Human Performance, 26,* 149–171.
15. March, J.G., & Simon, H.A. (1958). *Organizations.* New York: Wiley.
16. Mitroff, I. (1998). *Smart thinking for crazy times.* San Francisco, CA: Berrett-Koehler Publishers, Inc.
17. Vroom, V.H. (2000). Leadership and the decision making process. *Organizational Dynamics, 28* (4), 82–94.
18. Ibid.
19. Ibid.
20. Cited in Field, R.H., & House, R.J. (1990). A test of the Vroom-Yetton model using manager and subordinate reports. *Journal of Applied Psychology, 75* (3), 362–366.
21. Judson, A.I., & Cofer, C.N. (1956). Reasoning as an associative process, *Psychological Reports, 2,* 469–476. Maier, N.R.F., & Burke, R. J. (1967). Response availability as a factor in the problem-solving performance of males and females. *Journal of Personality and Social Psychology, 5,* 304–310. Tversky, A., & Kahneman, D. (1981). The framing of decisions and psychology of choice. *Science, 211,* 453–458.
22. Taken from Jones, M.D. (1998). The thinker's toolkit. New York: Three Rivers Press.
23. Volkema, R.J. (1986). Problem formulation as a purposive activity. *Strategic Management Journal, 7,* 267–279. Tversky, A., & Kahneman, D. (1981). The framing of decisions and psychology of choice, *Science, 211,* 453–458.
24. Senge, P.M., Kleiner, A.M., Roberts, C., Ross, R.B., & Smith, B.J. (1994). *The fifth discipline fieldbook* (p. 90). New York, NY: Doubleday.
25. Adapted from *What is systems thinking* (2006), Pegasus Communications. Pegasuscom.com
26. Adapted from Senge, P.M., Kleiner, A.M., Roberts, C., Ross, R.B., & Smith, B.J. (1994). *The fifth discipline fieldbook* (p. 90). New York, NY: Doubleday.
27. Adapted from Hammond, J.S., Keeney, R.L., & Raiffa, H. (1999). *Smart choices: A practical guide to making better decisions.* Boston, MA: Harvard Business Press.
28. Ibid.
29. Mullen, B., Johnson, C., & Salas, E. (1991). Productivity loss in brainstorming groups: A meta-analytic integration. *Basic and Applied Social Psychology, 12* (1), 3–23.
30. Paulus, P.B., & Yang, H. (2000). Idea generation in groups: A basis for creativity in organizations. *Organizational Behavior and Human Decision Processes, 82* (1), 76–87.
31. Thompson, L. (2003). Improving the creativity of organizational work groups. *Academy of Management Executive, 17* (1), 96–111.
32. Jackson, S.E. (1992). Team composition in organizational settings: Issues in managing an increasingly diverse workforce. In S. Worchel, W. Wood, & J.A. Simpson (Eds.), *Group process and productivity* (pp. 138–173). Newbury Park: Sage.
33. Sweetman, K.J. (1997). Cultivating creativity. *Harvard Business Review,* March-April, 10–12.
34. Ibid.
35. Nutt, P.C. (2004). Expanding the search for alternatives during strategic decision-making. *Academy of Management Executive, 18* (4), 13–28.
36. Whetten, D.A., & Cameron, K.S. (2005). *Developing management skills.* Upper Saddle River, NJ: Pearson Education.
37. Russo, J.E., & Schoemaker, P.J.H. (1989). *Decision traps: Ten barriers to brilliant decision making and how to overcome them.* New York: Simon & Schuster.

38. Nutt, P.C. (2004). Expanding the search for alternatives during strategic decision-making. *Academy of Management Executive, 18* (4), 13–28.

39. Cosier, R.A., & Schwenk, C.R. (1990). Agreement and thinking alike: ingredients for poor decisions. *Academy of Management Executive, 4* (1), 69–74.

40. Slovic, P. (1987). Perception of risk. *Science, 236,* 280–285.

41. Argyris, C., & Schon, D.A. (1978). *Organizational learning: A theory of action perspective.* Reading, MA: Addison-Wesley.

42. Veiga, J.F., Golden, T.D., & Dechant, K. (2004). Why managers bend company rules. *Academy of Management Executive, 18* (2), 84–90.

43. McCabe, D.L., & Trevino, L.K. (1996). What we know about cheating in college. *Change, 28,* 28–34.

44. Kidder, R.M. (1995). *How good people make tough choices* (p. 51). New York: Simon & Schuster.

45. Ibid. Here we rely heavily on the outstanding work of Kidder (1995). Kidder has framed ethical dilemmas as "right versus right" and "right versus wrong" and provides excellent examples.

46. Jones, T.M. (1991). Ethical decision making by individuals in organizations: An issue-contingent model. *Academy of Management Review, 16,* 366–395.

47. Casio, W. (2005). Strategies for responsible restructuring. *Academy of Management Executive 19(4)* 39–50.

48. "American seeks to weather the airline dip." (2004, September 13). National Public Radio.

Chapter 4

1. Vroom, V. (1964). *Work and Motivation.* New York: Wiley. Locke, E., & Latham, G. (1968). Toward a theory of task motivation and incentives. *Organizational Behavior and Human Performance, 3,* 157–189. Adams, J. (1963). Toward an understanding of inequity. *Journal of Abnormal and Social Psychology, 67,* 422–436.

2. Blumberg, M., & Pringle, C.D. (1982). The missing opportunity in organizational research: Some implications for a theory of work performance. *Academy of Management Review, 7* (4), 560–569.

3. Vroom, V.H. (1964). *Work and Motivation.* New York, NY: Wiley.

4. Maslow, A. (1943). A theory of human motivation. *Psychological Review, 50,* 370–396.

5. Adams, J.S. (1965). Inequity in social exchange, in Berkowitz, Leonard (Ed), *Advances in Experimental Social Psychology, 2,* Academic Press, New York, 267–299.

6. Adams, J. (1963). Toward an understanding of inequity. *Journal of Abnormal and Social Psychology, 67,* 422–436.

7. Huseman, R., Hatfield, J., & Miles, E. (1987). A new perspective on equity theory: The equity sensitivity construct. *Academy of Management Review, 12,* 222–234.

8. Markey, S. (2003, September 17). Monkeys show sense of fairness, study says. *National Geographic News.*

Brosnan, S.F., & de Waal, F.B.M. (2003). Monkeys reject unequal pay. *Nature, 425,* 297–299.

9. Miles, E., Hatfield, J., & Huseman, R. (1994). Equity sensitivity and outcome importance. *Journal of Organizational Behavior, 15,* 585–596.

10. Stecklow, S. (2001, January 2). Finnish drivers don't mind sliding scale, but instant calculation gets low marks. *The Wall Street Journal.*

11. McClelland, D. (1975). *Power: The inner experience.* New York: Irvington.

12. McClelland, D.C. (1966). That urge to achieve, *Think,* IBM, 82–89.

13. Stuart-Kotze, R. (2006). Motivation theory. http: www.managementlearning.com

14. McClelland, D. (1983). *Human motivation.* Boston MA: Addison-Wesley.

15. Locke, E., & Latham, G. (1984). *Goal setting: A motivational technique that works.* Englewood Cliffs, NJ: Prentice Hall. Locke, E. & Latham, G. (1990). *A theory of goal setting and task performance.* Englewood Cliffs, NJ: Prentice Hall.

16. Ibid.

17. Rubin, R.S. (2002, April). Will the real SMART goals please stand up? *The Industrial-Organizational Psychologist, 26–27.*

18. See, for example, Locke, E. & Latham, G. (1990). *A theory of goal setting and task performance.* Englewood Cliffs, NJ: Prentice Hall. Latham, G. (2002). The reciprocal effects of science on practice: Insights from the practice and science of goal setting. *Canadian Psychology, 42,* 1–11.

19. Earley, P., & Kanfer, R. (1985). The influence of component participation and role models on goal acceptance, goal satisfaction, and performance. *Organizational Behavior and Human Decision Processes, 36,* 378–390.

20. Thorndike, E.L. (1911). *The elements of psychology.* New York: Seiler. Skinner, B.F. (1974). *About behaviorism.* New York: Random House.

21. Kerr, S. (1975). On the folly of rewarding A, while hoping for B. *Academy of Management Journal, 18,* 769–783.

22. *BusinessWeek.* (1971, December 18).

23. Bateman, M., & Ludwig, T. (2004). Managing distribution quality through an adapted incentive program with tiered goals and feedback. *Journal of Organization Behavior Management, 75* (23), 33–55.

24. Hantula, D., Rajala, A., Kellerman, E., & Bragger, J. (2004). The value of workplace safety: A time-based utility analysis model. *Journal of Organization Behavior Management, 75* (21), 79–98.

25. Rohn, D., Austin, J., & Lutrey, S. (2004). Using feedback and performance accountability to decrease cash register shortages. *Journal of Organization Behavior Management, 75* (22), 33–46.

26. Ludwig, T.D., Biggs, J., Wagner, S. & Geller, E.S. (2002). Using public feedback and competitive rewards to increase the safe driving behaviors of pizza deliverers, *Journal of Organizational Behavior Management, 21,* 75–104.

27. Nelson, R. (1994). *1001 Ways to Reward Employees.* New York, NY: Workman Publishing.

28. Nelson, B. (1999, June 25). Recognition plans can be simple, yet effective. *Charlotte Business Journal.*

29. Easterlin, R. (2000). Income and happiness: Towards a unified theory. *The Economic Journal,* 111, 465–484. Easterlin, R. (2001). Life cycle welfare: Trends and differences. *Journal of Happiness Studies, 2,* 1–12.

30. Whetten, D., & Cameron, K. (1998). *Developing management skills.* (4th ed.). Reading, MA: Addison-Wesley.

31. Podsakoff, P.M., Bommer, W.H., Podsakoff, N.P., & MacKenzie, S.B. (2006). Relationships between leader reward and punishment behavior and subordinate attitudes, perceptions, and behaviors: A meta-analytic review of existing and new research. *Organizational Behavior and Human Decision Process, 99,* 113–142.

32. Hackman, J., & Oldham, G. (1980). *Work Redesign.* Reading, MA: Addison-Wesley.

33. Workman, M., & Bommer, W.H. (2004). Redesigning computer call center work: A longitudinal field experiment. *Journal of Organizational Behavior, 25,* 317–337.

34. From www.newport.com.

35. Ranky, P.G. (2004). *Total quality control and JIT management in CIM.* Ridgewood, NJ: CIMware.

36. From www.wainwrightindustries.com

37. From www.phelpscountybank.com

38. Milliman, J., Zawacki, R., Norman, C., Powell, L., & Kirksey, J. (1994). Companies evaluate employees from all perspectives. *Personnel Journal, 73,* 99–103.

39. Miles, E., Hatfield, J., & Huseman, R. (1994). Equity sensitivity and outcome importance. *Journal of Organizational Behavior, 15,* 585–596. Huseman, J., Hatfield, J., & Miles, E. (1985). Test for individual perceptions of job equity: Some preliminary findings. *Perceptual and Motor Skills,* 61, 1055–1064.

Chapter 5

1. Fournies, F.F. (2000). *Coaching for improved work performance.* New York, NY: McGraw Hill.

2. Delaney, J.T., & Huselid, M.A. (1996). The impact of human resource management practices on perceptions of organizational performance. *Academy of Management Journal, 39* (4), 949–969. Huselid, M.A. (1995). The impact of human resources management practices on turnover, productivity, and corporate financial performance. *Academy of Management Journal, 38* (1), 635–672. Welbourne, T.M., & Andrews, A.O. (1996). Predicting the performance of initial public offerings: Should human resource management be in the equation? *Academy of Management Journal, 39* (4), 891–919.

3. Cohen-Charash, Y., & Spector, P.E. (2001). The role of justice in organizations: A meta-analysis. *Organizational Behavior and Human Decision Processes, 86* (2), 278–321.

4. Huselid, M.A. (1995). The impact of human resources management practices on turnover, productivity, and corporate financial performance. *Academy of Management Journal, 38* (1), 635–672.

5. Kram, K.E. (1985). *Mentoring at work. Developing relationships in organizational life.* Glenview, IL: Scott, Foresman.

6. Dougherty, T.W., Tuban, D.B., & Callender, J.C. (1994). Confirming first impressions in the employment interview: A field study of interviewer behavior. *Journal of Applied Psychology, 79,* 659–665. Dipboye, R.L., & Gaugler, B.B. (1993). Cognitive and behavioral processes in the selection interview. In N. Schmitt, & W. Borman (Eds.), *Personnel selection in organizations* (pp. 135–170). San Francisco: Jossey-Bass.

7. Anderson, C.W. (1960). The relation between speaking times and decisions in the employment interview. *Journal of Applied Psychology, 44,* 267–268.

8. Kluger, A.N., & Denisi, A.S. (1996). The effects of feedback intervention on performance: Historical review, a meta-analysis and a preliminary feedback intervention theory. *Psychological Bulletin, 119,* 254–284.

9. O'Reilly, C.A., Chatman, J.A., & Caldwell, D.F. (1991). People and organizational culture: A profile comparison approach to person–organization fit. *Academy of Management Journal, 34* (3), 487–516. Kristof, A.L. (1996). Person–organization fit: An integrative review of its conceptualizations, measurement, and implications. *Personnel Psychology, 49,* 1–49.

10. Ledeen, M. (2002). The real Bobby Knight. *American Enterprise, 7,* 24–27.

11. Breaugh, J.A., & Starke, M. (2000). Research on employee recruitment: So many studies, so many remaining questions. *Journal of Management, 26* (3), 405–434.

12. Ibid.

13. Ibid.

14. Phillips, J.M. (1998). Effects of realistic job previews on multiple organizational outcomes: A meta-analysis. *Academy of Management Journal, 41* (6), 673–690.

15. Meglino, B.M., Ravlin, E.C., & DeNisi, A.S. (2000). A meta-analytic examination of realistic job preview effectiveness: A test of three counterintuitive propositions. *Human Resource Management Review, 10* (4), 407–434.

16. Rynes, S.L., Brown, K.G., & Colbert, A.E. (2002). Seven misconceptions about human resource practices: Research findings versus practitioner beliefs. *Academy of Management Executive, 16* (3), 92–103. Terpstra, D.E. (1996). The search for effective methods. *HRFocus,* 16–17.

17. Schmidt, F., & Hunter, J.E. (1998). The validity and utility of selection methods in personnel psychology: Practical and theoretical implications of 85 years of research findings. *Psychological Bulletin, 124* (2), 262–274. Hurtz, G.M., & Donovan, J.J. 2000. Personality and job performance: The big five revisited. *Journal of Applied Psychology, 85* (6), 869–879.

18. Judge, T.A., Higgins, C.A., & Cable, D.M. (2000). The employment interview: A review of recent research and recommendations for future research. *Human Resource Management Review, 4,* 383–406.

19. Harris, M.M. (1989). Reconsidering the employment interview: A review of recent literature and suggestions

for future research. *Personnel Psychology, 42,* 691–726. Judge, T.A., Higgins, C.A., & Cable, D.M. (2000). The employment interview: A review of recent research and recommendations for future research. *Human Resource Management Review, 4,* 383–406.

20. Schmidt, F.L., & Zimmerman, R.D. (2004). A counterintuitive hypothesis about employment interview validity and some supporting evidence. *Journal of Applied Psychology, 89* (3), 535–561.

21. Van der Zee, K.I., Bakker, A.B., & Bakker, P. (2002). Why are structured interviews so rarely used in personnel selection? *Journal of Applied Psychology, 87,* 1, 176–184.

22. Campion, M.A., Palmer, D.K., & Campion, J.E. (1997). A review of structure in the selection interview. *Personnel Psychology, 50,* 655–702.

23. For grounding in the situational interview, see Latham, G.P., & Saari, L.M. (1984). Do people do what they say? Further studies of the situational interview. *Journal of Applied Psychology, 69,* 569–573. For theory regarding the behavioral interview, see Janz, T. (1989). The patterned behavior description interview: The best prophet of the future is the past. In R.W. Eder, & G.R. Ferris (Eds.), *The employment interview: theory, research and practice* (pp. 158–168). Newberry Park, CA: Sage.

24. Huffcutt, A.I., Weekley, J.A., Wiesner, W.H., & Degroot, T.G. (2001). Comparison of situational and behavior description interview questions for higher-level positions. *Personnel Psychology, 54,* 619–644.

25. McDaniel, M.A., Whetzel, D.L., Schmidt, F.L., & Maurer, S.D. (1994). The validity of employment interviews. A comprehensive review and meta-analysis. *Journal of Applied Psychology, 79,* 599–616.

26. Strauss, S.G., Miles, J.A., & Levesque, L.L. (2001). The effects of videoconference, telephone, and face-to-face media on interviewer and applicant judgments in employment interviews. *Journal of Management, 27,* 363–381.

27. Ibid.

28. Rowe, P.M. (1985). Unfavorable information and interview decisions. In R.W. Eder, & G.R. Ferris (Eds.), *The employment interview: Theory, research and practice* (pp. 77–89). Newberry Park, CA: Sage.

29. Heilmann, M., & Saruwatari, L. (1979). When beauty is beastly: The effects of appearance and sex on evaluation of job applicants for managerial and nonmangerial jobs. *Organizational Behavior and Human Performance, 23,* 360–370. Huffcutt, A.I., & Roth, P. (1998). Racial group differences in employment interview evaluations. *Journal of Applied Psychology, 83* (2), 179–189. Degroot, T., & Motowidlo, S.J. (1999). Why visual and vocal interview cues can affect interviewers' judgments and predicted job performance. *Journal of Applied Psychology, 84* (6), 968–984.

30. Waldman, D.A., & Kobar, T. (2004). Student assessment center performance in the prediction of early career success. *Academy of Management Learning & Education, 3* (2), 151–167.

31. Sackett, P.R., & Ostgaard, D.J. (1994). Job-specific applicant pools and national norms for cognitive ability tests: Implications for range restriction corrections in

validation research. *Journal of Applied Psychology, 79* (5), 680–684.

32. Ryan, A.M., & Ployhart, R.E. (2000). Applicants' perceptions of selection procedures and decisions: A critical review and agenda for the future. *Journal of Management, 26* (3), 565–606.

33. Rynes, S.L., Brown, K.G., & Colbert, A.E. (2002). Seven common misconceptions about human resources practices: Research findings versus practitioner beliefs. *Academy of Management Executive, 16* (3), 92–103.

34. Adapted from www.wonderlic.com/promotion/nfl_article.asp

35. Hurtz, G.M., & Donovan, J.J. (2000). Personality and job performance: The big five revisited. *Journal of Applied Psychology, 85* (6), 869–879.

36. Latham, G.P. (2004). The motivational benefits of goal setting. *Academy of Management Executive, 18* (4), 126–129.

37. Latham, G.P., & Wexley, K.N. (1994). *Increasing productivity through performance appraisal.* (2nd ed.). Reading, MA: Addison-Wesley.

38. Rynes, S.L., Gerhart, B., & Parks, L. (2005). Personnel psychology: Performance evaluation and pay for performance. *Annual Review of Psychology, 56,* 571–600.

39. Latham, G.P., & Wexley, K.N. (1994). *Increasing productivity through performance appraisal.* (2nd ed.). Reading, MA: Addison-Wesley.

40. Kluger, A.N., & DeNisi, A.S. (2000). Feedback effectiveness: Can 360-degree appraisals be improved? *Academy of Management Executive, 14* (1), 129–139.

41. Kluger, A.N., & DeNisi, A.S. (1996). The effects of feedback interventions on performance: Historical review, a meta-analysis, and a preliminary feedback intervention theory. *Psychological Bulletin, 119,* 225–284.

42. Ibid.

43. Nadler, D.A. (1977). *Feedback and organization development: Using data-based methods.* Reading, MA: Addison-Wesley.

44. Schein, E.H. (1999). *Process consultation revisited. Building the helpful relationship.* Reading, MA: Addison-Wesley.

45. Kluger, A.N., & DeNisi, A.S. (2000). Feedback effectiveness: Can 360-degree appraisals be improved? *Academy of Management Executive, 14* (1), 129–139.

46. Ilgen, D.R., Fisher, C.D., & Taylor, M.S. (1979). Consequences of individual feedback on behavior in organizations. *Journal of Applied Psychology, 64* (4), 349–371.

47. Hunt, J.M., & Weintraub, J.R. (2002). *The coaching manager: Developing top talent in business.* Thousand Oaks, CA: Sage.

48. Example taken from Schein, E.H. (1999). *Process consultation revisited. Building the helpful relationship* (p. 138). Reading, MA: Addison-Wesley.

49. London, M. (2003). *Job feedback: Giving, seeking and using feedback for performance improvement.* Mahwah, NJ: Lawrence Earlbaum Associates.

50. Colquitt, J.A., Conlon, D.E., Wesson, M.J., Porter, C.O.L.H., & Ng, K.Y. (2001). Justice at the millennium: A meta-analytic review of 25 years of organizational

justice research. *Journal of Applied Psychology, 86* (3), 425–445.

51. Buckingham, M. & Coffman, C. (1999). *First, break all the rules. What the worlds' greatest managers do differently.* Simon & Shuster, New York.

52. Adapted from Fournies, F.F. (2000). *Coaching for improved work performance.* New York, NY: McGraw Hill.

53. Bayer, R. (2000, September–October). Termination with dignity. *Business Horizons, 43,* 4–10.

54. Sussman, L., & Finnegan, R. (1998, March–April). Coaching the star: Rationale and strategies. *Business Horizons, 41,* 47–54.

55. Groysberg, B., Nanda, A., & Nohria, N. (2004, May). The risky business of hiring stars. *Harvard Business Review, 82*(5) 92–99.

56. Lombardo, M.M., & Eichinger, R.W. (2000). High potentials as high learners. *Human Resource Management Journal, 39* (4), 321–329.

57. Trank, C.Q., Rynes, S.L., & Bretz, R.D. Jr. (2002). Attracting applicants in the war for talent: Differences in the work preferences among high achievers. *Journal of Business & Psychology, 16* (3), 331–345.

58. Ibid.

59. McCauley, C.D., Moxley, R.S., & Velsor, E.V. (1998). *The center for creative leadership: Handbook of leadership development.* San Francisco, CA: Jossey-Bass.

60. Ashford, S.J., & Cummings, L.L. (1983). Feedback as an individual resource: Personal strategies of creating information. *Organizational Behavior and Human Performance, 32,* 370–398.

61. Example adapted from Sacco, J.M., Scheu, C.R., Ryan, A.M., & Schmitt, N. (2003). An investigation of race and sex similarity effects in interviews: A multilevel approach to relationship demography. *Journal of Applied Psychology, 88* (5), 852–865.

62. Adapted from Orth, C.D., Wilkinson, H.E., & Benfari, R.C. (2001). The manager's role as coach and mentor. *Organizational Dynamics, 16,* 66–73.

63. Flynn, G. (1995). Thirteen steps to a smoother termination. *Personnel Journal, 74* (10), 27–30.

Chapter 6

1. Granovetter, M.S. (1973). The strength of weak ties. *American Journal of Sociology, 78,* 1360–1380. Granovetter, M.S. (1994). *Getting a job: A study in contacts and careers.* (2nd ed.). Chicago: University of Chicago Press.

2. Montgomery, J.D. (1992). Job search and network composition: Implications of the strength-of-weak-ties hypothesis. *American Sociological Review, 57,* 586–596.; Montgomery, J.D. (1994). Weak ties, employment, and inequality: An equilibrium analysis. *American Journal of Sociology, 99,* 1212–1236.

3. Granovetter, M.S. (1994). *Getting a job: A study in contacts and careers.* (2nd ed.). Chicago: University of Chicago Press.

4. French, J.P.R. Jr., & Raven, B. (1960). The bases of social power. In D. Cartwright, & A. Zander (Eds.), *Group dynamics* (pp. 607–623). New York: Harper & Row.

5. Sherif, M. (1935). A study of some social factors in perception. *Archives of Psychology, 27* (187), 17–22. Asch, S.E. (1955). Opinions and social pressure. *Scientific American,* 31–35.

6. Bond, R., & Smith, P.B. (1996). Culture and conformity: A meta-analysis of studies using Asch's (1952b, 1956) line judgment task. *Psychological Bulletin, 119* (1), 111–137.

7. Falbe, C.M., & Yukl, G. (1992). Consequences for managers of using single influence tactics and combinations of tactics. *Academy of Management Journal, 35,* 638–652. Yukl, G., Kim, H., & Falbe, C.M. (1996). Antecedents of influence outcomes. *Journal of Applied Psychology, 81,* 309–317. Yukl, G., & Tracey, J.B. (1992). Consequences of influence tactics used with subordinates, peers, and the boss. *Journal of Applied Psychology, 77,* 525–535.

8. Ibid.

9. Fox, S., & Amichai-Hamburger, Y. (2001). The power of emotional appeals in promoting organizational change programs. *Academy of Management Executive, 15* (4), 84–94.

10. Ferris, G.R., Perrewe, P.L., Anthony, W.P., & Gilmore, D.C. (2000). Political skill at work. *Organizational Dynamics, 28* (4), 25–37.

11. Throughout this section, we relied heavily on Cialdini, R.B. (2001). *Influence: Science and practice.* (4th ed.). Boston: Allyn & Bacon.

12. Hosoda, M., Stone-Romero, E.F., & Coats, G. (2003). The effects of physical attractiveness on job-related outcomes: A meta-analysis of experimental studies. *Personnel Psychology, 56,* 431–462.

13. For a detailed review of this literature, see Eagly, A.H., Ashmore, R.D., Makhijani, M.G., & Longo, L.C. (1991). What is beautiful is good, but . . .: A meta-analytic review of research on the physical attractiveness stereotype. *Psychological Bulletin, 110,* 109–128.

14. Efran, M.G., & Patterson, E.W.J. (1974). Voters vote beautiful: The effects of physical appearance on a national election. *Canadian Journal of Behavioral Science, 6,* 352–356.

15. Hamermesh, D.S., & Biddle, J.E. (1994). Beauty and the labor market. *The American Economic Review, 84* (5), 1174–1194.

16. Dion, K., Berscheid, E., & Walster, E. (1972). What is beautiful is good. *Journal of Personality and Social Psychology, 24,* 285–290.

17. Ritts, V., Patterson, M.L., & Tubbs, M.E. (1992). Expectations, impressions, and judgments of physically attractive students: A review. *Review of Educational Research, 64,* 413–426.

18. Furnham, A. (1996). Factors relating to the allocation of medical resources. *Journal of Social Behavior and Personality, 11,* 615–624.

19. Drachman, deCarufel, & Insko, C. (1978). The extra credit effect in interpersonal attraction. *Journal of Experimental Social Psychology, 14,* 458–465.

20. Cialdini, R.B. (2001). Influence: Science and practice (4th ed.), 53. Boston: Allyn & Bacon.

21. Sherman, S.J. (1980). On the self-erasing nature of errors of prediction, *Journal of Personality and Social Psychology, 39,* 211–221.

22. Cialdini, R.B. (2001). *Influence: Science and practice.* (4th ed.). Boston: Allyn & Bacon.

23. Brehm, J.W. (1966). *A theory of psychological reactance.* New York: Academic Press.

24. Cialdini, R.B. (2001) Influence: Science and practice. (4th ed., p. 53. Boston: Allyns Bacon.

25. Bushman, B.J. (1988). The effects of apparel on compliance. *Personality and Social Psychology Bulletin, 14,* 459–467.

26. Deluga, R.J. (2003). Kissing up to the boss: What it is and what to do about it. *Business Forum, 26* (3/4), 14–18. Jones, E. (1990). *Interpersonal perception.* New York: Freeman. Michener, H., Plazewski, J., & Vaske, J. (1979). Ingratiation tactics channeled by target values and threat capability. *Journal of Personality, 47,* 35–56.

27. DeVries, M.F.R. (2001). *The leadership mystique,* p. 94. London: Financial Times/Prentice Hall.

28. Hegarty, W. (1974). Using subordinate ratings to elicit behavioral changes in supervisors. *Journal of Applied Psychology, 59,* 764–766. Tourish, D., & Robson, P. (2003). Critical upward feedback in organizations: Processes, problems, and implications for communication management. *Journal of Communication Management, 8* (2), 150–167.

29. Nutt, P. (1999). Surprising but true: Half the decisions in organizations fail. *Academy of Management Executive, 13,* 75–90.

30. Atwater, L., Waldman, D., Atwater, D., & Carrier, P. (2000). An upward feedback field experiment: Supervisors' cynicism, reactions, and commitment to subordinates. *Personnel Psychology, 53,* 275–297.

31. Becerra, M., & Gupta, A.K. (2003). Perceived trustworthiness within the organization: The moderating impact of communication frequency on trustor and trustee effects. *Organization Science, 14,* 32–44.

32. Corman, S., & Poole, M. (2000). The need for common ground. In S. Corman, & M. Poole (Eds.), *Perspectives on organizational communication: Finding common ground* (pp. 3–16). New York: Guilford Press.

33. Cable, D.M., & Judge, T.A. (2003). Managers' upward influence tactic strategies: The role of personality and supervisor leadership style. *Journal of Organizational Behavior, 24,* 197–210. Pater, R. (2005, January). High-level persuasion: Influencing up, down, and sideways. *Occupational Health & Safety, 74* (1), 24–30.

34. Krone, K. (1992). A comparison of organizational, structural, and relationship effects on subordinates' upward influence choices. *Communication Quarterly, 40,* 1–15.

35. McCall, M.W., & Lombardo, M.M. (1983). *Off the Track: Why and How Successful Executives Get Derailed. Technical Report 21.* Greensboro, NC: Center for Creative Leadership. Leslie, J., & Van Velsor, E. (1996). *A look at derailment today: North America and Europe. CCL No. 169.* Greensboro, NC: Center for Creative Leadership.

36. Ibid.

37. Cross, R., & Parker, A. (2004). *The hidden power of social networks.* Boston: Harvard Business School Press.

38. Cross, R., Davenport, T., & Cantrell, S. (2003). *Rising above the crowd: High performing knowledge workers differentiate themselves.* Accenture Institute for Strategic Change working paper.

39. Adapted from Johnson, C. (2000, July 30). *The Washington Post.*

40. Pfeffer, J. (1994). *Managing with power.* New York: Random House.

Chapter 7

1. Bass, B.M. (1990). *Bass and Stogdill's handbook of leadership: Theory, research, and managerial applications.* New York: The Free Press.

2. Ibid.

3. See Bass, B.M. (1990). Bass and Stogdill's handbook of leadership: theory, research, and managerial applications. New York: Free Press for a highly detailed account.

4. Pfeffer, J. (1996). Competitive advantage through people. Cambridge, MA: Harvard Press.

5. Amazon search conducted in June 2005. www.amazon.com

6. Hogan, R., & Hogan, J. (2001). Assessing leadership: A view from the dark side. *International Journal of Selection and Assessment, 9,* 40–51.

7. Avolio, B.J. (1999). *Full leadership development: Building the vital forces in organizations.* Thousand Oaks, CA: Sage Publications.

8. Bass, B.M. (1990). *Bass and Stogdill's handbook of leadership: Theory, research, and managerial applications.* New York: The Free Press.

9. Hughes, R.L., Ginnett, R.C., & Curphy, G.J. (1993). *Leadership: Enhancing the lessons of experience.* Burr Ridge, IL: Richard D. Irwin, Inc.

10. Allison, S.T., & Eylon, D. (2005). The demise of leadership: Death positivity biases in posthumous impressions of leaders. In D. Messick, & R. Kramer (Eds.), *The psychology of leadership: Some new approaches.* New York: Erlbaum.

11. Kouzes, J., & Posner, B. (1997). *The leadership challenge.* San Francisco: Jossey-Bass.

12. Fleishman, E.A. (1973). Twenty years of consideration and structure. In E.A. Fleishman, & J.G. Hunt (Eds.), *Current developments in the study of leadership.* Carbondale: Southern Illinois University Press.

13. Hersey, P., & Blanchard, K.H. (1982). Leadership style: Attitudes and behaviors. *Training & Development Journal, 36,* 50–52.; Hersey, P., & Blanchard, K.H. (1969). Life cycle theory of leadership, *Training & Development Journal, 23,* 26–34.

14. Dansereau, F. Jr., Graen, G., & Haga, W.J. (1975). A vertical dyad linkage approach to leadership within formal organizations: A longitudinal investigation of the role making process. *Organizational Behavior and Human Performance, 13,* 46–78.

15. Wayne, S.J., Shore, L.M., & Liden, R.C. (1997). Perceived organizational support and leader-member exchange:

A social exchange perspective. *Academy of Management Journal, 40*, 82–111. Liden, R.C., Sparrowe, R.T., & Wayne, S.J. (1997). Leader-member exchange theory: The past and potential for the future. In G. Ferris (Ed.), *Research in Personnel and Human Resources Management* (pp. 47–119). Greenwich, CT: JAI Press.

16. Podsakoff, P.M., Bommer, W.H., Podsakoff, N.P., & MacKenzie, S.B. (2006). Relationships between leader reward and punishment behavior and subordinate attitudes, perceptions, and behaviors: A meta-analytic review of existing and new research. *Organizational Behavior and Human Decision Process, 99*, 113–142.

17. Ibid.

18. Bass, B.M. (1990). *Bass and Stogdill's handbook of leadership: Theory, research, and managerial applications.* p. 14 New York: The Free Press.

19. Podsakoff, P.M., MacKenzie, S.B., Moorman, R.H., & Fetter, R. (1990). Transformational leader behaviors and their effects on followers' trust in leader, satisfaction, and organizational citizenship behaviors. *Leadership Quarterly, 1*, 107–142.

20. Podsakoff, P.M., MacKenzie, S.B., & Bommer, W.H. (1996). Transformational leader behaviors and substitutes for leadership as determinants of employee satisfaction, commitment, trust, and organizational citizenship behaviors. *Journal of Management, 22*, 259–298.

21. Onnen, M.K. (1987). The relationship of clergy and leadership characteristics to growing or declining churches. (Doctoral dissertation, University of Louisville, KY).

22. Barling, J., Weber, T., & Kelloway, E.K. (1996). Effects of transformational leadership training on attitudinal and financial outcomes: A field experiment. *Journal of Applied Psychology, 81*, 827–832.

23. Geyer, A.L.J., & Steyrer, J.M. (1998). Transformational leadership and objective performance in banks. *Applied Psychology: An International Review, 47*, 397–420.

24. MacKenzie, S.B., Podsakoff, P.M., & Rich, G.A. (2001). Transformational and transactional leadership and salesperson performance. *Journal of Academy of Marketing Science, 29* (2), 115–134.

25. Podsakoff, P.M., MacKenzie, S.B., & Bommer, W.H. (1996). Transformational leader behaviors and substitutes for leadership as determinants of employee satisfaction, commitment, trust, and organizational citizenship behaviors. *Journal of Management, 22*, 259–298.

26. Frese, M., Beimel, S., & Schoenborn, S. (2003). Action training for charismatic leadership: Two evaluations of studies of a commercial training module on inspirational communication of a vision. *Personnel Psychology, 56*, 671–697.

27. Organ, D.W. (1988). *Organizational citizenship behavior: The good soldier syndrome.* Lexington, MA: D.C. Heath.

28. Kouzes, J., & Posner, B. (1997). *The leadership challenge.* San Francisco: Jossey-Bass.

29. Rosenthal, R., & Rubin, D. B. (1971). Pygmalion reaffirmed. In J.D. Elashoff, & R.E. Snow (Eds.), *Pygmalion reconsidered* (pp. 139–155). Worthington, OH: Jones Publishing.

Chapter 8

1. Katzenbach, J.R., & Smith, D. (1993). *The wisdom of teams.* Cambridge, MA: Harvard Business School Press.

2. Freiberg, K., & Freiberg, J. (1998). *Nuts! Southwest Airlines' crazy recipe for business and personal success.* New York: Bantam Paperbacks.

3. Dumaine, B. (1993, September 5). The trouble with teams. *Fortune,* 86–92.

4. Adapted from Thompson, L.L. (2004). *Making the team: A guide for managers.* Upper Saddle Ridge, NJ: Pearson Prentice Hall.

5. Maier, N.R.G. (1967). Assets and liabilities of group problem solving: The need for an integrative function. *Psychological Review, 74*, 239–49. Leavitt, H. (1975). Suppose we took groups seriously. In E.L. Cass, & F.G. Zimmer (Eds.), *Man and work in society.* New York: Van Nostrand Reinhold.

6. Hackman, J.R. (1990). *Groups that work and those that don't.* San Francisco, CA: Jossey-Bass.

7. Katzenbach, J.R., & Smith, D. (2001). *The discipline of teams.* New York: Wiley. Cohen, S.G., & Bailey, D.E. (1997). What makes teams work: Group effectiveness research from the shop floor to the executive suite. *Journal of Management, 23*, 239–290. Guzzo, R.A., & Dickson, M.W. (1996). Teams in organizations: Recent research on performance and effectiveness. *Annual Review of Psychology, 47*, 307–338. Campion, M.A., Papper, E.M., & Medsker, G.J. (1996). Relations between work team characteristics and effectiveness: A replication and extension. *Personnel Psychology, 49*, 429–452.

8. Katzenbach, J.R., & Smith, D. (1993). *The wisdom of teams.* Cambridge, MA: Harvard Business School Press.

9. Wicker, A.W., Kermeyer, S.L., Hanson, L., & Alexander, D. (1976). Effects of manning levels on subjective experiences, performance and verbal interaction in groups. *Organizational Behavior and Human Performance, 17*, 251–274. McGrath, J.E. (1990). *Groups: Interaction and performance.* Upper Saddle River, NJ: Prentice Hall.

10. Deutschman, A. (2004, August). Inside the mind of Jeff Bezos and his plans for Amazon. *Fast Company,* 52–58.

11. Stevens, M.A., & Campion, M.J. (1994). The knowledge, skill and ability requirements for teamwork: Implications for human resource management. *Journal of Management, 20*, 503–530.

12. Stevens, M.J., & Campion, M.A. (1999). Staffing work teams: Development and validation of a selection test for teamwork settings. *Journal of Management, 25* (2) 207–228.

13. Chen, G., Donahue, L.M., & Klimoski, R.J. (2004). Training undergraduates to work in organizational teams. *Academy of Management Learning and Education, 3* (1), 27–40. Stevens, M.J., & Campion, M.A. (1999). Staffing work teams: Development and validation of a selection test for teamwork settings. *Journal of Management, 25* (2) 207–228.

14. Neuman, G.A., & Wright, J. (1999). Team effectiveness: Beyond skills and cognitive ability. *Journal of Applied Psychology, 84*, 376–389.

15. Katzenbach, J.R., & Smith, D. (1993). *The wisdom of teams.* Cambridge, MA: Harvard Business School Press.

16. Ibid.

17. Pritchard, R.D., Jones, S.D., Roth, P.L., & Stuebing, J., & Ekeberg, S.E. (1988). Effects of group feedback, goal setting and incentives on organizational productivity. *Journal of Applied Psychology, 73,* 337–58.

18. Anderson, D.C., Crowell, C.R., Doman, M., & Howard, G.S. (1988). Performance posting, goal setting and activity-contingent praise as applied to a college hockey team. *Journal of Applied Psychology, 73,* 87–95.

19. Zander, A., & Newcomb, T. (1967). Group level of aspiration in United Way Fund campaigns. *Journal of Personality and Social Psychology, 6,* 157–162.

20. Ibid.

21. Tuckman, B.W. (1965). Developmental sequence in small groups. *Psychological Bulletin, 63,* 384–399.

22. Argote, L. (1989). Agreement about norms and work-unit effectiveness: Evidence from the field. *Basic and Applied Social Psychology, 10* (2), 131–140.

23. Miller, L.K., & Hamblin, R.L. (1963). Interdependence, differential rewarding, and productivity. *American Sociological Review, 28,* 768–778. Wageman, R. (1995). Interdependnece and group effectiveness, *Administrative Science Quarterly, 40,* 145–180. Fan, E.T., & Gruenfeld, D.H. (1998). When needs outweigh desires: The effects of resource interdependence and reward interdependence on group problem solving. *Basic and Applied Social Psychology, 20* (1) 45–56. Thompson, L.L. (2004). *Making the team: A guide for managers.* Upper Saddle Ridge, NJ: Pearson Prentice Hall.

24. Adapted from Parker, G., McAdams, J., & Zielinski, D. (2000). *Rewarding teams: Lessons from the trenches.* San Francisco: Jossey Bass.

25. Ibid.

26. Ibid.

27. Steiner, I. (1972). *Group process and productivity.* New York: Academic Press.

28. Adapted from Thompson, L.L. (2004). *Making the team: A guide for managers.* Upper Saddle Ridge, NJ: Pearson Prentice Hall.

29. Darley, J.M., & Latane, B. (1968). Bystander intervention in emergencies: Diffusion of responsibility. *Journal of Personality and Social Psychology, 8,* 377–383.

30. Baumeister, R.F. (1984). Choking under pressure: Self-consciousness and paradoxical effects of incentives on skillful performance. *Journal of Personality and Social Psychology, 46,* 610–620.

31. Staw, B.H. (1976). Knee-deep in the big muddy: A study of escalating commitment to a chosen course of action. *Organizational Behavior and Human Decision Processes, 16* (1), 27–44.

32. Keysar, B., & Henly, A. (2002). Speakers' overestimation of their effectiveness. *Psychological Science, 13* (3) 207–212.

33. Ibid.

34. Gigone, D., & Hastie, R. (1993). The common knowledge effect: Information sharing and group judgment. *Journal of Personality and Social Psychology, 65* (5) 959–974.

35. Shaw, M.E. (1981). *Group dynamics: The psychology of small group behavior.* (3rd ed.). New York: McGraw-Hill.

Stasser, G., Stewart, D.D., & Wittenbaum, G.M. (1995). Expert roles and information exchange during discussion: The importance of knowing who knows what. *Journal of Experimental Social Psychology, 31,* 244–265.

36. Kravitz, D.A., & Martin, B. (1986). Ringelmann rediscovered: The original article. *Journal of Personality and Social Psychology, 50* (5), 936–941.

37. Ringelmann's research as cited in Forsyth, D. (1990). Group dynamics. Pacific Grove, CA: Brooks/Cole

38. Williams, K., Harkins, S., & Latane, B. (1981). Identifiability as a deterrent to social loafing: Two cheering experiments. *Journal of Personality and Social Psychology, 40,* 303–311.

39. Asch, S.E. (1951). Effects of group pressure upon the modification and distortion of judgments. In Guetzkow, H. (ed.) Groups, leadership, and men (pp. 177–90). Pittsburgh: Carnegie Press.

40. Janis, I.L. (1982). *Groupthink: Psychological studies of policy decisions and fiascoes.* (2nd ed.) Boston: Houghton Mifflin.

41. Harvey, J. (1974). The Abilene paradox: The management of agreement. *Organizational Dynamics, 3* (1) 63–80.

42. Watson, W.E., Kumar, K. & Michaelson, L.K. (1993). Cultural diversity's impact on interaction process and performance: Comparing homogenous and diverse task groups. *Academy of Management Journal, 36* (3) 590–602.

43. Jehn, K.A., Northcraft, G.B., & Neale, M.A. (1999). Why differences make a difference: A field study of diversity, conflict and performance in workgroups. *Administrative Science Quarterly, 44,* 741–763.

44. Harrison, D.A., Price, K.H., & Bell, M.P. (1998). Beyond relational demography: Time and the effects of surface- and deep-level diversity on work group cohesion. *Academy of Management Journal, 41* (1), 96–107.

45. Hambrick, D.C., Davison, S.C., Snell, S.A., & Snow, C.C. (1998, Spring). When groups consist of multiple nationalities: Toward an understanding of the implications, *Organization Studies, 19,* 181–205.

46. Raines, C. (2003). *Connecting generations: The sourcebook for a new generation.* New York: Crisp Publications.

47. Tannen, D. (1990). *You just don't understand: Women and men in conversation.* New York: William Morrow.

48. Boiney, L.G. (2001). Gender impacts virtual work teams. *Graziado School of Business Report, Pepperdine University, 1* (4).

49. Kraiger, K., & Ford, J.K. (1985). A meta-analyses of race effects in performance ratings. *Journal of Applied Psychology, 70,* 56–65.

50. Mullen, B., & Cooper, C. (1994). The relation between group cohesiveness and performance: An integration. *Psychological Bulletin, 115,* 210–227. Berkowitz, L. (1954). Group standards, cohesiveness and productivity. *Human Relations, 7,* 509–519.

51. Brawley, L.R., Carron, A.V. & Widmeyer, W.N. (1988). Exploring the relationship between cohesion and group resistance to disruption. *Journal of Sport and Exercise Psychology, 10* (2), 199–213.

52. Mullen, B., & Cooper, C. (1994). The relation between group cohesiveness and performance: An integration. *Psychological Bulletin, 115,* 210–227. Berkowitz, L.

(1954). Group standards, cohesiveness and productivity. *Human Relations, 7,* 509–519.

53. Cascio, W.F. (2000). Managing a virtual workforce. *Academy of Management Executive,* 14 (3), 81–90.

54. Haywood, M. (1998). *Managing virtual teams: Practical techniques for high technology managers.* Boston: Artech House. Henry, J.E., & Hartzler, M. (1998). *Tools for virtual teams: A team fitness companion.* Milwaukee, WI: ASQ Press.

55. Coutu, D. (1998, May–June). Trust in virtual teams. *Harvard Business Review, 76* (3) 20–21.

56. Dennis, A., & Reinicke, B. (2004). Beta vs. VHS and the acceptance of electronic brainstorming technology. *MIS Quarterly, 28* (1), 1–20.

57. Benn, K.D., & Sheats, P. (1948). Functional roles of group members. *Journal of Social Issues, 4,* 41–49.

58. Mosvick, R., & Nelson, R.B. (1996). *We've got to start meeting like this: A guide to successful meeting management.* Indianapolis, IN: Park Avenue. Whetton, D.A., & Cameron, K.S. (2005). *Developing management skills.* (6th ed.). Upper Saddle Ridge, NJ: Pearson Prentice Hall.

59. Ibid.

Chapter 9

1. Lax, D.A., & Sebenius, J.K. (1986). *Manager as negotiator.* New York: The Free Press.

2. Jehn, K. (1994). Enhancing effectiveness: An investigation of advantages and disadvantages of value-based intragroup conflict. *International Journal of Conflict Management, 5,* 223–238.

3. Amason, A. (1996). Distinguishing the effects of functional and dysfunctional conflict on strategic decision-making: Resolving a paradox for top management teams. *Academy of Management Journal, 39* (1), 123–148.

4. Ibid.

5. De Dreu, C.K.W., & Weingart, L.R. (2003). Task versus relationship conflict and team effectiveness: A meta-analysis. *Journal of Applied Psychology, 88,* 741–749. Jehn, K.A., & Mannix, E. (2001). The dynamic nature of conflict: A longitudinal study of intragroup conflict and group performance. *Academy of Management Journal, 44,* 238–251.

6. Simons, T. (1995). Top management team consensus, heterogeneity, and debate as contingent predictors of company performance: The complementarity of group structure and process. *Academy of Management Best Proceedings,* 62–66.

7. De Dreu, C.K.W., & Weingart, L.R. (2003). Task versus relationship conflict and team effectiveness: A meta-analysis. *Journal of Applied Psychology, 88,* 741–749.

8. Jehn, K. A. & Mannix, E. (2001). The dynamic nature of conflict: A longitudinal study of intragroup conflict and group performance. *Academy of Management Journal, 44,* 238–251.

9. Jainism and Buddhism. *Udana* 68–69.

10. Hottes, J.H., & Kahn, A. (1974). Sex differences in a mixed-motive conflict situation. *Journal of Personality, 42,* 260–275.

11. Bergmann, T.J., & Volkema, R.J. (1994). Issues, behavioral responses, and consequences in interpersonal conflicts. *Journal of Organizational Behavior, 15* (5), 467–471.

12. Sherif, M., Harvey, O. J., White, B. J., Hood, W. R., & Sherif, C. W. (1954). *Experimental study of positive and negative intergroup attitudes between experimentally produced groups. Robber's Cave Study.* Norman: University of Oklahoma Press.

13. Ibid.

14. Lee, K.N. (1982, Spring). Defining success in environmental dispute resolution. *Resolve,* 1–6.

15. Bazerman, M.A., & Neale, M.H. (1991). *Negotiating rationally.* New York: Free Press.

16. Adapted from Yourdon, E. (2004). *Death march.* Upper Saddle River, NJ: Prentice Hall.

17. Fisher, R., & Ury, W. (1981). *Getting to Yes: Negotiating agreement without giving in.* New York: Penquin Books.

18. Lewicki, R. Barry, B., Saunders, D., & Minton, J. (2003). *Essentials of negotiation.* Burr Ridge, IL: McGraw-Hill.

19. General Electric Co., 150 NLRB 192, 57 LRRM 1491 (1964), *enf'd sub nom,* NLRB v. General Electric Co., 418 F.2d 736, 72 LRRM 2530 (2d Cir. 1969), *cert. denied,* 397 U.S. 965, 73 LRRM 2600 (1970).

20. Colosi, T. (1983, November–December). Negotiating in the public and private sectors. *American Behavioral Scientist, 27,* 229–253.

21. Ibid.

Chapter 10

1. Deutschman, A. (2005, May). Change or die. *Fast Company,* 54–62.

2. Lewin, K. (1951). *Field theory in social science; selected theoretical papers.* (D. Cartwright, Ed.). New York: Harper & Row.

3. Porras, J., & Berg, P. (1978) The impact of organization development. *Academy of Management Review, 3,* 249–266.

4. Katzell, R.A., & Guzzo, R.A. (1983). Psychological approaches to productivity improvement. *American Psychologist, 38* (4), 468–472.

5. Golembiewski, R., Proehl, C., & Sink, D. (1982). Estimating success of OD applications. *Training and Development Journal, 72,* 86–95.

6. Jick, T.D. (1995). Accelerating change for competitive advantage. *Organizational Dynamics, 24* (1), 77–82.

7. Kanter, R., Stein, B, & Jick, T. (1992). *The challenge of organizational change: How companies experience it and leaders guide it.* New York: The Free Press.

8. Bridges, W. (1980). *Transitions: Making sense of life's changes.* New York: Perseus Books.

9. Kotter, J. (1996). *Leading change.* Boston, MA: Harvard Business School Press.

10. Kotter, J., & Cohen, D. (2002). *The heart of change.* Boston, MA: Harvard Business School Press.

11. Kanter, R., Stein, B.A., & Jick, T. (1994). *The challenge of organizational change.* New York: Free Press.

12. Block, P. (2002). *Flawless consulting: A guide to getting your expertise used.* San Francisco: Jossey-Bass/Pfeiffer.

13. Kanter, R., Stein, B, & Jick, T. (1992). *The challenge of organizational change: How companies experience it and leaders guide it.* New York: The Free Press.

14. Schaffer, R.H. (2002). *High-impact consulting: How clients and consultants can work together to achieve extraordinary results.* San Francisco: Jossey Bass.

15. Kaplan, R.S. (2005, July–August). Add a customer profitability metric to your Balanced scorecard. *Balanced Scorecard Report, 7* (4).

16. Golembiewki, R., Proehl, C., & Sink, D. (1982). Estimating success of OD applications. *Training and Development Journal, 72,* 86–95.

17. Schein, E.H. (1999). *Process consultation revisited: Building the helping relationship.* Reading, MA: Addison-Wesley.

18. Cooperrider, D., & Srivasta, S. (1987). Appreciative inquiry in organizational life. In R. Woodman, & W. Pasmore (Eds.), *Research in organizational change and development, vol.1* (pp. 129–169). Greenwich, CT: JAI Press.

19. Ibid.

20. Schwartz, R. (2002). *The skilled facilitator.* San Francisco: Jossey-Bass.

21. Nadler, D. (1977). *Feedback and organization development. Using data-based method.* Reading, MA: Addison-Wesley.

22. Raisel, E. (1999). *The McKinsey way: Using the techniques of the world's top strategic consultants to help you and your business.* New York: McGraw-Hill.

23. Schaffer, R.H. (2002). *High-impact consulting: How clients and consultants can work together to achieve extraordinary results.* San Francisco: Jossey Bass.

24. Dalton, C.C., & Gottlieb, L.N. (2003). The concept of readiness to change. *Journal of Advanced Nursing, 42* (2), 108–117.

25. Cummings, T.G. & Worley, C.G., (1997). Organization development & change. (6th ed.). Cincinati, OH: Southwestern Publishing.

26. Bolman, L., & Deal, T. (1991). Reframing organizations. Artistry, choice, and leadership. San Francisco: Jussy-Bass Publishers.

27. Cheng, Y.C. (1994). Principal's leadership as a critical indicator of school performance: Evidence from multi-levels of primary schools. *School Effectiveness and School Improvement: An International Journal of Research, Policy, and Practice, 5* (3), 299–317. Wimpelberg, R.K. (1987). Managerial images and school effectiveness. *Administrators' Notebook, 32,* 1–4.

28. Bolman, L., & Deal, T. (1991). *Reframing organizations. Artistry, choice, and leadership.* San Francisco: Jussy-Bass Publishers.

29. Block, P. (2002). *Flawless consulting: A guide to getting your expertise used.* San Francisco: Jossey-Bass/Pfeiffer.

30. Kotter, J. (1996). *Leading change.* Boston, MA: Harvard Business School Press.

31. Kotter, J.P., & Schlesinger, L.A. (1979 March–April). Choosing strategies for change. *Harvard Business Review, 57* (2), 106–114.

32. McClough, A.C., Rogelberg, S.G., Fisher, G.G, & Bachiochi, P.D. (1998). Cynicism and the quality of an individual's contribution to an organizational diagnostic survey. *Organization Development Journal, 16,* 31–41.

33. Katzenbach, J.R., & RCL Team. (1995). *Real change leaders.* New York: Random House.

34. Kriegel, R., & Brandt, D. (1996). *Sacred cows make the best burgers.* New York: Warner Books.

35. Adapted from Price Waterhouse Change Integration Team. (1994). *Better change: Best practices for transforming your organization.* Burr Ridge, IL: Irwin Professional Publishing.

Conclusion

1. Buckingham, M., & Coffman, C. (1999). *First, break all the rules: What the world's greatest managers do differently.* New York: Simon & Schuster.

2. General Electric Company. (2001). *GE 2000 Annual Report.* http://www.ge.com/annual00/letter/index.html.

3. Quoted in Mintzberg, H. (2004). *Managers not MBAs: A hard look at the soft practice of managing and management development.* San Francisco: Berrett-Koehler.

4. Pfeffer, J. (1998). *The human equation: Building profits by putting people first.* Boston: Harvard Business School Press.

5. Ibid.

6. Huselid, M.A. (1995). The impact of human resource management practices on turnover, productivity, and corporate financial performance. *Academy of Management Journal, 38,* 635–672. Huselid, M.A., & Becker, B.E. (1997). The impact of high performance work systems, implementation effectiveness and alignment with strategy on shareholder wealth. *Academy of Management Best Paper Proceedings,* 144–148.

7. MacDuffie, J.P. (1995). Human resource bundles and manufacturing performance. *Industrial and Labor Relations Review, 48* (2), 197–221.

8. Welbourne, T., & Andrews, A. (1996). Predicting performance of initial public offering firms: Should human resource management be in the equation? *Academy of Management Journal, 39* (4), 891–919.

9. Arthur, J.B. (1992). Effects of human resource systems on manufacturing performance and turnover. *Academy of Management Journal, 37,* 670–687.

10. Dunlop, J.T., & Weil, D. (1996) Diffusion and performance of modular production in the U.S. apparel industry. *Industrial Relations, 35* (93), 334–355.

11. Pfau, B., & Kay, I. (2002). *The human capital edge: 21 people management practices your company must implement (or avoid) to maximize shareholder value.* New York: McGraw-Hill.

12. Pfeffer, J. (1998). *The human equation: Building profits by putting people first.* Boston: Harvard Business School Press.

13. Pfeffer, J. (1998, Spring). The real keys to high performance. *Leader to Leader,* (8), 23–29.

14. Buckingham, M., & Coffman, C. (1999). *First, break all the rules: What the world's greatest managers do differently.* New York: Simon & Schuster.

15. Ibid.

Glossary

A

ABC method   Prioritization method used to rank job tasks in terms of their importance and urgency.

Abilene Paradox   This is a paradox through which a particular situation forces a group of people to act in a way that is counter to their actual preferences. It is a phenomenon that occurs when groups continue with misguided activities which no group member desires because no member is willing to raise objections.

Ability   A capacity to successfully perform job tasks.

Absolute subjective assessment   Involves comparing an employee's performance to that of a model or set performance standard.

Accommodation   Conflict style in which individuals neglect their own concerns to satisfy the concerns of others.

Active listening   Communication technique in which an individual confirms his/her understanding of content and feelings of the person speaking.

Activity-based goals   Describes solely the activities by which success will be determined.

Adverse impact   Legal term referring to normally unintentional discrimination caused by the use of certain types of selection tests.

After action review   Technique used to learn from a group's successes and failures by thoroughly reviewing the process and outcomes of an exercise or project.

Analogies   A well-tested technique for improving creative problem solving by helping make the strange familiar or the familiar strange.

Anchoring and adjustment bias   Tendency to use a number or value as a starting point and then adjust future judgments based upon the initial value.

Appreciative inquiry   An approach that seeks to identify the unique qualities and special strengths of an organization.

Articulating a vision   Behavior that allows the leader to identify new opportunities for his or her group and talk positively about what that means for them.

Assertive communication   Clearly and respectfully expressing one's needs to others.

Assessment center   Method for assessing and developing managerial capabilities consisting of a series of behavioral exercises.

Authority   The rights inherent in a managerial position.

Availability bias   The tendency for people to base their judgments on information that is readily available or easy to bring to mind.

Avoidance   Conflict style in which individuals circumvent their own concerns or those of the other person.

B

Balanced scorecard   A method for tracking business results across a number of critical areas including financial, customer, internal process, and employee factors.

BATNA   The BATNA, or Best Alternative to a Negotiated Agreement, is what alternative a person will be left with if they cannot reach a negotiated agreement with another party.

Behavioral intentions   The motivation and thoughts that are immediate precursors of a person's actual behavior.

Behavioral interviews   Interview technique that requires candidates to recount actual instances from their past work or relevant experiences relative to the job at hand.

Behaviorally anchored rating scales (BARS)   Performance evaluation technique that compares job behaviors with specific performance statements on a scale from poor to outstanding.

Benchmarking   Technique used to compare one organization's practices with another, usually successful organization's practices.

Big Five   The five basic dimensions of personality which include extraversion, agreeableness, conscientiousness, emotional stability, and openness to experience.

Black or white fallacy   The tendency to assume that a solution to a problem is limited to two distinct possibilities.

Bounded rationality   Limiting decision making to simplified solutions that do not represent the full complexity of the problem.

Brainwriting   Technique used to generate solutions to a problem which allows participants time to generate ideas on their own, record them and then share with the group.

C

Career orientation   A preference for a specific type of occupation and work context.

Change agent   An individual who possesses knowledge and power to guide and facilitate an organizational change effort.

Choking   Slang term used to describe the phenomenon that the presence of others often hinders individual performance.

Coercive power   Power base that draws upon an individual's ability to control the distribution of undesirable outcomes.

Cognitive ability   The capacity to learn and process cognitive information such as reading comprehension, mathematical patterns, and spatial patterns.

Collaboration   Conflict style in which individuals work to find an alternative that meets all parties concerns.

Communicating high performance expectations Behavior that demonstrates the leader's expectations for excellence, quality, and high performance on the part of followers.

Competition Conflict style in which individuals pursue their own concerns relatively aggressively, often at the expense of other people's concerns.

Competitive team rewards Situation in which a team is rewarded based upon each individual's contribution and each member's reward varies according to his individual performance.

Compromise Conflict style in which individuals pursue a mutually acceptable solution that partially satisfies everyone involved.

Confirmation bias Tendency to seek information that verifies past or current beliefs while ignoring information that contradicts past or current beliefs.

Conflict The process in which one party perceives that its interests are being opposed or negatively affected by another party.

Conformity Loyal adherence by individuals or group members to group or societal norms.

Consultative coaching Helping an employee develop or solve problems by exploring alternatives and challenging the employee's thinking through asking questions.

Contingent punishment behavior Leader behavior that administers a negative outcome to a subordinate based upon the performance of the subordinate.

Contingent reward behavior Leader behavior that provides a positive outcome to a subordinate based upon the performance of the subordinate.

Contracting A process in which a change agent establishes a relationship with key stakeholders and agrees to the process for change.

Convergent thinking Group problem-solving which is oriented toward deriving the single best answer to a clearly defined question.

Cooperative team rewards Situation in which a team is rewarded as a group for its successful performance, and each member receives exactly the same reward.

Core job dimensions The key characteristics of any job: skill variety, task identity, task significance, autonomy, and feedback.

D

Daily hassles Frequent minor annoyances or events that contribute to an individual's overall stress level.

Daily uplifts Frequent unexpected positive events which can reduce an individual's overall stress level.

Deductive argument Based on a structure which moves from the general assertion to the specific evidence supporting the assertion.

Deep-level diversity Differences among people reflected in underlying attitudes, beliefs, knowledge, skills, and values.

Dependence The power attributed to one individual in a relationship when he/she possess something that another individual desires.

Devil's advocate A person who advocates an opposing or unpopular cause for the sake of argument or to expose it to a thorough examination.

Diffusion of responsibility A condition whereby members feel their personal responsibility is limited because others will step up and act.

Directive behavior Leaders define the roles and tasks of the followers and supervise them closely.

Disparate treatment Legal term referring to intentional discrimination caused by the selection preferences or practices of a manager or organization.

Divergent thinking Involves producing multiple or alternative answers from available information. It requires making unexpected combinations, recognizing links among remotely associated issues, and transforming information into unexpected forms.

Downsizing Terminating large numbers of employees to recapture losses or gain some form of competitive advantage.

E

80/20 rule This rule states that for many phenomena, 80% of the consequences stem from 20% of the causes.

Emoticons An evolving set of symbols for expressing emotions in e-mail communications.

Emotional intelligence The ability to accurately detect and manage emotional information in oneself and others.

Equality rule Process by which resources and rewards are distributed so that each employee gets the same outcome regardless of contributions.

Equifinality A condition in which different initial conditions lead to similar effects.

Equity rule Process by which resources and rewards are distributed to employees with respect to their abilities or contributions.

Equity sensitivity Those high in equity sensitivity are more outcome-oriented and want more than others for the same level of inputs. Those low in equity sensitivity pay more attention to their inputs and are less sensitive to equity issues.

Equity theory Refers to an individual's perceptions of the fairness of outcomes he/she receives on the job.

Escalation of commitment The phenomenon where people increase their investment in a decision despite new evidence suggesting that the decision was probably wrong. Such investment may include money (known informally as "throwing good money after bad"), time, or other resources.

Ethical commitment Level of dedication or desire to do what is right even in the face of potentially harmful personal repercussions.

Ethical competency Skillful consideration of ethics in each stage of the problem-solving process.

Ethical consciousness   The ability to understand the ramifications of choosing less ethical courses of action.

Ethos   Greek term used to describe the acceptance of a communicator's arguments on the basis of the communicator's perceived competence, ethical or professional character.

Eustress   Positive, desirable form of stress.

Expectancy   The understanding of what performance is desired and the belief that effort will lead to a desired level of performance.

Expectancy theory   The level of an individual's motivation depends on the strength of his/her expectation that work behavior will be valued by others and followed by an outcome that is attractive to the individual.

Expert coaching   Helping an employee develop or solve problems by dispensing advice, instructing or prescribing recommendations.

Expert power   Power base that draws upon an individual's special skills or knowledge.

Extinction   The gradual disappearance of a behavior that occurs after the termination of any reinforcement of such behavior.

Extraversion   A personality dimension that characterizes people who tend to be outgoing, talkative, sociable, and assertive.

Extrinsic outcomes   Outcomes obtained from sources external to the individual including pay and benefits.

F

Filter   Selectively listening to some content from a communicator and not to others.

Five bases of power   Major forms of both formal and personal power that managers possess to a greater or lesser extent; reward, legitimate, referent, expert, and coercive power.

Five S's   A simple, five-step process that can guide an individual preparing a persuasive presentation. The five S's are: strategy, structure, support, style, and supplement.

Force field analysis   Lewin's model of system-wide change that helps change agents diagnose the forces that drive and restrain proposed organizational change.

Forming stage   In this stage of group development, a primary concern is the initial entry of members into a group. Individuals ask questions as they begin to identify with other group members and with the group itself.

Fostering the acceptance of group goals   Behavior on the part of the leader aimed at promoting cooperation among employees and getting them to work together toward a common goal.

Four frames model   An approach to change suggesting that four frames exist in organizations of every kind: structural, human resource, political, and symbolic. The four frames can be respectively likened to factories, families, jungles, and theaters or temples.

Full range of leadership   An approach to leadership using transactional leader behaviors to establish a good relationship and then utilizing transformational leader behaviors to get "performance beyond expectations."

Fundamental attribution error   The tendency of a decision maker to underestimate or largely ignore external factors and overestimate internal factors.

G

Gap analysis   Tool used to evaluate the relationship between an organization's current practices and its desired future practices.

Graphic rating scale   Performance evaluation technique in which managers rate a particular employee behavior on a predetermined graduated scale.

Groupthink   A pattern of faulty decision making that occurs in groups where members seek agreement at the expense of decision quality.

Growth need strength   The need to want to grow or develop in one's job.

H

Hasty generalization fallacy   Tendency to draw an inappropriate general conclusion from a single specific case.

Hearing   The physical reality of receiving sounds; it is a passive act that happens even when we are asleep.

Histogram   A graphic bar-chart display of data (on the X axis) tracked against some important standard (on the Y axis).

Hypotheticals   A theoretical suggestion or comment that lets you explore creative possibilities with less pressure and helps both parties think through issues they may have not previously considered.

I

Identifiability   A strategy for reducing social loafing by making member contribution to a task explicit.

Inductive argument   Based on a structure which moves from specific evidence to a general assertion supported by the evidence.

Influence tactic   Behavior that attempts to alter another individual's attitude or behavior.

Information richness   The potential information-carrying capacity of a communication channel, and the extent to which it facilitates developing a common understanding between people.

Innocent bystander effect   When a person sees others are present, they will be more likely not to get involved, assuming that others will take care of the problem. This is the effect caused by a diffusion of responsibility.

Inquiry skills   Skills used to surface others' assumptions by asking questions about a problem.

Instrumentality   An individual's subjective belief about the likelihood that performing a behavior will result in a particular outcome.

Intrinsic outcomes   Outcomes that stem from sources internal to the individual including a sense of accomplishment and satisfaction.

Introversion   A personality dimension that characterizes people who tend to be quiet and solitary.

Intuition   A sense of something not evident or deducible; an impression or gut feeling.

J

Jargon   Technical language and acronyms as well as recognized words with specialized meaning in specific organizations or groups.

Job analysis   The process of collecting information about the tasks, knowledge, skills, and abilities required for a job.

Job Characteristics Model (JCM)   Description of the potential motivation level inherent in various jobs.

K

Kotter's eight stages of change   An eight-step framework that is a useful way to think about the critical elements necessary to create successful change interventions. (Increase urgency, create a guiding coalition, get the vision right, communicate for buy-in, empower action, create short-term wins, consolidate gains and don't let up, anchor change in your culture.)

L

Ladder of inference   A common mental pathway in which people observe events or information and ultimately form misguided beliefs based upon their perception of the events or information.

Leader-member exchange   Refers to the quality of the relationship between a manager and his or her subordinate.

Leadership   The ability to influence people to set aside their personal concerns and support a larger agenda.

Legitimate power   Power base that relies on a position in the formal hierarchy of an organization.

Listening   An active process that means a conscious effort to hear and understand. To listen we must not only hear but also pay attention, understand, and assimilate.

Logos   Greek term for logical arguments presented by a speaker including facts, figures, and other forms of persuasion.

M

Maslow's hierarchy of needs   Depiction of five basic needs that motivate behavior arranged in a hierarchy from lower order (physiological) to highest order (self-actualization).

MECE   This is an abbreviation for mutually exclusive and collectively exhaustive. The MECE approach says that data should be divided in groups which do not overlap and which cover all the data. This is desirable for the purpose of analysis, because it avoids both the problem of double counting and the risk of overlooking information.

Mental models   The broad worldviews that people rely on to guide their perceptions and behaviors.

Mentor   A more experienced person who provides assistance and guidance as part of a long-term relationship.

Mentoring   An intense, long-term relationship between a more experienced individual (mentor) and a less experienced individual (protégé).

Mixed-motive situation   Situations in which an individual is motivated to both compete and cooperate.

Model of transitions   A change model that depicts individuals experiencing three stages of transition while undergoing change; endings, neutral zones, and beginnings.

Modeling   Learning by imitating the behavior of others.

Moral imagination   Ability to cognitively remove oneself from a problem and see the possible ethical problems present, imagine other possibilities and alternatives, and evaluate new possibilities.

Moral intensity   The degree to which an issue demands the application of ethical principles.

Motivating force   In expectancy theory, the total drive toward action that a person experiences. Consists of the multiplicative product of expectancy, instrumentality, and valence. Generally represented by the formula $MF = E \times I \times V$.

Motivation   Psychological factors that determine the direction of an individual's behavior, effort and persistence.

Motivation potential score (MPS)   Predictive index suggesting the motivating potential in a job, derived from the Job Characteristics Model.

Multi-source feedback   Feedback provided by many sources other than one's self, such as from a boss, co-worker, customer, or subordinate.

N

Need for achievement   Degree to which an individual has a desire to achieve in relation to a set of standards and strive to succeed.

Need for affiliation   Degree to which an individual has a desire for friendly and close interpersonal relationships.

Need for power   Degree to which an individual has a desire to influence or control other people.

Need rule   Process by which resources and rewards are distributed to an employee or employees who need them most.

Negative reinforcement   Eliminating an undesirable outcome when an individual performs a desired behavior.

Norming stage   The point at which the group begins to come together as a coordinated unit.

Norms   The informal rules and expectations that groups establish to regulate the behavior of their members.

O

Objective assessment   Evaluation technique based on results or impartial performance outcomes that are easily identifiable, representing employee output that is visible and/or countable.

Occupational fit   The degree to which a match exists between an individuals' career preferences and their current job and organization.

Operant conditioning   The process of learning that links desired consequences to desired behaviors.

Organizational behavior modification   An application of reinforcement theory to increasing an individual's motivation and performance.

Organizational citizenship behavior (OCB)   Discretionary behaviors (not required to perform one's job) beneficial to the organization but that are not explicitly recognized by the formal reward system.

Organizational cynicism   A feeling of distrust toward an organization. Usually associated with prior misdeeds by the organization whereby the trust of the employees has been undermined.

Organizational development (OD)   A system-wide strategy intended to change the beliefs, attitudes, values, and structure of organizations so that they can better adapt to new technologies, markets, and challenges.

Outcome-based goals   Describes the specific results by which success will be determined.

Overconfidence bias   Tendency to be overly optimistic or confident in one's decisions.

P

PADIL   Acronym to describe the five key steps in the problem solving process: problem, alternatives, decide, implement, and learn.

Pareto efficient   Represents an outcome in which no other possible agreement results in both parties being better off.

Pathos   Greek term for appeals that rely on emotion to persuade.

Performance management cycle (PMC)   The key steps involved in managing employee performance; selecting, assessing, and managing performance.

Performance tests   Employment tests designed specifically to measure hands-on skills that are highly predictive of future job performance.

Performing stage   The emergence of a mature, organized, and well-functioning team.

Personality   Represents the pattern of relatively enduring ways in which a person thinks, acts, and behaves.

Platinum rule   Variant of the golden rule, treat others how *they* wish to be treated.

Positive reinforcement   Providing a desirable outcome for an individual who performs a desired behavior.

Positive self-talk   A self-management tool intended to create a frame of mind that energizes your self-confidence and gets you beyond self-defeating and negative feelings that can accompany learning difficult tasks.

Power   The capacity of a person, team, or organization to influence others.

Power bases   The sources of power for an individual.

Power distance   The worldview that values economic and social differences in wealth, status, and well-being as natural and normal.

Preferences   Choices we make, mostly unconsciously, to navigate the world.

Professionalism   A level of behavior that is consistent with the current standards and practices of individuals in organizations.

Protégé   A junior, less experienced person in an organization that forms a relationship with a mentor.

Providing an appropriate model   Behavior on the part of the leader that sets an example for employees to follow that is consistent with the values the leader or the organization espouses.

Providing individualized support   Behavior that indicates the leader respects followers and is concerned about their personal feelings and needs.

Providing intellectual stimulation   Behavior on the part of the leader that challenges followers to re-examine assumptions about their work and rethink how it can be performed.

Prudence   The practical wisdom to make the right choice at the right time.

Psychological hardiness   The ability to remain psychologically stable and healthy in the face of significant stress.

Psychological reactance   Phenomenon that when a person's choice is limited or threatened, the need to retain freedom makes the person want that option more than if the choice had not been limited or threatened in the first place.

Psychological states   The personal states experienced by an individual that are employed in the job characteristics model.

Punishment   Providing an undesirable outcome for an individual who performs a desired behavior.

Pygmalion effect   Based on the premise that we form expectations of others, then we communicate those expectations through our behavior, and as a result people tend to respond to our behavior by adjusting their behavior to match our expectations. This is also called a self-fulfilling prophesy.

R

Ranking technique   Relative performance evaluation method whereby a manager lists all employees from best to worst.

Realistic job preview (RJP)   Presentation to applicant regarding both the positive and negative aspects of a job.

Reciprocal determinism   In Bandura's Social Learning theory any new behavior is the result of three main factors—the person, the environment, and the behavior—and they all influence each other.

Referent power   Power base that relies on the possession by an individual of desirable resources or personal traits.

Reframing   To explore organizational issues through multiple lenses or frames and to use those frames to uncover new opportunities and options in confusing or ambiguous situations.

Reinforcement theory   Set of principles based on the notion that behavior is a function of its consequences.

Relationship conflict   Conflict that arises from incompatible or strained personal interactions.

Relative subjective assessment   Performance evaluation technique that compares an employee's performance against that of another employee's performance.

Representative bias   Tendency to classify something or someone according to how similar it is to a typical case or to previous situations in the past.

Reversing the problem   In problem solving, this refers to the process of turning a problem around to try to come up with creative solutions. An example would be rather than looking at why some people are getting ill, look at why most people are staying healthy.

Reward power   Power base that relies on the ability to distribute rewards that others view as valuable.

Ringelmann effect   Describes the situation in which some people do not work as hard in groups as they do individually.

Risky shift   Phenomenon that groups tend to make riskier decisions than the average of each group member's risk propensity would suggest.

S

Satisficing   Settling for the first alternative that meets some minimum level of acceptability.

Self-management   The ability to manage one's own, behavior, cognitions, emotions, and impulses.

Self-observation   The ability to determine when, why, and under what conditions an individual should engage in certain behaviors.

Self-serving bias   Tendency of an individual to attribute favorable outcomes to his/her internal factors and failures to his/her external factors.

Situational interview   Interview technique that requires candidates indicate how they would respond to various hypothetical job scenarios.

Situational leadership   An approach to leadership suggesting that the appropriate leader behavior depends upon the development level of the employees.

Small wins   Small but meaningful milestones in order to build self-confidence in completing a large task.

SMART goals   Acronym representing key characteristics of effective goals. SMART represents specific, measurable, attainable, relevant, and time-bound.

Social conformity   Involves social pressures to conform to the perceived wishes of the group.

Social contracting   A strategy for trying to actively reduce loafing by addressing the issue before it happens. Before a goal gets set, a task assigned, or work divided, the team might discuss and agree upon the consequences for members who do not pull their own weight.

Social influence   The ability to influence others without formal authority.

Social influence weapons   Set of influence tactics described by Cialdini which include friendship/liking, commitment and consistency, scarcity, reciprocity, social proof, and appeals to authority.

Social learning theory   Perspective that people learn the best through direct observation and experience.

Social loafing   A situation in which people exert less effort when working in groups than when working alone.

Social network   An extended group of people with similar concerns who rely on each other for advice and support and share resources that benefit those involved.

Stakeholder   Shareholders, customers, suppliers, governments, and any other groups with a vested interest in the organization or problem.

Storming stage   This is a period of high emotion and tension among the members while the group is still in its relatively early stages of development. Hostility and infighting between members may occur, and the group typically experiences some changes.

Stress   An individual's response to a situation that is perceived as challenging or threatening to the person's well-being.

Strong ties   Direct personal connections between people.

Structured interview   Interview technique in which interviewers ask the same set of predetermined questions to all job applicants.

Subdivision   The process of breaking things, such as problems, products, or services, into their smallest component parts or attributes.

Subjective assessment   Performance evaluation methods that involve human judgments of performance.

Suboptimization   The pursuit of goals that ignore other important objectives (not formally covered by goals) and may do things outside the spirit of the goals, even unethical behavior, to achieve the goals.

Superordinate goal   A common objective that transcends individuals needs and can serve as a unifying purpose.

Supportive behavior   Leaders pass day-to-day decisions, such as task allocation and processes, to the follower and provide encouragement to complete the task.

Surface-level diversity   Differences among people reflected in easily seen physical characteristics, including gender, age, race, and national origin/ethnicity.

Swiss Cheese Method   Refers to poking small holes in important projects. In this way, work is being accomplished toward the larger objective and progress is being made.

System   A perceived whole whose elements hang together because they continually affect each other over time and operate toward a common purpose.

Systemic structure   A pattern of interrelationships among the system components that sustains behavior.

T

Task conflict   Conflict that arises from disagreements of ideas or project content.

Team   A group of two or more people who have a high degree of interaction and interdependence and are mutually accountable for achieving common objectives.

Topgrading   Also known as forced distribution and requires the manager to assess employees based on pre-determined evaluation categories and to force employees into these categories to form a desired distribution.

Transactional leadership   Leadership behaviors based on exchange that motivate followers to achieve by rewarding them for good performance and reprimanding them for poor performance.

Transformational leadership   Leadership behaviors based on appealing to higher level needs that motivate followers to achieve beyond expectations by inspiring them to transcend personal interests.

U

Unfreeze - change - refreeze model   Unfreezing is the first part of the change process whereby the change agent produces disequilibrium between the driving and restraining forces. Change refers to when the change intervention is started and ongoing. Refreezing is the latter part of the change process in which systems and conditions are introduced that reinforce and maintain the desired behaviors.

Unstructured interview   Interview technique in which the interviewer and applicant have an unscripted conversation.

V

Valence   The value a individual places on received outcomes.

Value system   An individual's values arranged in a hierarchy of preferences.

W

Weak ties   Indirect personal connection between people. An example would be a "friend of a friend."

Win-lose negotiation   Negotiation approach in which an individual seeks to win the negotiation thereby causing the other party to lose.

Win-win negotiation   Negotiation approach in which an individual works to seek a mutually acceptable solution to the conflict.

Work sample   Employment test whereby an applicant performs an actual component of the job for which he/she has applied.

Z

Zero-sum game   Describes a situation in which a person's gain or loss is exactly balanced by the losses or gains of the other people. It is so named because when the total gains of the people are added up, and the total losses are subtracted, they will sum to zero.

Name Index

Note: Page numbers in *italics* indicate material in figures and their captions; numbers followed by *t* indicate material in tables; numbers followed by *n* indicate source citations and endnotes.

A

Acheson, Dean, 62
Adams, J. S., 374*n*
Adams, Jack, 192
Adams, Scott, 85, 241
Albrecht, Karl, 310
Alexander, D., 379*n*
Alge, B. J., 372*n*
Allen, David, 32, 35, 371*n*
Allison, Scott T., 234, 378*n*
Alpert, M. I., 372*n*
Amason, A., 381*n*
Amichai-Hamburger, Y., 377*n*
Anderson, C. W., 375*n*
Anderson, D. C., 380*n*
Andrews, A., 375*n*, 382*n*
Ang, Soon, 20, 370*n*
Angelou, Maya, 13
Annan, Kofi, 319
Anthony, W. P., 377*n*
Argote, L., 380*n*
Argyris, Chris, 75, 110, 373*n*, 374*n*
Aristotle, 49
Arpey, Gerard, 118
Arthur, J. B., 382*n*
Asch, Solomon E., 207, *207*, 380*n*
Ash, Mary Kay, 144
Ashcroft, John, 234
Ashford, S. J., 377*n*
Ashkanasy, N. M., 370*n*
Ashmore, R. D., 377*n*
Assael, H., 372*n*
Attila the Hun, 88
Atwater, D., 378*n*
Atwater, L., 378*n*
Auerbach, S. M., 371*n*
Augustine, N. R., 372*n*
Austin, J., 374*n*
Avnet, T., 372*n*
Avolio, B. J., 378*n*

B

Bachiochi, P. D., 382*n*
Bachmann, Sherri, 293
Bailey, D. E., 379*n*
Bakker, A. B., 376*n*
Bakker, P., 376*n*
Baldry, C., 370*n*–371*n*
Baldwin, James, 13
Baldwin, T. T., 369*n*
Ballou, Roger, 149
Bandura, Albert, 10, 11, 12, 13, 244, 369*n*
Barker, R. T., 372*n*
Barling, J., 379*n*
Barna, L. M., 372*n*
Barr, Roseanne, 277
Barrick, M. R., 370*n*
Barron, F., 369*n*
Barry, B., 381*n*
Bartz, Carol, 244

Bass, Bernard M., 238, 241, 369*n*, 378*n*, 379*n*
Bateman, M., 374*n*
Baumeister, R. F., 380*n*
Bayer, R., 377*n*
Bazerman, Max H., 373*n*, 381*n*
Beatty, R. W., 371*n*
Becerra, M., 378*n*
Becker, B. E., 369*n*, 382*n*
Becker, R. A., 372*n*
Beimel, S., 379*n*
Bell, M. P., 380*n*
Benfari, R. C., 377*n*
Benn, K. D., 381*n*
Bennett, Eddie, 262
Bennis, Warren, 229, 239, 250
Berg, P., 381*n*
Bergmann, T. J., 381*n*
Berkowitz, L., 380*n*–381*n*
Berlo, D. K., 48*n*
Berra, Yogi, 140, 219
Berscheid, E., 377*n*
Bezos, Jeff, 28, 77, 249, 261
Biddle, J. E., 377*n*
Biggs, Jay, 142, 374*n*
Blanchard, Ken H., 236, 378*n*
Bledsoe, Beth, 7
Block, Peter, 281*n*, 334, 344, 382*n*
Bloomberg, Michael, 117
Blumberg, M., 374*n*
Boiney, L. G., 380*n*
Bolman, Lee, 342, 382*n*
Bommer, W. H., 369*n*, 370*n*, 375*n*, 379*n*
Bond, R., 377*n*
Bormann, E. G., 372*n*
Bossidy, Larry, 181
Boulware, Lemuel R., 314
Bowerman, Bill, 51
Bozek, P. E., 372*n*, 373*n*
Bragger, J., 374*n*
Brandon, J. E., 371*n*
Brandt, D., 382*n*
Branson, Richard, 140, 247
Brawley, L. R., 380*n*
Breaugh, J. A., 375*n*
Brehm, J. W., 378*n*
Bretz, R. D., Jr., 377*n*
Bridges, William, 330, 331*t*, 381*n*
Briggs, Katherine, 22–23
Bright, Grant, 236
Brin, Sergey, 113
Brooks, Herb, 262
Brosnan, Sarah F., 133, 374*n*
Brothers, Joyce, 217
Brown, K. G., 375*n*, 376*n*
Bruning, N. S., 371*n*
Bucholz, Steve, 259
Buckingham, Marcus, 188, 356, 356*n*, 365, 369*n*, 371*n*, 377*n*, 382*n*
Buda, R., 372*n*
Buffett, Warren, 67, 262
Burke, L., 370*n*

Burke, R. J., 373*n*
Bushman, B. J., 378*n*
Bushyhead, J., 373*n*
Byrne, Robert, 359

C

Cable, D. M., 370*n*, 375*n*, 376*n*, 378*n*
Caldwell, D. F., 375*n*
Callans, Michael, 176
Callender, J. C., 375*n*
Cameron, K. S., 369*n*, 373*n*, 375*n*, 381*n*
Campion, J. E., 376*n*
Campion, M. A., 262*t*, 376*n*, 379*n*
Cantrell, S., 378*n*
Capone, Al, 145
Carens, K., 369*n*
Carlin, George, 204
Carlson, J. R., 372*n*
Carnahan, Melvin (Mel), 234
Carnegie, Andrew, 1, 172
Carnegie, Dale, 51
Carpenter, Bill, 125
Carrier, P., 378*n*
Carron, A. V., 380*n*
Carty, Don, 118
Caruso, David R., 19, 370*n*
Cascio, W. F., 381*n*
Casio, W., 374*n*
Casperson, Dana, 221
Casson, Herbert, 14
Chabris, C. F., 70*n*
Chaiken, S., 372*n*
Chambers, John, 1, 257
Channing, William Ellery, 320
Chatman, J. A., 375*n*
Chen, G., 379*n*
Cheng, Y. C., 382*n*
Christensen-Szalanski, J., 373*n*
Churchill, Winston, 14, 216, 229
Cialdini, Robert B., 51, 211, 214, 372*n*, 377*n*, 378*n*
Ciardi, John, 59
Cicero, 52
Clemens, Samuel (Mark Twain), 36, 116, 212, 272, 299, 369
Clifton, D. O., 371*n*
Clutterbuck, D., 371*n*
Coats, G., 377*n*
Cofer, C. N., 373*n*
Coffman, Curt, 188, 356*n*, 369*n*, 371*n*, 377*n*, 382*n*
Cohen, D., 381*n*
Cohen, S. G., 379*n*
Cohen-Charash, Y., 375*n*
Colbert, A. E., 375*n*, 376*n*
Collins, D. B., 369*n*
Collins, Jim, 164
Collins, Matt, 325
Colosi, T., 381*n*
Colquitt, J. A., 376*n*–377*n*
Coney, K. A., 371*n*

Subject Index

Note: Page numbers in *italics* indicate material in figures and their captions; numbers followed by *t* indicate material in tables; numbers followed by *n* indicate source citations and endnotes.